Rebuilding

RebuildingBooks
For Divorce and Beyond

THIRD EDITION

REBUILDING

When Your Relationship Ends

DR. **BRUCE FISHER**
DR. **ROBERT ALBERTI**

FOREWORD BY VIRGINIA M. SATIR

Impact **Publishers,®** *Inc.*
ATASCADERO, CALIFORNIA

ATTENTION ORGANIZATIONS AND CORPORATIONS:
This book is available at quantity discounts on bulk purchases for educational, business, or sales promotional use. For further information, please contact Impact Publishers, Inc., P.O. Box 6016, Atascadero, California 93423-6016. Phone: 1-800-246-7228, Fax: 805-466-5919, e-mail: info@impactpublishers.com.

Library of Congress Cataloging-in-Publication Data

Fisher, Bruce, 1931-
    Rebuilding: when your relationship ends / Bruce Fisher; foreword by Virginia M. Satir. -- 3rd ed.
       p. cm.
    Includes bibliographical references and index.
    ISBN 1-886230-17-X
      1. Divorce--Psychological aspects. 2. Man-woman relationships.
I. Title.

HQ814.F53 1999
306.89--dc21   99-049480

Impact Publishers and colophon are registered trademarks of Impact Publishers, Inc.
Cover design by Sharon Schnare, San Luis Obispo, California.
Illustrations by Sharon Schnare and Emilie Kong, North Hollywood, California.
Page 264 illustration by Anne Bain, Boulder, Colorado.
Printed in the United States of America on acid-free paper.
Published by **Impact ⓘ Publishers®, Inc.**
POST OFFICE BOX 6016
ATASCADERO, CALIFORNIA 93423-6016
www.impactpublishers.com

Dedication

❦

This book is dedicated to...

...the thousands of people that, while I was attempting to teach them in the Rebuilding Classes, taught me much of what I've written in this book;

...my children, Rob, Todd, and Sheila, who often through their love gave me more reality, feedback, and truth than I was ready to hear;

...my parents, Bill and Vera, because the more I understand life, families, and myself, the more I appreciate the gifts of life and love they gave me;

...my wife, Nina, who, with her love, often gave me what I needed instead of what I wanted.

Finally, a word of thanks to my co-author, editor and publisher, Bob Alberti, who helped it turn out the way I wanted it to.

— Bruce Fisher (1931-1998)

...my parents, Carita and Sam, who showed me — long before I had any formal training in psychology — that divorce, while painful, can be a growth experience for adults and children, and that we all can be healthier and happier at the end of the day.

...and to Bruce, who showed us all how to make that happen.

— Bob Alberti

Contents

Foreword
Virginia M. Satir, M.S.W.

❦

Divorce is a metaphorical surgery which affects all areas of life of the individual. I have often said that the roots of divorce are in the circumstances and hopes at the time of marriage. Many, many, many people marry with the idea that life is going to be better. Perhaps only a fool would enter into marriage thinking that would not be the case. The depth of disappointment at the time of divorce will depend upon how much more one wants to get out of life or how much more one feels it necessary to add someone to one's life to make life worthwhile.

For many people, divorce is a broken experience, and before they can go on with their lives, they need to be able to pick up the pieces. This period often includes deep emotional feelings of despair, disappointment, revenge, retaliation, hopelessness and helplessness. They need to develop a whole new orientation to the life that will come. And they need time to mourn what was hoped and to realize that the hope will not manifest itself.

Many books on divorce talk only about the problems. Of course, there are the injury to the ego, diminished feeling of self-worth, constant nagging questions about what went wrong, and many fears about the future. Dr. Fisher has given a very practical and useful framework within which to examine the brief period, to take a look at where one is, and to point directions for the future. He offers step-by-step guides to getting oneself in a position to enjoy the life that comes after the divorce. He presents it as a period in which one can learn from the past, get to know oneself better, and also to help to develop new parts of the self that were previously unknown. An apt analogy would be that of a convalescence which occurs after any kind of surgery.

The emotional levels one needs to work through during and following divorce are very much parallel to the stages one goes through at the time of death. At first, there is a denial of the events that have taken place and a consequent feeling of wanting to isolate oneself from the whole situation. Then anger, wherein one blames someone else for one's predicament. The third level is bargaining; a kind of situation in which one wants to look at the ledger to see that things are equal. This is often manifest over the custody of children and property settlements at the time of divorce. Then comes a period of depression, which is where much self-hatred, self-blame and feelings of failure are present. Finally, after all of this, one comes to the acceptance of the situation and an acceptance of the self. Out of this comes hope for what can happen. I believe Bruce Fisher's book makes it possible for people to work through these various levels, stage-by-stage. It is important to give this *rebuilding* period the time it needs, to awaken parts of the self that have been paralyzed, repressed, or unknown. Let each self — in this case the divorced person — come into the next part of life with hope rather than failure !

Menlo Park, California
September 1980

Editor's Note: Virginia Satir (1916-1988) was one of the most well-loved and highly respected contributors to the field of marriage and family therapy. She was recognized as a founder of family systems theory. Her many books, including her best-seller PEOPLEMAKING, were influential in establishing the framework for family therapy, and comprise a major component of the foundation of the profession as it is currently practiced. Ms. Satir wrote this foreword for the first edition of REBUILDING.

Introduction
to the Third Edition
Robert E. Alberti, Ph.D.

It was a growing experience to have known Bruce Fisher for nearly two decades as a psychotherapy colleague, as a prolific and creative writer, as a friend...

It was a challenge, back in 1980, to help him develop his "lesson plan" for a ten-week divorce workshop into the book that is *Rebuilding*...

And now it is my privilege to honor his wish that I carry on his work into a third revised edition as his co-author.

In more than a quarter-century as a psychologist, marriage and family therapist, and a writer and editor of popular and professional psychology books, I have known hundreds of human service professionals whose messages were important and influential in the lives of thousands of clients and readers. In all that time, however, I have not known any to have been *more* influential, *more* powerful, *more* downright practical than was Bruce Fisher. Bruce and I often struggled to "get it right," his creative and open-to-new-experience energy wrestling with my scientifically trained, strict-grammarian, "will-it-sell-books?" pragmatism. Yet the result was always what Bruce wanted, and evidently – some three-quarters-of-a-million copies later – what his readers wanted as well. So many readers – more than for any of the hundred-or-so books I've published – have said, "How did he know *exactly* what I'm feeling?"

Before you skip the rest of this sentimental commentary and go on to the meat of this book, let me give you one bit of advice: *pay attention as you read this book*. A word-of-mouth success like *Rebuilding* (Amazon.com bestseller; selling better after two decades than when first released) happens only when it *works*. Countless divorced men and women have bought and worked their way through this book – many of them several times — after their friends have said, "You're going through a divorce? You have to read *Rebuilding!*"

It will take you a while. You can read the book, of course, in a few hours. But the process of divorce recovery is another matter altogether. Use this book well, and use it for a year or more, because that's likely to be what it will take. You'll take a few steps forward, then a step back. You'll make faster progress if you take part in a divorce recovery seminar based on the book. But whatever else you do, allow yourself the time it will require to work through what Bruce liked to call "the divorce process." His research showed that it can take two years or more. I know that's not what you wanted to hear, especially in the age of "one-minute" and "chicken soup" cures. But in the real world you won't go from married person to divorced person to fulfilled independent person in a few weeks, or even a few months.

During Bruce's last months, before cancer stole him from us in the spring of 1998, he and I often discussed the future of this book, and the changes and updates he wanted for it. He remained committed to the nineteen-step "rebuilding blocks" model, and wanted changes only when they were warranted by the evidence. And for Bruce, *evidence* came directly from the thousands of clients who participated in the divorce seminars he taught — and trained others to teach — for a quarter century. I've tried very hard to make this third edition of *Rebuilding* the book Bruce wanted it to be. As it turned out, the changes from the second edition are often subtle, but I can assure you they come straight out of the real world of women and men who've put their lives back together after divorce.

So prepare yourself for a journey. Pack up your energy, your optimism, your hopes for the future. Discard your excess baggage. Put on a sturdy pair of shoes. Colorado's Rocky Mountains were an important part of Bruce's life. California's Sierra Nevadas have been an important part of mine. And the Rebuilding mountain lies ahead for you. Let's get ready to climb together.

The Rebuilding Blocks

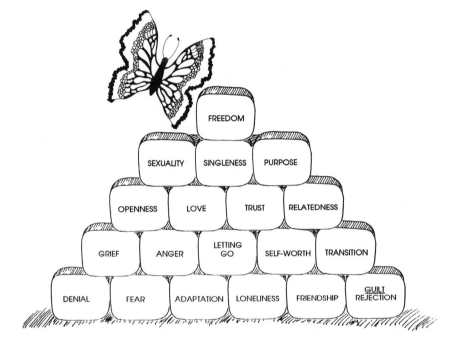

You are probably experiencing the painful feelings that come when a love relationship ends. There is a proven 19-step process of adjustment to the loss of a love. This chapter provides an overview and introduction to the Rebuilding Blocks which form that process.

Chapter 1

Are you hurting? If you have recently ended a love relationship, you are. Those who appear not to hurt when their love relationships end have either already worked through a lot of hurt, or have yet to feel the pain. So go ahead, acknowledge that you're hurt. It's natural, expected, healthy, even *okay* to hurt. Pain is nature's way of telling us that something in us needs to be healed, so let's get on with the healing.

Can we help? We think so. We can share with you some of the learning that takes place in the divorce process seminars Bruce conducted for over 25 years. The growth that takes place in people during a ten-week seminar is remarkable. Maybe by sharing with you some of these ideas and some of the feedback we've had from the hundreds of thousands of readers of the first edition of this book, we can help you learn how to get through the hurt also.

There is an adjustment process after a divorce — with a beginning, an end, and specific steps of learning along the way. While you're feeling some of the pain, you're more anxious to learn how to be healed. If you are like most of us, you probably have had some destructive patterns of behavior for years — maybe since your childhood. Change is hard work. While you were in a love relationship you might have been comfortable enough that you felt no need to change. But now there is that pain. What do you do? Well, you can use the pain as motivation to learn and to grow. It's not easy. But you can.

The steps of the adjustment process are arranged into a pyramid of "Rebuilding Blocks" to symbolize a mountain. Rebuilding means climbing that mountain, and for most of us it's a difficult journey. Some people don't have the strength and stamina to make it to the top; they stop off somewhere on the trail. Some of us are seduced into another important love relationship before learning all that we can from the pain. They too drop out before reaching the top, and they miss the magnificent view of life that comes from climbing the mountain. Some withdraw into the shelter of a cave, in their own little worlds, and watch the procession go by — another group which never reaches the top. And, sadly, there are a few who choose self-destruction, jumping off the first cliff that looms along the trail.

Let us assure you that the climb is worth it! The rewards at the top make the tough climb worthwhile.

How long will it take to climb the mountain? Studies with the *Fisher Divorce Adjustment Scale* indicate that on the average it takes about a year to get up above the tree line (past the really painful, negative stages of the climb), longer to reach the top. Some will make it in less time, others in more. Some research suggests that a few in our climbing party will need as long as three to five years. Don't let that discourage you. Finishing the climb is what counts, not how long it takes. Just remember that you climb at your own rate, and don't get rattled if some pass you along the way. Like life itself, the process of climbing and growing is the source of your greatest benefits!

We've learned a great deal about what you're going through by listening to the people in the seminars, and by reading hundreds of letters from readers. People sometimes ask, "Were you eavesdropping when my ex and I were talking last week? How did you know what he (she) was saying?" Well, although each of us is an individual, with unique experiences, there are similar patterns that all of us go through while ending a love relationship. When we talk about patterns, you will likely find it will be more or less the pattern you're experiencing.

These patterns are similar not only for the ending of a love relationship, but for any ending crisis that comes along in your life. Frank, a participant in one of Bruce's seminars, reports that he followed the same patterns when he left the priesthood of the Catholic Church. Nancy found the same patterns when she was fired from her job, Betty when she was widowed. Maybe one of the most important personal skills we can develop is how to adjust to a crisis. Probably there will be more crises in our lives, and learning to shorten the pain time will be a highly valuable learning experience.

In this chapter we'll briefly describe the trail that we will be taking up the mountain. In the following chapters we will get on with the emotional learning of actually "climbing" the mountain. We suggest that you start keeping a journal right now to make the climb more meaningful. After the journey is over, you can re-read your journal to gain a better perspective on your changes and growth during the climb. More about journals at the end of this chapter.

The rebuilding blocks model graphically shows nineteen specific feelings and attitudes, arranged in the form of a pyramid to symbolize the mountain that must be climbed. The adjustment process can be as difficult a journey as climbing a mountain. At first the task is overwhelming. Where to start? How do I climb? How about a guide and a map to help us climb this difficult mountain? That's what the rebuilding blocks are — a guide and a map prepared by others who have already traveled the trail. As you climb, you'll discover that tremendous personal growth is possible, despite the emotional trauma you've experienced from the ending of your love relationship.

In the first edition of this book, published in 1981, Bruce described just fifteen rebuilding blocks. His work since then, with thousands of people who've gone through the divorce process, has led to the addition of four new blocks, and some changes in the original fifteen. He's grateful to those whose lives touched his, through this book and through the classes. Much has been learned from them, and we'll be sharing their experiences with you in these pages.

Throughout the book you will find specific ways of dealing with each rebuilding block to prevent it from becoming a stumbling block. (You have probably already stumbled enough!) People often report that they can immediately identify their blocks which need work. Others are unable to identify a problem block because they have effectively buried their feelings and attitudes about it. As a result, at some higher point on the climb, they may discover and explore the rebuilding blocks they overlooked at first. Cathy, a volunteer helper in one of the seminars, suddenly recognized one during an evening class: "I've been stuck on the Rejection and Guilt rebuilding block all along without realizing it!" The following week she reported considerable progress, thanks to identifying the problem.

On the following pages is a pre-journey briefing on the climb, presenting the blocks as they come on the trail up the mountain. Beginning at the bottom, we find *denial* and *fear,* two painful stumbling blocks which come early in the process of adjustment. They can be overwhelming feelings, and may make you reluctant to begin the climb.

Denial: "I Can't Believe This Is Happening to Me"

The good news is we humans have a wonderful mechanism that allows us to only feel as much pain as we can handle without becoming overwhelmed. Pain that is too great is put into our "denial bag" and held until we are strong enough to experience and learn from it.

The bad news is some of us experience so much denial that we are reluctant to attempt recovery — to climb the mountain. There are many reasons for this. Some are unable to access and identify what they are feeling and will have difficulty adjusting to change of any sort. They must learn that "what we can feel, we can heal." Others have such a low self-concept, that they don't believe they are capable of climbing the mountain. And some feel so much fear that they are afraid to climb the mountain.

How about you? What feelings are underneath your denial? Nona talked hesitantly about taking the ten-week seminar, and finally was able to describe her hesitation. "If I took the divorce seminar, it would mean that my marriage is over, and I don't want to accept that yet."

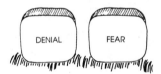

Fear: "I Have Lots of It!"

Have you ever been in a winter blizzard? The wind is blowing so hard that it howls. The snow is so thick you can see only a few feet ahead of you. Unless you have shelter, it feels — and it can be — life threatening. It's a very fearful experience.

The fears you feel when you first separate are like being in a blizzard. Where do you hide? How do you find your way? You choose not to climb this mountain because even here at the bottom you feel overwhelmed. How can you find your way up when you believe the trail will become more blinding, threatening, fearful? You want to hide, find a lap to curl up in, and get away from the fearful storm.

Mary called several times to sign up for the seminar but each opening night came and went without her. As it turned out, she had been hiding in her empty apartment, venturing out only for an occasional trip to the grocery store when she ran out of food. She wanted to hide from the storm, from her fears. She was overwhelmed with fear; coming to opening night of the divorce class was way too scary for her.

How do you handle your fears? What do you do when you discover your fears have paralyzed you? Can you get the courage to face them so you can get ready to climb the mountain? Each fear you overcome gives you strength and courage to continue your journey through life.

Adaptation: "But It Worked When I Was a Kid!"

Each of us has many healthy parts: inquisitive, creative, nurturing, feelings of self-worth, appropriate anger. During our growing-up years, our healthy parts were not always encouraged by family, school, church, or other influential experiences, such as movies, books, and magazines. The result was often stress, trauma, lack of love, and other hindrances to health.

A person who is not able to meet his or her needs for nurturing, attention, and love will find ways to adapt – and not all adaptive behaviors are healthy. Examples of adaptive responses include being over-responsible for others, becoming a perfectionist, trying to always be a people-pleaser, or developing an "urge-to-help." Unhealthy adaptive behaviors which are too well-developed leave you out of balance, and you may try to restore your balance through a relationship with another person.

For example, if I am over-responsible, I may look for an under-responsible love partner. If the person I find is not under-responsible enough, I will *train* her to be under-responsible! This leads me to "polarize" responsibility: I become more and more over-responsible, the other person becomes more and more under-responsible. This polarization is often fatal to the success of a love relationship and is a special kind of co-dependency.

Jill stated it clearly: "I have four children — I'm married to the oldest one." She resents having all of the responsibility, such as keeping track of the checkbook and writing all of the checks. Instead of blaming Jack for not being able to balance the checkbook, she needs to understand that the relationship is a system, and as long as she is over-responsible, chances are Jack will be under-responsible.

Adaptive behaviors you learned as a child will not always lead to healthy adult relationships. Does that help you understand why you need to climb this mountain?

The next few blocks represent the "divorce pits" — *loneliness, loss of friendships, guilt & rejection, grief, anger, letting go.* These blocks represent difficult feelings, and pretty tough times. It will take a while to work through them before you'll start feeling good again.

Loneliness: "I've Never Felt So Alone"

When a love relationship ends, the feeling is probably the greatest loneliness you have ever known. Many daily living habits must be altered now that your partner is gone. As a couple, you may have spent time apart before, but your partner was still in the relationship, even when not physically present. When the relationship is ending, your partner is not there at all. Suddenly you are totally alone.

The thought, "I'm going to be lonely like this forever," is overwhelming. It seems you're never going to know the companionship of a love relationship again. You may have children living with you and friends and relatives close by, but the loneliness is somehow greater than all of the warm feelings from your loved ones. Will this empty feeling ever go away? Can you ever feel okay about being alone?

John had been doing the bar scene pretty often. He took a look at it and decided that, "I've been running from and trying to drown my lonely feelings. I think I'll try sitting home by myself, writing in my journal to see what I can learn about myself." He was beginning to change feeling lonely into enjoying aloneness.

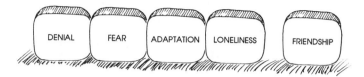

Friendship: "Where Has Everybody Gone?"

As you've discovered, the rebuilding blocks that occur early in the process tend to be quite painful. Because they are so painful, there is a great need for friends to help one face and overcome the emotional pain. Unfortunately, many friends are usually lost as one goes through the divorce process, a problem that is especially evident for those who have already physically separated from a love partner. The problem is made worse by withdrawal from social contacts because of emotional pain and fear of rejection. Divorce is threatening to friends, causing them to feel uncomfortable around the dividing partners.

Betty says that the old gang of couples had a party this weekend, but she and her ex were not invited. "I was so hurt and angry. What did they think — that I was going to seduce one of the husbands or something?" Social relationships may need to be rebuilt around friends who will understand your emotional pain without rejecting you. It is worthwhile to work at retaining some old friends, and finding new friends to support and listen.

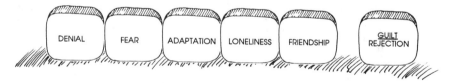

Guilt/Rejection: Dumpers 1, Dumpees 0

Have you heard the terms *dumper* and *dumpee* before? No one who has experienced the ending of a love relationship needs definitions for these words. Usually there is one person who is more responsible for deciding to end the love relationship; that person becomes the dumper. The more reluctant partner is the dumpee. Most dumpers feel guilty for hurting the former loved one. Dumpees find it tough to acknowledge being rejected.

The adjustment process is different for the dumper and the dumpee, since the dumper's behavior is largely governed by feelings of guilt, and the dumpee's by rejection. Until our seminar discussion of this topic, Dick had maintained that his relationship ended mutually. He went home thinking about it, and finally admitted to himself that he was a dumpee. At first, he became really angry! Then he began to acknowledge his feelings of rejection, and recognized that he must deal with them before he could continue the climb.

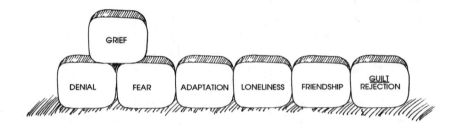

Grief: "There's This Terrible Feeling of Loss"

Grieving is an important part of the recovery process. Whenever we suffer the loss of love, the death of a relationship, the death of a loved one, or the loss of a home, we must grieve that loss. Indeed, the divorce process has been described by some as largely a grief process. Grief combines overwhelming sadness with a feeling of despair. It drains us of energy by leading us to believe we are helpless, powerless to change our lives. Grief is a crucial rebuilding block.

One of the symptoms of grief is a loss of body weight, although a few people do gain during periods of grief. It was not surprising to hear Brenda tell Heather, "I need to lose weight — guess I'll end another love relationship!"

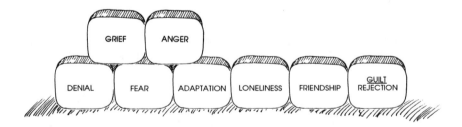

Anger: "Damn the S.O.B.!"

It is difficult to understand the intensity of the anger felt at this time unless one has been through divorce. Here's a true story from the Des Moines *Register* that helps us find out if an audience is primarily composed of divorced or married people: While driving by the park, a female dumpee saw her male dumper lying on a blanket with a new girl-friend. She drove into the park and *ran over* the former spouse and his girlfriend with her car! (Fortunately the injuries were not serious; it was a small car.) Divorced people respond by exclaiming, "Right on! Did she back over them again?" Married people, not understanding the divorce anger, will gasp, "Ugh! How terrible!"

Most divorced people were not aware that they would be capable of such rage because they had never been this angry before. This special kind of rage is specifically aimed towards the ex-love partner and — handled properly — it can be really helpful to your recovery, since it helps you gain some needed emotional distance from your ex.

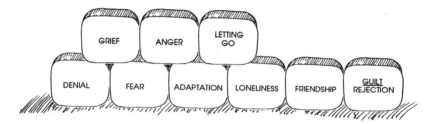

Letting Go: Disentangling is Hard to Do
It's tough to let go of the strong emotional ties which remain from the dissolved love union. Nevertheless, it is important to stop investing emotionally in the dead relationship.

Stella, whom you'll meet again in chapter 10, came to take the seminar about four years after her separation and divorce. She was still wearing her wedding ring! To invest in a dead relationship, an emotional corpse, is to make an investment with no chance of return. The need instead is to begin investing in productive personal growth, which will help in working your way through the divorce process.

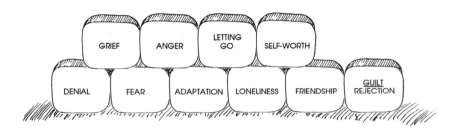

Self-Worth: "Maybe I'm Not So Bad After All!"

Feelings of self-worth and self-esteem greatly influence behavior. Low self-esteem and a search for stronger identity are major causes of divorce. Divorce, in turn, causes lowered self-esteem and loss of identity. For many people, self-concept is lowest when they end the love relationship. They have invested so much of themselves in the love relationship that when it ends, their feelings of self-worth and self-esteem are devastated.

"I feel so worthless I can't even get out of bed this morning," reports Jane. "I know of no reason for doing anything today. I just want to be little and stay in bed until I can find a reason why I should get up. No one will even miss me so what's the use of getting up?"

As you improve your feelings of self-worth, you're able to step out of the divorce pits and start feeling better about yourself. With improved self-worth also comes the courage you'll need to face the journey into yourself which is coming up.

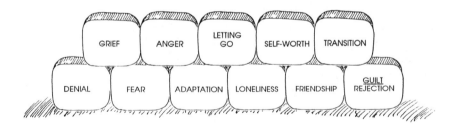

Transition: "I'm Waking Up and Putting Away My Leftovers"

You want to understand why your relationship ended. Maybe you need to perform an "autopsy" on your dead relationship. If you can figure out why it ended, you can work on changes that will allow you to create and build different relationships in the future.

At the Transition stage of the climb, you'll begin to realize the influences from your family of origin. You'll discover that you very likely married someone like the parent you never made peace with, and that whatever growing-up tasks you didn't finish in childhood, you're trying to work out in your adult relationships.

You may decide that you're tired of doing the "shoulds" you've always done, and instead want to make your own choices about how you'll live your life. That may begin a process of *rebellion,* breaking out of your "shell."

Any stumbling block that is not resolved can result in the ending of your primary love relationship.

It's time to take out your trash, to dump the leftovers which remain from your past and your previous love relationship and your earlier years. You thought you had left these behind; but when you begin another relationship, you find they're still there. As Ken told Bruce, "Those damn neuroses follow me everywhere!"

Transition represents a period of transformation, as you learn new ways of relating to others. It is the beginning of becoming free to be *yourself.*

The next four blocks are hard work, but highly satisfying, as you face yourself, learn about who you really are, and rebuild your foundation for healthy relationships. *Openness, love*, and *trust,* will take you on a journey into yourself. *Relatedness* will ease you back into intimate contact with others.

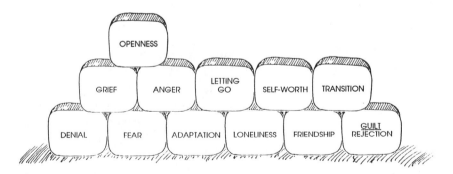

Openness: "I've Been Hiding Behind a Mask"

A mask is a feeling or image that you project, trying to make others believe that is who you are. But it keeps people from knowing who you really are, and sometimes even keeps you from knowing yourself. Bruce remembered a childhood neighbor who always had a smiling face: "When I became older, I discovered the smiling face covered up a mountain of angry feelings inside the person."

Many of us are afraid to take off our masks because we believe that others won't like the real person underneath the mask. But when we do take off the mask, we often experience more closeness and intimacy with friends and loved ones than we believed was possible.

Jane confided to the class that she was tired of always wearing the Barbie Doll® happy face. "I would just like to let people know what I am really feeling instead of always having to appear to be happy and joyful." Her mask was becoming heavy, which indicates she might be ready to take it off.

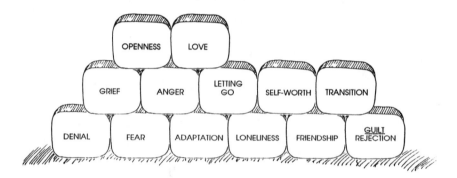

Love: "Could Somebody Really Care for Me?"

The typical divorced person says, "I thought I knew what love was, but I guess I was wrong." Ending a love relationship should encourage one to re-examine what love is. A feeling of being *unlovable* may be present at this stage. Here's how Leonard put it: "Not only do I feel unlovable now, but I'm afraid I never *will* be lovable!" This fear can be overwhelming.

Christians are taught to "Love thy neighbor as thyself." But, what happens if you don't love yourself? Many of us place the center of our love in another person rather than in ourselves. When divorce comes, the center of our love is removed, adding to the trauma of loss. An important element in the rebuilding process is to learn to love yourself. If you don't love yourself – accepting yourself for who you are, "warts and all" — how can you expect anybody else to love you?

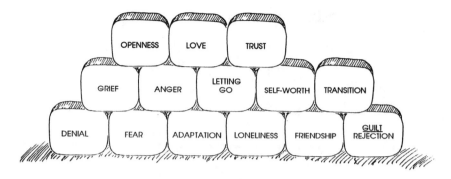

Trust: "My Love Wound is Beginning to Heal"

Located in the center of the pyramid, the Trust rebuilding block symbolizes the fact that the basic level of trust, within myself, is the center of the whole adjustment process. Divorced people frequently point their fingers and say they cannot trust anyone of the opposite sex. There is an old cliché, which fits here: when you point a finger at something, there are three fingers pointing back to you. When divorced people say they don't trust the opposite sex, they are saying more about themselves than about the opposite sex.

The typical divorced person has a painful love wound resulting from the ending of the love relationship, a love wound which prevents him/her from loving another. It takes a good deal of time to be able to risk being hurt and to become emotionally close again. Incidentally, keeping that distance can be hazardous, too! Lois says that when she returned home from her first date, there was a mark on the side of her body caused by the door handle on the car — she was attempting to get as far away from him as possible!

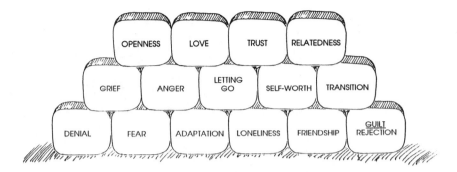

Relatedness: "Growing Relationships Help Me Rebuild"

Often after a love relationship has ended, one finds another relationship — one which appears to have everything the previous union lacked. The feeling sounds like this: "I believe I've found the one and only with whom I will live forever. This new relationship appears to solve all of my problems, so I'll hold onto it very tightly. And I believe the new partner is the one who is making me happy."

This person needs to realize that what feels so good is that she is becoming who she would like to be. She needs to take back her own power and take responsibility for the good things she is feeling.

The new relationship after a breakup is often called a "rebound" relationship, a label which is partly true. When this relationship ends, it is often more painful than when the primary love relationship ended. One symptom of that pain: about twenty percent of the people who have signed up for the divorce class didn't enroll after their marriages ended; they enrolled after their rebound relationships ended.

You may not be quite ready to think about the next block just yet. But it's time.

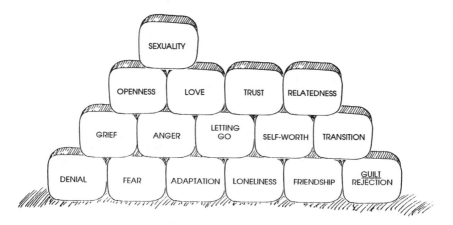

Sexuality: "I'm Interested, but I'm Scared"

What do you think of when the word *sex* is mentioned? Most of us tend to react emotionally and irrationally. Our society over-emphasizes and glamorizes sex. Married couples often imagine divorced people as oversexed and free to "romp and play in the meadows of sexuality." In reality, single people often find the hassles of sexuality among the most trying issues in the divorce process.

A sexual partner was available in the love relationship. Even though the partner is gone, sexual needs go on. In fact, at some points in the divorce process, the sex drive is even greater than before. Yet most people are more or less terrified by the thought of dating — feeling like teenagers again — especially when they sense that somebody has changed the rules since they dated earlier. Many feel old, unattractive, unsure of themselves, and fearful of awkwardness. And for many, moral values overrule their sexual desires. Some have both parents telling them what they should do, and their own teenagers who delight in parenting them! ("Be sure to get home early, Mom.") Thus, for many, dating is confusing and uncertain. No wonder sexual hang-ups are so common!

As we near the top of our climb, the remaining blocks offer comfort, and a feeling of accomplishment for the work you've done to get this far: *singleness, purpose,* and *freedom*. Here at last is a chance to sit down and enjoy the view from the mountain top!

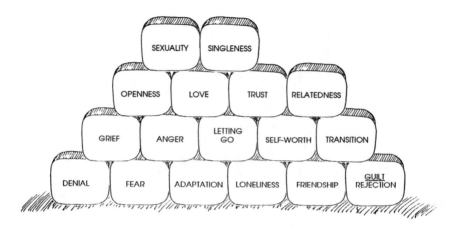

Singleness: "You Mean It's Okay?"

People who went directly from their parental homes into "marriage homes," without experiencing *singleness,* often missed this important growth period entirely. For some, even the college years may have been supervised by "parental" figures and rules.

Regardless of your previous experience, however, a period of singleness — growth as an independent person — will be valuable now. Such an adjustment to the ending of a love relationship will allow you to really let go of the past, to learn to be whole and complete within yourself, and to invest in yourself. Singleness is not only *okay*, it is necessary!

Joan was elated after a seminar session on singleness. "I'm enjoying being single so much that I felt I must be abnormal. You help me feel normal being happy as a single person. Thanks."

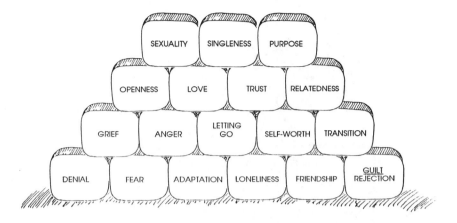

Purpose: "I Have Goals for the Future Now"

Do you have a sense of how long you are going to live? Bruce was very surprised during his divorce when he realized that at age forty he might be only half-way through his life. If you have many years yet to live, what are your goals? What do you plan to do with yourself after you have adjusted to the ending of your love relationship?

It is helpful to make a "lifeline" and take a look at the patterns in your life, and at the potential things you might accomplish for the rest of your time. Planning helps bring the future into the present.

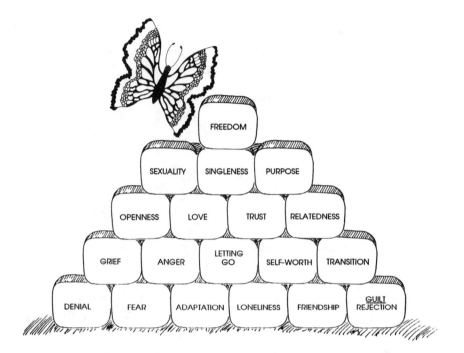

Freedom: From Chrysalis to Butterfly

At last, the top of the mountain!

The final stage has two dimensions. The first is freedom of choice. When you have worked through all of the rebuilding blocks that have been stumbling blocks in the past, you're free and ready to enter into another relationship. You can make it more productive and meaningful than your past love relationships. You are free to choose happiness as a single person or in another love relationship.

There is another dimension of freedom: the freedom to *be yourself.* Many of us carry around a burden of unmet needs, needs which may control us and not allow us freedom to be the persons that we want to be. As we unload this burden and learn to meet needs that were formerly not met, we become free to be ourselves. This may be the most important freedom.

Looking Backward

We have now looked at the process of adjustment as it relates to ending a love relationship. While climbing the mountain, one occasionally slips back to a rebuilding block which may have been dealt with before. The blocks are listed here from one to nineteen, but you won't necessarily encounter and deal with them in that order. In fact, you're likely to be working on all of them together. And a big setback, such as court litigation or the ending of another love relationship, may result in a backward slide some distance down the mountain.

Rebuilding Your Faith

Some people ask how religion relates to the rebuilding blocks. Many people working through divorce find it difficult to continue their affiliation with the church they attended while married, for several reasons. Some churches still look upon divorce as a sin or, at best, a "falling from grace." Many people feel guilty within themselves, even if the church doesn't condemn them. Many churches are very family oriented, and single parents and children of divorced people may be made to feel as if they don't belong. Many people become distant from the church since they are unable to find comfort and understanding as they are going through the divorce process. This distance leaves them with more loneliness and rejection.

There are, happily, many churches which are actively concerned for the needs of people in the divorce process. If your church does not have such a program, we urge you to express your needs. Organize a singles group, talk to an adult class, let your minister know if you feel rejected and lonely. Ask your church leaders to help you educate others about the needs of people who are ending their love relationships.

The way each of us lives reflects our faith, and our faith is a very strong influence on our well-being. Bruce liked to put it this way: "God wants us to develop and grow to our fullest potential." And that's what the rebuilding blocks are all about – growing to our fullest potential. Learning to adjust to a crisis is a spiritual process. The quality of our relationships with the people around us, and the amount of love, concern, and caring we're able to show others are good indications of our relationship with God.

Children Must Rebuild Too

"What about the children?" Many people ask about how the rebuilding blocks relate to children. The process of adjustment for kids is very similar to that for adults. The rebuilding blocks apply to the children (as they may to other relatives such as grandparents, aunts, uncles and close friends). Many parents get so involved in trying to help their kids work through the adjustment process that the parents neglect to meet their own needs.

If you're a parent who is embarking on the Rebuilding journey, we recommend that you learn to take care of yourself and work through the adjustment process. You will find that your children will tend to adjust more easily as a result. The nicest thing you can do for your kids is to get your own act together. Kids tend to get hung up in the same rebuilding blocks as their parents, so by making progress for yourself, you will be helping your children, too.

In our discussion of each rebuilding block in the chapters to come, we will take up the implications of that stage for the kids. Appendix A may become the basis for you to set up and implement a "Children of Divorce" workshop in order to help your children do a better job of adjusting to the divorce.

Homework: Learning by Doing

Millions of people read self-help books looking for answers to problems in living and relationships. They learn the vocabulary and gain awareness, but don't really learn at a deep emotional level from the experience. Emotional learning includes those experiences which register in your feelings, such as: mothers are usually comforting; certain kinds of behavior will bring punishment; ending a love relationship is painful. What we learn emotionally affects our behavior a great deal, and much of the learning we have to do to adjust to a crisis is emotional relearning.

Some things you believed all of your life may not be true and you'll have to relearn. But intellectual learning – thoughts, facts, and ideas — is of value only when you also learn the emotional lessons that let it all make sense in your life. Because emotional learning is so important, we have included in this book exercises to help you relearn emotionally. Many chapters have specific exercises for you to do before continuing your climb up the mountain.

Here's your first set of homework exercises to get you started:

1. *Keep a journal or a diary* in which you write down your feelings. You might do it daily, weekly, or whenever it fits your schedule. Start a lot of the sentences in the journal with "I feel" — that should help you write more feelings. Writing a journal will not only be an emotional learning experience that will enhance your personal growth, but it will also provide a yardstick to measure your personal growth. People often come back months later to read what they wrote and are amazed at the changes they have been able to accomplish. Every report we've heard from those who have kept a journal has described it as a worthwhile experience. We

suggest you start writing the journal as soon as you finish reading this chapter. You may want to write in your journal after reading each chapter, or perhaps once a week, or on some other regular schedule. But "regular" or not, do make this a part of your rebuilding process.

2. *Find a person you trust and can ask for help, and learn to ask.* Call someone you would like to get to know better and start building a friendship. Use any reason you need to get started. Tell the person about this homework assignment if you like. You're learning to build a support system of friends. Make that connection when you're still feeling somewhat secure, so that when you are down in the pits (It's tough to reach out when you're down there!), you will know you have at least one friend who can throw you an emotional life-line.

3. *Build a support group for yourself.* Because a support system is so important, this is a key part of your first homework assignment. We suggest you find one or more friends, preferably of both sexes, and discuss the rebuilding blocks with which you're having difficulty. This sharing may be easier for you with a person who has gone or is going through the divorce process himself/herself, because many married people may have difficulty relating to your present feelings and attitudes. Most important, however, is your trust in that person.

If you choose to form a discussion group of supportive friends, you may find this book a helpful guide. We do caution you to be aware that not all "support groups" are supportive. Choose carefully the others with whom you work through this process. They should be as committed as you are to a positive growth experience, and willing to maintain confidentiality of personal information.

4. *Answer the checklist questions.* At the end of each chapter, you'll find a series of statements, most of them adapted from Bruce's *Fisher Divorce Adjustment Scale,* which we have included as checklists for you. Take the time to answer them, and let your responses help you decide how ready you are to proceed to the next rebuilding block. (If you would like to take the complete *Fisher Divorce Adjustment Scale,* contact a professional counselor or psychologist, who can administer, score, and interpret the Scale for you.)

5. You may find it helpful to *listen to Bruce's audio cassette(s),* (see page 293), as you make your way up the mountain. The tapes summarize the ideas in the book, and may help you focus your attention on the material in the chapters.

How Are You Doing?

Here is the first set of checklist statements for you to respond to before you start reading the next chapter. Assess your response to each question as satisfactory, I need to improve, or unsatisfactory.

1. *I have identified the rebuilding blocks that I need to work on.*
2. *I understand the adjustment process.*
3. *I want to begin working through the adjustment process.*
4. *I want to use the pain of this crisis to learn about myself.*
5. *I want to use the pain of this crisis as motivation to experience personal growth.*
6. *If I am reluctant to grow, I will try to understand what feelings are keeping me from growing.*
7. *I will keep my thoughts and feelings open to discover any rebuilding blocks that I may be stuck in at the present time.*
8. *I have hope and faith that I can rebuild from this crisis and make it into a creative learning experience.*
9. *I have discussed the rebuilding blocks model of adjustment with friends in order to better understand where I am in the process.*
10. *I am committed to understanding some of the reasons why my relationship ended.*
11. *If I have children of any age, I will attempt to help them work through their adjustment process.*

How to Use this Book

On Your Own. Most readers of *Rebuilding* are recently-divorced individuals who are reading this book on their own. If that description fits you, we suggest you start at the beginning and take it one chapter at a time. Do each chapter's homework before going on to the next chapter. The chapters are arranged in the approximate order you will experience them.

On the other hand, we have found many readers want to devour the whole book first, then go back and work their way through it and do all of the homework. Whichever approach you choose, we suggest you use a highlighter as you read the book in order to better understand the information. Some readers have found it helpful to use a different colored highlighter each time they read the book. Each time you read it, you will find new and different concepts that you missed before. You hear only what you are ready to hear — depending upon where you are in your personal growth process.

There are many different reactions from individuals who read this book. Some readers are overwhelmed with some of the information. You may, for example, realize you left your relationship too soon and need to go back and work on some of the unfinished business with your love partner. George (a member of the Fisher divorce class a few years ago) told Bruce that after he had read the first chapter, he experienced so much anger that he threw the book against the wall as hard as he could!

In a Group. Even better than reading the book on your own is to form a small group to discuss a chapter per week together. It takes a minimum of leadership to do this and you will be pleased to discover how much support you get, and how much more you learn from the book by discussing it with others. Many churches have implemented such a discussion group as part of their singles ministry.

Experience has shown that the most personal growth and transformation comes in groups which follow the *Rebuilding Workbook* and the *Rebuilding Facilitator's Manual* that explain how to implement a ten-week divorce recovery class. The ten-week program uses this book as a textbook. The *Rebuilding Workbook* and *Rebuilding Facilitator's Manual* have lesson plans for each of the ten sessions, explain how to use the *Fisher Divorce Adjustment Scale* as a test to give you feedback about your adjustment, and describe the use of "volunteer helpers" — graduates of the class selected and asked to come back to support the present class participants. The workbook and manual have information designed to answer any question you might have in implementing the ten-week seminar.

Most people are amazed at the transformation that takes place in the participants in the ten-week class. Although it's usually called a "Divorce Recovery Program," it's really about helping people take control of their lives and learn to make "loving choices" in the way they live. Research suggests that this is the most helpful form of treatment you can experience when you're putting your life back together after the ending of a love relationship — even more helpful than individual therapy.

Caution. It is rewarding to see that many churches and other groups have developed programs for divorce recovery. In some such programs, however, the book is accompanied by an "expert" lecture each week on a related topic. With this method, you not only must adjust to your crisis, but also to a new viewpoint each week. Instead of giving you an opportunity for active discussion and learning from your peers — a "laboratory" in how to take control of your life — the lecture approach keeps you listening passively to someone else's ideas. Such an emphasis on information can keep your group from bonding and connecting with each other the way you can in a participation-centered program such as the Fisher Rebuilding Class.

Don't get us wrong here. There is nothing wrong with gaining lots of information about the divorce process. There are many excellent books — including others in the "Rebuilding Books" series from our publisher — and we encourage you to read and broaden your knowledge of the complexities of divorce and divorce recovery and life after divorce. But information alone will just put "band-aids" on your pain; it doesn't allow you to really heal and transform your life.

If you are a part of an information-centered group, we urge you to take control of your life and assertively ask the group leaders to investigate the Fisher Rebuilding Class by getting copies of the *Rebuilding Workbook* and the *Rebuilding Facilitator's Manual.* Thousands have found this participation-centered class a powerful and helpful way to make this crisis into a creative emotional recovery experience. (See the back of this book for information on how to order the *Workbook* and *Facilitator's Manual.*)

We don't claim to have all the answers, but we do know that the program described in this book works. It has been successful for hundreds of thousands of individuals going through the divorce process, and it can help you deal effectively with your crisis and take control of your life. We believe you'll find in these pages strong practical support for your desire to learn, to grow, to heal, to become more nearly the person you would like to be. We wish you every success in climbing the mountain!

Denial
"I Can't Believe This Is Happening to Me!"

Ending a love relationship may be the greatest emotional pain you will ever experience. The pain is so great, in fact, you may react with denial or disbelief. This only prevents you from facing the important question, "Why did my love relationship have to end?" There are rarely simple answers, so it will take some time and effort. Until you can accept the ending, you will have difficulty adjusting and rebuilding.

Chapter 2

⁢⁀⁊

Owl is crying forlornly in the dark,
I heard him calling to his mate last night.
I waited with him to hear the familiar answering cry,
And my heart fell with his
as the silence fell, louder than a cry.
He is still calling tonight,
Only to be answered by longer silences.
I have never seen the owl.
I have only heard him calling
And waiting...

— Nancy

Look at the big crowd gathered at the trailhead waiting to climb the mountain! There are so many kinds of people waiting — all sizes and colors, all ages, both men and women, some wealthy, some poor. Some people think that only losers get divorced, but many of these look like winners. Some are eager to start the climb and are doing calisthenics. Some look in shock — as though they have just witnessed a death. There are some who look up the mountain and act overwhelmed, as though they expect never to be able to climb to the top. Many are waiting around, expecting their former love partners to pick them up so they won't have to make the climb.

Many act confused and disoriented. John is shaking his head and mumbling, "I thought we had a good marriage. I had been the captain of the football team in high school, she was a cheerleader. Everyone predicted we would be perfect together. Then last week she dropped the bombshell on me. She said she was unhappy, that she didn't love me, and she wanted a divorce. She left with our two children to stay with her parents. I was dumbfounded. I thought it would never happen to me."

Mary is impatient to start the climb. She is telling a passerby, "I was so unhappy in our marriage. I wanted a divorce but was afraid to initiate any actions. Then he was killed in a train wreck, and everyone thought I was weird because I felt so little grief. But his death left me free to climb this mountain. "When do we start?"

We hear Rita saying, "He has left me and is living with another woman, but I know in my heart that he will always be my husband. God made this marriage and God will have to end it. I refuse to climb this mountain and will stay married until I die. Maybe when we get to Heaven we will be together again."

David is warming his feet by stomping on the ground and appears to be cold and in shock. "I had a good marriage. We never fought. But last night she told me she had fallen in love with my best friend and she was packing her bags to leave. I went in the bathroom and was sick. This morning I called my lawyer and asked him to start divorce proceedings."

Maria is a gray-haired grandmother. "I lived with him and gave him my whole life. I planned to share the harvest of our years in old age with him. But he left without giving any reasons. My harvest is destroyed and I am too old to plant another crop."

We could fill this whole book with stories similar to these. Similar, yet unique stories of people who are reacting in many different ways to the ending of their love relationship.

It is hard for anyone to be comforting when you are hurting so much. The most help we can offer at this point is to listen to your reality of the crisis. You feel as though you have failed, as though you have been hit in the stomach and had your emotional wind knocked out, as though you had just experienced death even though you are still living. The initial shock is easier for those of you who made the decision to leave and who were more prepared for this crisis, but the ending is still painful no matter what the circumstances.

Why Did It Have To End?

The big question you may be asking is "Why?" You feel a strong need to understand what went wrong, to perform an "autopsy" on the dead relationship. You want to know why, yet denying the pain often prevents you from accepting the results of this emotional autopsy. To understand why helps to overcome the denial, so in this chapter and the next we'll discuss some of the reasons love relationships die.

It's fun to start a talk with teenagers by asking them, "How many of you plan to get married?" Usually about half of them raise their hands. Then the next question: "How many of you plan to get divorced?" There are never any raised hands after this question.

No one plans to get a divorce. And most of us deny it at first if it does happen. We want to bury our heads in the sand like ostriches to avoid the storm. But, like the ostrich, we have problems in our love relationships which are more obvious to others than they are to us.

There are three entities in a love relationship — two individuals and the relationship between them. It is analogous to a bridge: the two people are the foundations at each end of the bridge; the relationship is the span that connects the two foundations. When change occurs in one or both of the foundations at the end of the bridge, it strains the bridge itself. Some changes are too great for the bridge to handle, and it falls into the river. In people, such changes may result from personal growth, education, religious experiences, attitude change, illness, anxiety, anger, relocation, or maybe a reaction to stress or trauma.

(One way to prevent such stress on a relationship is to never grow or change — not a very healthy way, is it?)

You may recognize that you or your love partner recently went through a period of change and personal growth, and that upset the system of your love relationship — tumbling your bridge into the river.

If you need to doubt and question yourself and your abilities, you may feel that you *should* have been able to adjust to this stress resulting from change. If you were, you would be unusual. Two of the most important abilities we need to learn in our lives are how to build and maintain the bridge between two people in a love relationship, and how to parent our children. And where do we receive education and training for these two important roles? From our parents, mostly. And TV. And other adults. Not always helpful or well-informed sources. In a talk to a group of about a hundred women, Bruce asked them how many would like to have a marriage like that of their parents. Only one raised her hand! Did the rest receive good training from their families on how to have a happy love relationship? Did you receive good training and education on how to adjust to a strain in your love relationship?

Perhaps relationship counseling would have helped you to adjust? Perhaps. We are terrific marriage counselors when both parties want to work on the relationship, but lousy marriage counselors when only one wants to work!

What was the reality in your love relationship? Were both you and your partner wanting to work and improve the system, or did only one of you want to work on the relationship? If only one is willing, then it is not very likely that the relationship will improve. A team of horses will not pull a very big load when one of the horses is lying down.

You may be punishing yourself with feelings of failure in your love relationship by playing the *if only* game: "*If only* I had listened more; *if only* I hadn't become so angry; *if only* I had made love to her every time she wanted to; *if only* I hadn't been such a bitch."

We hope by now you have satisfied your need to punish yourself. We suggest you let it go. Your hindsight is much better now. You have learned a great deal about life and about yourself since the troubles began in your love relationship. Your awareness and your insights are much improved. How about using the new awareness and insight as a basis for further *growth*, rather than self-punishment? Do something for the *rest* of your life, not the past. Try saying, "I did the best I could with what I knew and what I had to work with," and leave it at that. Now, you're going to work on today, and tomorrow, and the next day, and the next...

Maybe your relationship failed because there was a third party involved. It is easier to be angry at that third party than it is to be angry at your former love partner or yourself. There is a "Catch-22" in being angry at your former love partner "you're damned if you do, and damned if you don't." How can you be angry at the person you loved? It is easier to be angry at the person who came in and "took your spouse away from you."

There are many reasons why one partner leaves a relationship to become involved with another. You may feel that the other person had something to offer that you didn't have. That may be true in some cases. But every love relationship has some cracks in its foundation, and in many cases – and for many reasons — these cracks may result in a breakup. Patterns of development and interaction start long before love relationships end. If there were such serious cracks in your relationship, it may be difficult for you to see and understand them at this time.

Here's an example. Many people have not freed themselves from their parents' influence when they marry. They don't have identities of their own, separate from being children of their parents. Such a person may later decide to dump a love partner. But when you examine what is really going on, you see that he or she is actually dumping the parents' control and influence. To rebel against the spouse may be, in reality, to rebel against the parents.

So the crack in your relationship may have begun even *before* you married. And if there was a crack in your relationship, it is easy for a third party to become involved by filling that crack. It often is easier — or seems easier — for a person outside of the relationship to fill the deficiency than it is for a person who is part of the relationship. A good marriage counselor may be able to help you to explore and understand some of the cracks and deficiencies in your past love relationship.

There is another important phenomenon that frequently contributes to the demise of a marriage. Many couples make the mistake of investing all of their time and energy into a project external to the love relationship. Examples might be building a new house or business or going to school. This external project may keep the couple so occupied they have little energy or time to invest in their love relationship. In fact, the project may become a method of avoiding each other. When the house is finished, the couple finds they have nothing in common anymore, and the new house becomes a monument to their divorce.

Why Did It Begin in the First Place?

Many people ask, "Why did so-and-so get a divorce?" Sometimes a more relevant question is, "Why did that couple marry?"

(Bob recalls a college paper he wrote which began, "The basic cause of divorce is marriage." Not profound, perhaps, but not far off when we look at the facts surrounding most divorces.)

Many people marry for the wrong reasons, among them 1) to overcome loneliness, 2) to escape an unhappy parental home, 3) because they think that everybody is expected to marry, 4) because only "losers" who can't find someone to marry stay single, 5) out of a need to parent, or be parented by, another person, and, 6) because they got pregnant, 7) because "we fell in love," …and on goes the list.

We'll talk more about love in another chapter, but let it suffice for now that there are many levels of love and not all are mature enough to provide a sound basis for getting married. It's common to develop an idealized image of another person, and to fall in love with that *image* rather than the real person. When the honeymoon is over (a long time passes before reality hits), disillusionment follows; that person is not living up to the idealized image. Perhaps "falling in love" is an attempt to fill some emptiness, rather than a sound basis on which to build a marriage.

Those who get married for these wrong reasons (including "falling in love") might be described as half-people who are trying to become whole, and trying to find happiness by getting married. Even the usual wedding vows talk about "two people becoming one." During a talk with a group of ministers, one asked if Bruce thought the marriage vows were contributing to divorce. When he replied, "Yes," the discussion was lively, and a few of the ministers began to consider changing the vows in the marriage ceremony.

Similarly, Bob has often objected to the common marriage ritual in which two candles (representing the two partners) are used to light a single candle (representing the relationship) — OK so far! — but then *the two are extinguished!* What happens to those individual partners when their "candle" goes out?

When you are ready to face life alone and have found happiness as a single person, then you are ready to face life together with another person. Two whole people who have climbed the mountain of personal growth and self-awareness will tend to have a much more dynamic relationship than two half-people joining together in an attempt to become whole.

Most of the wrong reasons may be summarized by stating that the unhappy person expects that getting married will bring happiness. Do you remember the movies we saw about marriage in the *old days* — the '30s, '40s and '50s? (Television has seen to it that no one is too young to remember them!) The movie was all about the *courtship* of the couple. When they married, the movie ended. The subtle message was that you became married and without effort lived "happily ever after." Such a fairy tale!

Bruce's son Todd writes his ideas and thoughts on paper and often they are profound. As a young man, he described a good reason for getting married:

"At some time in the future during my growth toward becoming a full person, there will come a day when my cup runneth over so profusely that the need will arise for another person to soak up the excess."

When It's Over... It's Over

Recognizing the ending of an unhappy and unproductive relationship may help you look at your divorce as a decision reflecting good mental health. Take a look at your former relationship, your former partner, and yourself. Set aside for a moment all of society's reasons why you were "meant for each other." This is the time for painful honesty. Ask yourself:

Were you and your partner friends?

Did you confide in one another?

What interests did you share? Hobbies? Attitudes toward life? Politics? Religion? Children?

Were your goals for yourself, for each other, for the relationship, similar/compatible?

Did you agree on methods for solving problems between you (not necessarily the solutions, the methods)?

When you got angry with each other, did you deal with it directly, or hide it, or try to hurt each other?

Did you share friendships?

Did you go out together socially?

Did you share responsibilities for earning money and household chores in a mutually-agreed-upon way?

Did you make at least major decisions jointly?

Did you allow each other time alone?

Did you trust each other?

Was the relationship important enough for each of you to make some personal sacrifices for it when necessary?

We hope these questions were not too painful for you. Your honest answers will probably help you recognize that your relationship really was "in most cases" at an end, even before the formal separation/divorce. It is tough to acknowledge some of those shortcomings. It is even tougher to accept that you were part of the problem (easy enough to blame my partner, or society, or...). Acceptance, however, is the all important positive side to this first rebuilding block called *Denial.*

Take some time with this. And remember: You do not have to take on a load of guilt in order to accept that your relationship is over! Stay out of the "if only" game. The reasons, the contributing factors are as complex as those structures which support a bridge. It takes a great deal of analysis of *known* forces and stresses and loads and strength of materials to build a successful bridge. How infinitely more complex is a successful love relationship! And how little most of us really *know* about the interpersonal forces and stresses and loads and strength of our own materials!

You'll learn much more as the journey up our mountain continues. For now, take a deep breath and say it "My love relationship has ended."

Now let yourself cry for a while.

From Denial to Acceptance

Now that you are up to your tears in the reasons why relationships end, and you have taken a hard look at the cracks in your own former love relationship, you may be feeling "sadder but wiser." And maybe a bit down on yourself. You are not alone at this point either.

A computer uncovered a key aspect of learning to accept that a love relationship is ending. One subtest on the *Fisher Divorce Adjustment Scale* was designed to measure how well you had accepted the ending of your love relationship. When the statistics had been analyzed by the computer, the items of the *acceptance* subtest had disappeared! An investigation to find where they had gone revealed that many of the items were related to feelings of self-worth. The data are clear, and confirmed by others: the better your feelings of self-worth, the easier it is for you to accept the ending of your love relationship.

If you have difficulty starting the journey up this mountain because you refuse to accept the ending of your love relationship, you may need to work on improving your self-concept. When you are in the shock of a recent ending, telling you to improve your self-concept is like blowing in the wind — it does not change much. Still, you will find it true. Especially after we deal with self-concept more in chapter eleven, you will experience the difference for yourself as you discover more of your own value.

As you come closer to standing alone, to accepting that your relationship has really ended, the emotional pain will get pretty intense. And the pain you are feeling is real. Divorce and death of a spouse are probably the two most painful experiences you will feel in your life. Millions of other people have felt the same things you are feeling as your relationship ends. It hurts. And even knowing you're not alone helps only a little. But we need to use our pain to learn. To flow with the pain rather than denying it. To use it as motivation to grow and make the crisis into an opportunity, rather than an experience that leaves us with wounds that never heal. We can use the pain as an excuse to remain bitter, angry, unhappy; or we can use the pain to grow. Which do you choose to do?

Those of you who believe that you will be getting back together with your former love partner probably feel there is no reason to climb this mountain of adjustment. In Colorado about 20 to 30 percent of the people who file for divorce do not obtain a final decree (the percentage varies from year to year). We do not know what happens to these couples, but it can be assumed that many resurrect their love relationships, and get back together again.

What's the best plan of action for those of you who want to get back together? Do you have to climb this mountain of adjustment? If your relationship has become fractured to the point of physical separation and you are talking about divorce, you may need time apart to change the old patterns of interaction. You may need to close off the bridge to traffic while you shore up the foundations. Experience individual personal growth before you start working on the bridge. It's pretty easy just to move in together again, but it's difficult to make the old *relationship* more meaningful and productive unless the *people* go through changes. You may need to climb the mountain before you go back to your former love partner!

Suffer the Children

There are three areas relating to denial that cause problems for kids. First is that children of divorce will continue to maintain some sort of a fantasy image of their parents getting back together again, with much emotional investment in that dream. They have difficulty accepting the reality that their parents' relationship is over. It may be a surprise to learn how strong this fantasy is in your children. You continually need to present them with the reality that the relationship is over, so they don't continue to invest in this fantasy. Kids may use all kinds of manipulative behavior trying to get the two of you back together again, trying to have you spend time together, or trying to get you talking to each other. Your kids have a large emotional investment in not accepting the ending of their parents' relationship, and in hoping that their parents will get back together again. Respond gently but firmly and persistently with your own decision — that the marriage is over.

An important second aspect with kids and the denial/acceptance block is their belief that they did something to cause their parents' breakup. The last time that they disobeyed — when they didn't go to bed or clean up their food at mealtime or do their household chores — they think this led to their parents' fight and then to their divorce. Try

Thoughts About Friends and Lovers

I want to become somewhat parental and talk to you about how vulnerable you are to becoming involved in another love relationship as a way of making your pain go away. My belief is that you need *friends* rather than *lovers* right now.

Have you read Homer's *Odyssey*? The Greek myth tells of sailors on a journey filled with various obstacles. One of these obstacles is an island where beautiful female sirens attempt to seduce the sailors into stopping. (The sailors have been forewarned that stopping will lead to their destruction). They prevent the sirens from tempting them by tying themselves to the mast and blindfolding themselves.

Like Homer's sailors, you will need to tie yourself to the mast of self-discipline and avoid becoming too deeply involved in another love relationship until you have healed some of the emotional pain. Almost always a relationship which is started when you are in deep pain will add to your misery in the long run. But friendships are helpful; and if you can build friendships rather than love relationships, it will be more productive, for the present.

Imagine a circus tightrope act. The platform at one end represents the security you had in the love relationship. The platform at the other end represents the security you need to find within yourself. You need to walk across the tightrope in your adjustment process to find that inner security. You can fall off one side by withdrawing into your apartment or home and not making any friends.

You can fall off the other side by becoming deeply involved in another long-term, committed love relationship — if you're investing more in the relationship than you are in your own personal growth. You wake up one morning and discover you're trying to please the other person and trying to make the relationship work, but you're not trying to become the person you wish to be.

The balance pole is having friends that help you keep your balance as you walk across the tightrope. They give you honest feedback that is not biased by a need to have your love. Friends are more objective than lovers, and you need objectivity at this point in your life. Set yourself a goal: learn to be happy as a single person before you become coupled again!

— Bruce

hard to help your kids see that it's not their fault and that divorce is a grown-up problem.

A third aspect has to do with the children's fear that now that they have "lost" one parent, will they lose the other parent? They tend to be very clinging and dependent upon the parents, and they need a lot of reassurance that the parents will not leave. Parents do divorce each other, but they do not divorce their children. You need to reassure your children that even though Mom and Dad are divorced from each other, *you will never divorce the children.*

How Are You Doing?

You may be making this journey even though you don't want to, even though you are still married in your heart. The emotional pain is so great that you know you have to climb. It will benefit you to learn as much from this journey as possible, so decide to make it a positive experience, rather than a begrudging one.

In the next chapter, we'll continue our exploration of why love relationships end. Before you go on, however, take time to complete this chapter's checklist, to help you decide if you are ready to move on to the next portion of the trail. Use it to check out your progress. No one is grading you, so be very honest with yourself.

1. *I am able to accept that my love relationship is ending.*
2. *I am comfortable telling my friends and relatives that my love relationship is ending.*
3. *I have begun to understand some of the reasons why my love relationship did not work out, and this has helped me overcome the feelings of denial.*
4. *I believe that even though divorce is painful, it can be a positive and creative experience.*
5. *I am ready to invest emotionally in my own personal growth in order to become the person I would like to be.*
6. *I want to learn to become happy as a single person before committing myself to another love relationship.*
7. *I will continue to invest in my own personal growth even if my former love partner and I plan to get back together.*

Fear
"I Have Lots of It!"

Fear can be paralyzing until you're able to recognize it as a part of you that is your friend. Fear then becomes a motivator and a way to learn more about yourself. Fears are a major part of the feelings you experience when you are in the pits of divorce.

Chapter 3

❦

*Fear was my biggest obstacle. I was afraid of all the changes
I had no control over, and at the same time, I was afraid nothing
would ever change. My whole life was being influenced by my
fears! I was afraid of being alone, and at the same time isolating
myself, afraid of never really being loved again and yet pushing
love away when it got too close... I was completely stuck,
paralyzed by my own fear... It wasn't until I admitted my fears,
listed them and talked about them openly, that they lost their
power over me.*

— Jere

*I spent thirty-three years as a homemaker, raising a large family.
I had the security and comfort of upper-middle-class living. When
I became a single parent, with responsibility for our youngest child
and faced with the task of becoming self-supporting (with few if
any marketable skills), I was literally paralyzed with fear.*

— Joanne

The trail looks a bit intimidating, doesn't it? Some would-be climbers are showing their fears with comments like these: "Don't take that trail; you'll fall off the side of the mountain!" "The trail is too steep. I'm afraid I can't climb it." "I don't know what kind of wild creatures will jump out at me while I'm climbing." "I don't think I want to do this." "I'm afraid of what I'll learn about myself if I make this climb."

Ending a love relationship results in fears of all kinds. Some fears you didn't know you would ever feel. Some are old fears you've had most of your life but had been successfully denying.

It's easy to allow fears to immobilize you. You feel too afraid to make the climb, and become almost paralyzed by your fears. A little fear can be motivating. But too many fears makes it difficult to function and to get on with your life. There are a couple of key things we've learned about fears which can be helpful in learning to deal with them. The first is that fears not yet identified can be the most powerful. When you identify them, take a look at them, and face them, you'll find they aren't as scary and powerful as you thought. One simple thing you can do which really helps is to make a list of your fears. Identify the things you're afraid of, so you can get in touch with just what you're feeling.

Another useful insight about fears is that *feared situations which you don't face are the very ones that are likely to occur.* If I'm afraid of being rejected, I find many ways of avoiding rejection. I may become a people-pleaser, or develop an over-responsible part, or avoid expressing anger. While these behaviors might appear to insulate me from rejection, they actually can increase my chances of being rejected. People sense I am not being real, honest, authentic, and may reject me for that. Until we face our fears, what we are afraid of will most likely happen to us. So, as you become aware of your fears, it's best not to deny them, but to face them openly. That alone may be enough to chase some of them away!

What Are YOU Afraid Of?

Let's take a look at some of the common fears we've heard people express in the past. This list of fears which come up often in the divorce process will help you access and identify your own fears. How many of these fears are you experiencing?

One of the greatest fears is fear of *the unknown future.* I don't know what the trail up this mountain is like. I don't know what I'll learn about myself or about others. I can't visualize how I'll be able to make it as a single person.

These fears about the unknown are based in our formative years. Like the ghosts you thought you saw when you woke up in the middle of the night, the fear is real, but the objects aren't really there; they're figments of your imagination. You need to learn that you can face the ghosts of the unknown future, and live one day at a time. You can learn to trust the process and know that you'll be able to face eventually every new experience that occurs as you experience the ending of a love relationship.

There is a common fear of *becoming a divorced person.* What will people think? They'll discover what a failure I am. If I can't work out the problems in my love relationship, what is there left for me? It's as if I spilled food on my clothes while eating and now everyone is shouting, "Look at that person who is so stupid and foolish that she spilled food all over herself." I feel embarrassed, awkward, found out, ashamed, and afraid people won't like me anymore.

It is fearful *to have everyone discover our family secrets.* Often we haven't thought about it but many of our family secrets are not secret anymore.

When we were together, I could have a fight with my love partner but no one knew about it. We felt ashamed of having problems in our marriage, but at least the whole world didn't know about it then. When you separate, it's hard to keep the kids' teachers from knowing. Friends soon discover there is another phone number to reach my ex. The post office found out right away that her mail was to be forwarded to another address. The utility company had to be notified that the bill wouldn't be paid until some of the financial decisions had been made. It seems everyone in the whole world knows about the dirty linen that only the two of us knew about before.

I feel fearful because I don't know *how to make the decisions I have to make*. What lawyer do I contact? What therapist will I go see? How do I decide which bills to pay when I won't have enough money to pay them all? My spouse handled the checkbook. Now how do I learn to manage the checking account? I don't have any idea of how to have my car serviced. I'm sure the men at the repair shop will take advantage of me because I never had to take the car in before. Just learning all I need to know so I can make good decisions is a full-time job. I'm too overwhelmed emotionally to care much about my car.

I am fearful about *money*. How can I make it financially when there are now two houses to maintain? I'm afraid I'll be fired because all I do is cry at work. I can't concentrate and do an adequate job. Why would anyone want to have me work for them when I'm so inefficient? I don't know where I'll find enough money to pay the bills and feed my children.

And speaking of children, I'm afraid of *being a single parent*. I'm barely functioning on my own and I just don't have the patience, courage, and strength to meet the needs of my kids by myself. I no longer have a partner to take over when I'm overwhelmed. I have to be there for my kids 24 hours a day, seven days a week. I want to crawl into bed and hide my head under the covers. I wish there were someone whose lap I could crawl up in, someone who would hold me, instead of me having to pretend I'm strong enough to hold my kids on my own lap.

I'm afraid of *losing my kids*. My ex-partner is talking about going for custody. I've always been the significant parent for my kids and they say they want to be with me. But my ex has more money and is able to buy the things the kids want. I'm sure my kids will be swayed by the promise of so many material things that I can't provide; surely they'll want to live with him. If we have a custody hearing, what will my kids say? Will they talk about how distraught mom is and that she's too busy and upset to spend any time with them?

I'm afraid about *whom to talk to*. I need someone to listen to me but will anyone understand? Most of my friends are married and have not been through a divorce. Will they gossip about what I share with them? Will they still be my friends now that I'm divorced? I must be the only person in the whole world feeling these feelings. No one else can possibly understand me when I can't even understand myself.

I'm afraid of *going to court*. I've never been in court before. I thought only criminals or those who have broken the law go to court. I have heard the "war stories" of what's happened to others in court when they were going through a divorce, and I'm afraid some of the same things will happen to me. I know my ex-partner will find the best barracuda attorney around, and I'll lose everything. I don't want to be mean and nasty but I am afraid I'll have to be in order to protect myself. Why does the court have so much power over what happens to me, my family, my children? What have I done to deserve this kind of treatment?

I'm afraid of *anger*. I'm afraid of my own anger and of my partner becoming angry. As a child I used to feel terror when my parents were angry and fighting. I learned to avoid being around anger. My partner and I never fought or showed anger in any way. I find myself feeling angry sometimes and it really frightens me. What if I became angry? It would take away any chance of getting back together again. I feel angry a lot of the time but it's not safe or right for me to get angry. I do feel depressed and I wonder if there is a connection between my anger and feeling depressed.

I'm afraid of *being out of control*. The anger feelings are so great inside of me. What if I were like my parents when they got angry and lost control? I hear stories of people doing violent actions when they are divorcing. Might I do something violent if I get out of control?

I'm afraid of *being alone and living alone*. If I'm alone now, who will take care of me when I am old? I have seen couples take care of each other and avoid going to a nursing home or retirement center. But with no one to take care of me, I'll spend my old age alone. And what if I get ill? I might just die in my empty apartment and no one will know. There's no one to take care of me when I'm ill, and no one to find me if I become so sick I can't function or call for help.

I also fear *discovering I am unlovable*. If my ex-partner, who knows me better than anyone, doesn't want to live with me, I must be unlovable.

How can I live the rest of my life alone and feeling unlovable? I was always afraid of being abandoned and now I feel I have been abandoned. I've been discarded like a toy that isn't wanted anymore.

I feel afraid I am *becoming mentally ill.* I feel crazy enough to be admitted to a mental hospital. I feel crazy enough that the idea of being taken care of completely in a psych ward, with even my meals provided, is almost appealing. Never before in my life could I imagine being crazy enough to think a psych ward would sound desirable. But it does in a way. I want to be little and have someone take care of me, even if I have to go to a psych ward to have it happen.

I'm afraid of *being hurt even more than I have been hurt.* I never knew I could hurt so much. The person I loved — and I thought loved me — has hurt me more than anyone else has ever hurt me in my life. I want to hide so I won't be hurt anymore. I hurt so much I found myself feeling numb, as though I had calluses on my feelings. I'm afraid I will crack and not be able to survive being hurt again.

I am afraid of *change.* What changes are going to happen to me? Will I have to move from my home? Will I have to find a new job? Will I have to make new friends? Will I have to make changes in myself and my personality in order to survive? These unknowns are pretty frightening; I don't know what changes I will have to make as a result of this crisis.

The thought of *dating and being with another person* is so fearful that I don't allow myself to even think about it.

Allowing Fear to Become a Friend.
A few people deal with their fears by doing risky and dangerous things. They want to face their fears and find that taking risks allows them to feel their fears. As part of the divorce process, they will climb cliffs, drive their cars dangerously, or put themselves in other dangerous situations which cause them to feel fearful. Rarely are such extreme behaviors productive. Instead of trying to push the limits of fear, it's more valuable to let fear become a friend.

Therapists often ask those who are feeling a great deal of fear to think of the worst thing that could happen. Are you going to die from this crisis? Are you going to become ill? Are you going to be sent off to prison? Usually the worst thing is that you're going to live with a lot of hurt for a while. The most likely outcome is that the crisis will lead to being transformed and experiencing life in a deeper more profound way.

Fear is a normal part of each of us, and we can make it a friend. It keeps us from taking unnecessary risks, putting ourselves in situations that are dangerous to us, exposing ourselves and becoming vulnerable. Without fear, we might not live very long, because we would expose ourselves to situations which are life-threatening. We need fear to help protect us. You suffer a physical burn from a fire and learn to respect and fear the fire; you know it can hurt you. The same thing is true with an emotional burn. When you're hurt, you learn to protect yourself from becoming too intimate until you have healed the emotional burn.

Fear also can be a motivator. It can motivate us to develop coping skills in order to survive. It can motivate us to develop better defenses. It can motivate us to become stronger emotionally and physically. We can use fear as a motivator to work through the adjustment process. For example, I may say to myself, "I don't want to be in this much pain. I want to work through the process and overcome my fears."

The best way to overcome fears is to allow yourself to feel them. "The only way out is through." You need to discover your fears, to be committed to overcoming them, and to use them as an avenue into understanding yourself better. The things you're afraid of lead you to knowing yourself better.

You may, for example have fears about parenting and dealing with your children. Working through this crisis can result in your being a far better parent than you were before the crisis. Facing and dealing with your fears allows you to have more time and energy to devote to personal growth, career development, developing better relationship skills, becoming a better parent.

Dealing with Fear

When you are feeling fear, it can help a lot to pay attention to your body so you can determine where you are experiencing the fear. Most people experience fear in the solar plexus, that area just above your belly button. But you can feel it in various places in your body, such as accelerated heartbeat, or tension down the backs of your legs. Identifying where in your body you are experiencing fear helps you to accept and start to deal with the fearful feelings.

Here's an exercise that can help. Find a comfortable place to sit or lie down and do some deep breathing exercises. Breathe in as much air as you can. Fill your lower lungs with air by doing belly breaths — inhaling deeply into your abdomen and exhaling slowly. Get the oxygen flowing in your blood, especially to your head.

Now relax. Allow all the muscles in your body, from your toes to your forehead, to release tension and become deeply relaxed. Keep breathing deeply as you relax more and more fully. Close your eyes for a few minutes and imagine yourself in a very calm relaxing scene (on the beach, in a mountain meadow,...).

Then begin to visualize your fear. Think: Is this fear life threatening? Where did I learn this fear? Is it a present concern or a remnant from my past? For example, when my partner in exile is expressing anger toward me, does it remind me of how fearful I felt when my father became angry when I was a child? Does my fear remind me of a time when I was emotionally or physically hurt in the past? What would be appropriate action for me to do when I am feeling this fear? Is the fear I am feeling going to overwhelm me or can I use it as a method of better understanding myself?

Keep breathing deeply as you consider these questions. Come "back to the room" slowly and open your eyes when you're ready. Use this deep relaxation exercise often as a way to discover more about your fear(s), and to deal with them more effectively. Processing your fear in this way will help you to allow fear to become your friend and help you to take more control of your life. The more choices you can make, the less fear will control you.

You can experience a great deal of personal growth and transformation because of the crisis of ending your love relationship. Facing and overcoming your fears can help you make the crisis into a creative experience.

Your Children Are Even More Scared than You

"After I told my eight-year-old daughter I was leaving, I went in to pack my clothes. When I came back to kiss her good-bye, she was hiding under the bed. She was so scared she doesn't remember this and denies to this day that she was hiding." (Bruce)

Imagine the fears children feel when their parents divorce! Their whole world is threatened: Do my parents still love me? Where will I live? Will I go with mommy, or with daddy? What will my friends think? Will I even have any friends? What's going to happen to me?

Children often fear that they'll be left alone: "Mommy is leaving me; will Daddy leave too?" "I didn't have anything to say about my daddy moving out. I wonder when my mommy will move out and leave me all alone."

The message we need to give our children is that *parents may divorce each other, but they will never divorce their children.* The marriage may end, but parenting is forever. Reassurance on this point, *in words and actions*, is extremely important at this time.

Fears are extremely powerful. Children, like adults, can learn to identify their fears, talk about them, and handle them more comfortably. All of us need to recognize that it's okay to be afraid; everybody is sometimes.

Incidentally, the relaxation and deep breathing methods described in this chapter are very valuable for kids, too. If they learn them early, they can apply them in all kinds of life situations which bring up anxiety and fear (e.g., exams, public speaking).

How Are You Doing?

Here is a checklist to help you determine if you have completed this part of the journey. It will be hard to really climb the mountain of adjustment until you have become courageous enough to deal with your fears.

1. *I have identified and made a list of my fears.*
2. *I have found a friend or a helping person with whom I can share my list of fears.*
3. *I am learning that fear can be one of my friends.*
4. *I am changing fear from a paralyzing into a motivating feeling.*
5. *I am learning more about myself by facing my fears directly.*
6. *I am practicing deep relaxation regularly as a way to help deal with my fears and with everyday stress.*

Adaptation
"But It Worked When I Was a Kid!"

Growing up, we all learned a variety of ways to adapt when our needs for love and attention were unfulfilled. Some of those strategies may have helped us get by as children, but they are excess baggage for grown-ups. An over- or under-responsible style for example, is not effective in adult relationships. The process of rebuilding offers many opportunities to change your unhealthy parts into authentic, relationship-enhancing behaviors.

Chapter **4**

⟨◦⟩

In my first marriage I was the parent taking care of him. In my next love relationship I would like to have a parent to take care of me and nurture the little girl inside of me. And then in my third love relationship maybe I can become balanced and have a healthy relationship.

— Janice

You're still trying to figure out why your love relationship ended, aren't you?

Before we continue our climb up the mountain of rebuilding blocks, let's take some time to explore that question. Almost everyone going through the divorce process wants to find out more about why their love relationships ended; this chapter will help you answer that question.

Nothing is 100 percent when you are ending a love relationship. When you were considering divorce, your feelings were probably about 80 percent favorable to the divorce and 20 percent against it. When you are in crisis, it is confusing — but quite normal — to hear these competing voices inside of you.

Each of us has many parts. When you drive by the ice-cream store, one voice says, "Let's stop and get an ice cream cone." Another voice says somewhat critically, "Do you remember your New Year's Resolution to lose twenty pounds? You won't do it by eating ice cream all the time!" Best of all is a mediating voice that says, "It's okay to have a small ice cream cone once a week as a reward for being such a good person."

Listen to your self-talk and you will better understand your different sub-personalities. As you listen to the different voices inside yourself, try to identify the parts that are represented. If you're like a lot of people going through a divorce, there may have been an "internal war" among the parts that eventually became an "external war" with your love partner and resulted in the ending of the relationship.

Getting in touch with the diverse parts of yourself can be of great benefit to your healing process, and will also improve the self-understanding you'll need for building more solid relationships in the future.

Healthy Relationships

Why do so many people, when they have a choice between a healthy relationship and an unhealthy one, often choose the unhealthy one? What does health look like, anyway? How does it feel? How can we create healthy relationships with ourselves and with others?

Let's begin to deal with those questions by looking first at what might be called healthy personality parts.

Each of us has a *feeling part*, which some refer to as the "inner child." It's important to be able to access and identify feelings. There is evidence of a correlation between how much one can *feel* and how much one can *heal*. The person who isn't able to access and talk about feelings will take much longer adjusting to a crisis.

We also have a *creative part* that thinks of new ways of doing things or thinking about things. The creative part is a wonderful gift that allows us not only to be artistic, but original, unique, individual, and self-actualized. Being creative feels good and leads us to be more human and less robot-like.

The *magical part* reads garden seed catalogues and believes that the seeds we plant will produce flowers and plants that look like the catalogue pictures. This part enjoys going to see *Aladdin* movies and believes we too could fly with a magic carpet. The magical part allows us to balance out our serious and rational sides so we can have fun and not always have to be eating bran, broccoli, and other things that are good for us.

We have a *nurturing part*, but often we become unbalanced with our nurturing. We nurture others quite easily but neglect to nurture ourselves. We bought the idea that it is better to give than to receive, and then often pay the price of giving ourselves away. The healthy part is to give both to others and to ourselves.

We have a *spiritual part* that allows us to connect through faith to whatever our supreme being looks like. This is often more of a childlike part because faith may not be rational, intellectual, and adult. The spiritual child part allows us to surrender to a power greater than we, but at the same time to use our free will to make loving choices in our lives.

Can you name other parts of you that are healthy parts? Take some time and think about it. Write down a list of other healthy parts.

Did You Grow Up Healthy?

We have some important questions for you to think about. How much did your family, your childhood home, encourage your healthy parts? Were you, particularly if you are a male, encouraged to cry? If you're female, were you encouraged to be appropriately angry — and to show it? Were you encouraged to be inquisitive and creative? Were you encouraged to be independent and think for yourself or were you told to "do as I say because I'm your parent"?

How about other influences in your childhood, such as school? Were you encouraged to be creative or did being different cause you problems? Were you encouraged to be angry? To cry? To talk about feelings? What grades did you receive for being nurturing, spiritual, believing in magical fairy tales?

What about your religious training? Did your church encourage creative doubts in your beliefs? Did you find encouragement to be angry or was anger looked at as sinful and not religious? Was nurturing of yourself encouraged? Or were you taught it is better to give (and give, and give) than to receive?

Feedback from seminar participants indicates that some of us received more encouragement to acknowledge our healthy parts than others. Some of us grew up in families that allowed us to be creative, to believe in magic, to give and receive nurturing. Others had schools which, along with teaching the three R's, still allowed us to be individual and unique. Some families and schools and churches taught us how to be more loving, but too many emphasized fear and control to make us behave as we were "supposed to."

For a variety of reasons, many of us failed to learn how to acknowledge and encourage our healthy parts. As adults, we forget to pay attention to our feelings, to be creative, to take time for ourselves, to invest in our spiritual well-being. We internalized the rejection of these healthy parts in order to get along, to belong, to get grades, to make money, to be what others want us to be. Now, we feel more or less unloved, not nurtured, not okay. We may have low self-esteem, and look for ways of feeling better from our relationships instead of looking inside ourselves. No wonder we're uncomfortable when we find healthy relationships with others. We're uncomfortable with any healthy parts we may have *within* us.

Healthy and Unhealthy Adaptation Strategies

We humans are amazingly adaptive creatures. Our highly-developed intelligence gives us the ability to express our individuality, as well as to respond to an infinite variety of circumstances presented by our natural and social environments.

If life treated us well in our early years, our adaptive capabilities helped us to be creative, exploratory, self-expressive, loving, and responsible.

Those of us whose emotional and psychological needs were slighted in our formative years found it necessary to discover ways to adapt to those non-nourishing situations. We developed alternative — and often unhealthy — "adaptive behavior" parts that allowed us to survive in such conditions. The more stressful and traumatic a childhood was, the greater the need for such adaptive behavior parts. Let's take a look at what some of these unhealthy adaptation strategies look like.

Caren developed an *"urge-to-help"* part. If others in the family were unhappy, quarreling, angry, using drugs to excess, she felt better when she "helped" them. Her pain and discomfort was less when she focused on their pain and discomfort. Now in her adult relationships, whenever she sees someone needing help, she wants to pitch in: picking up hitch-hikers along the road; talking to anyone in the grocery store who appears to be feeling sad or irritable; finding stray cats and bringing them home. She may choose to marry someone in need, because she's looking for someone who needs help to balance out her "urge-to-help" part.

Gerald learned an adaptive *over-responsible* behavior. An oldest child, he changed his siblings' diapers, baby-sat the younger ones, helped with preparing meals. These activities gained him recognition, attention, and love. He grew up continuing to take care of the rest of the family — just what he had resented doing as a child. And he found someone to marry who is under-responsible (and when she wasn't under-responsible enough, he "trained" her to be more under-responsible!)

Lots of us grew up with adults who were very critical. Joe was given the job of taking care of the yard at an early age. He learned that if he mowed every blade of grass off evenly with no long stems sticking up, if he trimmed around each tree and along the sidewalk, mowed the grass diagonally so it looked like a major league baseball diamond, he might receive less criticism. He gave up early on looking for any "atta-boys," praise, or encouragement. He found the only way he could receive compliments was to go to the neighbors: his father often bragged about his son to others, but never praised him directly.

When Joe grew up, it was very difficult to go shopping with him because he had a great deal of difficulty making up his mind what to buy. He was afraid of making the wrong decision because he had internalized a part of his father which might be called an *inner critic* part. Many of us have a big adaptive "inner critic" part which keeps reminding us that we should strive to be perfect and we are definitely not behaving as perfectly as we "should." All decisions, even what to buy when we go shopping, should be the best decision possible. Like Joe, we strive to be perfect so the inner critic will not shout so loudly inside.

What does this adaptive behavior perfectionist look for in a partner? Maybe a people-pleaser who will continually please the inner critic, which easily becomes an "outer-critic" in our adult relationships. The only thing more difficult than living with another person who is a perfectionist is living with one's own internal perfectionist part. Some perfectionists marry an opposite — like the "Pig-Pen" comic strip character — so the perfectionist can continually find something to criticize in the other person's messy behavior.

Charles grew up with a lot of chaos in his childhood home: family members always coming home drunk, being off-the-wall emotionally, behaving irrationally, or just angry and emotional all of the time. Charles made a choice to always be rational, logical, sensible, intellectual, and to avoid feelings of any kind. He learned to adapt to the chaos by being completely *intellectual and unfeeling*, because when he got into feelings, he was hurt, criticized, and felt not-okay. He learned to stuff feelings of any kind, particularly any angry feelings he might have. Becoming angry was okay for the "big people" but not for him.

What kind of person would a buried-feelings person like Charles look for in a relationship? He had become unbalanced by being all intellect and with no feelings so he needed a partner who would balance him out — a person who was very emotional and expressive of her feelings! (It seems to be easier for males to become non-feeling people but it can be either sex. Often the female is the more feeling person because growing up female in our society usually means learning to be aware of and to trust feelings.)

When emotional individuals marry their non-feeling opposites like Charles, the emotional partners keep trying to draw feelings of any kind out of their reluctant mates. And the harder they try, the more the other person becomes focused on thinking rather than feeling. And the more one is thinking, the more emotional the other becomes. Such relationships may become polarized, with one person carrying virtually all of the thinking parts, and the other carrying all of the feelings for the relationship.

Most folks think they married because they "fell in love." There's an argument to be made that "falling" in love is actually an unstable condition — maybe even an emotional illness! Oftentimes it has to do with *the way the partners are unbalanced*, rather than having anything to do with love. Some of us marry our disowned or disused personality parts and call it "falling in love."

Why Relationships End

What do adaptation strategies have to do with the ending of relationships?

Think about personality as a car with one of the unhealthy adaptive behavior parts in the driver's seat. Other people in the person's life are going to have to put up with the way that part is driving, particularly if the "driving" part is a rigid adaptive behavior. And the more unmet needs there are which led to the unhealthy adaptive behavior style, the more rigid and controlling the adaptive behavior is likely to be. If the driver is over-responsible, for example, everyone will have to deal with a lot of controlling behavior, and will learn to be under-responsible (if they elect to stay in the relationship). On the other hand, if the personality in the driver's seat is a people-pleaser, everyone will have to tell the driver how and where to drive — people-pleasers don't like to make any decisions on their own.

Everything can work okay for a while with an unhealthy adaptive personality part in control. Sooner or later, however, one partner is likely to grow tired of the imbalance.

Nancy was an over-responsible person (O-R) who tired of always being in control. She developed a lot of resentment at Jack, her partner, because he was a walking example of that part of her which she didn't want to own or admit. Nancy saw Jack having more fun, being less responsible, and not carrying his share of the load. She became angry and resentful because Jack couldn't even handle the checkbook; checks were bouncing all over town because of insufficient funds. Sometimes Jack never got the checks written or the bills paid until the phone calls started coming. Nancy decided to end the relationship.

Like Nancy, over-responsible partners quite frequently become tired of the role and leave the marriage. As for Jack and other under-responsible people (U-R), the crisis can be an opportunity to wake-up and become more responsible. If not, they will look for another mommy or daddy to marry so they can carry on the same pattern in the next relationship.

Had Jack decided to take more responsibility, he might have resented Nancy for not "allowing" him to grow up; he may have decided to end the relationship. U-R's often become rebellious, frustrated, irritable and angry, and want to get away from the O-R's smothering behavior.

If Nancy doesn't take the opportunity to look at herself and her adaptation strategy, she will probably seek out and find another stray cat to take care of so her O-R part can keep driving the personality car.

When people are asked to identify when they first noticed an event that upset the system in their love relationship, many mention things like a baby being born, the wife starting to work outside of the home, the husband being transferred to a new job, a grandparent becoming ill or dying, being in and barely surviving a major flood. If asked how they were able to adjust to this change in the relationship, they usually say the relationship was too rigid to adjust. The major life change was the beginning of the end of their relationship.

Did you have an event that upset your system which resulted eventually in your relationship ending?

The Bridge Across Responsibility
Here is a metaphor to help you think about this over/under-responsible relationship. Imagine the love partners (Jack and Nancy; you and your partner) as the ends of a bridge. The two of them are supporting the relationship bridge: it is the connection between them. The over-responsible person (Nancy) is the bridge sweeper who keeps the whole bridge clean — all the way across to Jack's end of the bridge. The under-responsible person (Jack) is sitting on his end of the bridge with a fishing pole. Nancy resents Jack fishing all of the time instead of keeping his end of the bridge swept. Fisherman Jack resents Nancy never taking time to enjoy fishing herself, not to mention her scaring away the fish with her persistent sweeping.

We're discussing this particular over/under responsible adaptive behavior more than some of the others because it was the most common unhealthy adaptation strategy with the 2,000 people Bruce taught personally in the divorce class. The over/under responsible pattern seems to be a major cause of divorce. It might be called a parent-child relationship, caretaker/taker relationship, or an alcoholic/enabler relationship. It is a specific form of co-dependency, in which each person is dependent upon the other to keep the system in balance. (Or rather, *imbalance*.) What kinds of adaptive behaviors have you developed? Are they driving your personality car? Would you like to be better able to choose which of your parts you want to be driving? How will you go about changing and taking charge of your life?

Feelings Underneath Adaptive Behavior

Over-responsible people are usually giving to others what they would like to have someone give to them. They have unmet needs — usually from an unsatisfying childhood — which lead them to develop unhealthy adaptive behavior so they'll feel better and more comfortable. The same is true of the other adaptation strategies. The way to take charge of your life is to learn how to meet the needs which were not met in your formative years. This starts with understanding some of the feelings underneath adaptive behavior.

Julie developed an unhealthy adaptive behavior pattern because, "I don't want to feel *rejected* and *abandoned*. If I take care of him, he won't dare leave me. He'll feel obligated to not reject me." She takes care of others so she will feel less rejected.

Wayne takes care of Susan because, he told the class, "I would feel *guilty* if I didn't. If I do things for myself, my inner critic starts telling me how selfish I am. How I never do enough for others. How I need to be more loving. By giving to Susan, I feel less guilt."

Fear of criticism is one of the most common feelings behind adaptation strategies. Bill tells it this way: "I learned to feel somewhat anxious inside because of the large amount of criticism I heard from one or more of the significant adults in my childhood. I need to make my world as perfect as possible because I feel *fearful* when my external world is not perfect. I've developed my adaptive behavior so I will feel less fear."

Here is Edward's story: "The only time I feel worthwhile is when I am doing something for others. I don't have much *self-esteem*, but I feel better when I am doing my adaptive behavior. I didn't feel loved as a child and I learned to be seen and not heard. So I am a people-pleaser because I feel worthless if I am not pleasing you."

"I feel *angry*," Alec admitted, "and I don't know how to express it or even allow myself to feel it. So I become very critical of you as a way of adapting. I saw my father as being angry but never showing it openly. But he was very critical of others. I become critical and controlling as a way of disguising my dis-owned anger."

Jennifer grew up with an all-too-common experience: "As a female I saw my mother being the caretaker of the family so my unhealthy adaptive behavior was learned from her *modeling* — take care of others."

Michael also learned from parental *modeling*: "As a male I saw my father being the breadwinner of the family so the adaptation strategy I learned is to make enough money to be as good a breadwinner as my father was. It is more important to me to work long hours than it is to spend time with my family."

Making Peace with My Inner Critic

Most of us have a well-nourished and thriving "inner critic" part, which often has been the part driving our "personality car." The inner critic is good at finding ways of controlling us, just as critical people in childhood found ways of controlling us.

When the members of one class were asked to think of a name for their inner critics, most gave them the name of one of their parents. Most of us developed our inner critics from the criticism we heard from one or both of our parents.

"I've often thought of the inner critic as me, or as *who I am*," Beverly told the class. We pointed out to her that it is important to identify it as just *one* of the many parts of her personality, and to put up some internal boundaries between the essence of who she is and the part of her that is critical. When we understand that the inner critic is just one of many parts, we have begun to diminish the power it has over us. *My inner critic is smaller than I am, and I can be bigger than it is.* Many of us tend to respond to our inner critics in much the same way we did to our parents. If we believed our parents' criticism, which often resulted in lower feelings of self-esteem, we similarly believe our inner critics and allow the criticism to continually lower our esteem. Those of us who rebelled against our parents may well rebel against our inner critics.

We must remember that we are controlled if we always *obey* one of our parts. But we are also controlled if we are forced to always *rebel against* one of our parts. If we tuned out our parents and didn't listen, we probably will tune out the inner critic voice as well.

How do you react to the voice of your inner critic? Do you react the same way as you did to your parents? Do you want to react differently? How will you do that?

Instead of trying to dis-own or dis-use your inner critic by not listening to it or by ignoring it or by believing it, start listening to what it is saying. Think of it this way: if you keep ignoring a person sitting next to you, she will probably try harder and harder to get your attention. She might even start shouting at you, or inflict some physical pain or discomfort.

The inner critic is even more powerful than that frustrated person at your elbow, and it's harder to keep ignoring it when it lives inside your head! Consciously make a decision to start listening to that part. You might even write down what you hear it saying. It probably has been talking with "you" messages: "You are really dumb." "Can't you ever do it right?" Acknowledge it, and eventually it will start softening the words it uses. When it is feeling heard, feeling important, and feeling understood, it will start changing from "you" messages to "I" messages: "I didn't like the way I handled that situation." Notice how much more constructive that statement is, and how much more valuable to you when you accept it as your own.

When your critic is finished each time, you may respond with a simple, "Thank you."

What is really happening is that you are making peace with your "inner-parent." The inner critic is usually very much like the admonitions of your parent(s) when you were a child. As you listen to and begin to own your inner critic, it becomes a new and healthy "good-parent."

Homework to Help You Take Charge of Your Life.

Among the major goals of this *Rebuilding* book and the ten-week class are to help you understand what went wrong with your past relationship, and to help you learn how your unhealthy adaptive behavior keeps you unbalanced. Here's a homework assignment designed to help you start becoming more balanced.

(If you want to try to change your relationships either with your past love-partner or with a new partner, we suggest you read Bruce's follow-up book, *Loving Choices,* which emphasizes the next stages of relationship, and teaches key communication skills. You'll find more information in the back of this book.)

If your adaptive behavior in the past relationship was *over-responsible,* you were probably a good giver and a poor taker. You were responsible for others, but were not responsible for yourself. You need to become balanced in your giving and receiving so you can do each one equally well.

Here's your homework assignment: First, ask someone to do something for you. (I can just hear some of you saying, "I can't do that." Not ready to let go of your unhealthy adaptive behavior, huh?) There is a second part of the homework: Say "no" when someone asks you to do something for him. Do you see the value of this homework exercise? It can help you to balance out your giving and receiving. The important thing for you be aware of when you do this homework is which one of the six feelings you experience when you do the homework: rejected, guilty, fearful, angry, low self-worth, or unable to stop doing the modeled behavior?

If your adaptive behavior in your past relationship was *under-responsible*, you will need to put your money where your mouth is and carry out specific changes in responsible behavior.

Dave shared an example of his homework. In the past his former wife was over-responsible. After they were divorced, he would ask her what their teen-age daughters would like for their birthdays. She, of course, was over-responsible and able to state exactly what they would like. He continued his under-responsible behavior by purchasing for the girls exactly what his ex-wife recommended. She was happy to continue her over-responsible behavior. His daughters were happy to get what they wanted for their birthdays. And Dave was still in his under-responsible behavior. He shared his homework with the class: "I decided on my own what my daughters would like for birthday presents, and I got it for them without asking anyone what I should buy. It wasn't anything they'd asked for, but they seemed thrilled anyway!"

If your adaptive behavior in your past relationship was being a *perfectionist*, your homework is to not make your bed when you get up this week. ("Oh, I can't do that. I will be thinking about the messy bed all day and not get anything done at work. The room looks really messy when the bed isn't made. What if the plumbing should break down and someone would come and see the messy bedroom?" Still not ready to change, huh?)

Remember to ask yourself what are you feeling when you do the homework so you can become aware of the feelings underneath your adaptive behavior.

If your adaptive behavior in your past relationship was being a *people-pleaser*, your homework is to do something that displeases someone. It might be saying "no" to a request for a favor, or not doing something that you have been resenting doing but were afraid if you didn't, they would be displeased. The problem here is that, if we suggest homework, you might do it to please us. So it may be valuable for you to create your own homework instead. Be aware of the feelings underneath as you do the homework.

If your adaptive behavior in your past relationship was being the *thinking, non-feeling person*, your homework is to write ten "I-feel messages" each day for the next week. (An "I-feel message" is simply a statement of your *feelings* — not what you *think*, what you *feel* — at any moment. "I feel angry." "I feel confused." NOT "I feel that you're being unfair." That's an opinion, a thought.) And be aware of how it feels to talk about your feelings!

If your adaptive behavior in your past relationship was being *unorganized* as a way of hiding under the mess, then your homework is to start a "to be done today" list. Be aware of feelings underneath.

If your adaptive behavior in your past relationship was being *rebellious*, your homework is to make a list of ten "I-am statements." ("I-am" statements are self-descriptions without the usual social roles: "I am a person who hates rules" fits this assignment; "I am a resident of Ohio" does not.) This is designed to help you gain an individual identity of your own instead of allowing someone else to be in charge of your life — which is what happens when you feel you *must* rebel.

If your adaptive behavior in your past relationship was *whatever you decided*, then you will have to decide what your homework will be also!

Learning to Nurture Yourself

This is homework for everyone — even if you haven't determined if you have any unhealthy adaptive behavior: Do something nice for yourself, something that will make you feel good. Stop and get an ice cream cone and eat it all before you pick up the kids. Take a long bubble-bath. Read a book that you have been wanting to read for a long time. Develop a new hobby. Have a full body massage. Have someone take care of and nurture you for a whole evening. Write twenty things you like about yourself on recipe cards and post them where you can read them until you believe them.

Children and Adaptation

This part of the trail is especially important for children. As we have seen in this chapter, it is the formative years — and usually in response to parents — when unhealthy adaptive behaviors develop: when we're not getting our needs met; when we feel frightened; when we need more attention and love.

Not surprisingly, the need to develop adaptive behavior is even greater when our parents are separating and divorcing. Ever notice how the oldest daughter becomes a pseudo-mom when she is with dad? Or how the boy becomes the "man of the house" when he is with mom? How often children become over-responsible when the parents are in the divorce pits and are behaving under-responsibly!

We adults often encourage our children to develop unhealthy adaptive behaviors by our own need to be little. We have difficulty working through our own process, and want somebody "big" around because we don't feel we can do it ourselves. It's understandable, but not a good idea. We need to be careful not to use our children to meet our own needs.

Let's encourage our children to become independent as they grow and develop — to be themselves instead of being caretakers for their parents. Let's help them build their creative and inquisitive parts. Let's help them make peace with the inner critic, and learn how to use it as a friendly guide to a responsible and independent life.

How Are You Doing?
The crowd on the trail is growing restless. Most want to get on with the journey. Before you go, check out the following questions to see if you're ready to move ahead.

1. *I have become aware of my adaptive behavior part(s).*
2. *I am committed to becoming more flexible and balanced by doing self-nurturing.*
3. *I have identified and completed the homework designed to help me take charge of my unhealthy adaptive behavior.*
4. *I have become aware of the feeling or feelings underneath my adaptive behavior.*
5. *I have made a list of healthy parts that I would like to encourage within myself.*
6. *I have a better understanding of why my love relationship ended.*

Loneliness
"I've Never Felt So Alone"

It is natural to feel extreme loneliness when your love relationship ends. But healing can come from the pain, if you listen to it. You can learn how to grow through loneliness to the stage of aloneness — where you are comfortable being by yourself.

Chapter 5

Loneliness is a disease
That grows slowly and
Undetected. Its symptoms
Are terrifying.
Loneliness is a dark,
Unseeing veil that covers
You with sadness, and a
Desperate race to conquer the
Complete spiritual and
Emotional emptiness. . .
In an unmerciful world.

I am experiencing this
Disease, and wish I could
Find a cure —
But even a ray of sunlight
Is a blessed thing.
For loneliness demands; it takes
Everything from you and
In return gives you nothing
But solitude; as if you
Were the only person

— Elaine

As we observe others climbing this mountain of rebuilding blocks, we see a lot of lonely people. There are those who have withdrawn into their "caves," just peering out once in a while, looking very sad and dejected. And there are the lonely people who insist on being with somebody else, so they're always holding hands or following somebody around. And then there are the busy ones — always busy doing this and that so they never have to face their loneliness. Some express their loneliness like a vacuum -- "sucking up" everyone around in order to fill the void. For others it's like an iceberg — trying to gain warmth by staying as close as possible to whomever they can.

Loneliness is pain. But it is a pain which tells us we have something important to learn.

The formerly married do not have a corner on the loneliness market. Untold numbers suffer from the affliction. For many, it began in childhood and persisted through the marriage and into divorce. (Another cause of divorce, for those of you who are keeping a list.) This may be a crucial part of the climb for you if loneliness has been a stumbling block for years.

The loneliness that comes when that special person is gone is often more intense than any you have ever felt. Suddenly, you have no one with whom to share meals, bed, or the special moments in your children's growth. Used to having the sounds, smells, and touch of that other person in the home, you now know nothing but silence. There is a strange emptiness in the house – even a house full of children — as though a gong was struck and produced no sound. You can find no one in the whole world to see, hear, or feel as you do. Friends who do try to reach out seem distant, even as you most need them to be close and real.

A voice within you may warn, "Withdraw, withdraw, and you won't be hurt again!" You want seclusion — like the wounded dog who retires to parts unknown until its wound is healed. At the same time, you crave emotional warmth, to be a child, to have a "mommy" care for you.

Some who have been lonely in marriage are actually relieved to end the relationship. But there is now a different kind of loneliness. They were never really emotionally close to the loved one; life with that person may have been painful, angry, frustrating, distant – and lonely. (Another cause of divorce — are you keeping track?) Ending the relationship was a relief, but the new loneliness is there nonetheless.

Stages of Loneliness

Many of the rebuilding blocks have a three-stage pattern. For loneliness, the first stage is *withdrawal;* one may withdraw or fantasize about it. Some hide in empty apartments and brood, so that others will not suspect their fear. Another approach is to play the "poor-little-me" game, hoping that someone will come along and feel sorry. The goal is to keep others from seeing how much one hurts, while at the same time letting the former partner know.

Quiet is a constant reminder during this stage that the other person is gone — really gone. The silence can be crushing. Inability to concentrate makes reading impossible. TV is boring. Nothing is exciting! There is a nagging, restless desire to do something — but what?

Withdrawal may be appropriate for some during this period because — let's face it — the lonely are not very good company. Their need for emotional warmth is insatiable. The need often stifles friends, engulfs them, and denies them space to be themselves, to be friends. There is an old nursery story about millions and billions and trillions of cats who began to eat each other up until there were no cats left. Close friends in this stage can "eat each other up" until there is nothing left of either!

Life is often like a pendulum, swinging from one extreme to the other. Seeking ways to escape this loneliness, many people escape their withdrawal and enter a second stage, *becoming "busyholics,"* with an activity for each night of the week and two on Saturdays and Sundays. They work long hours and find all kinds of excuses to keep working rather than coming home to emptiness. (They also may have been workaholics while married — perhaps to keep from coming home to a lonely marriage. Add that one to your list.) They go out with people they really do not enjoy just to avoid being alone. A party for singles may last all night — no one wants to go home to be alone!

They are running from themselves — as though a frightening ghost lurked inside, a ghost of loneliness. For those who have really been lonely, the ghost may have begun to seem real! They never take time to stop and look at what they are doing or where they are going because they are so busy running. Instead of climbing up the mountain, they are running around it in circles! (Sound familiar?)

This busy-loneliness varies in length and intensity from person to person. Some may only feel that they want to be busy; others may become so busy that they have to walk on tiptoes to keep their posteriors from dragging. Eventually all get tired and begin to realize that there must be more to life than running from the ghost of loneliness. Then they begin to slow down into the aloneness stage.

And Then You're Alone

Aloneness — what one friend called the "all-oneness" stage — is finally achieved at the point of being *comfortable* by yourself. You may *choose* to be at home alone by the fire with a book, rather than going out to be with people you really do not like. Development of your inner resources leads to interests, activities, thoughts, and attitudes that make it comfortable to be alone with yourself.

"How do I get there from here?" Start by facing the ghost of loneliness and realizing that it is a ghost! You have run from it, feared it, avoided it. But when you turn to that ghost of loneliness and say "Boo!" often the ghost loses its power and control. You have accepted loneliness as part of being human, and thereby become more comfortable being alone.

Accept also that loneliness has healing qualities. A period of time alone with yourself allows introspection, reflection, growth and development of the inner self. Hollowness and emptiness are replaced by inner fullness and strength. You have made a giant step toward independence when you are comfortable by yourself, no longer dependent on the company of others.

We encourage you to go slowly in seeking new relationships at point on the trail. You really need to learn to be alone with yourself. What's more, choosing to be with another person to escape loneliness is a very unhealthy reason to begin another love relationship. There is tremendous therapeutic value in being by yourself, even lonely for a time, before you start another love relationship.

Time really is the best healer. A period of loneliness – and self-discovery — is part of the remedy you need. This is an important growth stage in your life. Then, when the time is right, you can *choose* to enter into the next relationship, rather than *needing* the next relationship to overcome loneliness.

A mentally healthy person maintains a balance between being with others and being alone. You need to find the proper balance for you.

All the Lonely Children

Children suffer loneliness too after their parents are divorced. They have the same kind of empty feelings inside them that parents have. They have the same need to be with others to fill up that loneliness, but they also fear being close to others.

Kids may feel they are the only divorced kid in school. In one community, divorce was so prevalent that when one youngster told school friends that his parents were getting a divorce, the other kids said, "Your parents are finally getting with it, aren't they?" In another community, divorce can still be so "wrong," so unusual, that the child might be the only divorced kid in the grade.

Daily living habits are altered just as are those of the parents. At home, there is only one parent to spend time with, to play with, to put them to bed. And the kids feel the loneliness of a new house when one or both parents move. At the home of the noncustodial parent, there may not be familiar toys or books to play with. Often the other parent's new home is not set up for children, and may be located in a new neighborhood, away from friends.

The kids need to work through this loneliness — just as the parents do — in order to develop their own healthy feelings of aloneness. Kids need to learn that they have the resources within themselves to spend time alone without having to have another person around.

Many kids may have been lonely before the divorce because the interaction within the family did not help them to feel that they belonged. Divorce tends to increase this feeling of not belonging or not being okay. However, perhaps the crisis itself can be used to help deal directly with the problem.

This is a special time for parents to help the children feel that they belong, that they are loved, and that they are an important part of a new (restructured) family. They need help in learning to live with a single parent, two parents living apart, new step-parent(s) and/or step-siblings. (Again, we caution you not to develop serious new relationships too soon!)

As with all of the rebuilding blocks, when you're dealing with your own loneliness, it is very difficult to have enough emotional time and energy left to devote to the kids' needs. Like putting your own oxygen mask on first in an airplane emergency, it may be necessary for you to work through your own rebuilding blocks first; then you'll be better able to help your children.

How Are You Doing?

Do some work *now* on your own capacity for being alone. If you can honestly answer "yes" to most of the items listed below, you have developed a healthy *aloneness*, and you are ready to move on up the mountain. If more than three or four of these areas need work, spend some time going over this chapter, so you can become more comfortable being by yourself.

1. *I am taking time for myself rather than keeping too busy.*
2. *I am not working such long hours that I have no time for myself.*
3. *I am not hiding from loneliness by being with people I don't enjoy being with.*
4. *I have begun to fill up my time with activities important to me.*
5. *I have stopped hiding and withdrawing into my home or apartment.*
6. *I have stopped trying to find another love relationship just to avoid being lonely.*
7. *I am content doing activities by myself.*
8. *I have stopped running from loneliness.*
9. *I am not letting the feelings of loneliness control my behavior.*
10. *I am comfortable being alone and having aloneness time.*

Friendship
"Where Has Everybody Gone?"

The support you receive from life-line friends is very important and can shorten the time it takes you to adjust to the crisis. Friends are more valuable to you than lovers right now. You can develop friends of both sexes without becoming romantically and sexually involved. Divorce is threatening to many married people, so your married friends may slip away from you.

Chapter 6

❦

Maria and I had lots of friends and family around all the time. Most weekends we'd have a barbecue or go over to her sister's place or take a picnic with two or three other couples. Since we split up none of those people ever call me or drop by. How come married people don't seem to want us around when we're single?
— Jose

As we climb the mountain, notice the different ways people handle the problems of friendship. While going through the pain of separation, some people insist on walking alone. They tend to withdraw, and they feel uncomfortable being with anybody else. You will notice others who are continually clinging to each other, as though they cannot be alone for a single minute. Always walking arm in arm, they even plan ahead so that they have no part of the journey to walk by themselves. Note also how few people continue to have any communication with friends from the days of their love relationship.

It appears that we have to find new friends as we journey up the path. On this stage of our climb, finding friends seems to be a very difficult problem.

"Ain't It Great to Be Single?"

Did you ever, when you were married, look at your divorced friends with envy and wish you could be part of all of those interesting activities they were into? That you could go to the exciting events that your spouse was reluctant to go to? Well, now you are free! What do you think about the "glamorous" single life now? For most of us, especially when we first separate, the single life is not glamorous — in fact it is downright lonely and scary.

It is lonely, in part, because we tend to lose the friends we had when we were married. There are four main reasons:

• When you are ending a love relationship, you suddenly become an eligible love partner and a possible partner for one of the people in a marriage. Thus, whereas you were formerly invited to all the parties as a couple because you were safe, now you are a single person and a threat. Suddenly people are looking at you as eligible, and invitations to married friends' parties diminish accordingly.

When Bruce was first divorced, he was working side-by-side with a married woman. One day, three months after his separation, he walked by her desk and she said, "You're sure a lot more sexy now that you are separated and getting a divorce!" He responded, "I don't really believe I've changed very much, but you're looking at me differently now. It makes me feel like an object rather than a person." Though flattered by her interest, he was uncomfortable as a potential threat to her marriage.

• The second reason we tend to lose friends is that a divorce is very polarizing. Friends tend to support either the ex-husband or the ex-wife, rarely both. Thus, we tend to lose the friends who have sided with our former spouse.

• The third reason is probably the most important: the fear that "If it can happen to you, it can happen to me." Your divorce is very threatening to many marriages around you, so married "friends" slip away. Although you may feel rejected, actually it is their problem, and a reflection on them rather than on you. It is likely true that the shakier your friends' marriage, the quicker they will leave you. So, instead of feeling rejected, understand that the divorce has caused them to feel very insecure about their marriage. They withdraw from the friendship because they fear divorce may be a contagious disease!

• There is a fourth aspect of friendship which is important to understand while you are going through divorce. Married people are considered to be part of the mainstream, accepted, couple-oriented society that is the cornerstone of our way of life. Divorced people, however, become part of the singles subculture — a part of our society that is less acceptable to many. This singles subculture may not be evident until you become a single person yourself. To be pushed out of the mainstream couples culture into the singles subculture is a difficult adjustment.

There are different standards of mores and values in the singles subculture. People live a little bit "looser," a little bit freer, as if a large fraternity or sorority. At a singles gathering, "I'm divorced" becomes a valuable conversation opener, rather than a turn-off. If, as is often the case, the other person is also divorced, suddenly you have something in common and you can start talking to each other. Because the standards and mores are different, formerly-coupled people are not quite sure how to behave in the singles subculture and their first reaction can be somewhat of an emotional shock. You think, "Somebody's changed the rules, and I don't know the new rules!'"

Building Friendships
As you begin to work at rebuilding your friendships, you will find a three-stage process. In the first stage, you are so hurt, lonely, and depressed that you *avoid friends* unless it is very safe to be with them. The second stage begins when you can at last take the risk of *reaching out* to people, even when the fear of rejection looms large. The third stage is *becoming comfortable* with people, finding out that you are okay, and beginning to enjoy people without fear of being rejected.

Recently divorced persons frequently ask: "How do I make friends after a divorce? Where can I find someone to date?" The problem is that many formerly married people are out looking desperately for another love relationship, instead of just enjoying the people around them. Your goal for now should be to get to know people; some of these new acquaintances *may* become special friends or even lovers. But be patient, and go slowly. Start by expanding your "pool" of acquaintances. You can meet new people wherever you go – the grocery store; church; classes in computers, tennis, ceramics, cooking, language, personal growth; community groups; volunteer service organizations; the library; work; or just out walking the dog.

As you do begin to explore ways to make new friends, you'll find that when you are genuinely interested in the people with whom you come in contact, you are sending out "vibrations" that make people want to respond. But if you are coming across as lonely, desperate, and needy, people will not want to be around you.

The vibrations we're talking about include your body movements, the way you walk, the tone of your voice, your eye contact, your style of dress, and all the subtle ways you show how you are feeling. Experienced people in the singles subculture can often tell if you are single by your non-verbal signals. Note that even if you do not intend to do so, you are sending out some sort of signals. Are you inviting others to get to know you?

When you are ready to make friends and feel comfortable doing so, there are some specific steps you might want to take. The people who enroll in classes or groups such as the Fisher divorce and personal growth seminar have found one way to handle the rebuilding block of friendships. Participating in such a seminar may help you find deep and meaningful friendships you never thought possible. Check with local churches, colleges, Y's, mental health centers, marriage counselors, and psychologists.

If you don't find such a seminar, you may want to start a group of your own with five to ten people of both sexes who are interested in reading this book and discussing the ideas. Meet in each others' homes. Have a time for work and a time for play; spend some time in group discussion and some time just socializing with each other. Share your common concerns and feelings. It may be advantageous to have people who do not know each other, so you will not get into old patterns of gossip. This kind of discussion group can provide some of the most memorable and enjoyable evenings in your divorce process. There are literally hundreds of divorce process groups around the country (and in other countries as well) which meet weekly and use this book as a discussion guide.

Let us offer one caution in this age of "instant electronic friendships." You will find hundreds of on-line opportunities to "meet" other people: chat rooms, interest groups, singles sites... Computer friendships can be seductive, but they may keep you from making connections close to home – and that's where you really need them. (Remember that "You've Got Mail" worked out because Tom Hanks and Meg Ryan were following a screen play!) We've all read and seen films about e-mail romances, and no doubt there are a (very) few that have actually worked out beyond the virtual world. But research shows that the chances are slim that a successful face-to-face relationship will result from an on-line connection, and the energy (and fantasy) you invest there are likely to detract from your real-world growth. Use the Internet for information, for sharing ideas, for broadening your horizons. But don't let it be your primary source of friends. (And avoid it altogether as a source of romance, when the time comes for that.) Face your fears and seek out friendships in the world around you. In the long run, they will be much more satisfying, and much more likely to last.

It's Not Time for Romance Yet!

There is one concept we feel so strongly about that we want to give it special emphasis:

We suggest you not get involved in another long-term, committed love relationship until you have emotionally worked through the ending of the past love relationship!

Getting involved too soon results in carrying emotional garbage from the past relationship into the next one. You would likely marry someone just like the one you left, or someone just the opposite. Either way, the chances of the same problems occurring in the next relationship are great.

A healthy process of divorce is well described as "learning to be a single person." Many people never learned to be independent individuals before they were married. They went directly from their parental home to the marriage home. If you have not learned to be a single person, it is easy for you to *hide* in another relationship. Because your emotional needs are great when you are ending the love relationship, the comfort of another love relationship is appealing. Nevertheless, there is truth in the paradox that when you are ready to face life alone, then you are ready for marriage.

But you do need friends, and relationships with potential love partners based upon friendship. If you can build open, trusting, honest relationships with good communication and opportunities for both persons to experience personal growth, then you will probably work through the divorce process more rapidly.

Sometimes it is hard to tell whether a current relationship is limiting personal growth. The best criterion might be to ask, "Am I learning to be a single person?" If you feel you are losing your identity because of your love relationship, then you probably need to back off from it. (This is easier said than done in many instances! But we stress again how important it is to *get yourself together first!*)

We'll have more to say about growing relationships in chapter 16.

Can't We Just Be Friends?

Here is an exciting concept that you may learn for the first time: It is possible to develop a close, nonsexual, nonromantic friendship *with a member of the opposite sex!* This may be the way it happens for you: you tentatively make friends, but you are very cautious because of your fears of closeness and intimacy. The friendship becomes important, and you suddenly realize that you want very badly to maintain this friendship because it feels so good. You have a feeling down inside somewhere that if the quality of the friendship changes to a romantic, sexual one, it will be less meaningful, and it will become not so special anymore. Then you realize that you want to keep this friendship very much, and will go to great lengths to invest emotionally so that it will continue to grow. Such a friendship brings a free and exhilarating feeling. It also destroys the myth about never becoming a friend with a member of the opposite sex.

There was an old wives' tale about this kind of friendship destroying marriages, which you will now recognize as pretty phony logic. There are just as many kinds of friends as there are vegetables; and trying to make a tomato into a zucchini is difficult, if not impossible! You have learned something that will enrich your next marriage if you choose. To have friends of both sexes is one indication of a healthy relationship.

While you are working to develop new friendships, you may also be hearing a barrage of negative comments about marriage in the singles subculture. There are people who rant and rave and shout from the hilltops that they will never get married again. They compile long lists of all the painful and negative aspects of marriage. And if there is someone who decides to remarry, they even send cards of *sympathy* to the couple! You need to realize that these people are as threatened by marriage as some people are threatened by divorce. Perhaps a bad marriage led to feelings that they could never have a happy marriage, so they project their unhappy biases about marriage onto others.

There *are* a lot of unhappy married people. But much of that is due to individual personalities. Some folks would be unhappy wherever they are; the marital situation may have little to do with it. A marriage, after all, can be no happier than the two individuals in it.

Building a support system of life-line friends will shorten the time it takes you to adjust to a crisis. We all need friends who can throw us a life-line when we feel we are "drowning." A friend whom we can talk with is a *real* "life-saver" during a crisis. If you have not developed such a support system, then you need to start doing so — it may save your life.

Children Need Friends Too

Children have a problem with friendships also, often feeling isolated and "different." In some communities, they may think they are the only children of divorce in the whole school. They may not know anybody else whose parents are divorced, partly because children often don't *talk* about their parents getting divorced — it is a painful experience for them, after all. Of course, a youngster may go to school and say, "Guess what? My parents are getting divorced!" And these days, other kids are likely to respond, "Welcome to the club!"

Just as their parents tend to become friends with only formerly married and single people, children may begin to seek out friendships from families with single parents. Some children may withdraw, just as parents withdraw, and shut out all friendships whatsoever. Children who are going through the pain of their parents' divorce really need friends to talk to, but they may find it difficult to seek them out or to discuss personal concerns. Schools are concerned about this, and many are providing some sort of counseling service to help kids who shut themselves off, whether because of their parents' divorce or for other reasons. It is a valuable service for children experiencing emotional trauma. (What's more, it may go a long way toward helping prevent some of the tragic acting-out behaviors that have devastated many communities in recent years.)

Parents can help their children find somebody to talk to. Maybe it is the time for other relatives to get involved. (Caution: relatives – or friends or neighbors — who are highly emotional and who may have unresolved concerns themselves are *not* good people for the children to talk to. They are likely to be more concerned with meeting their own needs.) Also, while it is often helpful for children to talk to adults, this is the time that they need to talk to other children of divorce if possible.

We need to be aware and supportive of the needs of our kids as they are going through this process. We can encourage them to become involved with others through after-school activities and community programs. Having friends to talk with will shorten children's adjustment time, just as it does for the adults involved.

How Are You Doing?

Now might be a good time to sit down off the trail, rest for a moment, and take a look at the people around you. How long has it been since you have taken time to act interested in them, to see them as persons rather than as married, potential lovers, or people to be afraid of? Do any look interesting enough to have as a friend? You'll find it easier to make the rest of the climb up this mountain if you have a friend to hold your hand, to give you a hug, and to catch you when you slip. Why not take time right now to invest emotionally in some friendships? If you worry about rejection, remember that that person may want a friend just as much as you do!

Use the check list below to assess your progress with friendships, before you go on to the next chapter. Remember too, that friendship does not just *happen* — like anything worthwhile, it takes continuous effort !

1. *I am relating with friends in many new ways since my crisis.*
2. *I have at least one life-line friend of the same sex.*
3. *I have at least one life-line friend of the opposite sex.*
4. *I am satisfied with my present social relationships.*
5. *I have close friends who know and understand me.*
6. *People seem to enjoy being with me.*
7. *I have both single and married friends.*
8. *I have discussed ideas from this book with an important friend.*
9. *I communicate frequently about important concerns with a close friend.*

Guilt / Rejection:
Dumpers 1, Dumpees 0

Dumpers end the love relationship, while dumpees have it ended for them. The adjustment process differs since dumpers feel more guilt and dumpees feel more rejection. Dumpers start their adjustment while still in the love relationship, but dumpees start adjusting later. For the mutuals, people who jointly decide to end the relationship, the adjustment process is somewhat easier.

Chapter 7

❧

I laughed so hard.. .
It was the funniest joke I ever heard;
"He doesn't love you."
And it was even funnier
When you told it yourself;
"I don't love you. "
And I laughed so hard
That the whole house shook,
And came crashing down upon me.

— Nancy

As we begin this segment of our climb through the rebuilding blocks, let us explain where we are headed in the pages ahead. The four key concepts of this chapter are so closely intertwined that it may get confusing at times. We will be viewing the two main characters in the divorce drama as *dumper* and *dumpee*. And we will take a look at two of the very strong feelings which accompany the trauma of divorce — *guilt* and *rejection*.

We notice different groups of people on this portion of the trail. There are those who are in shock, lying on the ground trying to get their emotional wind back. Some are walking around looking guilty and trying not to look at those on the ground. Then there are others who are walking around holding hands with their former lovers! (What are *they* doing here, anyway?) Everyone looks sad.

On the ground are the *dumpees*, who were walking the pathway of life and enjoying their love relationships when their partners announced they were leaving. Sometimes the dumpees had some warning; sometimes they had none. They have a great deal of difficulty accepting the ending of their relationships. Those looking guilty are the *dumpers*. They had been thinking about leaving the relationship for some time, maybe a year or two, trying to get their courage up because they knew it would hurt their dumpees a great deal. They avoid looking at the dumpees because that makes them feel more guilty. They are usually better climbers because they had been thinking about the climb while still in the love relationship.

The ones holding hands — the *mutuals* — have decided jointly to end the relationship. Notice how few of them there are! Many people ask them why they are ending the relationship if they are such good friends. They may be very unhappy *together*, and want to end the relationship for the benefit of both. They are good climbers because they do not keep tripping each other as often as the dumpers and dumpees do. Mutuals do not enjoy the game going on between dumpers and dumpees: "Don't-let-my-ex-climb-faster-than-me."

To get us started up this portion of the trail, here is an over-simplified summary of the chapter:

Dumpers are the partners who leave the relationship, and they often feel considerable guilt; dumpees are the partners who want to hang on to the relationship, and they often experience strong feelings of rejection.

Of course it is not really as simple as that! We will get into much more detail in the pages ahead, but that gives you an advance look at the topography of the area we are about to enter.

Rejection Really Hurts

Nearly everyone has been a *dumpee* in some relationship, and no one enjoys rejection. After being rejected I become very introspective, continually examining myself to see what fault causes people to reject me. Such a self-examination can help me see myself more clearly — perhaps I will want to change the way I relate to other people. In any case, to accept the fact that feeling rejected is an expected part of the ending of a relationship — particularly a love relationship — is helpful in itself.

One step toward overcoming those feelings of rejection is to learn that the breakup of the love relationship perhaps is not my fault. As we've explored on earlier stages of the climb, everyone brings much of the past into a love relationship, and the past often determines the course of events in the relationship. Because the love relationship ended does not necessarily mean that *I* am inadequate or inferior or that there is something wrong with me. Relationships do end. Maybe that ending is not an indication of inadequacy at all!

The goal is to say, "If we have a problem, it's not because there is something terribly wrong with me. If we can't work it out, then he (she) has as much to lose as I have — maybe more." Feeling that good about yourself is a difficult goal to reach emotionally. Don't be discouraged if it takes quite a period of time to admit that the responsibility is mutual, not yours or your ex-partner's alone.

You are a worthwhile person, capable of loving and being loved. You have something special to offer to others, and that is your own unique individual self. You really ought to believe that. You could even get to feeling so good about yourself that you might believe that anyone who dumps such a neat person must have a problem!

A Little Guilt Goes a Long Way

Let us look now at guilt. It may sound strange, but the ideal may well be to have "the right amount of guilt" in your personality. If you feel no guilt at all, nothing other than being caught deters you from doing harmful things to yourself or to others. A sense of guilt is helpful in making decisions about the way one chooses to live. Unfortunately, many people experience so much guilt that they become very inhibited and controlled, unable to do the productive things which can bring happiness. The happy balance is "just enough" guilt to help maintain a sense of direction without severely restricting one's options.

Ending a love relationship tends to make one deal realistically with guilt feelings. The dumper especially, feels a large amount of guilt and says, "I'm feeling very bad about hurting somebody I love, or used to love, and I wish I could meet my needs without feeling so guilty." Guilt — or the tendency to feel it — appears to be deeply ingrained in the personality and it is difficult to overcome. The best solution appears to be rational thinking about the breakup: Listen to your head right now, not your heart (and its guilt feelings!). To end a love relationship may be *appropriate* because it has been destructive for *both* people. Under those conditions, instead of sitting around feeling guilty, those involved may be able to say, "This is probably the best decision for both of us."

One way to resolve guilt is to be punished. Bruce recalls, as a middle-school teacher, marching a misbehaving seventh-grade boy to the hall and giving him such a lecture that he began crying. Bruce felt somewhat mean and hurtful until, after school that day, the boy came to the classroom and acted as though Bruce were his long-lost friend. By punishing him, Bruce helped him overcome his guilt, and he appreciated that. Someone had cared enough to set limits for him, to pay attention when he misbehaved, and to balance the scale of justice by exacting a penalty for his behavior.

When we're feeling guilty, we often seek ways of punishing ourselves to relieve the guilt. If you see you are trying to punish yourself by setting yourself up to experience pain in relationships, maybe you should look for feelings of guilt which may be motivating your behavior.

Guilt is usually a result of not living up to some standard of behavior. If the standard is one you have freely chosen for yourself, and if it is a *possible* one, it is probably healthy to feel some guilt about falling short. But if the standard is someone else's, or society's, or the church's, and not one you have adopted for your own, your guilt feelings are not productive. Give yourself a break! It is tough enough to live up to your own standards, you can't expect to please everyone.

"But," you tell me ruefully, "staying married *is* one of my standards. I feel guilty because I didn't make the marriage work, so I failed one of my own standards." We hear you, and we understand that feeling. What we hope for you is that you can come to accept your own humanness. Nobody is perfect! Maybe you could take another look at that feeling of guilt, and consider a more useful response to the situation.

Try this one on for size: "My love partner and I aren't able to make our love relationship meet our needs and provide us happiness. It appears that, somehow or another, we didn't learn enough about loving and communicating with another person."

Remember in school, taking a test you hadn't prepared for? You probably did poorly on the test, and felt pretty bad. But you didn't fail the whole course! As an adult, you feel bad because your love relationship didn't work. Maybe you can learn from this experience so you can do better the next time. You might even help your ex learn something positive. Maybe, if you can accept your guilt as appropriate for this situation, you can change yourself into a better person who could build a productive, meaningful relationship in the future.

All Guilt is Not the Same

Let's compare two types of guilt: *appropriate guilt*, and the large reservoir of *free-floating guilt* that seems to reside within each of us. Appropriate guilt is the feeling that comes when you do something wrong or do something to hurt somebody, and feel bad about it. You've broken one of your own standards or values. When a love relationship ends, it's very appropriate to feel bad about hurting somebody else or hurting yourself. Appropriate guilt is a current process that you can work through.

Some people, however, carry long-standing guilt, usually from childhood: a large reservoir of unexpressed guilt feelings. When an event comes along and taps this reservoir of guilt, the result is such a strong sense of guilt that the person feels anxious, afraid, and fearful.

The guilt may feel overwhelming because it does not seem to be attached to anything or related to anything. It just feels huge and enormous.

If you have this sort of free-floating guilt within you, you may need help from therapy to work through and minimize the guilt and get it under control. Again, maybe the crisis of divorce will motivate you to work on something you have needed to do for a long time.

Acceptance is an important aspect of dealing with rejection and guilt. In the Fisher divorce seminars, the emotional atmosphere values acceptance of one's own feelings, and strong mutual support among the members. Being with people who help you feel accepted and supported can heal feelings of rejection rapidly. If you can find warm, supportive, accepting friends, and/or a supportive group, you will be able to heal feelings of rejection.

Rejection and guilt are closely tied to feelings of self-worth and self-love, which we will discuss further up the trail. You will find that as you improve your feelings of self-worth and self-love, you will be less devastated by life's inevitable rejections.

"Wicheryoo?"

In Bruce's classes, approximately half of the people state that they were dumpees, a third state they were dumpers, and the rest believe it was a mutual decision. We don't know if this is true of the general population of divorced people. Theoretically, of course, we would expect an equal number of dumpers and dumpees in society. However, in some situations, one person feels like a dumpee, and the other (usually a dumper who doesn't want to feel guilty) feels it was a mutual decision.

The divorce process is different in many ways for dumpers and dumpees. Research with the *Fisher Divorce Adjustment Scale* indicates that dumpees experience more emotional pain at the point of separation, especially in the areas of letting go and anger. However, if dumpers' pain could be measured while they were still in the love relationship, they would very likely show more emotional pain than the dumpees. The dumpers began to let go before they left the relationship, so they have been able to back off from being lovers to being friends with the dumpees. The dumpee, however, is usually still deeply in love with the dumper when the relationship ends. (Mutuals tend to score like dumpers, but they experience less grief.)

Occasionally there are persons who have a strong negative reaction to the words "dumper" and "dumpee." They fail to see any humor in the words. They usually have not been able to accept their divorces, and definitely have not been able to accept the idea of being a dumper or a dumpee. Despite such strong reactions, it helps to use the terms because we each need to accept the reality of a dumper and a dumpee in nearly every dissolution. You can climb the mountain of rebuilding more rapidly if you accept your role.

You may not know if you are a dumper or a dumpee. First of all, you may not have thought about it. Second, the roles may switch back and forth.

George and Margaret, for example, were childhood sweethearts who married soon after graduating from high school. During the courtship and marriage, George was continually going out with other women, leaving home for short periods of time, and acting like a dumper wanting out of the relationship. Finally, Margaret reached her "martyr's tolerance limit" and filed for divorce. Immediately George's behavior and vocabulary became those of a dumpee. Margaret and George had switched roles.

It may occur to you to ask if the person who files for dissolution in court is the dumper. Not always; filing is not the deciding factor. And you may ask if there are more male or female dumpers. We don't know about the general population, but in the divorce classes there is exactly the same percentage of male and female dumpers!

The Language of Dumping
Language is an important clue to whether you are a dumper or dumpee. It is often possible to identify someone as a dumper or dumpee just by the question he or she asks. Questioners are surprised to be recognized ("Are you a mind reader?"), until we point out that there are dumper and dumpee vocabularies.

Dumper vocabulary goes like this: "I need some time and space to get my head on straight. I need to be out of this relationship in order to get this time and space. I care for you, but don't love you enough to live with you. Don't ask me why I don't love you — I just know that I need out. I feel bad for hurting you, but there is nothing I can do about that because staying with you would also hurt you. Can we be friends?"

Dumpee vocabulary goes like this: "Please don't leave me! Why don't you love me? Tell me what is wrong with me and I will change. There must be something wrong with me, and I don't know what it is. Please tell me what I did wrong. I thought we had a good love relationship and I don't see why you want to leave. Please give me some more time before you leave. I want to be friends but I love you. Please don't leave me."

The dumper may reply: "I have been trying for a long time to tell you that I was unhappy in the relationship and that we needed to change. You just wouldn't listen. I have tried everything. I don't have any more time. You keep hanging onto me and I just want to be friends."

Dumpees at this point are likely to be hurt and to cry. They become introspective and try to understand what went wrong: "Why am I unlovable?" and "Why did our relationship have to end?" Often there is denial of feelings while the dumpee gains time to recover from the shock. The emotional pain is great for the dumpee.

The vocabulary seems universal; almost all dumpers and dumpees use the same words. The problem of timing is evident. The dumper claims to have been trying for "months and years" to do something about the problem, during much of that time thinking about leaving. The dumpee has not heard this dissatisfaction, perhaps because he or she had been "in denial" long before the dumper actually left. But when the dumper makes the announcement, the dumpee really starts denying and refusing to believe there is anything wrong. "We had such a good relationship!"

Notice the difference in priorities. The dumper wants to work on personal growth: "I have to get my head on straight." The dumpee wants to work on the relationship: "I need more time and feedback about what I need to change." Listen carefully to the words the dumpee is saying to reflect the hurt. Can you hear the anger beneath the words? But the dumpee does not express these words because the divorce is still in its honeymoon period.

During this period, the dumper is feeling much guilt, acting super-nice, willing to give the dumpee anything. The dumpee is feeling rejected, anxious for the dumper to come back, and afraid to express anger for fear it will drive the dumper even further away. The dumpee is acting super-nice also. Eventually anger replaces the feelings of guilt in the dumper and the feelings of rejection in the dumpee. Then the "divorce honeymoon" ends. This phase often begins around three months after the separation, but the timing may vary a great deal. "Good court settlements" are often negotiated while dumpers feel so guilty they will give up everything, and while dumpees will settle for anything in hopes of getting the dumper back. Dumpers: "I want out so badly that I don't care about property or money. Dumpees: "I won't ask for anything because all I want is for her (him) to come back."

There is a strategy to change the honeymoon period in case you are interested. Both parties feel better and can speed up the adjustment process when the dumpee can express anger quickly. Dumpers feel less guilty when dumpees express anger because the anger helps them deal with guilt. And dumpees feel less depression by expressing anger quicker because some depression is the result of unexpressed anger. But it is not always possible to shortcut the process because the dumper may have a need to feel guilty for a while, and the dumpee may have a need to feel rejected and depressed for a while. Working through feelings takes time.

There is an exercise that will help you understand this dumper-dumpee concept better. Find a friend to role-play with you — one of you as dumper, the other as dumpee. Begin in the middle of a room, then have the *dumper* walk out of the room saying dumper vocabulary. The dumpee should follow after, trying to keep the dumper from leaving the room by using dumpee vocabulary and behavior. Change roles so you can experience being both a dumper and a dumpee.

The symbolism of the exercise is good. The dumper is looking toward the door and trying to get out. The dumpee is looking at the back of the dumper and trying to figure out a way to prevent the leaving. (There have been dumpees who follow the partner out of the room, out to the car, and then hang on the car as the dumper drives off.) How does it feel to be a dumper in the exercise? Did you feel guilty? Did you feel the other person was hanging onto you to keep you from leaving? Did you feel reluctant to look back at the other person? Did you try to keep looking at the door? Did you feel like walking faster or maybe even running?

How does it feel to be a dumpee in the exercise? Did you want the other person to look at you? Did you feel the desire to physically grab the other person? Did you want to cry and plead with him/her not to leave? Did you feel rejection and loneliness as the other person left the room? Did you feel anger?

Good News, Bad News

At the risk of confusing this discussion further, we want to introduce a further breakdown in the dumper-dumpee categories. The words are strong and somewhat judgmental, but they are helpful in understanding better the dumper-dumpee concept. There are *good-dumpers* and *bad-dumpers*, and *good-dumpees* and *bad-dumpees*.

The good-dumper is a person who has tried to work on the love relationship in order to make it last. A good-dumper was willing to make changes, invest emotionally in trying to change, and go for marriage counseling if appropriate. But finally the dumper realized that the relationship was destructive to both people, and that it is better to end an unhealthy relationship than to continue to destroy each other. This person has the courage and strength to end the relationship, and it often takes a great deal of courage and strength.

Bad-dumpers are very similar to runaway kids. They believe the grass is greener on the other side of the fence, and all that is needed for happiness is to get out of the relationship. There is often another love relationship waiting in the wings. The bad-dumper avoids dealing with feelings and avoids looking inside at attitudes that might need to be changed. Bad-dumpers often leave quickly without even a "goodbye" conversation or explanation of their intent to end the partnership.

Good-dumpees are open, honest, willing to work on the relationship, and willing to go for counseling if appropriate. They seldom have had an affair, and have likely worked hard on communicating. They are not "innocent victims" in the sense that they too have done things to hurt the relationship. They are basically at the wrong time and place when the internal explosion and the need to be out of the relationship take place in the dumper.

Bad-dumpees are people who want out of the relationship but do not have the courage and strength to be a dumper. They make it miserable for the other person who then is forced into being the dumper.

There are few who fit perfectly into these four categories. Most of us are a combination of both good and bad dumpers or dumpees.

"Maybe I'll Come Back After All"
Another important phenomenon in the dumper-dumpee relationship is the "pain cycle." The dumper is not hurting as much when the relationship ends, but the dumpee's pain is great and motivates rapid growth and adjustment. When the dumpee is reaching a good emotional adjustment, the dumper frequently comes back and begins talking about reconciliation. This really blows the dumpee away. Gordon exclaimed, "I devoted all my emotional energy to learning to accept the ending of the relationship and I'd given up completely the hope that Juanita would come back. And then she called me!" There are many different

ways to interpret this phenomenon: Perhaps the dumper, in contrast to the sense of euphoria when she/he first left, has found it so scary out there in the single world that the security of the old love relationship looks good. "There ain't nothing out there but turkeys, and the old lover looks better all the time." Another interpretation is illustrated by dumpee anger, "She made me the dumpee. Now she wants to make me the dumper, to share the guilt!" Perhaps the best explanation comes from observing that the dumper comes back around the time the dumpee is "making it" successfully. Maybe when Juanita no longer felt the guilt and responsibility of having Gordon cling with dependency, she felt free to come back into a more equal relationship.

The typical dumpee reaction is not to take the dumper back. Dumpees find that they can make it on their own, that being single has advantages, and that it feels good to experience the personal growth they have been experiencing. If you get a dumpee to talk long enough, you will learn what was wrong with the relationship. It is only during the first period of denial that the dumpee maintains there was nothing wrong with the relationship. "Now I can see what was happening all those years! Besides, I don't see that much change and personal growth in Juanita, so why should I want the old relationship back?" At this point the dumper usually gets dumped!

Down in the Dumps
It is no wonder that dumpers and dumpees have trouble working together! The timing is different, with the dumper often starting the adjustment process while still in the relationship. The feelings are different, with the dumper tending to feel more guilt and the dumpee tending to feel more rejection (although you may experience both, whether you were a dumper or a dumpee). The attitudes are different for the two people because the dumper feels pressure to leave the relationship (wanting "personal growth" of some sort), and the dumpee fears the relationship ending. The dumper has already let go much more than the dumpee, causing problems in communicating and interacting. These different attitudes and behaviors add to the trauma of adjusting to the ending of a love relationship.

One last note on the terms *dumper* and *dumpee*. Despite differences in timing and attitudes, the two people are not that much different. Most times, both have contributed fairly equally to the relationship not working. Even differences in their attitudes are not major. Once a dumpee begins talking about the love relationship, he or she will say almost the same things about the problems that the dumper was saying, using dumpee vocabulary of course. *Timing* remains the essential element that separates the dumper from the dumpee.

This discussion of dumpers and dumpees may be a bit confusing at first (you'll want to read it over again), but it will help you to see that feelings of guilt and rejection are part of the process. Intellectual understanding is often the first step of awareness that leads to emotional understanding. Feelings of guilt and rejection are normal and typical during the ending of a love relationship — in fact you may have been experiencing these feelings before. But the ending of a love relationship tends to magnify and emphasize feelings, so you can be more aware of them and thus learn to deal with them more adequately.

Don't Dump on Your Children

The concept of dumper and dumpee has interesting implications for the children of divorce. Often the children are very angry at the parent who decided to leave, and they have a great deal of difficulty maintaining a relationship with that person. They blame the breakup on the dumper, so they take out their pain and frustration on that person. They probably fail to see that there is not that much difference between the dumper and dumpee, since both of them contributed to the ending of the relationship, only in different ways.

Almost always, the children of divorce could be looked upon as dumpees. They had very little to do with the decision, thus may feel the same frustration and anger that dumpees do. Kids, however, are not like dumpees in the sense that they often recognize that the marriage is ending — sometimes before the parents do!

Kids have a definite problem with rejection and guilt. Youngsters may have problems with guilt when they feel they are responsible for their parents' marriage not working out. The youngsters may need help in seeing that it is not their fault, that divorce is a grown-up problem.

Kids frequently feel a tremendous amount of rejection because it seems one parent is leaving and rejecting the child. The rejection a child feels is often long-lasting and can even persist into adulthood. Adults who have never fully accepted their parents' divorce find that their own love relationships can be adversely affected.

Children must be assured that they are not guilty, they are not responsible for their parents' divorce, and they are not being rejected. If the parents can maintain a quality relationship with the children after their separation and divorce, the children will be able to deal with these feelings.

How Are You Doing?

Let's rest from our climb for a while. You may want to think about the differences between dumpers and dumpees, and try to understand the feelings and attitudes on both sides of the issue. Maybe you have changed your mind about whether you are a dumper or a dumpee after reading this chapter. In any case, take time now to consider the different perspectives partners get of *what happened* during a dissolution. We hope this chapter has helped you gain a better view of the end of your own relationship. After completing the check list below and treating yourself to some time to think about these ideas, you'll be ready to move on up the mountain!

1. *I am no longer overwhelmed by feelings of guilt and/or rejection.*
2. *I can accept that I was a dumper or a dumpee or that we made a mutual decision.*
3. *I have thought about whether I was a good/bad dumper/dumpee.*
4. *I can accept that being a dumper may not necessarily mean one should feel guilty.*
5. *I can accept that being a dumpee may not necessarily mean one should feel rejected and unlovable.*
6. *I am aware of the differences in feelings and behavior between dumpers and dumpees.*
7. *I realize that both dumpers and dumpees feel emotional pain even though it may differ in timing and intensity.*
8. *I understand that in some areas I was a dumper and in other areas I was a dumpee, since this is typical of most relationships.*
9. *I understand the concept of dumper/dumpee is most meaningful at the point of separation; as I grow it becomes less and less important.*
10. *I have looked at my life patterns to see if rejection or guilt feelings have controlled much of my behavior.*
11. *I am working to overcome the influence of rejection and guilt in my life.*

Grief
"There's This Terrible Feeling of Loss"

Grief is an important part of your divorce process. You need to work through grief's emotions in order to let go of the dead love relationship. An intellectual grasp of the stages of grief can help you become emotionally aware of grief. Then you can do the grieving that you may have been afraid of before.

Chapter 8

Weekends are...
All the lonely hours poured into remembering,
All the lonely thoughts poured into trying to forget,
The harder we try to forget, the easier it is to remember.
The past can't die and the future can't live,
But the present exists.

If silence is deafening, then what is quiet?
Quiet is weekends and weekends are hell.
Wake up and face reality — why?
Weekends enforce reality, weekdays subdue it.

Saturday — it's a world of two plus two,
Where one has no meaning and no value.
Sunday — the body rests,
But where's the "off button" for the mind?

— "Honey"

We are now entering one of the most difficult and emotionally draining parts of the climb. All along the path sit people who are crying mournfully. Some will stop crying for a while, then suddenly start in again. Other people are trying to comfort them, but seem uncomfortable and not quite sure what to do. What is happening?

These people are experiencing grief. Whenever there is a loss of someone or something important in our lives, we suffer grief. Perhaps you — like many of the people participating in the divorce seminar — had not been aware that grieving is a part of the divorce process. For death, there is a set ritual with a funeral, casket, and acceptance that grieving is important. For divorce, there is no prescribed ritual other than the court hearing, and grief is often not acknowledged or accepted. But, the death of a love relationship is more than enough cause for us to grieve.

The Many Faces of Grief

Many forms of loss occur when we end a love relationship. Most obvious, of course, is the loss of the love partner, which many people do grieve. There are other losses: the *future plans* as a pair; the love *relationship*; the *role* of husband or wife or lover; the *status* associated with being a couple. Many changes occur as one progresses from being married through the transition to being single. For some people the loss of the relationship is as important as the loss of the partner.

There is the loss of the future. Married "till death do us part," there were plans, goals, joint careers, and a house that had become a home. Now all of these future parts of your life are no longer there. The future is a very difficult loss to accept, and many will need to grieve that loss for a long time.

The pain of ending a love relationship often forces us to look at past pain. Many people have not properly grieved a loss in the past, such as the death of a loved one. Re-experiencing a past pain intensifies the grieving process. For those who carry an unresolved loss from the past, divorce grief will be especially painful and difficult.

Similarly, a history of unfulfilled emotional needs — perhaps childhood deprivations — may become prominent during divorce grief. Dan reported that he dreamed frequently about childhood experiences on the farm while he was working through his divorce. As we talked about grief in the seminar, he realized that he was grieving the unhappiness he experienced during his lonely childhood.

Many divorced people are forced to move from the house they lived in while in the love relationship, and they may have to grieve the loss of that house. Single parents may have to grieve the loss of children when they are with the other parent. And the children must also grieve the loss of a house, a parent, a family — which are all part of their divorce process.

A Fable of Grief: The Check Mark

A favorite device of Bruce's, useful in understanding grief, is known as the "check mark" theory. It goes like this:

Once upon a time, there was a little creature called Jot, living a good life, oblivious to the Black Cloud hovering over it. Suddenly, the Black Cloud let loose, and Jot's lover went away. In the anguish of lost love, Jot tumbled down a huge slide, so long that Jot could not see the bottom of it. There were no handles to hold on the way down the scary slide, and the ride was painful, but Jot finally landed on a soft rainbow. Looking around, Jot spied stairs that led up into the sunlight again. The stairs were very difficult to climb at first, but became easier and more exciting as Jot neared the sunshine and began to feel completely renewed.

You might like to know what Jot's trip was like, since you will have to take the grief trip someday.

I hurt. This looks like a tough climb!
Why me? Wow, it's a long way up, but I'm gaining strength.
I'm so lonely. Maybe I'll slow down to catch my breath.
I'm so unlovable. It's great to have a few friends to help out.
Won't someone hold me? I'm going to make it.
Sadness is my only friend. Look at the new me.
I sigh a lot. I'm OK — you're OK.
I don't want to eat. Two steps up, sometimes one step back.
I think about her(him) all the time. Look at my new friends.
He (she) better be hurting too! I'm beginning to like myself again.
Damn the S.O.B.! It's great to be alive! I'm renewed!

Some of Jot's friends see a mean Giant Dragon with fangs who's breathing fire at the top of the slide. The dragon frightens them right past the slide. Instead, they bury their heads, and imagine they read on the Dragon's T-shirt such things as: "Don't go down the slide — you must control your emotions — don't cry or show weakness — you aren't strong enough to take any more pain — you may end up crazy!" They stay in this self-chosen hell until they somehow muster the courage to confront the Giant Dragon, only to discover that the sayings on the Dragon's T-shirt are only myths. At last Jot's friends risk the slide and they too discover the steps leading to the warm sunshine.

Are you like Jot? Do you see a Dragon? What do you see on the T-shirt? Are you willing to risk the slide into pain, in order to gain access to freedom?

This check mark offers a good perspective on the divorce grief process, and illustrates many of our fears about grieving. An intellectual understanding of the grief process may help us to emotionally understand our feelings as well. Eventually, however, each of us must allow ourselves to experience grief, not just talk about it.

Symptoms of Grief

Let's see what we can learn from a head trip. As a beginning, a list of the grief symptoms commonly felt during divorce will help you see that your feelings are much like those of others.

Many people talk continuously about their situation until they drive away their friends, and they need to seek new ones (the *"verbal diarrhea"* stage). The grieving person needs to stop talking about irrelevancies and begin to express the genuine feelings of grief. (If you find — or friends tell you — that you continually repeat yourself, this is a likely indication of a need to *express* your feelings rather than talking *about* them.) Later in this chapter you'll find some help with this.

Grief has a *push-pull effect*. Having been hurt, you have a big, empty feeling in your gut; and you expect friends to help you fill it. You try to talk with friends and get close to them, but at the same time this empty feeling — like a big wound — is very vulnerable to being hurt again. When people get too close, you tend to push them away to prevent further emotional pain. Thus, you pull people toward you emotionally, but push them away when they get too close. Quite a mixed message for your friends!

With grief, *feeling emotionally drained* and *not sleeping* are frequent problems. Many people in grief have trouble falling asleep at night without using drugs or alcohol. Often they wake up very early in the morning, unable to go back to sleep, yet too tired to get up. At a time when sleep is needed most, they have difficulty sleeping, and the hard emotional work has them tired all day long. Grief is hard work, and you will likely feel tired continuously until you have finished your grief process.

Eating is a problem during grief. You may have a feeling of tightness in your throat and find swallowing difficult. Sometimes your mouth will be very dry, also making eating difficult. You may not even have any appetite and may have to force yourself to eat. An empty feeling may occur in your stomach as though you were hungry, but you do not feel hungry. For these and other reasons, most people lose a great deal of body weight during the grief process. (Although a small percentage may actually gain appetite and weight.) During a break in one divorce seminar, several participants were comparing their loss of body weight during divorce grief. Of the six people present, all had lost at least 40 pounds! While the amount may not always be so dramatic, the unanimity is not surprising.

One of the most useful questions in the *Fisher Divorce Adjustment Scale* asks about *sighing often*. People are often not aware that they are sighing, but it is an indication to others that the person is grieving a great deal. Not only does the sigh itself release body tension, but also the deep breathing of the sigh seems to "carry feelings from the gut" that need release.

Rapid mood changes are typical during divorce grief. You have moved from the black pits of grief and finally feel good. Then, without apparent reason, you are out of control emotionally, unable to keep from crying. The whole sudden mood swing may have been triggered by a conversation with a friend or acquaintance who said something to you or did something for you. You were feeling fine and in control until then. Your change to the depths of grief again leaves that person confused and sad, not understanding what he or she did to upset you. For your part, the downer is made even worse because you feel bad about feeling so out of control. The incident is a clear sign that you have not completed your grief work yet.

There may be a sense of *loss of reality,* of being in a daze, in an unreal world. You observe the environment as though watching a movie, remote and detached from the events happening around you. You are unable to wake up from this dream to the real world.

You may experience a period of *lack of contact with your emotions.* You are afraid to trust your feelings because of your inability to control them. The emotional pain is so great, you have to protect yourself from feeling too much by deadening your emotions. You may sense an emotional "numbness."

Many people experience quite a bit of *fantasizing* during grief. You may fantasize that you see the former love partner, or that you hear his/her voice. You may fantasize that a part of your body is missing, as though your heart were removed, symbolizing the loss of the other person. This fantasizing may be frightening if you do not recognize it as a normal part of grief.

Loneliness, lack of concentration, weakness and helplessness, depression, guilt, lack of interest in sex, and perhaps even a *feeling of impotence or frigidity* may accompany grief. *Self-criticism* — a need to continually question your errors and how you would relive the past differently — persists.

Anger is a part of grief that results from the apparent unfairness of the loss. Anger directed toward the former love partner may approach rage in its intensity. We will look at it in detail in the next chapter.

Suicidal feelings are common during divorce grief. Approximately three-fourths of the participants in the divorce seminars admit to having experienced some suicidal thoughts during their grief periods. Research indicates a much higher than normal rate of actual suicides occurs among persons engaged in the divorce process.

All of these feelings can be overwhelming. *Uncontrollable mood swings, loss of reality, fantasies, depression, suicidal feelings...* one may wonder fearfully, "Am I going crazy?" For most people this is a difficult fear to discuss. And holding that fear inside makes it even scarier, even more crazy-feeling. The "craziness" is a real feeling, but is related to the situation rather than to a permanent psychological diagnosis. You may well be experiencing a normal grief reaction if you feel you are going crazy.

These grief symptoms may be handled by acknowledging them, accepting that they indicate grief work to be done, allowing yourself to feel the pain without denial. Crying, shouting, and writhing are other nondestructive actions to express your grief. Make a decision to manage the grief by deciding on an appropriate time and place to do grief work. On the job, for example, is not the time to cry and grieve. At work you must put the grief aside — "on the shelf," so to speak — and concentrate on your job. Because you have set aside time to grieve, your emotions become easier to control at other times, and you do not become caught in the grieving. But be sure you do grieve during the time you have set aside for grieving! If you do not manage the grief, it will manage you.

If you do not do your grief work, your body may express the feelings of grief in symptoms of illness. You may have simple ailments like headaches, or you may develop ulcerative colitis, arthritis, asthma, or ulcers. Unresolved grief puts a great deal of stress upon your body, and may increase your medical and hospital bills.

Often people are reluctant to take the divorce class because they do not want to experience the pain and crying of grief again. This reluctance may be translated as their need to complete grief work. Somewhere deep inside, you will know when the grief work is completed because of the feeling of letting go that you experience. You cannot be pulled down into the grief pits again!

Stages of Grief: The Work of Elisabeth Kubler-Ross

In this part of the climb it will be helpful to identify the five stages of grief. An intellectual overview will help us to work through the five stages emotionally. We are all greatly indebted to Dr. Elisabeth Kubler-Ross for her fine work in helping to clarify the stages of the grief process.

Stage 1. The first reaction to the sense of loss is *denial:* "This isn't happening to me. If I just wait a while, everything will be okay and my lover will come back." There is often a state of emotional shock, numbness, and denial of any feelings. One may enter into a robot-like phase, acting as though nothing is happening, repressing anger and becoming depressed. Best manners are extended toward the former love partner, in the hope that it is all a bad dream and that person will not really leave! No one wants to tell friends and neighbors that a love relationship is ending. Indeed, we don't want to tell ourselves!

Stage 2. As one gradually begins to accept the ending of a love relationship a feeling of *anger* develops. The anger that has been turned inward, contributing to depression, is now turned toward others. Expressing the anger feels good, but there is also concern that the other person will not return because of the anger, thus some guilt and ambivalence. The frustrations that have existed in the relationship for years begin to come out. Friends may wonder how you have tolerated that person when you have been so emotionally upset in the love relationship for so long. In turn, you may go to great lengths to convince others how terrible your former partner was, resulting in a "Catch-22" situation: you lose both ways. If you talk about how good that person is, how do you stay angry? But if you say how terrible that person is, then the question becomes why you chose to love such a terrible person in the first place! You have started working through the grief process when you admit and express the grief anger.

Stage 3. Beginning to face the fact that the love relationship is ending, yet reluctant to really let go, one may start *bargaining:* "I'll do anything if you'll just come back. I'll change my ways, and put up with anything. Just take me back!" This stage is dangerous for the divorce process because many people do get back together, for the wrong reasons — to avoid the loneliness and unhappiness of ending the love relationship. They are not choosing to live successfully with the former love partner, but rather choosing the "lesser of two evils."

Stage 4. Stage four of grief is a final *letting go* of the love relationship, and is, in a sense, the darkness before the dawn. Depression is typical during this stage, but the depression is different from that of stage one. This depression is a "blahs" feeling: "Is this all there is to life?" There is much internal dialogue about the meaning of life: "Why am I here on earth? What is the purpose of my life?" This is a stage of personal growth to build a stronger identity, to find a deeper purpose for living, and to make life more meaningful.

A number of people feel suicidal during this stage: "I've tried so long and worked so hard, and here I am down in the pits again. I don't want to let go!" Because the stage sometimes comes so long after the actual separation, people are surprised to feel so depressed again. It is discouraging to have worked so hard but feel so little progress. People who are aware of this stage tend to get through it much easier. They are comforted to realize that there is a purpose for the depression they are feeling, that it will not last long, and that it is different from that of early-stage grief.

Stage 5. This is the stage of *acceptance* of the loss of the love relationship. The person has begun to feel free from the emotional pain of grief and to feel no need to invest emotionally in the past relationship. Now one can begin to move on up the mountain toward fuller personal freedom and independence.

It is critically important to work through these five stages of grief before one enters into another love relationship.

Allow the Children to Grieve

Children, too, must grieve an important loss, although sometimes it is difficult for us as parents to let them do the grieving they need to do. We see them starting to cry because they miss their noncustodial parent, and we want to take away that pain and reassure them, "Now don't cry, it's okay. Your father (mother) will be back. You will get to see him (her) in the future." Reassurance is not necessarily what kids need, rather they need some sort of acceptance: "I know you feel very sad to have your father missing. You feel very sad living away from your father you love so much." It is easy for us to get our own emotions and guilt involved instead of allowing the child to express his or her feelings and emotions. Children will tend to cry and grieve more naturally than adults until we take away the permission and start interfering with the process.

The same may be true with the anger part of grief. The child may be very angry about being separated from a parent and having a lifestyle change. When children start expressing their anger, adults often try to take that anger away by saying, "Well, you just need to grow up and understand. Someday you'll see that what we did was normal, natural, and healthy." It is important to *allow* the children just to be angry; try saying, "I can see that you feel very angry toward your father for being gone."

Children will go through Kubler-Ross' five stages of grief. They will start out by denying that their parents are separated and believing the parents will get back together again. As they proceed through the stages of anger, bargaining, and so on, children need to be *allowed* to work through all five stages. The exercises described above, plus the check list at the end of this chapter, can be very helpful for children as well as for their parents.

Obviously, there is a difference in the children's loss because parents do not divorce the children. The relationship between child and parent will persist, it is hoped, although in many cases the child does not see the noncustodial parent much, if at all.

As with all other feelings, a parent who *shows* the child how to grieve is far more influential than the parent who *tells* children about grieving. Children will emulate a grieving parent, and will gain much from experiencing that healthy and needed release.

We hope you are helping your children of divorce to grieve, rather than hindering them by not giving permission or not showing them it is OK. Try to allow your children to work through the process described in this chapter.

Working Through Your Grief

There is a process of grief. Many people are afraid of grieving because it could show weakness, or maybe even signs of "going crazy." It is reassuring to find that other people experience many of the same feelings and symptoms of grief. We may emotionally work through the grief stages effectively, overcome our fear of grief, and feel safer in our grief work. This process gives us permission to grieve with a minimum of fear and anxiety.

goodbye

goodbye to the New House that I spent endless afternoons and weekends looking for ~ making sure that it met all the rigid requirements. I'll probably never find another house like that again. It was so much more than a house ~ it represented an end to looking, an achievement of a goal; a new beginning of the beginning. So very far away from that place I'd worked so hard to get to. God, I was so tired of searching and so grateful to have found it, and now I've lost it all.

goodbye to the home we were making for our future. goodbye to the tulips we planted in the Fall but that we never saw together in the Spring when it came time for them to bloom. goodbye to the plans we made for the nursery and fixing up the old cradle for the baby we never had.

goodbye to all that potential our new beginning was bringing us.

goodbye to the confidence and satisfaction I felt as "your mate" ~ the well defined role; knowing what was expected of me.

goodbye

I've wanted so badly to say goodbye. To let go of you. to push you swiftly and completely from my life as you have done with me.

What is it that I'm holding onto?

Promises

the good old "as-soon-as-we" promises...
degrees...
travel...
jobs...
honeymoon...
money...
funny how they changed to "as-soon-as-I" promises

I loved you because you were the other half of a marriage that I needed very badly in order to feel whole because you were the future father of our family because I needed someone to care for, to nurture, to parent; you made me feel needed.

I guess I've already said goodbye in more ways than I would have thought possible. You've been gone for a year and a half. Somehow I'm still here; all here; and no where, not even on the final decree, does it say that I am now only half a person with only 50% of the purpose, of the value that I once had. I am not trying to say goodbye to my self-worth or dignity ~ I've not really lost that ~ but rather I am trying to say goodbye to my need for your credibility stamp on those feelings in order to make them valid.

The last goodbyes are the positive ones. For they are goodbyes to the negatives.

goodbye to the feelings of enslavement

goodbye to the picky little dislikes:
    onions, mushrooms, olives and
    my flannel nightgown and
    getting up early and
    Joni Mitchell and
    my friend Alice and
    going to the zoo.

goodbye to your lack of direction and
    your lack of creativity and
    your lack of appreciation and
    your lack of sensitivity

goodbye to your indecisiveness and
    your stifled, dried-up emotions and
    your humorless sense of humor

goodbye to feeling ashamed of getting angry and showing it,
    feeling embarrassed for being silly
    feeling guilty when I knew the answer and you did not.

goodbye

Trisch

Take time now to get out your handkerchief and see if you can let go of some more grief while you rest on the trail. Now that you understand the grieving process and have permission to grieve as a mentally healthy activity, you may feel freer to do some needed grieving (maybe including some past loss also). Call upon a trusted friend, family member, clergyperson, or counselor to provide support (without interference) while you allow yourself to express the depths of your grief.

An important experiential homework assignment from the seminars that you may find helpful is to write a letter of "good-bye" to one of the areas of grief mentioned earlier in the chapter. It may be good-bye to your home, to the relationship, or to a past loss. The letter is intended to help you actually do the emotional grieving and letting go. It is a difficult assignment, so we suggest you start with one of the more superficial losses. Eventually, you can write a letter of good-bye to the major loss. The letter may or may not be mailed to another person. It is really for your own benefit. In most cases, you will not want to share the letter with the person you are grieving about.

On the preceding two pages is an excerpt from a letter of good-bye that a woman in the divorce class wrote. It will give you insight into her thoughts and feelings, and maybe it will help stimulate you to write your own letter of good-bye. Read it thoughtfully, then begin work on your own letter(s).

Now, dry your eyes and read on. As before, please be sure you have dealt thoroughly with this rebuilding block before you go on. Grief is a tough and painful stage. Do not just bury it! And do not try to get through it in the time it took you just to read this chapter. Use your lifeline friends (see chapter 6) for help as you work through your grief. The mountain will still be yours to climb when you are ready.

How Are You Doing?

Here again is a checklist for your review. Take a few minutes to answer these questions honestly, and to consider how much grief work you may have to complete before you move on up the mountain.

1. *I have given myself permission to grieve if I need to.*
2. *I am not burying the grief sadness but am trying to express it.*
3. *I now have physical and emotional energy from morning until night.*
4. *I have stopped feeling depressed most of the time.*
5. *I have no trouble concentrating.*
6. *I no longer feel like crying most of the time.*

7. *I have overcome the feeling that I am in a daze.*
8. *My emotions and moods are back in my control.*
9. *I have no trouble going to sleep and sleeping all night.*
10. *I rarely sigh now.*
11. *I notice my body weight has stabilized.*
12. *My appetite is good.*
13. *I no longer feel mechanical in my daily living habits.*
14. *I have outgrown the feeling that I am losing my mind.*
15. *I have stopped talking continuously about my crisis.*
16. *I have no thoughts of attempting suicide.*
17. *I have no more lump in my throat.*
18. *My stomach feels relaxed and at ease.*
19. *I am beginning to be emotionally close to people again.*
20. *I feel emotionally alive rather than emotionally dead.*
21. *I understand the grief process.*
22. *I have identified which of the five stages of grief I am in.*
23. *I have identified any past grief that I have not experienced and worked through.*
24. *I have identified what I need to grieve (person, relationship, future).*
25. *I am comfortable talking about my feelings of grief with a friend.*
26. *I have written a letter of good-bye to the loss I am experiencing now.*

Anger

"Damn the S.O.B.!"

You'll feel a powerful rage when your love relationship ends, whether you're the dumpee or the dumper. Those angry feelings are a natural, healthy part of being human. How you express them makes all the difference. Don't bottle your feelings up inside, but you needn't get aggressive either. You can learn to express both your divorce anger and your "everyday" anger constructively. And you can learn to reduce your anger altogether.

Chapter 9

❦

I don't know what came over me. I saw his car in the parking lot and I knew he had met his girlfriend and left in her car. I went over and let the air out of all four tires. Then I went behind the building and waited until they returned so I could watch them find his car with the tires flat. I watched them trying to solve their problem and I felt so good. I've never done anything like that before in my life. Guess I didn't know how angry I could get.

— Jean

You're approaching a point in the trail where fire is a very real danger. The hazards of anger are great during the divorce process, and if you don't deal with it effectively, your anger might start a fire that can spread to the other rebuilding blocks and keep you from making progress on the trail.

Divorce anger is extreme. Rage, vindictiveness, and overpowering bitterness are common feelings when a love relationship is ending. It is a special kind of anger that most of us have never experienced before. Married friends don't understand the strength of it unless they too have ended a love relationship.

You may be like a lot of angry folks who try to keep their anger inside and not express it. One possible result: you may become more depressed.

(Bruce's view – and that of many therapists – is that anger not expressed is an important cause of depression. The divorce process can be pretty depressing anyway, and people who fail to express their anger during the early stages of divorce often get even more down. Bob — like many therapists from a different school of thought — sees anger and depression as separate emotions. What's important to you is the major point we agree on: like other emotions, *anger needs to be expressed in healthy ways.*)

Dumpers tend not to express anger because they feel so guilty, and dumpees don't express it because they fear the other person won't come back if they do. Both are "nice" for a while, and both feel a lot of depression during the breakup.

Anger may be expressed in violent ways, of course. Given the opportunity while they are angriest, some people do commit acts of violence during the divorce process. You're lucky if you are able to restrain yourself and find more suitable methods of expressing these feelings of rage and vindictiveness.

There are more constructive ways to express anger than to destroy yourself with depression, headaches, body tension, ulcers, and the like. Also, since the fires of anger can spread to other rebuilding blocks, working through this block will result in much less trouble on other parts of the trail.

Three Phases of the Anger Rebuilding Block

The anger rebuilding block — like many of the others — falls rather naturally into three phases.

• The first phase is learning to *accept that it's okay to feel angry* — it's part of being human. There are many myths in our society that say that to be angry is to be weak, childish, destructive, and sacrilegious. (Christian tradition teaches us to "turn the other cheek." But Christ became angry and drove the money changers out of the temple! Why can't we be angry like that?)

Many of us learned growing up that it's not permissible to feel angry. Now we have to relearn that it is okay after all. This may be easy to do in your head, but it is much more difficult to do emotionally. The strong emotional reactions of others when you've become angry may make you very reluctant to accept your angry feelings now. Just remember there is a difference between your *feelings* of anger and the way you act to *express* it!

• The second phase, after acknowledging that you're human and can feel anger, is to *learn as many positive ways of expressing anger as possible* — ways that will not be destructive to yourself or to those around you. It can be done with humor, physical exercise, and other ways that we will explore in this chapter.

Let us add a caution here: One of the most destructive things that happens to many people during the divorce process is the use of children as a vehicle for expressing anger at the former spouse. Corinne makes the children into spies when they come back from visitation. Annette will not allow Russ to see the kids until he pays child support; Russ will not pay child support until Annette allows visitation. We forget about what's best for the children because we are so intent on "getting" that other person. Getting back through the kids is hitting below the belt.

For the sake of the children, if for no other reason, learn constructive methods of dealing with your anger.

• The third phase of anger is to *learn forgiveness and other ways to minimize your anger.* Those of you in the first two stages may react emotionally with a big outburst now — "I will never forgive! " Well, it's not just forgiving the other person but learning to forgive yourself as well.

Whose Anger Is It, Anyway?

You are responsible for your anger; it's your feeling, not someone else's. Although projecting blame for anger onto someone else may be a part of the process, when you get further along you must learn to take responsibility for that anger yourself.

There is a powerful anger item in the *Fisher Divorce Adjustment Scale:* "I blame my former love partner for the ending of our love relationship." People who have not yet dealt with their anger will answer "Yes" to that question. Those who have worked on their rebuilding enough to have dealt with the anger begin to realize that failure, blame, and responsibility are two-way streets. What happened was part of a complicated interaction that did not work, rather than the fault of one person.

Taking responsibility for anger takes a long time for some of us. It requires a great deal of maturity and strength to do that. It's so much easier to blame the other person! The stage of forgiveness is actually learning to forgive ourselves, and letting go of our anger.

Appropriate vs. Aggressive Anger

Have you thought about how appropriate it is to feel very angry when your love relationship ends? "What," you may ask, "is *appropriate* anger?" Anger that is related to the present situation is appropriate. Harry is frustrated because someone ran into his new car; Jan feels angry because someone has said something mean to hurt her; Sharon may become angry when she is unable to accomplish a simple task, such as threading a needle. Appropriate anger is realistic for the situation; the feeling fits the event.

Aggressive anger is out of proportion to the event. Bea is driving and, when the light turns red, she also turns red. A chance remark is made and Bart starts a fist fight. The response is not consistent with the importance of the event. Often this person is bringing up past anger that was buried, sometimes way back in childhood.

"Back When I Was a Kid..."

What about childhood and its relationship to anger? We start our lives in the womb, truly the center of our own universe. All of our needs are met while we remain completely passive. The first big trauma is birth, when we are thrust into the "cold, cruel world." We suddenly have to start bawling and screaming to get fed and changed. During the process of maturing we become more and more responsible for meeting our own needs, often a frustrating experience. Thus maturity is reached, in part, through a process of frustration and anger.

If your angry feelings were validated when you were a child, and/or if you were taught to express your angry feelings freely and in constructive ways, you're not likely to accumulate and "sandbag" anger. But if your anger was punished, and you weren't allowed to express anger in constructive ways (such as those I'll describe later in this chapter), or if you grew up among very angry people or others who pushed your normal frustration up to abnormal levels, you probably accumulated what might be called *childhood rage.*

Anger which accumulates in childhood becomes like layers around the gut, and any small event may trigger inappropriate behavior. You won't have to think very long to imagine someone you know whose anger expression is always out of proportion. Look out for such people during the divorce process. They sometimes do violent things, like running over people with cars!

Beneficial Anger

A few pages back we said it was appropriate to feel angry when your love relationship ends. In fact, it is not only appropriate but it is beneficial and productive. "What?" you say, "Anger is beneficial?" Yes, because anger helps us to let go and become emotionally distant from the former love partner. People who are unable to express anger will prolong the letting go process. They often experience a great deal of depression, stay stuck, and are unable to end the strong feelings they have for that former love partner.

Because people who divorce are likely to have had trouble expressing anger in their marriages, they have a lot of unexpressed anger. That's the bad news. The good news is that learning to express divorce anger often frees the person to express other anger from the past as well.

Victor posed a question in the seminar, "Why do we have to go through a divorce to talk about the problems that occurred five or ten years ago?" The answer is because it took the divorce anger to get those buried problems out in the open.

Why Do We Bury Our Anger?

Anger is like a fire that must be burned up into the ashes of forgiveness. Burying your anger can be like throwing more logs on the fire; you keep it smoldering, never letting it burn down to the ashes of forgiveness. You may need to learn methods of direct -- assertive, not aggressive -- expression in order to get your divorce anger fire to go out.

Many people find that obstacles from the past block the trail for them in this section, keeping them from learning about the positive aspects of anger. Theresa had been badly abused as a child and had accumulated a great deal of childhood rage. We were trying to help her express her anger and asked her what would happen if she expressed it with the therapist. Theresa was silent for a long while, and then admitted that she was afraid he would hurt her. The fear of retaliation keeps many of us from expressing anger.

Anthony came into the office with a "Buddha smile" on his face. His son was flunking out of school by doing nothing, and his daughter was running away. The smiling Buddha face is often a mask for anger. Anthony, a self-ordained minister, was unable to express his anger because he had an image to maintain: "ministers don't act angry." But his anger came out with his children through physical abuse. His children reacted with appropriate angry *feelings,* but their *behavior* was harmful and not constructive. The children needed to learn positive ways of expressing anger, but emotionally they were learning from Anthony to abuse their future children instead.

It is clear that we often learn to express anger the same way our parents did. We may learn to express it in *non-assertive* (passive) ways, *aggressive* or hostile ways, or *assertive* (direct-but-non-hostile) ways. Sometimes it is a reaction to our parents' anger that we learn. Jim saw his father throwing temper tantrums and acting childish, and he decided that he would never be like his father by acting childish around his children. So when he felt angry he became the stoic who put on the stone-face mask, like Anthony's "Buddha." His face would look like granite, but he would never admit that he was feeling angry.

Scapegoats, Martyrs and Other Anger Targets

Poor Jeannette — she was the *scapegoat* in her family. Some families have an unhealthy interaction style, whereby they need someone to blame for everything that goes wrong. They find a scapegoat and dump all of the blame upon him/her.

Bruce dealt with families like this when he was a probation officer. He was tempted at first to remove the scapegoat from the home for placement in a foster home. But he learned that if you remove the scapegoat there are two possible reactions: either the caseworker becomes the scapegoat, or another member of the family becomes the scapegoat. There will always be a scapegoat until the members of the family learn to take responsibility for their own feelings rather than projecting their unhappiness onto another. A person who has been a scapegoat in his or her family (were you?) will have great difficulty expressing anger. This person will have a great deal of childhood rage.

There is a scapegoat in almost every divorce seminar, because the scapegoat is prone to divorce. Scapegoats have to do a great deal of emotional relearning before they can overcome the feeling that they are so worthless that they do not have the right to be angry. Being the scapegoat is so destructive that one may need to seek professional counseling to escape this destructive role.

And, oh! We must not forget the *martyr*. Almost every divorce seminar has someone in it who was either a martyr or the victim of a martyr. Martyrs try to live through other persons. They completely sacrifice themselves to "helping" others. Martyrs will give to others, seemingly without limit, at great personal cost to themselves. The feeling behind martyrdom may well be genuine, but the giver does things whether he or she feels like giving or not. There is a deep, subtle process going on. The giver is not giving because he or she cares, but from the fear of losing the other person, or because giving is a way of interacting that the martyr learned at an early age. This giving, for what turn out to be selfish reasons when we look closely, will cause resentment in the other person. But the other person will find it very difficult to express this resentment and anger because the martyr's self-denying style generates a nurturing response.

The principle operating underneath this relationship is that martyrs do not have identities of their own. They try to find their identities through other people. Living through others is what makes the martyr relationship so destructive and harmful to both people. (In chapter 15 you will find an exercise which may help clarify the martyr role.)

How do you escape being a martyr if you are one yourself? Or how do you help another person to escape being a martyr? The martyr who doesn't have an identity of his or her own needs to work at finding that identity; to stop exclusively giving; to learn to accept from others as well; to feel good about himself or herself; to find an identity through relationships, activities, interests, goals; and to escape the martyr role.

Some of us have been on the receiving end of martyrdom, and we have learned so much guilt that we have difficulty expressing our anger. Quite possibly if you have been on the receiving end of the martyr relationship, you have already begun to express your anger toward that other person. But many people who have been on the brunt end have kept their anger turned in and have become martyrs themselves to the people around them. In many cases, we learn how to be martyrs by living with a martyr parent.

For some of us, learning about martyrs may be an emotionally heavy situation. Trudy watched and learned about martyrs in the seminar one evening. She went home, did not sleep all night, and called a friend to talk to the next day because it overwhelmed her to see that she had been a martyr in her marriage and had controlled her husband by making him feel guilty.

If you're a martyr, or the partner of a martyr, find a friend or a therapist to talk to so you can begin to work through your guilt feelings about martyrdom. It can also be helpful to observe that your anger may be so powerful that it is covering up other feelings, such as frustration, rejection, inferiority, hurt, or unlovableness. It can be difficult to get in touch with these feelings. Anger just seems to come more easily for many of us, even though we feel bad about it. Let learning about your anger open the door to discovering other feelings as well.

Push-Button Anger – What Triggers Yours?

A helpful exercise in the divorce seminars has been to have people list their pet peeves. What really gets *you* angry when someone pushes one of your buttons?

Elaine, so angry about Steve's efforts to gain custody of the children in court, may be feeling doubts about her abilities to parent. Charles may be so angry about Marie leaving the marriage because he is re-experiencing feelings of rejection from the past when his mother died. What are some of your pet peeves? And what are some of the feelings underneath that push your buttons and make you angry? It is worth a break on the trail to think about it for a time.

Dumpees, as we have discussed, tend to feel more anger than dumpers. That may be easier to understand if we look for other feelings underneath the anger. Consider, for example, the frustration of being out of control. Most of the power is in the hands of the dumpers. They hold the cards, and the dumpees have to take whatever hand is dealt. It is frustrating to feel out of control, and frustration can lead to anger.

How about rejection? Dumpees usually are still in love, and the people they love are suddenly saying they do not love them anymore. That is deep rejection and often leads to anger.

How about the future? The dumpee may have thought the future was all planned. Then suddenly he/she has to face being alone (and lonely), and has to develop a new life plan. This may be accompanied by fear of making it financially, which is difficult and frustrating. The dumpee feels afraid — often *really* afraid. Anger can seem to be a beautiful way to fight being afraid, and may be one way to get the adrenaline going to overcome the fear. Dumpees thus tend to feel more anger, and their scores on the *Fisher Divorce Adjustment Scale* tend to reflect that. Each person is an individual, of course, and there are some dumpers who feel a great deal of anger because of their unique situations.

Venting Divorce Anger vs. Expressing Everyday Anger

Okay, enough about how we got to this point. Now let's take a look at some constructive ways to get your anger out. The focus here will be on positive ways to express anger; ways that will not be harmful to you or to others.

We want to start by reemphasizing the important difference between the special *divorce anger* you may feel about your dissolution, and your *everyday anger* in connection with other life situations.

Keep this in mind: Divorce anger needs to be *vented and released* (by yourself or in therapy) in nondestructive ways. Everyday anger — in future relationships with friends, family, lovers, children — needs to be *expressed constructively,* directly, firmly, honestly, to encourage communication and deeper relationships.

First we'll present some methods for constructively expressing the divorce anger, then some ways for you to express your anger *whenever* it occurs in your relationships.

What Can You Do With All That Divorce Anger?

It is tempting to act on your strong desire to take your anger out on your former spouse directly. Most of us want to call up the ex and do what we can to hurt, get back, be vindictive, and vent our anger directly. *This is not helpful in most cases.* When you throw a few logs on the divorce anger fire, your ex may throw a few logs back in retaliation. Pretty soon the fire is consuming both of you. We suggest that you express your anger in other ways, such as those suggested here, rather than taking it out on your former spouse.

There are couples who have learned to express anger to each other in their relationships and are able to continue to express this anger as they go through the divorce process. However, if you — like most of us — were not able to express anger in your marriage, how do you expect to express it constructively now?

Humor is a very effective way of expelling angry feelings. Harriet was the comedian of one class. She would come to the group and say, "I don't know what to tell people when they ask me where my ex is. I don't want to tell them that he's off with another woman." One week she arrived with a big smile, "I finally decided that the next time a person asks me, I'll tell them that he croaked!" She laughs and the whole class laughs, and everybody has vented angry feelings through laughter. A sense of humor is always valuable in life, but it is especially valuable in dealing with anger.

One of the most effective ways of expressing anger is to *call a friend* and say, "I need to talk about this anger that I'm feeling toward my former spouse. I know I may not make sense sometimes. I know that I may become very emotional. And I know that some of the things that I say may not be what I'm really feeling all of the time. But right now I'm feeling really angry, and I need you to listen to me talk about my anger." A life-line support friend who will help you through these times is one of your best tools for dealing with anger.

Many people who experience divorce anger are able to use *fantasies* to help them express it. Sandy was an expert at this. She would fantasize the following incident: "I would go to the garden store and buy a sack of hot lawn fertilizer. Then in the middle of the night I would go over to my ex's house and write obscene four-letter words with the fertilizer in front of his house. Then he would read them every time he had to mow his lawn all summer long!" We have to keep remembering these are fantasies and that we should not act them out! If you do not have much self-control, possibly you should not use fantasies because you may tend to act on them, which is likely to be destructive in most cases.

Physical exercise of any sort is usually helpful. Physical games, jogging, house cleaning, beating on a rug, or anything like that is especially helpful. Anger is a source of energy and it's important to use up the energy. Physical activity is a good way. You can be more effective in expelling anger through physical exercise if you use other techniques along with it. For example, when you play a game of golf or tennis, you can fantasize that the ball is that person's head. In addition, if you can do some grunting and groaning, using your vocal cords along with physical exercise, that would be more effective. When you go jogging, with each step you can mentally picture his or her face on the ground in front of you, and you can add grunts and groans.

If you feel comfortable using *cuss words,* this can be an effective way to vent strong feelings of divorce anger. Using your vocal cords provides a vehicle for getting your gut feelings to literally come out your throat and mouth and be expelled from your body.

Try getting your feelings out by screaming. Many of us would not be comfortable screaming with people around, but maybe you can find a place to go and scream alone. Charlene was able to do this by driving her car to a private place. Then she could park for a while and do the screaming, crying, and yelling that she found so helpful to get out her anger. Her kids became aware of it and when Mother was getting upset they would say, "Mom's about ready to go to her screaming place again!"

Tears are another way which helps some people to express divorce anger. Crying is a positive, honest expression of feelings. Many people, especially males, have difficulty crying. You need to "give yourself permission to cry" — it will help you feel better. Crying is a natural body function for expressing sadness or anger.

Another effective way of getting anger out is to *write a letter* saying all of the things that you would like to say to that former lover. Write it in really big letters; maybe use a piece of crayon and write it with lots of anger. But after you have written the letter, *do not mail it.* Instead, take the letter to the fireplace and burn it up. You have both expressed and symbolically burned up your anger.

You can use the *"empty chair,"* an effective Gestalt therapy technique. Imagine that the person sitting in a vacant chair is your former love partner, and say everything that you would like to say to that person. If you are good enough at imagining, you can even switch chairs and say the things that person would say back to you. Then go back to your chair and say the things that you would like to say again.

So you see there are many ways for you to vent your *divorce anger.* You will not find all of these ways helpful to you — in fact, you may have a great deal of resistance to some and be completely unable to use them. But you are only limited by your own creativity, ingenuity, and inhibition in finding ways for anger expression.

And once again, remember that these are ways to release some of your divorce anger. We do not recommend *any* of the above methods as healthy ways to express everyday anger. We'll get to that in a moment.

Incidentally, some people are not able to express anger because of a "need" to keep it. It is like a companion. If you let go of that anger, you will not have it as a tool for punishing the other person. So you may have some sort of payoff or reward for keeping the anger. The question for you to think about is: What kind of person would you like to be? Do you like being an angry person, or would you like to let go of the anger?

Only You Can Prevent Block Fires

Anger is one of the most important rebuilding blocks because it spreads to the feelings in the other rebuilding blocks. If the fires of divorce anger are burning out of control in you, then you will have trouble working your way up the trail until you get them under control.

A great sense of relief will result from working through your anger until there is nothing but ashes left. It will free energy for other areas in your life. You can forgive yourself and the other person for the love relationship not working out. You have stopped blaming yourself; you have stopped feeling like a failure; you have found the internal peace that comes from letting go of everything that was painful. You find that you can talk to the former love partner in a calm and rational manner without becoming emotionally upset. Now you can deal with friends — either your partner's or yours — without becoming irritated. You suddenly wake up and find there is sunshine in your life instead of the stormy cloud of anger. You realize that things just happened the way they happened, and that there is no point in blaming somebody.

Zack, a fellow in the divorce class, picked up a slogan that is very useful when you work through the divorce process: "It just doesn't matter." So many things that seemed important to us before just are not anymore. Once you have reached the stage of forgiveness, you no longer need to punish or be vindictive toward the other person.

Beyond Divorce: Expressing Your Everyday Anger

We hope the preceding material has helped you learn to express your divorce anger. Now, we're going to discuss everyday, "garden variety" anger — the kind we all experience in response to the ups and downs of daily life.

First, notice that how we act (our behavior) is not the same as how we feel (our emotions). Feelings and behavior are really two different parts of who we are.

Anger is a *feeling*. Assertion and aggression are types of *behavior*. Remember Jean at the beginning of this chapter? She's the one who let the air out of her ex's tires. Jean was feeling such strong anger that her behavior was definitely aggressive. It would have been possible for her to express her anger in other ways as well. For instance, she could have been even more aggressive and acted in some violent way toward her ex himself — maybe by physically attacking him. Or she could have taken an assertive approach to expressing her anger by confronting him directly and telling him exactly how she felt: "I'm so mad at you I feel like letting the air out of your tires! You've been unfair and unreasonable...!" Of course, that is the special situation we have advised against, but you get the idea: angry *feelings* can be expressed in many different *behaviors*. Put yourself in the following situations:

You have been waiting in line for concert tickets for two hours. Two "friends" of the man in front of you walk up and say, "Hey, Joe, how about letting us in here?"

The child support check is two weeks late, and you really need the money to buy clothes for the kids before school starts next week. When you call your ex, the answer is, "Well, I had a lot of expenses from my trip to Hawaii, and I won't be able to pay you until next month."

You read in the newspaper that your state legislature has just voted itself a 20 percent raise — and voted to cut support for education by 10 percent.

Angry? Well, you should be! These situations and a thousand other examples of unfairness, abuse, thoughtlessness, and other mistreatment are good cause for anger. Never mind what you were told as a child — anger is natural, normal, healthy, and human! We all feel it at times. (If you think you *never* get angry, maybe you have already forgotten the difference between feelings and behavior. Go back and reread the paragraphs above!)

The question now is, "What *do* I do about my anger?" We have already discussed some ideas for releasing the strong feelings of divorce anger — humor, fantasies, exercise, screaming, crying, and others. These ways are helpful while you are getting rid of that powerful anger toward your former partner. But they do not give you much help for dealing with your anger in everyday situations because they are designed to release pent-up anger in a situation you are no longer in. We need methods to use in situations involving on-going relationships.

"I–Messages" and Other Fair Fighting Methods

Because anger expression is such a common problem in marriages, divorces, and remarriages, one of the important topics in the "Relationships After Divorce" seminars is to help the participants learn to express anger constructively through the techniques of "fair fighting." A number of fair-fight techniques were developed in the late 1960s by psychotherapist George Bach. Many other professionals have contributed to these procedures, and one of our favorites is the use of "I messages," first introduced as a part of the Parent Effectiveness Training programs of psychologist Thomas Gordon.

"I-messages" start with the word "I," and place the responsibility for your feelings on you, rather than blaming the other person for your anger. "I-messages" allow you to get anger and other strong feelings out of the way so that closeness, intimacy, and love may come into the relationship. "I-messages" also help you identify what it is you are feeling, rather than covering up your feelings by blaming the other person.

Learning to use "I-messages" will help you communicate with all of the loved ones around you — lovers, children, friends, relatives. We suggest you start practicing "I-messages" as a way of improving your interactions with others, and as a way of expressing anger constructively. A simple example: instead of "You *make* me mad! " try "I *get so mad* when you… !" The difference may seem subtle, but notice that, when you say "I get so mad," you accept responsibility for your own feelings. And you take back control over your feelings, rather than giving that power to someone else.

(Note that "I-messages" are great for expressing *positive* feelings as well!)

Expressing anger constructively is probably as important as anything you can do to make your love relationship productive and keeping it clear of all the garbage that accumulates. (Another cause of divorce — how many is that now?) Anger left unexpressed will grow like a volcano until it erupts. Talking out anger is the relief valve that keeps the relationship from exploding. And talking out anger usually leads to intimacy (and often to good sex). It is worth it!

Assertive Anger Expression

Anger expression has been a special interest of Bob's for many years. The assertiveness training bestseller, *Your Perfect Right,* that Bob co-authored with Michael Emmons offers a system for positive, constructive anger expression. It takes some effort, but you and your relationships will benefit a great deal. The following steps are adapted, with permission, from *Your Perfect Right:*

Before you get angry:
- *Get to know yourself and the attitudes, environments, events, and behaviors which trigger your anger.*
- *Don't set yourself up to get angry.*
- *Reason with yourself.*
- *Learn to relax.*
- *Save your anger for when it's important.*

When you get angry:
- *Develop several coping strategies for handling your anger (relaxation, physical exertion, counting to ten, calming self-talk.)*
- *Take a few moments to consider if this situation is really worth your time and energy, and the possible consequences.*
- *Decide if you want to work it out with the other person, or resolve it within yourself.*
- *Express your anger assertively. (Be spontaneous; don't let resentment build; state your anger directly; use honest, expressive language; let your posture, face, gestures, voice convey your feelings; avoid sarcasm, name-calling, put-downs, physical attacks, one-upmanship, hostility).*
- *Express concern verbally. ("I'm very angry." "I strongly disagree." "That's unacceptable to me.")*
- *Schedule some time to work things out.*
- *State your feelings directly, and accept responsibility for them.*
- *Stick to specifics and to the present situation.*
- *Work toward resolution of the problem.*

Righteous Anger

Before we end this chapter, a brief word is in order about the religious beliefs that prevent many people from showing anger. Many believe that we should "turn the other cheek," and that expressing anger is somewhat "sinful." We believe that expressing anger in a positive manner and freeing yourself from that anger is often the most spiritual thing you can do. God doesn't want us to be controlled by buried anger any more than by any other strong emotion.

Forgive and Forget

As we have noted in this chapter, not all anger is justified (appropriate), and not all anger must be expressed. Sometimes an act of forgiveness is the healthiest thing you can do. We're not saying "turn the other cheek" all the time, nor are we going back on our advice to express your anger and keep your life clear. What we're saying here is that you must make a choice as to where you're going to spend your life energy. You can't address all the wrongs in the world, nor even in your own life. Sometimes, as the old saying goes, discretion really is the better part of valor. Take a moment to decide if the situation is worth making the effort to express your anger. If it is (e.g., someone has treated your child unfairly), by all means do so assertively. If not (e.g., someone has cut you off on the freeway), take a deep breath and get on with your life.

"Smoke Gets In Your Eyes"

Don't stop climbing when you feel the fires of anger starting within you. This chapter has given you permission to feel angry, offered you ways of expressing anger positively and constructively, so you can have nothing left but ashes. The fire may smolder for a long time, but it is better to let it burn out so that you can be free. Take your time in this part of the trail, with forest fires raging around you, and be careful. It is important that you get through without destroying the people in your environment or destroying yourself. Uncontrolled anger can be very destructive.

Bruce's research indicates that the average person going through the divorce process stays angry at their ex-spouse for three years. How long will you choose to be angry at your former partner?

Children Get Angry Too!

Children of divorce experience the same type of extreme divorce anger that parents do. The daughter of one divorced parent became uncontrollably angry at her father in the swimming pool one day. She screamed at him about some very minor oversight. The anger was far stronger than the situation warranted, and was apparently a direct result of a feeling of abandonment, for which she blamed her father.

It is very easy for divorced parents not to allow their children to be angry. The custodial mother will many times try to establish a good relationship between her children and their father, even though he has not kept visitation appointments and appears to be involved in activities without the children much of the time. The mother may try to help the children to accept their father without being angry. But it is appropriate for children to be angry at the noncustodial parent who lets them down.

It is also easy for us to withdraw love when our children express anger. We may be so emotionally uptight ourselves that when children get angry, we immediately become unaccepting: "Go to your room until you can learn to behave properly!" We need to find that extra energy to listen to and accept our children's anger. But we also need to see that they do not become aggressive, have temper tantrums, or break things. Allow the children to express their anger in the same positive, constructive ways explained in this chapter. When they say that they are very angry at their father (mother) for not coming, just accept that and say, "I think it's right for you to feel angry in this situation. "

Most of us learned our emotional blocks for expressing anger through some interaction with our parents. We were punished for being angry, or we were not allowed to be angry, or we were sent to our rooms and had feelings of rejection and loss of love. It is far better for children to learn that anger is part of being human and that it is okay to express anger in a positive way.

How Are You Doing?

Check yourself with these statements before you go on. Remember to be honest with yourself!

1. *I can communicate with my former love partner in a calm and rational manner.*
2. *I am comfortable seeing and talking to my former love partner.*
3. *I no longer feel like unloading my feelings of anger and hurt on my former love partner.*
4. *I have stopped hoping that my former love partner is feeling as much emotional pain as I am.*
5. *I no longer feel so angry at my former love partner.*
6. *It is not important any more that my family, friends, and associates be on my side rather than on my former love partner's side.*
7. *I have outgrown the need to get even with my former love partner for hurting me.*
8. *I no longer blame my former love partner for the failure of our love relationship.*
9. *I have stopped trying to hurt my former love partner by letting him/her know how much I hurt emotionally.*
10. *I have overcome my anger and have begun to accept the things my former love partner has been doing.*
11. *I am expressing my anger in a positive manner that is not destructive to me or to those around me.*
12. *I am able to admit it when I feel angry rather than denying my angry feelings.*
13. *I understand the emotional blocks that have kept me from expressing anger in a positive manner.*
14. *I am able to express my anger constructively rather than venting it inappropriately.*
15. *I am reaching a stage of forgiveness rather than remaining angry.*

Letting Go
Disentangling is Hard to Do

You need to stop investing emotionally in your dead love relationship. It is easier to let go if your own life-bucket is full rather than empty. Dumpers tend to let go more quickly, often because they have let go even before they left. Failure to let go may be a symptom that you are not facing some painful feelings within yourself.

Chapter 10

❦

Stella:	*"Harry left me four years ago and he immediately remarried."*
Counselor:	*"I notice you are still wearing a wedding ring."*
Stella:	*"Yes, it's very important to me."*
Counselor:	*"And you wrote me a check for the therapy with Harry's name still on the bank account!"*
Stella:	*"I guess I just can't let go."*

Did you ever get a song in your brain that you keep humming over and over? How many songs can you think of that have to do with letting go? Here are a few to get you started:

"The Way We Were"

"Time to Say Goodbye"

"Whatcha Gonna Do (When She Says Goodbye)?"

"I Stopped Loving Her Today"

Most of us have ended a love relationship at one time or another in our lives, even if it was when we were teenagers and dating. It is interesting that this common phenomenon has been researched so little. We seem to depend a lot on the poets and song writers to teach us about ending a love relationship.

What Is This Thing Called "Disentanglement"?

Let's start with a clear idea of just what letting go is. Try this: Clasp your hands together with the fingers loosely intertwined, then pull your hands apart while you continue to clasp. That gives you an experiential description of what we mean by "disentanglement." It involves the painful letting go of all your strong emotional feelings for that other person.

The feeling of being in love is not the only thing that's hard to give up. There are also anger, bitterness and feelings of vindictiveness. A person who still talks about the former love partner a great deal, whether in endearing or angry terms, has not let go of strong feelings for the ex.

It's common for people to claim that they want to continue being friends during the "honeymoon period" of the divorce process. Then when the dumper guilt and dumpee anger set in, the desire to stay friends begins to disappear. But many people strive so hard to remain friends that they fail to let go — and fail to allow the anger to come and help them do it. As a result, it is advisable not to maintain the friendship during that early stage; wait until after you have disentangled. Trying to be friends may prolong the process and even endanger the possibility of being friends later on. (That doesn't mean you shouldn't be civil, or even cordial, just not friendly.)

Another aspect that needs to be mentioned is the "runaway syndrome." Most divorced people at some time in the process have a strong urge to run away. They want to get into a new community, away from where the former spouse is living, to avoid the pain of running into the former spouse or mutual friends.

Coleen had been married to a college professor who left her when he became involved with a young student. Driving her car down the street, Coleen saw him in his car with the younger woman. Before she could stop her car, she vomited. Needless to say, it is very painful to see that former love partner with a new mate.

If you are running toward something, such as a new job, a former home with a support system of family or friends, or anything that is an advancement in your life, maybe the move is advisable. If you are running away from dealing with the unpleasant situation, you should reconsider. You are already under a stressful situation, and a major move will only add to the stress.

Difficult as it will probably be, there may be advantages to staying in the present community and dealing with the painful feelings of seeing your former spouse and his or her friends. ("So you were married to the president of the Chamber of Commerce? I know him well.") People who move may just be burying and denying the process of letting go. Those who stay and tough it out will likely be able to see and talk with the former spouse sooner without becoming emotionally upset. They will have dealt with the disentanglement rebuilding block more effectively by confronting it.

There appears to be a connection between three key rebuilding blocks: *denying* that the love relationship is ending; *grieving* the loss; and *letting go* of the dead relationship. As we climb the trail, we may be working on all three interconnected blocks at the same time.

Don't Drag It Out

We want to talk to you dumpers for a moment. (You dumpees may listen in if you want, because we'll be talking about you.)

Dumpers often want to "be kind" to the dumpee to avoid feeling guilty, but this only prolongs the process. If you are going to be a dumper, do it with strength, courage, and firmness. It is far kinder than being timid about dumping.

Richard thought he would be a kind dumper, and made it a point to take Barbara (the dumpee) out to dinner every week, supposedly to make her feel better. But each time he did it, it was like throwing a few crumbs to a hungry cat. It kept the cat from finding other places to eat, and it kept the cat at a starvation level. Barbara failed to let go as long as there seemed to be some hope of reconciliation. Bluntness may be far kinder than "kindness" to the dumpee. Richard was being "kind" only to himself — easing his guilt feelings.

There are other situations that prolong letting go. Lengthy court hearings will drag things out. Children and pets that have to be exchanged at regular intervals may prolong the process, as may continuing to live close to each other. (The same town is okay; next door is not!) A joint business that forces you to keep dealing with each other is another delaying factor. (Business matters often do make disentanglement more difficult; weigh carefully any decisions in this area. You'll want advice from your attorney and tax advisor.)

Another problem in letting go has to do with in-law relationships. Divorce usually includes separation from the ex-partner's family as well. While in most cases the ties with in-laws are broken or much loosened at the time of divorce, the breakup may have the opposite effect. In some situations, the in-laws' emotional ties remain closer to their son- or daughter-in-law than to their own son or daughter.

All fifty states have laws that give grandparents visitation rights with their grandchildren regardless of who has custody, making it possible for many to maintain the bonds of the "family by a former marriage." (In its 1999-2000 term, the U.S. Supreme Court is reviewing a case in Washington State.)

Disentangling Is Hard Work

With or without all of these complications, the big question remains — *how* do you let go? For many of us, "How do I stop loving that person?" is the tough issue. It is much easier to let go, of course, if you have other things going for you. A good job, a good support system, friends and relatives who are helpful and supportive, some sort of internal fullness rather than emptiness — all of these will help fill the void created when the beloved person is removed.

There are some specific things you can do to help yourself let go. Start by going through the house and removing all of those things that tend to keep you thinking about your former love partner. Pictures, wedding gifts, birthday gifts, and similar mementos can be removed so that they are not a constant reminder. You may need to rearrange the furniture in the house, perhaps even to make the house look as different as possible from the way it was when you were living there as a married couple. The marriage bed is often an especially important symbol. You may need to get a new spread, move the bed to a new spot in the bedroom, put it in another room, sell the bed or even give it away.

You may want to make a collection of all those reminders of your former love relationship and store them in a box in the garage or basement. Some weekend you may choose to do some *implosive grieving,* whereby you bring out all of these mementos and set aside a period of time to grieve as heavily as possible. This heavy grief period will probably be very depressing, and we suggest you have another person around for support. Becoming as much out of control as possible in your grieving may help you to let go more rapidly. By increasing the intensity of the grief, this implosive grieving may shorten the number of weeks or months it takes you to let go fully.

Another area that is a problem for many people is dealing with phone calls, letters, and visits from — and/or for — the former love partner. If it is evident that he or she is hanging on, you may feel irritated. But the fact that you keep allowing it to happen may indicate that you have not let go either! It takes two to keep this game going. If you simply refuse to play the game, it will be easier on everyone in the long run. You will have to become assertive, or perhaps even to start hanging up the phone or returning letters unanswered and unopened.

You also can make a decision to control your thinking and fantasizing about the former love partner. Whenever you find yourself weeping about that person, think about something painful or something unpleasant in the love relationship. That will lead you to stop thinking about the person. As an alternative, you may simply choose another image or subject to concentrate on, instead of focusing on the past love.

Letting Go of Your Fears

There is a more abstract answer to the problem of letting go. Often a pattern of behavior has at its core a specific feeling — such as fear of rejection, guilt, fear that one is not lovable, or low self-worth and lack of confidence. It is surprising how often we set up our lives to feel the feeling we are most afraid of! If we fear rejection, we either consciously or unconsciously set it up to be rejected. If we have a need to feel guilty, we set up situations that make us feel guilty.

When Teresa and Patrick came for marriage counseling, his pattern of behavior was to seek rejection, and hers was to feel guilty. Their neurotic needs fit together perfectly! They went through years of marriage with her feeling guilty because he felt rejected. She set up reasons to feel guilty, thus feeding his feelings of rejection.

When love relationships end, we tend to respond with the feeling which is at the root of our behavior. If it is rejection, we feel rejected; if guilt, we feel that. Unfortunately, such a feeling may be so great that one is not strong enough to endure it and let go at the same time.

If you are having a difficult time letting go, ask yourself, "What feeling would I feel the strongest if I did let go of my ex-love?" Maybe your reluctance to let go is actually covering up your inability to face yet another painful feeling. For instance, you may be afraid to let go because it will force you to deal directly with your feelings of rejection. So, you avoid feeling rejected by not letting go. You will probably have to face that feeling directly before you will be able to let go. Get help from a life-line friend or a counselor if you feel the need for support.

Invest in Yourself

The goal of working through this rebuilding block is to emotionally invest in your own personal growth instead of in the dead relationship. There is no return on an investment in the relationship's emotional corpse. The greatest possible return comes from investment in yourself.

Helping the Children to Let Go

Children of divorce deal with letting go by letting go of the old concept of the two-parent family. Suddenly it is a one-parent family, with a custodial and a noncustodial parent. Even if there is joint custody, the children still have to deal with different lifestyles. It is hoped that the children will not have to let go of a quality relationship with both parents.

The child may have difficulty, however, in dealing with the parents' ability to let go or not. This may become an important rebuilding block for children if they continually hear from one parent about all of the good things (or bad things) the other parent is doing. If the parents have not let go of the relationship, the children will tend to get caught in either the positive or negative feelings between the parents. This will prolong the adjustment process for the children.

How Are You Doing?

Take time on the trail now to stand still and shake off those feelings from the past that keep you investing in the dead relationship. Jump up and down to feel strong inside, shake off the heavy burden you have been carrying, and find the free feeling that comes from not carrying that dead love relationship on your back.

Finally, check yourself out on the items listed below. Have you really let go?

1. *I think of my former love partner only occasionally now.*
2. *I rarely fantasize about being with my former love partner.*
3. *I no longer become emotionally upset when I think about my former love partner.*
4. *I have stopped trying to please my former love partner.*
5. *I have accepted that my former love partner and I will not get back together.*
6. *I have stopped finding excuses to talk to my former love partner.*
7. *I rarely talk about my former love partner with friends.*
8. *I have outgrown any feelings of romantic love for my former love partner.*
9. *I no longer wish to continue a sexual relationship with my former love partner.*
10. *I have given up my emotional commitment to my former love partner.*
11. *I can accept my former love partner having a love relationship with another person.*
12. *I feel like a single person rather than a person in a committed love relationship with my former love partner.*
13. *I am no longer angry at my former love partner.*

Self-Worth

"Maybe I'm Not So Bad After All!"

It is okay to feel good about yourself. You can learn to feel better about yourself, and thus gain strength to help you adjust better to a crisis. As you successfully adjust to a crisis, you will feel even better about yourself! If you are experiencing a personal identity/rebellion crisis, you may be seriously straining your love relationship.

Chapter 11

❦

When I was a child, my father continually warned me about getting a "big head" and becoming "stuck on myself." Then I went to church and learned that I had been born sinful. At school it was the jocks and the brains that got all the attention. Finally I married so there would be someone who thought I was worthwhile. It made me feel good that someone cared. But then she became a pro at pointing out my faults. I finally reached a point where I began to believe I was truly worthless. It was then that I decided to leave the marriage.

— Carl

Wow! This self-worth portion of the trail is crowded with people who appear unable to continue the climb. Some sit on rocks, dejected, without energy left to climb. Some are lying on the ground like door mats, expecting everyone to walk on them. The faces of some show the effects of criticism and feelings of worthlessness. Some seem almost invisible, as if a shield surrounds them, blending them into the background.

Notice those people who are followed everywhere by a black cloud! Rain falls on them, but not on those around them. That woman over there seems to have misplaced her black cloud for a while. She is anxiously peering over her shoulder, stumbling over rocks — can she be searching for the lost cloud? Sure enough, the cloud has caught up with her and is raining on her again, and she actually seems more content now.

The Importance of Self-Worth

In this portion of the climb, learning more about self-worth and ways to improve it are our main concerns. Self-worth — also known as "self-concept" and "self-esteem" — refers to the way you see yourself — your core beliefs about your value as a human being. Heavy stuff.

Growing up, Bruce thought he alone suffered from an affliction called "inferiority complex," never realizing that the term was used so often because many others were feeling inferior also! (Indeed, wasn't everybody?)

When the participants in the divorce seminars are asked to raise their hands if they want to improve their self-esteem — usually *all* hands go up! Do you see how important this rebuilding block is?

Have you ever wondered whether self-concept exists at birth or if it is learned later? These days, psychologists believe it's about fifty-fifty. Apparently we are born with certain tendencies, and then we learn much of how we feel about ourselves during the early years from the significant people around us, including parents and siblings, teachers, ministers, and relatives. This basic level of self-concept is later influenced strongly by peers — especially during the teen years. As an adult, a love partner becomes a primary source of validation and feedback, and greatly affects one's feelings of self-worth.

Many marriages that end in divorce developed a pattern of interaction destructive to the self-concept of one or both of the parties involved. In fact, some become so destructive that the parties may not be able to end the marriage: "I don't even deserve a divorce!" For example, a battered wife may think she *deserves* to be emotionally and physically abused. She may be unable to risk leaving the marriage because she's convinced she would not be able to make it on her own. Many people suffer serious erosion of their self-esteem in bad marriages before finally seeking relief in divorce.

But when the physical separation comes and the love relationship ends, self-concept hits an all time low. So much of a person's identity is involved in the love relationship that when the marriage fails, the identity suffers.

Bruce asked recently separated people to complete the *Tennessee Self-Concept Scale* (a paper-and-pencil psychological test designed to measure feelings of self-worth). It would be hard to find another group of people whose average score was as low as theirs. Ending a love relationship can be devastating to self-concept. In fact, feelings of self-worth at this time may be the lowest ever experienced. A low self-concept immobilizes some people emotionally, making them unable to function in their jobs, in their parenting of children, or in their interaction with others.

Further study of the self-concept scores of this same group of people showed that people with a good self-concept were better able to adjust to the ending of their love relationship. The research confirms what our common sense tells us: a good self-concept makes adjustment to a life crisis easier.

Obviously feelings of self-worth are very important to the way we live. Since ending a love relationship is usually detrimental to self-concept, most of us need to improve our feelings about ourselves after experiencing a major life crisis such as this. It is reassuring to know that self-concept can be enhanced. That is an exciting and optimistic viewpoint — you can relearn, grow, and change! You don't have to be saddled with old feelings of low self-worth.

Eleven Steps to Greater Self-Esteem
In the divorce and personal growth seminars which Bruce taught continuously for a quarter-century, changes in self-worth were among the most significant outcomes for participants during the ten weeks. What techniques are used? How do people make such big changes? Let us share with you some tools you may use to improve your own self-esteem. These are not magical, and your attitude toward yourself will certainly not change overnight, but we hope you'll try them. We think you'll be pleasantly surprised.

• **Step one** seems obvious, but is often overlooked. You must *make a decision to change*. A few years ago, it seemed that several of Bruce's clients were being followed by little black clouds — like the woman we met earlier on the trail. When there was progress in therapy, these folks would become uncomfortable, look for the cloud, and expect rain to fall!

Frustrated, Bruce decided to take a solitary walk in the mountains, hiking up the Big Thompson Canyon in the Rocky Mountains. Near the top of the trail is a little sign pointing out a Douglas fir tree uprooted by the wind. The tree had been lying on the ground long enough for the end of the trunk to bend around and continue growing toward the sunlight. The new growth was pointing toward the sky for about 20 feet. Because the old trunk's roots stick mostly out of the ground, you have to wonder how the tree could keep growing for so many years! Besides the trunk, several branches also reach from the upper side of the trunk to the sky. One of these branches is more than 30 feet high.

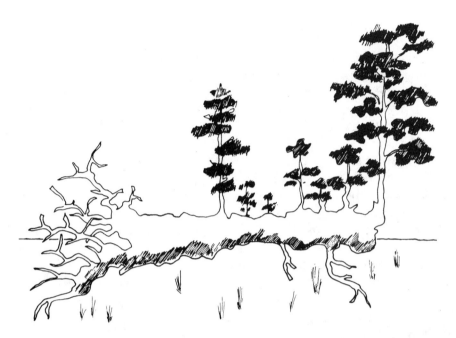

BF: "I thought to myself, as I studied this tree, that it was uprooted in its life just as a person's life is uprooted by a crisis such as a divorce. The tree sought its own fullest potential, continuing to grow and reach for the sky. I was greatly moved by the sight of this tree. I realized that there is a force within each of us that will help us to reach our full potential after a crisis has uprooted our lives. The tree's continuing reach for the sky led me to develop my belief in changing self-concept."

We need to find and listen to that inner source of emotional energy which encourages the development of our potential. If you get in touch with that source — whether it be called a religious soul, a psychological ego, the inner source, or the life force — you will be capable of making the changes that you desire. Look within yourself for this source of strength and use it to become the person you would like to be.

If you make a decision to improve your self-concept, almost everything in your life will be affected: your work; your relationships with other people; the way you parent your children; your choice of a partner in a future love relationship; and, most of all, the way you feel about yourself. Enormous changes may occur in your personality and your life if you proceed to improve your self-concept. The decision is the first and perhaps the most difficult step. If your commitment is firm, the steps which follow will come much more easily.

• **Step two** is to *change the way you look at yourself.* Most people can easily list twenty things they do not like about themselves. Why not make a list of twenty positive things you *do* like about yourself? When this assignment is given in the divorce seminars, there are groans and comments such as, "How about two instead of twenty?" One late-night phone call from a class participant started with, "Damn you! I came home from teaching school and started the list of things I like about myself. It took me an hour to come up with the first one. It took almost that long for the second one. Now it is 11 p.m. and I only have five things on my list!" That was the most important homework for him in the whole ten weeks.

This is an important task; take time to do it. Be sure to write the list down so you can do the next step.

• **Step three:** *Say positive things about yourself aloud to others.* Good things may be easier to write to ourselves than to say out loud. All the old messages inside start screaming, "Don't act stuck up and conceited!" Ignore those messages; take your list and share the comments with a friend. Get your courage up and break the negative pattern. It is *okay* to make good comments about yourself. It does take courage to say them out loud. Remember, changing your self-concept is *not* easy!

Those voices that scream inside us are especially loud if a critical person influenced us when we were growing up. In class Russ said that he could not do step three because his parents had told him so often "not to get a big head." He was a good athlete in high school, and the exercises could have helped him to build confidence in himself. But the parent voices were louder, and he had learned to be "humble." As an adult he could not say good things out loud about himself because he still felt his parents would be unhappy! That statement may sound ridiculous to you, but not to Russ. He was finally able to read his list aloud in the seminar, although with a look of pain on his face. When he finished, everyone applauded; and he said, "Boy, I feel good!"

• **Step four** is a tough one: *re-examine your relationships with others, and make changes which will help you break destructive patterns and develop the "new you."*

Much of your self-concept is validated by feedback that you get from others. Take a hard look at your relationships. Which are constructive for your self-concept? Which are really more harm than good? If you see that some of your relationships with other people are destructive to your self-concept, choose either to end those relationships or to make them more productive and positive for you. Old and established patterns of interaction are hard to change. Nevertheless, to remain in a comfortable relationship which reinforces a poor self-concept is to choose to keep a major obstacle in your own path of growth.

As a probation officer, Bruce often heard people say that a certain juvenile in trouble "only needed to find a new peer group" to solve all the problems. In reality, it's not that simple. Troubled teens generally need to change both their peer group and their feelings about themselves. They tend to seek feedback from others that basically agrees with their own self-concept. Peer group relationships powerfully reinforce the present level of self-concept. This happens partly because the group was chosen as a reflection of the self-concept: "I really feel at home with these people."

Changing your relationships may be very difficult due to your tendency to follow the old patterns and find relationships that reinforce your present level of self-esteem. But if you sincerely want to feel better about yourself, you will need to invest in positive relationships — those which help you feel good about being you!

• **Step five:** *Get rid of the negative self-thoughts in your head.* We all hear messages playing in our heads. Much of this self-talk may have originated from parents or from teachers, ministers, or other significant adults: "Be careful and don't let this success go to your head. Remember that it is sinful to be conceited and selfish. You think you're smart, don't you?" Such messages are destructive, and prevent you from improving your self-concept. They were originally designed to discipline and control. Unfortunately, they turn out to be neither helpful nor productive to us.

As adults, we choose whether we want to continue to listen to those messages or not. Say your own "tapes" out loud and write them down. Think about whether they are appropriate. Analyze these "parental" or "childish" messages from an "adult" viewpoint to see if they are rational and healthy at this time in your life. Then rid yourself of those that prevent progress toward feeling better about yourself.

You may need to express these feelings of not being okay in a counseling or therapy session, with life-line friends, or perhaps in self-introspection. Write these messages down or tape record them. You need to somehow "carry out the emotional garbage of the past," so you can stop letting it control and burden you now. Allow yourself to air, ventilate, express, and verbalize those old not okay messages. Then let go of them: move them out of your path toward improving your self-concept.

• **Step six** may sound like a silly activity, but it worked for Trudy, a member of one divorce seminar. *Write positive notes to yourself and pin them up around the house in prominent places*: on a mirror or on the refrigerator, for example. These notes might be compliments such as, "You have a pretty smile." The notes could come from the list of twenty positive things that you like about yourself.

Trudy came to a weekend seminar and was like an emotional corpse. She had a great deal of difficulty paying attention, but somehow this exercise rang a bell for her. She reported the next week that she had written about 100 notes to herself, even placing one on the toilet! She became a different person; her self-concept improved almost miraculously! Writing notes to herself appeared to make the big difference. Such a dramatic change is rare, but shows the potential power of *active effort*.

• **Step seven:** Open yourself up to hearing positive comments from others. People tend to hear only what they want to hear. If you have a low sense of self-worth, you will hear only the negative comments that other people make. When somebody praises you, you deny it, ignore it, or rationalize it by saying, "Oh, they're just saying that. They don't really mean it." Some people protect themselves from hearing anything positive because their basic self-concept says that those positive comments do not fit. The next time a person praises you or compliments you, try to let that compliment soak in, rather than defending yourself against hearing it. This may be hard for you to do. But it is very important to break your negative pattern of hearing. When you can hear positive comments, you will feel better about yourself.

• **Step eight:** *Make a specific change in your behavior.* Determine a part of your personality which you want to change. Maybe you would like to say "hello" to more people, or to be on time to work or school, or to stop putting off small jobs, like making your bed each morning. Decide to change that behavior every day this next week. Make the change easy so that you can accomplish it and feel successful. Don't set yourself up for failure by deciding to make an impossibly big change the first week.

Perhaps you'll want to mark a check on the calendar to reward yourself a little each day. At the end of the week you can look back and say, "I accomplished it! I've changed something! I'm different *in this particular area* of my personality." After you've accomplished this first step, take a second step during the following week — another small change — and begin! If you do this for several weeks in a row, you will notice that you can make significant changes which will improve your self-esteem.

• **Step nine** is one of the most fun. *Give and get more hugs!* There has been almost a fear in our society about touching other persons to show affection, probably related to our undue emphasis and Victorian attitudes toward sex; some comes from fear of rejection; some from discomfort about invading another's personal space. Many people are not aware of the difference between affectionate and sexual touching, and many avoid touching and hugging altogether. Many other societies have overcome (or never had) this hang-up and are more comfortable with affectionate touch.

A warm and meaningful hug from a friend reinforces far more than spoken words can. A hug helps heal emotional wounds, and can help improve self-concept rapidly. It frees us, warms us inside, improves our feelings of self-worth. "I'm worthwhile enough to be hugged!" may be the warmest message we can hear. If you can overcome your fear of touching and even ask for a hug (if you are not getting enough), you will make a big step toward improving your regard for yourself — and you will enjoy the process!

• **Step ten** suggests you *work hard at meaningful communication with another person.* Some of the most significant growth people experience after a divorce is accomplished while communicating with close friends. Ask for and give honest feedback about each other. Say things that you never said to anyone before. Call it as you see it! Such a dialogue provides a mirror for you to see yourself as others see you.

• **Step eleven** has to do with professional help. You may *choose to enter into a therapy relationship* in order to enhance your self-concept. It is a safe place to talk about anything you want to. Guidance from a professional may shorten the time it takes to change your self-concept. Therapy does not have the stigma that it once did. Most therapy now is personal-growth oriented, or aimed at resolving specific life issues, such as stress, rather than healing "mental illness."

If you work diligently at these exercises, you may be able to make some of the same changes that participants in the seminar are able to make. All you have to lose is your poor view of yourself! Make this part of the trail an important part of your growth. This rebuilding block will probably affect more aspects of your total life than any of the others.

Children: The Most Fragile Self-Concepts

Be aware that divorce can be very damaging to a child's self-concept also. Suddenly life has been uprooted. Children feel rejected, lonely, alienated, and perhaps guilty, questioning what they did wrong that contributed to their parents' divorce.

Children's adjustment to divorce may be complicated if they are also going through certain growth stages which are, of themselves, threatening to self-concept. As a prime example, there is some evidence that the junior high years are the most difficult years in growth and development for most children. We have listened to many adults talk about the painful difficulties of their junior high years. Puberty means dramatic changes in the body: height; weight; sexual characteristics; body hair; and voice. Suddenly, their identity — or who they *thought* they were — is also changing. They are experiencing new attitudes and feelings, such as attraction to the opposite sex. Relationships with peers have become much more important. This rapid period of change is a real strain upon a teenager's self-concept, even under the best of conditions. So youngsters who are going through these extreme changes in themselves are also faced with the stress of their parents' divorce, the children's self-concepts are more likely to be affected.

The exercises in this chapter are helpful to share with your children. In fact, doing the exercises together is a good way to increase family communication. We suggest that you parents of divorced children take these eleven steps toward improving your own self-concept, and assist your children in following the same steps.

How Are You Doing?

Here is your checklist for this portion of the trail. Once again, allow yourself adequate time to deal with this important area. When you are comfortable with most of these items, you are probably ready to resume the climb. Take care!

1. *I am willing to work hard to improve my self-concept.*
2. *I want to improve my self-concept even though I understand that it will change many aspects of my life.*
3. *I like being the person I am.*
4. *I feel I am an attractive person.*
5. *I like my body.*
6. *I feel attractive and sexually desirable.*
7. *I feel confident most of the time.*
8. *I know and understand myself.*
9. *I feel good being a woman/man.*
10. *I no longer feel like a failure because my love relationship ended.*
11. *I feel capable of building deep and meaningful relationships.*
12. *I am the type of person I would like to have for a friend.*
13. *I'm attempting to improve my self-concept by using the 11 steps listed in this chapter.*
14. *I feel what I have to say is important to others.*
15. *I feel I have an identity of my own.*
16. *I have hope and faith that I can improve my self-concept.*
17. *I am confident that I can solve the problems facing me.*
18. *I am confident that I can adjust to this crisis.*
19. *I can listen to criticism without becoming angry and defensive.*

Transition
"I'm Waking Up and Putting Away My Leftovers"

Early experiences are extremely influential in our lives. The attitudes and feelings you developed in childhood, and in relationships with family, friends, and lovers, are bound to carry over into new relationships. Some of these attitudes and feelings are helpful, others are not. Other common leftovers which cause problems for adults, include an unresolved need to rebel against prior constraints (such as parental rules), and power struggles over control. Recognize the valuable leftovers, so you can keep and nourish them; work at changing those which get in the way.

Chapter **12**

❧

"When I was a child, I spoke as a child, I understood as a child, I thought as a child; but when I became a man, I put away childish things."

— St. Paul (I Cor. 13:11)

We're well over halfway up the mountain now, and it's time to make a careful inspection of our packs before we proceed on the climb. Many of us may be carrying extra, unneeded weight. Bob remembers his first backpacking trip, when he carried a quart of water to the campsite at 11,000 feet in the Sierra Nevada Mountains in California. When he arrived at the top, he realized that he had been carrying an extra two pounds of water while climbing through five miles of snow!

Are you lugging an unnecessary load of leftovers from earlier days? You may have extra weight from your past marriage, or perhaps from relationships with parents, school friends, or others while you grew up. It's time now to put away those unneeded burdens! In this chapter, we'll take a look at the most common leftovers, where they come from, and how to deal with them.

Bruce has found that very few participants in the divorce seminars understand the importance and power of four key leftovers from their pasts: their *family of origin issues*, the influences of their *childhood experiences*, the confusing period of *rebellion*, and the frustration and hopelessness of the *power struggle*. These factors often contributed directly to the ending of the primary love relationship.

The four influences overlap and are difficult to separate from each other, but we can divide them roughly this way: Events that happened in your parental family before you were born are *family of origin* influences. Events that happened from the time you were born until you moved away from your parental home are *childhood* influences (these include events happening outside of the home such as school, church, and society). Your attempt to find an individual identity separate from the expectations of family and society is the period of *rebellion*. The *power struggle* is a combination of all the unresolved issues from all areas including the above three.

(This chapter extends the work we did in chapter 2, and is designed to help you further understand why your relationship died. If you want to learn how to make a love relationship work, we suggest you read Bruce's follow-up book, *Loving Choices*.)

Family of Origin Influences

Your *family of origin* is the family in which you grew up. Your parents, siblings, grandparents, aunts and uncles, all were important influences shaping your view of "how a family should be." Most of the ideas you gained during those years were probably healthy, some were not.

Now think about the beginning of your own love relationship. If you could imagine the bride's "significant parent" married to the groom's "significant parent," you would have an idea of what your marriage would be like in later years. (For example, Bruce's father married to his ex's grandmother. They never met but if they had, it would have been disastrous!) There is hope: we can grow beyond our family of origin patterns of interaction. But many of you can see that it was your parents in you and your partner who were divorcing each other.

Bruce asked audiences from many different countries the following question. "How many of you would like to have a marriage basically like your parents' marriage? Raise your hand." Fewer than five percent of the people raise their hand. If we don't want a marriage like our parents, what kind of marriage do we want?

Some of the family of origin influences are easy to see and understand. We tend to belong to the same political party as our parents, to join the same religious organization, to live in the same community. Some of us rebel, striking out on our own and choosing a completely separate path. Even in rebellion, however, the family of origin is an important element.

There are many other subtle influences. Bruce observed: "My love partner came from a family of powerful females; I came from a family of powerful males. One of our family of origin issues was to make a compromise as to which gender was going to be the boss. (She says I won and I say she won.)"

Another issue is how you handle money. Here's Bruce's experience: "My mother came from a family where the males were very irresponsible in handling money. She learned to be the saver and controller of money. She, of course, lived out her family of origin influences by marrying a man who was, like the men she grew up with, under-responsible in handling money." Many people married thinking they were escaping the family influences only to discover they had perpetuated them.

"That doesn't seem to fit," you observe. "If your father was the dominant and stronger personality, why was your mother the one who controlled the money?" The answer shows up in sociological studies of families, and may have been true in your house as well. The "woman of the house" often was more powerful than it appeared but *she exercised her power in a subtle and indirect manner*. Dad appeared to be in charge, but Mom held the purse strings.

It is confusing, when you thought you were marrying the father or mother you didn't have, to end up *being* a father or mother. Do you recall the explanation in our discussion of adaptive behavior patterns in chapter 4? Most of us learned to adapt when we didn't get all of our needs met in the childhood formative years. Often the adaptive behavior was to become a "father" or "mother," which resulted in giving to others what we were hoping to get.

Skeptical about family of origin influences? Here's an exercise you'll find helpful: make a list of how your most significant parent dealt with the various human emotions: anger, guilt, rejection, loneliness, fear, intimacy. Then make a similar list for yourself. When you compare the lists, you'll have a better idea of just how independent you are from the influence of your significant parent. Until we question and grow beyond the influence of our families of origin, we tend to deal with emotions in much the same way as our most significant parents.

Incidentally, when people who've made such a list are asked to identify their "most significant parent," those who are in the process of divorce quite frequently list an adult other than mother and father. When one parent was not there physically or emotionally, many of us found another "pseudo-parent" to compensate for the loss.

Those of us who didn't receive enough good parenting tend to make our partners responsible for making it up to us. There is a part in each one of us that wants our love partner to provide the parenting we didn't receive from our mothers and fathers. For some this part is large, for others it is small. When this happens in a love relationship, it often contributes to the demise of the relationship. Few love partners are happy to change diapers and nurse and make up for the parenting we didn't receive when we were little.

Family of origin issues, of course, are extremely complex and pervasive in our lives. A full discussion is beyond the scope of this book. Such issues as birth order, scapegoating, boundaries, family triangles, rituals and traditions, secrets, substance abuse, and many others are powerful influences on who we are, and how we relate to our love partners. For now, let's agree that we all need to wake up to the important effects of these family of origin leftovers, and to learn how to deal with them in our future relationships.

Healing the Influences of the Family of Origin

Linda offers one typical example of an unresolved family of origin issue. When she began to realize she married Noah because he was like the parent she had not finished making peace with, it was the beginning of the end of the relationship. This concept can be expressed in one of two ways. Linda might have married someone like her disliked parent because that relationship was comfortable and familiar, even though it was stressful and painful. Or perhaps she did *not* marry someone *like* the parent, but when she began the process of healing that parental relationship, she put Noah on the stage so she could work through the unfinished business. She told him, "you're always telling me what to do, just like my father did." It may not be true but her old anger at father for being so domineering makes it *seem* as if Noah is bossy also.

When one or both partners begins waking up and realizes the marriage is much like their parents' marriages, they have a problem. Either they have to accept their parents' marriages (instead of disdaining them), or they have to change their own marriage into what they want it to be. Without one or the other they'll probably feel their marriage is a failure. (Actually the *marriage* didn't fail; the process of healing family of origin influences was not successful.)

Childhood Influences

In the first years of life, we adopt many beliefs about ourselves, about the world, and about relationships. We learn how we feel about ourselves and our self-worth. We learn whether the world is safe, and if we can trust the people around us. We learn to feel loved and, when we don't feel loved enough, we learn to adapt. We may develop fears of rejection and abandonment. We learn if we are "OK" or "not OK."

Have you ever tried to compliment a not-OK person, one with low self-esteem? It usually goes like this: "I like your hair." *"Oh, I just washed it and can't do a thing with it."* "Such a pretty dress you have on tonight."

"What, this old thing? I found it at the Goodwill store." Complimenting such people causes them discomfort because their inner-child does not agree! They've adopted, at an early age, a belief that they are "not OK."

Any part of your growth and development that you didn't complete during your formative years, you are at some level attempting to grow through in your adult relationships. People who learned low self-worth at an early age want to improve their feelings of self-worth in their marriages. But they prevent learning what they want to learn because they don't believe the partner's compliments. "You tell me you like my hair, but you are just saying that to make me feel good."

It takes more than a few compliments to change a person's "inner-child" beliefs. If low self-esteem is a central theme of your inner child, we hope you paid special attention to chapter 10. You may want to go back to that point in the trail and do some more work. (And we urge you to carry out the homework assignments.)

Another example of a lasting childhood influence is the emotional bonding that ideally takes place in the first year of a person's life. Parents who are comfortable being intimate and who are able continually to hold their babies closely and look them in the eyes, help their children learn to be intimate. Those who didn't learn early to bond emotionally often are attempting to finish the process with adult love partners. But they may not even be aware of what emotional bonding is and may actually distance partners who attempt to become intimate. They want intimacy but "check out" — one way or another — when they begin to experience it.

Healing the Influences of Childhood

There are many examples of attempts to heal negative childhood influences. A man who has remained childlike and under-responsible may resent his partner's parental behavior; he finds another relationship or starts having an affair. But when you look at it closely, he has found another mother figure to serve his need for the mothering he didn't receive as a child. The third-party relationship may not be the problem. The inability to heal the unmet needs in the inner-child is where the person needs to heal.

If you'd like to learn more about how family of origin issues and early childhood experiences influence the adults we become, we strongly recommend Virginia Satir's classic book, *Peoplemaking* (see the Bibliography).

Rebellion: The Rocky Road to Adulthood

One of the most common leftovers we carry from our earlier experiences is the unresolved need to establish ourselves as independent persons by rebelling against our parents and their rules for us. If you or your partner carried that particular burden into your love relationship, it may have seriously jeopardized your chances of success.

There is a period of rebellion in each teenager's growth when the not-quite-adult is seeking an individual identity. Although it is a necessary part of young adult development, it causes a tremendous strain in the family relationship. Let's take a look at these key developmental stages we all must grow through on our journey toward independent adulthood. Bruce has labeled them the *shell stage*, the *rebel stage (external and internal)*, and the *love stage*.

• **The Shell stage** occurs when we are young, conforming and trying to please our parents. During these years, children have the same moral and political values, belong to the same church, and more-or-less behave in ways expected of them by their parents. The shell stage child is basically a reflection of the parents, similar to the egg that is laid by a chicken, with no identity of his/her own. Vocabulary of people in the shell stage is full of inhibitions: "What will people think? I must be careful to do what I'm supposed to do. I should follow the rules and regulations of society. I must conform to what society expects from me."

In the teen years, or sometimes later, a person begins a period of rebellion, breaking out of the shell. This process includes changing behavior patterns, doing what one "should not" do, pushing against the limits, and trying to find out how far one can go. It is very experimental at this stage, and the person is trying out different kinds of behavior. The little chicken inside is growing, beginning a life of its own, and starting to pick its way out of the shell. Vocabulary of the adult who's still working through the rebel stage is: "I've got to do it on my own. I don't need your help. If it weren't for you, I would be able to be the person I want to be. Please leave me alone!" The rebellion occurs in two stages: *external rebellion* and *internal rebellion*.

• **Rebel stage — external:** The rebellion identity crisis usually begins when the person starts being overwhelmed with feelings of internal pressure and stress — the point where the burden of carrying around the "shoulds" from family of origin, childhood, and society become too great. Having learned such behavior as over-responsibility, perfection, people pleasing, or avoiding feelings, the person is like Atlas who carried the world on his shoulders: tired of the whole situation. The rebellious partner wants to run away and may begin to act like a rebellious teenager, searching for an identity separate from the identity given by parents and society.

The behavior of people in rebellion is predictable. (Isn't it interesting that non-conforming rebellion is so predictable and conforming?) Here are some of the behaviors typical of external rebellion.

1) These people feel unhappy, stressed, smothered, and caged in. They believe their partners are responsible for their unhappiness and they project by saying things like, "As soon as you change, I will be happy." They project their unhappiness upon others and especially their love partner.

2) They like doing all the things they didn't feel comfortable doing before. They start having fun and don't understand why people don't appreciate the things they are doing because it feels so good to be doing it. Their partners say, "This isn't the same person that I married."

3) They like being under-responsible after feeling so over-responsible for all of their lives. They take a less responsible job or quit work if possible. One partner of a person in rebellion said, "I have four kids and I'm married to the oldest one."

4) They find someone they can talk to. They tell their partners, "I could never talk to you. But I found this person who understands me and really listens to me." Such people are usually younger and potential love partners. It looks like an affair but persons in rebellion will usually deny having an affair. Often everyone believes they have a sexual relationship but quite often it is platonic.

5) The vocabulary of external rebellion often goes like this:

"I care for you but I don't love you. I thought I knew what love was but now I don't know. I'm not sure I ever did love you."

"I need to be out of this relationship so I can find myself. I need emotional space away from you. I need to find my own world and I don't want to continue to be sucked into your world. I want to be me."

"You remind me of my parent and I don't want to be around anyone who is parental. I can smell a parent a mile away."

If all of this behavior is happening in a love-relationship, is it any wonder that the relationship ends? The partner usually buys into each one of the rebellious behaviors above, takes it personally, and gets bent out of shape emotionally and psychologically. Instead what they need to do is sit back and watch the show and become aware of how much growth and change can be taking place in their rebel partners. They need to realize it is an internal process going on with a person in rebellion and has very little to do with themselves. The rebels are trying to get rid of people and relationships from the past, but often dump their love partners in the process.

• **Rebel stage — internal:** When people in the process of rebelling gain enough courage and insight to look at themselves, they may be able to evolve into internal rebellion. This is when they realize the battle is within themselves and is basically a battle between their "should" part and their "want" part. They realize they are trying to separate from the expectations of their family of origin and society, and the battle is within themselves rather than against their love partners and other parental figures.

The partner of someone in rebellion often decides to wait until the rebel comes "back to sanity" again, believing that the relationship will then work. The partner considers the rebel to be the "patient," and doesn't accept any responsibility for finding a solution to the difficulty.

On the other hand, partners of rebels often become emotionally drained and bent out of shape. They have bought into the behavior of their rebellious partners, assigning them all the blame. They don't recognize that the love partnership is a system, and that they share responsibility for its problems. People who adopt this attitude toward the love relationship usually don't have the courage and emotional strength to do the personal work they need to do.

Rebellion is not an accident. The partner of a person in rebellion is usually parental. The partner has, at some level — maybe unconsciously — found a partner who needs parenting. "I know what's best for my partner, if he would only listen!" Their need for control makes it difficult for these folks to accept the rebel when he or she seems "out of control."

Instead of waiting for the storm to blow over, the partner of a person in rebellion needs to take the opportunity to look inward, and to experience as much personal growth as possible.

• **Love stage:** Eventually rebels begin to gain individual identity. This leads to being able to make choices about life based upon love instead of being based on doing the "shoulds." They feel more self-love and love for others — especially their parents.

The vocabulary of the love stage includes words of acceptance and understanding. "My parents did the best they could. They made mistakes and many times I was angry and upset with them, but they've tried hard and I understand and accept them for who they are."

This adult period is the "love stage" because the person has an independent identity, and is capable of loving another person as an adult rather than because of childish expectations. In the shell stage, one does what one *should do*; in the rebel stage, what one *should not do*; and in the love stage, what one *wants to do*. Many times behavior in the love stage will be similar to behavior in the shell stage, but the motivation behind it is entirely different. Instead of trying to please somebody else, the person is trying to please her- or himself.

Shell, Rebel, Love: A Summary

Figure 12-1 is a summary of the progression through these three stages. The chart shows some typical characteristics of the stages: vocabulary, behavior, and growth steps one may find helpful. Please recognize that these are highly individual. Although some patterns exist, each individual will be unique!

Figure 12-1. "BECOMING AN ADULT" IN THREE NOT-SO-EASY STAGES

	SHELL ○	REBEL	LOVE
VOCABULARY	"What should I do?" "I'll do whatever you want." "Take care of me." "You're everything to me." "I only want you to be happy."	"If it weren't for you..." "I don't need your help!" "Leave me alone!" "I'll do it anyway." "If it feels good, do it!"	"I've considered the alternatives." "I'll take responsibility for my choice." "It may not work, but I want to try." "You and I can both enjoy ourselves."
BEHAVIOR	Compliant, obedient. Caregiving [obliged]. Consistent, predictable. Careful, non-risking. Obligations, not choices.	Self-centered, selfish. Irresponsible, blames others. Erratic, unpredictable, careless. Childish, "plays" with young folk. Sports cars, flashy clothes, sex.	Self-enhancing, respects others. Responsible, flexible, open. Willing to risk, learns from mistakes. Makes choices based on facts.
GROWTH STEPS **self**	Begin to trust self. Begin to take risks. Begin to communicate openly. Begin to accept responsibility. Begin to try new behavior.	Try positive growth activities: classes, recreation, exercise, friendships, hobbies, community. Enter therapy [with spouse?]. Talk to spouse, friend, therapist. Maintain moral, ethical balance.	Work at self-awareness. Work at self-acceptance. Work at open, honest communications Develop close, non-romantic friends. Express anger assertively.
partner	Encourage partner's growth. Lessen dependence on partner. Cooperate in therapy if needed. Prepare for turbulence when "rebellion" starts!	Maintain stability, patience. Allow partner to grow up. Be available to talk with partner. Encourage joint therapy. Recognize rebellion is against shell, not you!	Maintain balance of independence and interdependence in close relationships.

Members of the divorce classes over the years have provided many examples of the shell/rebel/love phenomenon.

Eloise came to class very angry one night because her ex, Larry, was going through the rebel stage and causing her a lot of unhappiness. Larry had been a school principal when he was in the shell stage; but because he was looking for less administrative responsibility, he returned to full-time teaching. He developed a relationship with a woman involving "a lot of communication," helping him to find out "who he was." Larry, of course, was very excited about this new relationship. After his young son came to visit, Larry sent him home with a suitcase full of clothes and a note explaining to Eloise how great his new relationship was. Needless to say, this made her extremely angry! As it happened, we were discussing the rebel stage that week in the seminar. Eloise began to understand what was happening with Larry and his attempt to grow up and leave some of the old leftovers. She was able to let go of some of her anger as she gained an understanding of what was happening.

Gretchen became very excited as the concept was explained in class. Her husband had been a college professor and had proceeded to run off with one of his students while he was in the rebel stage. The whole thing seemed insane to her, until she heard the shell/rebel/love theory of growth and development. When she recognized that Charles was trying to get free from past expectations and become a person of his own identity, Gretchen was able to see that there was some sanity in what had appeared to be insanity. (It didn't save the marriage, but she at least felt she understood!)

Bill told the group that three years ago his marriage suffered a crisis while his wife was going through the rebel stage. When he and Charlotte went for marriage counseling, the therapist put a damper on the rebel stage and pushed Charlotte to "behave as she should" — in effect telling her to remain in the shell stage. Bill said he felt this was a mistake at the time. The marriage lasted another three years until suddenly Charlotte's growth pressures and need to rebel surfaced again, and she became "completely irresponsible," leaving the marriage and the home without even taking any clothes! Bill did not hear from Charlotte for three weeks. Looking back on those painful events, Bill observed that maybe people need to be concerned about what stage of growth and development their *therapists* are in!

Many people ask, if so many marriages end when one person is going through the rebel stage, is there any way to have the relationship *last* when a person is going through the rebel stage? The rebel who can focus inward and realize the internal interaction going on between him- or herself and the parental figures of the past may be able to deal directly with the *shoulds*, the *oughts*, and the expectations. To talk about one's rebellion rather than acting it out will be much less destructive to those near and dear at the present!

It is possible for a person to find the emotional space *within* a marriage to rebel, perhaps by becoming involved in therapy, college classes, community service, recreational or sports programs, or other creative activities. The rebel needs opportunities to experiment with behavior, to try new styles of relating, and to interact with people other than the spouse. If the couple can understand directly what is happening — that the rebel is working on an internal conflict which has little to do with the spouse — it can free the work of growth and development to be done within the person, rather than strain the love-relationship.

Rebelling love partners need to accept that their process of rebellion is an internal one and not the responsibility of other people. Their partners need to work on healing their own "inner-child," because their parenting and controlling behavior patterns result from unmet needs.

The Stormy Seas of the Power Struggle

Many couples find themselves arguing over the correct way to squeeze the toothpaste tube and which way to unroll the toilet paper. And the issues they argue over never become resolved, even if they think they are. Each person feels he or she has no power or control in the relationship. Both feel hopeless, helpless, and tired of fighting. The war may be a hot war with a lot of shouting, anger, and verbal abuse. Or it may be a cold war with the silent treatment, walking out, pouting, and other such passive ways of attempting to gain control and power.

The two people involved have stopped talking about or sharing feelings. They talk using "you" messages at each other. They have given up on finding any intimacy other than the pseudo intimacy they feel while fighting. Neither wants to lose, so both use any method they can to win the war.

The power struggle is like a pot of stew boiling over on the stove. The ingredients in the stew are all of the unresolved issues within each partner that are projected out into the relationship. The heat under the stew is a belief that someone else is responsible for one's happiness or unhappiness. They married with the belief that they would live happily ever after. It worked fine as long as the honeymoon lasted and they were happy. But when the honeymoon was over and they sometimes were less than happy, the person who was responsible for their happiness is now responsible for their unhappiness. They gave away their power when they began to believe someone else was responsible for their happiness or unhappiness.

Calming the Rough Seas of the Power Struggle

The power struggle changes into growing-pains when each person takes ownership for the unresolved problems within them. It may be concerned with the shell/rebel/love stumbling blocks discussed above, but the unresolved issues can come from anywhere in their lives or their personality. It is truly an internal power struggle projected out upon the relationship. The problems each person is unable to face and overcome become projected out into the relationship and the pot keeps boiling over.

The power-struggle is diminished when:

• each person learns to talk about feelings,
• each person starts using "I" messages instead of "you" messages,
• each person takes ownership for their unresolved problems,
• each person looks at the other person as their relationship teacher trying to help them learn more about themselves instead of projecting the hurt and blame upon the other person.

Leaving Leftovers Behind

As with any life transition, this stage of the climb is very uneven and quite difficult. Waking up and understanding why your past relationship died is usually not an easy process. It may even be quite painful: it is much easier for me to see the splinter in your eye than it is to see the log in mine.

As a juvenile probation officer, Bruce typically referred a family a week for family counseling. When each person was going to counseling to discover what they could learn and change about *themselves*, the counseling was usually helpful and successful. But when each person in the family was going for counseling because *the other person* needed to change, family counseling was usually unsuccessful.

Next time you see a person on the trail acting like a teenager, rebelling and always angry at parental, authoritative figures, you can be understanding. You know that rebel is trying to grow up emotionally, to gain an independent identity, and to become free from past expectations and controls. Even though you may want to become parental and tell the rebel how to behave, maybe you need to back off, remain adult yourself, and say, "I think that's probably the best thing for where he or she is right now." Indeed, perhaps you are still in the shell stage yourself, needing to start some rebellion of your own to improve your sense of self-worth and to find a better identity!

Do you notice that you are really making progress in the climb up the mountain? The fact that you are able to face and deal with leftovers is an indication that you are getting a much broader perspective of life and yourself. You probably could not have done much about carrying out the leftovers when you were at the bottom of the mountain trying to survive emotionally.

Children and Transition

As with their parents, most children will have some difficulty with their parents' leftovers: family of origin issues, childhood experiences, rebellion, and power struggles. A child's view of the actions of others is based on only a few years of life, and a limited repertoire of experience.

A very strong influence on children during this process is the feeling of internal pain. The growing child will interact with other significant adults as he or she learned to do with the parents, until some healing learning takes place. (Children are, after all, going through their own family of origin and childhood experiences.) If a new stepparent comes into the picture, for example, the child will tend to have the same problems with that stepparent as he/she had with his/her natural parent. This will change only when the child learns — perhaps with loving support from understanding adults — how to deal effectively with those old emotions (e.g., without destructive adaptive behaviors), and how to develop new ways of relating to adults.

Homework to Ease Your Transition

• Describe what a relationship between your partner's most significant parent and your most significant parent would be like. Would your past relationship be anything like that imaginary relationship?

• How did your family of origin influences affect the ending of your love relationship?

• Make a list of the ways your family of origin reacted to anger, love, fear, guilt, rejection, intimacy, and conflict. Make a list of the way you react to these same emotions.

• Do you perceive your former love-partner to be like one of your parents? Did your marriage begin to resemble your parent's marriage? Are you wanting a marriage that is different from your parent's marriage? How would you go about creating such a marriage?

• Do you believe you really bonded emotionally with your parents in your childhood? Are you comfortable being intimate with another person? Did you develop good feelings of self-worth in your childhood? Did you have a good relationship with both of your parents? Is your relationship with your love-partner anything like the relationship with one or both of your parents?

• This chapter identified the stages of rebellion as 1) Shell stage, 2) Rebel stage (External and Internal), and 3) Love stage. In which of these stages are your parents? Your former love partner? You?

• Did the process of rebellion have anything to do with your love relationship ending?

• Were you and your partner in a power-struggle when you ended the relationship? Did you believe that when you became married, you would live happily ever after? Do you believe someone else is responsible for your happiness and/or unhappiness? Have you identified any of the unresolved issues within you that contributed to you and your partner having a power struggle? For example: (Woman) Did you start standing up to your husband like you wished you had stood up to your father? (Man) Did you start being responsible for yourself instead of letting your wife smother-mother-do everything for you?

• What did you learn in this chapter that you need to work on before you can create a healthy relationship in the future?

How Are You Doing?

After you make sure you are ready by responding to the checklist below, go on to the next part of the journey. After a discussion of the importance of open and honest communication, we will take a look at that elusive but ever-present phenomenon, love.

1. *I am aware of the leftovers I am carrying from past relationships.*
2. *I am working on my leftovers rather than blaming others for them.*
3. *I am building relationships that will help me eliminate my leftovers.*
4. *I understand that I will have to change attitudes and awareness within me in order to rid myself of leftovers.*
5. *I am avoiding becoming emotionally involved with stray cats.*
6. *I have identified whether I am in the shell, rebel, or love stage in my growth and development.*

7. *I have thought about my spouse's growth and development in terms of the shell, rebel, and love stages.*

8. *I have thought about my parents' development in terms of the shell, rebel, and love stages.*

9. *I have identified positive ways of rebelling in contrast to more negative, destructive forms of rebelling.*

10. *I can understand and accept those elements of my spouse's behavior which were related to the rebel stage.*

11. *I realize the shell, rebel, and love stages are something that may happen several times in my life.*

12. *I am attempting to do the self-care needed to remain strong and stable.*

13. *I will attempt to get rid of as many leftovers as possible before I get into another long-term, committed love relationship.*

Openness
"I've Been Hiding Behind a Mask"

A mask is a false face — a feeling projected to others that's different from what you're really feeling. Some masks are appropriate; others are inappropriate. Masks may protect you from emotional pain you feel or fear, but wearing masks takes a great deal of emotional energy. Masks distance you emotionally from others, keeping you from building intimate relationships. When you remove your masks appropriately, you find intimacy rather than emotional pain.

Chapter **13**

After my divorce, looking for ways to meet new people, I took a small part in a little theater production. One night at rehearsal I suddenly realized that's what I'd been doing in my marriage — reciting lines. I wasn't myself, I was a character in a romantic comedy-tragedy.

— Scott

At this point in our climb most of us have learned a lot about ourselves and our former love relationships. You probably have a good idea of what happened, and we hope you're starting to think about how you'll avoid similar mistakes in the future.

One key element in successful love relationships is *openness*. Were you really honest with your partner? Are you really even honest with yourself? Or do you often hide behind a mask of "everything is okay"?

Masks and Openness

All of us wear masks at times. Sometimes you just don't want others to know what you're feeling, and a "mask" is a convenient way to hide what's going on inside — a protective shield. So the mask projects a different attitude or feeling on the surface, protecting you from the pain underneath. The pain may be fear of rejection, fear of somebody not liking you, fear of feeling inadequate, or maybe just a feeling that nobody really cares.

Young children don't wear masks as adults do — that's one of the reasons it's enjoyable and delightful to be with them. We develop our masks as we mature and become "socialized." It's not a conscious effort to deceive, the idea is simply that the masks will help us to interact with people more effectively.

However, some masks are not productive in helping us to connect with others. Instead, they keep us at a safe emotional distance from the other person. Openness, after all, can be pretty scary at times.

What Color Is Your Mask?

What are some examples of the masks we're talking about?

There are some people who, as you become emotionally close to them, immediately start making jokes and cracking humor — the *humor mask*.

A similar mask is the *"Barbie® Doll face"* mask. Whenever you start getting real with such a person and start talking about something important, you immediately see the happy, smiling, unchanging face that looks like a Barbie® Doll.

Many people going through divorce put on the mask of *"I'm so strong."* They project an image that they are going to be in control at all times and never show any weakness. But underneath lies the real turmoil of confusion and helplessness.

Like nearly all divorced people, Connie had been close to the fire of emotional intimacy. When she was married to Chris, he made her feel really warm. Then she was burned by the fire, and she grew afraid to become emotionally close to warmth from another person again. Now she distances other people emotionally in all kinds of sophisticated ways. Her *"don't mess with me"* angry mask has a reputation for miles around; it's very effective in keeping others at arm's length.

Who's Masking What from Whom?

Some masks are not very productive. In wearing them, we fight against the very things we long for: closeness, intimacy, a feeling of being safe with another person. But because we've been hurt, we're also afraid of that same intimacy and closeness.

Marian projected a mask and thought she was fooling people, that they didn't know what she was really feeling. She learned, however, that not only did others see through the mask, they saw her more clearly than she saw herself. That's one of the strange things about masks: we often fool ourselves more than we fool other people. The mask Marian thought nobody could see through allowed others to know — better than she knew herself — the pain she was feeling underneath.

A mask may keep you from getting to know yourself, rather than keeping somebody else from getting to know you. You are actually denying your own hurt from yourself. It's kind of like the ostrich: with his head in the sand he thinks no one can see him, just because he can't see them.

Masks Can Be a Burden!

Sometimes we invest a great deal of emotional energy in wearing our masks.

You're carrying around a great big burden all the time by trying to act the way you think you "should" act, rather than just being yourself. Emotional energy that is put into carrying a mask is sometimes almost overwhelming. You spend more energy carrying the mask than you do in learning about yourself, achieving personal growth or doing anything more productive.

Think about how lonely it is behind a really big, thick mask. A person is more or less living in his or her own world, and there is no one else who really knows and understands the lonely person down inside the big mask. And often the more lonely you feel the more mask you create around that loneliness. There seems to be a direct connection between the amount of loneliness you feel and the thickness of the mask you're wearing.

Anybody who has been carrying around a really heavy mask and then takes it off — in counseling or in sharing and talking with a friend — discovers a great feeling of freedom after unloading the burden. It leaves a lot more energy to do other things in life.

Jeff started wearing a mask as a child. He learned early that he had to exhibit certain "acceptable" behavior in order to get the love or the strokes or the attention that he needed. He learned to take care of other people when he really wanted to be taken care of himself. He learned to excel in school, even though he really didn't care whether he got A's or not. He learned to keep all his feelings inside rather than open up and share himself with others. Jeff grew up with the idea that love was not related to being himself. It came to him when he wore his "good boy" mask. He sure learned well not to value openness.

We develop most masks because we have not felt loved unconditionally just for being ourselves.

"Let's Do Lunch: My Mask Will Call Your Mask"

Imagine somebody trying to kiss you when you have a mask on. That's a good image for how hard it is to get close to another person when either of you is wearing a mask. It gives an idea of what a mask does for the communication between you and another person. Think of all the indirect and devious messages that are sent because of our masks! So much for openness!

There are *appropriate* masks and *inappropriate* masks, of course. An appropriate mask is one that you wear at work while dealing with other people. You project the feeling of efficiency, of competence, of "I'm here to serve you" — an evenness and a calmness that makes your work with other people more effective. But when you get off work and go home to be with a friend or a loved one, the same mask becomes inappropriate. It emotionally distances you from your partner, prevents straight communication, kills openness, and doesn't allow either of you to be yourselves. That could be appropriate when you need time just for yourself, but it's tough on intimacy!

A Matter of Choice

A mask that *you choose* to wear is probably an appropriate mask, but the mask that *chooses you* is probably inappropriate. It chooses you because you are not free to expose the feelings that are underneath. And in that sense the mask controls you. Many times you are not aware that you're wearing a mask that controls you.

Are You Ready To Take Off Your Mask?

How does one decide to take off a mask?

Some time along in the divorce process it becomes appropriate to take down some of the masks you've been wearing — to try openness instead. Is that time now?

What would happen if you took your mask off? Why not try it with some safe friends? Take off a mask and see how many times you find acceptance from those friends, rather than the rejection you expected. See how many times you become closer to somebody rather than being hurt. See how many times you feel freer than you felt before.

Here's an example of how to take off a mask with a friend you can trust. You might say something such as this: "You know, there have been times when I've not been very honest with you. When you come close to me, I become a joker. The 'joker mask' is a defense I use to protect myself from getting hurt. When I'm afraid or feel that I'm about to get hurt, I start making jokes. When I make jokes at inappropriate times it keeps me from knowing you and you from knowing me. I want you to know about my mask. When I tell you, it destroys some of the power of the mask. I'm trying to take off the mask a bit by sharing this with you." (Later in this chapter, we'll give you an exercise in "lifting the mask.")

Some friends may hurt you when you take the mask off. Those people are not able to handle the feelings you've been covering up with the mask. But, if you had your choice, which would you choose? To continue to wear the mask and not get to know that person? Or take off the mask, be open, and risk being hurt or rejected? If you are at a point emotionally where you can think ahead to a possible love-relationship in the future, what kind of a relationship would you like to have? One that would include openness, intimacy and trust? Or one where both of you wear masks of one kind or another? You *do* have the choice!

If you are wearing a mask because of the pain underneath, then part of removing the mask must be to deal with that pain. As counselors, we prefer to help our clients try to get in touch with the pain behind the mask and to express and verbalize it. While she was going through divorce, Sharon was trying to be the strong person, always in control. Her therapist encouraged her to talk about the pain and confusion she was feeling underneath, and she did, hesitantly. She learned that maybe it is appropriate to be confused when one is going through a confusing situation, and that taking down the mask and dealing with that confusion is productive. It took her several sessions in therapy to fully acknowledge her pain, and to build some constructive coping strategies which allowed her to keep the mask off.

Many who have been hurt at the end of a love relationship put on more masks than they were wearing before. Part of climbing the divorce process mountain is learning to take off some of the masks you may have put on to cover the pain of ending your love relationship.

Your Self Behind the Mask

We all have a little "S" inside of us — the "Self" — the real person down inside. We all develop our personalities — the face we show to the rest of the world — around this essence of Self. We communicate outward from that Self down inside, through the personality, to the people around us. Ideally, the communication is two-way, from one Self to another.

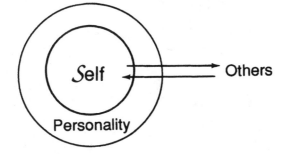

When you develop a thick shell or facade or mask to "protect" your inner Self, your communication is blocked by the mask. Instead of Self-to-Other-to-Self, your messages go from mask-to-Other-to-mask. (Of course, the other person may be wearing a mask also!)

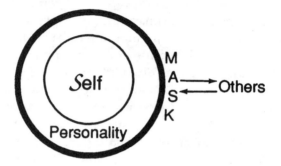

In this situation, your Self is not really involved in the communication. If you keep the mask up, your inner Self becomes starved and never sees the sunshine and never finds anything that will help it grow. Your inner Self becomes smaller — or at least less influential — until it is such a small S that you may not even be able to find your own identity. Meanwhile the shell around you grows thicker and harder all the time.

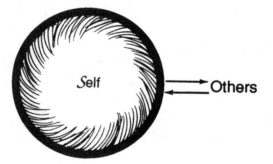

There's another variation on this theme: you may mask certain areas of your personality but not others. In the example below, there are thick spots in parts of your personality that prevent communication through them, but there are other parts of your personality through which you do communicate to other people.

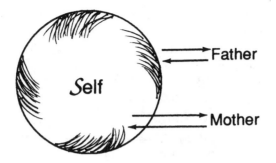

As a probation officer, Bruce found some juveniles very easy to work with, while others felt very defensive around him. After a while he noticed a pattern: a juvenile who was easy to work with usually had a good relationship with his father. He was able to communicate well with his probation officer, who was somewhat of a father figure. A young man who felt uncomfortable relating to Bruce probably also had been uncomfortable with his father. He had grown a powerful protective mask which prevented communication between his inner Self and adult males in authority. This same juvenile might find it easier to work with a female probation officer, particularly if he had learned to relate well with his mother.

Who Are You?

Do you know yourself? Are you pretty sure of your own identity? Many people use masks because they lack a sense of identity. They can't be open because they don't know who they are or what they're really feeling. They start wearing masks, and the masks begin to get thicker and thicker and the Self inside gets even harder to identify. Pretty soon these people have lost touch with their identities completely. They have support and encouragement that it needs in order to grow.

If you want to take down the masks, then you need to get as many things into the open area as possible. When you share things about yourself that you have not shared with anybody before, you are actually taking down a mask. And when you ask for feedback from other people, you often find out things about yourself that you did not know before, and this takes down some of the mask that you have used to keep you from knowing yourself.

To get rid of some of the inappropriate and unproductive masks that you are carrying around, begin to open yourself as much as possible to other people. Develop some relationships with other people that have a great deal of open, *meaningful* communication (not just talking about yourself endlessly!). These connections with others will help you take off the masks, allow your inner Self to grow, and place all your relationships on a foundation of honesty and openness — with yourself and with those you care about.

There are many people whose little boy or girl inside is extremely frightened and fearful of coming out. If you're experiencing that kind of fear, you'll find it helpful to enter into a professional counseling relationship. Counseling is a safe place to let your scared little boy or girl out — to get open with yourself.

Homework to Help You Move from Masks to Openness

• Sit down and write a list of all of the masks that you use. Look at these masks that you have listed and identify the few that are appropriate and those that are inappropriate. Identify the masks that you would like to take off because they are inappropriate.

• Focus deep inside yourself and try to get in touch with your feelings. See if you can locate the fear and/or pain underneath the masks that you wear. Why is it important to protect yourself from intimacy with others? The masks are probably hiding fear of some sort. Look at those fears and see if they are rational or perhaps fears you have developed from interacting with other people in unproductive ways.

• Find a friend or a group of friends with whom you feel safe — friends you can trust. Describe this exercise to them and let them know that you are going to try to share some of your masks with them. Explain that by revealing your mask it will not have the same power over you as it has had in the past. Share with these friends some of the fearful feelings you have found that have kept you from being open and honest and intimate with others. Ask the other people to do the same thing with you. Open, meaningful communication between you and your friends will help you get free from the masks you've been carrying around, and will help you recover some of the emotional energy they've required.

The Masks of Children

How open and honest are you with your children? Have you shared the important things happening in your relationship that directly affect them? How did you tell your children when you were ready to separate? How consistent have you been with them? Can they depend upon you to do what you say you will? In short, can they trust you?

In one Children of Divorce Workshop, a thirteen-year-old girl, when asked what kind of an animal she felt like, said, "That's easy. When I am with dad, I am one person. When I am with mother, I'm another person. I try to please both of them so they won't be so upset. I'm a chameleon."

It is so hard for us to really listen to our children when we are caught up in our own pain. We can easily be hurt and upset by their comments. No wonder they walk around on thin ice, being careful what they say and do. They often feel so responsible for us, so sympathetic with us, so afraid they will upset us even more.

Children should be encouraged to speak their truth and their thoughts and feelings, even when it's hard for us to hear. If you can't listen without judgment or criticism or getting upset, help them to find another person — someone more detached and more objective — whom they can talk to.

Their whole world has been shattered. They wonder what will happen next. When they have open and honest communication with their parents — or at least with one understanding adult — they begin to feel a part of the solution, instead of being to blame.

How Are You Doing?

Before you go on to the next portion of the climb, answer the following self-evaluation review for yourself:

1. *I'm beginning to recognize the masks I've been wearing.*
2. *I'd like to be more open with the people I care about.*
3. *I'm willing to face the fears behind my masks, even though it's scary.*
4. *I've risked sharing with a trusted friend a fear I've been hiding.*
5. *I've asked a trusted friend for some honest feedback about myself.*
6. *I'm beginning to understand the value of openness in relationships.*
7. *Openness is becoming more natural for me.*
8. *I can choose to wear an appropriate mask when it's important.*
9. *My masks don't control me any more.*

Love
"Could Somebody Really Care for Me?"

Many people need to relearn how to love, in order to love more maturely. Your capacity to love others is closely related to your capacity to love yourself. And learning to love yourself is not selfish and conceited. In fact, it is the most mentally healthy thing you can do. There are a number of specific steps you can take to increase your self-love.

Chapter **14**

❧

Love is like a bouquet of roses: you don't remember the work to get them; you only remember the love in her eyes when she received them.
Love is like sitting with my back to the fireplace. I can feel the warmth without ever seeing the fire.
Love is the greatest gift you can receive. But you have to give it to yourself.

— Ed

As we make our way up the mountain, we observe graffiti on the rocks, written by poets commenting about love. Most of what we learn about love is from the poets. Who had any homework in school concerning the nature of love? Would you take time right now to do some "homework?" In the space below write your definition of what love is. (We are talking about love between two people in a romantic relationship, not about parental love, spiritual love, or love for humankind.)

Love is:

Okay, when you are finished, turn the page and let's continue up the trail.

Thousands of people have done this exercise in the divorce adjustment seminars. It is a very difficult assignment for divorced people — or for anyone, for that matter. A typical divorced person says, "I thought I knew what love is, but I guess I don't." Many people feel inadequate about the definition of love. Love is like a diamond. You can view it from many different directions, and there is no right or wrong way of defining it. There is only the way you feel about love.

In our society many people have stereotyped love to be something you do for somebody or to somebody. Very few people have learned that love is something that should be *centered within you,* and that the basis for loving others is the love you have for yourself. Most of us recall the instruction in the Bible to "Love thy neighbor as thyself." But what if you don't love yourself?

Here is a somewhat cynical definition upon which many relationships are based: "Love is the warm feeling that you get toward somebody who meets your neurotic needs." This is a definition of neediness rather than love. Because we are not whole and complete people, but have emotional deficiencies, we try to fill those emotional deficiencies by "loving" another person. What we lack in ourselves we hope to find in the other person. In other words, many of us are "half-people" trying to love someone in order to become whole. Love coming from a whole person is more mature, and more likely to be lasting.

"Falling in Love with Love"
Perhaps you have heard the expression "warm fuzzies with a fish hook in them." A "warm fuzzy" is a nice gesture that you give somebody — such as saying, "I love you." Unfortunately, many of us are still struggling to fulfill *ourselves.* If your own life bucket is nearly empty when you say, "I love you," to another person, it probably means, "Please love me." The other person finds the warm fuzzy, swallows it, and is hooked. Saying "I love you" from an empty bucket tends to be manipulative, while love from a full bucket allows others to be themselves and to be free.

Another problem with love in our society is that falling in love is the most acceptable reason for getting married. However, "falling in love" may have more to do with loneliness than with warmth toward the other person. Falling in love to overcome loneliness is not actually love. It is rather a feeling of warmth which comes from breaking down the barriers that have kept us from being intimate with other people.

Sometimes one does not love the other person, but loves instead the idealized image of that person. When the difference is realized, one becomes disillusioned, falls out of love, and the relationship is dissolved. If a couple can grow past the stage of loving their idealized images of each other, there is a possibility that they will be able to love in a more mature manner. For some, this growth will occur in the love relationship, and their love for each other will mature. For others, maturity comes only after dissolution of an immature relationship.

We see many people loving with an immature love: Love equals doing something to somebody or for somebody; Love equals taking care of someone; Love equals achieving; Love equals always being in control; Love equals "never having to say you're sorry;" Love equals always being strong; Love equals being nice.

Shirley had believed that love equals being nice, and she was trying to improve an unhealthy love relationship. Ken asked her in class why it was not working for her to be nice. Shirley replied, "I guess I just wasn't nice enough."

Unconditional Love: "Warts and All"

Many (most?) of us, while growing up, have not received enough *unconditional* love — love that was given by parents or others just because we were, not because we earned it by being "good." We adopt *immature* forms of love toward others because we have not been loved unconditionally. That's a tough history to overcome. Nevertheless we can come to realize that mature love equals loving yourself for being who you are, and likewise loving another person for whom he or she is. When we can feel such unconditional no-matter-how-you-act love, we have learned *mature* love. Mature love allows you fully to be yourself with the loved one.

For many people it is difficult to give up the immature forms of love. That is the way they have always received their strokes, attention, and good feelings. Yet, eventually they recognize that they had to keep striving harder in order to earn the love they were seeking. It is like settling for second best, taking whatever strokes we can, rather than going all the way to get really good strokes by learning to love ourselves.

The need to be loved unconditionally is not met very often. As a child, parents' love can be seen as unconditional. After all, most parents are able to provide the basics of food, clothing, shelter, care, and physical affection. The child's limited awareness makes this seem to be unconditional love. The child has no question that this love is infinite and omnipotent.

However, with age, maturity, and awareness, one recognizes that any human being may at any point stop loving another for any reason. Or the love may be ended by death. For adults it is difficult emotionally to accept *unconditional* love.

Perhaps you can attack the problem from another direction: by learning to love yourself unconditionally. Sound like "pull yourself up by your bootstraps"? Actually it is simply an acceptance of yourself for who you are: a unique individual, with no one else like you. You can begin to feel that you are an *okay* person, and begin to feel love for yourself.

It is difficult to love yourself if you have not been loved as a child.

This is where a spiritual faith can become very important. Belief in a Supreme Being who offers the unconditional love that you have difficulty giving yourself can bring you one of the greatest benefits of spiritual life. The person who has developed a spiritual relationship with a God who loves us for what we are — not for what we do to or for somebody — can in turn feel loved unconditionally. He or she will also have the potential to love others in the same way.

The widespread problem of mental illness in our society gives us yet another perspective on love. One way of looking at mental disorders is that they are all ways of compensating for lack of unconditional love. If we could peel all of the psychological diagnoses down to the heart and core, we would find that many emotional problems stem from lack of loving and being loved.

We tend to teach our children the same concept of love that we learned ourselves. Thus, if you have developed an immature form of love, your children may tend to develop an immature form of love also. If you want to teach your children to love in a mature way and to make them feel loved unconditionally, you will have to learn to love yourself! Then you can develop the capacity to love your children so that they feel loved unconditionally.

We are emphasizing unconditional love so strongly because it is such a very vital quality for human growth. To know that you are valuable enough — just because you are you — to be loved regardless of how you act, is the greatest gift you can give yourself and your children.

(Please understand that we are not advocating irresponsible or antisocial behavior, but acknowledging our universal humanness and imperfection, and urging you to learn to accept yourself fully, "warts and all.")

"... As You Love Yourself"

Look at the definition of love that you wrote at the beginning of this chapter. In the divorce classes, most people include in their definition of love something that makes the love other-centered — centered in the other person rather than within themselves. Many people write that love is caring and giving and making that other person happy. Very few people include in their definition of love a mature idea of self-love.

Let's examine that. If the center of your love is in your partner and the relationship dissolves, the center is suddenly removed; as we considered earlier, this makes divorce even more painful. What might it be like if you had become a whole person and learned to love yourself? If divorce came, there would still be pain and trauma. But it would not be so devastating; you would still be a whole person.

Divorce is especially traumatic for those who have not centered their love within themselves and learned to love themselves. They end up feeling unlovable, or that they are incapable of loving another person. Many spend a great deal of time and energy trying to prove to themselves that they are lovable. They may search for another love relationship immediately, because that helps to heal the wound. They may become sexually promiscuous, developing all kinds of relationships with anybody who comes along. Many of these people have confused sex and love, feeling that if they go out and find sex, with it will come the love they have been missing and needing. It sometimes seems it would be more appropriate for them to say, "I sex you," rather than, "I love you"!

As we discussed in chapters 2 and 6, it is wiser to go easy on love relationships during this difficult time. Invest in friendships instead, until you have made good progress at learning to love yourself. More on this in chapter 16, also.

So many people have never really learned to love and to be loved. Sometimes it seems easier to love others, and not allow oneself to be loved. By "wanting to love another person," you may really be hiding your own need to be loved.

How Warm Is Your Love?

BF: "I would like to share a personal experience that happened to me as I was working through the divorce process. I was taking part in a meditation exercise. We sat with our eyes closed and meditated to bring a flow of energy through the different levels of our bodies until it reached the tops of our heads. I was able to follow this meditation and feel a warm flow of energy within me, gradually rising higher in my body. When the guided fantasy had reached the level of our chests, the leader said, 'Many of you at this point will be feeling that the flow of energy is leaking out the front of your chests. If you are feeling such a leak, then imagine a cover over the front of your chest so that the warm flow of energy will not leak out.' She was describing exactly the way I felt! I was amazed!

"After the guided fantasy was over, I asked, 'How did you know how I was feeling when I was sitting there with my eyes closed, not talking?' She replied that many people have the feeling that the flow of energy is leaking out the front of their chests. She related it to be belief that love is doing something to somebody or for somebody, and that it is other-centered rather than centered within ourselves. Thus the flow of energy leaks out toward others. We emotionally drain ourselves by putting the love into others, rather than filling our own bucket of life.

"I thought about this a great deal and decided that my goal was to learn to love myself in a more adequate manner. I decided that I would like to have my love be a warm glow, burning within me, warming me and the people with whom I came in contact. My friends would be warm without having to prove that they were lovable. They simply would feel warm by being close to my fire!

"Since a special, committed love relationship involves being very close, that special person gets an extra flow of warmth from my fire."

How about you? Do you have a fire going within you? Or has your fire gone out? It is important for us to care for the fire within us and make sure that we have a glow that warms us and also allows the people around us to be warm.

Styles of Loving

Our lives express our definition of love. If we believe that love is translated as making money, then that is how we spend our time. We act out our definition of love in our behavior. How have you been acting out your definition of love? What has been the important priority in your life? Are you satisfied with the definition of love you show by your behavior, or do you want to change? Think about it.

An interesting paradox exists about the way we love others. While each of us has a unique style of loving, each person tends to believe that his or her style is *the only way there is* of loving! It is difficult for us to see that there are styles other than our own.

When you enter into a love relationship it's important to be aware of your own style and that of the other person. Perhaps by examining some of these styles we can better understand ourselves and others. We're impressed with the work of University of Toronto sociologist John Alan Lee, who has researched the subject rather thoroughly and identified nine "types of love." We've simplified the list a bit, and offer the following six for your thoughtful consideration:

• The *romantic* style of loving has a lot of warmth, feeling, and emotion. It is the "electricity" type of love, sending all kinds of tingly feelings through your body when you see the beloved person (you actually do have physiological changes in your body, such as increases in heart beat and body temperature). This tends to be an idealistic type of love, leading you to search for and find the "one and only" person for whom you can feel it. Many of our popular songs refer to this style of love. The romantic lover tends to love deeply and to need a sexual relationship along with romantic love. Withholding sex from a romantic lover is sometimes compared to withholding food from a baby. It is an important part of this style of loving. Because it is so loaded with feeling and emotion, romantic love may not be as stable as some of the other styles of loving.

• *Friendship* love is not as loaded with emotion and feeling. The relationship starts with a liking for each other, and then the liking "just sort of grows" into something more, which might be called love. It is cooler, lacking the passion of romantic love. Sex is not as important to the friendship lover, often developing long after the relationship has started. This is one of the most stable styles of loving, and it is not unusual for people who get into this style of loving to remain good friends even if they divorce. Their loving was based upon mutual respect and friendship rather than strong emotional feelings.

• *Game-playing* love regards the love relationship as a game with certain rules to follow. Game players are not as interested in intimacy as romantic lovers. In fact, they may have several simultaneous love relationships in order to *avoid* closeness and intimacy. Game-playing love is like the old popular song that says, "When I'm not with the one I love, I love the one I'm with." Game-playing lovers tend to make up their own special rules, and their sexual relationships will follow whatever rules are most convenient.

• There is a *needy* style of loving that tends to be full of possessiveness and dependency. This style of loving is very emotional, and the need to be loved makes it very unstable. The people involved tend to have difficulty maintaining the relationship; and they feel a lot of jealousy, possessiveness, and insecurity. Many people who have been through the divorce trauma adopt this style of loving because it reflects the neediness resulting from the divorce pain. Especially typical of the first relationship after the separation: "I've got to have another love relationship in order to be happy." This is an immature style of dependent and possessive love.

• The *practical* lover takes a realistic look at the love partner and decides, on a rational and intellectual basis, if this love is appropriate. This type of person will make sure that there is similarity in religious beliefs, political beliefs, ways of handling money, views on raising children… The lover may look into deficiencies in the person's family by considering socioeconomic status, characteristics, and genetic makeup. The practical lover will choose to love someone whom it "makes good sense" to love.

• There are *altruistic* lovers, who may be somewhat other-centered and very willing to meet the needs of the other person. Carried to the extreme, the altruistic lover may become a martyr, trying to meet his or her own "empty-bucket" needs. There is, however, an authentic altruistic lover: a person who has a full bucket and enough inner strength to be able to love another person in a very unselfish manner. Many altruistic lovers have strong religious beliefs, and find a relationship with a Supreme Being keeps their own buckets full.

A couple in marriage counseling had a great deal of difficulty because he was a friendship lover and she was a romantic lover. She felt that his cool love was not love, and he felt that her romantic love was unstable. His style of loving was to take care of her, provide for her needs, and stay with her in the marriage; and he felt that this was proof of his love for her. Her request was for him to say, "I love you," and to express different forms of romantic thoughts that would make her feel loved and romantic. His friendship love was not a good mix with her romantic love. They had difficulty in communicating and understanding each other's viewpoints because their basic beliefs about what love was were not compatible.

Each person obviously is a mixture of the styles, and there is no one style that fits anyone at all times. Understanding your own mix of styles is very important when you get into a love relationship with another person.

Learning to Love Yourself

As people move up the trail in the divorce seminars, the question often arises, "How do we learn to love ourselves?" As we have seen, the answer is not easy. Here is a specific exercise that will *help* with learning to love yourself, however:

Think of a time in your life when you started to make changes. It may have been when you first had difficulties in your marriage, when you first separated from your beloved, or perhaps when you started reading this book. Make a list of the changes that you have made, the personal growth you have experienced since that time, and the things you have learned about yourself, others, and life. Consider the feeling of confidence you have gained by learning these things and getting more in control of your own life. That confidence is what gives you the good feelings. The length of your list may surprise you.

The late esteemed psychotherapist Virginia Satir devised another method of helping people learn to gain more self-love. Make a list of five adjectives that could describe you. After you have listed these five adjectives, go through and put a plus or minus sign after each word to indicate whether you think each is a positive or negative adjective. After you have done this, look at the minus adjectives and see if you can find anything positive about each particular adjective, quality, or aspect of your personality.

A woman in the class listed the adjective "bitchy." When questioned about it, she stated that her husband constantly referred to her as bitchy. As she began to talk about it, she realized that what he called bitchiness, she recognized as *assertiveness* — a positive way to stick up for herself. Once she understood that difference of labels, she was able to accept that as a part of herself and to feel good about it.

After all, that's what self-love is: learning to accept ourselves for what we are. As renowned psychologist Carl Rogers observed, when you learn to accept yourself as you are, that gives you permission to grow, change, and become more the person you *want to be*. As long as you don't accept a part of who you are, you have trouble changing that part! Does that sound like a strange paradox?

We all need to discover that "it's okay to not be okay" in certain areas. We have all had traumatic experiences that have left us wounded someplace, incidents when we did not feel loved, experiences that have left us less than whole. But those experiences are part of life and part of living. We are not perfect; we are human beings. And when we can learn to accept some of the non-okay things about ourselves, then we begin to feel more okay. And that's a step toward self-love.

Have you thought about how we learn to love another person? What causes the feelings of love for that other person to begin suddenly – or slowly? Perhaps it was a kind and thoughtful deed he or she did; maybe by doing something that met your needs, she or he helped you feel good. What would happen if you did kind and thoughtful deeds to yourself? If you would set aside a period of time tomorrow to do something that really felt good and made you feel okay about yourself, that could be a way of learning to love yourself more fully and more completely. After all, it would be *you* who was capable of doing something kind and lovable for you!

Perhaps the most important method of learning to love yourself is to *give yourself permission* to love yourself. If you can decide that it is okay, and not selfish or self-centered, to love yourself, maybe you can allow yourself to go ahead and have feelings of self-love!

The growth you have achieved is something that no one has done for you, so no one can take it away from you. Your life is in your control, through knowledge of yourself and others. To that extent, you are not at the mercy of others anymore. Let the good feelings of your growth soak into your body, and let yourself feel the warmth of what you have achieved. Let yourself feel love for yourself for a while. It is okay to love yourself. No — it's more than okay — *it is the way life is meant to be!*

Let the Children Know They Are Loved

While everyone is concerned about what love is, children may feel somewhat unlovable because one parent has left. Many suffer from the fear of losing the other parent as well. At the very time children need a great deal of parental love, parents are undergoing their own trauma and often are incapable of giving as much love to the children as they would like. Awareness of this problem and special efforts to overcome it — especially through much honest conversation with youngsters about what is going on, and reassurance that they are much loved by both parents — are much needed at this crucial time.

A mother recently told a delightful story, one of those little vignettes in life that seem to make everything worthwhile. Her three-year-old son came down one morning and sat on the davenport. He was sitting there thinking and meditating, and suddenly popped up with, "What do you know? It seems like everybody loves me. Isn't that nice!" Those are special moments in life. As parents, a major goal for us is to try to help children of divorce feel that same way, even though we are going through a period of feeling unlovable ourselves.

How Are You Doing?
Check out your own self-love before you proceed to the next chapter:
1. *I feel I am lovable.*
2. *I am not afraid of being loved.*
3. *I am not afraid of loving another.*
4. *I have an understanding of what I believe love is.*
5. *I am living a lifestyle that is congruent with my definition of love.*
6. *I feel comfortable meeting my own needs rather than feeling selfish.*
7. *I am able to accept love from others.*
8. *I am able to express love to others in a way that makes them feel loved.*
9. *I am able to love myself.*
10. *I have experienced a great deal of personal growth since my crisis began.*
11. *I am trying to develop my immature, needy, dependent parts of love into a more mature style of loving.*

Trust

"My Love-Wound is Beginning to Heal"

If you say, "You can't trust men (women)!" you are saying more about yourself than about the opposite sex. Love relationships after divorce often are attempts to heal your love-wound, so many of them will be transitional and short-term. In your new relationships with others, you may be reworking and improving the way you got along with your parents. By building a basic level of trust within yourself, you can experience satisfying emotionally close and intimate relationships.

Chapter **15**

꩜

I was doing just fine and enjoying myself. Then he said, "I love you."
I panicked and told him to get up, put on his clothes, and go home.
— Ann

On this *trust* part of the trail, you will notice people who walk some distance away from members of the opposite sex. They are like wild animals that come close, hoping to get some food, yet run for cover the minute you move toward them. These people talk about relationships a great deal of the time, and they seem to want to date and be with the opposite sex. But as soon as someone makes a move toward them, they run and shout, "Stay away!" They wear T-shirts with a motto saying, "You can't trust men (women)!" They have severe *love-wounds*.

A love-wound is the internal pain felt after the end of a love relationship, but it may originate much earlier in life. Many of the teenagers Bruce worked with as a juvenile probation officer suffered from love-wounds. They had learned that "love equals getting hurt." If they were put in a warm, loving foster home, they would run away. People who have painful love-wounds will hold others at a distance emotionally until the love-wound is healed. It may take months or even years for some people to heal — to be able to be emotionally close again.

There Are Relationships, and then There Are Relationships

Relationships are important to people after divorce. When the seminar participants are asked what topics they want to discuss, every class picks "relationships" as the most important topic.

(Have you ever noticed at a gathering of singles how often the word *relationship* is used? One woman suggested that the word be censored with a "bleep," she was so tired of hearing it! We use it a great deal in this book and in the seminars, simply because we don't know a better word with that meaning! Needless to say, as an editor of psychology books as well as a psychologist, Bob hates to admit that!)

It is often assumed that the only way to prove that you're okay is to become involved in another love relationship. In fact, some experts in the divorce field consider remarriage an indication of divorce adjustment. A research study using the *Fisher Divorce Adjustment Scale* demonstrated the inadequacy of that assumption. A large number of remarried people have not adjusted to the past divorce.

The idea that another relationship will "prove you are okay" leads many people to start immediately to find a new one-and-only. The healthiest early relationships after divorce have the goal of healing the love-wound. They are *transitional* — rather than long-term, committed — relationships. (More on this in chapter 16.)

You may have seen the poster that says, "You have to kiss a lot of frogs before you find a prince." It seems to be healthier to conclude, "You have to kiss a lot of frogs before you *become* a prince/princess." If you can make this transition in your thinking, you can free these early relationships from expectations, pressures, and a futuristic outlook. Don't let the all-important question be, "Can I live with this person for the rest of my life?" Try instead, "Can this person and I benefit from some time together?"

Allow your new relationships to flow in the present and to help heal your love-wound (and perhaps the other person's love-wound also). Sit back and enjoy the sunsets each day, stop to "smell the roses," let yourself heal, and realize that many of these early relationships will be short-term because they are built during a needy time in your life. Let these early transitional relationships help you clear the confusion. You have plenty of time later to rebuild another permanent relationship when you have rebuilt a good foundation within yourself.

The divorce adjustment process may be viewed in two major steps. The first is *learning to be a single person,* ready to face life alone, with the rubble of the past cleared away. The second step is *learning to love again* after you have rebuilt your strength to carry the burden of a long-term committed relationship. If you complete step one first, step two will be easier!

Styles of Relationship: A "Body-Sculpture" Exercise

Here is an exercise which will help you examine your own *style* in relationships. It is called *body sculpturing* and is derived from the work of famed family therapist Virginia Satir. You'll need a friend to help. The diagrams illustrate different body positions which show various types of love-relationships that people have. Let's look at the body sculptures and consider the feelings underneath each style:

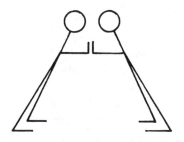

1. A-Frame Dependency Relationship

In the dependency relationship, two people lean on each other. Dependency upon another person sometimes feels good, but it's somewhat confining. When one person wants to move, change, or grow, it upsets the other who is leaning on him/her. Try this sculpture with another person and then put into words some of the feelings that you have while you are assuming this position.

2. Smothering Relationship

Here is a position quite frequently seen in teenage relationships. The vocabulary for this relationship is, "I can't live without you. I want to spend the rest of my life with you. I will devote myself completely to making you happy. It feels so good to be close to you." Many lovers start out by smothering, then gradually release the strangle hold on each other to allow more room for growth. This smothering pattern may be particularly significant during the honeymoon stage of a new love. The smothering relationship feels good for a while, but eventually the partners begin to feel trapped.

3. Pedestal Relationship

This "worshipful" relationship says, "I love you not for who you are, but for who I think you are. I have an idealized image of you and I'd like to have you live up to that image." It is very precarious on top of the pedestal because there are so many expectations to live up to. You can see the problems of communication here. In love with the person's idealized image, the worshipper is looking up to and trying to communicate with that image instead of with the real person. There is a great deal of emotional distancing inherent in this relationship, and it is difficult for the two people to become close.

4. Master/Slave Relationship
The master acts and is treated according to these ideas: "I'm the head of this family. I'm the boss. I'll make the decisions around here." Do not assume that this relationship necessarily places the male as the boss and head of the family. There are many females who are masters, making all of the decisions for their families.

In most relationships one of the partners has a personality which is at least a little stronger than the other, and that is not necessarily bad. It is when a relationship becomes rigid and inflexible, and one person is set up to make virtually *all* of the decisions, that emotional distancing and inequality take place. Maintaining one person as master and the other as slave tends to take a great deal of emotional energy, and often results in a power struggle that interferes with the communication and intimacy of the relationship.

5. Boarding House: Back-to-Back Relationship
Linked by their elbows, these two have some sort of contract or agreement that they are going to live together. There is no communication in this relationship. The typical thing is for people to come home and sit down and watch TV while they are eating, then retire to their own living habits for the remainder of the evening. There is no expression of love toward each other. Notice as you try this position, that when one person moves forward, changes (i.e., grows and matures), the other person is linked to that change. Back-to-back is a very confining relationship. Many persons recognize this as the pattern that existed just before their relationship ended.

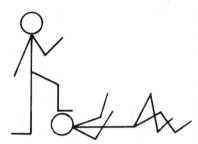

6. Martyr Relationship

Here is the person who completely sacrifices by trying to serve others. Always doing things for other people, never taking time for self, the martyr goes about "asking" to be stepped on. But don't let the lowly posture fool you! The martyr position is very controlling. Note that when the person lying down moves, the other person — who has a foot on the martyr — is thrown off balance.

How does the martyr gain control? You guessed it — through guilt. How can you be angry at a person who is doing everything for you, who is taking care of you completely? The martyr is very efficient at controlling people. It is very difficult to live with a martyr because you feel too guilty to express your own needs and angry feelings. Perhaps you have a martyr parent, and can recognize ways of dealing with that parent by understanding the martyr relationship.

7. Healthy Love-Relationship

Two people who are whole and complete have happiness within themselves. Standing upright, not leaning on or tangled up with the other person, they are able to live their own lives. They have an abundance of life to share with the other person. They choose to stay together because they are free to be individuals who are sharing their lives together. They can come close together and choose the smothering position temporarily; they can walk hand-in-hand as they might do in parenting their children; they can move apart and have their own careers, their own lives, and their own friends. Their choice to stay together is out of love for each other rather than needing to stay together because of some unmet emotional needs. The healthy love-relationship gives both people the space to grow and become themselves.

Again, let us urge you to try these different body-sculpture exercises with a friend and see how you feel in each instance. Talk or write about the feelings you were experiencing while in each body position. Which of these positions describes your past love-relationship? Many people in the classes say that they think that their love-relationship went through almost all of the unhealthy body positions!

Did you learn more causes of divorce from the body sculpturing? The unhealthy relationships seem to suggest a half-person looking for another half-person. As you become more of a whole person (do we ever become completely whole?), your chances of developing a healthy, healing relationship are greatly increased.

Feelings Into Actions
We tend to act out our internal feelings in our relationships. If you are angry, you probably express anger in your relationships. If you are lonely, you tend to be possessive in the relationship in order to keep the other person from leaving you and making you lonely again. If you are in deep emotional pain, you'll likely have a relationship full of pain. If you have a love-wound, you will emotionally distance others to avoid bumping your love-wound.

Many of us seek relationships with persons who have qualities we are missing in ourselves. If you are introverted and want to be more comfortable around people, you may marry an extrovert. Lacking confidence, you marry a person who exudes confidence. To meet your need to feel guilty, you develop a relationship with someone who will make you feel guilty.

And of course, the coin also has a positive side. If you are happy, confident, and feel lovable, you marry to act out those feelings in your relationship. We can learn much about ourselves by looking at our relationships. What feelings are you expressing in your relationships? Is there a pattern? (Do you always bring home a stray cat?) Do your relationships reflect good feelings within, or do they reflect neediness?

Is Your History Repeating Itself?
Another major factor in relationship styles is one we've mentioned before: the interaction we had with our parents. Each of us learned how to respond to love, anger, rejection, and intimacy from our own parents. If your parents fought, then you are likely to have a very tough time with fights. If your parents were cold and untouching, then you may find it difficult to touch and to handle warm emotions. Many a marriage is not satisfactory because the partners are interacting like their parents did.

Jeff put it this way, "Marriage may be like a pot of stew. If you don't make it right the first time, you keep doing it over until you get it right. In my first marriage, I was acting out the unproductive patterns I learned as a child. I didn't change internally after my divorce, so I continued to act out those patterns in my second marriage!"

If you can use each relationship to learn about yourself and how you are acting out your internal feelings in your relationships, you can then use each relationship to become more the person you want to be. It is possible to grow from each relationship, and that is a positive way of looking at more than one marriage.

After divorce, we often regress and interact the way we did earlier in life. This can be positive: becoming a healthy person emotionally is like climbing a slide in the playground. You progress up so far, then lose your grip and slide back down. Then the next time you are able to climb to a higher point. Although each relationship that ends may put you back down the slide, when you climb again, you know how to climb higher and become more healthy. In their relationships after divorce, many people are reworking the patterns of interaction they learned from their parents in order to make those patterns more productive.

We hope the body sculpturing and this discussion of various concepts of relationships are helping you carry out the rubble and make room to rebuild yourself. The problem of trust is largely internal rather than external, and understanding your past is helpful in understanding where you are now. The first step of growth is to become aware of ourselves, our patterns of interaction, and our methods of relating with others.

Enough of carrying out the rubble — let's start rebuilding!

"Where Do I Meet Someone?"

This is one of the questions formerly married people ask most frequently. The simple, almost absurd, answer is "Right where you are!"

People go to bars, singles groups, and ceramics classes (amazing how many formerly-marrieds do that!) in their attempts to meet people. We don't quarrel with going places where single people gather. But take care! The "bar scene," for example, typically includes many lonely people who can't relate until they are slightly under the influence. And the bar hoppers are often game-players out to practice and improve their games of interaction, frequently with sex being the goal of the game. Singles groups, too, may have a certain amount of desperation and loneliness, and usually consist predominantly of women.

The question, "Where do I meet someone?" often indicates that the asker is looking for a committed, long-term partner. Perhaps somewhat desperate and sending out desperate vibrations with body language, vocabulary, and "the look in their eyes," these persons tend to drive people away. Others fear that they will become sucked in by the neediness; some call the needy ones "vacuum cleaners!"

How often have you heard it said, "There ain't nothing but *turkeys* out there?" Of course, it is partly true. Many formerly married people are hurting, and are not especially attractive dates during the rough periods. But have you thought about what you would do if an *eagle* landed near you? You would probably run like mad! A person who is eligible and looks like a possible marriage partner scares the hell out of you if your love-wound is still very painful. Maybe you are *looking* for turkeys because they are safe? Maybe you are still hurting, and more or less a turkey yourself? Turkeys do tend to hang together, you know. Maybe, if there "ain't nothing but turkeys out there," you haven't rebuilt yourself to the status of an eagle.

When you have blinders on and see only potential marriage partners, do you realize how many people you are *not* seeing out there? When you start becoming interested in getting to know the people around you, then you start making friends. And some of those friends might become lovers, but *looking* for lovers keeps both friends and lovers away!

It bears repeating: Your goal (for now) is to get acquainted and develop friendships with the people around you. Pay no attention to whether or not they are "eligible singles"; notice only if they are *interesting people* you would like to get to know. Develop as many positive relationships with people of both sexes as you can. You can get to know these potential friends wherever you are. When you go to the grocery store and send out positive vibrations and act interested in others, you attract people like flies to honey. At parties, if you forget about trying to find a bed partner or someone to go home with after the party, you might get to know a number of interesting people. If you've found happiness within and send out those vibrations, people will enjoy being with you.

We are fully aware of the difference in the numbers of formerly married males and females. The ratio is unfair; there are many more females than males. Women live longer than men; for each year of life there are more females than males living. Also, there are many males who remarry someone much younger, often a woman not married before. (It may be small compensation to women, but it is true that women adjust to living alone much better than do men.)

Ginger posed another issue frequently discussed in the seminars, "Every time I go to a singles gathering, it becomes a game of 'my place-or-yours?'" There are many singles who have not learned to deal with the opposite sex other than sexually, but that doesn't mean you have to narrow yourself the same way. Keep developing your personality and broadening yourself. The more interests you develop, the more interesting people you will find.

Rebuilding Trust

Some ideas which have grown out of the divorce seminars may help you overcome problems of trust.

Try this one: *Be really honest the next time you go out.* If you are hurting, and have a painful love-wound, explain to the person that you want to spend time with him/her, but you fear you'll be a wet blanket. Don't try to put on the mask of cool and sophisticated, when in reality you're scared to death. When you explain your fears to others, you might be surprised to learn they were feeling the same way! After all, we're *all* human. And you'll both be relieved to be able to be yourselves instead of the "Joe Cool" you thought you had to be.

Have you thought about learning to trust with friends rather than lovers? If you find someone of the opposite sex with whom you can be a friend, that person is much safer for you than a lover. When you add romance to the ingredients of a friendship, it adds instability to the relationship, and makes it harder to take risks and learn to trust.

We project our lack of trust upon others. Many parents believe that their teenagers are not to be trusted. Valerie's parents, for example, feared their daughter would become pregnant, so they wouldn't allow her to date, even though she was a junior in high school. It turned out that the mother had become pregnant as a teenager, and was projecting her lack of trust in herself upon Valerie.

A similar event often occurs in marriage counseling. Tess admitted that her husband Andre kept checking on her to make sure she was not having an affair. Then she discovered that Andre was having the affair and projecting his lack of trust upon her! Like so many other feelings, lack of trust may become a self-fulfilling prophecy. Valerie said she felt she *should* become pregnant because that was what her parents seemed to believe was going to happen. And Tess felt she *might as well* have an affair if that was what Andre suspected anyway!

A severe love-wound leads to fear of trusting. As appealing as the warmth may be, to become close is to risk being burned again. Relationships after divorce are controlled by this lack of trust. The purpose of these relationships ought to be to learn trust again and to heal the love-wound. Thus many such connections are short-term.

Trying to make them into something long-term often does nothing but increase the love-wound and prolong the adjustment process.

We have all learned how to interact from our love-relationships and from our parents. As adults, we may choose to improve the styles of interaction that we learned. Becoming aware of one's style is an important first step. It may also take several friendships and love-relationships to help one develop healthier styles.

We have to take risks to learn to trust. Risks may backfire and lead to rejection or misunderstanding, but risks are necessary if one is to become close and experience intimacy again. The rewards are worth the risk.

Trust and the Children

The problem of trust is especially difficult for those children who did not know what was going on with their parents' divorce, so the children are now adjusting to a parent's absence with little or no direct communication with that parent. If the father, for example, suddenly leaves the family, and doesn't communicate why he is leaving or the problems that the parents are having, the child may feel deserted, and have trouble trusting that absent, noncustodial parent.

Kids really are tougher than you think, and can handle an awful lot of direct communication and reality if parents will just take the time to communicate with them. Parents who hide their heads and feel they cannot share the reality of their situation with their children often create a great deal of mistrust in the children, and lose a potentially valuable source of love and support for themselves! It is a very unusual — or very young — child who does not know that the parents are going to get a divorce before the parents tell him/her. The more you can communicate and level with your children, the more they will trust what you have to say.

How Are You Doing?

Here are some items to see how you are doing and if you are ready to continue the climb. We are nearing the top, so take care not to rush here — this rebuilding block must be securely in place before you proceed.

1. *I can trust members of the opposite sex.*
2. *I have begun to understand that men and women are much more alike than different in their responses to feelings such as love, hate, intimacy, and fear.*
3. *I can trust myself and my feelings.*
4. *I trust my feelings enough to act on them.*
5. *I am not afraid of becoming emotionally close to a potential love-partner.*
6. *I am aware of the ways that I distance people.*
7. *I am building relationships that will help me to heal my love-wound.*
8. *I am building healing and trusting relationships with friends of both sexes.*
9. *I communicate with others where I am emotionally rather than giving mixed messages.*
10. *I understand that not everyone is capable of being trusted.*
11. *I am capable of trusting someone when it is appropriate.*
12. *I want to heal my love-wound and experience intimacy.*
13. *I am trying to live in the present in my relationships.*
14. *I realize that many of the early relationships after divorce may be short-term.*
15. *I am taking risks in my relationships by exposing my true feelings and thoughts.*
16. *I am truly interested in the friends around me rather than desperately looking for another love-relationship.*

Relatedness

"Growing Relationships Help Me Rebuild"

It's okay to have an important relationship after your primary relationship has ended. You need support, companionship, and feedback from others to help yourself rebuild. These relationships are often short-term, so you need to learn how to have "healthy termination." You need to take credit for creating these relationships as part of your growing process. And you need to become aware of how you can make these relationships as growing and healing as possible.

Chapter 16

∽

Have I had a growing relationship? Not one, but four. Each seemed healthier than the one before. I guess I learned something from each one.

— Susan

I had one with a woman who had a great built-in `crap-detector.' When I was sorting through my stuff, I could bounce off her and she would tell me what parts of me were authentic and what parts of me were crap. I think I found the perfect partner to have a growing relationship with.

— David

Many people climbing the mountain decide to pair off, to help support each other in the difficult climb. They appear to enjoy each other's company very much for a while, but often they part ways and continue the climb alone.

It helps to have another person's support for a while, but sooner or later one or both of them realize they need to make this climb alone. When they part, one or both of them feel very sad for a while. They often have to rework some of the blocks they had already gone through, such as grief and anger. Both appear to make rapid progress while they are together, but when this new relationship ends, their progress slows down considerably.

What Is a Growing Relationship?

We call these unions *growing relationships*. Other professionals have variously labeled them "transitional relationships," "rebound relationships," "experimental relationships," and "healing relationships." Psychiatrist Martin Blinder for example, in his book *Choosing Lovers,* describes the various types in some detail, and asserts that each type is unique, meeting particular needs of the partners. Later in this chapter, we'll discuss a couple of the more common types.

Growing relationships, because they help folks manage the climb better for a while, can be very healthy for both partners. But it's not enough just to let them "happen." It's important to understand them and how they work, so they can be made more growth-enhancing, longer lasting, and — just maybe — hurt less when they end.

Among the typical characteristics of growing relationships:

• They often occur after a marriage or love relationship has ended, but they can occur at any time.

• They often are with a potential love partner, but they can be with a friend, a family member, a therapist, or even with your primary love partner.

• They usually are temporary, but they can become a more permanent, long-lasting relationship.

• They are usually very healing, but they can be destructive.

• They usually occur when you are in a personal growth or transformation period in your life.

• They are an attempt to find new ways of creating and building relationships with yourself and with others.

• They can end with a "healthy termination," rather than the painful, destructive endings you may have experienced in the past.

• They typically involve good communication. Usually the two people spend a great deal of time talking with each other about important topics such as personal growth and the meaning of life.

• These relationships are based upon honesty and openness — with each other if not with their primary love partners — and the people often share themselves in ways they have never shared before. Instead of "dressing up and putting on good clothes" — to put on their best facade for the new partner (as most of us did in the old "courting" system) — these people strip to the bare emotional essentials, so they can present their true essence in ways that allow them to feel excited about their new behavior.

• They are growth-oriented, not stagnant. There is a difference between this type of healing relationship and the one that is simply a summer re-run of old shows. The male who needs mothering is often married to an enabler/over-responsible person. He often leaves that relationship and marries another enabler/over-responsible person (often with the same or a similar first name!). The female who needs to take care of someone may marry another "stray-cat" so she can continue her old pattern. In contrast, the growing relationship is dedicated to developing a new and different relationship — a laboratory for personal growth — not to perpetuating old patterns.

Are We Talking Affairs Here?

Sometimes a person in a primary love relationship has a third-party relationship and calls it a growing relationship. Such a union can take the form of an affair. We've worked with clients who have been able to make their third-party relationships into healing experiences, using them to enrich their primary relationships and make them stronger. That usually is possible only if the new pairing is a *friendship,* rather than a romantic affair. Romantic third-party involvements typically have long-term consequences, and make it difficult for the people involved to heal the pain of the affair.

The old childhood parent-tapes about sex and marriage come back and say, "When you talk about relationships outside of marriage that may include sex, aren't you encouraging affairs or promiscuity?" Not necessarily; these relationships don't have to be romantic or sexual. If your values — religious or moral — are such that you don't want a relationship that is sexual outside of marriage, you can still learn and heal tremendously by having a non-sexual friendship.

A growing relationship must fit your moral values while it focuses in on the learning and the lessons that you need to learn.

Why Are Some People More Likely to Create Growing Relationships?

There are some groups of people who are more likely to have growing relationships:

• Dumpers after a divorce will tend to get into other relationships quicker than dumpees.

• Men will tend to get into other relationships more quickly after a divorce than women.

• Women are more likely than men to create a growing relationship with a friend.

• Extraverts are more likely than introverts to use the growing relationship to heal. From research with the *Myers-Briggs Type Indicator* (a psychological test which describes people by personality types), we learn that extraverts heal better with other people, introverts heal better by themselves.

• People who are able to be emotionally open and vulnerable will more likely create a healing growing relationship than emotionally closed-down people who can't talk about feelings.

- People in rebellion will usually have a growing relationship. (See chapter 12 on Transition for more on rebellion).
- Younger people are more inclined to develop growing relationships than older people.
- People who are involved in divorce recovery classes or seminars will almost automatically develop growing relationships with the other participants in the class. This is one of the great "side benefits" of participation in a class. The friendships you make in such a class will probably last for a long time, maybe for the rest of your life. And the friendships will be more healthy and growing than many of the relationships you have had in the past. Remember that you can create the same kind of relationships outside of class that you have created with other class participants.
- Many people will not want to start such a relationship because it could become more than they can handle. They want something safe that won't become long term. It's important to be clear and communicate your intentions, needs and desires directly and openly with a potential partner. You can decide how to control your future involvement and not let the relationship become more than what you want it to be.

Fifteen to twenty percent of the participants in the divorce class don't enroll after their marriage has ended. They enroll in the divorce class when their growing relationship *after* their divorce has ended. The first relationships after a marriage has ended usually don't last very long. The emotional pain is often greater when these relationships end than when the marriage or primary love relationship ended.

As the 21st century begins, growing relationships appear to be one of the myriad social transitions taking place in society. Learning more about these types of relationships will increase the chances of them becoming more healing. Toward that end, let's take a look at two of the most common types of growing relationships: the *passionate* and the *therapeutic*.

Passionate, Emotional Relationships

Perhaps the most common of the several types of growing relationships which occur after a primary love relationship has ended is the passionate type, with its emphasis on romantic love. Here at last — or so it seems — are all of those qualities which were missing in the late marriage: passion, honesty, good communication, empathy, understanding! No wonder the new partners want it to last forever, hang onto it tightly, and talk about their future together.

But commitments for the long term might not be healing for either party at this stage. Let's consider some of the potential pitfalls and benefits of the passionate emotional relationship:

Pitfall: *Making the other person responsible for your excitement and passion.* Have you made this new attachment too important in your life? It feels so good when you are on the rough seas of your transition that you want to make it last forever. You think you can't live without this exciting new partner. What you need to remember is that *you're in the process of recovery.* Take responsibility for creating this relationship yourself. You have just begun to be the person you want to be; give yourself the time it takes to finish the job. It does feel good to be with that other person. But don't give away all your power by making another person responsible for your happiness.

Benefit: *Your personal growth is an important reason for this relationship.* The lesson for you to learn in this relationship is to heal, to become, to be free, to be yourself. Take advantage of the lesson, and take credit for what you are learning. You have created an environment in which you can grow.

Pitfall: *Putting your new partner on a pedestal.* That mistake will almost surely limit the healing potential of this relationship. Try acting out this pedestal relationship by doing what the late family therapist Virginia Satir called "body-sculpture" (you'll recall the discussion and illustrations in chapter 15). You and another person describe how your relationship feels by arranging your bodies in a sculpturing position. Let your partner stand on a pedestal (a chair, stool, small table) while you stand on the floor. Talk to each other. Give each other a hug. Become aware of how it feels. The partner on the pedestal usually feels lonely, precarious, and uncomfortable.

Pitfall: *Focusing too much on the future.* Because the relationship feels so good, you start thinking about the future, and what it would be like to be married to this person forever. Living in the future inhibits healing, while living in the present maximizes healing, Living in the present is an indication of a self-actualized person. You need to enjoy the sunset each day in this relationship. You need to live each day as though it were your last. You need to communicate about everything you are feeling now, and let go of dreaming about the future or how long this relationship is going to last.

Benefit: *Communication is usually good in such a relationship.* You often share things about yourself and become more vulnerable than you have ever been. You treasure being open, vulnerable, and intimate. Realize that an important lesson in this relationship might be learning to be intimate and vulnerable. Remember that the communication skills and the feeling of vulnerability you are learning in this relationship will always be available to you in other relationships.

Pitfall: *You believe you'll never have another relationship with such a wonderful person again.* Part of the reason you hang on to this relationship so tightly is that you see this person as your "one and only." (An expectation you learned from society?) Any other person will be dull and unexciting after this person. There is some truth in this. But the excitement you feel is not because of the other person. It is because of your own process of growth. You are living in the present, being vulnerable, feeling new feelings. Much of the excitement you feel is because you are coming out of your shell, finding yourself, "coming home" emotionally.

While you may never feel this same excitement — becoming free of your shell — again, you have the potential of feeling the joy and excitement of intimacy, being emotionally close, and feeling loving and being loved in your future relationships which may have more meaning than the good feelings you experience in this relationship when you are coming out of your shell.

Benefit: *You find out how good it feels to be healthy.* As you grow and become you, you can allow yourself to be vulnerable with the resulting feelings of intimacy, to feel more secure with an identity of your own. The really important point for you to learn here is that *you can feel this way in many relationships and with many people.* So stop believing this is the only person that you can have such a relationship with. You will be able to have other healthy relationships if you choose, because you are learning to have a better relationship with yourself. But you may not feel as intense in another relationship because it won't have the neediness.

Benefit: *An adult relationship can be a laboratory for growth.* Remember the themes from chapters 4 and 12, on family of origin and childhood influences? You can rework and relearn the things you learned as a child. This growing relationship might be as good a "laboratory" for growth as any relationship you have had or will ever have. This new relationship is very likely much different from the relationships you built with your family of origin and with ex-love partner. This may partly explain why this relationship feels so good.

Pitfall: *An imbalance of emotional investment.* It is very easy to invest 80% or more of your emotional time and energy into this relationship and neglect investing in yourself. That inhibits your healing and your growth, contributes to the relationship ending, and makes it much more painful when it does end. If you want to maximize the healing possible in this growing relationship, discipline yourself to keep investing as much into yourself as you are investing in the relationship. This will help you keep your individual identity rather than losing it in your exciting, new, passionate love relationship.

Keep track of your time. How much of your free time is spent in improving yourself, such as hobbies, taking classes, time by yourself or with your friends? And how much time are you spending with the other person doing relationship activities?

Learn all you can, heal all you can, and stop holding the precious butterfly in your hands so tightly that it can't fly and be free. The energy you spend holding on tightly to the other person and to the relationship keeps you from climbing your own mountain and completing your own healing.

Friendship and Therapeutic Relationships

A growing relationship doesn't have to be with a love partner. In fact, there are tremendous advantages in having a growing relationship with a person who is not a love partner. You can have the same healing with a good friend or a trusted family member. You can still talk about feelings, be vulnerable, share parts of yourself that you have never shared with another. This friendship doesn't have the same thrills, excitement, and passion as the love relationship. But it is safer, seldom ends with the emotional pain present in ending romantic relationships, and can have just as deep healing. It can also be the laboratory for growth to change past patterns of relationships just as the passionate love relationship can be.

It is easy for participants in the Rebuilding class to identify with growing relationships based upon friendship. The participants are open and honest, share important aspects of themselves, feel a closeness and intimacy with others, and realize the relationships are special and often more healthy and healing than what they have known in the past. Learning to develop these kind of friendship growing relationships can be one of the most valuable learning experiences for the participants in divorce recovery classes.

Therapy can also be a growing relationship, depending upon the therapist and the style of therapy. But the same type of growth can take place and with the safety that comes from clear boundaries, paying for the therapy, and keeping it professional. A therapy relationship that helps you to become fully yourself can be one of the most valuable experiences you will have.

Can a Growing Relationship Last?

Does every growing relationship have to end? Each relationship has a foundation that is unique, both to that relationship and to where you are emotionally when you start the relationship. The foundation for the growing relationship is built for growth and healing; that's its purpose. A long-term committed relationship has a foundation built for longevity. What's the difference?

When you are building a growing relationship, you are in process — unstable, continually growing and changing, healing the wounds of the past. You are different today from what you were yesterday. And you will be different tomorrow. During this period of rapid change, your foundation needs to be flexible, adaptable, changeable — allowing you to be different as you change. That isn't a suitable foundation for a long-term relationship.

The "contract" when you started the growing relationship probably wasn't written, or even spelled out verbally, but it was there. "I need this relationship so I can find out who I am" was probably in the contract. The foundation for a long-term relationship is more stable and more permanent (although not rigid). Long-term unions require commitment, purpose, and stability.

If a growing relationship is to become a long-term one, it needs to be jacked up and a new foundation put under it. This can be done in various ways. Some couples have had a healthy "termination" of their relationships so one or both of them could be the "young colt" — out running around the pasture investing in themselves rather than investing in the relationship. Then they got back together and built a relationship with a more permanent foundation.

Changing the relationship can also can be done with good communication. Both partners must become aware of the costs and benefits of changing to a committed relationship. Each must take ownership of his or her feelings, contribution, and role in a long-term relationship. And communication must be open and honest. If you and your partner talk it out thoroughly, with awareness and ownership, and decide that the relationship needs to be changed from a growing one to a longer, more committed one, it can be done.

There is another problem. If you are truly changing, you might be a different person than you were when you started the relationship. Maybe your attraction and reason for entering into the relationship was to be with a person who was entirely different than your parents, former lovers, former friends. And when the need for a contrasting person is met, maybe you will want relationships with people more like your parents, former lovers, and former friends. So when the need for the different person passes, you may want to end the relationship. Many people in growing relationships outgrow the relationship for a variety of reasons.

Don't move too quickly to try to convert a growing relationship into one of long-term commitment. Both partners must be ready to accept themselves where they are now, and to move ahead into a more stable future.

Why Do I Have to Have so Many?

Sometimes people ask why they have to have so many growing relationships. A very good question. There are several explanations:

• The relationships may have had only a fraction of the healing power that is possible because you loaded them down with the future, rather than focusing on the present.

• You didn't pay enough attention to your own recovery and healing process because you were so infatuated with how great the other person was.

• You terminated the relationship with a lot of pain because you weren't aware of how to do a healthy termination. (This pain increases the need for another relationship to heal the pain of ending that one.)

• You may just simply have a lot of healing needing to be done from your family of origin and childhood experiences, and it takes several relationships to accomplish that.

• You've been working through issues that have been described in the previous chapters, but you weren't aware of what these issues were. Awareness increases the healing possible in a relationship a great deal.

• Another reason you have had so many relationships is because of the passion possible in these relationships. They become so physical that the real teaching of the relationship becomes obscured. You can escape very easily into passionate sex, and not ever wake up on the awareness level.

• You and your partner may not have been able to connect effectively on an emotional level. If you are not living in the present, if you do not give your complete attention to the relationship, if you avoid intimacy rather than seek it, then you never reach closeness, connectedness, intimacy, healing in the relationship. You may have been reluctant to end it because it in essence was never complete on an intimate level.

Each relationship contributes to your growth, and it might be helpful for you to identify and be thankful for each relationship, and each person with whom you have been in relationship. The homework at the end of the chapter suggests you write the things you learned and healed in each of your growing relationships.

Please be gentle with yourself. If you beat yourself up with your inner critic each time you enter into or end a relationship, you again have negated the healing. Give yourself a warm fuzzy for each growing relationship you have created; you'll maximize the healing that has taken place.

Making Your Primary Love a Growing Relationship

One of the exciting ways to have one of these healing-relationships is to make your marriage or primary love relationship into a growing relationship! It takes the same concepts to make it work: living in the present, good communication, no future expectations, and ownership (individually that you are responsible for your own feelings and attitudes, and jointly for carving out this new relationship).

You may find helpful material in the chapters on rebellion and healing separations to help you carve out a new relationship within your marriage. It won't be easy, but most primary love relationships can be jacked up and have a new foundation put under them. Bruce's follow-up book with Nina Hart, *Loving Choices*, is designed to help you create a growing relationship within your committed love relationship.

Learning Good Communication Skills

The growing relationship needs good communication, and the quickest way you can improve your communication skills is to learn to use "I" messages instead of "you" messages. (You may recall we introduced the concept of I-messages in chapter 9, when we were talking about expressing anger.)

You-messages are like poisoned darts that you throw at another person, who either becomes defensive or starts thinking what to say (throw) back at you. I-messages let others know that you are accepting responsibility for (owning) your own feelings and attitudes.

I-messages may be difficult for you because you haven't always thought about what is going on inside of you. Here's an easy way to start using I-messages: Start each sentence with "I" when you are doing important communication with yourself and with others. Try using these four kinds of communication: "I think _____," "I feel _____," "I want _____," and "I will _____." It is helpful to separate your thoughts from your feelings and to use different kinds of communication for each. Think about what you hope to achieve with your message. If you don't *say* what you want, you probably won't *get* what you want. And you need to finish your communication with a commitment about what action *you* will take. Taking responsible action to help achieve what you want is really putting your money where your mouth is.

Men frequently have difficulty accessing and talking about feelings. Using "I feel" statements may help them overcome this handicap. On the other hand, women can often tell you what the other people around them want or need but they can't tell you what they themselves want or need.

This material on I-messages builds on the work of Dr. Thomas Gordon, California psychologist who developed the highly successful "Effectiveness Training" programs for parents, teachers, and leaders. (*Loving Choices* describes a more complicated communication model using the same foundation. If you want to learn more about how to better communicate with yourself and others, you may want to read the communication chapters in that book.)

Healthy Termination
Another key part of growing relationships is *healthy termination*. Because most of these relationships will end, they will be more growth-enhancing for both parties if you learn how to do a healthy termination. It's an inherent problem in these relationships: you try to make them last longer than is healthy because you've started laying the expectations of a future on them.

By trying to stretch a short-term relationship into something longer than its "natural life," you make it unduly stressful. When you finish stretching it till it breaks, it snaps back at you like a rubber band — and hurts more than it has to.

If you could back it off into friendship before it gets stretched too far, you are more likely to have a healthy termination. If you live in the present, you'll notice when the "present" is less meaningful than it was. The needs that created the relationship have changed. That's the time to start terminating. Talk about your needs being different. Own what is happening with your changes, how your needs are different, and share your valuable learning from the relationship. Healthy terminations end with a fraction of the pain that could be there from trying to stretch the relationship into something it is not.

The healthy termination has its roots in openness and honesty about the needs and desires of both partners when you started the relationship. Pete was an Army chaplain who stated it well. "I told her I was a wet little kitty, and needed someone to take care of me and lick me dry like the mother cat does. And I also told her I didn't know whether I would want a relationship with her when I finally was dry. We were able to terminate the relationship with a minimum of pain because we had been open and honest from the beginning."

So here are the characteristics of a healthy termination. We encourage you to build them into your growing relationships:

• Openness and honesty in communication.

• Living in the present. Taking one day at a time, rather than making plans for an uncertain "future" together.

• Taking responsibility — ownership — for your own feelings, and expressing them openly. Avoiding games like, "I'm fine. Nothing's wrong."

• Seeing this from the beginning as a short-term relationship. "Commitment" is not part of a growing relationship, unless it becomes a long-term union.

• Talking about your needs. Listening to your partner's needs.

Watch for clues which tell you it's time to move on. Let your partner know when they start to show up.

Planning for the highly-probable termination of the relationship. Discuss how you'll handle it when the time comes (e.g., Will alternate living arrangements be needed? Transportation? Are children involved? Will you continue as friends? How about mutual friends?).

This concept of a healthy termination applies to all relationships. Each relationship has its natural cycle of growth. Some are short-term annuals, and others are long-term perennials. It's not easy to recognize just what the life-span of the relationship is. Ownership — acceptance of responsibility for yourselves, your feelings, and what's going on with each of you individually — is a tremendous help in allowing the relationship to find its own natural cycle.

A great deal of the pain in our lives comes from holding on to something too long when we need to let it go. If you believe your happiness is someone else's responsibility, you'll have difficulty letting a relationship have its natural length of life.

Do You Need a Growing Relationship?

There are a number of ways to heal without having a growing relationship. However, it does feel good to have someone's hand to hold while you are waking up. And someone to talk to while you are learning about yourself. They contribute much to the healing experience.

If you can understand that these relationships are a place you can put into practice all the skills that you have read about and learned while reading this book, you'll see the benefits of this relationship even more. We hope that the awareness you've gained from reading this book — and doing the exercises we've suggested — will help you pursue real healing in these kinds of relationships, instead of allowing them to repeat old patterns.

Children and Relatedness

Your children will probably develop growing relationships also. They may suddenly be good friends with other children whose parents are divorcing. They will find they can talk to these friends better than the "married kids" who had been their friends.

You may be surprised to find yourself feeling judgemental toward kids whose parents are divorcing. You may even not want your kids to associate with them. Surprise! You have found some of your own biases and prejudices toward divorce. Remember your children are going through the divorce process also, and finding friends who are in a similar situation may be helpful. As you have learned, anyone can go through a divorce; it doesn't help to persist in critical attitudes toward people who are ending relationships.

If you are involved in your own growing relationship, where does your child fit in? It depends upon the type of relationship you are creating. If you have a therapy relationship, it may be helpful to share this with your children. They will be more open to talking with others if they realize you are talking to someone. If your growing relationship is with a friend or family member, you may choose to involve your children in this relationship by sharing with them how good it feels to have a special person to talk to.

If your relationship looks like the passionate love affair kind of growing relationship, however, then you need to decide carefully how much to include your child in this relationship. Your child has been observing the arguments between you parents and you may want to expose your child to a more peaceful and loving relationship. However, it's very easy for the excitement of the new relationship to cloud your thinking; you may find yourself wanting to include the children in this relationship more than is appropriate. Having your new partner spend the night while the kids are there will usually be difficult for your children to deal with.

As we've discussed in this chapter, the chances of a growing/transitional relationship lasting and becoming long term are not high. Your children will very likely have to deal with the rending of another of your relationships. Keep that in perspective as you consider how much you want to involve your children in your growing relationship.

Take responsibility for creating this growing relationship as part of your adjustment process. Awareness of this may help your children to put the relationship in better perspective. You take control of your life by making more aware, loving choices; your children can — and will — follow your example.

Homework for a Growing Relationship
Write responses to the following questions in your journal.

1. What is your response to this chapter? Does this discussion square with your experience?

2. If you have had one or more growing relationships, describe them. How were they healing? How were they harmful? What did you learn in each one? Were they with a friend, lover, therapist, or a family member? How could you make the next one more healing and healthy?

3. If you have not had a growing relationship, do you want to? Are you afraid of becoming vulnerable? Are you unable to communicate? Are you afraid of being hurt again?

4. If you are in a primary committed love relationship and having a healing separation, do you think it is possible to experience a growing relationship with your partner? Is this a new concept for you?

Bruce has observed hundreds of couples create a new and loving relationship from the painful ashes of a dead relationship. If that is your goal, a good way to start is for both partners to read and work your way through this book. Do as much of the homework as you have time to do. Encourage and nurture each other because this process takes commitment, self-discipline, and confidence. And there are no guarantees.

How Are You Doing?

Before you go on the the next chapter, take advantage of this brief self-assessment. It will help you to determine if you're ready to head on up the trail.

1. *I'm ready to forgive myself for relationships in the past where I made the other person responsible for my joy and happiness.*
2. *I am making a list of what I learned in each of my past growing relationships.*
3. *I will choose, using my present awareness, what kind of growing relationship I want to have in the future.*
4. *I will take ownership for creating growing relationships as part of my healing process.*
5. *I will take ownership of good feelings in my growing relationships; I am becoming the person I choose to be.*
6. *I will put into practice all of the relationship skills I am learning in this book (and as a participant in the Rebuilding Class, if I took part). I will use these skills in all of my future relationships.*
7. *I am being open and honest, and using good communication skills, in my current relationships.*
8. *I am trying out new healthy behaviors, breaking old patterns, and making my relationships as growing and healing as possible.*

Sexuality

"I'm Interested, but I'm Scared"

When you're first separated, it's normal to be extremely fearful of sex.
During the adjustment process, you can learn to express your unique
sexuality according to your own moral standards. Many singles follow a
conventional moral code: no sexual relationships outside of marriage.
Others like the "singles subculture," and adopt its emphasis on
authenticity, responsibility, and individuality. It's time to discover what
you believe. (Whatever you decide, remember that if there is to be any
sex, it must be safe sex.)

Chapter 17

❦

Being Divorced and Middle-aged Is:
...Not taking out the garbage for fear you'll miss that obscene
*   phone call.*
...Standing out in the middle of the dark parking lot and shouting,
*   "Hey you muggers, the muggee is here!"*
...Telling the guy who frisked you and demanded all your money
*   that you have no money but if he'll frisk you again, you'll write*
*   him a check.*
...Putting a sign on your gate that reads, "All trespassers will be
*   violated."*
...Looking under the bed and hoping someone is there.
                                                    — Lois

Everyone looks forward to this portion of the climb with great expectations. You may have turned to read this chapter first. Maybe you have been anticipating this chapter on sexuality since the original discussion of the rebuilding blocks in chapter 1. Either way, we urge you to slow down, take a deep breath, and try to put sex in its proper perspective. (At least read chapter 1 first!)

Before We Begin...

We'd like to open this chapter by acknowledging the very wide range of attitudes and beliefs people hold about sex. We know that our readers' views span the spectrum, from "no sex outside marriage" to "if it feels good, do it." Sexuality and morality are closely connected in our society, and we respect those who have adopted a strong moral position, as well as those who have chosen non-conventional lifestyles.

A very large percentage of those who take part in the divorce seminars do so under the auspices of a church or religious organization, and many religious groups maintain that a sexual union belongs only within committed marriage relationship. Some readers who hold that view may find that portions of this chapter will offend their beliefs. We regret that, but we would consider it irresponsible to ignore a subject so central to the concerns of people going through the divorce recovery process.

Because we believe that decisions in the realm of sexual morality are very personal, we have elected not to take a position on the moral issues involved. In short, we do not advocate sexual relationships after divorce, nor do we condemn them. Whatever your moral stance, we believe you'll find this chapter a useful examination of the issues in developing a sexual relationship — or not. (Still, some readers may prefer to skip this chapter.)

Take It One Stage at a Time

I've had a conflict about having sexual relations while I am single. One part of me says that sex is important to my personal growth, and the other part says that I feel guilty having sex with a woman I'm not married to. What do I do?

— Tom

On this part of the climb up the mountain you'll want to find your own pathway. Each of us has an individual morality that will largely determine our direction. Because this area requires an effort not only to climb, but also to find your way, you may feel more hesitant and less confident. Take your time and make sure the path you choose really suits you. Of course, you can change paths if one isn't working for you. But some people have paid a tremendous price — emotionally and physically — because they experimented with behavior that was not really compatible with their own values.

There are three typical stages in this rebuilding block: *lack of interest*, the *horny* stage, and the *return to normal*. Each of the stages has powerful effects on the adjustment process. However, not everybody going through the divorce process goes through all three stages of the sexuality process. Some people do not go through the lack of interest stage, and some do not experience the horny stage. However, the stages are very common occurrences which need to be recognized.

You had a sexual relationship – for better or for worse — for all those years that you were married, but now your love relationship is no longer available. You are faced with all of the emotional and social adjustments of ending a love relationship, including what to do with your sexual desires.

"I Wish I Were Single… ?"

When you were married did you wonder if all those "free" singles were the sexual athletes they were rumored to be? And did you fantasize what it would be like to have a date with a different and exciting person each night of the week?

Now you are single. (We trust that, by this point on the trail, you have accepted the reality of your situation.) Look at the people around you. Many are spending evenings alone. Many are out pretending to have fun at singles parties — when in reality they are just plain bored. You may find yourself spending an evening with a person who makes your ex look attractive and desirable — and you never thought anyone could be worse than your ex. And everyone you know seems to be going with someone and then breaking up — you can't even keep track of who is dating whom. The contrast between your fantasy of the wild single life and what it actually is adds greatly to the trauma of divorce.

"A Date? Well, I Don't Know…"

Take heart — the first part of this sexuality climb is the steepest and most difficult — it gets easier after you become accustomed to being single. You have not been "out on a date" for years, and the first person you ask turns you down. You attend a singles party petrified that no one will ask you to dance — and equally petrified that someone will. At the first contact with the opposite sex you feel like an awkward junior-high kid on a first date. And wow! If someone should make a pass at you — the thought is enough to make you stay home, alone, forever.

Just what is appropriate behavior for an adult who hasn't dated in years? There may have been rules and chaperons at your teenage parties. Your parents probably told you what time to be in. Now you have no one to set the limits but yourself, and your feelings are so confused and uncertain that you can't even rely on them. You envied the freedom of singleness, and now you would give anything to have the security of marriage again. And what about the moral and health issues involved?

Later on in the process, when you've found your individual pathway, things will be more comfortable. After you have overcome your confusion and uncertainty, you'll find that you can express yourself through dating and relationships with the opposite sex. There may be a freedom that you didn't have when you were a teenager doing what was expected of you — or what was not expected.

"I'm Glad You Asked That Question"

In the Fisher divorce seminars, sexuality is one of the last of the sessions. This is not to save the "best" for last, but to give people time to become comfortable discussing such a personal and emotional issue. To help people become more comfortable, they're asked to *write down* their questions about sexuality — you know, the ones that they always wanted to ask but were afraid to. The questions are directed to either men or women, and the facilitator reads the questions aloud to ensure anonymity. These questions give us insights into the concerns of formerly married people.

Some questions recently separated people frequently ask include: (1) "What do you find attractive and desirable in the opposite sex?" (2) "What do you call going out? I hate the word *date!*"; and (3) "How do I tell the person I'm going out with that I don't want anything heavy?"

Later on in the process, people might ask other questions: (4) "What do men think about a woman who has sex early in the relationship?" (5) "How do women feel about having more than one sexual relationship at the same time?" (6) "Why don't men call again after we've gone to bed together?" and (7) "I refuse to consider having sex outside of marriage — would you want to go out with me?"

The adjustments resulting from the changing sex roles cause difficulty for both men and women: (8) "What do men think about a woman who asks you out?" (9) "Just what do women want? I hold the door open for one woman and she gets irritated. The next woman waits for me to open the door. What am I supposed to do?" (10) "I always felt comfortable making complimentary comments to a woman and asking her out. This week, a woman told me she liked my legs, and asked me if I would like to go out with her. What do I do?" (11) "Who do you think should pay for the date?" (12) "Whose responsibility is it for birth control?" (13) "Is everybody but me comfortable about using condoms?"

Questions about kids can be difficult, too: (14) "Who pays for the babysitter?" (15) "Who takes the babysitter home?" (16) "What do you think about a member of the opposite sex spending the night when children are present?" (17) "My children don't want me to date. What do I do?" (18) "What do I say to my teenager when she tells me to get home early?" and (19) "What do I do when the kid answers the doorbell, sees me, and shuts the door in my face?"

Most formerly married people are frightened about AIDS, VD, and other sexually-transmitted diseases: (20) "I would like to have sex but I'm deathly afraid of STDs. How can I be sure to avoid getting a disease?" (21) "How do I find out if the person may be infected with AIDS before we have sex?" and (22) "What is herpes? Is it really dangerous?"

Formerly married people have many understandable concerns about sexuality. These questions reflect only a few of their anxieties. Dorothy reflected the emotional impact of sexuality, reporting, "I became extremely depressed last week when I realized I was 40 years old, divorced, and might never get laid again!"

We don't claim to have answers to all these questions, but we think the discussion in this chapter will help you clarify your own issues around sexuality.

"Not Tonight, Thanks"

The first step of the process, while you are in deep grief, is a lack of interest in sex, or maybe a complete inability to perform sexually. Women tend to be completely uninterested in sex, men often are impotent. Just when you are feeling a great deal of emotional pain, the fact that you are uninterested or unable to perform sexually adds to the pain. Many people in the seminars say, "I was already hurting so much, and now I find that I can't perform sexually. It feels like hitting rock bottom." When they learn that it is perfectly normal and natural to be uninterested in sex while in deep grief, they feel greatly relieved.

Honk If You're...

I became so horny after my separation that I called my friend asking for suggestions of what I could do. Having sex with someone I was not married to was out of the question for me.
— Raquel

Somewhere along the divorce process, perhaps near the end of the Anger rebuilding block, you get through this stage of not being able to perform sexually. At that point, you will probably go to the other extreme and reach the *horny* stage. Your sexual desires may be greater than you have ever known in your whole life. It is almost frightening. Because the needs and desires of this stage are so strong, it is important to understand your feelings and attitudes as much as possible. Among the many feelings present in the horny stage is a need to prove that you are okay, personally and sexually. It is as though you are trying to solve not only your sexual problems but all of the other rebuilding blocks as well, using sex as the method. You are trying to overcome loneliness, to feel lovable again, to improve your self-concept, to work through some anger, to develop friendships — and all of these things are concentrated in the sexual drive. It is as though your body is trying to heal itself through sexual expression alone. Some folks find their behavior at the horny stage to be somewhat "compulsive" because of this.

One-night stands are one way people try to solve this horny stage. We see this approach commonly portrayed in books and movies about divorce. The need to go out and "prove that you are okay" may be so great that some people will do something sexually that they have never done before — without much thought for the moral or health issues.

Another important understanding about the horny stage is that there is a great need for touching during this stage. As you go through the divorce process, you will probably experience a heightened need to be physically touched. Touch has remarkable, healing qualities. Depending upon the warmth and closeness of your relationship, you likely received much physical touching in your marriage. Now that touching is not there anymore. Many people will try to meet their need for physical touching with sex, not realizing that there is a very real difference between physical touching and sexual touching. Although the two are entirely different, you can resolve much of your need for sexual contact by getting the physical touching that you need in non-sexual ways (e.g., hugs, massage, holding hands, walking arm-in-arm…).

You can resolve the needs of the horny stage by methods other than direct sexual contact. If you understand that a part of the compulsive drive behind the horny stage is to prove that you are okay, and to feel good about yourself again, then you can work directly on that. Building your identity and self-confidence, and understanding that you are lovable can overcome the loneliness and take away some of the pressures of the horny stage. And if you can reach your "quota" of hugs, this will also take away some of the pressures. Together, these steps may go a long way toward resolving your needs at this difficult time.

The stereotype about the divorced person being sexually an "easy mark" results from the horny stage. During this period, the divorced person may be an "easy mark." The sexual drive is tremendous. Many people going through the divorce process have sexual relationships somewhat promiscuously — not a recommended practice in the age of widespread AIDS, chlamydia, papilloma, and other sexually transmitted diseases.

Getting Back to Normal

Sex in our marriage was not good. We separated and experienced sexual relationships with other people. Then when we came together again, we were surprised that sex with each other was good. It seemed to free us to be apart and to be with others.

— Mike and Jane

Eventually you will overcome the horny stage and get into the third stage of post-divorce sexuality in which your normal sex drive resumes. (There is, of course, a great deal of variation in sex drive from one person to another, and remember that everyone does not experience all three stages.) Because the horny stage is so compulsive and so controlling, people often find it a relief to be back to their normal sexual desires.

During the early stages of sexuality you are doing what you *should* do; then you go through a stage of doing what you *want* to do. Most people going through the divorce process experience the evolution of becoming free sexually, in the sense that they are suddenly aware of who they are and what their sexual nature is. This is another growth aspect of the divorce process.

Most people were sexually monogamous in marriage because that is what they believed they should be. Then when they go through the horny stage, they may have many sexual relationships.

Finally, they decide to be monogamous again because this is what they want to be. Consider the impact of this process on future love relationships. The need for sexual experience outside of a committed relationship is much less when one arrives at this third stage. As long as you are in the *should* mode sexually, there is always the temptation to do what you *should not* do. But when you reach this third stage, doing what you want to do and expressing who you really are, the temptation for sex outside a love relationship is greatly diminished.

There's More to Life

I've agreed with everything you have said until now, but when you state that experiencing sexual relationships while single can be a personal growth experience, I have to strongly disagree. Sex is sacred, and should occur only between two people in a sacred marriage.

— Father John

We have blown sex out of proportion in our society, perhaps because we hid it and denied it for so long. The "media view" of sex appears not to have much to do with the real world. Advertising is full of sex in order to sell products. Youth — and the supposed beauty, aliveness, and sexuality of youth – are revered. With such a daily overdose in the media, it's tough to keep a realistic perspective on sexuality when it comes to love relationships and marriage.

Usually missing from popular presentations is the spiritual dimension of human sexuality. Sex is one way of transcending our normal means of expressing ourselves, and it allows us to show our love and concern for another person in a very special and positive way. Sex can be a method of transporting oneself to levels beyond everyday, to become something greater than what one normally is. But this spiritual dimension that is present in sexuality is also present in overcoming anger, in our ability to communicate, in learning to like another person, and in learning to accept and deal with all of the human emotions. Sexuality, when placed in perspective, may be seen as only one of the many normal healthy elements of our connectedness with our fellow humans.

Our society, with its historical roots in religious belief, has traditionally placed great emphasis on having a sexual relationship only with a marriage partner. Yet the messages are mixed and quite confusing. Many divorced people are amazed to learn that they can have very enjoyable and beautiful sex without being in love with the person. Those who hold more traditional moral and/or religious beliefs may feel a great amount of guilt if they have non-marital sexual relationships. And there are a number who have adopted a morality concerned only with not catching a disease and not becoming pregnant.

Healthy divorce adjustment requires that you grow beyond an undue emphasis on physical sex and arrive at the point where you can understand the beauty of your sexuality as a special way of sharing and communicating with another person. A personal style of sexuality which is (a) a genuine expression of your individuality, uniqueness, and morality, (b) equally concerned with the needs and well-being of your sexual partner, and (c) not hurtful to anyone else or the larger community, is socially responsible, self-fulfilling, …and human.

Each person has to develop a personal and individual sexual morality appropriate for her or his own beliefs, values, personality, background, attitudes, experiences, and partner. Many people will choose to have no sexual relationships outside of marriage — a very appropriate choice for them. Others may find sexual experiences an effective way of resolving the horny stage and a way of healing themselves after ending the love relationship.

Most divorced people are comfortable with only one sexual relationship at a time. In fact, the evidence seems pretty clear that most people need an emotional relationship to support a sexual relationship.

When two people have communication, trust, understanding, and respect for each other, they are comfortable having a sexual relationship, if that is within their moral value system. If you are able to reach this level of self-actualization in your sexual relationship, you will find less need to have relationships outside of marriage if you remarry in the future.

Can We Talk About It? Open Communication About Sex

Let's now look at some of the other adjustment problems that you may experience as you end a love relationship and enter the formerly married subculture.

Women often complain that all men are interested in is going to bed with them. Yet we find that very few formerly married people are genuinely able to enjoy cheap and casual sex. There are, unfortunately, many people in our society who have not developed ways of interacting with the opposite sex beyond the sexual area. It can be and often is the easiest avenue open for contact and, after all, is one where the potential payoff is great, if temporary. Nevertheless, there are many aspects of relationship other than sexual, and your life will be so much richer if you fully develop your range of choices. (In the previous chapter we looked at developing friendships with the opposite sex that are non-romantic and non-sexual.)

It is interesting that, on the seminar questionnaires asking people what they would like to talk about, the number two choice (after relationships) differs between men and women. The second choice for women is sexuality in almost all classes, and the second choice for men is love in almost all classes. Surprised? There's more. Not only are women more interested in talking about sex, they are much more comfortable talking about it than men are. After one sexuality class, Burt confided that he went home and was unable to go to sleep because he was so shocked by how freely the women in the class talked about sexuality.

We believe that openness is a very healthy style of interaction with others. (You'll recall our discussion in chapter 13, dealing with dropping our masks and being more open in our communication.) Sexuality used to be virtually impossible to talk and communicate openly about, so people were prevented from understanding and dealing with their sexual attitudes and feelings. Now, because of greater openness, we are able to understand and develop our sexual feelings just as we understand and develop all of the other human emotions we feel.

Openness in sexual matters opens up another avenue that is very freeing. When you are dating in the formerly-married society, you can discuss sexual concerns openly and early in the relationship, minimizing all of the little games that go on concerning, "Are we going to bed or not?" Many of the dating relationships that you have will never include sexual intimacy; it will simply not be appropriate. By discussing this and getting it out in the open, it frees you to allow the relationship to develop more naturally and normally, free of the games that go along with not knowing where you stand sexually with the other person.

If you are early in the rebuilding process, and the idea of having sexual relationships is extremely frightening, you can share this with the other person: "I really need to get out and be with a friend, but anything beyond friendship is more than I can stand emotionally at this point." You'll be surprised at the favorable response from others after you have shared yourself openly like this. Most will understand and accept you because they are going through the divorce process and have experienced some of the same feelings themselves.

Without Using Each Other

There are a considerable number of lonely — even desperate — people, who introduce another problem to the formerly married subculture. They make the whole problem of sexuality even more difficult because they are basically looking for somebody to use. If you are a kind and caring person, seeing all of the needy people around you may tempt you to help them meet their needs, some of which may be sexual.

The great loneliness and neediness out in the formerly married subculture causes special adjustment problems for those who are caught in the *compassion trap* — the need to nurture and give to others in response to their apparent needs. If you tend to be that way, you will have to learn to be somewhat selfish. (In this case, "selfish" is also arguably the responsible path.)

There is no way you can meet the needs of all those who are desperate and lonely. You must meet your own needs and take care of yourself first, and do so without using other people or allowing others to use you. Do everything you can to feel good about yourself and to grow within yourself so you can become as complete and whole as possible, and can overcome your own loneliness and neediness. That will provide you a solid foundation for future relationships, and for helping others who are in genuine need.

Roles and Rules: Who Does What to Whom?

Another big problem for many people entering the formerly married subculture is the question of rules. You may feel as if you are a bewildered teenager, not exactly understanding and knowing how to behave. There has been a great deal of change in our society regarding sexual behavior and attitudes. Most of this change is a freeing from set rules of conduct prescribed by the courting game into a freedom to be ourselves. Freedom to be yourself is very difficult if you do not know who "yourself" is! You'll need to find your way, and follow your own unique style as you go. To become open and honest with who you are, and to express that unique individuality as much as possible, will be much more difficult than just following the established rules of dating that were prevalent before. Needless to say, of course, an important part of who you are is defined by your moral values.

Another challenge results from the fact that gender roles have changed, and women are initiators in everything much more than before, including sex, and this is very upsetting for people of both sexes. Women in class during the sexuality discussion ask, "How do men feel about women being the initiators?" The typical male response is that they find it very freeing to have the woman be the initiator. They have had to deal with all the fears of rejection that have been inherent in asking and initiating with women. They say that it feels good to have women now deal with the risk of being turned down, and that they are free from the burden of being the initiator all the time.

Despite such comments from men in the seminars, women report that in the real world, many men are threatened by assertive women. Although men say they like to be asked out, often they are uncomfortable when the actual situation arises. It appears that *intellectually* men like women to initiate, but *emotionally* men have more difficulty handling sexually assertive women.

The problem is not limited to males. Females report confusion also. The woman may say she would like to ask the man out, but when the time comes the old roles takes over and the woman never gets around to asking. For many women there is a double adjustment process happening — adjustment to becoming single, and adjustment in finding a new identity as a woman.

It's not easy to question the old roles and try out new behavior when you are rebuilding after the loss of a relationship. On the other hand, it is an appropriate time to do it. Everything else in your life is changing. Why not try out some changes in gender roles at the same time?

It appears that the end result of changing gender roles will be more equality between the sexes and more freedom for individuals to be themselves. But nothing stays the same; we see the pendulum of social mores swing back and forth. In the late 20th century, the movement was strongly toward sexual freedom and gender equality. As we begin the new millenium, more traditional values have re-emerged. It's not a smooth road, and the period of change causes much uncertainty and confusion. Now more than ever, perhaps, it is necessary to know yourself, to adopt values which are both self-fulfilling and respectful of others, and to act in accordance with those values.

Let's Be Careful Out There

If you have decided to be open to new sexual relationships, let us pass along a couple of words of advice: *be safe!*

Safe sex is really important today. AIDS (acquired immunodeficiency syndrome) has made a major impact upon sexual behavior around the world. Although there was a plateau for a few years, the number of people in all walks of life who are dying from AIDS appears once again likely to increase into the 21st century. Science and medicine will continue to seek ways to deal with the disease, but in the meantime each of us will have to take responsibility for preventing AIDS — along with Herpes, Hepatitis B, chlamydia, papilloma, and other sexually transmitted diseases — by adopting safe sex practices. Many are choosing to be much more selective and/or to curtail their sexual activity.

Impact Publishers Statement on Safe Sex

Impact Publishers, Inc. recognizes safe and healthy approaches to sexual expression as one of the principal health and social issues of our time. We offer the following statement for your serious consideration:

Sexual expression is a basic, normal, positive, intensely personal and highly satisfying human activity. Although sexual practices are often publicly regulated by social mores, religious values, and law, individuals and couples decide privately how they will live their sex lives.

In addition to important choices about personal moral values, responsible sexual practice requires good information, including knowledge of the fundamentals of human sexuality, responsible family planning, contraceptive choices, and protection against sexually transmitted diseases.

Sexually transmitted diseases, such as Acquired Immune Deficiency Syndrome (AIDS), Chlamydia, various forms of Herpes, Hepatitis B, and the several Venereal Diseases, are serious and widespread public health problems, both in the United States and throughout the populated world.

"Safe sex" — minimizing the risks of sexually transmitted diseases — includes at minimum the following:

• an absolutely certain, long-term, exclusively monogamous relationship, or ALL of the following:

• regular periodic physical examinations;

• conscientious unfailing use of condoms (preferably with spermicides) during intercourse;

• awareness and avoidance of common risk factors in STD's (e.g., intravenous drug use, high-risk populations);

• honest and open discussion of sexual habits and preferences with potential partners; infrequent changing of partners.

Each individual — married or single — has the right to freedom of choice in sexual expression, so long as the practice involves consenting adults and consciously avoids physical or psychological harm to any person.

No one is obligated to have a sexual relationship with another person — including a marriage partner — unless he or she wishes to do so.

The following AIDS facts are reproduced from the brochure, *Understanding AIDS: A Message from the Surgeon General*, released in 1988 by C. Everett Koop, M.D. Then Surgeon General of the United States, Dr. Koop is now the principal medical advisor to America Online:

- *Who you are has nothing to do with whether you are in danger of being infected with the AIDS virus. What matters is what you do.*

- *There are two main ways you can get AIDS. First, you can become infected by having sex — oral, anal, or vaginal — with someone who is infected with the AIDS virus. Second, you can be infected by sharing drug needles and syringes with an infected person.*

- *Your chances of coming into contact with the virus increase with the number of sex partners you have.*

- *You won't get AIDS through everyday contact… a mosquito bite… saliva, sweat, tears, urine, or a bowel movement… a kiss… clothes, a telephone, or from a toilet seat.*

- *A person can be infected with the AIDS virus without showing any symptoms at all.*

- *The AIDS virus may live in the human body for years before actual symptoms appear.*

- *Condoms are the best preventative measure against AIDS besides not having sex and practicing safe behavior.*

RISKY BEHAVIOR
   Sharing drug needles and syringes.
   Anal sex, with or without a condom.
   Vaginal or oral sex with someone who shoots drugs or engages in anal sex.
   Sex with someone you don't know well (a pickup or prostitute) or with someone you know has several sex partners.
   Unprotected sex (without a condom) with an infected person.

SAFE BEHAVIOR
   Not having sex.
   Sex with one mutually faithful, uninfected partner.
   Not shooting drugs.

If you know someone well enough to have sex with, then you should be able to talk about AIDS. If someone is unwilling to talk, you shouldn't have sex.

It is extremely important to communicate with potential sexual partners the need for safe sex practices even if it is difficult to do so. Take control of your life in the area of sexuality, and make careful loving choices. Never was the old adage, "better to be safe than sorry," more appropriate.

Impact Publishers, which publishes a number of books on relationships and divorce (including this book and others in the Rebuilding Books series), has prepared the statement on the preceding pages regarding sensible safe sex. We encourage you to read it and to consider carefully how it may apply in your life.

Children and Sex

Children of divorce also have the rebuilding block of sexuality to deal with. When their parents' relationship ends, where do children find role models for relationships, sexuality, becoming an adult man or woman and a mature person?

It is often confusing for children to see their parents get involved in another love relationship. Somehow children sense that it may include sex. (Kids know more about which parents are going to bed and which are not than the parents believe!) And if the parents are in the horny stage and sending out all of the sexual vibrations which accompany that stage, what do the children do with that? How do they handle this new behavior in their parents?

Communication may sound like an old answer, but it is critically important at this point. When parents talk with their children frankly and openly about sexuality — at a level appropriate to each child's ability to understand — it is very helpful for the kids and for the parents. Although there is much anxiety and insecurity in the children's lives, that very turmoil can be the beginning of learning. Children may well gain a far deeper understanding of sexuality — including their own maturation — as their parents go through this stage of rebuilding.

Children can find role models in relatives, grandparents, and their parents' male and female friends. As one teenager stated to me, "I've got more role models around now than I ever had before!"

How Are You Doing?

We have covered a lot of ground in this chapter, and there is much we have not explored. Sex is often a stumbling block for the divorced person, so be sure you have dealt thoroughly with these issues before you go on. Here are some trail markers for assessing your progress.

1. *I am comfortable going out with potential love partners.*
2. *I know and can explain my present moral attitudes and values.*
3. *I feel capable of having a deep and meaningful sexual relationship when it becomes appropriate.*
4. *I would feel comfortable being intimate with another love partner.*
5. *My sexual behavior is consistent with my morality.*
6. *I am satisfied with my present dating situation.*
7. *I am behaving morally, the way I would like to have my children behave.*
8. *I feel satisfied with the way I am meeting my sexual needs.*
9. *I take responsibility for my interaction with others.*
10. *I have learned that male and female sexual attitudes and values may be more alike than different.*
11. *I feel comfortable being with the opposite sex.*
12. *I am secure enough to behave the way I want even if it does not conform to the expectations of others.*
13. *I am not letting the compulsive needs of the horny stage control my behavior.*
14. *I am solving the neediness of the horny stage in a manner that is acceptable to me.*
15. *I understand and accept that many people will have no desire and may be unable to perform sexually while in deep grief.*
16. *I am getting my "quota" of hugs every week.*

Singleness
"You Mean It's Okay?"

Singleness — a time to invest in your own personal growth rather than in other relationships. A period of singleness enables you to build confidence in yourself so you can experience and enjoy being single as an acceptable alternative lifestyle, not as a time to be lonely. It is easy, however, to become stuck in this rebuilding block as a means of avoiding another intimate love relationship.

Chapter 18

❧

I've become aware that living as a single person is an affirmation of strength and self — not an embarrassing admission of failure. I'm more relaxed in the company of others — I'm no longer wasting emotional energy being a social chameleon. Post-marital guilt, self-doubts, and questions like "Will I ever love again?" are greatly diminished. I am happy as a single person — something I had not thought possible before.

— Larry

You'll notice a number of people walking by themselves during this part of the climb. They've gained enough confidence in their climbing ability that they're choosing to walk at their own pace, rather than following the crowd. Some of these folks have chosen time alone as a way of investing in themselves. Others simply want and need to be by themselves, with their own thoughts, and to enjoy the view alone. This is the stage of *singleness.*

Were You Ever Really Single Before?

Many people never learned to be single persons before they married. They went from parental homes to marriage homes, never even considered that one could be happy living as a single person, and never questioned the myth of "happily ever after."

Mona lived with her parents until she married Joe. She went from pleasing one man, her father, to pleasing another man, her husband. When Joe first talked about leaving, she clung to him because the thought of living alone was terrifying. She had never learned to please herself. She had always been a dependent person, and now the thought of being independent, although challenging, was frightening to her. She was embarrassed because it really sounded silly to her that a woman of 35 did not know her own mind, or know what to do with her life.

Only gradually did she adjust to being alone. At first she searched for other relationships, something/someone to lean on. As she became more and more confident, she began doing more things for herself and enjoying it. She wallpapered a whole bedroom; sawed the boards and pounded the nails for a new patio fence; started going out to movies and concerts by herself while the kids were with Joe. She invited the whole neighborhood in for a party. These activities left her feeling exhilarated, knowing that she did not need anyone. She became a good example of what it means to be an independent person.

Jim represents the male side of this same coin. He had been well cared for by his mother. His clothes were always washed and ironed, meals were on time, and even his room was kept clean. He could devote his time to school, school activities, and his job. When he entered college, he lived in a dorm. Again his meals were provided and he had a minimum of housekeeping chores. When he married Janet, she took over all the things his mother had always done. He felt independent and didn't realize how dependent he actually was. He found out when he left Janet. He was helpless in the kitchen, even in preparing the simplest meal. He had very little understanding of how to wash his clothes, and ended up with pink underwear when he put them in the wash with his red shirt! You can pay for car maintenance, but it is difficult — and very expensive — to hire a full-time cook and housekeeper.

Gradually Jim's self-prepared meals improved. Finally he got brave enough to invite a woman friend to his home to eat, and she was delighted with the meal he prepared. His clothes began to look more cared for. He was very pleased and proud when he learned to iron his own shirts! Learning to care for himself was like growing up — and each accomplishment gave him a feeling of success and achievement.

"Me and My Shadow"

The singleness we're talking about is much more than learning to do the tasks that someone else has done for you, of course. It's a whole way of life.

Independence in the realm of dating and love relationships is a good example. A typical comment from a recently-separated person might be, "I'll never make it as a single person; I need another love relationship." During the singleness stage, the same person might say, "Why get remarried? I can come and go as I please. I can eat whenever I feel like it. I don't have to adjust my daily living habits to another person. Being single sure feels good!" Before the singleness stage, one may be looking for the "lost half." But during this stage one reaches the point of comfort in going out alone. No longer is a "date" necessary to avoid embarrassment or a feeling of failure. The quality of relationships improves: now you're choosing the person you go out with, rather than taking whoever seems available, just to be with someone. And the whole evening out may be spent sharing rather than needing. Other persons may be encountered and enjoyed for who they are, rather than as potential lifetime companions.

Single and Loving It
One of the homework assignments in the divorce seminars has to do with developing new interests in the singleness stage. Many have spent their free, recreational time in the past doing what the spouse wanted or what they had learned to do with their parents. Your assignment now is simply to take the time to develop a new interest, or to pursue something you may have wanted to do for a long time. It might be to learn to play the guitar, to paint, to drive a car, or to play a new sport. Seminar participants who take this homework seriously find many new activities that *they* really enjoy; they no longer settle for what someone else enjoyed.

Singleness is a time for being a responsible adult. The roles each of us play in our relationships with others are linked to our internal attitudes and feelings. Surprisingly, the link is a two-way street! As you change your actions and your ways of relating to others, you'll find your attitudes begin to change. ("Hey, I'm finding out I can get along well as a single person. Look what I'm accomplishing on my own!")

It's easier to make these changes toward independence in the singleness stage than when you were in a permanent love relationship. A neutral environment facilitates both internal and external changes. The singleness stage is a great opportunity to make the internal changes in attitudes and feelings — and the external changes in behavior and relationships — necessary for your growth toward becoming a whole person by yourself.

"I'm Glad To Be Single Again… Or Am I?"
Not everything is rosy in the singleness stage, of course. Research shows that single people — particularly women — do not fare well economically. Single persons are passed over for promotions in some career fields. They're looked upon as fair game romantically and sexually. Despite strengthened laws against sexual harassment, single women in particular may be pressured in the workplace, expected to trade sexual favors for promotions and other opportunities. (Just one example: Ford Motor Company recently joined a long list of major corporations which have settled sexual harassment law suits.) Although

there is discussion in Congress (as we go to press with this Third Edition in late 1999) of doing away with the "marriage penalty," the tax laws still favor married couples who file income tax jointly. Big changes have been made in obtaining credit for single people; nevertheless, there remain many forms of economic discrimination against singles.

There are other situations that create discomfort for single people. Alexa complained about her child's Sunday School class. When the teacher asked the children to draw pictures of their families, Alexa's son drew a picture of himself, his sister, and his mother — which was his family. The teacher made him draw a picture of a man in the family because, "We all know that a family consists of both a father and a mother!" Alexa was hurt, disappointed, and angry, and expressed her negative feelings directly to the minister of the church.

Ursula went to church on Mother's Day and the sermon was about marital love. Ursula and a dozen or more other single moms felt completely left out of the sermon. It was a depressing day in church for her. She wrote a letter to the minister explaining her feelings. In this case, he responded very favorably, meeting with the single mothers, and offering a special sermon — with a broader view of motherhood — a couple of weeks later.

Schools are often an irritating problem when you are a single parent. The PTA chairperson calls and asks that Johnny's parents run the dart show. The single-parent father explains that would be happy to take part — but that he'll be alone. The chairperson informs him that it takes two to run the show and she will ask someone else to handle it. PTA meetings themselves are often couple-oriented; you can feel really single and alone when you attend without a partner.

You come alone to a parent-teacher conference, and the teacher informs you that "all of the 'problem children' in the room have just one parent," and that's why she wanted to see you. Your child may not be getting "the parenting she needs," and perhaps that's why she is doing so poorly in her school work. What's more, your daughter is "so boy crazy for a fifth-grader!" It is implied that if Mom had a "permanent" relationship with one man, Janie would have a better attitude toward males. You feel angry, vulnerable, and defenseless. What can you say?

You can develop some assertive responses for the most common put-downs and discriminatory acts. You can help to educate others, while maintaining your own integrity, by responding firmly. You'll feel better inside, too, rather than going away fuming!

Here's an example: in response to the teacher who insists Janie would be better off in a two-parent household, you might try something like this, "You're right — being a single parent isn't easy. In fact, former Vice President Dan Quayle called single mothers 'genuine heroes.' But Janie and I are doing fine these days, and I don't agree that her school performance is suffering because of my divorce. I'll be glad to work with you on special homework or tutoring or other efforts to improve her schoolwork. What suggestions do you have for her study habits? Will you give her extra assignments?"

That way, you're not accepting her put-down, or letting her blame your personal life for Janie's school problems. The responsibility for school work is focused back where it belongs — on teacher-student-parent cooperation, not on your love life.

Successfully Single

It often takes a great deal of inner security to handle the singleness stage successfully. Much of the discussion in this chapter concerns the feelings singles experience in response to society's attitudes. If you have worked your way through the prior rebuilding blocks successfully, it is likely that you will be able to experience a sense of peacefulness and calmness in the singleness stage. You may become slightly upset about the attitudes of others, but you'll be strong enough to handle them. Learn from the external prejudices and use them to become more secure in your own internal feelings.

Singleness can be one of the most productive stages you go through in the climb, in the sense that the old wounds can really be healed. Dealing with the external discrimination may help you to become stronger inside.

One caution: Singleness is an easy stage in which to become stuck. If you have not worked through all of the leftovers concerning marriage and intimacy, you may use the singleness stage as a place to hide. It may sound like the singleness stage when you hear someone say, "I'll never marry again." But in many ways that is the opposite of genuine singleness. Fear of intimacy, avoidance of feelings, and opposition to marriage as though it were the worst institution in our society — all indicate that the person is stuck. The goal is to be free to *choose* singleness or remarriage, not to stay single forever.

Singleness has become an acceptable alternative in our society. A generation or two ago, a single person was looked upon in the community as somewhat weird, one who just did not quite make it to the altar. It was "patriotic" to be married because, after all, the family was the cornerstone of society. Attitudes are changing; at a talk on love relationships, one woman wanted to know why we had to keep talking about *relationships.* Was not it just as valid to talk about remaining single? Did we have to keep looking toward being in a relationship as the ideal?

The fact that there are approximately a million divorces in the United States each year makes singleness more acceptable for many. The large number of formerly married people in our society has brought about many changes in attitudes toward singleness. Perhaps we are becoming more accepting of individual differences? Let's hope so!

Children and Singleness

Singleness is an important rebuilding block for children, too. They need to learn to be single, individual, independent-from-parents people before they marry for the first time. If children can see and understand the importance of singleness, it will give them a much better chance to develop successful love relationships in their futures.

Parenting is different during the singleness stage. In earlier stages parents frequently bend themselves out of shape trying to make sure they are lovable, datable, and okay in many other ways. The kids often suffer; their needs are put on the "back-burner." In the singleness stage, parents usually are more responsive to the needs of the kids. Susannah had been volunteering in the seminars because she "needed" to feel worthwhile by helping others. When she began to reach the singleness stage, she resigned as a volunteer because she wanted to spend more time with her children. Parents in the singleness stage have begun to rise above their own emotional needs.

How Are You Doing?

At this point in our climb up the mountain we've gained a big reward: the view from above the timberline. You can see forever! And the singleness stage is definitely above the timberline. You can see the world much more clearly from here. You can know yourself much better. You understand others, and your interactions with others, much better. Your viewpoint of life is much broader. At the singleness stage, we're almost to the top. Let's hurry and see the view from the peak!

Here are some items to check yourself with before the final climb.

1. *I am comfortable being single.*
2. *I can be happy as a single person.*
3. *I am comfortable going to social events as a single person.*

4. *I see being single as an acceptable alternative lifestyle.*
5. *I am becoming a whole person rather than a half-person looking for my other lost half.*
6. *I am spending time investing in my own personal growth rather than looking for another love relationship.*
7. *I can look at my friends as people I want to be with rather than as potential love partners.*
8. *If I have children and family, I can spend time enjoying being with them rather than begrudging the time they take from my personal life.*
9. *I have found internal peace and contentment as a single person.*

Purpose
"I Have Goals for the Future Now"

Recently separated people tend to live in the past, and tend to be very dependent upon others. After they have worked through the divorce process, they begin to live more in the present and to be less dependent upon others. Now you can plan for your future as an independent person, with or without a new love relationship.

Chapter 19

⟨⟩

When I started this divorce seminar I dreamed I was driving a car that went off a mountain road and I was balancing on the edge of a cliff, too scared to move. When I completed this divorce seminar, I dreamed I was in a big, dark pit with my car but there was a cement ramp at the end of the pit where I could drive my car out.
— Harry

Take a look back down the trail. Hasn't this been a rewarding climb? Your highest priority, back in the divorce pits at the bottom of the mountain, was to survive. You weren't thinking about setting any goals for the future. You were getting along from hour to hour, day to day.

Things have changed a lot as we've "gained altitude," haven't they? It was hard work climbing the divorce process trail, but now that you're almost at the top, you have some perspective. You can look back at your past to see how you got to where you are today. You can look at your present situation and recognize how much you have accomplished. You can look at your future, and know that you can determine for yourself who you will become.

Looking at Your Past, Present, and Future Life
The trauma of divorce motivates us to take a good hard look at our lives. We tend to go back into the past and dwell a great deal upon the things that we would have done differently if we could live our lives over again. We tend to be so engrossed in the present scene that we are unable to think about the future.

It is time now for you to get out of some of the past thinking and the present pain and to start thinking about goals and decisions for the future.

People in a great deal of emotional pain cannot easily make plans and set goals for the future, and if you are still in a great deal of emotional pain, then you may find it difficult to read this chapter on setting goals. If you've read this book too fast and haven't allowed all of the emotional learning to take place, then you may need to set aside this chapter for now, take some time to go back over the previous material, and do the emotional learning that you need to do.

As we discussed in chapter 11, Bruce's research shows that people who have recently separated have very low scores in the *Tennessee Self Concept Scale*. Other research using the *Personality Orientation Inventory* indicated that recently separated people, and especially dumpees, have a great deal of "living in the past" in their thinking and attitudes. People in the divorce pits have very little hope and goals for the future. They feel they have entered Dante's *Inferno,* where the words above the gates read, "All Hope abandon, ye who enter here."

But chances are, if you have worked your way carefully through each of the preceding chapters over a period of weeks or months, you are ready to get on with your life. In this chapter, you'll be building on your successful climb up the mountain and doing some goal setting for your future.

Let's get started!

Your Lifeline: An Exercise in Setting Goals

Here's an experiential exercise that will help you to look at your past, your present and your future life: we want you to draw your own "Lifeline." This lifeline is a graphic "time line," drawn across a sheet paper from left to right, showing the ups and downs of your life. (Illustrated on page 246 is an example of one person's lifeline, to give you an idea of how the finished work might look.)

Keep in mind that this project is only for *yourself;* it's not an art project, and you won't be graded! (Although there will be questions on the "test" at the end of the chapter.) Erase and/or start over as you need to. Make the final product realistic and valuable for *you.* Here's a step-by-step guide to the process:

• The first step is to find as big a piece of clean paper as you can find. The bigger it is, the more freedom it gives you to draw your lifeline. A few feet of butcher paper is ideal.

• Next, think about your present age and then think about how long you expect to live. Most people, when they think about it, will have a feeling about how old they are going to be when they die. They may feel they are going to live to be very old, or they may feel they are going to die young. Get in touch with this feeling and see what kind of a life expectancy you have for yourself. Then think about your present age, what percent of your life you've already lived, and what percent of your life you've got left to live. For example, if you feel that you may live to be 80 and you are presently 40, you have lived half your expected life.

• Take your clean sheet of paper and draw a vertical line that will signify to the left of the line how much life you've already lived and to the right of the line how much you've got left to live. If you've lived half of your life, the line would be in the middle. If you've lived a third of your life, the line would be a third of the way across the paper. Think about how many years you've probably got left to live compared to how many years you've already lived. What are you going to do with the remaining years of your life?

• Think about whether your life has been basically happy or basically unhappy so far. Draw another line horizontally on the paper reflecting your basic level of happiness. If you have been basically unhappy all your life, draw the line lower down on the page. Now you're ready to start drawing your lifeline.

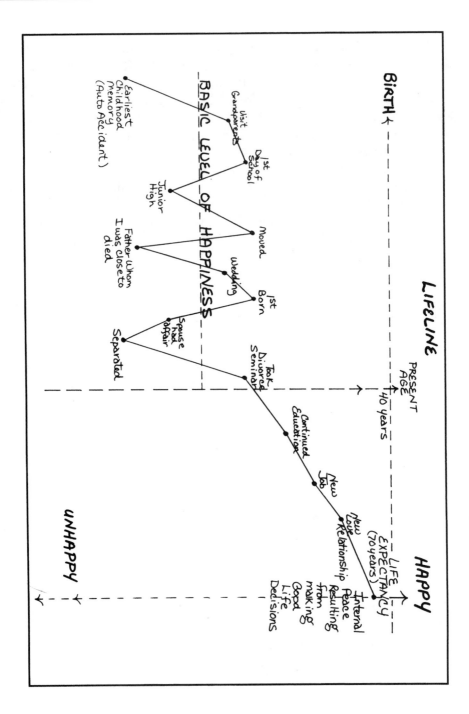

Your Lifeline: The Past

• Start your lifeline by trying to remember the earliest childhood memory that you have. Think about this early childhood memory for a little bit. It may tell you a great deal about yourself and about the rest of your life. Begin your lifeline so it reflects the happiness and unhappiness of this earliest childhood memory. The more unhappy this earliest memory was, the lower you start on the page.

• Next, think through the important things you can remember in your early childhood. Identify them in your mind and mark them on your lifeline. If there was an extremely happy event that you remember, mark that on your lifeline, putting it higher on the paper. If there were extremely unhappy things such as loss of somebody in your family through death, mark that as something more unhappy. Keep working through your life as you enter grade school, junior high, high school, and keep marking the important milestones that stand out in your memory. Think of doing this lifeline as though you were telling a story to a friend and you were to tell them about the important things that have happened to you in your life. Include your marriage, and any children that you may have.

Your Lifeline: The Present

• Now think about your divorce, and your present emotional situation. Many people who have recently separated will draw their lifelines with the divorce crisis as the lowest point in their lives. This kind of leaves you at a bad place in your lifeline, but remember that you still have all of the future left to work on it, and to improve yourself to become the kind of person you would like to be. Draw your lifeline to show your level of happiness at your divorce and since.

Your Lifeline: The Near Future

• Now you've passed the present, and it's time to start thinking about the future. Make some short-term goals of what you are going to be doing next month, the next three months, the next six months. Predict what you are going to be doing, and how you are going to be feeling, in your life. Is it going to be a happier or less happy time than the present? Do you still have some pain to work through, such as the trauma of the final hearing of the divorce decree, a property settlement, a poor financial condition with many financial obligations and very low income? Draw the next few months on your lifeline as realistically as possible.

Your Lifeline: The Long-Term Future

• Start making longer-term goals. Ask yourself, "What am I going to be doing a year from now? Five years from now? What am I going to be like in my old age? Is my face going to reflect the happiness that I've known in my life, or is my face going to reflect sadness, bitterness, anger, or negative feelings of some sort? How will retirement affect me? Will I be ready for retirement? Will I be able to handle the adjustment of not working any more? Have I taken care of my financial needs in old age? How do I feel about major illnesses occurring in my future life? Do I feel as though I have developed a healthy life style that will prevent me from having major illnesses? Is my life full of negative feelings that are going to be turned into physical illness as I become older?"

You have planted your life into a seed-bed and you're going to grow and mature and harvest the crop. What kind of crop are you going to harvest with your life? Are you going to look back and say, "I've lived the type of life that I wanted to live and I am ready to die." Or are you going to look back and say, "Life has somehow or other passed me by. I'm not ready to die yet."

What about the person you will be living with? Is it important for you to have another love relationship? To share your life with somebody else as you become old? Or would you like to live as a single person and enjoy all of the freedom of being single?

What is important to you in your life? Is it important to make money, to become famous, to have good health, to be successful? And what does "success" mean to you? What would you do with your life to make it successful? Will you be comfortable with your answers to these questions: "What contributions will I be remembered for?" "Will I leave the world a better place?"

Are you becoming the type of person that you'd like to be? When are you going to start changing and becoming that person? Today, next week, next month? Or are you never going to get around to being the person you want to be? Today would be a good time to start.

Kids Need Goals Too!

Children feel very confused when their parents are divorcing. While the parents are going through their own pain in the divorce process, the needs of the children are often overlooked. They have no idea where they are going, what's going to happen to them, how they'll feel tomorrow. They often feel lost, without any goals or direction.

Children have their own stumbling blocks to change into rebuilding blocks (see Appendix A). If they are given a chance to work through the process themselves, they can begin to develop goals for themselves and for their new family structure. If not, they probably feel they are going nowhere.

A structured personal or group growth program, such as the "Rebuilding Blocks" process described in Appendix A, can be very valuable for children at this time. Such experiences develop children's skills for dealing with their parents' pain, and for meeting their own needs.

The lifeline exercise in this chapter can be adapted for children also, particularly those of upper elementary age and older. They don't have the same perspective of time that you have as an adult, but it can be valuable for them to think about their future, and to set some goals (typically shorter term than yours) for themselves.

Divorce is an uncertain and unstable time for kids. It's particularly important that we help them to maintain hope for the future, and that we give them opportunities to develop their own goals.

How Are You Doing?

Now that you've thought about your life and your future, and completed your lifeline chart, take a few moments to assess your progress before you go on to the mountain top. It's tempting to sprint to the top when you're this close, but after all your work to get this far, it's worth maintaining a steady pace. Answer these few questions, then go on to the top-of-the-mountain chapter:

1. *I have worked my way through each of the rebuilding blocks on the climb up the mountain.*
2. *I have thought about my life and drawn a lifeline chart.*
3. *I have set some achievable goals for my future, and have a tentative plan for reaching them.*
4. *I have gone back over the blocks which were problems for me, and feel I've dealt with the issues.*
5. *I'm ready to accept the joys and responsibilities that Freedom can bring!*

Freedom
From Chrysalis to Butterfly

Freedom is being able to be fully yourself. By working through the rebuilding blocks, you are building a more fulfilled life and more meaningful relationships in your future. You're becoming free to choose your path to a self-actualized life as a single person or in another love relationship.

Chapter **20**

〜〜

I felt many times in my marriage that I was trapped in a prison of love. It was hard to be myself when there were so many demands and expectations placed upon me. When I first separated I felt even worse. But now I have found that I can fly. I can be me. I feel as if I left the chrysalis and have become a butterfly. I feel so free.

— Alice

Wow! Would you look at that view from here on top of the mountain!

After this page, we want you to stop reading for a moment and take time to go on a fantasy trip. Imagine being on top of a mountain with a view of other peaks and valleys below. Smell the pine trees; let the clear, bright high-altitude sun warm your skin. Notice the clouds lower than you are, and feel the cool breeze blowing off the snow glaciers. Notice how far away the horizon is out over the plains, and how far you can see. Think back about the climb. What was the most enjoyable and interesting portion for you? What was the most difficult part? The most painful? Can you identify the many changes that have taken place within you? Have you really reached the top emotionally or are you only at the top in your mind? Think about how it feels at the top, having worked so hard in your climb of personal growth.

Take as much time as you want with this fantasy before you go on reading. When you have thought about your fantasy carefully, turn the page and continue reading.

How Far You Have Come!

On the singleness portion of the trail, we hope you found not only that it feels good to be single, but that it may have been the most productive lifestyle for you during the climb. Now you are ready to consider whether you want to begin to develop love relationships again. How did the process of working your way through these rebuilding blocks affect the way you deal with others? The way you react to loneliness, grief, rejection, guilt, anger, and love significantly determines how you handle your daily life and your interactions with those around you.

If you really work at the rebuilding process, overcoming each stumbling block — including the ones you've had a lot of trouble with — you'll be able to enter into another love relationship (if that's your choice) and make it more productive than the last one. You'll be prepared to meet your own needs, and the needs of your loved one, much better than you have in the past. Rebuilding not only helps you to survive the crisis, but it also develops your life skills for living alone or in a new love relationship.

A Word to the Widowed

Perhaps you were widowed and were satisfied with the happiness you felt in your last relationship. Research indicates that people who were widowed, and elect to marry again, have remarriages which are more likely to last. Being widowed is a painful and very difficult adjustment process, and most of the rebuilding blocks are helpful to those who are going through that crisis. Many widowed persons, however, do not have to deal with one of the toughest parts of the adjustment — a previous, unhappy love relationship.

The Air Is Pretty Thin Up Here

For many people, the climb is so difficult that they feel like quitting before reaching the top. Over the years, Bruce heard countless people say, "I want to stop climbing and take a rest! I'm tired of growing." And many do stop along the way because they are tired, frightened, or feel unable to handle the changes. At such a point, it's time to sit and rest, get your energy back, then keep on climbing. The view at the top is worth it.

Support, hope, and a belief that you can make it are helpful. But it's up to you in the end. Probably the best evidence of the difficulty of the climb comes from the small percentage of people at the top. Do you have the self-discipline, desire, courage, and stamina to make it?

Now comes the "truth in packaging" disclaimer: We cannot promise that you will be happier, or wealthier, or more fulfilled if you complete the climb. We can assure you that there are fewer turkeys and more eagles at this altitude, but we can't promise that you will find an eagle for yourself (except when you look in the mirror!). The plain hard fact is that you will not necessarily find another "just right" person with whom to create a lasting relationship. What you will find is that you like yourself better, you can enjoy being alone and single, and the people you meet up here will be pretty special — after all, they made this tough climb, too!

It is true that there are fewer persons here from which to choose. An awful lot of folks just did not make it this far — indeed, many are still at the base camp, playing social games, hiding behind emotional walls, and finding excuses not to undertake the climb. The lack of numbers here may make the process of finding new friends and potential lovers more difficult. But relationships with others at the top have such a higher quality that quantity is not so important. When you're really at the top, giving off those good vibrations, there are many people attracted to you. (In fact, you may need to be careful — after all, you're an eagle now, and you look really good!) Actually, the top of the mountain is not as lonely as parts of the trail were on the way up. And if you are still feeling lonely, maybe you haven't reached the top emotionally. (Have you gone through the book too fast?)

Take a Deep Breath...

You may get discouraged at times when you realize that the old patterns have crept back and you really haven't changed as much as you thought. Do you normally put on your right or left shoe first? Try to reverse your routine this next week and put on the other shoe first. We'll bet you forget and go back to the old way. It's difficult to make changes in your daily living habits, and even harder to make changes in your personality. Keep up your determination and you will make it. Don't get discouraged — it may come slowly!

You may greatly fear the unknown future. You're not alone! It may be learning to be single; it may be not knowing what to expect or what is expected of you. How do you feel the first time you drive or ride in a new city that is unfamiliar to you? Confused, lost, uncertain? How about the way you feel the first time you go to a singles party? There is a certain amount of comfort in the known. (Your old relationship may look good even if it was like living in hell.)

We doubt you'll want to go back to your old relationship at this point, but if you do, it will be for more positive reasons than fear of the unknown future!

Beyond Singleness

We've talked a great deal during the climb up the mountain about the importance of learning to be single. Let us get in a last word about the importance of relationships. You can become whole by emotionally working hard at it, but we believe there is a part of each of us that needs another person to help us become completely fulfilled. A love relationship is more than icing on the cake, but that analogy seems to fit: the cake is whole without icing, but ever so much sweeter with it! We think each of us needs another person to help us become completely fulfilled, and to make life sweeter!

Becoming Free

When you were in the pits of the crisis, you gave no thought to plans and goals for the future. Part of your grief was concerned with loss of future, since you had to give up the plans and goals you had in that love relationship. But when you came out of the pits, you began looking to the future and making plans again.

Ernie, a member of one of the seminars who worked in a hospital, told the group one evening, "It's like the process in the hospital psych wards. There's a crafts room where the patients spend time. When patients first are admitted, they have no energy to work on crafts. But when they begin to be really interested in crafts, this is a good indication that they're ready to be discharged. I felt ready to be discharged from the divorce pits when I started making plans for the future!"

Research has found that recently separated people, and especially dumpees, are very much "living in the past," thinking mostly about how it "used to be." Further along in the process, people stop living in the past and start living in the present, enjoying the sunsets. We hope by now you have stopped living in the past, and are living in the present and making plans for your own future.

Recently separated people, and again especially dumpees, are very dependent upon others. As people grow further in the process, they gain more independence. We hope you have found a good balance between dependence and independence.

The Children of Freedom

Children need to work their way through the rebuilding blocks, and to learn the freedom to be themselves, free from all the unhealthy needs that control so many people. They need to be free to choose marriage when that time comes in their future. Quite frequently children of divorce say that they will not get married because they saw how devastating divorce was to their parents. Children need freedom of choice in what they will do with their lives, rather than to follow or contradict their parents' pattern.

All children are not the same, nor do they have the same needs. Although we generalized a great deal about children in each of the rebuilding blocks chapters, remember that each child is a unique human being, and that it is as important for them as it is for adults that they be respected and treated as such! Their differing needs depend upon age, sex, cultural background, number of children in the family, health, availability of extended family and/or friends and neighbors, physical environment, conditions at school, and the nature of their parents' breakup, as well as the individual personal characteristics of each child.

Kids are stronger than you think, and can grow through the rebuilding process right along with you. We encourage you to help them do so! You'll find the material in Appendix A helpful if you take this charge seriously.

How Are You Doing?

We thought you might like a self-evaluation report card to help you see how you are doing in your personal growth. You may wish to check yourself now and occasionally in the future, say once a month, or at least in two months, six months, a year. The list includes some important aspects of personal growth that you need to be aware of in order to keep growing. Most of these are areas we've talked about as we climbed the mountain together, and you may want to go back and review them in the book.

1. *I am able to put into words what I am feeling.*
2. *I am able to communicate to another person what I am feeling.*
3. *I have at least one life-line friend of each sex that I can ask for help when I feel I am "drowning in the river of life."*
4. *I can express my anger in a positive manner that is not destructive to me or to those around me.*
5. *I am keeping a journal of my feelings and attitudes as I adjust to my divorce crisis.*

6. *I have made at least one new friend, or renewed an old friendship in the past month.*

7. *I have invested quality time with at least one friend this past week.*

8. *I have identified which of the rebuilding blocks I need to work more on, and have made a plan to start my further work.*

9. *I have invested time in a personal growth experience this past week, such as reading a good book, taking an educational class, attending an interesting exhibit or lecture, improving my diet, watching an educational program on TV, looking for useful information on the Internet, beginning an exercise program…*

10. *I have seriously considered if I would benefit from a therapy relationship in order to enhance my personal growth or to speed up my adjustment process.*

11. *I have received my quota of hugs from my friends this week.*

12. *I have spent time by myself either in prayer, meditation, or solitary thought this past week.*

13. *I have nurtured myself with a kind deed this past week.*

14. *I pay attention to the aches, tensions, and feelings in my body to learn more about myself.*

15. *I exercise regularly.*

16. *I have made at least one change in my daily living habits that I feel good about this past week.*

17. *I nourish my body with a healthy diet (low fat, high fiber, fresh fruits and vegetables, whole grains).*

18. *I have given emotionally of myself to at least one friend this past week.*

19. *I have invested in my spiritual growth this past week.*

20. *I Iike being the person I am.*

21. *I am making plans for my future.*

22. *I have let the "natural child" within me have fun this past week.*

23. *I am not carrying around pent-up feelings of anger, grief, loneliness, rejection, or guilt, but have learned to express them in positive ways.*

24. *I am much more in control of my life than I was when my past love relationship ended.*

25. *I am experiencing the feeling of freedom to be myself.*

26. *I am actively using the concepts learned from this book to help speed up my adjustment process.*

Well, how are you doing? Are you satisfied with your self-evaluative "report card?" Get it out again from time to time. It will help you keep track of your progress, and remind you of some of the important concepts we've talked about in this climb.

Are You Ready to Fly?
What is this freedom we all seem to be striving for?

Freedom is something you find inside you. And you find it by becoming free from unmet needs which control you, such as the need to avoid being alone, the need to feel guilty, the need to please a critical parent, or the need to get free from your own "parent within you."

The butterfly at the top of the mountain stands for the freedom to fly and land where you choose. You can become free of the bonds that have kept you from being the person you would like to be — the person you were meant to be — the person you are capable of being.

Your worst enemies are those within you, and it is those demons from which you need to free yourself.

Of course, your best friends are inside you as well. Climbing the mountain not only gives you the freedom of choice to seek happiness — either alone or in another love relationship — it also gives you the freedom to be yourself. And that makes the climb of personal growth worthwhile.

It's tough for us to end this book, because we know it represents just a beginning for you. The thousands of people who have gone through the rebuilding process have taught us a great deal about what it means to climb the mountain. You could help us learn even more by dropping Bob a note — by mail or e-mail, in care of Impact Publishers — to let us know how *Rebuilding* has helped you, and how we could make it even better in future editions. Please don't expect a personal reply, but be assured that your letter will be read, and you might even end up (under a disguised name, of course) in a future edition of this book!.

If you think it would help you to hear Bruce talk about the process, you might want to listen to the audio cassette he recorded. It's not a reading of the book, but a summary of the original 15 rebuilding blocks in a conversational style. The tape runs about 90 minutes, and is available from Impact Publishers (see page 293).

We hope you won't put this book away on a shelf, but that you'll use it as often as you need to as a tool to help you rebuild. Share it with a friend, or perhaps give your friend his or her own copy.

Most of all, we wish you success in your continuing personal growth. It's a lifelong challenge!

APPENDIX A

KIDS ARE TOUGHER THAN YOU THINK
The Rebuilding Blocks Process for Children
Bruce Fisher, Ed.D., and Robert Stewart, M.A.

"I thought everything in my life that could go wrong had. But now my kids are acting out. I really don't know what to do."

— Corinne

"Sure, single working mothers have problems — real ones. But what about fathers who have custody of their children after a divorce? If you're a man trying to work and raise a child alone, you get no support from anyone. Women are uncomfortable around you — they either think you're on the make, or they want to mother you and your child to death. You can't talk to other men: they think you're a little weird if you're worrying about toilet training, while they're planning a golf game or a camping trip.

As a single custodial father I didn't know:
  a) what to do when my son woke up screaming with a nightmare,
  b) how to go about finding a good baby-sitter,
  c) how to plan my son's birthday when he turned three,
  d) how to plan the weekly meals and bake cookies and cakes,
  e) how to answer questions like, `Why did she go? Where is she? Will I see her again? Does she love me? Will you leave me? Why do I have to go to the baby-sitter's?'
Harboring all of these insecurities, we both cried a lot."

— Bill

"Remember the good old days, Dad — the days before you left home?"

— Sheila

Children go through an adjustment process similar to the adult's process, but the feelings and attitudes in each rebuilding block may be somewhat different for children. It helps if we realize that our children are also in process, with a mountain of their own to climb.

As family therapists, we believe we are obligated not only to help children adjust to their parents' divorce, but also to help them adjust to the transformation that took place while the parents were reading the Rebuilding book or attending the Fisher ten-week Rebuilding seminar.

There is a great deal of research about the effect on children of their parents' divorce. Some say the children are scarred for life, others say the children can actually benefit from their parents' divorce. The Fisher books and workshop are designed to facilitate the latter.

The people who have done a good job of adjusting are typically better parents. Their children reinforce what much of the research says: children whose parents are adjusting well tend to adjust better also.

Thoughts on Children and Divorce

Many parents try to make up for the guilt they feel about hurting the children when they get divorced by playing "super-parent." This is usually not helpful to the children.

Kids tend to become stuck in the same building blocks as their parents. The nicest thing you as a parent can do for your child is to get your own act together — to work through your own adjustment process — so you can be the warm supportive parent you are capable of being.

Many times the children remain strong and supportive to the parents until the parents get their act together. Finally, when the children perceive their parents are strong enough, they take their turn at working through the adjustment process.

There are many reasons we were motivated to add this Appendix on children to the book. First, in almost every class at least one person is working through his or her parents' divorce of twenty to forty years earlier. We hope your children will not take that long to adjust to the ending of your relationship.

The second reason is important to us as marriage and family therapists. Participating in the ten-week class often results in tremendous personal growth. This can result in changes affecting the children. They not only have to adjust to their parents' divorce, but also to the changes one or both parents may have made. We need to do all we can to help our children adjust to what can be major changes in our lives.

We hope the material in this Appendix, together with the material on children in the chapters, will help both you and your children to make this crisis into a creative experience. We also hope this Appendix will provide an outline and some motivation to provide a workshop for children wherever the ten-week adult class is taught.

A Good Divorce Is Better than a Bad Marriage

When I [Bruce] was a juvenile probation officer in the early seventies, I at first thought one of the major reasons teenagers were in trouble was because their parents had divorced. This was reinforced by the fact that 48% of the children we worked with came from a home other than a two-parent family. After I went through my own divorce, I was able to understand that I had been guilty of prejudice against divorced families. It wasn't the divorce that was the major cause of kids having difficulties, it was the dysfunctional family which often ended up divorced.

Research is showing today that maybe a third of children whose parents divorced are doing above average in school and adjustment, another third are doing about average, and one-third are doing below average. In contrast, children who are living in a two-parent dysfunctional family are almost all doing below average.

I also have a bias about the adversarial process in our divorce courts. I saw the benefits of the adversarial process when I worked in the juvenile justice system, because the process helped find the truth and bring about justice. But after working for more than two decades with people going through the divorce court, I have decided that the adversarial process contributes to the anger and vindictiveness of the divorce process, and ultimately makes the adjustment much harder for the children of divorce — not to mention its effects upon their parents.

The judge in one case allowed the father to force five custody hearings for the three children over a two-year period. I viewed this as the court abusing the children. Again it may not be the divorce, but the court's handling of the divorce, that contributes to the children's adjustment difficulty. Children suffer minimal emotional and psychological damage when their parents have an amiable divorce. The children's pain is magnified several times when their parents divorce is acrimonious.

Fortunately, parents, and subsequently their children, have a much better opportunity of adjusting to the trauma of divorce today than they did in the forties. I went to the library and copied articles on divorce from a *Saturday Evening Post* of 1948. An example of one headline was, "Children are semi-orphaned by their parents' divorce." It is my hope that we are approaching the time when the possibility of children having four parents instead of two will be looked at favorably.

I don't want to minimize the difficult adjustment for children when their parents go through a divorce. The consequences of divorce can affect children for many years. Where do the divorced parents sit at the daughter's wedding? How do the children have a close relationship with grandparents when the parents are continuing the divorce battles? How much more likely is it that the children will divorce after they marry if their parents divorced when they were young?

I believe that: a good divorce is better for children than living with their parents in a bad marriage; if parents are able to adjust to their divorce, the chances of the kids adjusting are greatly increased; many adults are able to be better parents after the divorce and the children often benefit from this improved parenting; divorce is often the most traumatic event in a child's life, and we need to do what we can to minimize the emotional and psychological hurt and pain.

The Effects of Parental Adjustment on Children

We've been perplexed and amazed at this phenomenon for years: When we adults are in the divorce pits, why do all of our mechanical appliances break down? Does our washing machine and our car know we are going through divorce? I don't laugh anymore at my friend who gives the copy machine a small blessing before she uses it so it won't misfeed.

When we are in the stage of mechanical breakdowns all around us, our children are often emotionally supporting us more than we would like to admit. They often behave better so they don't upset us. They often are doing things for us they wouldn't have thought about doing when we were married. They don't let us know how much pain and anger they are feeling. They in essence put their adjustment process on hold because they don't want to upset us any more than they have to.

When we parents begin to sit back and relax because we think we are adjusted, feeling stronger, and over the divorce, look out! That's often when our children sense at some level they can start working through the rebuilding blocks; they don't have to walk around on tip-toes anymore. Corinne told the class, "I thought everything in my life that could go wrong has. But now my kids are acting out. I really don't know what to do." I pointed out to her that her kids may have been giving her a compliment! What the children are really saying might be, "You've adjusted and are strong enough that I can now work through my process. I need to cry, to be angry, and act out my hurt. I think you're finally ready to handle me while I work through my pain." I enjoy watching the parents' faces light up when I explain this because many times that is exactly what has happened to them and their children.

Kids are tougher than you think.

There Are Stumbling Blocks for Children

As your children make the climb up the divorce recovery mountain there are seven stumbling blocks they may encounter.

The first stumbling block your children may be experiencing is, *"I don't know what divorce is."* Your children may not know what the word "divorce" means or how it will work in your lives together. It's not uncommon for children to hold myths about divorce, or to drift toward believing their worst fears when left to discover things on their own.

The second stumbling block is, *"I don't like all the changes happening around me."* Divorce has brought a complete overhaul of life as your children knew it. There are many logistical changes your children may have needed to adjust to, (residence, neighborhood, school, friends, personal space,...) perhaps in a short period of time.

The third stumbling block is, *"I have all these different feelings stuck inside me."* Your children are most likely experiencing a wide range of emotional responses related to the divorce. They may be feeling sad, angry, worried, confused, relieved, and many other emotions without any knowledge of what to do with their feelings.

The fourth stumbling block is, *"I wonder if I am responsible for my parents' divorce."* Children feel responsible in a variety of ways. Some believe they actually did something bad to cause their parents to get divorced. Other children feel responsible to help their parents feel better about what has happened. Finally, some children believe there is something wrong with them that they do not get to see the non-custodial parent more often.

The fifth stumbling block is, *"I don't know if we are a family any more."* Your children may be wondering how to relate to you and your former partner now that the two of you are no longer in relationship. Some children wonder if it is okay to love both parents, or if they need to pick a side. Children also wonder what it means to be a family now that everyone no longer lives together.

The sixth stumbling block is, *"I wish my parents would get back together."* It is a fantasy your children may keep alive because they are unhappy with what divorce has meant for their lives. Many children kindle hope as a way of moderating the stress of watching their parents separate. Other children who are having difficulty with the other stumbling blocks may want to change what they are experiencing by wishing for something different.

The next stumbling block is, *"I think it will be all good, or all bad, if my mom or dad finds a new partner."* This block concerns your children's view of the future. Some children think if you find a new partner everything will be okay; somehow the family is incomplete until they have a new mommy or daddy. Other children resist their parent's interest in someone new because it is a concrete sign that their parents will not get back together. Children who view your finding a new partner through either the "all good" or "all bad" lens may be stuck at this block.

The last stumbling block is *"I feel like the only child in the world whose parents are divorcing."* During the divorce process, children often believe they are alone, and have no friends. They are lonely, usually have low feelings of self-worth (as they wonder what they did wrong to cause the divorce), and keep looking for new friends.

What Are the Rebuilding Blocks for Children?

Remember the analogy of tripping over a log? While the stumbling blocks trip children up, rebuilding blocks are the process of getting them back on their feet. The experience of divorce is accepted, and the foundation for recovery built, with the rebuilding blocks. The crisis becomes an experience that may actually encourage your children's growth and maturity. As children change each of the stumbling blocks into rebuilding blocks, they become stronger.

The first rebuilding block is, *"I know what divorce is and what it means for me."* At this block your children gain a clear understanding and definition of divorce. They also learn what it will and won't mean for their individual lives.

The second rebuilding block is, *"I'm finding out how to handle the changes I am experiencing."* Here, your children discover some healthy ways to cope with the various events taking place around them. They may not like the changes, but they are finding non-destructive ways to work with them.

The third rebuilding block is, *"I'm letting my feelings out without hurting myself or others."* At this block your children become more aware of their feelings, and discover appropriate ways of expressing them. To reach this block, children usually need to feel safe sharing their feelings with at least one parent.

The fourth rebuilding block is, *"I know divorce is a grown-up problem."* Your children are letting go of their need to take responsibility for what has happened between you and your former partner. Your children develop good boundaries, learning the difference between what they can and cannot control.

The fifth rebuilding block is, *"I can still love my mom and my dad."* Your children realize they do not have to choose sides between their parents. They have a new definition of family that includes both mom and dad, separately.

The sixth rebuilding block is, *"I'm accepting that my parents will not get back together."* Your children grow toward accepting that you and your former partner will not be back together. They learn to feel safe even as they acknowledge that their wish won't come true.

The seventh rebuilding block is, *"I can see things I will like, and things I won't like, if my mom or dad finds a new partner."* Your children are moving away from viewing your dating as either all good or bad. They find a balanced perspective on both the positive aspects and the challenges that will arise if you find a new partner.

The next rebuilding block is *"I'm learning to be a friend to myself through my parents' divorce."* A child who is able to say this has neared the end of the climb. The feeling of self-worth in this statement makes the climb worthwhile. At this stage, children have grown from loneliness into a feeling of emotional closeness with themselves and others.

The last rebuilding block doesn't have a corresponding stumbling block: *"I have the freedom to be myself."* When you and your child(ren) reach the top of the mountain, the view of yourself, others and life itself is spectacular. The personal freedom and intimacy both children and parents feel is great. Together you and your children have transformed the crisis into a creative experience.

Each of the rebuilding blocks represents an adjustment for children as they experience the stages of divorce recovery. It is likely that your children will gain in wisdom, strength, and maturity as they climb to the top of the mountain.

Rebuilding Together

One symbolic activity you could do with your children is to take them for a hike. This is especially good if you live close to mountains or foothills, so you can pick a trail and climb to the top. Shared outdoor activities can really bring children and parents together. You and your children already know that adjusting to divorce is a lot like climbing a mountain. All of you could gain powerful insights by physically hiking even part way up. In urban areas, you could plan a challenging course in a safe neighborhood, and include some stair climbing along the way. If you decide to do this activity, it will help if each of you pays attention to the feelings you notice on your journey. Which aspects of your hike were exciting? Which were frustrating? What challenges did you encounter? How did you feel at the end of your hike? How about when you reached your goal? What was it like for you and your children to accomplish this goal together? What are you learning about adjusting to the ending of your love relationship? What are you learning about your children? What are your children learning about you?

Divorce Recovery Mountain for Children

ANNE BAIN

APPENDIX B

THE HEALING SEPARATION
An Alternative to Divorce
Bruce Fisher, Ed.D.

"I have a vision of a relationship more beautiful and loving than both of us can imagine or know. It is truly a relationship that is a laboratory for growth, where we are able to grow and completely be ourselves, while still in relationship with each other. I am not a whole enough person to be able to have such a healthy relationship with you without building a better relationship with myself first. I think I will need to separate and live apart from you for a while. I love you."

— Nina

For many years, a popular "women's" magazine ran a monthly column called "Can This Marriage Be Saved?" which gave advice to couples who were really in trouble. There's a resurgence of interest in saving marriages these days, and I'd like to share with you one very powerful tool which has helped a number of relationships. While it's too early to call this a thoroughly tested and proven process, it has such promise that I urge you to give it thoughtful consideration if you've not yet actually divorced.

A Healing Separation is a structured time apart which can help a couple heal a relationship that isn't working. It can also help revitalize and renew a relationship that is working. The Healing Separation is designed to transform the basis of a love relationship — moving it from neediness to health. A successful Healing Separation requires that both partners be committed to personal growth, and to creating healthier relationships with themselves and each other. Such a framework will allow them to carve out a new and more fulfilling relationship than they've known in the past.

When a relationship is in trouble, the couple has essentially three choices: 1) continue as is, 2) end the relationship, or 3) carve out a new relationship. If the relationship is already crumbling, not many couples want to continue it as is. That leaves choices 2 and 3. Chances are they hadn't thought much about the third choice — it probably seemed impossible. What's more, they don't know know how to go about it. So their choice, almost by default, is to end the relationship. And up goes the divorce rate.

There is another alternative: partners can work out a new relationship with themselves and with each other. The Healing Separation offers a process within which to do just that.

What is a Healing Separation?
The Healing Separation, like the old-style "trial separation," involves living apart for a while, with the decision as to whether or not to end the relationship put off until some future time. Unlike unplanned and unstructured separations, however, the Healing Separation is a working separation, in which you and your partner dedicate yourselves to investing in your own personal growth. If you can create a

better relationship with yourself, that can allow different and healthier relationships with others. Sometimes your work during a Healing Separation may be on "the old relationship," and sometimes it may be on "the old you." The Healing Separation is a creative way to strengthen both partners and build a new relationship without dissolving the partnership.

A relationship between two people is analogous to a bridge. Each partner forms one end and provides half the support for the bridge. The connection between the two — the bridge — is the relationship itself. A Healing Separation gives the partners time to concentrate on themselves, on their own supportive end structures, rather than on the relationship. It's a scary process because neither person is tending the relationship bridge for a while — it could collapse. Nevertheless, it may be worth the risk. When the two ends eventually are rebuilt, the possibility exists for a new healthy relationship bridge to be built, supported by bridge ends which are now stronger.

What Are the Purposes of a Healing Separation?

The goals of a Healing Separation are more profound than simply whether you continue your love relationship. There appears to be a high correlation between the amount of personal growth each person does and the success of the Healing Separation. If both parties are committed and motivated to work on their self-relationship, the chance of their new relationship lasting is good.

The following list of purposes for a Healing Separation may help you determine if your own separation is successful:

• *To take the pressure off a troubled relationship.* A love relationship is a changing pattern of interaction between two people who themselves are changing as they develop emotionally, socially, physically, and spiritually. This evolution of the relationship may result in strains and pressures upon the relationship and a crisis may develop. During this crisis, it is difficult for the partners to make rational and objective decisions concerning their future. A time apart pending a final decision may be an advantageous alternative for the couple to consider.

• *To enhance your personal growth* so that you can work through the stumbling blocks mentioned in this book. Changing stumbling blocks into rebuilding blocks can be the end result of a successful Healing Separation.

• *To transform your relationship* into something more beautiful and loving than you ever thought possible. You could find yourself in a relationship that not only allows you to be yourself, but enhances your individual identity, and offers more love and joy than you ever imagined. You could deepen your definition of what love is, and create a relationship that has no boundaries or limits, one which has evolved and transformed to a level of love usually associated with spiritual love — a good imitation of God's love.

• *To end your love relationship on a positive note* and have the ending a creative and constructive experience. To reach this goal might mean the ending has a minimum of stress, anxiety, court battles, with everyone feeling good about the way it worked out. Remaining friends and being able to co-parent peacefully could be important by-products of this healthy ending.

Who Should Have a Healing Separation?

Here are some key characteristics of partners who might want to consider a Healing Separation:

• *You are experiencing sad and unhappy feelings,* or feeling suffocated, or experiencing tremendous pressures, or feeling depressed, possibly even suicidal. You need to separate in order to survive and continue living.

• *Your partner has refused to take any responsibility for the relationship difficulties* and has refused to become involved in counseling or other growth activities. The separation is one way to "hit your partner over the head with a two-by-four" in order to get his or her attention.

• *You are going through the rebellion process* identified in chapter 12. You feel the need for emotional space and decide to separate to relieve the internal pressures.

• *You are in the process of healing your childhood abuse and neglect* and need to be alone in order to complete the process.

• *You have begun an important personal transformation,* perhaps psychological or spiritual in nature, and you want to invest as much time and effort as possible into your own process. You find the time and effort spent in the relationship competes with and limits the amount of time you can spend with yourself.

• *You have not been able to gain enough emotional space* in the love relationship and need more space to survive, to grow, to evolve, or to transform.

• *You're caught in conflict:* wanting to continue the love relationship, but unable to break the old patterns. Living together encourages continuing the old patterns of interaction. You want to "divorce the old relationship" so you can carve out a new one that is more healthy and less needy. A time apart may allow you to create new ways of interacting by developing a new and different relationship with yourself.

• *You need an understanding of how it feels to be single.* You may have gone directly from your parental home to a marriage home without experiencing the single life. You missed experiencing one of the developmental stages of growth and development — that of being an independent adult. Many people wrongly believe the single life to be one of freedom with no responsibilities — an escape from the stress of living with a love partner. Having some time apart from the love partner may provide a more realistic view of the difficulties of living as a single person.

• *You may need to express your independence from your family patterns* for the first time. You may have built a love relationship bridge much like your parents' bridge. Now you're attempting to get free from your parents' influence, and you need to have distance from your love partner because your patterns with your partner are too similar to those you experienced with one or both parents.

• *You and your partner are projecting your unhappiness onto each other,* making the other "responsible" for your unhappiness. You have not learned to take individual ownership of your own feelings. Time apart — with a plan for personal growth — could help both of you learn to accept adult responsibility for your lives.

Dumpers and Dumpees Again: The 80-20 Rule

A separation is seldom started as a mutual decision. In the Fisher divorce classes, some 84% of couples ended their relationships when the dumper decided to leave. We estimate a similar division in the decision to have a Healing Separation; that is, one partner is the initiator and the other is reluctant perhaps 80% of the time. Sounds like quite an obstacle to the success of the Healing Separation, doesn't it? How can a couple overcome the differences in attitude, goals, and motivation of the initiator and the reluctant one?

First of all, couples must re-think the question of "Who's to blame?" When a relationship is not working as well as it should, *both parties are equally responsible for the malfunctions.* That statement is not easy to understand and really believe at first – even for therapists. But the longer we work with couples, the more we find that when you peel off the layers of pain and get to the core issues, the responsibility for the problems is equal. Thus the problems are mutual even though one person was the initiator in the separation. When you begin to understand and accept the notion of mutual responsibility for the problems, you have begun to build a foundation for a successful Healing Separation — and a successful new relationship.

Bruce's research on the divorce process indicates the dumpee experiences much more anger and painful feelings than the dumper. Probably the reluctant one in a Healing Separation will experience more emotional pain. Whatever strong feelings are experienced by either party will need to worked through before the separation truly becomes healing.

The parties in a Healing Separation have more alone time, to work on themselves, on their careers, on projects and hobbies. This can be a positive aspect and helpful to both parties. The reluctant one may learn to appreciate having extra time to work on personal growth and eventually appreciate the initiator's decision to have a Healing Separation.

When the reluctant one finally understands that the initiator had so much internal pain and emotional pressure that separation was a matter of survival, it helps the reluctant one to understand and accept the initiator's decision.

In the "Rebuilding Relationships" classes, it is usually the female partner who is more motivated to take the class. After about five weeks of the class, however, men admit, "I didn't think I needed this class. I was just taking it for her because I thought she needed it, but the learning of this past five weeks has helped me discover I needed the class more than she did." Education and awareness helps the reluctant one to appreciate the benefits of a Healing Separation.

Experience has shown that it is more likely for the initiator to be female. Among the reasons for this: 1) Research indicates married females are more unhappy than married males. 2) Females are more likely to be open to new ways of improving relationships. 3) The person who is experiencing personal change and transformation — perhaps one who is healing past abuse, usually female — will seek time and space to do that work. 4) The person who is going through a spiritual transformation is usually female. 5) The female partner, most often the submissive one in our male-dominated society, is more likely than the dominant one to seek equality. 6) When a relationship is not working, the male often will leave the relationship, not knowing or believing there is a possibility of changing it. If the female partner initiates the separation, the traditional "macho male" will often seek the ending of the relationship rather than agree to a Healing Separation. It takes a male who is sensitive, patient, caring, flexible, and open to change to participate in a Healing Separation.

Guidelines for a Successful Healing Separation

Following the guidelines below will improve the chances of success of your Healing Separation. They're not all absolute rules, but if you ignore more than one or two, your prospects will be hurt:

1) Probably the most important requirement for both of you is *a strong commitment to make the Healing Separation work.* Feelings of love and commitment are tremendously helpful to motivate you both.

2) *Make a list of what your ideal love relationship would be like.* Think of what aspects would be important to you. Allow yourself to develop a fantasy role model of what your relationship might be like after the Healing Separation. Share and discuss your lists with each other.

3) *Commit yourselves to communicating with each other in an open and honest manner.* Learn to use "I" messages rather than "you" messages. Communicate by stating, "I think _____," "I feel _____," "I want_____," "I need _____," and "I will _____." Learn to be as honest as you can be with yourself and with your partner. Learn to say what is true for you. Complete honesty may include owning that portion of the relationship problems for which you have been responsible. Are you part of the problem, or part of the solution?

4) *Do not file for divorce or start any court proceedings during the Healing Separation.* You must agree to not take any legal action without first conferring with the other person. The adversarial legal system is antithetical to the goals of a Healing Separation. Even the threat or the thought of the other person filing is enough to release the brakes of the train headed for dissolution, so you need to make it clear in the "separation agreement" that neither of you will consider undertaking any court action. The exception to this is when one or both of you needs to let the old relationship die by having a final decree stating you are divorced. You need to work toward obtaining the final decree together and avoid the adversarial court process. Anything you can do to help end the old relationship is helpful in the Healing Separation. This may be the step that really gets your partner's attention and let's the other person know you are serious in your need for emotional space.

5) *Quality time together might nourish this new relationship.* (See the following section.) It is helpful to think of the new relationship as a tender young plant just emerging from the seedbed. It needs frequent tender, loving care in order to grow and not be squashed by the storms of the Healing Separation.

6) *Continuing a sexual relationship may help nurture the relationship, but it could also hurt.* Review the material in chapter 17 for cautions.

7) Sometimes you will need to *talk out issues with another person* other than with your partner. You will need a good support system, or a therapy

relationship, or both, to resolve these issues without them being added to the storms that will most likely occur during a Healing Separation.

8) It is a great time to *keep a personal journal.* You will need a place to express and dissipate the strong feelings which are bound to emerge during this difficult time, and a place to sort out the many thoughts and feelings you are experiencing.

9) *Read, take classes, attend lectures and seminars.* Awareness can really help to put the brakes on your runaway relationship train. Reading and learning all you can will help make the process healing rather than destructive.

10) You will need to *do some self-care* so you don't become emotionally and physically drained. The whole process can be very draining emotionally, and sometimes you feel like giving up because you don't have enough energy to continue. What can you do to restore yourself and keep from becoming emotionally drained?

11) *Use the "Healing Separation Agreement"* in Appendix C — with modifications to suit your relationship needs — as a firm commitment to each other. A formal agreement such as this will give your Healing Separation the best chance of success.

12) *Seriously consider a (joint) ongoing therapy relationship* with an experienced licensed marriage and family therapist or psychologist.

Other Considerations

Quality Time Together. You may find it beneficial to set times to be together on a regular basis during the separation, as often as feels right and okay. It should be agreeable to both of you to spend "quality time" together. This quality time might include one or more of the following activities: a) important sharing and active listening, using good communication skills, b) verbal intimacy and/or sexual intimacy, if appropriate, c) time to nurture each other, d) trying out new patterns of interaction leading to carving out a new relationship, e) doing fun activities together, f) sharing your personal growth with the other person. When your old dysfunctional patterns of interaction start happening, you need to be apart rather than continuing the old unproductive patterns of behavior together. Remember to stay honest with each other!

Length of Separation. You may be asking, "How long are we going to be separated?" Part of the goal for this process is to encourage and support you to be as fearful and insecure as possible! It would be easy for you to make a commitment for three months, and then use that deadline as a way of not dealing emotionally with the problems. "I can put up with anything for three months," might be your attitude. We suggest that you agree on a time limit for your Healing Separation, but realize it needs to be flexible and may be re-negotiated. This insecurity of not knowing how long you will be separated may help to keep you on your toes, and you may be able to use the insecurity of no time limit as motivation to keep growing.

Insecurity about the future of your relationship can be frightening. You don't know how much to work on yourself, and how much to work on the relationship. (If you've been trying to change your partner, that may be one of the reasons you're having a Healing Separation!) Sometimes it feels as if you are walking on ice. One false step and down you go, into the icy water of loneliness, rejection, guilt, anger, and the other feelings of the divorce pits.

The Healing Separation will probably consume a year or so of your life.

Timing of When To Move Back Together. I've found the question of when to end the separation by moving back together to be crucial. Usually the couple is uncomfortable living apart, and the pain motivates them to move back together too quickly. One party is usually pushing to live together more quickly than the other. Males usually want to move back together sooner than the females. The reluctant partner usually wants to move back together before the initiator does. Time itself is a factor: early in the process, one or both are eager to move back together; the longer the separation lasts, the more hesitant both partners are to move back together.

It is very destructive to move back together too quickly and have the patterns of the old relationship come back. This increases the possibility of separating again, and each separation increases the chances of the relationship ending.

Take your time about moving back together. Beware of the "honeymoon phase." You may start to feel emotionally close, intimate; sexual satisfaction may improve (maybe because you have let go of sexual expectations); you want to live together again — but maybe for the wrong reasons. Wait until you both agree that you sincerely choose to be in relationship with each other, and to share the rest of your lives with each other. Paradoxically, when you both believe you can live alone the rest of your lives and be happy, it may be a good indicator you are ready to move back and live together again.

Outside Love Relationships. As a general rule, having an extra love relationship during a Healing Separation will diminish your chances of improving your relationship with yourself. Time and energy invested in the outside relationship diminishes the time and energy available to invest in your own growth as a person.

Partners who initiate the separation seeking personal growth, healing, or transformation, are so involved in their personal growth process that an extra relationship is often not of interest. They have a strong commitment to the Healing Separation, and are willing to risk everything in their relationship with their reluctant partners just so they can work toward becoming whole persons.

Reluctant partners have many opportunities for outside relationships, but they usually find out they are more "married" than they thought. Often they discover that a potential new partner has a multitude of new problems. Dating may leave them much more committed to the Healing Separation.

The person, male or female, who initiates a separation while in the rebellion process is much more likely to have an outside relationship which looks like an affair and may include sexual intimacy. He or she usually thinks of it as part of the process — the primary purpose is to have someone to talk intimately with — and does not think of it as an affair. This extra relationship may become a long-term union, but the chances of it becoming a healthy relationship are small.

Outside relationships usually have an adverse effect upon a Healing Separation because the people involved make the extra relationship more important than it is. A partner who is in rebellion finds it exciting and believes it has much promise for the future. (This excitement rarely lasts beyond the early or "honeymoon" stage.) The other partner will feel hurt, rejected, and angry about the extra relationship, and may decide to end the Healing Separation and let go of the relationship altogether.

Lack of Support. Another area of difficulty in a Healing Separation is your support system. Both partners need an emotional support system to help deal with the pressures of the difficult situation. The problem is that very few people have seen a Healing Separation work, and the view of many friends and relatives will be that the relationship is going to end. They don't believe there is such a concept as a Healing Separation. Thus when you need emotional support the most, your friends are urging you to end the relationship, saying things like, "You're still in denial. Can't you see that the relationship is over?" "Are you co-dependent? You don't seem to be able to disentangle." "You are just opening yourself to be taken into court with some shark attorney. You better get your partner before s/he gets you." "Why are you staying in limbo? You need to get on with your life." "Why don't you get rid of that bum?"

The idea of a Healing Separation is contrary to the values and beliefs of many people. A commitment "till death do us part" is a strong belief in our society, and a Healing Separation is somehow undesirable, not spiritually okay, a form of radical behavior. That's one of the reasons people are unable to support and accept the couple attempting this alternative to divorce.

You need your support friends, but it often makes you more insecure when your friends tell you the relationship is going to end. Continue to reach out and build your support system, but understand they may not always be there to help you make the Healing Separation succeed. Maybe having them read this Appendix will help them be more supportive of you.

Paradoxes of a Healing Separation. There are many paradoxes (and contra-dictions?) in Healing Separations. Here are some of the more important ones:

1) The person who initiates a separation often does it out of a need for emotional space. But the reluctant one often uses and benefits from the emotional space as much as or more than the initiator.

2) Initiators appear to be selfishly seeking ways of meeting their own needs, but often are providing an opportunity for their reluctant partners to meet their needs.

3) The initiator appears to be leaving the relationship, but may actually be more committed to the relationship than is the reluctant one.

4) As soon as initiators feel they have the emotional space they need, they reach out and ask for more closeness with the reluctant one.

5) The initiator wants the separation, but is not looking for another relationship. The reluctant one wants the relationship to continue, but is more likely to enter into another love relationship.

6) When the partners separate, they are often more "married" than they were when they were living together.

7) Most love partners project some of their hang-ups onto the other person. The Healing Separation makes these projections more obvious and identifiable. It's harder to blame another person for what happens when he or she doesn't live there any more!

8) One of the reasons initiators give for wanting a separation is so they can enhance their personal growth. But reluctant partners may experience as much or more personal growth during a separation.

9) The initiator may actually elect to have the marriage legally ended by a final court dissolution so the partners can begin again to build and create a new and different relationship.

10) The Healing Separation makes it look to others as if the relationship is not working, when in reality it may be the healthiest it has ever been.

11) In the process of seeking a clearer personal identity, the initiator may find a stronger sense of "relationship identity" — personal identity as part of a relationship.

12) Initiators often give reluctant partners what they need rather than what they want.

Is This a Healing Separation or Denial?
It is a time for action, not promises. If both parties are not actively engaged in working on themselves and rebuilding their ends of the relationship bridge, it is probably not a Healing Separation but a step toward the ending of the relationship.

Here are some important questions. Are you both working at this Healing Separation or is only one of you investing in your own personal growth? Are both parties involved in counseling? Are both parties reading self-help books? Are both parties spending time alone or are they continually with people in situations that are not growth-producing? Are both parties avoiding excessive drug and alcohol use? Are both parties investing in themselves or are they investing in another relationship outside of this one? Are the two people having any quality time together which includes good communication? Are both parties attempting to become more aware of their individual contribution to the difficulties in the relationship? Are both parties looking at how they can grow, instead of expecting the other person to make all the changes? Do both believe the partner is the problem and there is nothing one can do to change or grow until the other changes?

How does your Healing Separation rate on these questions? Are both of you working at the relationship? If only one is, then most likely you are in denial and your relationship is going to end.

Afterword
The structure of the Healing Separation is designed specifically for couples in a primary love relationship; the lessons are most relevant to their needs. Nevertheless, the lessons presented in this Appendix will work for many kinds of relationships, including friendships, family relationships, co-workers in a business setting, therapy. A "time out" is often helpful to allow the people involved to gain

breathing space and perspective — a chance to take a fresh look at what's actually happening in the relationship, and to build a foundation for a stronger partnership in the future.

Check List for a Healing Separation

We strongly recommend that both partners read this material about the Healing Separation, and complete the following check list.

1. *I recognize the reasons I entered into my past love relationship which contributed to my need for a Healing Separation.*

2. *I have identified and own some of my contributions to our need for a Healing Separation.*

3. *I am committed to working on my own personal growth and development during this Healing Separation.*

4A. *I am aware of my own personal process that has resulted in my need for more emotional space at this time of my life. OR*

4B. *I am aware of my own contributions to my partner's need for more emotional space.*

5. *I am working on my own personal growth so I will have a healthier relationship with myself.*

6. *I am committed to make this Healing Separation a creative experience.*

7. *I am committed to learning as much as possible from my relationship partner during this Healing Separation.*

8. *I am avoiding the behaviors which may lead this Healing Separation toward the rocks of divorce.*

9. *I am working on relieving the internal pressures which contributed to my need for more emotional space.*

10. *I have completed my part of the Healing Separation agreement form.*

11. *When the time is appropriate, I will communicate with my partner about ending the Healing Separation, either through ending the relationship or moving back and living together again.*

12. *I am avoiding blaming and projecting upon my partner.*

13. *I am avoiding the "helpless victim" role; I don't believe there is "nothing I can do" about my situation.*

14. *I will either read the follow-up book,* Loving Choices, *or enroll in the ten-week "Rebuilding Relationships" class, or both.*

APPENDIX C

HEALING SEPARATION AGREEMENT FORM

(A healing separation is a very challenging experience, which may result in increased stress and anxiety for both partners. Some structure and awareness can help improve the chances of success of the healing separation. Unplanned and unstructured separations will most likely contribute to the ending of the relationship. This healing separation agreement attempts to provide structure and guidelines to help make the separation a more constructive and creative experience, and to greatly enhance the growth of the relationship rather than contributing to its demise.)

A. Commitment to Do a Healing Separation

With the awareness that our love relationship is at a point of crisis, we choose to try a working and creative healing separation in order to obtain a better individual perspective of the future of our relationship. In choosing this healing separation, it is acknowledged there are aspects in our relationship which are destructive to us as a couple and as individuals. Likewise we acknowledge there are positive and constructive elements in our relationship which could be called assets and upon which we may be able to build a new and different relationship. With this in mind, we are committed to do the personal, social, psychological, and spiritual work necessary to make this separation a healing one.

At some future time, when we have experienced the personal growth and self-actualization possible in a healing separation, we will make a more enlightened decision about the future of our love relationship.

B. Goals of Our Healing Separation

Each partner agrees to the following goals for this separation:

1. To provide time and emotional space outside of the love relationship so I can enhance my personal, social, spiritual, and emotional growth.

2. To better identify my needs, wants, and expectations of the love relationship.

3. To help me explore what my basic relationship needs are and to help me determine if these needs can be met in this love relationship.

4. To experience the social, sexual, economic, and parental stresses which can occur when I have separated from my partner.

5. To allow me to determine if I can work through my process better apart than I can in the relationship.

6. To experience enough emotional distance so I can separate out my issues which have become convoluted and mixed up together with my partner's issues in our relationship.

7. To provide an environment to help our relationship heal, transform, evolve into a more loving and healthy relationship.

C. Specific Decisions Regarding This Healing Separation

1. Length of separation
We agree our separation will begin on _____ 19____, and end on _____, 19____.

(Most couples have a sense of how long a separation they will need or want. It may vary from a few weeks to six months or longer. The length of time agreed upon may be re-negotiated at any time by the initiation of either partner. The length of time would be a good topic for a communication exercise.)

2. Time to Be Spent Together
We agree to spend time together when it is agreeable to both parties. This time might be spent having fun, talking, parenting together, or sharing my personal growth process. We agree to meet for _____ hours _____ times the first week, and to negotiate the time together for each succeeding week. We agree to discuss and reach an agreement if this time together is to include a continuing sexual involvement with each other.

(A healing separation ideally should include some quality time together on a regular basis. Some people will enjoy their new-found freedom and desire very little such time. On the other hand when the person needing more emotional space separates, he or she may want even more time together. This may be confusing to the person who didn't want a separation. Partners who feel suffocated emotionally desperately want out. But when they get out of what feels like a tight place, the need for emotional space is decreased tremendously.

It is important that the time together be quality time and be spent creating a new relationship. When the old pattern starts occurring in whatever form that may take, one solution is to end the quality time together and be apart. There are arguments for and against a continued sexual involvement with each other. Ideally, sexual contact can enhance intimacy and make the separation less stressful and hurtful. Sex may, however, result in problems of the sort discussed in chapter 17, creating confusion for the potential dumpee if the dumper is just trying to "let him/her down easy.")

3. Personal Growth Experiences
Partner A (_____) agrees to participate in _____ individual counseling, _____ the Rebuilding class, _____ the Rebuilding Relationships class, _____ marriage counseling, _____ other growth experiences such as reading self-help books, keeping an individual journal, dream interpretation, exercise programs, diet programs, growth groups.

Partner B (_____) agrees to participate in _____ individual counseling, _____ the Rebuilding class, _____ the Rebuilding Relationships class, _____ marriage counseling, _____ other growth experiences such as reading self-help books, keeping an individual journal, dream interpretation, exercise programs, diet programs, growth groups.

(Ideally a healing separation would include as many personal growth experiences as feasible, practical, and helpful.)

4. Relationships and Involvements Outside of the Relationship

Partner A agrees _____ to develop a support system of important friends, _____ to become more involved socially with others, _____ to not date potential love partners, _____ to remain emotionally monogamous , _____ to remain sexually monogamous, _____ to become involved in clubs, church singles groups, etc.

Partner B agrees _____ to develop a support system of important friends, _____ to become more involved socially with others, _____ to not date potential love partners, _____ to remain emotionally monogamous , _____ to remain sexually monogamous, _____ to become involved in clubs, church singles groups, etc.

(Ideally a joint decision and compromise should be made concerning social involvement, romantic, and sexual relationships outside of this relationship.)

5. Living Arrangements

Partner A agrees to _____ remain in the family home, OR _____ move and find an alternative living arrangement, OR _____ alternate living with partner so the children can remain in family home.

Partner B agrees to _____ remain in the family home, OR _____ move and find an alternative living arrangement, OR _____ alternate living with partner so the children can remain in family home.

(Experience has shown that the in-house separation, with both parties continuing to live in the family home, results in a less creative experience. It seems to dilute the separation experience and keeps both parties from experiencing as much personal growth as is possible with separate living arrangements. It may not give enough emotional space to the person who needs it.)

6. Financial Decisions

Partner A agrees to _____ maintain joint checking account jointly, _____ maintain joint checking account separately, _____ open new checking account, _____ pay auto expenses, _____ pay household living expenses, _____ pay child support of $_____ monthly, _____ pay home mortgage and utilities, _____ pay medical and dental bills.

Partner B agrees to _____ maintain joint checking account jointly, _____ maintain joint checking account separately, _____ open new checking account, _____ pay auto expenses, _____ pay household living expenses, _____ pay child support of $_____ monthly, _____ pay home mortgage and utilities, _____ pay medical and dental bills.

(Some couples will decide to continue joint checking accounts, savings accounts, and payment of bills. Other couples will completely separate financial aspects of the relationship. Experience with divorcing couples indicates that many times one person will completely close out checking accounts and savings accounts without the other person's knowledge or consent. If there is any chance for potential disagreement, each person could take out half of the assets and open separate accounts.)

7. Motor Vehicles

Partner A agrees to operate _____ vehicle, and Partner B agrees to operate _____ vehicle.

(It is suggested ownership and titles not be changed until a decision has been made about the future of the love relationship.)

D. Children Involved in This Relationship

1. We agree to _____ joint custody, ___ solo or physical custody be given to _____.

2. We agree to the following visitation schedule.

3. The medical and dental expenses and health insurance will be the responsibility of partner _____.

4. We agree to the following suggestions, designed to help the healing separation be a positive experience for our children:

    a. Both parents remain committed to maintain a good quality relationship with each child involved. Each child should continue to feel loved by both parents.

    b. Parents be as open and honest with the children about the healing separation as is appropriate.

    c. The parents will help the children see and understand the physical separation is an adult problem and that the children are not responsible for the problems in the parent's love relationship.

    d. The parents will not express anger or negative feelings towards the other parent through the children. It is very destructive to children to become caught in the emotional crossfire of the parents.

    e. The parents will avoid forcing the children to take sides in the parental arguments concerning differing attitudes and viewpoints.

    f. The parents will not put the children in a position of spying and reporting on the behavior of the other parent.

    g. Both parents will remain committed to work with each other on parenting the children and to effectively co-parent with as much cooperation as possible.

(It is important when a couple does a Healing Separation to minimize the emotional trauma for the children involved.)

E. Signing the Agreement

We have read and discussed the above Healing Separation Agreement and agree to the above terms of the agreement. Each of us furthermore agrees to inform the other partner of any desire to modify or change any terms in the agreement, or to terminate the agreement.

Partner A   Date

Partner B   Date

Suggestions

I have found that reading this book helps couples to build and create more healthy relationships. Of even more help is enrolling in the ten-week Rebuilding Class. It is helpful to think about taking the Rebuilding class with the goal of the class participation to be "divorcing the old relationship" rather than divorcing your former love partner.

A Healing Separation is very difficult to pull off. Here are some resources that may help you make it successful: a) work with a qualified marriage and family therapist or psychologist, b) read *Loving Choices*, c) enroll in the "Loving Choices Seminar" ten-week class if it is offered in your community, and/or d) create a support system to help you grow through this difficult time. If you haven't been able to make your relationship work before the Healing Separation, you may have difficulty making it work without outside help, guidance, information, and support during the Healing Separation.

BIBLIOGRAPHY

Further Reading On Chapter Topics

The Divorce Process

Ahrons, C. (1994) *The Good Divorce.* New York: HarperCollins.

Berry, D. (1998) *The Divorce Recovery Sourcebook.* Los Angeles: Lowell House.

Bloomfield, H., Colgrove, M. & McWilliams, P. (1976, 1991) *How to Survive the Loss of a Love.* Los Angeles, CA: Prelude Press.

Everett, C. and Everett, S. (1994)*Healthy Divorce.* San Francisco: Jossey-Bass Publishers.

Limon, W. (1991) *Beginning Again: Beyond The End Of Love.* New York: Harper/Collins Publishers.

Smoke, J. (1985) *Growing Through Divorce.* Eugene, Oregon. Harvest House.

Walton, B. (2000) *101 Little Instructions for Surviving Your Divorce: A No-Nonsense Guide to the Challenges at Hand.* Atascadero, CA: Impact Publishers.

Wilson, C.A. & Schilling, E. (1990) *Survival Manual for Women in Divorce: 150 Questions & Answers.* Boulder, CO: Quantum Press.

Wilson, C.A. & Schilling, E. (1992) *Survival Manual for Men in Divorce: Straightforward Answers About Your Rights.* Boulder, CO: Quantum Press.

Fear

Beckfield, D. (1998) *Master Your Panic and Take Back Your Life! Twelve Treatment Sessions to Overcome High Anxiety* (second edition). Atascadero, CA: Impact Publishers.

Jampolsky, G. (1970) *Love is Letting Go of Fear.* Toronto: Bantam Books.

Jeffers, S. (1987) *Feel The Fear and Do It Anyway.* New York: Fawcett Columbine.

Adaptation

Abrams, J. (1990) *Reclaiming the Inner Child.* Los Angeles, CA: Jeremy P. Tarcher.

Berman, C. (1991) *Adult Children of Divorce Speak Out.* New York: Simon & Schuster.

Brissett, M. & Burns, R. (1991) *The Adult Child of Divorce.* Nashville: Oliver Nelson.

Kellogg, T. (1990) *Broken Toys, Broken Dreams: Understanding & Healing Boundaries, Codependence, Compulsion & Family Relationships.* Amherst, MA: Brat Publishing.

Paul, M. & Chopich, E. (1990) *Healing Your Aloneness: Finding Love and Wholeness Through Your Inner Child.* San Francisco, CA: Harper & Row.

Whitfield, C. (1989) *Healing The Child Within.* Deerfield Beach, FL: Health Communications.

Guilt/Rejection

Borysenko, J. (1990) *Guilt is the Teacher, Love is the Lesson.* New York: Warner Books.

Grief

Deits, B. (1992) *Life After Loss.* Tucson, AZ: Fisher Books.
Fintushel, N. & Hillard, N. (1991) *A Grief Out Of Season.* New York: Little Brown.
Kubler-Ross, E. (1969) *On Death and Dying.* New York; Macmillan.
Palmer, P. (1994) *I Wish I Could Hold Your Hand: A Child's Guide to Grief and Loss.* Atascadero, CA: Impact Publishers.
Tatelbaum, J. (1980) *The Courage to Grieve: Creative Living, Recovery, & Growth Through Grief.* New York: Harper & Row.
Westberg, G. (1962) *Good Grief.* Philadelphia, PA: Fortress Press.

Anger

Alberti, R. & Emmons, M. (1995) *Your Perfect Right: A Guide to Assertive Living* (seventh edition). Atascadero, CA: Impact Publishers.
Ellis, A. and Tafrate, R. (1997) *How to Control Your Anger Before It Controls You.* New York: Carol Publishing Group.
Lerner, H. (1985) *The Dance of Anger: A Woman's Guide to the Changing Patterns of Intimate Relationships.* New York: Harper & Row.
Tavris, C. (1982) *Anger: The Misunderstood Emotion.* New York: Simon & Schuster.
Williams, R. and Williams, V. (1993) *Anger Kills: Seventeen Strategies for Controlling the Hostility that Can Harm Your Health.* New York: Times Books (Random House).

Letting Go

Brodie, D. (1999) *Untying the Knot: Ex-Husbands, Ex-Wives and Other Experts on the Passage of Divorce.* New York: St. Martins.
Kingma, D.A. (1987) *Coming Apart: Why Relationships End and How to Live Through the Ending of Yours.* New York: Fawcett Crest.
Webb, D. (2000) *50 Ways to Love Your Leaver.* Atascadero, CA: Impact Publishers.

Self-Worth

Bloomfield, H. (1985) *Making Peace With Yourself: Turning Your Weaknesses Into Strengths.* New York: Ballantine Books.
Branden, N. (1983) *Honoring The Self.* Toronto: Bantam Books.
Palmer, P. and Froehner, M. (2000) *Teen Esteem: A Self-Direction Manual for Young Adults.* Second Edition. Atascadero, CA: Impact Publishers.
Powell, J. (1969) *Why Am I Afraid to Tell You Who I Am?* Allen, TX: Tabor Publishing.
Satir, V.A. (1988) *The New Peoplemaking.* Palo Alto, CA: Science & Behavior Books.
Wegsscheider-Cruse, S. (1987) *Learning To Love Yourself: Finding Your Self-Worth.* Deerfield Beach, FL: Health Communications.

Transition

Bridges, W. (1980) *Transitions: Making Sense of Life's Changes.* Reading, MA: Addison-Wesley Publishing Co.

Love

Buchler, R. (1987) *Love: No Strings Attached.* Nashville, TN: Thomas Nelson Publishers.

Keyes, K. (1990) *The Power of Unconditional Love.* Coos Bay, OR: Love Line Books.

Powell, J. (1978) *Unconditional Love.* Allen, TX Tabor Publishing.

Trust

Larsen, T. (1979) *Trust Yourself: You Have the Power.* Atascadero, CA: Impact Publishers. (Out of print, but available in many libraries.)

Relatedness

Beck, A. (1988) *Love Is Never Enough.* New York: HarperCollins.

Bloomfield, H. (1983) *Making Peace With Your Parents: The Key to Enriching Your Life and All Your Relationships.* New York: Ballantine Books.

Fisher, B. & Hart, N. (1995) *Loving Choices: A Growing Experience.* Boulder, CO: Family Relations Learning Center. (Available from Impact Publishers.)

O'Mara, P. (1991) *The Way Back Home: Essays on Life and Family.* Santa Fe, N.M: Mothering Publications.

Smith, R. & Tessina, T. (1987) *How To Be A Couple & Still Be Free.* North Hollywood, CA: Newcastle Publishing Co.

WelWood, J. (1990) *Journey Of The Heart.* New York: HarperCollins Publishers.

Woititz, J. (1985) *Struggle for Intimacy.* Deerfield Beach, FL: Health Communications.

Sexuality

Calderone, M. & Johnson, E. (1989) *The Family Book About Sexuality.* New York: HarperCollins.

Woititz, J. (1989) *Healing Your Sexual Self.* Deerfield Beach, FL: Health Communications.

Singleness

Larson, S. & Larson, H. (1990) *Suddenly Single: A Lifeline For Anyone Who Has Lost a Love.* San Francisco, CA: Halo Books.

Children of Divorce

Briggs, D. (1970) *Your Child's Self-Esteem.* New York: Doubleday.

Brown, L. & Brown, M. (1986) *Dinosaurs Divorce: A Guide for Changing Families.* Boston MA: Little Brown & Company.

Francke, L. (1983) *Growing Up Divorced.* New York: Fawcett Crest.

Lansky, V. (1989) *Vicki Lansky's Divorce Book for Parents: Helping Your Children Cope With Divorce And Its Aftermath.* New York: Signet Books.

Palmer, P. (1977) *Liking Myself.* Atascadero, CA: Impact Publishers.

Palmer, P. (1977) *The Mouse, The Monster and Me.* Atascadero, CA: Impact Publishers.

Ricci, I. (1980) *Mom's House, Dad's House: Making Shared Custody Work.* New York: Macmillan Publishing Co.

Rofes, E. (Editor) (1981) *The Kids' Book Of Divorce: By, For & About Kids.* New York: Vintage Books.

Stahl, P. (2000) *Parenting After Divorce.* Atascadero, CA: Impact Publishers.

Virture, D. (1988) *My Kids Don't Live With Me Anymore: Coping With The Custody Crisis.* Minneapolis, MN: CompCare Publishers.

Readings on Related Topics

Inspirational

Gibran, K. (1923) *The Prophet.* New York: Alfred A. Knopf, Publisher.

Miller, R. (Editors of *New Age Journal*) (1992) *As Above So Below: Paths to Spiritual Renewal in Daily Life.* Los Angeles: Jeremy P. Tarcher.

Peck, S. (1978) *The Road Less Traveled: New Psychology of Love, Traditional Values and Spiritual Growth.* New York: Simon & Schuster.

Stepfamilies

Burt, M., (ed.) (1991) *Stepfamilies Stepping Ahead: Eight-Step Program for Successful Family Living.* Lincoln, NE: Stepfamily Assoc. of America.

Einstein, E. (1982) *The Stepfamily: Living, Loving & Learning.* Boston: Shambhala.

Visher, E. & Visher, J (1979) *Step-Families: Myths and Realities.* New York: Citadel Press.

Women and Men

Keen, S. (1991) *Fire In The Belly: On Being A Man.* New York: Bantam Books.

Phelps, S. & Austin, N. (1997) *The Assertive Woman* (third edition). Atascadero, CA: Impact Publishers.

Wenning, K. (1998) *Men Are from Earth, Women Are from Earth.* New York: Jason Aronson.

Wetcher, K., McCaughtry, F., Barker, F. (1991) *Save The Males: Why Men Are Mistreated, Misdiagnosed and Misunderstood.* Washington, D.C: The PIA Press.

Divorce-Related Web Sites*

www.divorcesource.com
www.divorcesupport.com

These two sites are linked together and provide a mega-site with information dating from 1997-98, with links for fathers and mothers rights, domestic violence links, a list of publications for more information, bulletin boards and chats.

www.Divorcecentral.com

Good listing of FAQs about divorce and separation... along with a resource guide, message boards and chat.

www.divorcesupport.miningco.com

Newsletter format with articles and links to assorted divorce topics.

www.parentsplace.com/readroom

Parentsplace has a huge amount of information for parents — single or not, and links to various sites with single parent information.

www.divorceonline.com

Interesting site with online access to multi-disciplinary professionals — lawyers, accountants and therapists, for advice and Q&A.

www.divorcenet.com

This site has a number of chat support groups, an attorney resource center, and a listing of state by state legal provisions, as well as bulletin board discussion on a number of topics.

www.dudley-gateway.co.uk/cz/czindex.htm

This is a site for kids to e-mail a counselor and talk... some of the Q&A are posted. Most of the information and resources are England-based.

www.parentswithoutpartners.org

Parents Without Partners is generally acknowledged to be the granddaddy of support groups, mainly catering to divorced men and women when it first began in the late 1950s. There is a resource center open to all, as well as a directory of local chapters and a search device to help anyone find a chapter near them. A listing of local and international PWP events makes it easy for people to find out how they can get involved.

http://home.navisoft.com/solemom/index.htm

Sole Mothers International is a site that means business, putting a host of resources at the tips of the single parent's fingers. Experts await individual questions, "Operation: Net Support" places single parents in touch with child support enforcement agencies, and legal information from across the country is available with a single click.

www.nucleus.com/~jlassali

Maintained by Jill Lassaline
Single Parents World is one of the best sites I found for a list of links where everyone can find information relevant to his/her situation. Jill's page has links to the Single Fathers Lighthouse, Sole Mothers Resource, the Single Dad's Index, PWP, Single Mothers by Choice, and much more, in addition to her own personal observations.

rampages.onramp.net/~bevhamil/singleparentresourcece_478.html

Maintained by: Beverly Hamilton
Single Parent Resource Center. Beverly is a single parent from Texas who compiled this list of 19 links when she was searching for information and support during her own unexpected divorce. The amount of excellent information here is stunning, complete with legal resources on every topic from collecting child support through divorce, custody and how to choose a lawyer. There are lists of sites offering support to single moms, and others for single dads, organizations and publications to help single parents, and religious sources of all persuasions for those seeking a little outside guidance when times get tough.

---

* Courtesy of Barbara Walton, *101 Little Instructions for Surviving Your Divorce.* Reprinted by permission of the publisher.

INDEX

RebuildingBooks™
For Divorce and Beyond

101 Little Instructions for Surviving Your Divorce
A No-Nonsense Guide to the Challenges at Hand
Barbara J. Walton
Softcover: $12.95   *128 pages*
One-step-at-a-time guide to the divorce process.
Practicing attorney "holds reader's hand" through
the maze of divorce attorneys, court procedures,
custody, property settlement, and more.

50 Ways to Love Your Leaver
Getting on With Your Life After the Breakup
Dwight Webb, Ph.D.
Softcover: $14.95   *176 pages*
Psychologist's sensitive, compassionate, insightful guide
offers hope and encouragement to those in despair at the end
of an intimate relationship. Covers grief, intimacy and loss,
denial, letting go of blame and anger, much more.

Rebuilding Workbook
Bruce Fisher, Ed.D., and Jere Bierhaus
Softcover: $12.00   120 pages
For use with *Rebuilding: When Your Relationship Ends*,
in groups or on your own, it will enhance your progress
and assist in your adjustment process.

Loving Choices
A Growing Experience
Bruce Fisher, Ed.D., and Nina Hart
Softcover: $12.00   240 pages
Helps individuals and couples to develop healthy, healing
relationships. Especially useful for those who have gone
through divorce. Emphasizes good communication. Views
relationship as a laboratory for growth.

Ask your local bookseller, or call 1-800-246-7228 to order direct.
Impact Publishers®, Inc.
POST OFFICE BOX 6016 • ATASCADERO, CALIFORNIA 93423-6016
Visit us on the Internet at **www.impactpublishers.com** • Write for our free catalog.
Prices effective October 1, 1999 and subject to change without notice.

Since 1970 — Psychology You Can Use, from Professionals You Can Trust

Brief Contents

The Academic Writer

A BRIEF RHETORIC

Fourth Edition

Lisa Ede
Oregon State University

Chapter 7, "Doing Research: Joining the Scholarly Conversation," with
Anne-Marie Deitering
Oregon State University

 bedford/st.martin's
Macmillan Learning
Boston | New York

For Bedford/St. Martin's

Vice President, Editorial, Macmillan Learning Humanities: Edwin Hill

Editorial Director, English: Karen S. Henry

Senior Publisher for Composition, Business and Technical Writing, Developmental Writing:
    Leasa Burton

Executive Editor: Molly Parke

Executive Development Manager: Jane Carter

Senior Production Editor: Peter Jacoby

Media Producer: Melissa Skepko-Masi

Production Supervisor: Robert Cherry

Marketing Manager: Emily Rowin

Copy Editor: Kathleen Lafferty

Indexer: Sandi Schroeder

Photo Researcher: Angela Boehler and Krystyna Borgen

Permissions Editor: Hilary Newman

Senior Art Director: Anna Palchik

Text Design: Maureen McCutcheon

Cover Design: John Callahan

Composition: Jouve

Printing and Binding: LSC Communications

Manufactured in the United States of America.

1   0   9   8   7
f   e   d   c   b

For information, write: Bedford/St. Martin's, 75 Arlington Street, Boston, MA 02116
(617-399-4000)

ISBN   978-1-319-03720-8 (Student Edition)
ISBN   978-1-319-03724-6 (Instructor's Edition)

Acknowledgments

Text acknowledgments and copyrights appear at the back of the book on page 401, which constitutes an extension of the copyright page. Art acknowledgments and copyrights appear on the same page as the art selections they cover.

For students and teachers everywhere—and for Gregory

Preface for Instructors

What does it mean to be an "academic writer" in today's world? What is the role of print texts in a world that increasingly favors multimedia presentations? How can students strengthen their academic writing skills while also developing their ability to compose multimodal texts? How can students think critically and effectively evaluate the abundance of sources to which they now have access? How can students make informed decisions about how and where to access texts, whether in print or on a variety of devices, including smartphones, at a time when computing is increasingly mobile? In a world of YouTube, Facebook, Twitter, Snapchat, and other social media, what role does and should print communication play? Does writing really *matter* anymore?

Thinking Rhetorically: A Foundational Concept for the Book

The longer and harder I thought about the challenges and opportunities that contemporary writers face, the more I found myself wondering about the continued relevance of the **rhetorical tradition**. Could this ancient tradition have anything left to say to twenty-first-century students?

I concluded that it still has a *lot* to say. Some of the most important concepts in Western rhetoric were formulated in Greece during the fifth century B.C.E., a time when the Greeks were in the midst of a transition from an oral to an alphabetic/manuscript culture. It was also a time when principles of democracy were being developed. In Athens, an early limited democracy, citizens met in the Assembly to make civic and political decisions; they also served as jurors at trials. Those arguing for or against an issue or a person made public speeches in the Assembly. Because each case varied, rhetoricians needed to develop flexible, situation-oriented strategies designed to achieve specific purposes.

Modern rhetorical practices derive from these ancient necessities. A rhetorical approach to communication encourages writers to think in terms of *purpose* and *effect*. Rather than providing "rules" about how texts should be organized and developed, rhetoric encourages writers to draw on their commonsense understanding of communication—an understanding they have developed as speakers, listeners, writers, and readers—to make local, situated decisions about how they can best communicate their ideas. As the revised Chapter 2, "Reading Rhetorically," indicates, a rhetorical approach can also help students make appropriate decisions about how deeply they must interact with texts and how best to access them, given their rhetorical situation.

In keeping with these principles, the rhetorical approach in *The Academic Writer* encourages writers to think—and act—like problem solvers. In its discussion of rhetoric and of the rhetorical situation, *The Academic Writer* shows students how best to respond to a particular challenge, whether they are writing an essay exam, designing a Prezi presentation for work, reading a difficult text for class discussion, writing an email to their teacher or supervisor, or conducting research. "Thinking Rhetorically" icons that appear throughout the book highlight the rhetorical advice, tips, and strategies that will help them do so efficiently and effectively.

Organization

PART ONE, "WRITING AND RHETORIC IN ACTION," provides the foundation for the book. In addition to introducing the principles of rhetoric—with particular emphasis on the **rhetorical situation**—Part I focuses on two central concepts:

1. Writing as design
2. The rhetorical nature of reading

Increasingly, scholars of rhetoric and writing argue that the most productive way to envision the act of composing texts is to think of it as a kind of design process: Among other things, both activities are open-ended, creative, persuasive, and problem solving in nature. In fact, given the extent to which visual and multimedia elements are now routinely incorporated into composition classrooms and other writing spaces, the distinctions between what was traditionally conceived of as "design" and what was traditionally conceived of as "writing" are disappearing. *The Academic Writer* draws on this research, and it does so in a clear, user-friendly manner. This discussion creates bridges between students' self-sponsored writing on such social networks as Facebook and Pinterest (where they literally design self-representations) and the writing they undertake as college students. It also creates bridges between the diverse ways that students now create and consume texts—in print or on their smartphone, iPad, or computer—and the reading and writing they do as students.

A substantially revised chapter on reading rhetorically emphasizes the extent to which reading and writing are parallel processes. As with reading, students must learn to construct meaning within the context of the community by learning to embed themselves in the ongoing conversation in the disciplines. Doing so requires the same habits of mind needed to write successfully in college: curiosity, openness, creativity, engagement, persistence, responsibility, flexibility, and metacognition. *The Academic Writer* draws on current research in reading to provide students with a rhetorical context for reading as well as practical strategies they will need as they confront challenging academic texts.

PART TWO, "WRITING IN COLLEGE," focuses, as its title suggests, on the demands that contemporary students face. **Analysis, synthesis, argument,** and **research** are central to academic writing, and this section provides coverage of each of these topics as well as a chapter on **writing in the disciplines.**

PART THREE, "PRACTICAL STRATEGIES FOR COMPOSING TEXTS," provides concise, reference-friendly advice for students on the writing process: **invention, planning, drafting, revising, editing, and proofreading.** It also includes a new chapter on **multimodal composing,** with strategies that are versatile and eminently practical for writers producing texts in our fluid, ever-changing technological present.

Key Features

- **Every feature of the text, in every chapter, reinforces the book's primary aim: to help students learn to think rhetorically.** The text as a whole encourages transfer by emphasizing decision making over rules. In other words, as the old trope goes, it teaches students to fish rather than presenting them with a fish. **"Thinking Rhetorically" icons** flag passages where rhetorical concepts are explained and exemplified, and **"For Exploration," "For Collaboration,"** and **"For Thought, Discussion, and Writing"** activities encourage students to apply and extend what they have learned.

- **A wide range of model student essays** includes a multipart case study and eleven other samples of student writing—including a new essay by Elizabeth Hurley—that serve both to instruct students and to inspire them.

- **Thoughtful discussions of visuals and of writing as design** in Chapters 1, 2, and 11 suggest strategies for reading, writing, and designing multimodal texts.

- **Strong coverage of reading, research, and writing in the disciplines** in Chapters 1, 2, and 5 through 10 emphasizes the importance of consuming and creating texts rhetorically and enables students to succeed as academic readers and writers.

- **Guidelines and Questions boxes** present key processes in flowchart format, reinforcing the importance of decision making and active engagement in the processes of writing, thinking, and reading and helping students easily find what they need.

New to This Edition

- **Careful attention to multimodal composing is infused throughout the text** to help today's students employ all the resources available to them—words, images, design, media—effectively. In this edition, I have now also added a new Chapter 11, "Strategies for Multimodal Composing," to provide thoughtful strategies for analyzing the rhetorical situation when composing or creating multimodal texts, including considerations of design and the practical demands of composing with multiple modes and media.

- **A revised Chapter 2, "Reading Rhetorically," foregrounds the importance of reading rhetorically.** This chapter pulls together all the reading coverage from previous editions into a single chapter that focuses on helping students become active, critical readers by teaching them to develop and apply rhetorical sensitivity to their reading, to use practical strategies for reading actively and critically, and to "read" visuals in a rhetorically sensitive way. New to this edition is an extensive discussion of how medium and device influence the reading process and how students can make rhetorically appropriate decisions about their reading.

- **A new section on the habits of mind for academic success in Chapter 2 draws on the Framework for Success in Postsecondary Writing** developed by the National Council of Teachers of English, the Council of Writing Program Administrators, and the National Writing Project. Although habits of mind (such as curiosity, openness, flexibility, and responsibility) can help students become more active and reflective writers, they are particularly important in relation to reading because students encounter reading demands that are not only more stringent but are different in kind from what they experienced in high school.

- **New discussions of the role of kairos** (the ability to respond to a rhetorical situation in a timely or appropriate manner) now appear in Chapter 1, where I have added a discussion of kairos and the rhetorical situation; Chapter 3, which now includes a discussion of kairos and the appeals to logos, ethos, and pathos; and Chapter 5, where I include kairos as a tool for critical reading and analysis.

- **More attention to practical strategies for writing** now appears in Part Three. To make this text more useful to instructors and students using *The Academic Writer* on its own, I've added coverage of drafting, revising, and editing, with new emphasis on drafting paragraphs and proofreading, to Chapters 9 and 10.

- **Streamlined advice for conducting academic research** appears in Chapter 7, "Doing Research: Joining the Scholarly Conversation." This chapter was written in conjunction with Anne-Marie Deitering, an expert on research and learning technologies, who revised the chapter to highlight the importance of academic habits of mind to successful research and to provide up-to-date coverage of research tools, from using filters and facets of databases to staying organized with citation managers.

The Instructor's Edition of *The Academic Writer*

We have designed *The Academic Writer* to be as accessible as possible to the wide variety of instructors teaching composition, including new graduate teaching assistants, busy adjuncts, experienced instructors, and writing-program administrators. To that end, we provide detailed *Instructor's Notes*, written by Lisa Ede and Sara Jameson (also of Oregon State University). This material, bound together with the student text in a special instructor's edition (ISBN 978-1-319-03724-6), includes correlations to the Council of Writing Program Administrators' Outcomes Statement, multiple course plans, practical tips for meeting common classroom challenges and for teaching key concepts, detailed advice for working with each chapter in the text, and ten sample student writing projects. These new *Instructor's Notes* are also available for download by authorized instructors from the instructor's tab on *The Academic Writer's* catalog page at **macmillanlearning.com**.

Acknowledgments

Before I wrote *The Academic Writer*, acknowledgments sometimes struck me as formulaic or conventional. Now I recognize that they are neither; rather, acknowledgments are simply inadequate to the task at hand. Coming at the end of a preface—and hence twice marginalized—acknowledgments can never adequately convey the complex web of interrelationships and collaborations that make a book like this possible. I hope that the people whose support and assistance I acknowledge here not only note my debt of gratitude but also recognize the sustaining role that they have played, and continue to play, in my life and in my work.

I would like to begin by thanking my colleagues in the School of Writing, Literature, and Film at Oregon State University who supported me while I wrote and revised this text. I am indebted to my colleagues Chris Anderson, Vicki Tolar Burton, Anita Helle, Sara Jameson, Tim Jensen, and Ehren Pflugfelder for their friendship and their commitment to writing. I am especially grateful for Sara Jameson's and my ongoing collaboration on the *Instructor's Notes* for *The Academic Writer*. I also owe a great debt of gratitude to another friend and teacher, Anne-Marie Deitering, who is at the cutting edge of all things involving digital literacies, writing, research, and undergraduate learning. I am deeply grateful for her work on the chapter on research for *The Academic Writer*.

For this edition, I particularly thank the reviewers who advised me as I revised Chapter 2, "Reading Rhetorically," and wrote Chapter 11, "Strategies for Multimodal Composing": Alice Horning, Oakland University; Brittany Stephenson, Salt Lake Community College; Patricia Ericcson, Washington State University; and Jason Dockter, Lincoln Land Community College. Alice and Brittany provided much useful feedback and thoughtful criticism on the revisions I made to Chapter 2, and Patty and Jason were indispensable as I drafted the new Chapter 11 on multimodal composing. I also want to thank Janine Morris of Nova Southeastern University, who shared her dissertation research on reading in digital environments with me, and Rachel Chapman of Texas Christian University, who similarly shared her innovative multimodal composition course materials. Thanks to Janine and Rachel, and the previously mentioned reviewers, Chapters 2 and 11 are stronger and more pedagogically useful.

I would also like to thank the many dedicated teachers of composition I have worked and talked with over the years. By their example, comments, suggestions, and questions, they have taught me a great deal about the teaching of writing. A number of writing instructors took time from their teaching to look carefully at *The Academic Writer* as well as drafts of this edition. Their observations and suggestions enriched and improved this book. These reviewers include the following instructors: Thomas Bonfiglio, Arizona State University; Patricia DeMarco, Ohio Wesleyan University; Anita DeRouen, Millsaps College; Jason Dockter, Lincoln Land Community College; Martha Dolly, Frostburg State University; Joanne Hash, Whittier College; Emily Isaacson, Heidelberg University; Erica Jeffrey, Yuba Community College; Justin Jory, Salt Lake Community College; Lynn Kilpatrick, Salt Lake Community College; Joal Lee, Spokane Falls Community College–Pullman; Edie-Marie Roper, Washington State University; Jerald Ross, Southwestern Illinois College; Shillana Sanchez, Arizona State University; Ron Schwartz, Pierce College–Fort Steilacoom; Brittany Stephenson, Salt Lake Community College; April Strawn, Washington State University; Susan Waldman, Leeward Community College; Ivan Wolfe, Arizona State University; and Sam Zahran, Fayetteville Technical Community College.

Colleagues and students play an important role in nurturing any project, but so do those who form the intangible community of scholars that is one's most intimate disciplinary home. Here, it is harder to determine who to acknowledge; my debt to the composition theorists who have led the way or "grown up" with me is so great that I hesitate to list the names of specific individuals for fear of omitting someone deserving of credit. I must, however, acknowledge my friend and frequent coauthor Andrea Lunsford, who writes with me even when I write alone.

I wish to thank the dedicated staff of Bedford/St. Martin's. Any textbook is an intensely collaborative effort, and I count myself particularly fortunate in having had Jane Carter, executive development manager, as the development editor on this project. From start to finish, I have valued Jane's expertise and insight. In particular, I value her ability to keep the big picture always in view while also carefully attending to local details and to ask tough but essential questions. I am sure that *The Academic Writer* is a better book as a result. In addition, I want to thank senior project editor Peter Jacoby, whose patient attention to detail proved especially valuable; editorial assistant Suzanne Chouljian, who kept us organized and on track; acquisitions editor Molly Parke, whose frequent reminders about the needs of instructors and students were always appreciated; and marketing manager Emily Rowin, whose knowledge and enthusiasm for English composition informs this text.

Finally, I want to (but cannot adequately) acknowledge the support of my husband, Gregory Pfarr, whose passionate commitment to his own creative endeavors, and our life together, sustains me.

Lisa Ede

Get the Most Out of Your Course with *The Academic Writer*

Bedford/St. Martin's offers resources and format choices that help you and your students get even more out of your book and course. To learn more about or to order any of the following products, contact your Bedford/St. Martin's sales representative, e-mail sales support (**sales_support@bfwpub.com**), or visit the Web site at **macmillanlearning.com**.

CHOOSE FROM ALTERNATIVE FORMATS OF *THE ACADEMIC WRITER*

Bedford/St. Martin's offers a range of affordable formats, allowing students to choose the one that works best for them.

- *Paperback* To order the paperback edition, use ISBN 978-1-319-03720-8.
- *Popular e-book formats* For details of our e-book partners, visit **macmillanlearning.com/ebooks**.

SELECT VALUE PACKAGES

Add value to your text by packaging one of the following resources with *The Academic Writer*. To learn more about package options for any of the following products, contact your Bedford/St. Martin's sales representative or visit **macmillanlearning.com**.

Writer's Help 2.0 is a powerful online writing resource that helps students find answers whether they are searching for writing advice on their own or as part of an assignment.

- **Smart search**

  Built on research with more than 1,600 student writers, the smart search in Writer's Help 2.0 provides reliable results even when students use novice terms, such as *flow* and *unstuck*.

- **Trusted content from our best-selling handbooks**

  Choose *Writer's Help 2.0, Hacker Version*, or *Writer's Help 2.0, Lunsford Version*, and ensure that students have clear advice and examples for all their writing questions.

- **Adaptive exercises that engage students**

  Writer's Help 2.0 includes *LearningCurve*, a game-like online quizzing program that adapts to what students already know and helps them focus on what they need to learn.

Student access is packaged with *The Academic Writer* at a significant discount. Order ISBN 978-1-319-10953-0 for *Writer's Help 2.0, Lunsford Version*, or ISBN 978-1-319-10954-7 for *Writer's Help 2.0, Hacker Version*, to ensure your students have easy access to online writing support. Students who rent a book or buy a used book can purchase access to Writer's Help 2.0 at **macmillanhighered.com/writershelp2**.

Instructors may request free access by registering as an instructor at **macmillanhighered.com/writershelp2**.

For technical support, visit **macmillanhighered.com/getsupport**.

LaunchPad Solo for Readers and Writers allows students to work on whatever they need help with the most. At home or in class, students learn at their own pace, with instruction tailored to each student's unique needs. *LaunchPad Solo for Readers and Writers* features:

- **Pre-built units that support a learning arc**

  Each easy-to-assign unit is comprised of a pre-test check, multimedia instruction and assessment, and a post-test that assesses what students have learned about critical reading, writing process, using sources, grammar, style, and mechanics, and includes help for multilingual writers.

- **A video introduction to many topics**

  Introductions offer an overview of the unit's topic, and many include a brief, accessible video to illustrate the concepts at hand.

- **Adaptive quizzing for targeted learning**

  Most units include LearningCurve, a game-like adaptive quizzing program that focuses on the areas in which each student needs the most help.

- **The ability to monitor student progress**

  Use our Gradebook to see which students are on track and which need additional help with specific topics.

LaunchPad Solo for Readers and Writers can be packaged at a significant discount. Order ISBN 978-1-319-10952-3 to ensure your students can take full advantage.

Visit macmillanhighered.com/catalog/readwrite for more information.

Writer Key Built around best practices for feedback and revision, *WriterKey* puts student writers at the center of your course. Robust review tools allow you to quickly comment on assignments—using voice or text—and link to a flexible rubric and comment library all from one screen. Students use the same tools to reflect, ask for feedback on specific areas, and review one another's work. Powerful analytics, tied to instructor comments, show writers' strengths and areas for improvement. A side-by-side view of drafts lets students revise their work while they apply teacher and reviewer feedback. After revised drafts are submitted, instructors can compare drafts and view analytic data to see revision in action. For more information, visit **ml.writerkey.com/**.

INSTRUCTOR RESOURCES

macmillanlearning.com
You have a lot to do in your course. Bedford/St. Martin's wants to make it easy for you to find the support you need—and to get it quickly.

The *Instructor's Notes for The Academic Writer* is available bound into the instructor's edition of the text and as a PDF that can be downloaded from the Bedford/St. Martin's online catalog at the URL above. In addition to chapter overviews and teaching tips, the instructor's manual includes sample syllabi, correlations to the Council of Writing Program Administrators' Outcomes Statement, and classroom activities.

JOIN OUR COMMUNITY!

At Bedford, providing support to teachers and their students who choose our books and digital tools is our first priority. The Bedford/St. Martin's English Community is now our home for professional resources, featuring Bedford Bits, our popular blog site offering new ideas for the composition classroom and composition teachers. Connect and converse with a growing team of Bedford authors and top scholars who blog on Bits: Barclay Barrios, Steve Bernhardt, Susan Bernstein, Traci Gardner, Elizabeth Losh, Andrea Lunsford, Jack Solomon, Elizabeth Wardle, and Donna Winchell, among others.

In addition, you'll find an expanding collection of resources that support your teaching. Download titles from our professional resource series to support your teaching, review projects in the pipeline, sign up for professional development webinars, start a discussion, ask a question, and follow your favorite members.

Visit **community.macmillan.com** to join the conversation with your fellow teachers.

Contents

part

2 Writing in College

Writers' References

Writing Rhetorically

What does it mean to be a writer today? In a media-saturated world where visual images surround us, does writing still matter, and if so, how much? How has the increasing emphasis on the visual—and the availability of digital and online media—influenced how ordinary people communicate? One need only search Google to notice the power that images hold. While drafting this chapter, for instance, I typed *dog and owner photos* into Google's search box and promptly got more than 80 million hits. Clearly, dog owners are using the web to communicate how much they love their pets.

As a medium, photographs are not new, and neither is sharing them. Now, though, just about anyone with a smartphone or a computer and Internet access can establish a visually rich presence on the web. On social-networking sites such as Facebook, Pinterest, Instagram, Snapchat, and Twitter, on video-sharing sites like YouTube, and on many blogs, images and video or audio clips can be as important as the written text.

Courtesy of Angie Boehler

The power of images: The love people have for their pets — and the power images have to communicate — is reflected in the huge number of pet photos online.

Written language has hardly lost its power, however. If anything, the power of the written word has grown with writers' increased ability to reach readers. In a developed country like the United States, individuals with access to computers and online technologies are writing more than ever before. On the same day that I searched Google for photos of owners with their dogs, I also searched Amazon for the first book in Suzanne Collins's *Hunger Games* trilogy, and I found 23,933 customer reviews of this novel. Outside of school, many students read and write virtually all the time, via texting, tweeting, posting on Facebook, and so on.

Technology, of course, has engendered many changes in the kinds of texts produced, and the design of these texts has become increasingly important, with more and more written texts integrating video, photographs, music, and the spoken word. As an example, consider the website for the White House: Whitehouse.gov. The briefing room tab alone includes blog posts, infographics, videos, photos, and links to live events.

You may think that the writing you do for fun is irrelevant to the writing you do for your classes. It's not. All your experiences as a writer, reader,

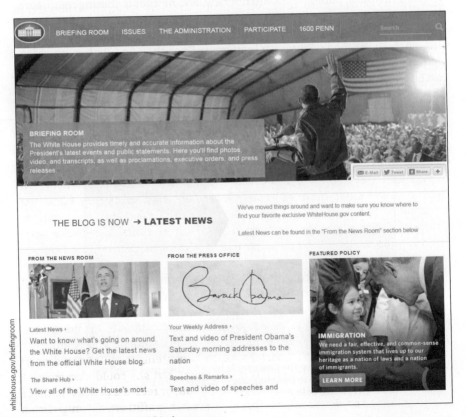

whitehouse.gov/briefingroom

The Briefing Room Page on Whitehouse.gov

speaker, and listener will help you learn how to meet the demands of academic writing. But to communicate effectively, you will need to develop your rhetorical sensitivity: your ability to make effective choices about your writing based on your purpose, your audience, and the genre and medium in which you're composing and presenting. As you well know, a text to a friend is very different from an essay for a history class. Learning how to recognize your rhetorical situation and to adjust your writing appropriately will play a powerful role in helping you transfer what you already know about writing to an academic setting. This chapter (and this book) will help you gain that understanding.

Understanding the Impact of Communication Technologies on Writing

One helpful way to understand the impact of technology on writing is to consider the history of the printed text. For centuries in Western Europe, the only means of producing texts was to copy them by hand, as scribes did in the Middle Ages. The limited number of manuscripts created meant that few people owned manuscripts and fewer still could read them. In 1440, Johannes Gutenberg invented the printing press, which could produce multiple copies of texts and therefore dramatically increased the availability of the written word. The rise of printing tended to deemphasize the role of visual elements, however, because the technologies for printing words and images were largely incompatible. In the 1800s, it became possible to print high-quality illustrated texts. Since that time, readers have come to expect increasingly sophisticated combinations of words and images.

The history of texts produced by individual writers differs from that of printed texts. The invention of the typewriter in 1868 enabled writers to produce texts much more efficiently than they could writing by hand, and by using carbon paper, they could even make multiple copies. But typewriters were designed to produce only words. Writers could manipulate spacing and margins, and they could underline words and phrases, but that was about it.

The development of the personal computer and of sophisticated software for writing, designing, and illustrating changed all that. Today anyone with a computer and access to the Internet can compose texts that have most, if not all, of the features of professionally produced documents, including integrated visual and auditory elements. An art history student who's convinced that graffiti represents an important genre of contemporary art could write a traditional print essay to make this argument, but she could also create a video, develop a PowerPoint or Prezi presentation, or record a podcast to make her point. If this student has an ongoing interest in graffiti art, she might even host a blog on this subject.

Take some time to think about — and list — all the kinds of writing you do, from tradi-tional print and handwritten texts such as essays, class notes, and to-do lists to texts, tweets, Facebook posts, and blog comments.

Now turn your attention to the media you use to write.

- In writing essays for your classes, do you first brainstorm and write rough drafts by hand and then revise at your computer; do you write entirely in a digital medium (on your computer, laptop, tablet, or smartphone); or do you switch back and forth, depending on the project and situation?

- How many programs do you typically have open on your computer, and how often do you move back and forth from your word processing program to Google, Facebook, or some other site as you compose?

- Does your smartphone play a role in your writing?

- Do you ever incorporate images or graphics (yours or other people's) into your informal or formal writing? Are design elements and visual images more impor-tant to some kinds of writing that you do than to other kinds?

Take a few more minutes to reflect about what — and how — you write. What insights have you gained from this reflection?

The ability to compose in diverse media (print, digital, and oral) and to integrate words, images, and sounds represents an exciting opportu-nity for writers—but opportunity can also bring difficulties and dilemmas. Consider the art history student writing an essay on graffiti as art. If she followed the conventions of traditional academic writing, she would double-space her essay and choose a readable font (like 12-point Times New Roman) that doesn't call attention to itself. If she's using headings, she might make them bold; she might also include some photographs. In general, though, her essay would look and read much like one written twenty, or even fifty, years ago.

Suppose, however, that in addition to assigning an essay her instructor required students to prepare a presentation on their topic using software like PowerPoint or Prezi. The student would still need to communicate her ideas in a clear and understandable way, but she might manipulate fonts and spacing to give her presentation an edgy, urban feel. Although she would hardly want to use a font like the graffiti-style BROOKLYN KID throughout, she might employ it at strategic points for emphasis and to evoke the graffiti she's writing about (see p. 5). She might choose visual examples of graffiti and arrange her images in prominent or unusual ways to create the kind of in-your-face feel that characterizes much graffiti. In each case the student is sharing her understanding of and enthusiasm for graffiti, but she is doing so in ways appropriate to her particular rhetorical situation.

Settings for GRAFFITI

→ Subways eliminated in the late 1980s as most popular venue

→ Moved above ground to walls and buildings

→ Freight trains took art across continent

Don Emmert/Getty Images

Tools for GRAFFITI

→ Paint cans using custom spray nozzles

→ Keith Haring's work with chalk

→ Markers and stickers

→ Cutouts and posters applied with glue

Andrew Burton/Getty Images

PowerPoint Slides from a Student Presentation

Writing and Rhetoric

One of the most powerful resources that students, and other writers, can draw upon is one of the oldest fields of study in Western culture: rhetoric. Rhetoric was formulated by such Greek and Roman rhetoricians as Isocrates (436–338 B.C.E.), Aristotle (384–322 B.C.E.), Cicero (106–43 B.C.E.), and Quintilian (35–96 C.E.). Originally developed to meet the needs of speakers, rhetoric came to be applied to written texts as well. Thanks to recent developments in communication technologies, students today are increasingly communicating via multiple media, not just print. In this world of expanded media and modes of communication, rhetoric continues to provide essential guidance. ✻

When you think rhetorically, you consider the art of using words, images, space and design elements, sounds, and gestures to engage—and sometimes to persuade—others. Writers who think rhetorically apply their understanding of human communication in general, and of texts in particular, to the decisions that will enable effective communication within a specific situation.

A rhetorical approach to writing encourages you to consider four key elements of your situation:

1. Your role as a *writer* who has (or must discover) something to communicate

2. One or more *readers* with whom you would like to communicate

3. The *text* you create to convey your ideas and attitudes

4. The *medium* (print, digital, oral) you use to communicate that text

The relationship among these elements is dynamic. Writers compose texts to express their meaning, but readers are equally active. Readers don't simply decipher the words on the page; they draw on their own experiences and expectations as they read. As a student, for instance, you read your economics textbook differently than you read a comic book or a popular novel, and you read an online newspaper differently than you do the print variety. You also know that the more experience you have reading certain kinds of writing—textbooks in your major or the sports or financial pages of the newspaper, for example—the more you will get out of them. ✻ (The same is true for viewers and listeners, of course.) Rhetoric is a practical art that helps writers make effective choices by taking each of these four elements into consideration within specific rhetorical situations.

Let's return to the student who wants to write an essay on graffiti as art. To analyze her situation, she would first consider her own position as a writer. As a student in a class, how much freedom does she have? In academic writing, this question leads immediately to the second element of the rhetorical situation: the reader. In academic writing, the reader is primarily the teacher, even when the student is asked to imagine another audience (an audience

✻ To learn more about multimodal composing, see Chapter 10.

For more about reading, see Chapter 2.

of interested nonexperts, for example). In an academic context, the student would also need to consider the nature of her assignment, such as how open it is and what statement (if any) the teacher has provided about format and expectations. But the writer would also want to draw on her general understanding of writing in the humanities. Instructors in the humanities often favor a conservative approach to academic writing; they want to make sure students can develop and express clear, logical, and insightful prose. So while this student might use headings and images in her research project, her safest bet would be to focus primarily on the clear and logical development of the ideas.

This student would have considerably more flexibility in approaching her PowerPoint or Prezi presentation. The conventions for presentations are more open than those of traditional academic writing. Moreover, instructors and students alike expect individuals who compose presentations to take full advantage of the medium. Since this presentation would be for a class, however, the student would still want to focus on the development of her ideas, and any visual and design elements would need to enhance and enrich the expression of those ideas.

In this example, the student's teacher has specified the media that should be used: a print essay and a presentation using PowerPoint or Prezi. For this reason, constructing a blog or creating a video would be an inappropriate response to the assignment, but the student could embed video clips of interviews with graffiti artists and images of their work in her presentation. If this student were writing an honors thesis on graffiti as art, for instance, she could create a blog to express and explore her ideas during the year that she works on this major project. At her thesis defense, she might share relevant blog posts and comments with her committee. As this example indicates, a rhetorical approach to writing encourages you to think in practical, concrete ways about your situation as a writer and to think and act like a problem solver.

Composing—and Designing—Texts

When you think and act like a problem solver, you use skills that have much in common with those used in the contemporary profession of design. There are many kinds of design—from industrial design to fashion design—but writing is especially closely allied with graphic design, thanks in large part to the development of the web and such software programs as Adobe InDesign and Adobe Photoshop. In fact, given ongoing developments in communication technologies, conventional distinctions between these two creative activities seem less and less relevant. While it is true that in the humanities the most traditional forms of academic writing emphasize words over images and other design elements, student writers—like all writers—are integrating the visual and verbal in texts more than ever before.

thinking rhetorically

In his influential book *How Designers Think*, Bryan Lawson lists the essential characteristics of design:

- Design problems are open-ended and cannot be fully specified.
- The design process is endless.
- There is no infallibly correct process of design; rather, design is a persuasive activity that involves subjective value judgments.
- The design process involves finding as well as solving problems.

These characteristics apply, Lawson argues, to all kinds of design, from product design to graphic design.

Like design, writing is a creative act that occurs within an open-ended system of opportunities and constraints, and the writing process, too, is potentially endless in the sense that there is no objective or absolute way to determine when a project is complete. Instead, writers and designers often call a halt to their process for subjective and pragmatic reasons: They judge the project to be ready when they believe that their audience or clients will be pleased or when they run out of time or money. Indeed, the open-ended nature of writing and design is typical of activities that require creativity.

Precisely because writing and design are creative processes, there is no infallibly correct process that writers and designers can follow. Experience enables writers and designers to determine the strategies appropriate to the task, but each project requires them to consider anew their situation, purpose, medium, and audience. As they do so, designers and writers do not just solve problems; they also find, or create, them. That may sound intimidating at first. "I don't want to find problems," you might think. "I want to solve them quickly and efficiently." Here's the rub: Often you can't do the latter until you do the former.

Let's say, for example, that two dormmates are frustrated because their room is always a mess. They talk it over and realize that the problem is that they just don't have enough storage space, so rather than put clothes and other items away in already overstuffed closets and chests, they leave them out everywhere.

To address this problem, they have to go beyond the general recognition that they need more storage space to pinpoint the problem more specifically. After reading a web feature on organizing and redecorating dorm spaces, they realize that the real problem is that they've neglected to consider systematically all their storage options. Once they've identified the crux of their problem, they can address it; in this case, they take measurements and head to the local discount store to look for inexpensive storage units that will fit the space. They've solved their storage problem in part by correctly identifying, or creating, it.

In writing and in design, as in everyday life, the better you are at identifying your problem, the better you will be at addressing it. In fact, the ability to create complex and sophisticated problems is one feature that distinguishes experienced from inexperienced writers and designers. A professional interior designer might develop solutions to the roommates' dorm room problems more quickly, and possibly more innovatively, than the students do. Furthermore, as

Lawson argues, design inevitably involves subjective value judgments and persuasion to convince clients to accept the designer's vision. One roommate, for instance, may argue for design purchases that reflect her commitment to sustainably produced products, while the other roommate may believe that the least expensive product that meets their needs is the best choice.

Both writing and design offer individuals the opportunity to make a difference in the world. Someone who redesigns wheelchairs and in so doing improves their comfort and mobility, for instance, will improve the quality of life for all who rely on this mode of transportation. It's easy to think of writers who have made a difference in the world. Most environmentalists agree, for example, that Rachel Carson's 1962 *Silent Spring* played a key role in catalyzing the environmental movement. But there are other, less visible but still important examples of the power that writing can have to effect economic, social, political, and cultural change. Writing is one of the most important ways that students can become members of a disciplinary or professional community. For example, in order to be recognized as professional civil engineers, engineering students not only need to learn how to plan, design, construct, and maintain structures; they also must learn to write like civil engineers. Besides playing a key role in most careers, writing also represents an important way that citizens express their views and advocate for causes (see the poster on p. 10). Think, for example, of the role that Twitter and blogs now play in politics and public affairs. In these and other ways, writing provides an opportunity for ordinary people to shape the future of local, regional, and national communities.

---

for **exploration**

Write for five to ten minutes in response to this question: What has this discussion of the connections between writing and design helped you better understand about written communication?

for **collaboration**

Bring your response to the preceding Exploration to class and meet with a group of peers. Appoint someone to record your discussion and then take turns sharing your writing. Be prepared to share your discussion with the class.

Developing Rhetorical Sensitivity

Both graphic designers and writers understand that to create a successful project they must do the following:

thinking
rhetorically

- Draw on all their resources, learning from their experiences, exploring their own ideas, and challenging themselves to express those ideas as clearly and powerfully as possible

Poster Advocating for a Cause

- Consider their audience—who they are, what they know and like, and what they value and believe
- Assess the purpose and goals of the project—the meaning they wish to communicate and their reasons for composing
- Make use of all the tools available to them (such as word processing, image and sound creation and editing, as well as specialized programs), given the medium in which they are working

In all of these activities, experienced writers and designers practice *rhetorical sensitivity*.

Designers and writers practice rhetorical sensitivity when they explore the four elements of rhetoric—writer/designer, audience, text/project, and medium—in the context of specific situations. The student writing about graffiti art, for example, drew on her rhetorical sensitivity in determining how best to respond to her assignment. She realized that as a student writing for a class she is constrained in significant ways and that her reader's (that is, her teacher's) expectations are crucial to her decision making. She also knew that the textual conventions governing essays are more conservative than those governing presentations and that differences in media—print versus Power-Point or Prezi—reinforce this distinction. As a result of her analysis, this student realized that she had more freedom to experiment with visual elements of design in her presentation than in her essay.

To respond to her assignment, this student consciously explored her rhetorical situation. Writers and designers are particularly likely to do this when they undertake an important assignment or work for a new client. At other times, this kind of analysis takes the form of rhetorical common sense. In your daily life, you already practice considerable rhetorical sensitivity. As you make decisions about how to interact with others, you naturally draw on your commonsense understanding of effective communication. When you interview for a job, everything you do before and during the interview—what you wear, how you act, and what you say—is in an effort to make it a success. Much of your attention will focus on how best to present yourself, given the company you are applying to. You would dress differently if you were interviewing at your local fitness center rather than at a bank or a law firm, for example. You would probably also recognize the importance of being well prepared and of interacting effectively with your interviewer. Savvy applicants know that everything they do is an effort to persuade the interviewers to hire them.

> **note for multilingual writers**
>
> It is more challenging to "read" a rhetorical situation when you are new to the context. You may find it helpful to consult your teacher or classmates, asking specific questions to better understand the rhetorical situation for a particular assignment.

You also employ rhetorical sensitivity when you "read" contemporary culture. As a consumer, for instance, you're bombarded with advertisements urging you to buy various products or services. Wise consumers know that ads are designed to persuade, and they learn ways to read them with a critical eye (even as they appreciate, say, a television commercial's humor or a magazine ad's design).

You read other aspects of contemporary culture as well. Much of the time, you may do so for entertainment: While watching sports or other programs on television, for instance, your primary goal might be to relax and enjoy yourself. If you find the plot of a detective show implausible or the action of the Monday night football game too slow, you can easily click to a more interesting program.

At times, however, you may take a more critical, distanced perspective on various forms of popular culture. After arguing with a friend about whether the video game *Mortal Kombat* advocates sexism and violence, you may read reviews of (and play) this game with a careful eye, ultimately making your own judgment. When you analyze a video game like *Mortal Kombat* to determine whether it advocates sexism and violence, you're analyzing its *rhetoric*.

thinking rhetorically

Rhetorical Sensitivity and Kairos

Writers and designers who think rhetorically understand that writing and reading do not occur in a vacuum. The language you grow up speaking, the social and cultural worlds you inhabit, and the technologies available to you, among other factors, all influence how you communicate. For example, wherever they come from, most students find that the writing they do in college differs considerably from the language they use in their everyday lives. The language that feels comfortable and natural to you when you speak with your family and friends may differ considerably from that required in academic reading and writing assignments. This is just one of many reasons why writing cannot be mastered via a handy list of rules. Instead, writers must consider their rhetorical situation; doing so is especially important when they are writing in a new or unfamiliar context.

thinking rhetorically

Writers must also consider what the Greek rhetoricians called *kairos*. *Kairos* refers to the ability to respond to a rhetorical situation in a timely or appropriate manner. You can probably think of some obvious examples of kairos in action. Consider, for instance, President Lincoln's Gettysburg Address, which was delivered on November 19, 1863, four and a half months after the Battle of Gettysburg—which Union soldiers won at a terrible cost—and the day that the new Soldiers' National Cemetery in Gettysburg, Pennsylvania, was to be dedicated:

> Four score and seven years ago our fathers brought forth, on this continent, a new nation, conceived in Liberty, and dedicated to the proposition that all men are created equal.
>
> Now we are engaged in a great civil war, testing whether that nation, or any nation so conceived and so dedicated, can long endure. We are met on a great battle-field of that war. We have come to dedicate a portion of that field, as a final resting place for those who here gave their lives that that nation might live. It is altogether fitting and proper that we should do this.
>
> But, in a larger sense, we can not dedicate—we can not consecrate—we can not hallow—this ground. The brave men, living and dead, who struggled here, have consecrated it, far above our poor power to add

or detract. The world will little note, nor long remember what we say here, but it can never forget what they did here. It is for us the living, rather, to be dedicated here to the unfinished work which they who fought here have thus far so nobly advanced. It is rather for us to be here dedicated to the great task remaining before us — that from these honored dead we take increased devotion to that cause for which they gave the last full measure of devotion — that we here highly resolve that these dead shall not have died in vain — that this nation, under God, shall have a new birth of freedom — and that government of the people, by the people, for the people, shall not perish from the earth.

President Lincoln was not the major speaker at the dedication, but his words have rung throughout subsequent history, while those of other speakers have not.

Historians generally argue that Lincoln's address, which lasted roughly two minutes, was so powerful because it took full advantage of its rhetorical situation and strongly appealed to kairos. In 1863, the war had been going on for two bloody years, and it would continue another two years before it ended in 1865. In his address, Lincoln shifted the terms of the war, redefining what had largely been viewed as an effort to save the union between the North and the South to one dedicated to ensuring human equality.

The Gettysburg Address represents a pivotal moment in the Civil War and in U.S. history. World leaders often draw on kairos when they respond to a crisis or argue for an initiative. Many arguments about the necessity of addressing global warming, and doing so immediately, rely on kairotic appeals. Kairos also plays a role in our daily lives. Advertisers recognize the power of kairos, even if they are not familiar with the term. For example, much of the advertising surrounding Black Friday, the day after Thanksgiving when brick-and-mortar retail stores advertise what are supposed to be their best sales of the year, draws on kairotic appeals as advertisers attempt to persuade people to embark on a day of frenzied bargain hunting.

As these examples suggest, those hoping to persuade an audience to value, believe, or do something must necessarily consider kairos. This is also true of academic writing, which often involves argumentation. For example, instructors in a writing course might ask students to identify and take a position on a campus issue that they believe needs to be addressed. A kairotic approach to argumentation would encourage students to explore the history of this issue so they could understand how best to resolve it and emphasize its urgency. It would also encourage them to pay careful attention to both explicit and implicit arguments made by others about this issue so they can better understand the most important areas of agreement and disagreement.

The first three chapters of this book will help you understand and apply a rhetorical approach to writing and reading. Chapter 4, "Academic

Writing: Committing to the Process," will help you learn how to manage the writing process so you can be successful as a college writer. You may have a clear understanding of both the rhetorical situation and kairos as they apply to an essay you are writing, but if you procrastinate and begin working on your essay the night before it is due, the odds of writing a successful essay are against you.

As a college student, you may at times feel like the new writer on the block. Both this book and your composition course will help you build on the rhetorical sensitivity you already have, so you can use all the resources available to you to make timely and appropriate choices about your writing.

---

note for multilingual writers

If you learned to write in a language other than English, you may sometimes feel frustrated when teachers ask you to stop speaking and writing in a way that feels natural to you and instead to adopt the conventions of academic writing in the United States. Many students who have grown up in the United States speaking English share this discomfort. Your goal as a writer should not be to abandon your first or home language; rather, it should be to become so fluent in the conventions of standard written English that you can write effectively in both languages and for both communities.

---

for exploration

Take a look at the advertisements for women's skin care products on p. 15. After carefully examining the two ads, respond in writing to these questions:

1. How do the designers of the ads use words, images, and graphics to persuade? Do some of these elements seem more important than others? Why?

2. In what ways do the ads reinforce Lawson's observation that design involves "subjective value judgments"? Do they, for instance, rely on culturally sanctioned stereotypes about women, beauty, and aging? If they do, how do these stereotypes reinforce the message?

3. In what ways do these ads demonstrate rhetorical sensitivity on the part of those who created them?

4. Advertisers often appeal to kairos in order to persuade consumers to buy something. In what ways do these two ads appeal to kairos?

thinking
rhetorically

Advertisement from Dove's Campaign for Real Beauty

Advertisement for an Anti-Aging Face Cream by L'Oreal

Image Courtesy of The Advertising Archives

Image Courtesy of The Advertising Archives

for **thought, discussion, and writing**

1. Take a few moments to recall an incident when you were called on to demonstrate *rhetorical sensitivity* and write a paragraph describing it. Then write a paragraph or two stating your current understanding of the terms *rhetoric* and *rhetorical sensitivity*. Finally, write one or two questions that you still have about these terms.

2. Write an essay in which you describe and reflect on the many kinds of writing that you do and the role that visual and design elements play in your writing. After writing the essay, create a text that uses words, images, and (if you like) graphics to convey the ideas you discuss. You can use any mix of photographs, drawings, text, or other material that will help others understand your experience.

3. Interview two or three students in your current or prospective major to learn more about writing in this field. Ask these students the following questions:

   ● What kinds of writing are students required to do in classes for this field?
   ● How would they characterize the role of images and other graphic elements in this writing? What roles, if any, do multimedia play in their writing?
   ● How is their writing evaluated by their professors?
   ● What advice about writing would they give to other students taking classes in this discipline?

   Your instructor may ask you to report the results of these interviews to the class and to write an essay summarizing and reflecting on the results of your interview.

4. Choose a print or online newspaper of interest to you. It could be a local, regional, or national newspaper or your school newspaper. Read the letters to the editor that are published each day in the newspaper and identify three letters that you believe depend strongly on appeals to kairos. In what ways do these letters attempt to persuade readers to value, believe, or do something through appeals to timeliness? Be prepared to share your examples and analysis with your classmates.

2

Reading Rhetorically

Why—and how—do people read? Not surprisingly, they read for as many different reasons and in as many different contexts as they write. They read to gain information to learn how to make the fullest use of all the features of their new smartphone, to decide whether to attend a movie, or to explore ideas for writing. They read for pleasure, whether checking Facebook, browsing a magazine, or enjoying a novel. They read to engage in extended conversations about issues of importance to them, such as climate change, U.S. foreign policy, or contemporary music. In all these ways, people read to experience new ways of thinking, being, and acting.

Reading and writing are in some respects parallel processes. The process of reading a complex written work for the first time—of grappling with it to determine where the writer is going and why—is similar to the process of writing a rough draft. When you reread an essay to examine the strategies used or the arguments made, you're "revising" your original reading, much as you revise a written draft. Because writing requires the physical activity of drafting, you may be more aware of the active role you play as writer than as reader. Reading is, however, an equally active process. Like writing, it is an act of *composing*, of constructing meaning through language and images.

Applying Rhetorical Sensitivity to Your Reading

thinking rhetorically

Reading, like writing, is a *situated* activity. When you read, whether you're reading print or digital texts, you draw not only on words and images (as well as video, animated graphics, and audio files for digital texts), but also on your own experiences to make cultural, social, and rhetorical judgments. The purposes you bring to your reading, the processes you use to scrutinize a text, your understanding of the significance of what you read, and other aspects of your reading grow out of the relationships among writer, reader, text, and medium. (To learn more about the rhetorical situation, see Chapter 3.)

UNDERSTANDING YOUR PURPOSES AS A READER

Imagine two students reading in a café. One student is reading excerpts from Aristotle's *Nichomachean Ethics*, a foundational work in philosophy, for her Introduction to Philosophy class; the other is taking a break from studying and is browsing blogs and online magazines (or e-zines) on his tablet. Both students are reading texts, but they are undoubtedly reading them in quite different ways.

The student reading excerpts from an ancient philosophical treatise knows that she will be expected to discuss the reading in class; she also knows that she can expect a question on this text to appear on her midterm exam. Consequently, she reads it slowly and with care. Because the writing is dense and many of the concepts and vocabulary are unfamiliar, she knows that she will need to look up terms she doesn't understand and do background research to grasp the important points. She also recognizes that she may need to read the text several times. Early readings focus on basic comprehension of the text; later readings allow her to interact with it via annotations that raise questions, note important passages, and articulate personal responses.

The student browsing blogs and e-zines, on the other hand, knows they can be put out by anyone with the time and inclination and can range from well-written and thought-provoking reflections on contemporary issues to poorly written diatribes. Before diving in, then, he skims the contents quickly to see if the topics are interesting and the writing worth reading. Because he has a personal interest in contemporary culture, he ends up spending a good deal of time on *Harlot: A Revealing Look at the Arts of Persuasion*, a well-written e-zine that explores the role of rhetoric in everyday life (p. 18).

UNDERSTANDING HOW GENRE AFFECTS YOUR READING

The differences between how these two people read reflect their purposes as well as their social and cultural understandings of the texts. These readers are also influenced by the texts' *genre*—that is, by the kind of text or the category to which each text belongs—be it textbook, blog, e-zine, scholarly article or book chapter, Facebook post, or newspaper article. When we recognize that a text belongs to a certain genre, we make assumptions about the form of the writing and about its purposes and subject matter.

For example, a businessperson reading a company's annual report understands that it is a serious document and that it must follow specific conventions, including those of formal written English. When the same person goes online to read *Book Stalker* (p. 19), a blog by writer and editor Julia Bartz about "the NYC lit scene," he brings quite different expectations to his reading. Everything about the site—from its title to its colorful,

Harlot: A Revealing Look at the Arts of Persuasion, an Online Journal (http://harlotofthearts.org)

playful design—suggests that the author will emphasize her personal voice (and personal opinions) as she shares her "unabashedly subjective" views about literature and the literary life in New York City. So he is not surprised by the blog's conversational tone, occasional use of slang, and humorous touches.

You will be a stronger, more effective reader if you are attentive to genre. The following are some common genres organized by the context in which they might be produced or consumed:

Personal writing: letters, Facebook posts, journal entries, personal essays, tweets, text messages

Screenshot from the Blog *Book Stalker* (http://bookstalker.tumblr.com)

Academic writing: textbooks, scholarly articles and books, lab reports, essay exams, research projects

Popular writing: articles in mass-market magazines, reviews, fan publications

Civic writing: editorials, letters to the editor, advocacy websites, public-service announcements

Professional writing: technical and scientific articles and books, job applications, business email

Creative or literary writing: poetry, stories, novels, graphic fiction, comics

When thinking about genre, it's important to remember two points. First, all genres have histories: They are not static forms, but rather are socially constructed responses to the specific needs of writers and readers.✱ Second, while some genres, such as lab reports, have changed little over time, others are more fluid. For instance, consider the variety of blogs that exist today, from personal blogs read only by a limited number of the author's friends and family members to blogs such as the *Huffington Post* that circulate widely in ways similar to more traditional media.

When we move through our daily lives, we intuitively understand many genre differences and respond appropriately as readers. For example, we read instructions for our new high-definition smart television differently than we read the news feed on Facebook or a scholarly article for class discussion or a research project. As a college student, however, you need to develop a sophisticated response to an array of academic genres. A textbook written for students in an Introduction to Sociology course is very different from a scholarly article or book published in this same area and thus requires reading strategies appropriate to the genre. As you take courses in various disciplines, you will find it helpful to ask yourself what the defining features are of the genre you are reading.

UNDERSTANDING HOW MEDIUM AND DEVICE AFFECT YOUR READING

Today, most college students have a variety of options about how and where to read texts: on paper or on-screen, and if on-screen, on a PC or Mac, desktop or laptop, tablet or smartphone. The question of how to best take advantage of these options can be complicated, however. For example, the student discussed earlier who is reading excerpts of Aristotle's *Nichomachean Ethics* could read this text on her smartphone, but should she? How people read, what they remember, how they see information, and even what reading is can be radically altered when the medium or device changes. Imagine a person reading a detailed graphic in a print magazine. In that medium, the graphic appears across two pages and can be taken in all at once. Now imagine reading that graphic on a smartphone (even one with a large screen): He'd have to scroll up and down and left and right, and still he'd only be able to see the image piecemeal. Now consider him reading it on a tablet or laptop, on which the once-static graphic of the print magazine may now include minilectures, animations, audio files, and other digital enhancements.

Some educators and critics worry that individuals who read texts on-screen are less likely to engage with the material with the same critical depth as individuals who read print texts. In his best-selling book *The Shallows: What*

✱ For more about the history of academic genres, see Chapter 8, pp. 234–61.

the Internet Is Doing to Our Brains, Nicholas Carr makes just such an argument. In a study grounded partly in his personal experience and partly in brain research, Carr argues that a reliance on the Internet is reducing users' capacity for concentration and for sustained deep thought. Others, such as Clay Shirky (author of *Cognitive Surplus: Creativity and Generosity in a Connected Age*), applaud the opportunities for collaboration and creativity afforded by the web and praise the opening up of reading to multiple media, devices, and apps. They point out, as just one of many examples, the enhancements available to texts—including college textbooks—designed to be read on digital platforms, such as zoomable art, embedded videos and lectures, and tools for sharing reading notes with classmates.

At this point, the jury is still out: The research available on this topic is limited, and more data is needed before we can determine whether those in Carr's camp or those in Shirky's will be proved correct. (It's possible, of course, that a less extreme position than either Carr's or Shirky's may be more helpful and accurate.) Still, most of us will be reading at least some texts online. Today, academic research, for example, often begins with an online search for scholarly articles accessed through academic databases, so it is important to develop the rhetorical sensitivity needed to make informed decisions about how best to access and interact with these sources.

thinking rhetorically

As a student negotiating the multiple demands of school, work, family, and friends, you must make decisions about how and when to access texts. (By the way, texts can include visual and auditory elements: Political cartoons, advertisements, and podcasts are all examples of texts.)✱ The student reading Aristotle's *Nichomachean Ethics*, for example, may need to review this text for an exam while doing her laundry and waiting for her wash to dry: It may not be the best device for the job, but if it's the device she has with her, it's better to review the material on her phone than not to review it at all. In a situation like this, the most pressing issue she faces becomes how she can use her mobile device to read actively and critically, taking a rhetorical approach to reading that recognizes the limits and opportunities afforded by the medium (and by programs or apps developed for that medium).

thinking rhetorically

The more aware you are of the impact of your own experiences and preferences, particularly in terms of reading in print and on-screen, the more you can build on strengths and address limitations. The following quiz will help you reflect on these issues.

This quiz can help you determine your preferences and habits as a reader. As you answer the questions, consider all the reading you do. Include your reading for school and work as well as the newspapers, magazines, fiction, comics or manga, blogs, wikis, websites, social media posts, and so forth that you read for your personal satisfaction.

For more help with reading visuals, see pp. 41–47 later in this chapter. ✱

Quiz: Reading on Page or Screen

1. As a reader, not just of academic writing but of all kinds of writing, how would you describe your preferences in terms of reading in print and on-screen?
   a. I still prefer print when possible.
   b. I prefer to read on-screen and on my e-reader when possible.
   c. I move back and forth from reading print to reading online and download texts depending on my situation, purpose for reading, nature of the texts, and so on.

   How do you think these preferences affect your ability to engage with academic texts critically and in depth?

2. If you selected option c, how do you decide which medium (print or digital) and device (computer, e-reader, laptop, tablet, or smartphone) to use for the different types of reading you do?

   _____
   _____
   _____

3. If you have a smartphone, how would you characterize your use of it? To what extent has it replaced your tablet, laptop, or desktop computer, and why?
   a. It's important in my daily life, but I use it mainly for communicating with others (texting, chatting on the phone, sending Snapchats, posting Facebook updates, and so forth).
   b. I use my smartphone for communicating but also for navigating, shopping, and streaming music.
   c. I use my smartphone for all the above purposes, but I also use it as a watch, a calendar, and an e-reader if the text isn't too complex.
   d. I pretty much use my smartphone for everything: to read assigned texts, study and prepare for exams, do online research, take notes, and so forth.

   How does your choice of medium and platform affect your reading experience?

4. What are the most important questions you have about your current practices as a reader?

   _____
   _____
   _____

5. What are the most important goals you would like to set for yourself as a reader and, especially, as a student reader of academic texts?

   _____
   _____
   _____

As a student reading academic texts, you need to read strategically, keeping in mind the constraints and opportunities of your rhetorical situation, including those of your chosen medium and (in the case of digital texts) device. Do you need to absorb names and dates (as for a history quiz), or do you need to synthesize information from a number of sources to get a sense of an academic research topic? What practical constraints are you facing, such as competing deadlines or the need to do laundry or shop for groceries while studying for a big test? Each of these purposes (and many others) will influence your approach to a text.

What should you take into consideration when you are deciding how to access and interact with an academic text? At the most general level, you would do well to remember that your instructors—whatever their discipline—share a strong commitment to a deep engagement with texts (whether scientific or humanistic) and to critical reading and writing, so your ability to interact with a text—whether in print or on-screen—is key. The kind, or genre, of text you are reading (and the reason you are reading it) is also important when determining how best to access and interact with texts. For example, if you're reading an op-ed for a research paper you are writing, using a smartphone makes sense. After all, op-eds are relatively short and nontechnical. If you decide that you might quote from the op-ed and thus need to take notes, you might want to read it on a device with a keyboard that makes note-taking easier. Reading an op-ed is a very different experience from that of reading a scholarly book or article that puts forward a complex argument, a novel like *War and Peace* that depicts complicated relationships and events and is peopled by characters with multiple names and nicknames, or a graphic novel that depends on the relationship between image, frame, and text for its meaning. When reading an academic text for the first time, you may want to read in print or on a large screen so that you can focus on, annotate, and critically engage with the text. When reviewing that same reading for a test, you might want the convenience of studying on your laptop or smartphone, especially if you are in the midst of a long commute to campus.

Another factor to consider is the complexity and importance of the work you need to read. The more intensively you need to read—the more challenging and complex the reading and the more central the reading is to your coursework or writing project—the greater the effect the medium can have. Some readers find, for instance, that they can more easily grasp the "big picture" of an argument and engage it deeply and critically when they read a print text rather than a digital one; they may learn better when they annotate a text by hand, or they may find it easier to focus when not tempted to surf the web or respond to a friend's latest text message. Others prefer to read a text on a device that allows them to look up the meaning of a word by clicking on it, zoom in on detailed images, watch a video of a process, or access a dictionary or other texts that can aid understanding.

note for multilingual writers

If you are a multilingual writer, you may especially appreciate some of the features of e-books, such as enhanced visuals and the inclusion of definitions, pronunciation guides, and audio options that allow readers to hear the text while reading. Features such as these can definitely enhance your experience as a reader and as a student.

When you are reading on-screen—whether on your phone, tablet, or laptop—be sure to take advantage of programs and apps such as Zotero and Mendeley that can make your life as an online reader, writer, and researcher easier.✳ If your instructor assigns an e-book as a textbook, take full advantage of its features, which may include embedded interactive video, 3-D capability, and hot links to glossary definitions.

Remember that research suggests that people often read quite differently on-screen than when they read texts printed on paper. People who read on-screen often do so erratically and selectively, skimming and scanning rather than reading intensively and critically. If you are reading important academic texts on your computer, laptop, tablet, reading device, or smartphone, you may need to consciously resist these behaviors by reminding yourself that whatever the discipline, your college instructors place a premium on engaged, critical reading. To help maintain your focus, close Facebook and other websites and programs that might distract you.

UNDERSTANDING THE TEXT'S RHETORICAL SITUATION

thinking
rhetorically

Successful college readers recognize that they need to consider their own rhetorical situation when they make decisions about how to approach texts, but they also recognize that they must consider the rhetorical situation of the text they are reading. Obviously, they can't get inside the mind of the writer of the text, but they can learn a good deal about his or her purposes and intended audience by asking a series of rhetorically oriented questions about them.

The questions on pp. 25–27 will help you understand how the rhetorical situation of the text affects you as a reader.

✳ For more about annotation, see pp. 34–37 later in this chapter.

Questions for Analyzing a Text's Rhetorical Situation

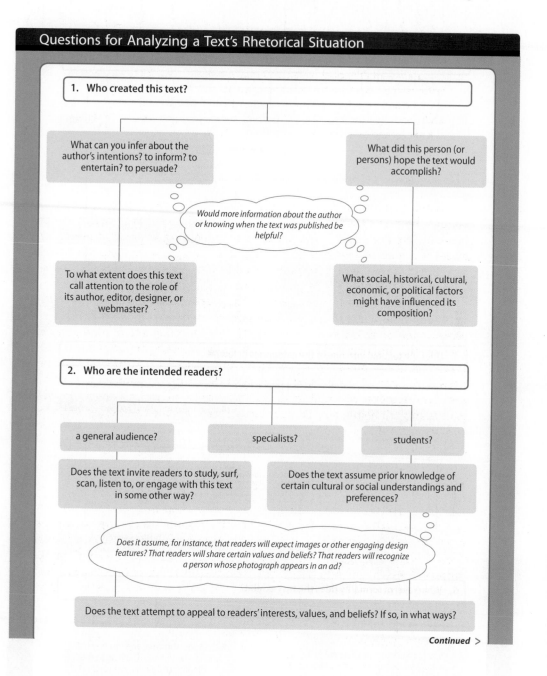

1. Who created this text?

What can you infer about the author's intentions? to inform? to entertain? to persuade?

What did this person (or persons) hope the text would accomplish?

Would more information about the author or knowing when the text was published be helpful?

To what extent does this text call attention to the role of its author, editor, designer, or webmaster?

What social, historical, cultural, economic, or political factors might have influenced its composition?

2. Who are the intended readers?

a general audience?

specialists?

students?

Does the text invite readers to study, surf, scan, listen to, or engage with this text in some other way?

Does the text assume prior knowledge of certain cultural or social understandings and preferences?

Does it assume, for instance, that readers will expect images or other engaging design features? That readers will share certain values and beliefs? That readers will recognize a person whose photograph appears in an ad?

Does the text attempt to appeal to readers' interests, values, and beliefs? If so, in what ways?

Continued >

Questions continued

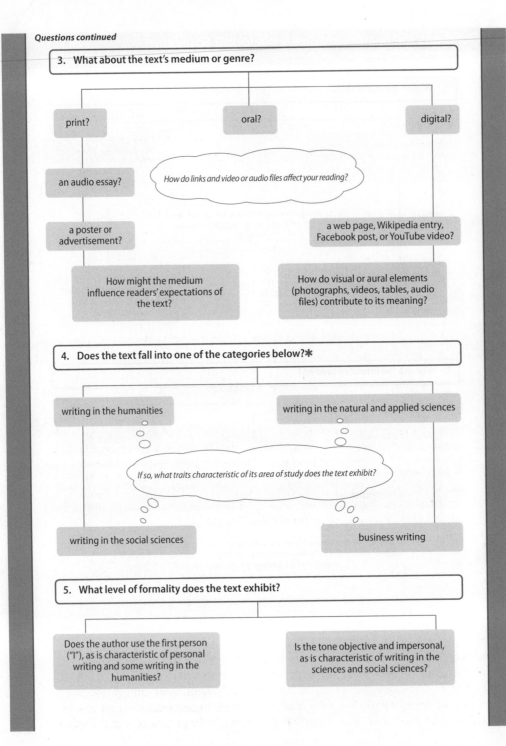

3. What about the text's medium or genre?

print?

oral?

digital?

an audio essay?

How do links and video or audio files affect your reading?

a poster or advertisement?

a web page, Wikipedia entry, Facebook post, or YouTube video?

How might the medium influence readers' expectations of the text?

How do visual or aural elements (photographs, videos, tables, audio files) contribute to its meaning?

4. Does the text fall into one of the categories below?✱

writing in the humanities

writing in the natural and applied sciences

If so, what traits characteristic of its area of study does the text exhibit?

writing in the social sciences

business writing

5. What level of formality does the text exhibit?

Does the author use the first person ("I"), as is characteristic of personal writing and some writing in the humanities?

Is the tone objective and impersonal, as is characteristic of writing in the sciences and social sciences?

✱ For descriptions of these broad generic categories, see Chapter 8, pp. 234–61.

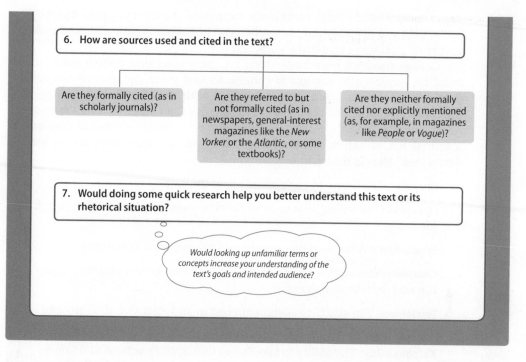

6. How are sources used and cited in the text?

Are they formally cited (as in scholarly journals)?

Are they referred to but not formally cited (as in newspapers, general-interest magazines like the *New Yorker* or the *Atlantic*, or some textbooks)?

Are they neither formally cited nor explicitly mentioned (as, for example, in magazines like *People* or *Vogue*)?

7. Would doing some quick research help you better understand this text or its rhetorical situation?

Would looking up unfamiliar terms or concepts increase your understanding of the text's goals and intended audience?

note for multilingual writers

If you have recently begun studying in the United States, it may be challenging to interpret texts that require extensive knowledge of American culture. You may also bring different rhetorical and cultural expectations to your reading from many of the other students in your classes. To better understand how you approach reading, reflect on how your background has influenced your expectations. It may be helpful to discuss these expectations with your teacher, your classmates, or a tutor in the writing center.

Developing the Habits of Mind Needed for Academic Reading

Learning how to draw upon and develop your rhetorical sensitivity can play an important role in your success as an academic reader, but you must also develop habits of mind appropriate to college-level expectations. When you were in grade school, your teachers emphasized first the ability to decode or read texts and later the ability to comprehend them. Your college teachers have something very different in mind, and their expectations are an important part of your rhetorical situation. Of course, college teachers still expect

thinking rhetorically

you to comprehend (and in some cases memorize) the texts you read. But they also expect you to go beyond comprehension to analyze, synthesize, and evaluate texts (including visual and aural texts).✳

College teachers have understood for some time that certain habits of mind are essential to success in college. Several years ago, representatives from three national organizations involved with the teaching of writing—the National Council of Teachers of English, the Council of Writing Program Administrators, and the National Writing Project—came together to develop a formal list of habits of mind essential to academic success across the disciplines.[1] Here is that list:

Curiosity: The desire to know more about the world

Openness: The willingness to consider new ways of being and thinking in the world

Engagement: A sense of investment and involvement in learning

Creativity: The ability to use novel approaches for generating, investigating, and representing ideas

Persistence: The ability to sustain interest in and attention to short- and long-term projects

Responsibility: The ability to take ownership of one's actions and understand the consequences of those actions for oneself and others

Flexibility: The ability to adapt to situations, expectations, or demands

Metacognition: The ability to reflect on one's own thinking as well as on the individual and cultural processes used to structure knowledge

These habits of mind can play a powerful role in helping you meet the challenges of academic reading (and writing).

It goes without saying that academic reading is often demanding. Whatever the subject—whether it's the history of post-Stalinist Russia or the development of French Impressionist art—you are being exposed to subject matter that is new and complex. Rather than reading a summary of Karl Marx's *Capital: Critique of Political Economics* for your Introduction to Political Science class, for instance, your instructor may ask you to read one or more sections of Marx's original text, published in 1867. If you are taking this class to fulfill a requirement and have not previously been interested in political science, you may find the text daunting. Even when you are reading a textbook designed to introduce students to a subject, lack of background and unfamiliarity with the concepts and vocabulary may still make it a difficult read.

---

[1] These habits of mind are discussed in *Framework for Success in Postsecondary Writing*, posted on the website of the Council of Writing Program Administrators, wpacouncil.org/framework.

· · · · · · · · · · ✳ Chapter 5 will help you learn to analyze and synthesize, Chapter 6 — to make and support claims,
· Chapter 7 — to evaluate the texts you read, and Chapter 11 — to compose multimodal texts.

How you respond to such challenges will influence your success as a student not only for a particular assignment or class, but throughout your college career. When you encounter reading that you experience as difficult and distant from your interests, one approach is to do the minimum and hope to get by, muttering to yourself that you never did like this or that subject and wish you didn't have to take the class. Another approach is to recognize that difficult readings represent an opportunity. If you have developed the habits of mind of *curiosity* and *openness*, for instance, you are able to recognize that, although the reading is challenging, you will learn new things and new ways of thinking and being in the world. Recognition of these benefits allows you to maintain a sense of *engagement* in your own learning and increases your motivation. When you are fully committed to your reading and learning, you are much more likely to be able to draw on and express your *creativity*, to take *responsibility* for your learning, and to demonstrate *persistence*. As a learner, your *flexibility* is increased, particularly if you take time to reflect on and learn from your experiences via *metacognition*. In sum, these habits of mind encourage you to be a productive and successful learner, whether you are taking an introductory course in a discipline new to you or are transitioning from introductory to advanced courses in your major. These habits of mind are also as applicable in the professional world as on campus.

As you work to develop these habits of mind, be sure to take advantage of the following resources:

- **Talk with your instructor.** If you are finding the readings in a course difficult, make an appointment (the earlier the better) with your instructor. Describe the difficulties you are experiencing, such as understanding the vocabulary or underlying concepts or keeping up with reading assignments, and ask for help. Your instructor may work with you to understand the reading or point you to additional resources that can help you enter the scholarly conversation. And here's something important to know about instructors: Most instructors enjoy talking with students about how they can succeed in their courses. Students are sometimes reluctant to ask their instructors for help, but think about it this way: Instructors are deeply committed to their discipline and to their students, so when a student indicates interest in a course, instructors are usually highly motivated to respond.

- **Take advantage of support services.** Many colleges provide services to help students transition from high school, or from years in the workforce, to college. In some cases, these services include peer mentoring, where you can meet with a more advanced student to talk about how you can respond to the challenges of college work, including college reading.

- **Visit your campus writing center.** Although writing centers generally focus on working with students on writing, many can also help you develop your skills as a reader, especially if the reading is connected with a writing assignment. If it's not clear whether your writing center can help you with the challenges and demands of reading academic texts, contact your center and explain your needs. Most writing centers are very student-oriented and will do all they can to help you succeed in college.

- **Use reference tools.** If you don't understand a word, look it up in a dictionary. An all-purpose dictionary like Merriam-Webster.com will be adequate in most situations, but for technical terms, you may need to consult a specialized dictionary for your discipline. (Most are now available through your library's online databases.) If you are reading a primary text by an author who is unfamiliar to you, use your library's reference databases to find specialized encyclopedias that can introduce you to this author's work, or Google the author to get some background.

Engaging in what the developers of the "Framework for Success in Post-secondary Education" refer to as *metacognition* is essential to your development as a reader. You might keep a reading journal, for instance, in which you reflect on the challenges—and successes—that you experience as a reader of academic texts. Or you might build in time for informal reflection and consider questions such as these: What are my strengths as a reader of academic texts? What are my limitations? How conscious am I of the various strategies I draw upon in reading different kinds of texts? How can I increase my repertoire of strategies?

When you encounter a particularly difficult reading, take the time to try to identify the sources of difficulty. Is it because of unfamiliar vocabulary and concepts, lack of clarity about the context in which the text was written (that is, its rhetorical situation), or inadequate background knowledge? Answering these questions can help you determine the most productive reading strategies to employ. After completing the reading, take a few minutes to ask yourself which strategies were particularly effective and which were less helpful.

---

for **exploration**

Think of a recent time when you were required to read a text that you experienced as difficult. Take five minutes to freewrite✱ about the sources of the difficulty. Then freewrite for an equal amount of time about how you approached this challenge. In retrospect, which of the strategies you used were productive? Which were not? Now take a few more minutes to write about what you have learned by reflecting on this experience. Conclude this exploration by identifying two positive ways that you could interact more productively with difficult texts.

for **collaboration**

Meet with a group of classmates to discuss your response to the previous For Exploration activity. Begin by having each person state two important things he or she learned as a result of the activity. (Appoint a recorder to write down each person's statements.) Once all members of the group have spoken, ask the recorder to read their statements

✱ For more information about freewriting — what it is and how to do it — see Chapter 9, pp. 263–65.

aloud. Were any statements repeated by more than one member of the group? Working as a group, formulate two suggestions for how to engage productively with difficult texts. Be prepared to discuss your conclusions with your classmates.

Developing Critical Reading Skills

Developing the necessary habits of mind can prepare you to engage college texts effectively. But you will also need to develop a repertoire of critical reading skills that you can employ depending on your rhetorical situation and the nature and complexity of the material you are reading. This section presents a number of useful strategies for engaging with texts. It also provides an opportunity for you to apply these strategies to a specific text, Frank Rose's "The Selfish Meme."

PREVIEWING

When you preview a text, you survey it quickly to establish or clarify your purpose and context for reading, asking yourself questions such as those listed on p. 32. As you do so, recognize that print, online, and visual sources may call for different previewing strategies. With print sources, for instance, it's easy to determine the author and publisher. To learn the author of a website, however, you may need to drill through the site or decipher the web address. When skimming a printed text, it's easy to see all the text at once; skimming an article in an online magazine, however, might require navigating a variety of web pages. It can also be challenging to determine how accurate and trustworthy informally published texts are. Whereas such print texts as scholarly journals and books have generally undergone extensive review and editing to ensure their credibility, that may not be the case with online sources, which may appear or disappear with alarming frequency.

---

note for multilingual writers

All readers benefit from previewing texts, but if you are a multilingual reader and writer, you will find previewing particularly helpful. It will give you valuable information that can help you read the text efficiently and effectively. As you preview a text, be sure to formulate questions about specialized terms or about the text's general approach.

---

for **exploration**

Using the Questions for Previewing a Text, preview "The Selfish Meme," an article by Frank Rose reprinted on pp. 33–34.

Questions for Previewing a Text

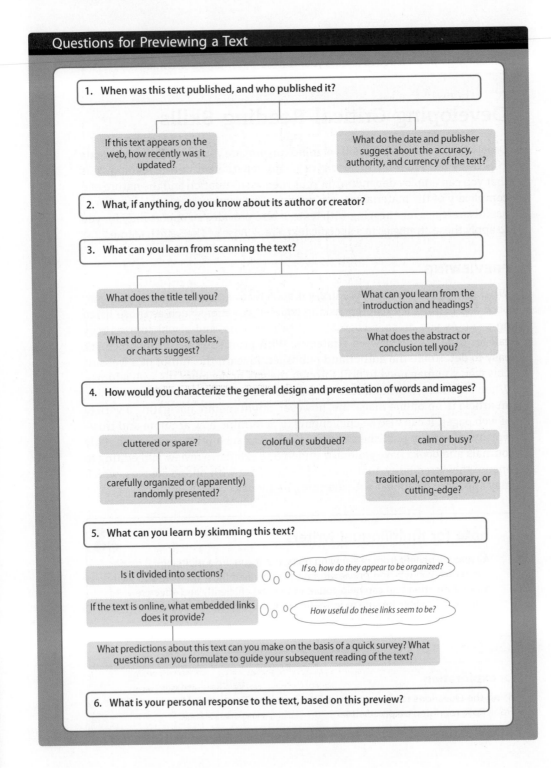

1. When was this text published, and who published it?

If this text appears on the web, how recently was it updated?

What do the date and publisher suggest about the accuracy, authority, and currency of the text?

2. What, if anything, do you know about its author or creator?

3. What can you learn from scanning the text?

What does the title tell you?

What can you learn from the introduction and headings?

What do any photos, tables, or charts suggest?

What does the abstract or conclusion tell you?

4. How would you characterize the general design and presentation of words and images?

cluttered or spare?

colorful or subdued?

calm or busy?

carefully organized or (apparently) randomly presented?

traditional, contemporary, or cutting-edge?

5. What can you learn by skimming this text?

Is it divided into sections?

If so, how do they appear to be organized?

If the text is online, what embedded links does it provide?

How useful do these links seem to be?

What predictions about this text can you make on the basis of a quick survey? What questions can you formulate to guide your subsequent reading of the text?

6. What is your personal response to the text, based on this preview?

The Selfish Meme

Twitter, dopamine, and the evolutionary advantages of talking about oneself

Nicholas Blechman

Frank Rose

This spring, a couple of neuroscience researchers at Harvard published a study that finally explained why we like to talk about ourselves so much: sharing our thoughts, it turns out, activates the brain's reward system. As if to demonstrate the thesis, journalists and bloggers promptly seized the occasion to share their own thoughts about the study, often at a considerable cost to accuracy. "Oversharing on Facebook as Satisfying as Sex?" the Web site for the *Today* show asked.

Well, not really. The study, which combined a series of behavioral experiments and brain scans, didn't suggest that anyone, in the lab or elsewhere, had found sharing on Facebook to be an orgasmic experience. What it did suggest was that humans may get a neurochemical reward from sharing information, and a significantly bigger reward from disclosing their own thoughts and feelings than from reporting someone else's.

The Harvard researchers — Diana Tamir, a grad student in psychology, and Jason Mitchell, her adviser — performed functional MRI scans on 212 subjects while asking them about their own opinions and personality traits, and about other people's. Neuroimaging of this sort can reveal which parts of the brain are being activated; in this case, the researchers found that the mesolimbic dopamine system — the seat of the brain's reward mechanism — was more engaged by questions about the test subject's own opinions and attitudes than by questions about the opinions and attitudes of other people. The system has long been known to respond to both primary rewards (food and sex) and secondary rewards (money), but this was the first time it's been shown to light up in response to, as the researchers put it, "self-disclosure."

What the study really illustrated, then, was a paradox: when it comes to information, sharing is mostly about *me*. The researchers weren't trying to answer the thornier question of *why* — why, as they wrote, our species might have "an intrinsic drive to disclose thoughts to others." The paper nonetheless points to an intriguing possibility: that this drive might give us humans an adaptive advantage.

Researchers have previously shown that certain online activities — such as checking your e-mail or Twitter stream — stimulate the brain's reward system. Like playing a slot machine, engaging in these activities sends the animal brain into a frenzy as it anticipates a possible reward: often nothing, but sometimes a small prize, and occasionally an enormous jackpot. The response to this unpredictable pattern seems to be deeply ingrained, and for the most basic of reasons: precisely the same cycle of suspense and excitement motivates animals to keep hunting for food. E-mail inboxes and slot machines simply tap into an attention-focusing mechanism that's perfectly designed to make sure we don't lose interest in Job No. 1, which is to keep ourselves alive.

However unrelated food and Facebook may seem, this foraging impulse sheds light on why, by one count, 96 percent of the country's online population uses social-networking sites: we get high from being on the receiving end of social media. But that's only half the story. The Harvard study helps clarify why we are so eager to be on the sharing side as well. "This would certainly explain the barroom bore, wouldn't it?" said Brian Boyd, the author of the literary Darwinist treatise *On the Origin of Stories*, when I asked him about the brain's response to acts of self-disclosure. What about estimates that, while 30 to 40 percent of ordinary conversation consists of people talking about themselves, some 80 percent of social-media updates fall in the same category? "Ordinarily, in a social context, we get feedback from other people," Boyd told me. "They might roll their eyes to indicate they don't want to hear so much about us. But online, you don't have that."

At first blush, the notion that the self-disclosure impulse is somehow good for the species might seem counterintuitive. If all we did was prattle on about ourselves, we'd soon bore one another to extinction. Why would we have evolved to get a rush of pleasure from hearing ourselves talk?

A closer look at the advantages conferred by storytelling offers some clues: by telling stories effectively, we gain status, obtain social feedback, and strengthen our bonds with other people. And on the flip side, all of this nattering — or tweeting — by our fellow humans ensures that we don't have to discover everything on our own. We have no end of people competing to tell us what's what. Hence the *real* paradox of sharing: what feels good for *me* probably ends up benefiting us all.

ANNOTATING

When you annotate a text, you highlight important words, passages, or images and write comments or questions that help you establish a dialogue with the text or remember important points. Some readers are heavy annotators, highlighting many passages and key words and filling the margins with comments and questions. Others annotate more selectively, preferring to write few comments and to highlight only the most important parts. In thinking about your own annotating strategies, remember that your purpose in reading should influence the way you annotate a text. You would annotate a text you're reading primarily for information differently than you would an essay that you expect will play a central role in an analytical essay you are writing for your history class.

One advantage of print texts is that there are an endless number of ways that readers can interact with them. If you look at three students' annotations of the same text, you might find that they look quite different but are equally effective in terms of engagement and critical thinking. Increasingly, electronic or downloaded texts offer similar opportunities for interaction. Many devices make it possible for readers to highlight, bookmark, search, tag, add notes, and draw and embed images. Popular programs and apps include iAnnotate, GoodReader, and Google Drive. These are just some of the many programs designed to increase the productivity of online reading and research, and new programs are being developed all the time.

Programs for note taking, sharing annotations, and making citations, as well as other tools for engaged reading, can help you read critically and deeply. The key is to choose a program that works for you, learn its strengths and limitations (depending on the complexity of the program, there can be a steep learning curve), and gain enough experience so that the benefits become real for you. Just as composing preferences vary,✱ so, too, can annotation preferences. One reader might love using iAnnotate, GoodReader, or Diigo to mark online texts, while another might find these apps cumbersome and prefer to annotate important texts by hand. Over time, as new programs are developed and your experiences change, your preferences as a reader may alter.

If you're working with print and have rented the text or prefer not to mark up your own copy, you can highlight and annotate a photocopy or scan or write questions and comments on a separate piece of paper or sticky notes. Some readers find it helpful to color code their annotations. For instance, you can underline main ideas in green and supporting evidence in orange. Color coding is easy to do in print, and many apps also allow for the use of color when annotating.

How can you know the most effective way to annotate a text? The Questions for Annotating a Text on p. 36 can help you make appropriate choices as you read and respond. In addition, see p. 37 for an excerpt from student Stevon Roberts's annotated copy of Amitai Etzioni's essay "Less Privacy Is Good for Us (and You)," which appears in Chapter 5 on pp. 117–20. Roberts's essay responding to Etzioni's work can also be read in Chapter 5 on pp. 129–34.

---

for **exploration**

Annotate "The Selfish Meme" by Frank Rose (pp. 33–34) as if you expected to write an essay responding to it for your composition class. If you do not want to write in your book, you can photocopy or scan and print the essay.

for **collaboration**

Working in small groups, compare your annotations of the article. List all the various annotating strategies that group members used. To what extent did group members rely on similar strategies? What can individual differences tell you about your own strengths and limitations as an annotator?

See Chapter 4, pp. 93–100, for more information on this topic. ✱ ● ● ● ● ● ● ● ●

Questions for Annotating a Text

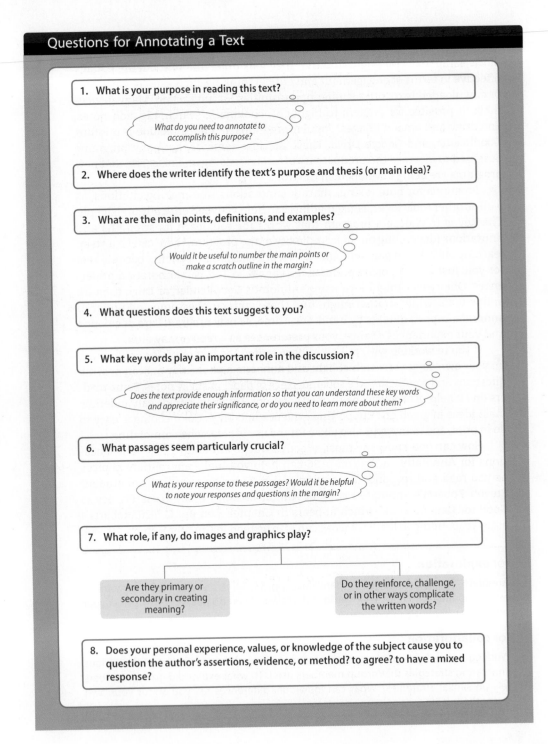

1. **What is your purpose in reading this text?**

   What do you need to annotate to accomplish this purpose?

2. **Where does the writer identify the text's purpose and thesis (or main idea)?**

3. **What are the main points, definitions, and examples?**

   Would it be useful to number the main points or make a scratch outline in the margin?

4. **What questions does this text suggest to you?**

5. **What key words play an important role in the discussion?**

   Does the text provide enough information so that you can understand these key words and appreciate their significance, or do you need to learn more about them?

6. **What passages seem particularly crucial?**

   What is your response to these passages? Would it be helpful to note your responses and questions in the margin?

7. **What role, if any, do images and graphics play?**

   Are they primary or secondary in creating meaning?

   Do they reinforce, challenge, or in other ways complicate the written words?

8. **Does your personal experience, values, or knowledge of the subject cause you to question the author's assertions, evidence, or method? to agree? to have a mixed response?**

Congress passed the buck by asking the Institute of Medicine (IOM) to conduct a study of the matter. The IOM committee, dominated by politically correct people, just reported its recommendations. It suggested that all pregnant women be asked to consent to HIV testing as part of routine prenatal care. There is little wrong with such a recommendation other than it does not deal with many of the mothers who are drug addicts or otherwise live at society's margins. Many of these women do not show up for prenatal care, and they are particularly prone to HIV, according to a study published in the American Health Association's *Journal of School Health*. To save the lives of their children, they must be tested at delivery and treated even if this entails a violation of mothers' privacy.

Recently a suggestion to use driver's licenses to curb illegal immigration has sent the Coalition for Constitutional Liberties, a large group of libertarians, civil libertarians, and privacy advocates, into higher orbit than John Glenn ever traversed. The coalition wrote:

I wonder if these groups would put themselves into these categories

inflammatory & dismissive

> This plan pushed us to the brink of tyranny, where citizens will not be allowed to travel, open bank accounts, obtain health care, get a job, or purchase firearms without first presenting the proper government papers.
>
> The authorizing section of the law . . . is reminiscent of the totalitarian dictates by Politburo members in the former Soviet Union, not the Congress of the United States of America.

maybe alarmist

Meanwhile, Wells Fargo is introducing a new device that allows a person to cash checks at its ATM machines because the machines recognize faces. Rapidly coming is a whole new industry of so-called biometrics that uses natural features such as voice, hand design, and eye pattern to recognize a person with the same extremely high reliability provided by the new DNA tests.

what's the cost & who pays for it. Is it worth it?

not likely

It's true that as biometrics catches on, it will practically strip Americans of anonymity, an important part of privacy. In the near future, a person who acquired a poor reputation in one part of the country will find it much more difficult to move to another part, change his name, and gain a whole fresh start. Biometrics are right through such assumed identities. One may hope that future communities will become more tolerant of such people, especially if they openly acknowledge the mistakes of their past and truly seek to lead a more prosocial life. But they will no longer be able to hide their pasts.

This is a fantasy!

Above all, while biometrics clearly undermines privacy, the social benefits it promises are very substantial. Specifically, each year at least half a million criminals become fugitives, avoiding trial, incarceration, or serving their full sentences, often committing additional crimes while on the lam. People who fraudulently file for multiple income tax refunds using fake identities and multiple Social Security numbers cost

speculation — sounds like someone is trying to sell me on something... (oh right, they ARE :")

Stevon Roberts's Annotations of "Less Privacy Is Good for Us (and You)"

SUMMARIZING

Never underestimate the usefulness of writing clear, concise summaries of texts. Writing a summary allows you to restate the major points of a book or an essay in your own words. Summarizing is a skill worth developing because it requires you to master the material you're reading and make it your own. Summaries can vary in length, depending on the complexity and length of the text. Ideally, however, they should be as brief as possible, certainly no longer than a paragraph or two. The guidelines on p. 39 offer suggestions for writing your own summaries.

for **exploration**

Following the guidelines on p. 39, write a one-paragraph summary of "The Selfish Meme" (pp. 33–34).

ANALYZING A TEXT'S ARGUMENT

Previewing, analyzing visuals, annotating, and summarizing can all help you determine the central points in a text. Sometimes the central argument is explicitly stated. In the last paragraph of "The Selfish Meme," Frank Rose answers the question he raises in the first paragraph of why we like to talk about ourselves so much. We do so because "by telling stories effectively, we gain status, obtain social feedback, and strengthen our bonds with other people. . . . Hence the *real* paradox of sharing: what feels good for *me* probably ends up benefiting us all."

Not all authors are so direct. Someone writing about current issues in health-care ethics may raise questions rather than provide answers or make strong assertions. Whether an author articulates a clear position on a subject or poses a question for consideration, critical readers attempt to determine if the author's analysis is valid. In other words, does the author provide good reasons in support of a position or line of analysis? The questions on p. 40 provide an introduction to analyzing the argument of a text. ✳

for **exploration**

Using the Questions for Analyzing a Text's Argument, analyze "The Selfish Meme" (pp. 33–34). Be sure to answer all the questions.

✳ For a fuller discussion of this and related issues, see Chapter 3's discussion of ethos, logos, and pathos (pp. 62–67); Chapter 5's coverage of analyzing and synthesizing texts (pp. 105-43); and Chapter 7's coverage of evaluating a text (pp. 183–233).

Guidelines for Summarizing a Text

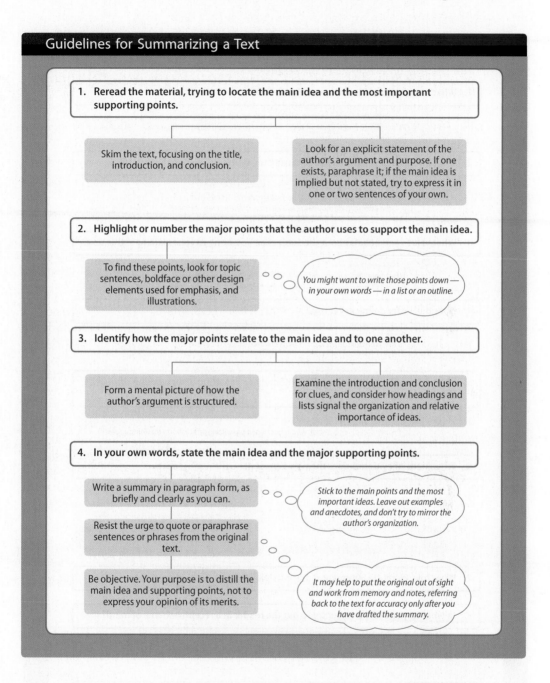

1. Reread the material, trying to locate the main idea and the most important supporting points.

Skim the text, focusing on the title, introduction, and conclusion.

Look for an explicit statement of the author's argument and purpose. If one exists, paraphrase it; if the main idea is implied but not stated, try to express it in one or two sentences of your own.

2. Highlight or number the major points that the author uses to support the main idea.

To find these points, look for topic sentences, boldface or other design elements used for emphasis, and illustrations.

You might want to write those points down — in your own words — in a list or an outline.

3. Identify how the major points relate to the main idea and to one another.

Form a mental picture of how the author's argument is structured.

Examine the introduction and conclusion for clues, and consider how headings and lists signal the organization and relative importance of ideas.

4. In your own words, state the main idea and the major supporting points.

Write a summary in paragraph form, as briefly and clearly as you can.

Resist the urge to quote or paraphrase sentences or phrases from the original text.

Be objective. Your purpose is to distill the main idea and supporting points, not to express your opinion of its merits.

Stick to the main points and the most important ideas. Leave out examples and anecdotes, and don't try to mirror the author's organization.

It may help to put the original out of sight and work from memory and notes, referring back to the text for accuracy only after you have drafted the summary.

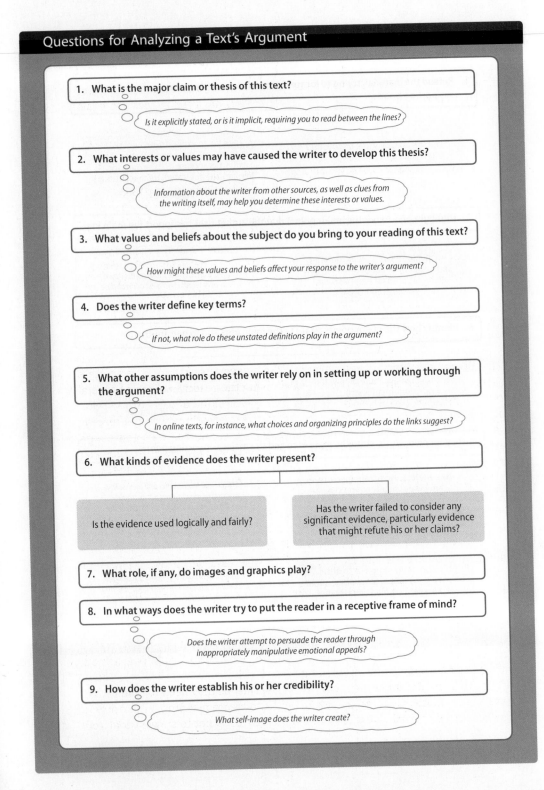

Questions for Analyzing a Text's Argument

1. **What is the major claim or thesis of this text?**

   Is it explicitly stated, or is it implicit, requiring you to read between the lines?

2. **What interests or values may have caused the writer to develop this thesis?**

   Information about the writer from other sources, as well as clues from the writing itself, may help you determine these interests or values.

3. **What values and beliefs about the subject do you bring to your reading of this text?**

   How might these values and beliefs affect your response to the writer's argument?

4. **Does the writer define key terms?**

   If not, what role do these unstated definitions play in the argument?

5. **What other assumptions does the writer rely on in setting up or working through the argument?**

   In online texts, for instance, what choices and organizing principles do the links suggest?

6. **What kinds of evidence does the writer present?**

   Is the evidence used logically and fairly?

   Has the writer failed to consider any significant evidence, particularly evidence that might refute his or her claims?

7. **What role, if any, do images and graphics play?**

8. **In what ways does the writer try to put the reader in a receptive frame of mind?**

   Does the writer attempt to persuade the reader through inappropriately manipulative emotional appeals?

9. **How does the writer establish his or her credibility?**

   What self-image does the writer create?

Reading Visual Texts

As noted at the start of this chapter, when you read rhetorically, you draw not just on the text before you but also on all aspects of your rhetorical situation. You think about your purpose as a reader: What are your immediate goals?

thinking rhetorically

---

note for multilingual writers

The Questions for Analyzing a Text's Argument reflect one approach that you can use as you read. If your first experience of reading is grounded in a language and culture other than North American English, some of these questions may strike you as odd. In some cultures, for instance, writers do not announce the major claim or thesis of their text in the introduction; doing so may seem overly obvious. As you read these questions, then, consider the extent to which they are culturally grounded. Remember, too, that everyone can learn from cultural differences, so think about the preferences in argumentation that you bring from your home (or parents') culture. You, your classmates, and your teacher will all benefit if you discuss these differences in class.

What do you need to "do" with your reading? Do you need to prepare for class discussion or an exam, or write an essay using the reading as one of several sources? You also think about issues of genre: What kind of text are you reading, and how might this constrain or facilitate your reading? Are you reading a genre with which you are already familiar, or are you reading a genre with unfamiliar and challenging content and conventions? And you also consider the medium. If you are reading a difficult text on your laptop, for instance, you may recognize that closing down multiple windows and programs will increase your ability to focus. Reading rhetorically means being an active, engaged reader, one who is not just reading passively to comprehend and absorb content but who is actively participating in the creation of meaning.

It may be easy for you to recognize the importance of reading rhetorically when you are reading traditional academic texts. Of course, the student reading excerpts from Aristotle's *Nichomachean Ethics* recognizes that this text requires her full attention, whether she is reading it in print or on her laptop. She also recognizes that to engage the reading critically she must read proactively, looking up new terms and learning more about concepts she needs to understand. If she is unfamiliar with the branch of philosophy called *ethics*, for instance, she might do some quick online research to familiarize herself with its origin, history, and significance.

It can be harder for students to realize that just as they need to read verbal texts—texts that emphasize the use of words to create meaning—rhetorically, they also need to read visual texts rhetorically. This is not to suggest that you should read all texts, whether primarily verbal or visual, with the same level of attention and engagement. If you are reading your grocery list, all you need to know is that the abbreviation *mayo* means you should buy mayonnaise. Some visual texts function in similar ways—traffic signs, for instance. At least when you are traveling in your home country: Anyone who has traveled abroad knows that even traffic signs, can require considerable cultural and rhetorical knowledge. To see why, enter the phrase "traffic signs around the world" in your browser and in Google images. You may be surprised by how much traffic signs in various countries can differ.

How well you need to read traffic signs depends on the specifics of your rhetorical situation. If you are planning a vacation in Germany and know you will be renting a car and driving on the notoriously fast Autobahn, all you need to do is be able to comprehend the most important traffic signs. If, however, you are a student in an anthropology class writing an essay on how various countries' traffic signs reflect broader cultural differences, you would have to read and analyze these countries' traffic signs quite differently and perhaps even undertake research on the history of traffic signs.

Reading and analyzing visual texts can be important in a variety of courses and disciplines. Students in art history are regularly asked to analyze reproductions of artwork; doing so is central to the discipline. Instructors in other disciplines may also create assignments that highlight the significance of visual texts. An instructor teaching an Introduction to Women's Studies

Image Courtesy of The Advertising Archives

Image Courtesy of The Advertising Archives

Two Magazine Advertisements from 1955

class might ask students to analyze the pair of 1955 magazine advertisements on the facing page to gain insights about this era. A historian teaching a class on the lives of the urban poor in Victorian England might present students with a series of photographs from pioneering photographer John Thompson's 1877 *Street Life in London*. Their assignment? To choose several photographs that help illuminate one of the readings for the course and write an essay explaining what they have learned via this analysis.

Analyzing one or more visual texts is also a common assignment in many writing classes. You may be asked, for instance, to choose an advertisement and analyze it. If you haven't done so before, writing about visual texts can seem intimidating. How can you get enough out of a photograph or advertisement to write about it? How do you go about understanding the relationship between text and image? The Questions for Analyzing Visual Texts below will give you a place to start.

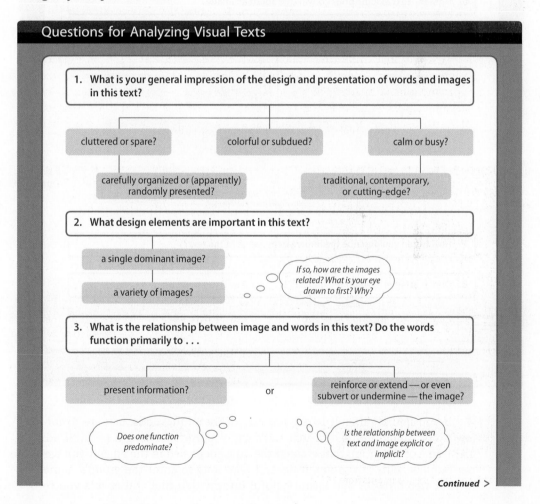

Questions for Analyzing Visual Texts

1. **What is your general impression of the design and presentation of words and images in this text?**

   cluttered or spare? colorful or subdued? calm or busy?

   carefully organized or (apparently) randomly presented? traditional, contemporary, or cutting-edge?

2. **What design elements are important in this text?**

   a single dominant image?

   a variety of images?

   If so, how are the images related? What is your eye drawn to first? Why?

3. **What is the relationship between image and words in this text? Do the words function primarily to . . .**

   present information? or reinforce or extend — or even subvert or undermine — the image?

   Does one function predominate?

   Is the relationship between text and image explicit or implicit?

Continued >

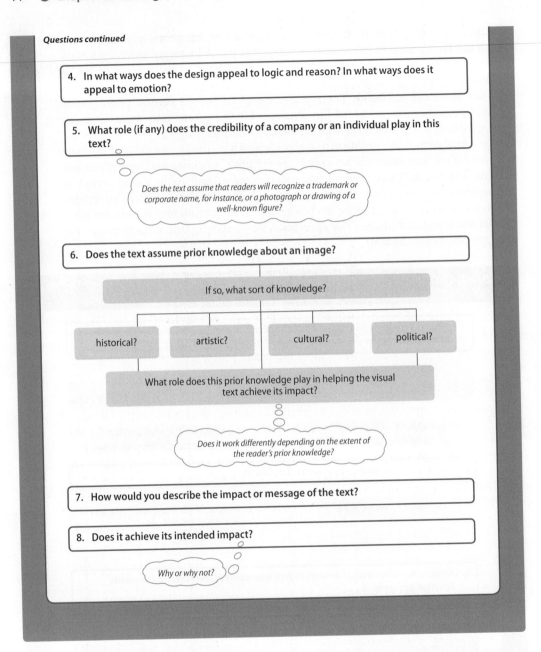

4. In what ways does the design appeal to logic and reason? In what ways does it appeal to emotion?

5. What role (if any) does the credibility of a company or an individual play in this text?

Does the text assume that readers will recognize a trademark or corporate name, for instance, or a photograph or drawing of a well-known figure?

6. Does the text assume prior knowledge about an image?

If so, what sort of knowledge?

historical?   artistic?   cultural?   political?

What role does this prior knowledge play in helping the visual text achieve its impact?

Does it work differently depending on the extent of the reader's prior knowledge?

7. How would you describe the impact or message of the text?

8. Does it achieve its intended impact?

Why or why not?

If you find it difficult to answer any of these questions, be sure to follow up by doing a little research. Let's say you are analyzing a political ad. The name of the group that created the ad is identified in the ad, but you are not familiar with this group. It doesn't take long to enter the group's name in your web browser and locate helpful information that will enable you to

Raising the Flag on Iwo Jima, February 23, 1945

MARKA/Alamy Stock Photo

determine the group's credibility. Online research can also help you fill in gaps in your prior knowledge about an image. You may be familiar with the well-known photograph of a group of soldiers raising the U.S. flag during the battle of Iwo Jima in World War II. You're aware that it is a famous photograph, but you know little about its historical, political, and cultural context. A quick web search can help you understand why this photograph became one of the most significant images of World War II. Depending on your purpose, this may be all the information you need. If you are writing a research paper on the role that news media played in World War II, however, you would need to learn more about the history of the photograph and the controversy surrounding it.

for **exploration**

Illustrations can play an important role in texts that rely primarily on linguistic elements for their meaning. Such is the case with Frank Rose's "The Selfish Meme," which appears on pp. 33–34. At the top of the first page of Rose's text is a simple image. A man and a woman are facing each other holding what are clearly smartphones. Above each head is a bubble: the bubble above the man's head contains an "m," and the bubble above the woman's head contains an "e." Together they spell "me."

Using the Guidelines for Analyzing Visual Texts, analyze the illustration that accompanies "The Selfish Meme." After you have responded to the guideline's question, take a few minutes to explain the extent to which you feel the illustration reinforces the message of Rose's essay.

© 2016 Artists Rights Society (ARS), New York/ADAGP, Paris

Ernesto "Che" Guevara, Photographed by Alberto Korda on March 5, 1960

Even apparently simple visual texts can have rich cultural histories. Here, for instance, is a well-known photograph of the Marxist revolutionary Che Guevara. An Argentinian by birth, Ernesto "Che" Guevara played a key role in the Cuban Revolution. This photo of Guevara was taken by photographer Alberto Korda on March 5, 1960, in Havana, Cuba. Korda recognized the power of the photo, but it was not distributed broadly until after Guevara's October 9, 1967, execution. After Guevara's death, this photograph quickly achieved near-mythic status.

Today, this image—and manipulations of it—persists in global culture as a powerful symbol of countercultural and political resistance. On p. 47, for instance, is a stylized version of the original photograph available as public domain clip art via www.wpclipart.com. In this rendering, the historical Guevara has become a widely recognized image, one that appears today in countless reproductions in every imaginable context, adorning posters, T-shirts, bumper stickers, Cuban currency, and even ice-cream wrappers, wine labels, and condoms.[2] Guevara's image has also become a popular tattoo, sported by Angelina Jolie and Mike Tyson, among many, many others. (For an entertaining sampling, try searching Google Images for "Che tattoo.")

---

[2] For additional examples accompanied by intelligent discussion, see Michael Casey's *Che's Afterlife: The Legacy of an Image*, Vintage Books, 2009.

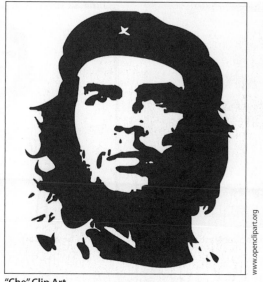

www.openclipart.org

"Che" Clip Art

Some uses of the image employ irreverence or outright mockery to resist the heroic image of Guevara promoted by his admirers. For example, *LiberaChe* by artist Christopher Nash (p. 48) morphs Guevara, usually the epitome of machismo, into a likeness of the flamboyant, rhinestone-bedecked entertainer Liberace, who was especially popular in the mid-twentieth century. (If you are not familiar with Liberace, who lived from 1919 to 1987, be sure to do a quick online search to learn more about him and his flamboyant dress and lifestyle.)

The widespread use of Guevara's image has also given rise recently to "meta" references to its popularity—that is, to uses of the image that make tongue-in-cheek reference to how frequently the image is used. For instance, a T-shirt sold online by the *Onion* depicts Guevara wearing a T-shirt with his own image. In a similar vein, the cartoon from the *New Yorker* on the next page depends on readers recognizing not only Guevara's iconic image but also that of Bart Simpson (an image that vies with Guevara's in terms of its ubiquity).

As meta references, these uses of Guevara's image call into question the ways in which the image has been and continues to be used. Rather than invoking Guevara as a symbol of countercultural and political resistance, they seem to suggest something about the image's commercialization and about its (mis)appropriation as a fashion statement and a means of perpetuating a consumer culture that the historical Guevara rejected.

LiberaChe, by Artist Christopher Nash

Christopher Nash

Cartoon: Che and Bart

Matthew Diffee/New Yorker Cartoon/Conde Nast

for **exploration**

Find a visual text that you believe has a rich cultural history. That history could be serious or humorous, high culture or pop culture. Take ten minutes to brainstorm everything you can think of about this visual text:

- What makes it interesting culturally?
- What are the specifics of its history?
- How has it been used in various contexts?
- What can it help writers better understand about how images and other visual elements create meaning?

Be prepared to share your visual text and brainstormed notes with others.

for **collaboration**

Bring your visual text and brainstormed notes to class. Meet with a group of peers, dividing the time your instructor has allotted for this collaborative activity so that each student has roughly the same amount of time to present his or her visual text and brainstormed notes. Be sure to reserve at least five minutes for general group discussion about what you have learned as a result of this activity. Appoint a recorder/reporter who will share your group's results with the class. What has this activity helped you better understand about analyzing visual texts?

Chapter 6 presents an extended case study of one student's analysis of a visual text, a public-service ad (PSA) for the National Center for Family Literacy. This case study shows student Daniel Stiepleman moving from his early explorations of this PSA through planning, drafting, and revising. Notice how much attention he pays to visual elements in his preliminary annotation and analysis of the PSA (p. 167). Daniel struggled at times with his analysis, as is clear from the two rough drafts included in the chapter, but his effort more than paid off. His final essay represents a thought-provoking and engaging analysis of a visual text, one in which image, text, and design work together in powerful ways. Daniel's case study appears on pp. 179–82.

Daniel's analysis of the PSA for the National Center for Family Literacy emphasizes the importance of being able to analyze the visual texts we encounter in our daily lives. After all, these images have come to play an increasingly important role in modern life. When driving down the street, watching television, skimming a magazine, or reading online—and in many other situations—we're continually presented with visual texts, most of which are designed to persuade us to purchase, believe, or do certain things. Often these texts can be a source of pleasure and entertainment, but informed consumers and engaged citizens recognize the value of being able to read them with a critical eye.

This chapter encourages you to recognize that reading, like writing, is best understood as a rhetorical activity. A rhetorical approach to reading encourages you to consider your rhetorical situation as an academic reader. It also encourages you to be aware of and take responsibility for your reading preferences and processes. Reading rhetorically means being an engaged reader who is actively participating in the creation of meaning.

---

for **thought, discussion, and writing**

1. For at least one full day, keep track of all the reading (in print and on screen) you do. Be sure to include both informal and formal material, from reading grocery lists—either handwritten or composed on a smartphone—to reading class assignments. Do you see any patterns in terms of preferences and habitual practices? Take a few minutes to write about what you have learned as a result of this inventory and reflection. Be prepared to share this writing with your classmates.

2. Write an essay in which you describe who you are as a reader today and how you got to be that way. Alternatively, create a poster-size collage that uses words, images, graphics, and even material objects to describe who you are as a reader today. For an example of such a collage, see Mirlandra Neuneker's collage on p. 90 portraying who she is as a writer.

   To prepare for this activity, spend at least an hour reflecting on your previous experiences as a reader. To do so, brainstorm responses to the following questions:

   ● What are your earliest memories of learning to read?
   ● Can you recall particular experiences in school or on the job that influenced your current attitude toward reading?
   ● What images come to mind when you hear the word *reader*?
   ● What kinds of reading do you enjoy or dislike?
   ● What kinds of reading do you do outside of school?
   ● How much of your outside-of-school reading is in print? How much is on screen?

- What do you enjoy most — and least — about the reading process?
- What goals would you like to set for yourself as a reader?

3. Interview either a professional in your intended major or (if that's not practical) an advanced student in your major. Ask that person about the reading he or she does for professional or academic work and about the other kinds of reading he or she does for different purposes and for relaxation. What devices does your interviewee use? What patterns emerge in his or her reading practices? What does that person see as the greatest challenges and opportunities for readers today? What advice would the interviewee give to a student just entering this area of study?

4. Choose an advertisement or a public-service announcement that interests you. Using the Questions for Analyzing Visual Texts (pp. 43–44), write a response to each question. Finally, write one or two paragraphs about what you have learned as a result of this analysis.

5. Earlier in this chapter you read "The Selfish Meme" by Frank Rose (pp. 33–34). Write an essay in which you respond to Rose's essay.

3

Analyzing Rhetorical Situations

As Chapters 1 and 2 emphasize, whenever you write—whether you're word processing an essay for your class or designing a website for a student organization—you are writing in the context of a specific rhetorical situation involving you as the writer, who you're writing for, what you're writing, and the medium you're using to share what you have written. Each rhetorical situation comes with unique opportunities and demands: A management trainee writing a memo to her supervisor, for example, faces different challenges than an investigative journalist working on a story for the *New York Times* or a student preparing a slide presentation for a psychology class. Successful writers know that they need to exhibit rhetorical sensitivity—an understanding of the relationships among writer, reader, text, and medium—to help them make decisions as they write and revise.

In this chapter of *The Academic Writer*, you will learn how to ask questions about your rhetorical situation, questions that will enable you to determine the most fruitful way to approach your topic and respond to the needs and expectations of your readers. You will also learn how to recognize the textual conventions that characterize different communities of language users. This kind of rhetorically sensitive reading is particularly helpful when you encounter new genres of writing, as is the case, for example, when you enter college or begin a new job.

Learning to Analyze Your Rhetorical Situation

Rhetoric involves four key elements: writer, reader, text, and medium. When you think about these elements and pose questions about the options available to you as a writer, you are analyzing your rhetorical situation.

thinking rhetorically

The process of analyzing your rhetorical situation challenges you to look both within and without. Your intended meaning—what you want to

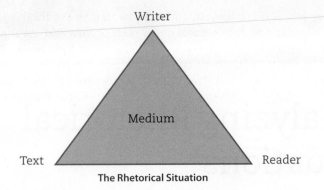

The Rhetorical Situation

communicate—is certainly important, as is your purpose for writing. Unless you're writing solely for yourself in a journal or notebook, though, you can't ignore your readers or the kind of text you're writing. You also need to consider which medium (print, oral, digital) is most appropriate given your rhetorical situation. Both at school and on the job, sometimes your medium will be predetermined; at other times you will have options. Analyzing your rhetorical situation helps you respond creatively as a writer and yet keeps you aware of limits on your freedom.

THE RHETORICAL SITUATION

In your daily life, you regularly analyze your rhetorical situation when you communicate with others, although you most often do so unconsciously and intuitively. Imagine, for instance, that you've been meaning to contact a close friend. Should you call, email, text, send a handwritten note, or contact him some other way? The answer depends on your situation.

note for multilingual writers

This chapter's approach to rhetoric and rhetorical sensitivity is grounded in the Western rhetorical tradition. Other traditions hold different values and assumptions about communication. For example, if part of your education took place in a non-Western culture, you may have learned an approach to communication that values maintaining communal harmony as much as (or more than) individual self-expression, which is highly valued in Western cultures. For some raised in non-Western cultures, English as it is written in school, business, and everyday contexts may seem abrupt and even rude. As a writer learning to communicate in different languages and communities, you need to understand the assumptions held by writers who are grounded in the Western rhetorical tradition, but you do not need to abandon your own culture's values. Your writing (and your thinking) will be enriched when you learn how to draw on *all* the rhetorical sensitivity you have gained as a speaker, listener, writer, and reader.

If you just want to let your friend know that you're thinking of him, you might choose to text him because of this medium's ease and informality. If your friend maintains a Facebook page, you might visit his wall, read some posts to see what he's been up to, and then leave a greeting. But what if you're writing because you've just learned of a death in your friend's family? The seriousness of this situation and its personal nature might prompt you to send a handwritten note instead.

USING YOUR RHETORICAL ANALYSIS TO GUIDE YOUR WRITING

Effective writers draw on their rhetorical sensitivity to determine the best ways to communicate with readers. Often, they do so without thinking. For example, the student deciding how best to get in touch with a friend didn't consciously run through a mental checklist; rather, she drew on her intuitive understanding of her situation. When you face the challenge of new and more difficult kinds of writing as you do in college, however, it helps to analyze your rhetorical situation consciously. The Questions for Analyzing Your Rhetorical Situation (pp. 54–55) can help you understand and respond to the constraints and opportunities.

---

for **exploration**

Imagine that you need to compose the following texts:

- An application for an internship in your major
- A flyer for a march you are organizing to protest a tuition increase
- A response to a film you watched in class, posted to an online discussion board
- A substantial research-based essay for a class you are taking
- A status update for your Facebook page

Spend a few minutes thinking about how you would approach these different writing situations. Then write a brief analysis of each situation, using the following questions:

thinking rhetorically

- What is your role as writer? Your purpose for writing?
- What image of yourself do you wish to present? How will you create this image?
- How will your readers influence your writing?
- How will the medium you use affect your communication?
- What role, if any, should images, design elements, and sound play?

SETTING PRELIMINARY GOALS

Before beginning a major writing project, you may find it helpful to write a brief analysis of your rhetorical situation, or you may simply review these questions mentally. Doing so can help you determine your preliminary intentions or goals as a writer. (Your intentions will often shift as you write.

Questions for Analyzing Your Rhetorical Situation

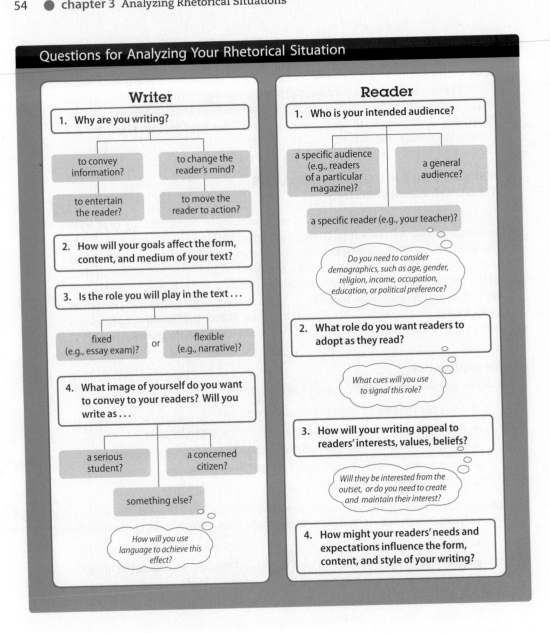

That's fine. As you write, you'll naturally revise your understanding of your rhetorical situation.) Despite its tentativeness, however, your analysis of your situation will give you a sense of direction and purpose.

Here's an analysis of a rhetorical situation by Alia Sands, whose essay appears on pp. 58–61. Alia analyzed her situation as a writer by using the Questions for Analyzing Your Rhetorical Situation above and on the facing page. She begins with some general reflections about her assignment.

Questions for Analyzing Your Rhetorical Situation

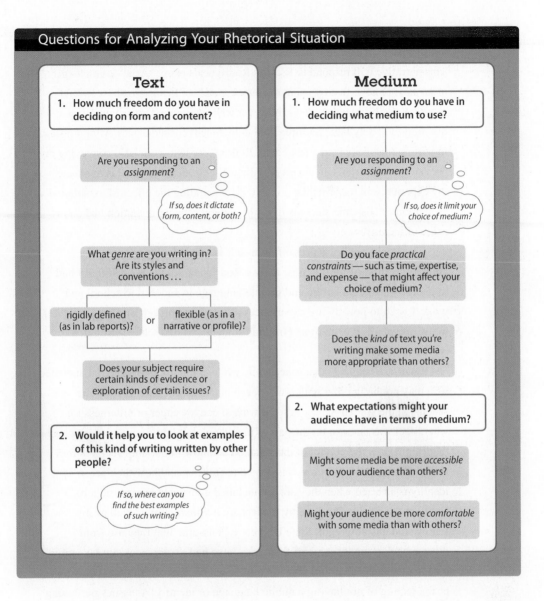

Text

1. How much freedom do you have in deciding on form and content?

Are you responding to an *assignment*?

If so, does it dictate form, content, or both?

What *genre* are you writing in? Are its styles and conventions . . .

rigidly defined (as in lab reports)? **or** flexible (as in a narrative or profile)?

Does your subject require certain kinds of evidence or exploration of certain issues?

2. Would it help you to look at examples of this kind of writing written by other people?

If so, where can you find the best examples of such writing?

Medium

1. How much freedom do you have in deciding what medium to use?

Are you responding to an *assignment*?

If so, does it limit your choice of medium?

Do you face *practical constraints* — such as time, expertise, and expense — that might affect your choice of medium?

Does the *kind* of text you're writing make some media more appropriate than others?

2. What expectations might your audience have in terms of medium?

Might some media be more *accessible* to your audience than others?

Might your audience be more *comfortable* with some media than with others?

ALIA SANDS'S ANALYSIS

I am writing an essay for my first-year writing class. The assignment asked us to read an essay by Richard Rodriguez titled "Aria." This essay is included in Rodriguez's literacy narrative *Hunger of Memory*. The assignment asked us to respond personally to Rodriguez's text but also to engage with and synthesize his assertions about bilingual education.

Writer: I am writing a personal narrative regarding my experiences as a half-Hispanic, half-Caucasian middle-school student in Marshalltown, Iowa. This narrative will respond to Richard Rodriguez's essay "Aria" from *Hunger of Memory*. I hope that by using my own experience I can show how special programs for bilingual students, however well-intentioned, raise complicated questions and may have multiple (and unintended) consequences. My purpose in writing this piece is to engage with Rodriguez's text while also conveying my own story. As I am not an expert on bilingual education, my goal is to situate my experience in its particular context, demonstrating the effect Marshalltown's separation of Hispanic students from the general school population had on my sense of identity.

The image I wish to present of myself is of particular concern to me. I am not the child of immigrants. Unlike Rodriguez, I have not felt that I had to choose between a public and private language to succeed in school and work. I wish to portray my experiences as unique to myself and decidedly *not* indicative of all or even most Hispanic students, as many have struggled in ways I have not.

I will use language that is academic while appropriate to a general audience who may not be familiar with issues faced by Hispanic students in public schools in the United States. I do not wish to convey anger or bitterness for what I feel was an error on the part of the school, but I do wish to use language that emphasizes the gravity of the situation and how important I feel it is for schools to recognize how much is denied to students and how their sense of identity is affected when they are not included in mainstream instruction.

Reader: I am assuming that my readers are my instructor as well as my fellow students at Oregon State University. I assume that they are from diverse backgrounds; some of them may have had experiences similar to my own, and some of them may be unfamiliar with issues of bilingual education or the feeling of not having a public language or identity. As issues pertaining to race and education are often sensitive ones, I'm hoping to communicate in a way that acknowledges differences in opinion while still taking a clear stance based upon my own experience and my understanding of Rodriguez's text. I am trying not to be reductive when it comes to complicated situations. I don't want to imply that I know what kind of education will be beneficial to everyone. I do hope to show how my experiences overlap with the ideas discussed by Rodriguez and how those experiences have led me to conclusions about what can happen when students are excluded, rather than included, in the use of public language.

Text: I only have a few pages to do the following: summarize Rodriguez's text, convey a meaningful story about my own experiences, and discuss the connections between the two. The length of the paper, then, will be a significant constraint. I will have to carefully edit my narrative, deciding on the most essential details to include, and also figure out what elements (examples, quotes, ideas) of Rodriguez's text I need to discuss. I will not be using multimedia or images, so I must engage my readers through my prose. I'll have to write clearly and succinctly because I have so little space, but I'll also need to use vivid language that will bring my experiences and other examples to life. (For example, I will be mentioning a movie, *Stand and Deliver*, that I was required to watch repeatedly in middle school. I will need to summarize its plot in order to convey its significance, but I'll also want to give readers a clear sense of what watching it felt like—the impression it made on me when I saw it for the first, second, third, etc., time.)

Medium: I currently am not choosing to include any images, graphics, or multimedia in my essay. If I were writing a research paper on this topic, I would probably include graphics or images that would help readers better understand the information I am presenting. As most of my paper will respond to and synthesize Rodriguez's work, I do not feel that images or graphics are necessary to help readers better understand my own experiences or those of Rodriguez.

Here is Alia's essay. As you read it, keep her analysis of her rhetorical situation clearly in mind. In what ways did her analysis inform the essay she wrote?

Sands 1

Alia Sands
Professor Rhoads
Writing 121
May 2, 2016

A Separate Education

Bilingual education and support for nonnative English speakers in classrooms are widely debated topics in academia today. While some argue that students benefit from learning in their native languages, others, like writer Richard Rodriguez, argue that bilingual education deprives students of a shared public identity, which is critical to their full participation in civic life. In middle school, as a half-Hispanic student who only spoke English, I was surprised to find myself in a special class for Hispanic students. My experience in the class brought Rodriguez's misgivings about the effects of separate education vividly to life: Being excluded from mainstream instruction even for a few class periods a week caused me to reevaluate my identity and question whether or not I was actually a member of the broader community.

In the essay "Aria" from *Hunger of Memory: The Education of Richard Rodriguez*, Richard Rodriguez discusses his own experience of second-language acquisition. Rodriguez, who describes himself as "socially disadvantaged—the son of working-class parents, both Mexican immigrants" (10), did not receive bilingual instruction and was actively discouraged by the nuns running his school from speaking Spanish at home. Though at first Rodriguez was reluctant to embrace English as his primary language because he could not believe "that English was [his] to use" (18), he grew increasingly comfortable with it. His experience learning English led him to believe that the common practice of separating students from mainstream classroom instruction and from that public language "dangerously . . . romanticize[s] public separateness and . . . trivialize[s] the dilemma of the socially disadvantaged" (27).

My story is different from Rodriguez's. My sister Hannah and I grew up in Marshalltown, Iowa, the children of a Hispanic mother and an

Sands 2

Anglo father, both college-educated. In school, I remember at some point checking off a box identifying myself as "Hispanic." In sixth grade, I received a small slip of paper instructing me to go to a basement classroom after lunch rather than to math class. When I arrived at the classroom, my older sister, Hannah, and about ten other students—all of whom were Hispanic—were already there.

There was a large Hispanic population in Marshalltown; many recent immigrants were employed in farming as well as in a local meat-packing plant. While there weren't many Hispanic students in my middle school, there were enough for the district to feel it necessary to send an instructor who said she would help us "integrate" more fully into the general school population. We were "at risk," she said. She promised to help us learn English and to value our home culture while also becoming meaningful parts of American culture.

Unfortunately, our instructor did not speak Spanish and assumed that none of us spoke English. In fact, more than three-fourths of the students in the class were bilingual, and those who weren't bilingual only spoke English. None of them spoke *only* Spanish. My older sister and I had never spoken Spanish; many of the other students were from Mexico and had only recently come to the United States, but they had improved their English throughout the school year attending regular classes and spoke enough English to understand what was said in classrooms. It was clear we were all being singled out based solely upon ethnicity. We had no idea that we were "at risk" until the instructor told us we were.

Statistics showed, she said, that most of us would not go to college. Many of us would drop out of school. She told us she sympathized with how uncomfortable we must be in class, not understanding English. Her first act as instructor was to go around the room pointing to objects and saying their names, drawing out the vowels slowly. Oooverhead projeeectoor. Blaaackboard. Liiight. She stopped in front of me and held up a pencil. My blank expression must have confirmed her suspicions about our substandard English skills, so she said "pencil" over and over again until I replied, "Uh, pencil?" hoping she would go away. One of the boys across the room laughed loudly and said something in Spanish.

When our instructor moved to the next student to teach "notebook," I leaned over to a girl sitting at my table.

"What did he say?" I asked, pointing to the boy across the table.

"He said that stupid woman can't tell you don't speak Spanish."

He was right—but that was not the only thing she didn't seem to understand. We spent the next few weeks watching the movie *Stand and Deliver* over and over. *Stand and Deliver* is the story of how Jaime Escalante began teaching a remedial math class in East Los Angeles and developed a program that led his students to take and pass the AP calculus exam. Our teacher would beam happily after showing us the movie and would tell us that this movie was proof that we didn't need to cheat to excel. She told us we could stay in school, not join gangs, and not get pregnant. The implication, of course, was that because we were Hispanic, we were somehow more likely than others to cheat, to join gangs, and to have unprotected sex. The teacher, and the school, attempted to "empower" us by using stereotypical and racist assumptions about our knowledge of English and our abilities.

In "Aria," Rodriguez argues that his mastery of English represented a social change, not just a linguistic one: It made him a successful student and participant in the larger community (32). Rodriguez emphasizes the "public gain" that comes with language acquisition, advising that people be wary of those who "scorn assimilation" and discount the consequences of not having access to the public language of power and the public community (27). These consequences had most likely been considered at some point by the students in the Hispanic class I was a part of; the fact that the native Spanish speakers were all bilingual indicated their awareness of the importance of speaking English in order to function in and become part of the Marshalltown community. The instructor, however, continued to emphasize our difference from the larger community.

Sands 4

Unlike Rodriguez, before that class I had always had a sense of myself as part of the public community. I assumed I would go to college: If my family could not afford to send me, I would get scholarships and jobs to fund my education. I assumed that being a native speaker of English guaranteed me a place in the public community. Being put in the basement caused me to question these assumptions. I learned what I imagine other students in the classroom may have already known—that even if you were bilingual or spoke English perfectly, there was no guarantee that you would be considered part of the public community.

Richard Rodriguez describes how becoming part of public society is a process with both benefits and costs. He asserts that "while one suffers a diminished sense of *private* individuality by becoming assimilated into public society, such assimilation makes possible the achievement of *public* individuality" (26). This process of developing a public identity is not always a simple one, especially when it involves changes in language or in relationships. As my experience and Rodriguez's demonstrate, schools play an active role in shaping students' sense of themselves as individuals. With increasingly diverse student bodies like the one in my middle school, educators face the difficult question of how best to educate students from a variety of backgrounds, while at the same time helping all students become members of a broader public community.

I don't think my middle school had the answer, and I'm not sure there is a one-size-fits-all solution. What I am sure about is this: Educators in every community need to honestly evaluate what they're doing now, and then, working with students and their parents, find ways to help students realize their full potential, both as individuals *and* as members of the larger society.

Work Cited

Rodriguez, Richard. "Aria." *Hunger of Memory: The Education of Richard Rodriguez,* Dial Press, 1982, pp. 9–41.

Note: In an actual MLA-style paper, Works Cited entries start on a new page.

---

for **exploration**

To what extent does Alia Sands's essay achieve the goals she established for herself in her analysis of her rhetorical situation? Reread Alia's analysis, and then reread her essay. Keeping her analysis in mind, list three or four reasons you believe Alia does or does not achieve her goals, and then find at least one passage in the essay that illustrates each of these statements. Finally, identify at least one way Alia might strengthen her essay were she to revise it.

Using Aristotle's Appeals

thinking rhetorically

Analyzing your rhetorical situation can provide information that will enable you to make crucial strategic, structural, and stylistic decisions about your writing. In considering how to use this information, you may find it helpful to employ what Aristotle (384–322 B.C.E.) characterized as the three appeals. According to Aristotle, when speakers and writers communicate with others, they draw on these three general appeals:

> *Logos*, the appeal to reason

> *Pathos*, the appeal to emotion, values, and beliefs

> *Ethos*, the appeal to the credibility of the speaker or writer

As a writer, you appeal to logos when you focus on the logical presentation of your subject by providing evidence and examples in support of your ideas. You appeal to pathos when you use the resources of language to engage your readers emotionally with your subject or appeal to their values, beliefs, or needs. And you appeal to ethos when you create an image of yourself, a persona, that encourages readers to accept or act on your ideas.

These appeals correspond to at least three of the four basic elements of rhetoric: writer, reader, and text. In appealing to ethos, you focus on the writer's character as implied in the text; in appealing to pathos, on the interaction of writer and reader; and in appealing to logos, on the logical statements about the subject made in your particular text. In some instances, you may rely predominantly on one of these appeals. A student writing a technical report, for instance, will typically emphasize scientific or technical evidence (logos), not emotional or personal appeals. More often, however, you'll draw on all three appeals to create a fully persuasive document. A journalist writing a column on child abuse might open with several examples designed to gain her readers' attention and convince them of the importance of this issue (pathos). Although she may rely primarily on information about the negative consequences of child abuse (logos), she will undoubtedly also endeavor to create an image of herself as a caring, serious person (ethos), one whose analysis of a subject like child abuse should be trusted.

This journalist might also use images to help convey her point. One or more photographs of physically abused children would certainly appeal to pathos. To call attention to the large number of children who are physically abused (and thus bolster the logos of her argument), she might present important statistics in a chart or graph. She might also include photographs of well-known advocates for child protection to represent the trustworthiness of her report's insights (and contribute to ethos). In so doing, the journalist is combining words, images, and graphics to maximum effect.

Kairos might also play a role in her column on child abuse. (Kairos, discussed in Chapter 1, pp. 12–14, refers to the ability to respond to a rhetorical situation in a timely or appropriate manner.) In presenting statistics about child abuse, for instance, the journalist might call attention to a recent substantial increase in the number of cases of child abuse reported to authorities. In so doing, she is appealing to kairos and encouraging readers to recognize that child abuse is an urgent problem that must be addressed. The journalist might also refer to several recent cases of child abuse that have been widely discussed in the media. Doing so also emphasizes the need to address a significant social and familial problem.

In the following example, Brandon Barrett, a chemistry major at Oregon State University, uses Aristotle's three appeals to determine how best to approach an essay assignment for a first-year writing class that asks him to explain what his major is and why he chose it. He also considers how his essay can take advantage of kairos.

In presenting the assignment, Barrett's teacher informed students that their two- to three-page essays should include "information about your major that is new to your readers; in other words, it should not simply repeat the OSU catalog. Rather, it should be your unique perspective, written in clear, descriptive language." The teacher concluded with this advice: "Have fun with this assignment. Consider your audience (it should be this class unless you specify a different audience). Remember Aristotle's three appeals: How will your essay employ the appeals of logos, pathos, and ethos? Remember the importance of kairos as a way of gaining the attention and interest of your readers. Finally, as you write, keep these questions in mind: What is your purpose? What do you hope to achieve with your audience?" Brandon's essay is preceded by his analysis of his rhetorical situation and of his essay's appeals to logos, pathos, ethos, and kairos.

thinking rhetorically

BRANDON BARRETT'S ANALYSIS

I'm writing this essay to explain how I made the most important decision in my life to date: what to major in while in college. I want to explain this not only to my audience but to myself as well, for bold decisions frequently need to be revisited in light of new evidence. There are those for whom the choice of major isn't much of a choice at all. For them, it's a *vocation*, in the strict *Webster's* definition of the word: a summons, a calling.

I'm not one of those people, and for me the decision was fraught with anxiety. Do I still believe that I made the right choice? Yes, I do, and I want my essay not only to reflect how serious I feel this issue to be but also to convey the confidence that I finally achieved.

Writer: I'm writing this as a student in a first-year writing class, so while the assignment gives me a lot of flexibility and room for creativity, I need to remember that finally this is an academic essay.

Reader: My primary reader is my teacher in the sense that she's the one who will grade my essay, but she has specified that I should consider the other students in the class as my audience. This tells me that I need to find ways to make the essay interesting to them and to find common ground with them.

Text: This assignment calls for me to write an academic essay. This assignment is different, though, from writing an essay in my history class or a lab report in my chemistry class. Since this is based on my personal experience, I have more freedom than I would in these other classes. One of the most challenging aspects of this essay is its limited page length. It would actually be easier to write a longer essay on why I chose chemistry as my major.

Medium: Our assignment is to write an academic essay. While I could potentially import graphics into my text, I should only do so if it will enrich the content of the essay.

After analyzing his rhetorical situation, Brandon decided to use Aristotle's three appeals to continue and extend his analysis. He also decided to consider kairos, making his essay timely.

Logos: This essay is about my own opinions and experiences and therefore contains no statistics and hard facts. What it should contain, though, are legitimate reasons for choosing the major I did. My choice should be shown as following a set of believable driving forces.

Pathos: Since my audience is composed of college students, I'll want to appeal to their own experiences regarding their choice of major and the sometimes conflicting emotions that accompany such a decision. Specifically, I want to focus on the confidence and relief that come when you've finally made up your mind. My audience will be able to relate to these feelings, and it will make the essay more relevant and real to them.

Ethos: The inherent danger in writing an essay about my desire to be a chemistry major is that I may be instantly labeled as boring or a grind. I want to dispel this image as quickly as possible, and humor is always a good way to counter such stereotypes. On the other hand, this is a serious subject, and the infusion of too much humor will portray me as somebody who hasn't given this enough thought. I want to strike a balance between being earnest and being human. I also need to write as clearly and confidently as I can manage. If I seem insincere or uncertain, then my audience may question the honesty of my essay.

Kairos: Thinking about kairos reminds me that even though I have analyzed logos, pathos, and ethos separately, they are really interconnected and work together to achieve the same effect: to turn an essay that could be boring into an essay that my classmates feel is timely and of interest. My use of humor is important in this regard, and so is my appeal to our shared experiences as college students. But the bottom line is that I have to persuade my readers that I have good reasons for my decision.

Barrett 1

Brandon Barrett
Professor Auston
Writing 101
Jan. 20, 2016

The All-Purpose Answer

When I was a small child, I would ask my parents, as children are apt to
do, questions concerning the important things in my life. "Why is the sky
blue?" "Why do my Cocoa Puffs turn the milk in my cereal bowl brown?"
If I asked my father questions such as these, he always provided detailed
technical answers that left me solemnly nodding my head in complete
confusion. But if I asked my mother, she would simply shrug her shoulders
and reply, "Something to do with chemistry, I guess." Needless to say,
I grew up with a healthy respect for the apparently boundless powers of
chemistry. Its responsibilities seemed staggeringly wide-ranging, and
I figured that if there was a God he was probably not an omnipotent deity
but actually the Original Chemist.

In my early years, I regarded chemistry as nothing less than magic
at work. So what is chemistry, if not magic — or a parent's response to a
curious child's persistent questions? Chemistry is the study of the elements,
how those elements combine, how they interact with one another, and
how all this affects Joe Average down the street. Chemists, then, study not
magic but microscopic bits of matter all busily doing their thing.

When all those bits of matter can be coerced into doing something
that humans find useful or interesting — like giving off massive quantities
of energy, providing lighting for our homes, or making Uncle Henry smell
a little better — then the chemists who produced the desired effect can pat
themselves on the back and maybe even feel just a little bit like God.

Chemists solve problems, whether the problem is a need for a new
medicine or a stronger plastic bowl to pour our Wheaties into. They
develop new materials and study existing ones through a variety of
techniques that have been refined over the decades. Chemists also struggle
to keep the powers of chemistry in check by finding ways to reduce

Barrett 2

pollution that can be a by-product of chemical processes, to curb the dangers of nuclear waste, and to recycle used materials.

Chemistry is a dynamic field, constantly experiencing new discoveries and applications—heady stuff, to be sure, but heady stuff with a purpose.

Chemistry isn't a static, sleepy field of dusty textbooks, nor does it—forgive me, geologists—revolve around issues of questionable importance, such as deviations in the slope of rock strata. Those who know little about chemistry sometimes view it as dull, but I am proud to say that I plan to earn my B.S. in chemistry. And from there, who knows? That's part of the beauty of chemistry. After graduating from college, I could do any number of things, from research to medical school. The study of chemistry is useful in its own right, but it is also great preparation for advanced study in other fields since it encourages the development of logical thought and reasoning. In one sense, logical thought (not to mention research and medical school) may seem a giant step away from a child's idle questions. But as chemistry demonstrates, perhaps those questions weren't so childish after all.

---

for **exploration**

Where can you see evidence of Brandon's attention to Aristotle's three appeals? Write one or two paragraphs responding to this question. Be sure to include examples in your analysis.

Analyzing Textual Conventions

When you analyze your rhetorical situation, you ask commonsense questions about the elements of the rhetorical situation: writer, reader, text, medium. As you do so, you draw on your previous experiences as a writer, reader, speaker, and listener to make judgments about the text's purpose, subject matter, and form. For familiar kinds of texts, these judgments occur almost automatically. No one had to teach you, for instance, that a letter applying for a job should be written differently than a quick text asking a friend to meet up for pizza: Your

thinking
rhetorically

social and cultural understanding of job hunting would cause you to write a formal letter. Similarly, if you are designing a flyer to announce an event—one that will be distributed both in print and online—you recognize that, although it is important to include basic information about the event, the visual design of the flyer and the images used in it will play a particularly important role in gaining the attention of your audience.

When faced with less familiar kinds of texts, you may have to work harder to make judgments about purpose, subject matter, and form. I recently received an email from a former student, Monica Molina, who now works at a community health center, where one of her responsibilities is to write grant proposals. In her email, she commented:

> It took quite a while before I could feel comfortable even thinking about trying to write my first grant proposal. Most of the ones at our center run 50 to 100 pages and seem so intimidating—full of strange subheadings, technical language, complicated explanations. I had to force myself to calm down and get into them. First I read some recent proposals, trying to figure out how they worked. Luckily, my boss is friendly and support-ive, so she sat down with me and talked about her experiences writing proposals. We looked at some proposals together, and she told me about how proposals are reviewed by agencies. Now we're working together on my first proposal. I'm still nervous, but I'm beginning to feel more comfortable.

Like Monica, those entering new professions often must learn new forms of writing. Similarly, students entering a new discipline will often have to work hard to master unfamiliar language or writing styles. Chapter 8, "Writing in the Disciplines: Making Choices as You Write," will help you make your way across the curriculum.

Indeed, writers who wish to participate in any new community must strive to understand its reading and writing practices—to learn how to enter its conversation, as the rhetorician Kenneth Burke might say. The forms of writing practiced in different communities reflect important shared assumptions. These shared assumptions—sometimes referred to as *textual conventions*—represent agreements between writers and readers about how to construct and interpret texts. As such, they are an important component of any rhetorical situation.

The term *textual convention* may be new to you, but you can understand it easily if you think about other uses of the word *convention*. For example, social conventions are behaviors that reflect implicit agreement among the members of a community or culture about how to act in particular situations. At one time in the United States, for example, it was acceptable for persons who chewed tobacco to spit tobacco juice into spittoons in restaurants and hotel lobbies. (In fact, the use of spittoons was at one time considered refined, compared to the frequently employed alternative of spitting directly on the ground, indoors or out.) This particular social convention has changed over time and is no longer acceptable.

If social conventions represent agreements among individuals about how to act, textual conventions represent similar agreements about how to write and read texts. Just as we often take our own social conventions for granted, so too do we take for granted those textual conventions most familiar to us as readers and writers. Even though many of us write more texts and emails than letters, we still know that the most appropriate way to begin a letter is with the salutation "Dear . . ."

Textual conventions are dynamic, changing over time as the assumptions, values, and practices of writers and readers change. Consider some of the textual conventions of texting and other electronic writing. If you're texting your mom, you may not start with "Dear Mom." Instead, you might begin with something like "Hi there" or just jump into your message with no greeting. (Note: Although leaving out a salutation is considered acceptable in electronic contexts, rhetorically savvy writers know that when they're writing a work- or school-related text or email to a supervisor or teacher, they should include a clear statement of their subject and adopt a more formal tone.) If you're texting a friend, you might use abbreviations, such as RU for "are you" because it's easier to type on your phone.

When you think about the kind of writing you are being asked to do, you are thinking in part about the textual conventions that may limit your options as a writer in a specific situation. Textual conventions bring constraints, but they also increase the likelihood that readers will respond appropriately to your ideas.

The relationship between textual conventions and medium can be critical. Students organizing a protest against increased tuition, for example, would probably not try to get the word out by writing an essay on the subject. To get as many students as possible to participate in the protest, they would more likely put together an inexpensive, attention-getting flyer that they could post online and around campus while also sending tweets using a newly created hashtag. After the protest march, they might draft a letter to the editor to summarize the speakers' most important points, they might set up a Facebook group or blog to post announcements and to encourage student participation, and they might even post a manifesto.

Some textual conventions are specific. Lab reports, for example, usually include the following elements: title page, abstract, introduction, experimental design and methods, results, discussion, and references. Someone writing a lab report can deviate from this textual convention but in doing so runs the risk of confusing or irritating readers.

Other textual conventions are more general. Consider, for instance, the conventions of an effective academic essay:

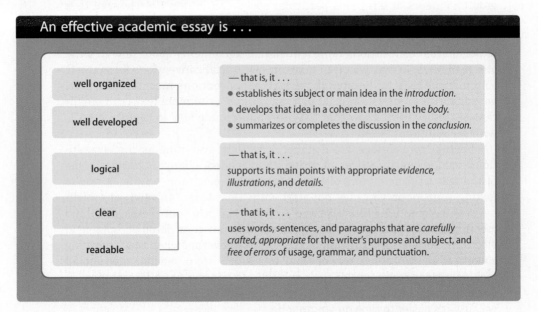

An effective academic essay is . . .

well organized
well developed

—that is, it . . .
- establishes its subject or main idea in the *introduction*.
- develops that idea in a coherent manner in the *body*.
- summarizes or completes the discussion in the *conclusion*.

logical

—that is, it . . .
supports its main points with appropriate *evidence*, *illustrations*, and *details*.

clear
readable

—that is, it . . .
uses words, sentences, and paragraphs that are *carefully crafted, appropriate* for the writer's purpose and subject, and *free of errors* of usage, grammar, and punctuation.

In writing an academic essay, you usually have more freedom in deciding how to apply the conventions than you do, say, when writing a lab report. For example, in an academic essay, an introduction is called for, but its specific form is not prescribed: How you begin depends largely on your audience, the reason you're writing, the disciplinary context in which you're writing, your chosen medium, and other factors.

Observing a Professional Writer at Work: Comparing and Contrasting Textual Conventions

One way to strengthen your own writing skills is to observe successful writers in action. Let's look at three texts by psychologist Jean M. Twenge to see how one writer tackles the problem of creating an effective and appropriate selection. Each text is based on Twenge's research on differences between earlier and current generations in the United States, a subject she investigated in her 2007 book, *Generation Me: Why Today's Young Americans Are More Confident, Assertive, Entitled—and More Miserable Than Ever Before*. Twenge's research is based on data from 1.3 million young people born between 1982 and 1999, a group sometimes characterized as the millennial generation and called "Generation Me" by Twenge. Her book *Generation Me* is addressed to a general audience, but she has also published a good deal of academic research on this same topic. In addition to her book publications, she has published more than one hundred scholarly articles in such journals as *American Psychologist*, *Journal of Personality*, and the *Journal of Personality and Social Psychology*. Twenge has also written for such publications as *Time*, *Newsweek*, the *New York Times*, *USA Today*, and the *Washington Post*.

The first selection (pp. 72–73) is an excerpt from the introduction to Twenge's *Generation Me*, a book written, as noted earlier, for a general audience. The second (pp. 74–75), "Generation Me on Trial," was published in the March 18, 2012, issue of the *Chronicle of Higher Education*, a weekly newspaper read by faculty, staff, and administrators at community colleges, colleges, and universities. This commentary reflects on the events that led to the suicide of Tyler Clementi, a student at Rutgers University. (Clementi committed suicide on September 22, 2010. On March 16, 2012, his roommate, Dharun Ravi, was found guilty on charges related to Clementi's suicide; Twenge's column was published two days later.) The third (pp. 76–77), an excerpt from an article titled "Generational Differences in Young Adults' Life Goals, Concern for Others, and Civic Orientation, 1966–2009," was coauthored with W. Keith Campbell and Elise C. Freeman and published in the November 2012 issue of the *Journal of Personality and Social Psychology*, a scholarly journal for psychologists.

Few academics attempt to reach such diverse audiences, and Twenge has clearly been successful in doing so. Her research has been featured on *Today*, *NBC Nightly News*, *Fox and Friends*, *Dateline NBC*, and National Public Radio, for instance. (For more information on Twenge, including access to her blog, see www.jeantwenge.com.) As a student writing in college, you won't write for such a broad range of audiences, but you will be writing for professors in a variety of disciplines, some of which can vary significantly in terms of textual conventions. Think, for instance, about the difference between writing a book review for your political science class and writing a lab report for your chemistry class. You can learn a good deal about what it means to be a rhetorically sensitive and an intellectually agile writer by studying these three Twenge selections.

Introduction

Linda was born in the 1950s in a small town in the Midwest. After she graduated from high school, she moved to the city and enrolled in secretarial school. It was a great time to be young: Free Love was in, and everybody smoked, drank, and had a good time. Linda and her friends joined a feminist consciousness-raising group, danced at the discos, and explored their inner lives at est seminars and through meditation. The new pursuit of self-fulfillment led Tom Wolfe to label the 1970s the Me Decade, and by extension the young people of the time the Me Generation.

Compared to today's young people, they were posers. Linda's Baby Boomer generation grew up in the 1950s and early 1960s, taught by stern, gray-suit-wearing teachers and raised by parents who didn't take any lip and thought that Father Knows Best. Most of the Boomers were well into adolescence or adulthood by the time the focus on the self became trendy in the 1970s. When Linda and her friends sought self-knowledge, they took the ironic step of doing so en masse—for all their railing against conformity, Boomers did just about everything in groups, from protests to seminars to yoga. Their youthful exploration also covered a brief period: the average first-time bride in the early 1970s had not yet celebrated her 21st birthday.

Today's under-35 young people are the real Me Generation, or, as I call them, Generation Me. Born after self-focus entered the cultural mainstream, this generation has never known a world that put duty before self. Linda's youngest child, Jessica, was born years after Whitney Houston's No. 1 hit song "Greatest Love of All" declared that loving yourself was the greatest love. Jessica's elementary school teachers believed that they should help Jessica feel good about herself. Jessica scribbled in a coloring book called *We Are All Special*, got a sticker on her worksheet just for filling it out, and did a sixth-grade project called "All About Me." When she wondered how to act on her first date, her

1

mother told her "Just be yourself." Eventually, Jessica got her lower lip pierced and got a large tattoo on her lower back because, she said, she wanted to express herself. She dreams of being a model or a singer, takes numerous "selfies" a day, and recently reached her personal goal of acquiring 5,000 followers on Instagram. She does not expect to marry until she is in her late 20s, and neither she nor her older sisters have any children yet. "You have to love yourself before you can love someone else," she says. This generation is unapologetically focused on the individual, a true Generation Me.

If you're wondering what all this means for the future, you are not alone. Reflecting on her role as a parent of this generation, *San Francisco Chronicle* columnist Joan Ryan wrote, "We're told we will produce a generation of coddled, center-of-the-universe adults who will expect the world to be as delighted with them as we are. And even as we laugh at the knock-knock jokes and exclaim over the refrigerator drawings, we secretly fear the same thing."

Everyone belongs to a generation. Some people embrace it like a warm, familiar blanket, while others prefer not to be lumped in with their age mates. Yet like it or not, when you were born dictates the culture you will experience. This includes the highs and lows of pop culture, as well as world events, social trends, technology, the economy, behavioral norms, and values. The society that molds you when you are young stays with you the rest of your life.

Today's young people speak the language of the self as their native tongue. The individual has always come first, and feeling good about yourself has always been a primary virtue. Everything from music to phone calls to entertainment is highly personalized, enjoyed on a cell phone instead of with the whole family. Generation Me's expectations are highly optimistic: They expect to go to college, to make lots of money, and perhaps even to be famous. Yet this generation enters a world in which college admissions are increasingly competitive, good jobs are hard to find and harder to keep, and basic necessities such as housing and health care have skyrocketed in price. This is a time of soaring expectations and crushing realities. Joan Chiaramonte, head of the Roper Youth Report, says that for young people "the gap between what they have and what they want has never been greater." If you would like to start an argument, claim that young people today have it (a) easy or (b) tough. Be forewarned: you might need referees before it's all over.

Generation Me on Trial

AP Photo/The Star-Ledger, John Munson, Pool

Dharun Ravi, shown waiting during a break in his trial last week, was convicted on Friday of invasion of privacy and hate crimes for using a Webcam to spy on his roommate.

By Jean M. Twenge | March 18, 2012

"I dare you to chat me between the hours of 9:30 and midnight. Yes, it's happening again," the Rutgers University student Dharun Ravi wrote on his Twitter account in September 2010. "It" was Tyler Clementi, Mr. Ravi's roommate, having a sexual encounter with another man — while Mr. Ravi and his friends watched on a Webcam. The next day, Mr. Clementi committed suicide. On March 16, Mr. Ravi was found guilty on charges related to the incident and faces up to 10 years in prison.

This was an explosive case, and the actions of one college freshman cannot be used to characterize an entire generation. Yet the incident echoes several distressing trends rippling through American culture — trends that often appear first among young adults who have never known a culture without reality TV and Facebook. Three seem the most relevant:

- An empathy deficit. In a study of more than 14,000 college students, Sara H. Konrath and her colleagues found that millennials (usually thought of as born between 1982 and 1999) scored considerably lower on a measure of empathy than previous generations. I call this group Generation Me, and my colleagues and I recently found a similar, though smaller, decline in empathy among high-school students on survey items such as "Maybe some minority groups do get unfair treatment, but that's no business of mine."

  Empathy was clearly lacking in the Rutgers incident. One of Mr. Ravi's tweets gleefully announced, "Roommate asked for the room until midnight. I went into molly's room and turned on my webcam. I saw him making out with a dude. Yay." Not "yay" as in, "I'm happy my roommate is getting some," but, "Yay, what a great opportunity to laugh at someone else's expense." Mr. Ravi is not alone; his voyeuristic joy is similar to the pleasure we get watching rich, attractive people fighting on a reality TV show. No matter how embarrassing, it's all on display for our amusement. In Ms. Konrath's study, the empathy decline was especially steep after 2000 — right around the advent of reality TV.

- A decline in taking responsibility. Since 1960, young Americans have become increasingly likely to say their lives are controlled by outside forces rather than their own efforts. Narcissism, a personality trait linked to blaming others for problems, has also increased among college students. Mr. Ravi's attorneys argued he was not guilty because he was young and immature; the attorneys of George Huguely V, convicted of beating his girlfriend to death at the University of Virginia, said he was drunk.

  These are extreme examples. Yet many university faculty and staff grapple almost daily with students who blame everyone but themselves when they do poorly or just don't bother to show up. The new twist, rarely seen until recently, is the parents who make excuses for the students. When we think we're fantastic, it must be someone else's fault when bad stuff happens — even when we did the bad stuff ourselves.

● More belief in equality for all. A third trend seems to contradict the incident at Rutgers — the growing acceptance of homosexuality, especially among the young. A recent Gallup poll, for example, showed 70 percent of Americans ages 18 to 34 now support gay marriage — nearly twice as many as among those over age 55.

However, a lack of prejudice is not the same as true empathy. Anyone who decides to broadcast someone else's sexual encounter, as Mr. Ravi did, is obviously not empathizing very well. Given the stigma and discomfort homosexuality still stirs among many people, telecasting a young gay man's sexual encounter is particularly callous. Mr. Ravi's actions reflect a common theme in many Generation Me mistakes: He seemed clueless that his actions would hurt someone more severely because that person belonged to a minority group. Mr. Ravi didn't seem to realize that Mr. Clementi's homosexuality made him more vulnerable. Treating people as equal, usually such a good thing, becomes harmful when individuals lose the ability to take someone else's perspective. "Tolerance" is not enough.

At the trial, students testified they had never heard Mr. Ravi say anything bad about gays. Mr. Ravi even wrote to Mr. Clementi, "I've known you were gay and I have no problem with it." Apparently Mr. Ravi didn't hate gays. He just thought watching them make out was funny.

A similar theme appeared in a February 2010 incident at the University of California at San Diego, when a fraternity sponsored a "Compton Cookout," where partygoers were asked to dress as pimps and "ghetto chicks." Many of the university's black students did not find that amusing, especially during Black History Month.

But to the fraternity brothers, it was just another theme party and just other costumes. Everybody's equal, right? It didn't seem to occur to them that making fun of a historically underprivileged group might cause offense, particularly on a campus where barely 2 percent of the students are black — and thus might feel isolated already. Like the case of Mr. Ravi and Mr. Clementi, it was cluelessness born of the combination of low empathy and the belief that we are all equal.

So should cluelessness and lack of empathy be prosecuted as a crime? Mr. Ravi's attorneys said he was simply an immature young man who played a prank. Although the decline in empathy is a worrying trend, and Mr. Clementi's death a true tragedy, it can still be debated whether cluelessness is a crime. The debate is likely to continue, but for now, the verdicts in New Jersey and Virginia are a reminder — to young people and to society as a whole — that cruelty has consequences.

Tolerance and equality are among Generation Me's greatest strengths, and should continue to be celebrated. But sometimes equality is not enough. For true peace and compassion, we need a healthy dose of empathy. It's not enough to realize that someone else is equal — we have to think about what it's really like to be him or her. That, perhaps more than anything else, is the lesson we must teach Generation Me — and ourselves.

Jean M. Twenge is a professor of psychology at San Diego State University. She is the author of *Generation Me: Why Today's Young Americans Are More Confident, Assertive, Entitled — and More Miserable Than Ever Before* (Free Press, 2006) and coauthor, with W. Keith Campbell, of *The Narcissism Epidemic: Living in the Age of Entitlement* (Free Press, 2009).

PERSONALITY PROCESSES AND INDIVIDUAL DIFFERENCES

Generational Differences in Young Adults' Life Goals, Concern for Others, and Civic Orientation, 1966–2009

Jean M. Twenge
San Diego Univeristy

W. Keith Campbell
University of Georgia

Elise C. Freeman
San Diego State Univeristy

Three studies examined generational differences in life goals, concern for others, and civic orientation among American high school seniors (Monitoring the Future; $N = 463,753$, 1976–2008) and entering college students (The American Freshman; $N = 8.7$ million, 1966–2009). Compared to Baby Boomers (born 1946–1961) at the same age, GenX'ers (born 1962–1981) and Millennials (born after 1982) considered goals related to extrinsic values (money, image, fame) more important and those related to intrinsic values (self-acceptance, affiliation, community) less important. Concern for others (e.g., empathy for outgroups, charity donations, the importance of having a job worthwhile to society) declined slightly. Community service rose but was also increasingly required for high school graduation over the same time period. Civic orientation (e.g., interest in social problems, political participation, trust in government, taking action to help the environment and save energy) declined an average of $d = -.34$, with about half the decline occurring between GenX and the Millennials. Some of the largest declines appeared in taking action to help the environment. In most cases, Millennials slowed, though did not reverse, trends toward reduced community feeling begun by GenX. The results generally support the "Generation Me" view of generational differences rather than the "Generation We" or no change views.

Keywords: birth cohort, generations, intrinsic and extrinsic values, civic orientation, concern for others

"People born between 1982 and 2000 are the most civic-minded since the generation of the 1930s and 1940s," say Morley Winograd and Michael Hais, co-authors of *Millennial Makeover: MySpace, YouTube, and the Future of American Politics*.... "Other generations were reared to be more individualistic," Hais says. "This civic generation has a willingness to put aside some of their own personal advancement to improve society."—*USA Today*, 2009

College students today show less empathy toward others compared with college students in decades before. With different demands at work—hours answering and writing e-mail—people have less time to care about others.—*USA Today*, 2010

American society has undergone significant changes during the past few decades. Opportunities for women and minorities have expanded, and beliefs in equality for all have become more common (e.g., Koenig, Eagly, Mitchell, & Ristikari, 2011; Thornton & Young-DeMarco, 2001). On the other hand, societal cohesiveness is on the decline, with more Americans saying they have no one to confide in (McPherson, Smith-Lovin, & Brashears,

2006) and more having children outside of marriage (U.S. Bureau of the Census, 2011).

How have recent generations been shaped by these trends? At base, generational differences are cultural differences: As cultures change, their youngest members are socialized with new and different values. Children growing up in the 1950s were exposed to a fundamentally different culture than children growing up in the 1990s, for example. Thus birth cohorts—commonly referred to as generations—are shaped by the larger sociocultural environment of different time periods (e.g., Gentile, Campbell, & Twenge, 2012; Stewart & Healy, 1989; Twenge, 2006), just as residents of different cultures are shaped by regional variations in culture (e.g., Markus & Kitayama, 1991).

Many previous studies have examined generational differences in personality traits and positive self-views (e.g., André et al., 2010; Gentile, Twenge, & Campbell, 2010; Stewart & Bernhardt, 2010; Twenge, Campbell, & Gentile, 2011). Fewer studies, however, have examined generational trends in values, life goals, and young people's relationships to their communities. For example, have young people's life goals changed to become more or less community focused? How concerned are they for others? How much do they wish to be involved in collective or civic action? These questions about community feeling are important, as they address crucial elements of social capital and group relations (e.g., Putnam, 2000). As the epigraph quotes illustrate, there is a great deal of interest in—and disagreement about—whether or not today's young people are higher or lower in community feeling. Community feeling is also a key element of what Kasser and colleagues (e.g., Grouzet et al., 2005; Kasser & Ryan, 1993, 1996) label intrinsic

This article was published Online First March 5, 2012.
Jean M. Twenge and Elise C. Freeman, Department of Psychology, San Diego State University; W. Keith Campbell, Department of Psychology, University of Georgia.
Correspondence concerning this article should be addressed to Jean M. Twenge, Department of Psychology, San Diego State University, 5500 Campanile Drive, San Diego, CA 92182-4611. E-mail: jtwenge@mail.sdsu.edu

Journal of Personality and Social Psychology, 2012, Vol. 102, No. 5, 1045–1062
© 2012 American Psychological Association 0022-3514/12/$12.00 DOI: 10.1037/a0027408

values, those important to inherent psychological needs that contribute to actualization and growth such as self-acceptance, affiliation, and community. These are on the opposite end of the same dimension as extrinsic values, those contingent on external feedback such as money, fame, and image. The current study seeks to expand the literature on generational differences by assessing changes in community feeling and the contrasting extrinsic values.

The literature on generational differences is limited in other ways as well. Most analyses have gathered data from other studies using cross-temporal meta-analysis instead of analyzing responses from large national surveys (e.g., Konrath, O'Brien, & Hsing, 2011; Malahy, Rubinlicht, & Kaiser, 2009; Twenge & Foster, 2010). Cross-temporal meta-analysis has the benefit of examining changes in well-established psychological measures but lacks the stratified, nationally representative sampling of large national surveys. However, these national surveys have limitations of their own. For example, the meaning of some items in large national surveys is unclear. Although most items are straightforward or behavioral—for example, civic orientation items about political participation, or concern for others items about community service or charity donations—others, especially those asking about life goals, are more ambiguous. For example, when a respondent agrees that being a "community leader" is an important life goal, does that reflect the value of community (an intrinsic value) or of wanting to be a leader (an extrinsic value)? Several observers (e.g., Greenberg & Weber, 2008; Pryor, Hurtado, Saenz, Santos, & Korn, 2007) have assumed it reflects community feeling, but this has never been confirmed by validating this item—or any other from these surveys—against psychometrically valid measures such as the Aspirations Index, the most established measure of life goals (Grouzet et al., 2005).

In the present study, we attempt to address these issues by (a) examining changes in community feeling across as many survey items as possible in (b) two very large national databases and (c) validating relevant items against existing measures, particularly those measuring community feeling and the larger dimension of intrinsic–extrinsic values. Before describing our research in detail, however, we discuss past research and commentary on generational changes in community feeling.

Opposing Views on Generational Changes in Community Feeling

Kasser and Ryan (1996) defined community feeling as helpfulness and wanting to "improve the world through activism or generativity" (p. 281). As the epigraph quotes show, the level of community feeling among today's young adults is in dispute. The arguments fall into three basic camps: the "Generation We" view, the "Generation Me" view, and the no change view.

In the "Generation We" view, Americans born in the 1980s and 1990s, often called GenY or Millennials, are more community oriented, caring, activist, civically involved, and interested in environmental causes than previous generations were (Arnett, 2010; Greenberg & Weber, 2008; Rampell, 2011; Howe & Strauss, 2000; Winograd & Hais, 2008, 2011). Winograd and Hais (2011) wrote, "About every eight decades, a new, positive, accomplished, and group-oriented 'civic generation' emerges . . . The Millennial Generation (born 1982–2003) is America's newest civic generation." Greenberg and Weber (2008) stated

that "*Generation We is noncynical and civic-minded.* They believe in the value of political engagement and are convinced that government can be a powerful force for good. . . . By comparison with past generations, *Generation We is highly politically engaged*" (pp. 30, 32; emphasis in original). Epstein and Howes (2006) advised managers that Millennials are "socially conscious" and that "volunteerism and giving back to society play an important role in their lives" (p. 25). The view that Millennials are unusually inclined toward helping others is so widely held that many companies have instituted recruiting programs for young workers involving volunteer service and helping the environment (e.g., Alsop, 2008; Epstein & Howes, 2006; Hasek, 2008; Lancaster & Stillman, 2010; Needleman, 2008).

The contrasting "Generation Me" view sees Millennials as reflecting an increasingly extrinsic and materialistic culture that values money, image, and fame over concern for others and intrinsic meaning (e.g., Gordinier, 2009; Mallan, 2009; Myers, 2000; Smith, Christoffersen, Davidson, & Herzog, 2011; Twenge, 2006). A few studies have found empirical support for this idea. American college students' scores on a measure of empathy for others declined between 1979 and 2009 (Konrath et al., 2011). Malahy et al. (2009) found an increase over the generations in the belief in a just world, or the idea that people get what they deserve and thus are responsible for their misfortunes. They concluded that more recent students are less likely to take the perspective of others in need and "less concerned with and less emotionally burdened by others' suffering and disadvantage" (p. 378). Narcissistic personality traits, which correlate with less empathy and concern for others, increased over the generations among college students in four datasets (Stewart & Bernhardt, 2010; Twenge & Foster, 2010).

A third view posits that generational differences do not exist, especially in representative samples, and that any perception of generational change is an illusion caused by older people's shifting frame of reference or a mistaking of developmental changes for generational changes (Trzesniewski & Donnellan, 2010). These authors analyzed a selected portion of items in the Monitoring the Future database of high school students and concluded that few meaningful generational differences existed (Trzesniewski and Donnellan, 2010; cf. Twenge & Campbell, 2010). Trzesniewski and Donnellan contended that young people in the 2000s are remarkably similar to those in the 1970s. They argued that previous studies finding generational differences were unreliable because they were not based on nationally representative samples.

The Current Research

Our primary goal in the present research was to assess generational changes in community feeling. To address the limitations of past research, we took several empirical steps. First, given previous concerns about sampling (Trzesniewski & Donnellan, 2010), we turned to two large, nationally representative samples of American young people collected over time: the Monitoring the Future (MtF) study of high school seniors conducted since 1976 ($N = 0.5$ million) and the American Freshman (AF) survey of entering college students conducted since 1966 ($N = 8.7$ million). Both include a large number of items on life goals, concern for others, and civic orientation.

Second, although much recent discussion has focused on the current generation of young people, we examine changes going back to the Boomer generation. . . .

---

for **exploration**

Read the Twenge selections (pp. 72–77) carefully, and write three paragraphs — one paragraph for each selection — characterizing their approaches. (Be sure to read the abstract and the footnote on the first page of the article from the *Journal of Personality and Social Psychology*, which provide important cues about Twenge's rhetorical situation and the interests and expectations of her scholarly readers.) Here are some questions for you to keep in mind as you read.

- How would you describe Twenge's tone in each selection?
- What kinds of examples are used in each selection, and what function do they serve?
- What relationship is established in each selection between writer and reader, and what cues signal this relationship?
- What assumptions does Twenge make in each selection about what readers already know?
- How would you describe the persona, or image of the writer, in each selection?

By glancing at the first pages of Twenge's three texts, you'll notice some important clues about the publications they appear in and about Twenge's expectations about their readers. For example, the first two pages of the introduction to Twenge's *Generation Me* begin with a story about Linda, who "was born in the 1950s in a small town in the Midwest." Even though the title of Twenge's book makes it clear that she will be generalizing about an entire generation, Twenge begins with a specific story, as if to say to readers that, although the author is a psychologist and is drawing on empirical research, this book will be relevant to them in their personal lives. Twenge is clearly aware that the market is flooded with books about a diverse range of topics, from how to survive a divorce to how to succeed in business. She knows that her introduction needs to invite readers into the story that she will tell in her book, and her introduction does just that. Twenge's introduction does not include any illustrations, but whether potential readers have looked at her book in a brick-and-mortar bookstore or on Amazon.com or some other online site, most of them will have already viewed its intentionally provocative cover.

In the remainder of the introduction to her book, Twenge describes how she became interested in the topic of generational differences and birth cohort studies. She informs readers about her own education as a psychologist and about the research that led to *Generation Me*. The story of her own engagement with her topic complements and enriches the story of Linda that begins the introduction. Twenge ends her introduction by referring to the years of library research and empirical data collection that are the foundation of her book and concludes with this simple but compelling statement: "This book tells that story" (15).

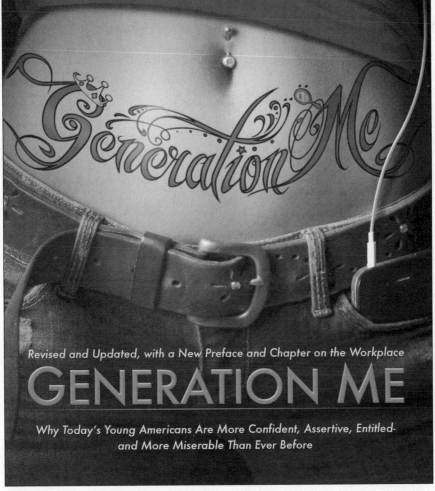

Twenge, Jean. Generation Me, rev. ed. Atria Books, 2014, pp. 1-2. ISBN 978-1476755564. Photo and cover design with permission of Tony Mauro.

Cover of Jean M. Twenge's *Generation Me* (2014)

thinking
rhetorically

Now consider Twenge's second text, an article titled "Generation Me on Trial" that was published in the *Chronicle of Higher Education*. This article is less visually dense than the introduction to Twenge's *Generation Me*, thanks to the increased use of white space and headings. The article also includes a photo of Dharun Ravi at the top of the page.

Subscribers to the weekly *Chronicle of Higher Education* represent a more specialized readership than that of the trade book *Generation Me*. They either work in or are interested in higher education. Still, the diversity within this readership—which includes faculty across the disciplines, administrators, and staff in various offices on campus—means many readers skim the *Chronicle* to determine what to read. Given that Dharun Ravi's conviction was a major news story, the publication of Twenge's column was quite timely and designed to gain the attention of readers. In grounding her discussion of her research on "generation me" in this highly publicized case, Twenge is clearly drawing upon kairos (timeliness or the opportune moment) to attract readers' interest.

In her *Chronicle* essay, Twenge seldom refers directly to the research on which her discussion is based. She assumes that readers will make a connection between the title of her book, *Generation Me*, and the title of her article, "Generation Me on Trial." She also assumes that readers will draw on the biographical information at the end of her piece, including her position as a professor of psychology at San Diego State University, to assess her authority to write about her topic. Twenge thus keeps the focus on her three main points: that Generation Me has "an empathy deficit," that it has seen a "decline in taking responsibility," and that it has "more belief in equality for all." Whereas in the first pages of the introduction to *Generation Me* Twenge focuses on creating a story that will draw readers in and make them care about her research, in her *Chronicle* article Twenge draws conclusions, including her final one: "For true peace and compassion, we need a healthy dose of empathy. It's not enough to realize that someone else is equal—we have to think about what it's really like to be him or her. That, perhaps more than anything else, is the lesson we must teach Generation Me—and ourselves."

Twenge's final text, "Generational Differences in Young Adults' Life Goals, Concern for Others, and Civic Orientation, 1966–2009," appears in the *Journal of Personality and Social Psychology*, a specialized publication that has the most cramped and least inviting first page. Twenge's article is coauthored with two other scholars, a common practice in the social sciences, where the nature and scope of research projects often require collaboration. Twenge, however, is the first author and the corresponding author (see the note at the bottom of the page), which indicates to colleagues reading the article that her contributions to the research have been particularly important.

Rather than using an attention-getting title, Twenge and her coauthors straightforwardly describe the focus of their research project. The article begins with an abstract and keywords designed to help readers decide whether they want to read the entire article.

Although the article begins with two attention-getting epigraphs, it quickly focuses on the most important research questions the authors wish to address. Twenge and her coauthors are careful to distinguish the research reported in this article from previous studies of generational differences. They assess some of the limitations of earlier studies, argue for the value of their own approach, contrast opposing views on generational changes, and establish their primary research goal.

Twenge and her coauthors' essay in the *Journal of Personality and Social Psychology* is seventeen densely argued pages long. In subsequent sections, the authors argue for the value of their methodology and examine three studies they undertook on generational differences in life goals. Their essay includes several tables that summarize and evaluate data, as well as graphs and other figures that help readers grasp the significance of their research. Clearly, the authors assume that scholars who choose to read their article will want the opportunity not only to understand and evaluate the authors' conclusions but also to critique their methodology. Twenge and her coauthors conclude their article by considering contradictory data from other sources, the strengths and limitations of their own studies, and their own conclusions, which remain tentative. As the authors note in their final sentence, how the attitudes and behaviors they discuss in their article "will shape the young generation and the country as more Millennials enter adult life remains to be seen" (1060).

Unlike in her commentary in the *Chronicle of Higher Education*, where Twenge reports some of the most important results of her research on generational differences, in the article in the *Journal of Personality and Social Psychology* Twenge and her coauthors take pains to make every step of their research process visible and available for other scholars to critique. Such critique might include efforts to replicate the studies described in the article. Clearly, Twenge expects much more of the readers of this scholarly article than she does of the readers of her commentary in the *Chronicle* or her popular book, *Generation Me*. She assumes that readers will be familiar with the many references she and her coauthors cite or will at least appreciate their inclusion. She also assumes that readers will have considerable prior knowledge of her topic, an assumption she cannot make about readers of her book or *Chronicle* commentary.

Twenge also understands that readers of the *Journal of Personality and Social Psychology* bring specific expectations to their reading of the journal. Like readers of the *Chronicle of Higher Education*, subscribers to the *Journal of Personality and Social Psychology* don't have time to read every article, but they don't make their reading choices based on inviting titles, illustrations, or opening anecdotes. Instead, they skim the table of contents, noting articles that affect their own research or have broad significance for their field. The abstract in Twenge and her coauthors' article matters very much to these readers; they can review it to determine not only *if* but also *how* they will read the article.

Some will read only the abstract, others will skim the major points, and others will read the entire article with great care, returning to it as they conduct their own research.

Although the excerpts of Twenge's three texts are grounded in the same research project, they differ dramatically in structure, tone, language, and approach to readers. Textual conventions play an important role in these differences. As shared agreements about the construction and interpretation of texts, textual conventions enable readers and writers to communicate successfully in different rhetorical situations.

---

for **exploration**

Take five to ten minutes to freewrite about your experience of reading the introductions to Twenge's three texts, as well as the subsequent analysis of them. What has this experience helped you better understand about the role that textual conventions — and rhetorical sensitivity — play in writing? If this experience has raised questions for you as a writer, be sure to note them as well. Be prepared to share your response to this For Exploration activity with your classmates.

---

note for multilingual writers

The conventions of academic writing vary from culture to culture. If you were educated in another country or language, you may have written successful academic texts that followed textual conventions that differ from those you have to follow now. Conventions that can differ in various cultures include the rhetorical strategies that introduce essay topics, the presence and placement of thesis statements, the kinds of information that qualify as objective evidence in argumentation, the use (or absence) of explicit transitions, and the use (or absence) of first-person pronouns. Given these and other potential differences, you may find it helpful to compare the conventions of academic writing in the United States with those of your home culture.

Using Textual Conventions

You already know enough about rhetoric and the rhetorical situation to realize that there can be no one-size-fits-all approach to every academic writing situation.

What can you do when you are unfamiliar with the textual conventions of a particular discipline or of academic writing in general? A rhetorical approach suggests that one solution is to read examples of the kind of writing you wish to do. Jean M. Twenge, whose selections you read earlier in this chapter, undoubtedly drew on her experience as a reader of the publications in which her work would later appear as she wrote these texts. Discussing these models with an insider—your teacher, a tutor in the writing center, or an advanced student in the field—can help you understand why these conventions work for such readers and writers. Forming a study group or meeting with a tutor can also increase your rhetorical sensitivity to your teachers' expectations and the conventions of academic writing.

Finally, a rhetorical approach to communication encourages you to think strategically about writing—whether personal, professional, or academic—and to respond creatively to the challenges of each situation. As a writer, you have much to consider: your own goals as a writer, the nature of your subject and writing task, the expectations of your readers, the textual conventions your particular situation requires or allows, and the medium in which to express your ideas. The rhetorical sensitivity you have already developed can help you respond appropriately to these and other concerns. But you can also draw on other resources, such as textual examples and discussions with teachers, tutors, and other students. As a writer, you are not alone. By reaching out to other writers, in person or by reading their work, you can become a fully participating member of the academic community.

for **thought, discussion, and writing**

1. From a newspaper or a magazine, choose an essay, an editorial, or a column that you think succeeds in its purpose. Now turn back to the Questions for Analyzing Your Rhetorical Situation on pp. 54–55, and answer the questions as if you were the writer of the text you have chosen. To answer the questions, look for evidence of the writer's intentions in the writing itself. (To determine what image or persona the writer wanted to portray, for instance, look at the kind of language the writer uses. Is it formal or conversational? Full of interesting images and vivid details or serious examples and statistics?) Answer each of the questions suggested by the guidelines. Then write a paragraph or more reflecting on what you have learned from this analysis.

2. Both Alia Sands and Brandon Barrett did a good job in anticipating their readers' expectations and interests. In writing their essays, they focused not just on content (what they wanted to say) but also on strategy (how they might convey their ideas to their readers). Not all interactions between writer and reader are as successful. You may have read textbooks that seemed more concerned with the subject matter than with readers' needs and expectations, or you may have received direct-mail advertising or other business communications that irritated or offended you. Find an example of writing that in your view fails to anticipate the expectations and needs of the reader, and write one or two paragraphs explaining your reasons. Your teacher may ask you to share your example and written explanation with your classmates.

3. Analyze the ways in which one or more of the following print advertisements (pp. 84–87) draw on Aristotle's three appeals: logos, pathos, and ethos.

Public Service Ad: "Dating Abuse Affects 1 in 3 Young People"

Public Service Ad: "You Don't Have to Be Perfect to Be a Perfect Parent"

Public Service Ad: "A Person Is the Best Thing to Happen to a Shelter Pet"

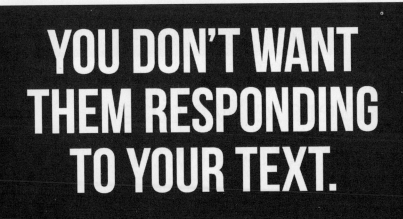

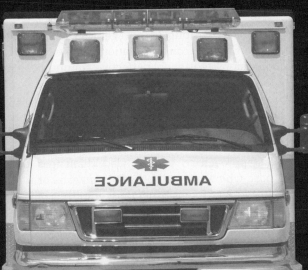

Source: Ad Council/National Highway Traffic Safety Administration (NHSTA), Concept Farm and the Ad Council

Public Service Ad: "You Don't Want Them Responding to Your Text"

4

Academic Writing: Committing to the Process

A rhetorical approach to writing encourages you to build upon and apply your understanding of human communication in general, and of texts in particular, to make decisions that enable effective communication. That is true whether you are writing an essay for your composition course, a lab report for your biology class, a memo for your employer, or an audio essay to share with family and friends. Rather than emphasizing rigid rules, a rhetorical approach to writing asks you to consider all the elements of your rhetorical situation: writer, reader, text, and medium.

A rhetorical approach to writing also challenges the common assumption that those who write well possess a magical or mysterious power. According to this view, people are either born with the ability to write well or not, and those who write well find writing easy: They just sit down, and the words and ideas begin to flow. Interestingly, people often feel the same way about those who work with images and graphics. They believe that designers and artists have a gift that enables them to create vivid and compelling designs, paintings, or other aesthetic objects.

In fact, most successful writers, designers, and artists study their craft for many years. What some would call "talent" or "a gift" might more aptly be characterized as interest, motivation, and commitment. Successful writers and designers know that their skills take time to mature. They also know that to develop their skills they must look for opportunities to practice them. As they practice, they reflect on the strengths and limitations not only of the products they produce but also of the processes they use to create them. This reflection, in turn, allows them to develop strategies to cope with the complexities of writing and design and thus to experience the satisfaction of a job well done.

As a student, you probably know from experience that your writing is most successful when you give yourself ample time to develop your thoughts, draft, and revise. If you're like most students, though, you don't always act on this knowledge. This chapter will help you gain insight into your own preferences as a writer, enabling you to commit to a writing process that works for you and that results in successful academic writing.

---

for **exploration**

Take some time to reflect on your own assumptions about writing and your experiences as a writer. Set aside at least half an hour, and respond in writing to the following questions. As you do so, be sure to reflect on both your academic and your personal writing and reading experiences.

1. What are your earliest memories of learning to read and write?
2. How were reading and writing viewed by your family and friends when you were growing up?
3. What role did reading play in your development as a writer? What kinds of texts were you drawn to: traditional print texts; visual texts, such as comics and graphic novels; a mix; or some other kind(s)?
4. Can you recall particular experiences in school or on the job that influenced your current attitude toward writing?
5. If you were to describe your history as a writer, what stages or periods in your development would you identify? Write a sentence or two briefly characterizing each stage or period.
6. What images come to mind when you hear the word *writer*? What images come to mind when you think of yourself as a writer?
7. Draw up a list of metaphors, such as "As a writer, I'm a turtle — slow and steady" or "As a writer, I'm a racehorse — fast out of the gate but never sure if I've got the stamina to finish." Write two or three sentences that use images or metaphors to characterize your sense of yourself as a writer.
8. What kinds of writing do you enjoy or dislike? What kinds of writing do you do outside of school? Do you regularly tweet or text, keep a personal journal, or blog? Do you write poetry, create podcasts, or design flyers? In answering these questions, be sure to include any print or multimodal texts that you regularly create simply because you enjoy doing so.
9. What do you enjoy most — and least — about the writing process?
10. What goals would you like to set for yourself as a writer?

for **exploration**

Using the notes, responses, and reflections generated by the previous For Exploration activity, write a letter to your classmates and teacher in which you describe who you are as a writer today and how you got to be that way. Alternatively, create a text that uses words and, if you like, images and graphics to describe who you are as a writer today. You can make it by hand or create it on the computer. (For her response to this assignment, student Mirlandra Neuneker created a collage, which is shown on p. 90.)   >

Mirlandra Neuneker

Mirlandra Neuneker's Collage, "Who I Am as a Writer"

for **collaboration**

Bring enough copies of the letter or visual text you created in response to the previous For Exploration activity to share with members of your group. After you have all read one another's texts, work together to answer the following questions. Choose one person to record the group's answers so that you can share the results of your discussion with the rest of the class.

1. To what extent are your attitudes toward writing and experiences as writers similar? List three to five statements all group members can agree with.

2. What factors account for the differences in your attitudes toward writing and experiences as writers? List two or three factors that you agree account for these differences.

3. What common goals can you set for yourselves as writers? List at least three goals you can agree on.

Managing the Writing Process

Successful writers know they must develop and commit to a writing process that enables them to succeed as students. But how do writers actually manage the writing process? Notice how differently the following students describe their process.

My writing starts with contemplation. I let the topic I have chosen sink into my mind for a while. During this time my mind is a swirl of images, words, and ideas. Sometimes I draw clusters or diagrams that show how my ideas relate; sometimes I make lists. Whatever works works. But this period of letting my ideas develop is essential to my writing. Gradually my ideas take shape—and at a certain point I just know whether I have the right topic or approach or not. If I think I don't, I force myself to start over. If I do, then I make a plan for my essay. I can't really write without at least a skeleton plan that I can refer to: It stresses me out not to know where I'm headed. Before I get very far into my draft I try to stop and ask myself whether I should write something that is straight text—a regular academic essay—or whether this is a project that needs visuals or graphics. By the time I'm done with my plan, I usually have a pretty clear idea of where I'm going. Next I write a draft, possibly several drafts, before I do a final revision.—**Sara Steinman**

Maybe it's just my personality, but when I get an assignment I have to leap right into it. It's hard to describe what I write at the beginning. It's part brainstorming, part planning, part drafting, part letting off steam. I just have to write to see what I think! I make notes to myself. What's the best evidence for this argument? Would an image, chart, or graph strengthen my point? What do I really think about this topic? I do most of this early writing by hand because I need to be able to use arrows to connect ideas, circle important points, draw pictures. At this point, no one but me could understand what I've written. I take a break if I can, and then I sit down and reread everything I've written (it can be a lot). That's when I move to the computer. Even at this point I still basically write without doing a lot of conscious planning—I'm going on intuition. The time comes when I've got to change gears and become my own harshest critic. That's when I do a kind of planning in reverse. I might outline my draft, for instance, and see if the outline makes sense. It takes a lot of time and work for me to get to the point where my ideas have really jelled, and even then I've often got several drafts ahead of me. —**Eduardo Alvarez**

As a writer, I am first a thinker and then a doer. I've always had to think my ideas out in detail before I begin drafting. Even though for me this is essentially a mental process, it still involves words and images. I can't really describe it—I just keep thinking things through. It's always felt like a waste of time to me to sit down to write without having a clear idea of what I want to say. Since I have two children and work part-time in public relations, I also don't have a lot of time to focus solely on my writing, so I try out different ideas while folding laundry, driving the kids to day care, after they're in bed. I'm a new media major, so part of my mental planning always involves thinking about media. If the assignment specifies the medium, then I always think how to make the best possible use of it. If it doesn't, then I run through all my options. Eventually I have a pretty clear sense of what I want to say and what medium will best convey it. Sometimes I make a plan before I get to work, especially if it's a long or complicated project. But sometimes I just begin writing. With some projects, my first draft is strong enough that I just have to edit it. Of course, that's not always the case. —**Wei Liao**

On the surface, these students' writing processes seem to have little in common. Actually, however, all involve the same three activities: planning, drafting, and revising. These activities don't necessarily occur in any set order. Wei Liao plans in her head and postpones making a written plan until after she has generated a rough draft, whereas Sara Steinman plans extensively before she writes her first word. To be successful, however, all these writers must sooner or later think rhetorically and make choices about their own situation as writers, their readers, their text, and the medium. Then they must try out these choices in their heads, on paper, or at the computer; evaluate the effects of these choices; and make appropriate changes in their drafts. Rather than being a magical or mysterious activity, writing is a process of planning, drafting, and revising.

thinking rhetorically

IDENTIFYING COMPOSING STYLES

When designers and writers take their own composing processes seriously, they attempt to build on their strengths and recognize their limitations. They understand that they must vary their approach to a project depending on the task or situation. A student who prefers to spend a lot of time developing written or mental plans for writing projects simply doesn't have that luxury when writing an in-class essay exam. For this reason, it's more accurate to refer to *writing processes* rather than *the writing process*. As a writer and designer, you must be pragmatic: You decide how to approach a project based on such factors as the nature and importance of the task, the schedule, the nature and demands of the medium, and the experience you have with a particular kind of writing. Most experienced writers and designers do have a preferred way of managing the composing process, however.

Heavy planners. Like Wei Liao, heavy planners generally plan their writing so carefully in their heads that their first drafts are often more like other writers' second or third drafts. As a consequence, they revise less intensively and less frequently than other students. Many of these students have disciplined themselves so that they can think about their writing in all sorts of places—on the subway, at work, in the garden pulling weeds, or in the car driving to and from school.

Some heavy planners write in this way because they prefer to; others develop this strategy out of necessity. Wei Liao, for instance, says that she simply has to do a great deal of her writing in her head because of the demands of her busy life As a result, she's learned to use every opportunity to think about her writing while she drives, cooks, or relaxes with her family.

Heavy revisers. Like Eduardo Alvarez, heavy revisers use the act of writing itself to find out what they want to say. When faced with a writing task, they prefer to sit down at a desk or computer and just begin writing.

Heavy revisers often state that writing their ideas out in a sustained spurt of activity reassures them that they have something to say and helps them avoid frustration. These students may not seem to plan because they begin drafting so early. Actually, however, their planning occurs as they draft and especially as they revise. Heavy revisers must often spend a great deal of time revising their initial drafts. To do so effectively, they must be able to read their work critically and, often, discard substantial portions of first drafts. For one example of heavy revision in action, see the accompanying photo of President Barack Obama holding a heavily revised text of one of his speeches.

thinking rhetorically

As you've probably realized, in both of these styles of composing, one of the components of the writing process is apparently abbreviated. Heavy planners don't seem to revise as extensively as other writers. Actually, however, they plan (and, in effect, revise) so thoroughly early in the process that they

President Barack Obama and Speechwriter Jon Favreau Editing a Speech on Health Care,
Sept. 9, 2009

often don't need to revise as intensively later. Similarly, heavy revisers may not seem to plan; in fact, though, once they write their rough drafts, they plan and revise simultaneously and, often, extensively.

Sequential composers. A third general style of composing is exemplified by Sara Steinman. These writers might best be called sequential composers because they devote roughly equivalent amounts of time to planning, drafting, and revising. Rather than trying out their ideas and planning their writing mentally, as heavy planners do, sequential composers typically rely on written notes and plans to give shape and force to their ideas. Unlike heavy revisers, however, sequential composers need to have greater control over form and subject matter as they draft.

Sequential composers' habit of allotting time for planning, drafting, and revising helps them deal with the inevitable anxieties of writing. Like heavy revisers, sequential composers need the reassurance of seeing their ideas written down: Generating notes and plans gives them the confidence to begin drafting. Sequential composers may not revise as extensively as heavy revisers because they generally draft more slowly, reviewing their writing as they proceed. Revision is nevertheless an important part of their composing process. Like most writers, sequential composers need a break from drafting to be able to critique their own words and ideas.

Composing Styles: Advantages and Disadvantages

Composing Style	Advantages	Disadvantages
Heavy planners	• The writer spends less time drafting and revising.	• The writer may lose her or his train of thought if unexpected interruptions occur. • The writer may miss out on fruitful explorations that result from reviewing notes, plans, or drafts. • The writer may face substantial difficulties if sentences and paragraphs look less coherent and polished on paper than they did in the writer's head.
Heavy revisers	• The writer generates words and ideas quickly and voluminously. • The writer remains open to new options because of the frequency with which he or she rereads notes and drafts.	• The writer may experience an emotional roller coaster as ideas develop (or fail to develop) through writing. • The writer must have the ability to critique her or his own writing ruthlessly. • The writer's work may suffer if he or she fails to allow adequate time for rewriting or, if necessary, for starting over.
Sequential composers	• The writer has more control over the writing process because so much time is spent planning, drafting, and revising. • Writers are unlikely to mistake a quickly generated collection of ideas or a brainstormed plan for adequate preparation.	• The writer may become too rigidly dependent on a highly structured writing process. • The writer may waste valuable time developing detailed plans when he or she is actually ready to begin drafting.

There is one other common way of managing the writing process, although it might best be described as management by avoidance, and that's procrastination. All writers occasionally procrastinate, but if you habitually put off writing a first draft until you have time only for a final draft (and this at 3 A.M. on the day your essay is due), your chances of success are minimal. Although you may tell yourself that you have good reasons for putting off writing ("I write better under pressure"; "I can't write until I have all my easier assignments done first"), procrastination makes it difficult for you to manage the writing process in an efficient and effective manner.

Is procrastination always harmful? Might it not sometimes reflect a period of necessary incubation, of unconscious but still productive planning? Here's what Holly Hardin—a thoughtful student writer—discovered when she reflected about her experiences as a writer.

> For me, sometimes procrastination isn't really procrastination (or so I tell myself). Sometimes what I label procrastination is really planning. The trouble is that I don't always know when it's one or the other.
>
> How do I procrastinate? Let me count the ways. I procrastinate by doing good works (helping overtime at my job, cleaning house, aiding and abetting a variety of causes). I procrastinate by absorbing myself in a purely selfish activity (reading paperbacks, watching TV, going to movies). I procrastinate by visiting with friends, talking on the telephone, prolonging chance encounters. I procrastinate by eating and drinking (ice cream, coffee, cookies—all detrimental). Finally, I procrastinate by convincing myself that this time of day is not when I write well. I'd be much better off, I sometimes conclude, taking a nap. So I do.
>
> Part of my difficulty is that I can see a certain validity in most of my reasons for procrastinating. There are some times of day when my thoughts flow better. I have forced myself to write papers in the past when I just didn't feel ready. Not only were the papers difficult to write, they were poorly written, inarticulate papers. Even after several rewrites, they were merely marginal. I would much rather write when I am at my mental best.
>
> I need to balance writing with other activities. The trouble is—just how to achieve the perfect balance!

Holly's realistic appraisal of the role that procrastination plays in her writing process should help her distinguish between useful incubation and unhelpful procrastination. Unlike students who tell themselves that they should never procrastinate—and then do so anyway, feeling guilty every moment—Holly knows she has to consider a variety of factors before she decides to invite a friend over, bake a batch of cookies, or take a much-needed nap.

note for multilingual writers

If your first or home language is not English, you may be familiar with alternate approaches to composing. Educational systems throughout the world have different approaches to writing and to the teaching of writing. In thinking about your writing process as a student in college, reflect on how your previous experiences as a writer enhance or interfere with your efforts to respond to the demands of academic writing in U.S. colleges. (Different approaches to revision may be especially relevant.) You may want to discuss the results of your reflection with your teacher or a tutor in the writing center.

ANALYZING YOUR COMPOSING PROCESS*

The poet William Stafford once commented that "a writer is not so much someone who has something to say as he is someone who has found a process that will bring about new things he would not have thought if he had not started to say them." Stafford's remarks emphasize the importance of developing a workable writing process—a repertoire of strategies you can draw on in a variety of situations. The quiz on pp. 98–99 can help you analyze your writing process.

thinking rhetorically

note for multilingual writers

If you are a writer whose first or home language is not English, think about how knowing one or more languages might affect your process when you compose texts in English. Do you typically think, freewrite, brainstorm, or make notes in your home language and then translate? Do you work directly in English? Or do you move back and forth between languages? How might this affect your writing process?

for **collaboration**

Meet with classmates to discuss your responses to the quiz on pp. 98–99. Begin by having each person state two important things he or she learned as a result of completing the quiz. (Appoint a recorder to write down each person's statements.) Once all members of your group have spoken, ask the recorder to read their statements aloud. Were any statements repeated by more than one member of the group? Working as a group, formulate two conclusions about the writing process that you would like to share with the class. (Avoid vague and general assertions, such as "Writing is difficult.") Be prepared to discuss your conclusions with your classmates.

For a case study of student Daniel Stiepleman's process of interacting with a text, exploring ideas, and developing an essay for a first-year writing class, see Chapter 6, pp. 166–82.

Quiz: Analyzing Your Composing Process

You can use the following questions to analyze your composing process. Your teacher may ask you to respond to some or all of these questions in writing.

1. **What is your general attitude toward writing?**
   a. love it
   b. hate it
   c. somewhere in between
   How do you think this attitude affects your writing?

2. **Which of the composing styles described in this chapter best describes the way you compose?**
   a. heavy planner
   b. heavy reviser
   c. sequential composer
   d. procrastinator
   If none of these styles seems to fit you, how do you compose?

3. **How long do you typically work on your writing at any one time?**
   a. less than an hour
   b. from one to two hours
   c. more than two hours
   Do you think you spend about the right amount of time at a given stretch, or do you think you should generally do more (or less)? Why?

4. **Are you more likely to write an essay**
   a. in a single sitting
   b. over a number of days (or weeks)
   Have you had success doing it this way? How do you think adjusting your approach would affect the essays you end up writing?

5. **Do you have any writing habits or rituals?**
   a. yes
   b. no
   If you answered "yes," what are they? Which are productive, and which interfere with your writing process? If you answered "no," can you think of any habits you would like to develop?

6. **How often do you import visuals, graphics, or sound files into texts you are composing?**
   a. sometimes
   b. never
   c. often
   If you do use visuals, sound, or graphics, do you enjoy doing so? find it a challenge? take it for granted? How have your instructors received your efforts?✳

7. **What planning and revising strategies do you use?**
   a. specific strategies (e.g., outlining, listing, etc.)
   b. general strategies (e.g., "I think out a plan, and I reread what I've written.")
   c. no strategies I'm aware of
   How do you know when you have spent enough time planning and revising?

8. **What role do collaborations or exchanges with others (conversations, responses to work in progress from peers or tutors) play in your writing?**
   a. an important role
   b. an occasional role
   c. little or no role
   Would you like to make more use of collaborations like these? Why or why not?

9. **How often do you procrastinate? (Be honest! All writers procrastinate occasionally.)**
   a. I procrastinate very little.
   b. I start later than I should, but I get the job done.
   c. I don't start until it's too late to do a good job.
   Do you need to change your habits in this respect? If you do need to change them, how will you do so?

10. **Thinking in general about the writing you do, what do you find most rewarding and satisfying? Most difficult and frustrating? Why?**
    _____
    _____
    _____

Writing is a *process*, and stopping to think about your own composing process can prove illuminating. One of my students, for example, formulated an analogy that helped us all think fruitfully about how the writing process works. "Writing," he said, "is actually a lot like sports." Writing—like sports? Let's see what this comparison reveals about the writing process.

See Chapter 10 for more about multimodal composing. ✳

Writing and sports are both performance skills. You may know who won every Wimbledon since 1980, but if you don't actually play tennis, you're not a tennis player; you're just somebody who knows a lot about tennis. Similarly, you can know a lot about writing, but to demonstrate (and improve) your skills, you must *write.*

Writing and sports both require individuals to master complex skills and to perform these skills in an almost infinite number of situations. Athletes must learn specific skills, plays, or maneuvers, but they can never execute them routinely or thoughtlessly. Writers must be similarly resourceful and flexible. You can learn the principles of effective essay organization, for instance, and you may write a number of essays that are well organized, but each time you sit down to write a new essay, you have to consider your options and make new choices. This is the reason smart writers don't rely on formulas or rules but instead use rhetorical sensitivity to analyze and respond to each situation.

thinking rhetorically

Experienced athletes and writers know that a positive attitude is essential. Some athletes psych themselves up before a game or competition, often using music, meditation, or other personal routines. But any serious athlete knows that's only part of what having a positive attitude means. It also means running five miles when you're already tired at three or doing twelve repetitions during weight training when you're exhausted and no one else would know if you did only eight. A positive attitude is equally important in writing. If you approach a writing task with a negative attitude ("I never was good at writing"), you create obstacles for yourself. Having a positive, open attitude is essential in mastering tennis, skiing—and writing.

To maintain a high level of skill, both athletes and writers need frequent practice and effective coaching. "In sports," a coach once said, "you're either getting better or getting worse." Without practice—which for a writer means both reading and writing—your writing skills will slip (as will your confidence). Likewise, coaching is essential in writing because it's hard to distance yourself from your own work. Coaches—your writing instructor, a tutor at a writing center, or a fellow student—can help you gain a fresh perspective on your writing and make useful suggestions about revision as well.

Experienced athletes and writers continuously set new goals for themselves. Athletes continuously set new challenges for themselves and analyze their performance. They know that coaches can help but that *they* are ultimately the ones performing. Experienced writers know this too, so they look for opportunities to practice their writing. And they don't measure their success simply by a grade. They see their writing always as work in progress. Successful athletes, like successful writers, know that they must *commit* to a process that will enable them to perform at the highest possible level.

Writing Communities

FINDING A COMMUNITY

For many people, one big difference between writing and sports is that athletes often belong to teams. Writers, they think, work in lonely isolation. In fact, this romanticized image of the writer struggling alone until inspiration strikes is both inaccurate and unhelpful. If you take a careful look at the day-to-day writing that people do, you quickly recognize that many people in business, industry, and other professions work as part of one or more teams to produce written texts. In many cases, these individuals' ability to work effectively with others is key to a successful career. Those who write for school, community-based projects, or even for personal enrichment also often turn to others for ideas and advice.

Even when writers do a good deal of their composing alone, they often find it helpful to talk with others before and while writing. A group of neighbors writing a petition to their city council requesting that a speed bump be installed on their street might well ask one person to compose the petition. To generate the strongest ideas possible, the writer would have to talk extensively with her neighbors. She would probably also present drafts of the petition for her neighbors' review and approval.

Most writers alternate between periods of independent activity (composing alone at a computer or desk) and periods of social interaction (meeting with friends, colleagues, or team members for information, advice, or responses to drafts). They may also correspond with others in their field, or they may get in touch with people doing similar work through reading, research, or online technologies. These relationships help them learn new ideas, improve their skills, and share their interest and enthusiasm.

Sometimes these relationships are formal and relatively permanent. Many poets and fiction writers, for instance, meet regularly with colleagues to discuss their writing. Perhaps more commonly, writers' networks are informal and shifting, though no less vital. A new manager in a corporation, for instance, may find one or two people with sound judgment and good writing skills to review important letters and reports. Similarly, students working on a major project for a class may meet informally but regularly to compare notes and provide mutual support.

Online technologies and the web have increased the opportunity for writers to work collaboratively. Using online spaces, from course websites to blogs and public writing communities such as Writing.com ("for writers and readers of all interests and skill levels"), writers everywhere are sharing their writing and getting responses to works in progress.

WORKING COLLABORATIVELY

Because you're in the same class and share the same assignments and concerns, you and your classmates constitute a natural community of writers. Whether your instructor makes it a requirement or not, you should explore the possibility of forming a peer group or joining one that already exists. To work effectively, however, you and your peers need to develop or strengthen the skills that will contribute to effective group work.

As you prepare to work collaboratively, remember that people have different styles of learning and interacting. Some of these differences represent individual preferences: Some students work out their ideas as they talk, for instance, while others prefer to think through their ideas before speaking. Other differences are primarily cultural and thus reflect deeply embedded social practices and preferences. Effective groups are pragmatic and task oriented, but they balance a commitment to getting the job done with patience and flexibility. They value diversity and find ways to ensure that all members can comfortably participate in and benefit from group activities.

Effective groups also take care to articulate group goals and monitor group processes. Sometimes this monitoring is intuitive and informal, but sometimes a more formal process is helpful. If you're part of a group that meets regularly, you might begin meetings by having each person state one way in which the group is working well and one way in which it could be improved. If a problem such as a dominating or nonparticipating member is raised, deal with it immediately. The time spent responding to these comments and suggestions will ensure that your group is working effectively.

Group activities such as peer response and collaborative troubleshooting can help improve your writing ability and prepare you for on-the-job teamwork. Remember, though, that groups are a bit like friendships or marriages. They develop and change, and they require care and attention. You have to be committed to keeping the group going, be alert to signs of potential trouble, and be willing to talk problems out.

Students juggling coursework, jobs, families, and other activities can sometimes find it difficult to get together or to take the time to read and respond to one another's writing. Getting together with classmates to share your writing is well worth the effort it takes. If it proves impossible, however, you may have one important alternative: a campus writing center. Many colleges and universities have established writing centers as places where you can go to talk with others about your writing, get help with specific writing problems, or find answers to questions you may have. If your campus does have a writing center, take advantage of the opportunity to get an informed response to your work.

Guidelines for Group Work

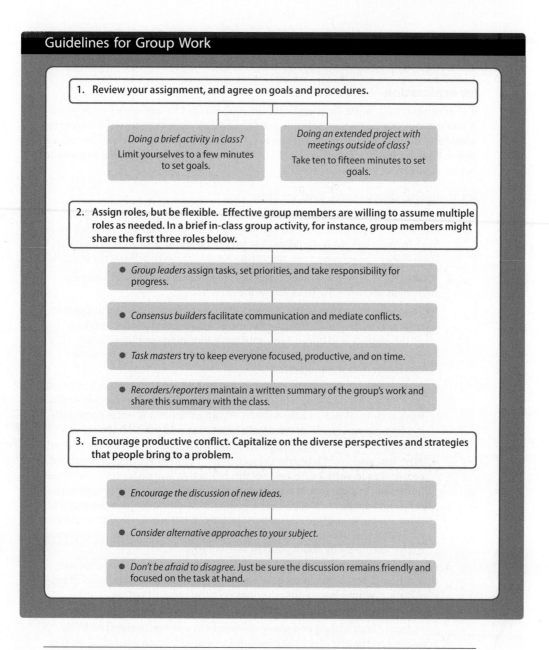

1. **Review your assignment, and agree on goals and procedures.**

   Doing a brief activity in class?
   Limit yourselves to a few minutes to set goals.

   Doing an extended project with meetings outside of class?
   Take ten to fifteen minutes to set goals.

2. **Assign roles, but be flexible.** Effective group members are willing to assume multiple roles as needed. In a brief in-class group activity, for instance, group members might share the first three roles below.

   ● *Group leaders* assign tasks, set priorities, and take responsibility for progress.

   ● *Consensus builders* facilitate communication and mediate conflicts.

   ● *Task masters* try to keep everyone focused, productive, and on time.

   ● *Recorders/reporters* maintain a written summary of the group's work and share this summary with the class.

3. **Encourage productive conflict.** Capitalize on the diverse perspectives and strategies that people bring to a problem.

   ● *Encourage the discussion of new ideas.*

   ● *Consider alternative approaches to your subject.*

   ● *Don't be afraid to disagree.* Just be sure the discussion remains friendly and focused on the task at hand.

for **collaboration**

Meet with your group to discuss how you can most effectively work together. Begin by exchanging names, phone numbers, and email addresses, and take time just to get to know each other. You might also see if your group can formulate some friendly rules to guide group activities. (You might all agree, for instance, to notify at least one member if you can't make a meeting.) Be sure to write these rules down, and consult them as you work together. Try to anticipate problems, such as coordinating schedules, and discuss how to resolve them.

for **exploration**

If your campus has a writing center, make an appointment to interview a tutor (sometimes also called a writing assistant or peer consultant) about the services the center provides. You may also want to ask the tutor about his or her own experiences as a writer. Your instructor may ask you to present the results of your interview orally or to write a summary of your discussion.

for **thought, discussion, and writing**

1. Now that you have read this chapter, make a list of several goals you'd like to accomplish in your composition class this term. What would you most like to learn or improve? What would you like to change about your writing process? Then write a paragraph or two discussing how you plan to achieve these goals.

2. You can learn a great deal about your own composing process by observing yourself as you write. To do so, follow these steps:

   ● Choose an upcoming writing project to study. Before beginning this project, reflect on its demands. How much time do you expect to spend working on this project, and how do you anticipate allocating your time? What challenges does this project hold for you? What strengths and resources do you bring to this project?

   ● As you work on the project, use a process log to keep track of how you spend your time. Include a record in this log of when you started and ended each work session, as well as a description of your activities and notes commenting on your process. What went well? What surprised you? What gave you problems? What might you do differently next time?

   ● After you have completed the project, draw on your prewriting analysis and process log to write a case study of this project. As you do so, consider these questions: To what extent was your prewriting analysis of your project accurate? How did you actually allocate your time when working on this project? What strategies did you rely on most heavily? What went well with your writing? What was difficult? Conclude by reflecting about what you have learned from this case study about yourself as a writer.

3. All writers procrastinate occasionally; some just procrastinate more effectively than others. After brainstorming or freewriting about your favorite ways of procrastinating, write a humorous or serious essay on procrastination.

4. The For Exploration activities on p. 89 encouraged you to reflect on your assumptions about writing and your experiences as a writer. Drawing on these activities and the rest of the chapter, write an essay in which you reflect on this subject. You may choose to write about pivotal incidents in your experiences as a writer, using particular occasions to support the general statements you make about your experiences.

5

Analyzing and Synthesizing Texts

A rhetorical approach to writing looks at the various contexts in which you write. Even if you are writing alone at your computer, you are writing in the context of a specific rhetorical situation. By analyzing that situation, you can identify your purpose and goals as a writer, develop an appropriate persona or voice, and respond to the expectations of your readers. You also can understand and implement the appropriate textual conventions for courses across the curriculum.

thinking
rhetorically

Understanding the Centrality of Reading to Academic Writing

One of the most important ways of recognizing and understanding the textual conventions appropriate to various disciplines is through reading. You already recognize that reading is central to academic writing. After all, as a student you are almost always writing in response to one or more texts. But you may not have realized that reading can help you understand how the methodologies that different disciplines are grounded in are reflected in their textual conventions. (Chapter 8 looks carefully at how the humanities, natural and applied sciences, social sciences, and business are reflected in each discipline's textual conventions.) Whatever kind of text you are reading—from a chapter in your sociology textbook to a poem in your literature class to a research report for psychology—the ability to read critically and to engage your reading at multiple levels is essential.

In this chapter, you will learn how to master two skills essential to all reading: analysis and synthesis. When you *analyze*, you determine how a text, an object, or a body of data is structured or organized; you also often assess its effectiveness or validity. Synthesis is a counterpart to analysis. When you *synthesize*, you explore connections and contradictions between two or more texts, objects, or bodies of data. Often, you also bring your own experience to bear on the subject under consideration, indicating where you agree and where you disagree with those whose words and thoughts you are exploring.

Considering Analysis and Synthesis in the Context of the Academic Community

Gaining an understanding of context is particularly important when you enter a new community of writers and readers. Accordingly, as you enter the academic community, you need to develop an insider's understanding of the conventions that characterize academic writing. Some of these conventions apply across the disciplines; for example, a successful academic argument must reflect an open, unbiased intellectual engagement with the subject, whether that subject is a Renaissance painting or the Federal Reserve System. Moreover, whatever your subject, the logic behind your conclusions and the evidence for them play key roles in any academic argument.

Most college instructors believe that *all* academic writing involves argument. But the model of argument they have in mind isn't about winning or losing a debate; rather, it involves using evidence and reasoning to discover a version of truth about a particular subject. I use the words *a version* here to emphasize that in academic writing what constitutes the "truth" is always open to further discussion. A political scientist or an economist who makes a convincing argument about federal policy on harvesting timber in national forests knows that others will add to, challenge, or refine that argument. In fact, having others respond to an argument is a sign that the writing has successfully raised questions that others consider important. In this sense, the scholarly work of the academy is a conversation rather than a debate.

Understanding Your Audience

Because your instructors are the primary readers of your college writing, you need to understand their values and their goals for you and other students. They all share a commitment to the ideal of education as inquiry. Whether they teach in business, liberal arts, agriculture, engineering, or other fields, your instructors want to foster your ability to think, write, and speak well. When they read your papers and exams, they're looking for evidence of both your knowledge of a subject and your ability to think and write clearly and effectively.

But your instructors will not necessarily bring identical expectations to your writing. Methods of inquiry and research questions vary from discipline to discipline, and textual conventions reflect these differences. Despite such disciplinary differences, college instructors generally agree that educated, thoughtful, and knowledgeable college students share certain characteristics.✱ They believe, for instance, that perhaps the worst intellectual error is oversimplifying. They want their students to go beyond simplistic analysis and arguments to achieve deeper and more complex understandings. Thus a historian might urge students to recognize that more was at stake in the American Civil War than freeing the slaves, and an engineer might encourage students to realize that the most obvious way to resolve a design problem isn't necessarily the best way.

Most college instructors want students to be able to do more than memorize or summarize information. Indeed, they strive to develop students' abilities to analyze, apply, question, evaluate, and synthesize information. What do instructors look for in students' writing? Most broadly, they want evidence of learning and a real commitment to and engagement with the subject. They also want you to adhere to academic standards of clear thinking and effective communication. More specifically, most instructors hope to find the following characteristics in student writing:

- A limited but significant topic
- A meaningful context for discussion of the topic
- A sustained and full development of ideas, given the limitations of the topic, time allotted, and length assigned
- A clear pattern of organization
- Fair and effective use of sources
- Adequate detail and evidence as support for generalizations
- Appropriate, concise language
- Conventional grammar, punctuation, and usage

The essay on pages 109–10, written by student Hope Leman for a class on politics and the media, meets these criteria. The essay was a response to the following assignment for a take-home midterm exam:

Journalists often suggest that they simply mirror reality. Some political scientists argue, however, that rather than mirroring reality journalists make judgments that subtly but significantly shape their resulting news reports. In so doing, scholars

See the discussion of academic habits of mind in Chapter 2, pp. 27–31. ✱

argue, journalists function more like flashlights than like mirrors. Write an essay in which you contrast the "mirror" and "flashlight" models of the role of journalists in American society.

Successful essays will not only compare these two models but will also provide examples supporting their claims.

Because Hope was writing a take-home midterm essay, she didn't have time to do a formal written analysis of her rhetorical situation. Still, her essay demonstrates considerable rhetorical sensitivity. Hope understands, for instance, that given her situation she should emphasize content rather than employ a dramatic or highly personal style. Hope's essay is, above all, clearly written. Even though it has moments of quiet humor (as when she comments on funhouses at the end of paragraph 2), the focus is on articulating the reasons the "flashlight" model of media theory is the most valid and helpful for political scientists. Hope knows that her teacher will be reading a stack of midterms under time pressure, so she makes sure that her own writing is carefully organized and to the point.

Leman 1

Hope Leman
Professor Roberts
Political Science 101
April 20, 2016

The Role of Journalists in American Society: A Comparison of the
"Mirror" and "Flashlight" Models

The "mirror" model of media theory holds that through their writing and
news broadcasts journalists are an objective source of information for the
public. This model assumes that journalists are free of bias and can be
relied on to provide accurate information about the true state of affairs in
the world. Advocates of the "flashlight" model disagree, believing that a
journalist is like a person in a dark room holding a flashlight. The light
from the flashlight falls briefly on various objects in the room, revealing
part—but not all—of the room at any one time. This model assumes that
journalists cannot possibly provide an objective view of reality but, at best,
can convey only a partial understanding of a situation or an event.

In this essay, I will argue that the "flashlight" model provides a
more accurate and complex understanding of the role of journalists in
America than the "mirror" model does. The flashlight model recognizes,
for instance, that journalists are shaped by their personal backgrounds and
experiences and by the pressures, mores, and customs of their profession.
It also recognizes that journalists are under commercial pressure to sell
their stories. Newspapers and commercial networks are run on a for-profit
basis. Thus reporters have to "sell" their stories to readers. The easiest way
to do that is to fit a given news event into a "story" framework. Human
beings generally relate well to easily digestible stories, as opposed to
more complex analyses, which require more thought and concentration.
Reporters assigned to cover a given situation are likely to ask "What is the
story?" and then to force events into that framework. Reality is seldom
as neat as a story, however, with neat compartments of "Once upon a
time . . . ," "and then . . . ," and "The End." But the story framework

dominates news coverage of events; thus the media cannot function as a mirror since mirrors reflect rather than distort reality (except in funhouses).

The "mirror" model also fails to acknowledge that journalists make choices, including decisions about what stories to cover. These choices can be based on personal preference, but usually they are determined by editors, who respond to publishers, who, in turn, are eager to sell their product to the widest possible audiences. Most people prefer not to read about seemingly insoluble social problems like poverty or homelessness. As a result, journalists often choose not to cover social issues unless they fit a particular "story" format.

In addition to deciding what to cover, journalists must determine the tone they will take in their reporting. If the "mirror" model of media theory were accurate, journalists wouldn't make implicit or explicit judgments in their reporting. But they do. They are only human, after all, and they will inevitably be influenced by their admiration or dislike for a person about whom they are writing or by their belief about the significance of an event.

From start to finish, journalists must make a series of choices. They first make choices about what to cover; then they make choices about whether their tone will be positive or negative, which facts to include or omit, what adjectives to use, and so on. Mirrors do not make choices—but a person holding a flashlight does. The latter can decide where to let the light drop, how long to leave it on that spot, and when to shift the light to something else. Journalists make these kinds of choices every day. Consequently, the "flashlight" model provides the more accurate understanding of the role that journalists play in American society, for the "mirror" model fails to take into account the many factors shaping even the simplest news story.

for **collaboration**

Working with a group of classmates, respond to these questions about Hope Leman's essay. Appoint a recorder to write down the results of your discussion, which your instructor may ask you to present to the class.

1. Hope begins her essay not by attempting to interest readers in her subject but by defining the "mirror" and "flashlight" models of media theory. Why might this be an effective way to begin her essay?

2. Writers need to have a working thesis, or controlling purpose, when they write.✱ Sometimes they signal this purpose by articulating an explicit thesis statement. Sometimes only subtle cues are necessary. (Students writing a personal essay might not want, for instance, to state their controlling purpose explicitly at the start of their essay but rather let readers discover it as they read.) In her essay, Hope includes an explicit thesis statement. Identify this statement, and then discuss the reasons that it is necessary in her particular situation.

3. Academic writing is sometimes viewed as dull and lifeless — as, well, *academic*. Yet even in this essay written under time pressure, Hope's writing is not stuffy, dull, or pompous. Examine her essay to identify passages where a personal voice contributes to the overall effectiveness of her essay. How does Hope blend this personal voice with the objective and distanced approach of her essay?

Understanding How Analysis Works

As a student, you must respond to a wide range of writing assignments. For an American literature class, you may have to analyze the significance of the whiteness of the whale in *Moby-Dick*, whereas a business management class may require a collaboratively written case study; you may need to write a lab report for a chemistry class and critique a qualitative research report for sociology. Although these assignments vary considerably, they all require and depend on analysis.

As noted earlier, analysis involves separating something into parts and determining how these parts function to create the whole. When you analyze, you examine a text, an object, or a body of data to understand how it is structured or organized and to assess its effectiveness or validity. Most academic writing, thinking, and reading involve analysis. Literature students analyze how a play is structured or how a poem achieves its effect; economics students analyze the major causes of inflation; biology students analyze the enzymatic reactions that comprise the Krebs cycle; and art history students analyze how line, color, and texture come together in a painting.

As these examples indicate, analysis is not a single skill but a group of related skills. An art history student might explore how a painting by Michelangelo achieves its effect, for instance, by comparing it with a similar work by Raphael. A biology student might discuss future acid-rain damage

See also Chapter 9, pp. 273–74. ✱ ⋯⋯⋯⋯

to forests in Canada and the United States by first defining *acid rain* and then using cause-and-effect reasoning to predict worsening conditions. A student in economics might estimate the likelihood of severe inflation in the coming year by categorizing or classifying the major causes of previous inflationary periods and then evaluating the likelihood that such factors will influence the current economic situation. Different disciplines emphasize different analytic skills.✱ But regardless of your major, you need to understand and practice analysis. You will do so most successfully if you establish a specific purpose and develop an appropriate framework or method.

ESTABLISHING A PURPOSE FOR YOUR ANALYSIS

thinking
rhetorically

Your instructors will often ask you to analyze a fairly limited subject, problem, or process: Lily Briscoe's role in Virginia Woolf's *To the Lighthouse*, feminists' criticisms of Freud's psychoanalytical theories, Mendel's third law of genetics. Such limited tasks are necessary because of the complexity of the material, but the larger purpose of your analysis is to better understand your topic's role within a larger context—for example, a literary work that you are analyzing or a political or philosophical theory. When you analyze a limited topic, you're like a person holding a flashlight in the dark: The beam of light that you project is narrow and focused, but it illuminates a much larger area.

Even though the purpose of your analysis is to understand the larger subject, you still need to establish a more specific purpose for your analysis. Imagine, for instance, that your Shakespeare instructor has asked you to write an essay about the fool in *King Lear*. You might establish one of several purposes for your analysis:

- To explain how the fool contributes to the development of a major theme in *King Lear*
- To discuss the effectiveness or plausibility of Shakespeare's characterization of the fool
- To define the role the fool plays in the plot
- To agree or disagree with a particular critical perspective on the fool's role and significance

Establishing a specific purpose helps you define how your analysis should proceed. It enables you to determine the important issues to address or the questions to answer.

There are no one-size-fits-all procedures for establishing a purpose for your analysis. Sometimes your purpose will develop naturally as a result of reading, reflection, and discussion with others. In other instances, it may help to draw on the invention strategies described in Chapter 9; these strategies help you explore your subject and discover questions to guide your analysis. Since writing and thinking are dynamically interwoven processes, you may at

✱　For more on what's required in different disciplines, see Chapter 8.

times need to *write* your way into an understanding of your purpose by composing a rough draft and seeing, in effect, what you think about your topic.

DEVELOPING AN APPROPRIATE METHOD FOR YOUR ANALYSIS

Once you have a purpose, how do you actually analyze something? The answer depends on the subject, process, or problem being analyzed. In general, however, you should consider the methods of inquiry characteristic of the discipline in which you're writing. While students studying *To the Lighthouse* or Mendel's third law may use the same fundamental analytic *processes*—for example, definition, causal analysis, classification, and comparison—the relative weight they give to these different processes and the way they shape and present their final analyses may well differ.

The questions below can help you develop an appropriate method for your analysis. If, after considering these questions and reflecting on your

thinking rhetorically

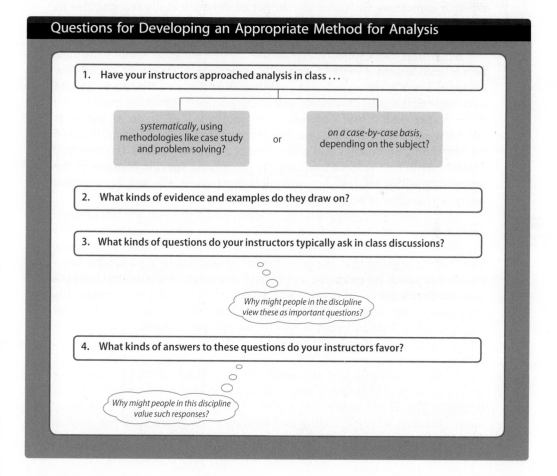

experiences in a class, you continue to have difficulty settling on an appropriate method, meet with your instructor to get help. You might ask him or her to recommend student essays or professional articles that clearly model the analytical methods used in the field.

Understanding the Relationship between Analysis and Argument

All academic writing has an argumentative edge, and sometimes that edge is obvious. If a student writes a political science essay arguing that the government should follow a particular environmental policy, that student is explicitly arguing that the government should do something. Essays that discuss whether something should or should not be done are easily recognizable as arguments, probably because they follow the debate format that many associate with argumentation.

But writers can express judgments—can present good reasons for their beliefs and actions—without explicitly endorsing a course of action. For example, a music theory student analyzing the score of a Beethoven sonata may argue that the second movement of the particular sonata is more daring or innovative than music historians have acknowledged. To do so, she must convince her reader, in this case her teacher, that she has a sophisticated understanding of the structure of the sonata. Analysis will play a particularly central role in this student's writing: By identifying specific features of the score and positing relationships among these features, she will demonstrate her understanding of Beethoven's use of the sonata form.

thinking
rhetorically

As this example demonstrates, analysis and argument are interdependent. Argumentation depends on analysis because through analysis writers clarify the logic of their thinking and provide evidence for their judgments. The student arguing that the government should follow a particular environmental policy, for example, would have to analyze the potential benefits and disadvantages of that policy and demonstrate that it's workable for his argument to be convincing. Similarly, analysis always carries an implicit argumentative burden because when you analyze something, you are in effect asserting "This is how I believe X works" or "This is what I believe X means."

Academic analysis and argument call for similar habits of mind. Both encourage writers to suspend personal biases, so they require openness and flexibility. This is not to say that academic writers are expected to be absolutely objective. Your gut feeling that "workfare" programs may not provide single parents with adequate support for their children may cause you to investigate this topic for a political science or an economics class. This gut feeling is a strength, not a weakness, because it enables you to find a topic that interests you. Once you begin to explore your topic, however, you need to engage it dispassionately. You need, in other words, to be open to changing your mind.

If you do change your mind about the consequences of workfare programs, the reading and writing you have done probably have given you a more detailed understanding of the issues at stake. To write a successful essay about this topic, you will have to describe these issues and analyze their relationships and implications, developing logical connections that make your reasoning explicit. In these and other ways, you will demonstrate to readers that you have indeed understood your subject.

The essay by Hope Leman that begins on p. 109 is a good example of academic analysis. In this essay, Hope is not arguing that something should or should not be done. Rather, she is attempting to understand whether the "mirror" or "flashlight" model best describes the role of journalists in American society.

ANALYZING ACADEMIC ARGUMENTS

Analysis plays a key role in all academic writing. It helps readers and writers understand the texts they encounter as they move across the disciplines and recognize, examine, and formulate arguments about them. In the world of academia, written, visual, and oral works—and even events, behaviors, and performances—can be considered "texts" susceptible to analysis. While written texts are still central to academic study, the ability to analyze texts that depend heavily on images, sounds, and graphics—whether they are television ads, multimedia presentations, or websites—has become increasingly important in our media-saturated culture. ✱

The analysis of any complex text will feel less intimidating if you address three basic questions:

thinking
rhetorically

- What question is at issue?
- What position does the author take?
- Do the author's reasons justify your acceptance of his or her argument?

DETERMINING THE QUESTION AT ISSUE

When you determine the question at issue, you get to the heart of any argument and distinguish major claims from minor elements of support. You can then identify the author's position and evaluate whether he or she has provided good reasons for you to agree with this position.

See Chapters 2 and 6 for advice on analyzing visuals (pp. 41–49) and a student's analysis ✱ of a public service ad (pp. 166–82).

Greek and Roman rhetoricians developed a method called *stasis theory* for determining the questions at issue in any argument. Stasis theory encourages readers to identify the major point on which a particular controversy rests. This method presents six basic questions at issue in argumentative writing.[1]

As you determine the kinds of issues addressed in a particular argument, you will draw on your rhetorical sensitivity. You do this naturally in your everyday life. Imagine that a friend has urged you to drive with her to a concert in a city an hour away. You'd like to attend the concert, but it's on a midweek work night. Depending on your situation, the primary question at issue may be one of *value*. If you value the concert enough, you can justify the time, expense, and late-night bedtime involved in attending the concert. On the other hand, the primary question at issue for you may be one of *consequence*: This would be the case if you couldn't justify time away from study, work, and family, especially on a weeknight.

On the next page is an argument by Amitai Etzioni about the advantages and disadvantages of traditional privacy protections in North America. Etzioni is a professor at George Washington University and former senior adviser to the White House. He has written over a dozen books, including *The Limits of*

Stasis Questions

QUESTIONS OF FACT arise from the reader's need to know
"Does _____ exist?"

QUESTIONS OF DEFINITION arise from the reader's need to know
"What is _____?"

QUESTIONS OF INTERPRETATION arise from the reader's need to know
"What does _____ mean?"

QUESTIONS OF VALUE arise from the reader's need to know
"Is _____ good?"

QUESTIONS OF CONSEQUENCE arise from the reader's need to know
"Will _____ cause _____ to happen?"

QUESTIONS OF POLICY arise from the reader's need to know
"What should be done about _____?"

---

[1]In this discussion of stasis theory, I employ the categories presented in John Gage, *The Shape of Reason: Argumentative Writing in College.* 3rd ed., Allyn and Bacon, 1991, p. 40.

Privacy, from which this excerpt is taken. As you read his analysis, consider which of the six stasis questions—fact, definition, interpretation, value, consequence, and policy—are most clearly at stake in his argument.

Less Privacy Is Good for Us (and You)

AMITAI ETZIONI

Poklekowski/ullstein bild via Getty Images

Despite the fact that privacy is not so much as mentioned in the Constitution and that it was only shoehorned in some thirty-four years ago, it is viewed by most Americans as a profound, inalienable right.

The media is loaded with horror stories about the ways privacy is not so much nibbled away as it is stripped away by bosses who read your e-mail, neighbors who listen in on your cell phones, and E-Z passes that allow tollbooth operators to keep track of your movements. A typical headline decries the "End of Privacy" (Richard A. Spinello, in an issue of *America*, a Catholic weekly) or "The Death of Privacy" (Joshua Quittner, in *Time*).

It is time to pay attention to the other half of the equation that defines a good society: concerns for public health and safety that entail some rather justifiable diminution of privacy.

Take the HIV testing of infants. New medical data—for instance, evidence recently published by the prestigious *New England Journal of Medicine*—show that a significant proportion of children born to mothers who have HIV can ward off this horrible disease but only on two conditions: that their mothers not breastfeed them and that they immediately be given AZT. For this to happen, mothers must be informed that they have HIV. An estimated two-thirds of infected mothers are unaware. However, various civil libertarians and some gay activists vehemently oppose such disclosure on the grounds that when infants are tested for HIV, in effect one finds out if the mother is a carrier, and thus her privacy is violated. While New York State in 1996, after a very acrimonious debate, enacted a law that requires infant testing and disclosure of the findings to the mother, most other states have so far avoided dealing with this issue.

1

Congress passed the buck by asking the Institute of Medicine (IOM) to conduct a study of the matter. The IOM committee, dominated by politically correct people, just reported its recommendations. It suggested that all pregnant women be asked to consent to HIV testing as part of routine prenatal care. There is little wrong with such a recommendation other than it does not deal with many of the mothers who are drug addicts or otherwise live at society's margins. Many of these women do not show up for prenatal care, and they are particularly prone to HIV, according to a study published in the American Health Association's *Journal of School Health*. To save the lives of their children, they must be tested at delivery and treated even if this entails a violation of mothers' privacy.

Recently a suggestion to use driver's licenses to curb illegal immigration has sent the Coalition for Constitutional Liberties, a large group of libertarians, civil libertarians, and privacy advocates, into higher orbit than John Glenn ever traversed. The coalition wrote:

> This plan pushed us to the brink of tyranny, where citizens will not be allowed to travel, open bank accounts, obtain health care, get a job, or purchase firearms without first presenting the proper government papers.
>
> The authorizing section of the law . . . is reminiscent of the totalitarian dictates by Politburo members in the former Soviet Union, not the Congress of the United States of America.

Meanwhile, Wells Fargo is introducing a new device that allows a person to cash checks at its ATM machines because the machines recognize faces. Rapidly coming is a whole new industry of so-called biometrics that uses natural features such as voice, hand design, and eye pattern to recognize a person with the same extremely high reliability provided by the new DNA tests.

It's true that as biometrics catches on, it will practically strip Americans of anonymity, an important part of privacy. In the near future, a person who acquired a poor reputation in one part of the country will find it much more difficult to move to another part, change his name, and gain a whole fresh start. Biometrics see right through such assumed identities. One may hope that future communities will become more tolerant of such people, especially if they openly acknowledge the mistakes of their past and truly seek to lead a more prosocial life. But they will no longer be able to hide their pasts.

Above all, while biometrics clearly undermines privacy, the social benefits it promises are very substantial. Specifically, each year at least half a million criminals become fugitives, avoiding trial, incarceration, or serving their full sentences, often committing additional crimes while on the lam. People who fraudulently file for multiple income tax refunds using fake identities and multiple Social Security numbers cost the nation between $1 billion and $5 billion per year. Numerous divorced parents escape their financial obligations to their children by avoiding detection when they move or change jobs. (The sums owed to children are variously estimated as running between $18 billion to $23 billion a year.) Professional and amateur criminals, employing fraudulent identification documentation to make phony credit card purchases, cost credit card companies and retail businesses an indeterminate number of billions of dollars each year. The United States loses an estimated $18 billion a year to benefit fraud committed by illegal aliens using false IDs. A 1998 General Accounting Office report estimates identity fraud to cost $10 billion annually in entitlement programs alone.

People hired to work in child care centers, kindergartens, and schools cannot be effectively screened to keep out child abusers and sex offenders, largely because when background checks are conducted, convicted criminals escape detection by using false identification and aliases. Biometrics would sharply curtail all these crimes, although far from wipe them out single-handedly.

The courts have recognized that privacy must be weighed against considerations of public interest but have tended to privilege privacy and make claims for public health or safety clear several high hurdles. In recent years these barriers have been somewhat lowered as courts have become more concerned with public safety and health. Given that these often are matters of state law and that neither legislatures nor courts act in unison, the details are complex and far from all pointing in one direction. But, by and large, courts have allowed mandatory drug testing of those who directly have the lives of others in their hands, including pilots, train engineers, drivers of school buses, and air traffic controllers, even though such testing violates their privacy. In case after case, the courts have disregarded objections to such tests by civil libertarians who argue that such tests constitute "suspicionless" searches, grossly violate privacy, and—as the ACLU puts it—"condition Americans to a police state."

All this points to a need to recast privacy in our civic culture, public policies, and legal doctrines. We should cease to treat it as an unmitigated good, a sacred right (the way Warren and Brandeis referred to in their famous article and many since) or one that courts automatically privilege.

Instead, privacy should rely squarely on the Fourth Amendment, the only one that has a balance built right into its text. It recognizes both searches that wantonly violate privacy ("unreasonable" ones) and those that enhance the common good to such an extent that they are justified, even if they intrude into one's privacy. Moreover, it provides a mechanism to sort out which searches are in the public interest and which violate privacy without sufficient cause, by introducing the concept of warrants issued by a "neutral magistrate" presented with "probable cause." Warrants also limit the invasion of privacy "by specification of the person to be seized, the place to be searched, and the evidence to be sought." The Fourth may have become the Constitutional Foundation of privacy a long time ago if it was not for the fact that *Roe v. Wade* is construed as a privacy right, and touching it provokes fierce opposition. The good news, though, is that even the advocates of choice in this area are now looking to base their position on some other legal grounds, especially the Fourteenth Amendment.

We might be ready to treat privacy for what it is: one very important right but not one that trumps most other considerations, especially of public safety and health.

for **collaboration**

After you have read Etzioni's argument, list the two most significant stasis questions (see p. 116) at stake in his argument. Find at least one passage that you believe relates to each question. Then meet with a group of classmates and share your responses to this assignment. (Appoint a timekeeper to ensure that all members of your group have a chance to share their responses.) To what extent did you agree or disagree with other group members on the stasis questions at stake in Etzioni's analysis? As a group, choose the two stasis questions that you believe best apply to Etzioni's argument, and agree on two or three reasons why each question is central to his argument. Be prepared to share the results of your discussion with your class.

IDENTIFYING AN AUTHOR'S POSITION ON A QUESTION

You may find it helpful to identify an author's position in two stages: *First, read the text carefully to determine the main question that the author has presented.* If you review the first three paragraphs of Etzioni's argument beginning on p. 117, for instance, you'll note that he observes in paragraph 1 that privacy "is viewed by most Americans as a profound, inalienable right" and goes on to argue in paragraph 3 that "[i]t is time to pay attention to the other half of the equation that defines a good society: concerns for public health and safety that entail some rather justifiable diminution of privacy." The remainder of the excerpt clarifies and supports his position on this issue.

After you have identified the author's position, you can read his or her argument critically. Reading critically doesn't mean simply looking for logical flaws, poor evidence, and so on. Rather, critical readers shift stances as they read to develop a complex understanding of the issues at hand.

The Questions for Critical Reading and Analysis below can help you become a more active and critical reader who reads both with and against the grain of an author's argument.

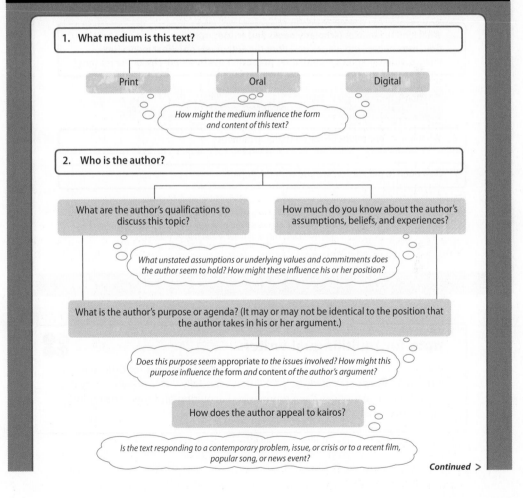

Questions for Critical Reading and Analysis

1. **What medium is this text?**

Print Oral Digital

How might the medium influence the form and content of this text?

2. **Who is the author?**

What are the author's qualifications to discuss this topic?

How much do you know about the author's assumptions, beliefs, and experiences?

What unstated assumptions or underlying values and commitments does the author seem to hold? How might these influence his or her position?

What is the author's purpose or agenda? (It may or may not be identical to the position that the author takes in his or her argument.)

Does this purpose seem appropriate to the issues involved? How might this purpose influence the form and content of the author's argument?

How does the author appeal to kairos?

Is the text responding to a contemporary problem, issue, or crisis or to a recent film, popular song, or news event?

Continued >

Questions continued

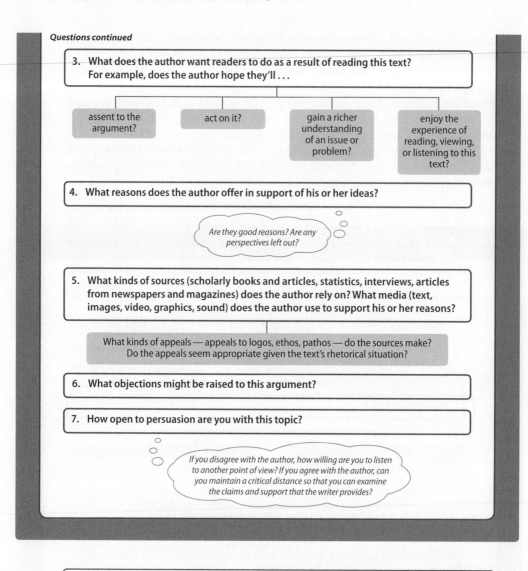

3. **What does the author want readers to do as a result of reading this text? For example, does the author hope they'll . . .**

assent to the argument?

act on it?

gain a richer understanding of an issue or problem?

enjoy the experience of reading, viewing, or listening to this text?

4. **What reasons does the author offer in support of his or her ideas?**

Are they good reasons? Are any perspectives left out?

5. **What kinds of sources (scholarly books and articles, statistics, interviews, articles from newspapers and magazines) does the author rely on? What media (text, images, video, graphics, sound) does the author use to support his or her reasons?**

What kinds of appeals — appeals to logos, ethos, pathos — do the sources make? Do the appeals seem appropriate given the text's rhetorical situation?

6. **What objections might be raised to this argument?**

7. **How open to persuasion are you with this topic?**

If you disagree with the author, how willing are you to listen to another point of view? If you agree with the author, can you maintain a critical distance so that you can examine the claims and support that the writer provides?

note for multilingual writers

If you are a multilingual writer you may find the Questions for Critical Reading and Analysis particularly helpful. This is especially the case if your previous educational experiences have emphasized acquiring and memorizing information over analysis and critique.

for **exploration**

Reread the excerpt from Amitai Etzioni's *The Limits of Privacy* (pp. 117–20). After doing so, respond to each of the Questions for Critical Reading and Analysis on pp. 121–22. What did this guided rereading of Etzioni's text help you better understand about it?

for **collaboration**

After you have analyzed Etzioni's argument with the help of the Questions for Critical Reading and Analysis, meet with a group of classmates to share your results. Appoint a timekeeper so that all group members have an opportunity to share their results. To what extent did other group members agree in their responses to the Questions for Critical Reading and Analysis? To what extent did they disagree? What did you learn as a result of this experience? Be prepared to share your responses with the rest of the class.

USING ARISTOTLE'S THREE APPEALS

As the Questions for Critical Reading and Analysis on pp. 121–22 suggest, you may agree with a writer's position on a subject but nevertheless question the support that he or she provides. One of the hallmarks of a critical reader, in fact, is the ability to maintain a critical distance from an argument, even when you have strong feelings for or against the author's position. Aristotle's three appeals, introduced on p. 62 in Chapter 3, can help you evaluate the strength and limitation of academic arguments.

In his *Rhetoric*, Aristotle determined that speakers and writers draw on three general appeals when they attempt to persuade others:

- *Logos*, the appeal to reason
- *Pathos*, the appeal to emotion, values, and beliefs
- *Ethos*, the appeal to the credibility of the speaker or writer

One way to analyze an argument is to determine which type of appeal the author draws on most heavily and his or her effectiveness in using it. When you consider appeals to logos, ask yourself if the author has articulated clear and reasonable major claims and supported them with appropriate evidence. Appeals to pathos raise different issues: Here you identify the strategies that the author has employed to appeal to readers' values and interests. Finally, appeals to ethos encourage you to consider the author's credibility and trustworthiness as demonstrated in his or her argument.

Appeals to logos are often considered especially trustworthy in academic contexts. Logical appeals include firsthand evidence—drawn from observations, interviews, surveys and questionnaires, experiments, and personal experience—and secondhand evidence—drawn from print and online sources. Critical readers do not automatically assume that support drawn from logical appeals is valid. After all, not all sources are equally valid, and facts can be outdated or taken out of context.✱

Critical readers look at all three of Aristotle's appeals in context. Appeals to pathos—to readers' emotions, values, and beliefs—can certainly be manipulative and inappropriate. We've all seen ads (like the one on the next page) that seem to promise one thing (youth, beauty, fitness) to sell another. Nevertheless, emotional appeals play key roles in many kinds of arguments, including academic arguments. A student writing about humanitarian issues growing out of the conflict in Syria might begin her essay by describing the loss of life, order, and basic material necessities that have resulted from the conflict. In so doing, she would be appealing to readers' emotions and emphasizing the importance of her topic. The same is true for appeals to ethos. While we might be skeptical when we see an ad in which a movie star or sports hero praises a product, this doesn't mean that all appeals to ethos are suspect.

In this regard, let's return to the excerpt from Etzioni's *The Limits of Privacy* (pp. 117–20). The biographical information that accompanies this excerpt provides information about Etzioni's experience and qualifications that can help readers determine whether Etzioni is an authority on issues of privacy. Critical readers will keep this knowledge in mind as they read his argument, but they'll also consider the credibility with which he makes his case. Does he use examples that are fair and reasonable? Does he develop a balanced, thoughtful argument? Does he seem to have society's best interest at heart, or is he pushing an agenda of his own personal assumptions and beliefs? By asking such questions readers can determine whether they should trust Etzioni's credibility as a thinker and writer. In short, critical readers respect relevant experiences and qualifications that authors bring to various issues, but they focus primarily on what the author does and says in the text that they are currently reading.

---

for **exploration**

Drawing on your understanding of Aristotle's three appeals, analyze the excerpt from Etzioni's *The Limits of Privacy* (pp. 117–20). What appeals does he draw on most heavily? How effective is he in using these appeals? (Be sure to comment on each of the three appeals.)

for **collaboration**

Meet with a group of classmates to share your responses to the previous Exploration. Appoint both a timekeeper and a recorder to summarize your group's responses. Begin by addressing this question: To what extent did members of your group agree about Etzioni's effectiveness in his use of Aristotle's three appeals?

✱   For a discussion of how to evaluate print and online sources, see Chapter 7, pp. 206–8.

After responding, develop a group position on Etzioni's use of Aristotle's three appeals. To do so, first agree on a statement that conveys your group's sense of how Etzioni employed each appeal. Then find one or two examples from his text that support your analysis. Be prepared to share the results of your discussion with the class.

The power of images: What is this ad promising viewers?

RECOGNIZING FALLACIES

When you analyze an argument, you should be aware of *fallacies* that may be at work. Fallacies are faults in an argument's structure that may call into question the argument's evidence or conclusions. Some fallacies are easy to recognize. If someone told you that Bono's position on the AIDS pandemic and poverty in Africa is ridiculous because he's just a celebrity, you would probably recognize that this assertion is illogical and unfair. Such a statement is an example of an *ad hominem* fallacy, in which an attack on someone's character or actions masquerades as a critique of his or her position. This fallacy, like all fallacies, tends to shut down, rather than encourage, communication.

To determine whether an argument is grounded in a fallacy, you need to consider it in the context of its specific rhetorical situation, including the place and time in which the argument was or is being made. Sometimes judgments about a person's character or actions are relevant to an argument, for instance. In other words, just because a writer or speaker grounds part of an argument in such a judgment doesn't mean that he or she is committing an *ad hominem* fallacy.

Since the time of Aristotle, rhetoricians have developed diverse ways of naming, describing, and categorizing various fallacies. Often the fallacies are categorized according to Aristotle's three major appeals of argument: ethical appeals (appeals to ethos), emotional appeals (appeals to pathos), and logical appeals (appeals to logos).

The guidelines on pp. 127–28 list some of the most significant fallacies that appear in arguments. As you read the brief descriptions, remember that the point of studying fallacies is not to discredit the ideas of others, but rather to thoughtfully evaluate the arguments of others and to develop fair, well-reasoned arguments of your own.

---

for **exploration**

Locate three of the fallacies described above in such popular media as political websites, the editorial pages of your favorite newspaper, or advertisements in print or online. Identify the fallacy, and explain how it functions in its particular context.

Putting Theory into Practice I: Academic Analysis in Action

Readers engage in academic analysis not to criticize or dissect another's argument but rather to understand that argument as fully as possible. When you analyze an academic argument, you attempt to go beyond your immediate

Guidelines for Identifying Fallacies

Ethical Fallacies

Writers who employ ethical fallacies attempt to discredit their opponents. Examples of ethical fallacies include the following:

AN *AD HOMINEM* attack is an unfair assault on a person's character or actions, one that diverts attention from the issue at hand.

> **"Any American who is in favor of gun control doesn't value our country's constitution."**
>
> *(A person's position on this topic does not indicate his or her commitment to the U.S. Constitution.)*

GUILT BY ASSOCIATION is an effort to damage a person's credibility by associating him or her with an unpopular or discredited activity or person.

> **"Hip-hop is bad because some hip-hop musicians have been involved in criminal activities."**
>
> *(The behavior of hip-hop musicians is separate from the music they create.)*

Emotional Fallacies

Emotional appeals can play a valid and important role in argumentation, but when these appeals are overblown or unfair, they distract readers from attending to the point that is being argued. Examples of emotional fallacies include the following:

A BANDWAGON APPEAL argues that readers should support a person, an activity, a product, or a movement because it is popular. This appeal is particularly common in advertising:

> **"Frosty Puffs™ is the best-selling cereal in America!"**

A SLIPPERY SLOPE fallacy occurs when writers exaggerate the consequences of an event or action, usually with an intent to frighten readers into agreeing with their conclusion.

> **"If we ban *Beloved* from our school library, the next thing you know, we'll be burning books!"**

Logical Fallacies

Logical fallacies are arguments in which the claims, warrants, or evidence are invalid, insufficient, or disconnected. Examples of logical fallacies include the following:

BEGGING THE QUESTION involves stating a claim that depends on circular reasoning for justification.

> **"Abortion is murder because it involves the intentional killing of an unborn human being."**

Continued >

Guidelines continued

(This statement is tantamount to saying, "Abortion is murder because it is murder." This fallacy often distracts attention from the real issues at hand because the question of whether a fetus should be considered a human being is complex.)

A HASTY GENERALIZATION is drawn from insufficient evidence.

> **"Last week I attended a poetry reading supported by the National Endowment for the Arts, and several of the speakers used profanity. Maybe the people who want to stop government funding for the NEA are right."**

(One performance doesn't constitute a large enough sample for such a generalization.)

A NON SEQUITUR is an argument that attempts to connect two or more logically unrelated ideas.

> **"I hate it when people smoke in restaurants; there ought to be a law against cigarettes."**

(Eliminating smoking in restaurants and the negative effects of secondhand smoke do not require the elimination of legal tobacco sales.)

A RED HERRING is an argument that misleads or distracts opponents from the original issue.

> **"How can you expect me to worry about global warming when we're on the brink of war?"**

(Whether or not we're on the brink of war is irrelevant to whether global warming is a problem.)

A STRAW MAN fallacy occurs when a misrepresentation, an exaggeration, or a distortion of a position is attacked.

> **"My opponent argues that drugs should be legalized without taking into consideration the epidemic that selling heroin in every drugstore would cause."**

(Arguing in favor of legalizing drugs does not mean that all drugs would be available over the counter.)

response—which often takes the form of binary-driven observations ("I agree/don't agree, like/don't like, am interested/not interested in X")—to achieve a fuller, more complex understanding of it.

On the next page is an example of a successful analysis of an academic argument. This essay by Stevon Roberts, a student at Oregon State University, analyzes the excerpt from Etzioni's *The Limits of Privacy* presented earlier in this chapter (pp. 117–20).

Roberts 1

Stevon Roberts
Dr. Mallon
Composition 101
Oct. 10, 2016

The Price of Public Safety

As a former senior adviser to the White House and author of *The Limits of Privacy*, Amitai Etzioni is a formidable advocate for revision of one of America's most cherished luxuries: protection of personal privacy. In "Less Privacy Is Good for Us (and You)," an argument excerpted from the above volume, Etzioni urges Americans to look critically at traditional expectations for personal privacy and to be prepared to sacrifice those expectations for increased public health and safety. Although the volume was published before the terrorist attacks on September 11, 2001, the events of that day give an increased sense of urgency to Etzioni's message and consequently might make Americans more receptive to protocols that afford protection from public risks in general.

Etzioni opens his argument by discussing recent HIV testing procedures in hospitals that may infringe on the rights of pregnant women. He then shifts gears and takes a brief look at public outrage from the Coalition for Constitutional Liberties regarding driver's license availability. Next, he gives us a crash course in "biometrics," a controversial new technology that could save billions of dollars lost to fraud every year. Finally, Etzioni addresses our fears (and those of other civil libertarians) that these and other procedures that are designed to increase our public health and safety will not be implemented justly and ethically. Etzioni admits, however, that a growing number of people and interest groups are not convinced that old laws—such as the Fourth Amendment, which protects the United States from becoming a military state—can protect us from new technology. We are left to wonder: Is Etzioni justified in making his unconventional claims despite such well-founded opposition?

After some brief media references, Etzioni's first substantial argument involves a real-world privacy dilemma facing pregnant women as well as

---

Margin annotations:

Identifies the argument and suggests its author is credible

Identifies Etzioni's position

Contrasts rhetorical situations of writing the piece and reading it

Summarizes Etzioni's argument fairly and introduces main question: Is Etzioni's argument legitimate?

Roberts 2

various health and legal groups. Specifically, he focuses on HIV testing of newborns. This is an excellent place to start because the reactions of these groups help shed light on our current attitudes toward privacy. Etzioni refers to the *New England Journal of Medicine*, which published evidence suggesting that infants born to HIV-infected women could ward off the disease with early diagnosis and treatment with AZT. In order for the infants to be treated, they must be tested. This becomes a privacy issue because testing infants for HIV also reveals whether "the mother is a carrier, and thus her privacy is violated" (117).

Notes major evidence Etzioni provides to support his claim

As Etzioni acknowledges, arguments in favor of required HIV testing of infants have met strong—and even "vehement"—opposition from civil libertarians, as well as from some gay activists. Indeed, the question of whether to test infants for HIV has been so contentious that most states, as well as the federal government, have avoided taking it on. In this regard, Etzioni chastises Congress for "pass[ing] the buck by asking the Institute of Medicine (IOM) to conduct a study of the matter" (118). This effectively illustrates Congress's lack of willingness to become involved. IOM's solution suggests that all pregnant women should consent to HIV testing as part of their routine prenatal care. However, Etzioni feels this would leave out many women who "are drug addicts or otherwise live at society's margins" (118). Such women, he argues, "do not show up for prenatal care, and they are particularly prone to HIV, according to a study published in the American Health Association's *Journal of School Health*" (118). A succinct sentence sums up his solution: "To save the lives of their children, they [infants] must be tested at delivery and treated even if this entails a violation of mothers' privacy" (118).

Establishes own ethos by signaling he's providing balanced assessment of Etzioni's argument

This is a well-documented and compelling argument. Other parts of Etzioni's text, however, are not so well rounded. Instead of taking seriously the arguments forwarded by civil libertarians and others who raise concerns about privacy, Etzioni focuses on the media, which he believes tell "horror stories" about "The Death of Privacy" (117). When

Roberts 3

he does address the views of other groups, he represents their concerns by
an inflammatory statement from the Coalition for Constitutional Liberties,
which accuses those in favor of the plan of pushing the country "to the
brink of tyranny" (118).

> Asserts first criticism of Etzioni's argument: Etzioni's representation of opposing viewpoints is not balanced

With this brief (and wholly unsuccessful) transition, Etzioni moves
from the Coalition's alarmist complaints to Wells Fargo's introduction of
"a new device that allows a person to cash checks at its ATM machines
because the machines recognize faces" (118). These machines rely upon a
new technology called biometrics, which, Etzioni explains, can use "natural
features such as voice, hand design, and eye pattern to recognize a person
with the same extremely high reliability provided by the new DNA
tests" (118). Etzioni acknowledges that biometrics is a controversial
technology, and he concedes that "it will practically strip Americans of
anonymity, an important part of privacy" (118). With this new technology,
people would find it difficult to change their names, move to another part
of the country, and gain a fresh start in life. His solution is a hope that
"future communities will become more tolerant of such people, especially
if they openly acknowledge the mistakes of their past and truly seek to lead
a more prosocial life" (118).

To his credit, Etzioni is quick to follow up the drawbacks of biometrics
with compelling statistics about the potential benefits. He says, "Above all,
while biometrics clearly undermines privacy, the social benefits it promises
are very substantial" (118). He refers to the $1 billion to $5 billion lost
annually to tax fraud, $18 billion to $23 billion annually in lost child
support, and $18 billion a year lost to fraud committed by illegal aliens
with false IDs. In addition to the potential economic benefits, he says sex
offenders who use false IDs would be more effectively screened and would
less easily find work at child-care centers or schools (119).

> Balances criticism of Etzioni's argument with praise

Etzioni's presentation of biometrics is, ironically, both calculated and
lacking in logic. His predominantly economic appeal doesn't mention the
cost associated with Wells Fargo's new face-recognizing ATM machines.

> Presents another major criticism of Etzioni's use of evidence

Roberts 4

Because he makes no attempt, even hypothetically, to weigh the cost of biometrics implementation against the savings from fraud protection or other liabilities, readers are left to assume that the overall results are beneficial, when that might not, in fact, be the case. For example, although he discusses credit card fraud, there is no mention of Internet credit card fraud. Biometrics countermeasures to combat this threat are likely to manifest as computer hardware add-ons, putting an unfair financial burden on lower-level consumers while taking the liability away from the credit card companies. It seems reasonable that while calculating the potential benefits, Etzioni should also calculate potential losses or system limitations, as he does when admitting that biometrics would not single-handedly wipe out abusers from child-care centers.

Raises questions about Etzioni's appeals to pathos and points out that Etzioni does not anticipate potential limitation to argument

Additionally, the author's appeals to pathos lack substance. In fact, his only olive branch to the human condition is a concession that biometrics may make it difficult for criminals seeking a new life. His solution to this problem is a touchy-feely dream in which everyone magically becomes more tolerant of criminals that repent and sin no more. Further, he makes no mention at all of persons seeking new lives for reasons other than legal trouble, such as women who have fled abusive husbands.

Etzioni concludes his argument by considering court trends in balancing the need to protect personal privacy with concerns about public health and safety. Etzioni observes that courts have tended to "privilege privacy and make claims for public health or safety clear several high hurdles" (119). More recently, however, the courts are lowering these barriers with growing concern for public interest. For example, the courts have mandated drug testing for those who "directly have the lives of others in their hands, including pilots, train engineers, drivers of school buses, and air traffic controllers, even though such testing violates their privacy" (119). Etzioni reports that the ACLU feels these new laws "condition Americans to a police state" (119).

Roberts 5

"All this," according to Etzioni, "points to a need to recast privacy in our civic culture, public policies, and legal doctrines. We should cease to treat it as an unmitigated good, a sacred right (the way Warren and Brandeis referred to in their famous article and many [other legal theorists have] since) or one that courts automatically privilege" (119). He feels that we should instead rely on the Fourth Amendment, which has built into its text safeguards that balance privacy and public security. His interpretation of the document's reference to "unreasonable" search protocols recognizes the difference between searches that "wantonly violate privacy" and those that "enhance the common good to such an extent that they are justified, even if they intrude into one's privacy" (120). Additionally, the amendment addresses sufficient cause by introducing warrants "issued by a 'neutral magistrate' presented with 'probable cause'" (120). Etzioni apparently believes interpretation of this document will be uniform from one court to the next. This assumption is problematic at best.

Challenges one of Etzioni's key assumptions

The author leaves us with a new vision of privacy as a "very important right but not one that trumps most other considerations, especially of public safety and health" (120). With this parting thought, the author packages a difficult and complex concept into a pill that is not terribly difficult to swallow. By the same token, however, his oversimplification may leave some readers feeling like something is missing.

Indeed, something is missing—the rest of Etzioni's book, from which this excerpt originates. Readers of this argument can only hope that Etzioni deals carefully and respectfully with the arguments of civil libertarians in other parts of his work, for he certainly does not do so here. His tendency to use only the most inflammatory statements from his opponents suggests he has no interest in fully addressing their respective concerns.

Adds to own ethos by acknowledging limitations of his perspective, as a reader not of the book but of the excerpt

All things considered, Etzioni begins his essay with a clear purpose and a logical, tangible starting point. Through the inclusion of several diverse public-interest groups, health organizations, courts, and

Roberts 6

governmental bodies, he initially appears to address all aspects of the moral dilemma. This is especially true in the obvious benefit to newborns with HIV who are diagnosed early. But in this excerpt, he distracts readers from the true opposition by focusing primarily on the media, while turning the Coalition for Constitutional Liberties and the ACLU into radical doomsayers that jeopardize public welfare. He marginalizes their concerns, argues for increased biometrics applications on the chance that billions of dollars might potentially be protected from fraud, and opposes legislation that would protect potential victims because society potentially could be more forgiving. Consequently, his venture into the hypothetical realm leaves opponents (and critical readers) unsatisfied.

Work Cited

Etzioni, Amitai. "Less Privacy Is Good for Us (and You)." *The Academic Writer: A Brief Guide*, 4th ed., by Lisa Ede, Macmillan Learning, 2017. 117–20.

Note: In an actual MLA-style paper, works-cited entries start on a new page.

for **exploration**

Now that you have read Etzioni's argument several times and have also read Stevon Roberts's analysis of it, reread Stevon's essay to determine its strengths and limitations. Identify two or three passages from the essay that strike you as particularly significant and helpful, and write several sentences of explanation for each passage. Next, identify one or more ways this essay might be even more successful.

for **collaboration**

Bring your response to the previous For Exploration to class to share with a group of peers. Appoint a timekeeper and a recorder. After all group members have shared their responses, answer these questions: (1) To what extent did other members of your group agree in their evaluation of Stevon Roberts's analysis? To what extent did they disagree? (2) Now that you have heard everyone's responses, what two or three passages does your group feel best demonstrate Stevon's analytical skills? (3) How might Stevon's essay be further strengthened? Be prepared to share the results of your discussion with the class.

Understanding How Synthesis Works

Analysis often is connected with and leads to synthesis. When you analyze something, you examine it critically to understand how it is structured and how the parts work together to create the overall meaning. When you synthesize something, you draw on ideas or information from sources, as well as from your own experience, to create meaning of your own.

In much academic writing, synthesis is an important counterpart to analysis, for it enables you to make connections and identify contradictions within a text or group of texts that you have analyzed. Synthesis is an essential part of the research process. For a good example of synthesis, take a look at Alletta Brenner's essay in Chapter 7 (pp. 223–32). There Alletta synthesizes a variety of sources as part of her exploration of the role that human trafficking plays in the American garment-manufacturing industry.

In a research project you typically draw on multiple sources; Alletta Brenner cites almost twenty. Sometimes, however, an instructor will ask you to engage a limited number of texts. Your writing instructor might ask you, for instance, to read and respond to two or more articles on the same or a related topic, with the goal of analyzing and synthesizing these texts while also articulating your own views.

You might think of this kind of synthesis essay as a chronicle of your intellectual journey as you explore a topic and readings related to that topic. This is not to say that your essay should be a narrative; in most cases, it is more likely to be an academic argument. But readers of your essay should be able to see that you have interacted at a serious level with the texts to which you are responding and that you have done so to promote your own independent analysis. In other words, it should be clear that as a result of reading and reflecting on these texts you have gained new insights and perspectives.

Synthesis requires both the ability to analyze and to summarize, and this book contains a number of resources that you might want to review before undertaking a synthesis assignment.✱ But it is equally important that you develop your own views on your topic. This may feel difficult at first: How can you engage the arguments of published authors when you are just a college student? The best way to work your way through this initial hesitation is to immerse yourself deeply in the texts to which you are responding.

As you begin your synthesis, focus on developing an understanding of the authors' positions, the reasons and evidence they use to support these positions, the contexts in which they are writing, and any motivating factors, such as their goals, interests, and priorities. Creating a chart in which you can record this information may help you keep track of what you are learning.

Chapter 2 covers summary and reading critically (pp. 31–40); Chapter 7 — summary and synthesis (pp. 211, 218–19). Elizabeth Hurley's essay in this chapter (pp. 138–42) is another good model of synthesis. ✱

(Chapter 7, p. 211, provides an example created by Alletta Brenner for the research project that appears at the end of that chapter.)

The Questions for Critical Reading and Analysis that appear on pp. 121–22 of this chapter will help you consider key aspects of the authors' rhetorical situation, such as each author's purpose or agenda and the values and beliefs that motivate him or her. The questions also encourage you to consider the reasons and evidence the authors provide, the objections that might be raised in response to the authors' positions, their use of evidence, and so forth. The Questions for Synthesizing Texts can help you synthesize the sources and develop your own approach to the issue.

Putting Theory into Practice II: Academic Synthesis in Action

Synthesis assignments represent an exciting opportunity for students to enter into conversation with others, whether they are nonprofessionals expressing their ideas or professional journalists, politicians, or scholars. Throughout your college career, and later at work, you will regularly be asked to synthesize ideas and texts. Your psychology teacher may ask you to read two articles taking different positions on whether it is possible to become addicted to social media, such as Facebook and Twitter, and to articulate your own views on this topic. Your business teacher may ask you to study two bids for a hypothetical project and to write a response that includes an evaluation of each bid and a recommendation. Once you graduate and join a company, you may find yourself writing an evaluation of two bids that are anything but hypothetical. In each of these cases, you must carefully and respectfully analyze the texts before you, and you must articulate your own position.

Here is an example of a successful essay analyzing and synthesizing two texts. This essay by Elizabeth Hurley, a student at Oregon State University, was written in response to the following assignment:

> Choose two readings included in the Optional Readings section of our syllabus that address the same general topic, and write an essay that analyzes and synthesizes these two texts. Be sure to analyze these texts carefully, paying attention to their arguments, evidence, and rhetorical situations. Recognize that your goal in writing this essay is not just to respond to the two texts but also to advance your own views on this topic.

Questions for Synthesizing Texts

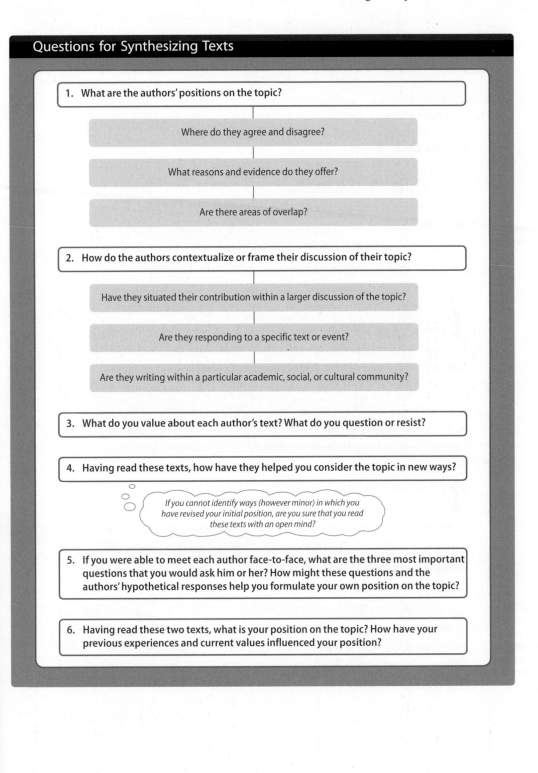

1. What are the authors' positions on the topic?

> Where do they agree and disagree?

> What reasons and evidence do they offer?

> Are there areas of overlap?

2. How do the authors contextualize or frame their discussion of their topic?

> Have they situated their contribution within a larger discussion of the topic?

> Are they responding to a specific text or event?

> Are they writing within a particular academic, social, or cultural community?

3. What do you value about each author's text? What do you question or resist?

4. Having read these texts, how have they helped you consider the topic in new ways?

> *If you cannot identify ways (however minor) in which you have revised your initial position, are you sure that you read these texts with an open mind?*

5. If you were able to meet each author face-to-face, what are the three most important questions that you would ask him or her? How might these questions and the authors' hypothetical responses help you formulate your own position on the topic?

6. Having read these two texts, what is your position on the topic? How have your previous experiences and current values influenced your position?

Hurley 1

Elizabeth Hurley
Professor Braun
WR 121
October 26, 2016

The Role of Technology in the Classroom: Two Views

As a student and a future teacher, I have spent quite a bit of time thinking about the role that technology has played in my education. In many ways, I know that I am fortunate to be a college student today. I have access to many resources — from word processing software to an almost endless number of online databases that I can consult when I'm researching a topic — that students as recently as twenty years ago could not have imagined. Thanks to course management systems like Blackboard and Canvas, I can easily submit assignments electronically, and I can even take classes (and complete entire degree programs) online. However, despite the many benefits that modern technology offers, there are potential disadvantages. One disadvantage that professors and students alike recognize is the role that devices like laptops, tablets, and smartphones can play in distracting students who should be engaged with lectures and discussions, causing some teachers to consider banning the use of such devices during class time.

As a student, I have to admit that these concerns are valid. Like many of my peers, I have been guilty of checking Facebook or texting a friend during a lecture, hoping that my instructor will assume that I am busily taking notes or looking through my backpack for a pencil. I have often felt conflicted about this, especially when I can sense how hard a professor is trying to make the material matter to me, but in the past I quickly forgot my momentary sense of guilt. Now that I have decided to major in education, I have started to think about this issue from a different perspective: that of the teacher. For these reasons, I was especially interested to read two blog posts on this topic: Clay Shirky's "Why I Just Asked My Students to

Introduces the topic of her essay

Connects the topic of her essay with her personal experience and identifies the two essays she will analyze

Hurley 2

Put Their Laptops Away" and David Croteau's "Banning Technology in Classrooms: The False Dichotomy and a Boring Call for 'All Things in Moderation.'"

Though Shirky and Croteau come from different fields of study, they are both professors who have spent a lot of time thinking and writing about the role of technology in contemporary life. A noted writer, professor of social media at New York University, and advocate for the benefits of emerging technologies, Shirky focuses his research on the way that social networks and digital communication technologies benefit our culture. He has published two well-received books on the advantages of new digital and online technologies: *Here Comes Everybody: The Power of Organizing without Organizations* and *Cognitive Surplus: Creativity and Generosity in a Connected Age.* In his post, however, Shirky narrows his focus to reflect on issues regarding technology and education that he faces as a classroom teacher. He begins by recounting changes that he has observed in his classrooms, concluding that his students have grown more distracted over the years. The culprit, he believes, is technology, and in his article, he explains why he now requires students to put their laptops, tablets, and phones away during class.

Provides background about Shirky and summarizes his position

Aware how odd this decision might seem coming from a self-described "advocate and activist for the free culture movement," Shirky states that

> I came late and reluctantly to this decision — I have been teaching classes about the internet since 1998, and I've generally had a *laissez-faire* attitude towards technology use in the classroom. This was partly because the subject of my classes made technology use feel organic, and when device use went well, it was great. . . . it's my job to be more interesting than the possible distractions, so a ban felt like cheating. And finally, there's not wanting to infantilize my students, who are adults, even if young ones — time management is their job, not mine.

Shirky's essay describes the gradual changes in his thinking about the role of devices in his classroom. He is clearly a believer in placing

Hurley 3

considerable responsibility for learning on the student, but he is also keenly aware that devices can lead to mass distraction in what he calls the "Nearby Peer Effect." Shirky ultimately argues that devices used by students in the classroom have been engineered to distract and that multitasking during a lecture can be detrimental to the learning experience. Later in his essay he adds that:

> The fact that hardware and software is being professionally designed to distract was the first thing that made me willing to require rather than merely suggest that students not use devices in class. . . . The industry has committed itself to an arms race for my students' attention, and if it's me against Facebook and Apple, I lose.

Croteau responds to Shirky in his subsequent post. As a professor at Virginia Commonwealth University; a sociologist studying the effects of media, social movements, and class; and a specialist in the VCU Office of Online Learning, he has also had extensive experience with technology in classrooms. Though he admits that Shirky has some valid points, Croteau worries that Shirky's decision, which got a lot of attention in the media, will cause instructors with similar concerns to focus on the narrow issue of whether professors should ban devices in the classroom rather than on the larger question of student engagement and learning. Croteau does not take a strong position about devices in the classroom, though he does observe that "I've never banned tech in the classroom and don't think I would in the future." But he goes on to add that he can understand why in some circumstances instructors might want to do so. His view might best be characterized as "promote engagement rather than ban distraction." He ends his piece by reinforcing the concept of "all things in moderation."

When I first read these two essays, I tried to fit them into a pro/ con framework: Shirky was against allowing students to use personal

Provides background on Croteau and summarizes his position

Hurley 4

devices in the classroom and Croteau was for it. But in rereading the articles, I realized that both authors' positions are more complicated — and closer — than I had originally thought. While Shirky spends a good deal of time explaining his decision to ban devices in the classroom, he concludes his article by noting that what is most important to him is not "a switch in rules, but a switch in how I see my role. . . . I'm coming to see student focus as a collaborative process." This comes very close to Croteau's emphasis on the importance of student learning and engagement. Croteau notes, for instance, that "stale PowerPoints and didactic lectures will likely be met with mental disengagement whether or not technology is present." In the end, both Shirky and Croteau argue that student engagement is central to effective learning.

> Discusses the evolution of her thinking and the relationship between Shirky's and Croteau's positions

As a future teacher, I am glad that I took the time to analyze Shirky's and Croteau's essays carefully. Doing so has reminded me that in the midst of constant change (the implementation of the Common Core, debates about the role of testing in education, etc.), some essentials remain. Though Croteau focuses more on the role of the instructor and Shirky emphasizes the way that technology has impacted students' concentration in the classroom, together they raised an important point for me: that both the student *and* the instructor have important roles to play in the student's education. After much deliberation, I now believe that student-teacher relationships and engaged learning remain the most important aspect of education despite all of the technological changes. And as Croteau reminds readers in the closing sentence of his article, this is hardly a new issue: "The daydream," Croteau observes, "is a timeless distraction from a dull classroom."

> Concludes by articulating what she has learned as a result of her analysis

Hurley 5

Works Cited

Croteau, David. "Banning Technology in the Classroom and a Boring Call for 'All Things in Moderation.'" *David Croteau*, 1 Oct. 2014, davidrcroteau.net/blog-post/banning-technology-in-classrooms-the-false-dichotomy-and-a-boring-call-for-all-things-in-moderation/.

Shirky, Clay. "Why I Just Asked My Students to Put Their Laptops Away." *Medium*, 8 Sept. 2014, medium.com/@cshirky/why-i-just-asked-my-students-to-put-their-laptops-away-7f5f7c50f368#.uip31nz3l.

for **thought, discussion, and writing**

1. Interview a junior or senior student majoring in your intended field of study or an area you are considering as a possible major. Ask this person the following questions, and record his or her answers:

   - What caused you to choose this area as a major?
   - What kinds of texts do students in this major typically read?
   - What analytical skills are required to succeed in this major?
   - How are these analytical skills taught and reinforced in courses in this area?
   - How do these analytical skills reflect this area's dominant methodologies?
   - What advice would you give to someone who is preparing to major in this area?

   Be prepared to report the results of this interview to the class. Your instructor may also ask you to write an essay summarizing and commenting on the results of your interview.

2. Find an editorial or opinion column that interests you in a newspaper or general news magazine, such as *The Week* or *Time*.

   - Use the Questions for Critical Reading and Analysis on pp. 121–22 to analyze the text you have chosen. If your analysis has raised questions for you as a reader, articulate them as well.
   - Use stasis theory (p. 116) to determine the most important questions at issue in this editorial or column. Write a brief summary of what these activities have helped you understand about your reading.

- Use Aristotle's three appeals (pp. 123–25) to further analyze the text you have chosen. After doing so, reread the summary you wrote earlier. What has this additional analysis helped you better understand about your reading?

Your teacher may ask you to write an essay analyzing or responding to the editorial or opinion column you have chosen.

3. In this chapter, you read Elizabeth Hurley's essay on the role of technology as discussed in two blog posts:

- Clay Shirky's "Why I Just Asked My Students to Put Their Laptops Away"
- David Croteau's "Banning Technology in the Classroom and a Boring Call for 'All Things in Moderation'"

Locate and print these posts; then use the Questions for Critical Reading and Analysis on pp. 121–22 and the Questions for Synthesizing Texts on p. 137 to analyze these two selections. Based on the insights you have gained as a result of this analysis, write an essay responding to and synthesizing Shirky's and Croteau's posts.

6

Making and Supporting Claims

As Chapter 5 emphasizes, analysis, synthesis, and argument are linked in powerful ways. To write an effective argument, you must analyze both your own ideas and those of others. But academic argument requires more than strong analytical skills. A successful academic argument also requires careful, well-supported reasoning that synthesizes or responds to ideas in sources and anticipates your readers' interests and concerns.

Understanding—and Designing—Academic Arguments

The first step in writing a successful academic argument is to understand the ways in which academic arguments are similar to and different from other kinds of arguments. Viewed from one perspective, all language use is argumentative. If you say to a friend, "You *have* to hear Adele's new album!" you're making an implicit argument that it's important (to be in the know, for sheer pleasure, or some other reason) to listen to that particular music. A sign that advertises the "Best Deep-Dish Pizza in Chicago" is also making an argumentative claim about the quality of the pizza relative to the competition. Even prayers can be viewed as arguments: Some prayers represent direct appeals to God; others function as meditations directed toward self-understanding. In either case, those who pray are engaged in an argument for change—either in themselves or in the world around them.

As these examples suggest, arguments serve many purposes beyond confrontation or debate. Sometimes the purpose is to change minds and hearts or to win a decision; this is particularly true in politics, business, and law. But winning isn't always the goal of argument—especially in the academy, where writers focus on contributing to the scholarly conversation in their fields. Given this focus, students who bring a debate model of argumentation to academic writing often encounter problems. Think about the terminology used in debate: Debaters *attack* their *adversaries*, hoping to *demolish* their *opponents'* arguments so that they can *win* the judge's approval and claim *victory* in the contest. In academic arguments, the goal is inquiry and not conquest. Your teachers aren't interested in whether you can attack or demolish your opponents. Rather, they value your ability to examine an issue or a problem from multiple perspectives. They want you to make a commitment not to "winning" but to using clear reasoning and presenting substantial evidence.

Not all scholarly arguments are identical, however. Because they reflect the aims and methods of specific disciplines, they can vary in significant ways. For example, interpretation—whether of literary texts, artwork, or historical data—is central to arguments in the humanities. Scholars in the social sciences often argue about issues of policy; they also undertake studies that attempt to help readers better understand—and respond to—current issues and events. For instance, a sociologist might review and evaluate recent research on the effects of children's gender on parents' child-rearing practices and then present conclusions based on her own quantitative or qualitative study. Argument is also central to research in the natural and applied sciences: Engineers who argue about how best to design and build trusses for a bridge or chemists who present new information about a particular chemical reaction are making claims that they must support with evidence and reasons.

Although scholarly arguments reflect disciplinary concerns, all scholars agree that the best arguments share the following traits:

1. They explore relevant ideas as fully as possible and from as many perspectives as possible.

2. They present their claims logically.

3. They include appropriate support for all significant claims.

These preferences distinguish academic arguments from other kinds of arguments. You and your friend might spend an hour on a Saturday night arguing about the merits of Adele's new album, but your discussion would undoubtedly be fluid and improvisational, with many digressions. In academic argument, great value is placed on the careful, consistent, and logical exploration of ideas.

In a way, what is true of design is also true of academic arguments. (See the discussion of writing as design in Chapter 1.) Most academic arguments are open-ended and cannot be solved once and for all. Philosophers have been arguing for centuries, for instance, about whether it is possible to justify warfare, just as historians continue to argue about the significance and consequences of specific wars. In this sense, those writing academic essays are participating in an ongoing scholarly conversation.

The process of identifying problems is central to writers of academic arguments, just as it is for designers. A literary scholar who believes that other critics of Toni Morrison's *Beloved* have failed to recognize the importance of religious imagery in that novel is describing a problem. Since literary texts—like other complex data sets—are open to multiple interpretations, this critic's argument—her response to the problem—will depend in part on subjective value judgments. The same occurs when a historian argues that previous accounts of the fall of Saigon near the end of the Vietnam War over-emphasize the Western media's role in this event.

Perhaps most important is that those composing academic arguments are, like designers, concerned with what might, could, and should be. A biologist proposing a new method for protecting wetlands, a sociologist reporting the results of a new study on children in foster care, and a historian reconsidering previous studies of the spread of the Black Death in medieval Europe are all composing writing that *matters*: writing that addresses complex problems, expands the scholarly conversation, and makes a difference.

Exploring Aristotle's Three Appeals

Academic writing places a high premium on logical appeals, or the quality of ideas, evidence, and organization—*logos*. This doesn't mean, however, that as a writer you should avoid emotional appeals (*pathos*) and ethical appeals (*ethos*).

All writers—whether they're composing a letter to a friend, an editorial for the student newspaper, or an essay for a history class—need to establish their ethos, or credibility. Academic writers generally do so by demonstrating knowledge of their subject and of the methodologies that others in their field use to explore it. They reinforce their credibility when they explore their subject evenhandedly and show respect for their readers. Writers demonstrate this respect, for instance, when they anticipate readers' concerns and address possible counterarguments. In these and other ways, academic writers demonstrate *rhetorical sensitivity*.✱

Just as all writers appeal to ethos, so too do they appeal to pathos—to emotions and shared values. Sometimes this type of appeal is obvious, as in requests for charitable contributions that feature heart-wrenching stories and images. Even texts that are relatively objective and that emphasize appeals to logos, as much academic writing does, nevertheless draw on and convey emotional appeals. An academic argument that uses formal diction and presents good reasons and evidence is sending readers a message based on pathos: "This subject is much too important for me to treat it frivolously. It requires the attention that only reasoned argument can give."

In academic writing, appeals to pathos can also emphasize just how much is at stake in understanding and addressing a problem or an event. Scholars writing about the Holocaust, for instance, often use vivid descriptions to encourage readers to connect personally with their texts. Moreover, to bring immediacy and impact to an argument, writers often employ figurative language, such as

✱   **For more on analyzing rhetorical situations and on Aristotle's three appeals, see Chapter 3.**

metaphors, similes, and analogies. (For example, some scholars who have written about the massacre that occurred when Nanking, China, fell to the Japanese on December 13, 1937, refer to this event as the Rape of Nanking.) They also may use images and graphics to lend visceral impact to their point.

Understanding the Role of Values and Beliefs in Argument

When you write an academic argument, you give reasons and evidence for your assertions. A student arguing against a Forest Service plan for a national forest might warn that increased timber harvesting will reduce access to the forest for campers and backpackers or that building more roads will adversely affect wildlife. This writer might also show that the Forest Service has failed to anticipate some problems with the plan and that cost-benefit calculations unfairly reflect logging and economic-development interests. These are all potentially good reasons for questioning the plan. Notice that these reasons necessarily imply certain values or beliefs. The argument against increasing the timber harvest and building more roads, for instance, reflects the belief that preserving wildlife habitats and wilderness lands is more important than the economic development of the resources.

Is this argument flawed because it appeals to values and beliefs? Of course it isn't. When you argue, you can't suppress your own values and beliefs. After all, they provide links between yourself and the world you observe and experience.

Suppose that you and a friend are getting ready to go out for breakfast. You look out the window and notice some threatening clouds. You say, "It looks like rain. We'd better take umbrellas since we're walking. I hate getting soaked." "Oh, I don't know," your friend replies. "I don't think it looks so bad. I heard on the radio that it wasn't going to start raining until the afternoon. I think we're OK." Brief and informal as this exchange is, it constitutes an argument. Both you and your friend have observed something, analyzed it, and drawn conclusions—conclusions backed by reasons. Although you each cite different reasons, your conclusions reflect your different personal preferences. You're generally cautious, and you don't like getting caught unprepared in a downpour, so you opt for an umbrella. Your friend relies on expert opinion and might be more of a risk taker.

If your individual preferences, values, and beliefs shape a situation like this one, where only getting wet is at stake, imagine how crucial they are in more complicated situations, such as determining whether a controversial government proposal is right or wrong, just or unjust, effective or ineffective. Argument necessarily involves values and beliefs, held by both writer and reader, that cannot be denied or excluded—even in academic argument, with its emphasis on evidence and reasoned inquiry. The student arguing against the Forest Service plan can't avoid using values and beliefs as bridges between reasons and conclusions. And not all these bridges can be explicitly stated; that would lead to an endless chain of reasons. The standards of academic argument require, however, that writers explicitly state and defend the most important values and beliefs undergirding their argument. In this case, then, the student opposing the Forest Service plan should at some point state and support his belief that preserving wildlife habitats and wilderness lands should take priority over economic development.

It's not easy to identify and analyze your own values and beliefs, but doing so is essential in academic argument. Values and beliefs are often held unconsciously and function as part of a larger network of assumptions and practices. Your opinions about the best way for the government to respond to the unemployed reflect your values and beliefs about family, the proper role of government, the nature of individual responsibility, and the importance of economic security. Thus if a political science instructor asks you to argue for or against programs requiring welfare recipients to work at state-mandated jobs in exchange for economic support, you need to analyze not just these **thinking** workfare programs but also the role your values and beliefs play in your **rhetorically** analysis. The guidelines on p. 149 will help you do so, thus enabling you to respond more effectively to the demands of academic argument.

At the same time, when you argue, you must consider not only your own values and beliefs but also those of your readers. The student writing about the Forest Service plan would present one argument to a local branch of the Sierra Club (an organization that advocates for protecting the environment) and a very different argument to representatives of the Forest Service. The student would expect members of the Sierra Club to agree with his major assumptions and therefore might focus on how the group could best oppose the plan and why members should devote time and energy to this project.

His argument to the Forest Service would be designed quite differently. Recognizing that members of the Forest Service would know the plan very well, would have spent a great deal of time working on it, and would likely be strongly committed to it, the student might focus on a limited number of points, especially those that the Forest Service might be willing to modify. The student would be wise to assume a tone that isn't aggressive or strident to avoid alienating his audience. He would articulate his most important assumptions and align them whenever possible with the beliefs and values of those who work for the Forest Service.

In the case of the arguments you'll write as an undergraduate, of course, your reader is generally your instructor. In this rhetorical situation, the most useful approach is to consider values and beliefs that your instructor holds as a member of the academic community. In writing for an economics or a political science instructor, the student arguing against the Forest Service plan should provide logical, accurate, and appropriate evidence. He should avoid strong emotional appeals and expressions of outrage or bitterness, focusing instead on developing a succinct, clearly organized, carefully reasoned essay.

Guidelines for Analyzing Your Own Values and Beliefs

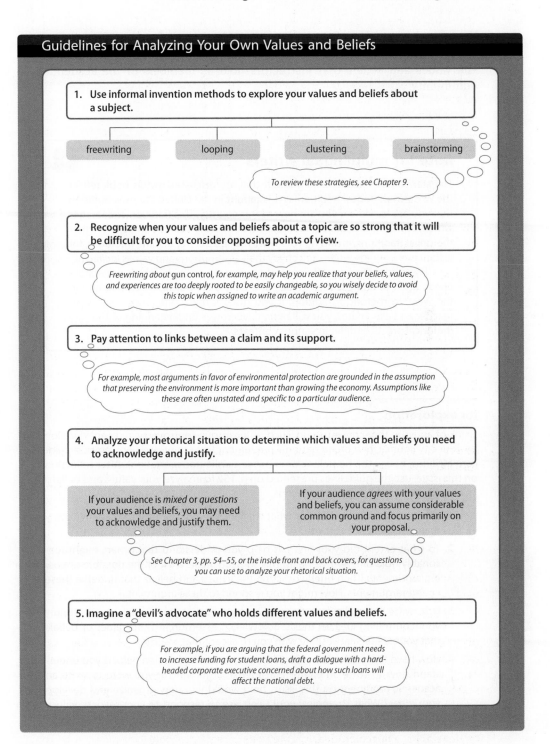

1. **Use informal invention methods to explore your values and beliefs about a subject.**

   freewriting   looping   clustering   brainstorming

   To review these strategies, see Chapter 9.

2. **Recognize when your values and beliefs about a topic are so strong that it will be difficult for you to consider opposing points of view.**

   Freewriting about gun control, for example, may help you realize that your beliefs, values, and experiences are too deeply rooted to be easily changeable, so you wisely decide to avoid this topic when assigned to write an academic argument.

3. **Pay attention to links between a claim and its support.**

   For example, most arguments in favor of environmental protection are grounded in the assumption that preserving the environment is more important than growing the economy. Assumptions like these are often unstated and specific to a particular audience.

4. **Analyze your rhetorical situation to determine which values and beliefs you need to acknowledge and justify.**

   If your audience is *mixed* or *questions* your values and beliefs, you may need to acknowledge and justify them.

   If your audience *agrees* with your values and beliefs, you can assume considerable common ground and focus primarily on your proposal.

   See Chapter 3, pp. 54–55, or the inside front and back covers, for questions you can use to analyze your rhetorical situation.

5. **Imagine a "devil's advocate" who holds different values and beliefs.**

   For example, if you are arguing that the federal government needs to increase funding for student loans, draft a dialogue with a hard-headed corporate executive concerned about how such loans will affect the national debt.

The essays by Hope Leman (pp. 109–10) and Stevon Roberts (pp. 129–34) that appear in Chapter 5 are excellent examples of arguments that respect the values and beliefs that instructors hold as members of the academic community.

---

note for multilingual writers

The standards of academic argument that are discussed in this book reflect the Western rhetorical tradition as it is taught in the United States, a tradition that you are learning if you are new to this country. This tradition encourages writers to clearly articulate and directly defend their values and beliefs. Other rhetorical traditions, including your own, may be different. Some traditions, for instance, encourage writers to convey their assumptions and values *indirectly*.

Try to identify any differences between the ways in which writers are encouraged to address their values and beliefs in your home culture and in the Western rhetorical tradition. If you discuss these differences with your teacher and classmates, you will enrich everyone's understanding of the way rhetorical practices differ in various contexts.

---

for **exploration**

Think of an issue that concerns you, such as a campus controversy, a recent decision by your city council, or a broad national movement (e.g., to provide on-campus child-care facilities, house the homeless, or improve public transportation). After reflecting on this issue, use the guidelines presented on p. 152 to analyze your values and beliefs. Then respond to the following questions.

1. Given your values and beliefs, what challenges would writing an academic essay on this subject pose for you?

2. To what extent did your analysis help you understand that others might reasonably hold different views on this subject? Make a list of the possible opposing arguments. Then briefly describe the values and beliefs that underlie these counterarguments. How might you respond to these arguments?

3. Now write the major assertions or arguments that you would use to support your controlling idea, or thesis. Below each assertion, list the values or beliefs that your readers must share with you to accept that assertion.

4. How have the guidelines on p. 152 and this For Exploration helped you understand how to write an effective academic argument? If you were to write an academic argument on this issue, how would you now organize and develop your ideas? What strategies would you use to respond to your readers' values and beliefs?

Mastering the Essential Moves in Academic Writing

Appeals to ethos and pathos play important roles in academic argument. For an academic argument to be effective, however, it must be firmly grounded in logos. The remainder of this chapter presents strategies that you can follow to meet the demands of academic writing. These strategies will help you to do the following:

1. Determine whether a claim can be argued
2. Develop a working thesis (an appropriately limited claim)
3. Provide good reasons and sound evidence for your argument
4. Acknowledge possible counterarguments
5. Frame your argument as part of the scholarly conversation
6. Consider whether visuals or other media would strengthen your argument

DETERMINING WHETHER A CLAIM CAN BE ARGUED

You can't argue by yourself. If you disagree with a decision to increase school activity fees, you may mumble angry words to yourself, but you'd know that you're not arguing. To argue, you must argue *with* someone. Furthermore, the person must agree with you that an assertion raises an arguable issue. If you like hip-hop music, for example, and your friend, who prefers jazz, refuses to listen to (much less discuss) hip-hop, you can hardly argue about her preferences. You'll both probably just wonder at the peculiarities of taste.

Similarly, in academic argument you and your reader (most often your instructor) must agree that an issue is worth arguing about if you're to argue successfully. Often this agreement involves sharing a common understanding of a problem, a process, or an idea. A student who writes an argument on the symbolism of Hester Prynne's scarlet A in *The Scarlet Letter*, for example, begins from a premise that she believes the teacher will share: that Hester's A has significance for the impact and significance of the novel.

The guidelines on p. 152 can help you compose an effective and arguable claim.

DEVELOPING A WORKING THESIS

Arguable claims must meet an additional criterion: They must be sufficiently limited so that both writer and reader can determine the major issues at stake and the lines of argument that best address them. In a late-night discussion with friends, you may easily slip from a heated exchange over the causes of the current unrest in world affairs to a friendly debate about whether Steph Curry or LeBron James is the better basketball player.

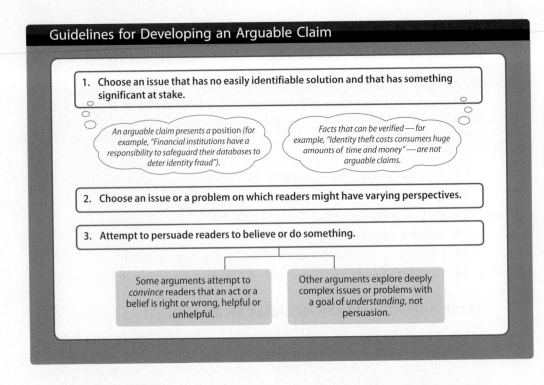

Guidelines for Developing an Arguable Claim

1. Choose an issue that has no easily identifiable solution and that has something significant at stake.

An arguable claim presents a position (for example, "Financial institutions have a responsibility to safeguard their databases to deter identity fraud").

Facts that can be verified — for example, "Identity theft costs consumers huge amounts of time and money" — are not arguable claims.

2. Choose an issue or a problem on which readers might have varying perspectives.

3. Attempt to persuade readers to believe or do something.

Some arguments attempt to convince readers that an act or a belief is right or wrong, helpful or unhelpful.

Other arguments explore deeply complex issues or problems with a goal of understanding, not persuasion.

In an academic argument, however, you must limit the discussion not just to a single issue but to a single thesis, a claim you will argue for. It's not enough, in other words, to decide that you want to write about nuclear energy or the need to protect the wilderness. Even limiting these subjects—writing about the Fukushima nuclear disaster in 2011 or the Forest Service's Land Management Plan for the White Mountain National Forest—wouldn't help much. That's because your thesis must be an *assertion*. In other words, it must be something to argue about.

An appropriately limited thesis makes it clear (for you and for your reader) what's at stake in your argument. For this reason, many instructors and writers suggest that academic arguments should contain an explicit thesis statement—a single declarative sentence that asserts or denies something about the topic. The assertion "The U.S. Forest Service's Land Management Plan for the White Mountain National Forest fails to protect New Hampshire's wilderness areas adequately" is an example of an arguable thesis statement.

Developing a clear, limited thesis statement can help you as a writer stay on track and include evidence or details relevant to the main point rather than extraneous or loosely related information. Readers—especially busy readers like your college instructors—also find thesis statements helpful. A clearly worded thesis statement helps instructors read your writing more efficiently and critically.

Here is the first paragraph of an essay written for a class on Latin American history. The thesis statement is highlighted. Notice how it clearly articulates the student's position on the topic, the role of multinational and transnational corporations in Central America.

> Over the past fifty years, Latin American countries have worked hard to gain economic strength and well-being. To survive, however, these countries have been forced to rely on multinational and transnational corporations for money, jobs, and technological expertise. In doing so, they have lost needed economic independence and have left themselves vulnerable to exploitation by foreign financiers.

A clear thesis statement can help both writer and reader stay on track as they "compose" or read an essay.

Often, thesis statements appear early in an essay. In her analysis of the "mirror" and "flashlight" models of the role of journalists in American society that appears in Chapter 5, Hope Leman articulates an explicit thesis statement at the beginning of the second paragraph of her essay: "In this essay, I will argue that the 'flashlight' model provides a more accurate and complex understanding of the role of journalists in America than the 'mirror' model does" (p. 109).

Stevon Roberts takes a different tack in his analysis of an excerpt from Etzioni's *The Limits of Privacy* in that same chapter. Stevon begins his essay by commenting on Etzioni's strong credibility as a writer and follows this by summarizing Etzioni's argument. Rather than introducing a thesis statement, Stevon concludes his second paragraph by raising the question that motivates and guides his analysis: "Is Etzioni justified in making his unconventional claims despite . . . [the] well-founded opposition" of civil libertarians and others concerned with privacy issues (p. 129)? As will be discussed more fully later in this chapter, Stevon spends the bulk of his essay carefully analyzing Etzioni's text, reserving final judgment until his concluding sentence, where he summarizes his analysis by arguing that ultimately the excerpt from Etzioni's text "leaves opponents (and critical readers) unsatisfied" (p. 134).

All three approaches represent thoughtful and effective responses to the writers' specific assignments. Hope Leman's assignment required her to take a position on her topic, so it made sense for her to present her thesis statement early on. (Hope was also writing under time pressure since she was completing a take-home midterm.) Stevon Roberts's assignment was more general: to respond to and evaluate the excerpt from Etzioni's book. It thus made equally good sense for him to defer his final judgment until he completed this analysis and demonstrated his ability to engage Etzioni's ideas via his own critique.

Sometimes you may develop a working thesis early in your writing process. This is especially likely if your assignment requires you to take a stand and specifies the options available to you, as Hope Leman's assignment did. At times, however, you may have to think—and write—your way to a thesis. In situations like this, you'll develop your thesis and gather evidence recursively as you deepen your understanding of your topic and your rhetorical situation. This chapter concludes with a case study of one student writer, Daniel Stiepleman, whose argument evolved in this way. Reading Daniel's prewriting and drafts will help you better understand how to work through the process of making and supporting claims in academic arguments. Often you will discover, as Daniel did, that you need to explore your ideas at considerable length before determining your thesis.

PROVIDING GOOD REASONS AND SUPPORTING THEM WITH EVIDENCE

To support a claim in a way that readers will find truly persuasive, you'll need to provide good reasons. Chapter 5 discusses two tools for analyzing and evaluating arguments: stasis theory (p. 116) and Aristotle's three appeals (pp. 123–25). You can use the same analytical tools to construct and revise your own arguments.

Let's say that you've drafted an argument challenging increased standardized testing in public schools. You're majoring in education, and you have strong feelings about federally mandated assessments. Your draft explores your ideas as freely and fully as possible. Now it's two days later—time to step back and evaluate the draft's effectiveness. So you turn to Aristotle's three appeals.

thinking rhetorically

As you reread your draft with the appeals of ethos, pathos, and logos in mind, you realize that you've gathered a lot of evidence about the limitations of standardized testing and thus made good use of appeals to logos. Your argument is much less successful in employing the appeals of ethos and pathos, however. Your rereading has helped you realize that the passion you bring to this subject caused you to write in a strident tone, which might make readers distrust your credibility and sense of fairness. You also haven't considered the advantages of standardized testing or the reasons that some people find it helpful and even necessary. Critical readers might well suspect that you've stacked the deck against standardized testing.

Clearly, you need to strengthen your argument's appeal to ethos. You revise your tone so that it's more evenhanded; you also consider multiple points of view by presenting and evaluating possible counterarguments. Perhaps in the process you'll discover some shared values and beliefs that can strengthen your argument. (You could acknowledge your opponents, for instance, for recognizing the importance of education as a national, and not just a local, concern.) You'll want to find as many ways as possible to demonstrate that you realize your subject is complex and that reasonable people might have different ideas on the best way to address it.

What about pathos? In rereading your essay, you realize that in gathering strong evidence to support your claim, you've failed to give your subject a human face. You've got plenty of statistics and expert testimony but little that demonstrates how standardized testing affects real students and teachers. Based on your own experiences and those of peers, you have good examples of how standardized testing can have a negative impact, so you write yourself a reminder to include at least one such example in your revised draft. You also look for other ways to remind readers that national debates over standardized assessment aren't about impersonal test scores but about the real-life learning and teaching experiences of students and teachers across the United States.

As this example suggests, such analytical tools as Aristotle's three appeals can play a key role in the construction of arguments. You may not use these tools to write the first draft of your argument, but once you have a rough draft you can use them to test your ideas and identify problems that need to be addressed and areas that need to be strengthened. The student who's arguing that increases in standardized testing threaten the quality of students' education, for instance, might find it helpful to identify the most important questions at issue in her argument. Are they questions of fact? definition? interpretation? value? consequence? policy?

In addition to using analytical tools, you can ask commonsense questions about the evidence that you include to support your claims. (See Questions for Evaluating Evidence, p. 156.)

---

for **exploration**

Think again about the issue you analyzed in response to the For Exploration on p. 150. Formulate a tentative, or working, thesis statement that reflects your current position on this issue. Articulate two or three reasons or claims that support your thesis, and then list the major evidence you would use to support these claims. Finally, write a brief statement explaining why this evidence is appropriate, given your thesis statement, the reasons or claims that you have written, and your intended audience.

ACKNOWLEDGING POSSIBLE COUNTERARGUMENTS

Since academic argument is modeled on inquiry and dialogue rather than debate, as a writer you must consider multiple sides of an issue. Responding to counterarguments demonstrates that you've seriously analyzed an issue from a number of perspectives rather than simply marshalled evidence to support your predetermined position.

Questions for Evaluating Evidence

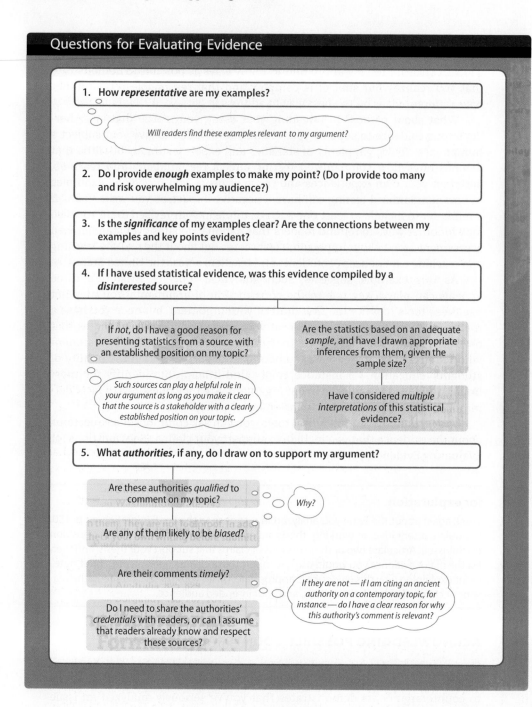

1. How *representative* are my examples?

   Will readers find these examples relevant to my argument?

2. Do I provide *enough* examples to make my point? (Do I provide too many and risk overwhelming my audience?)

3. Is the *significance* of my examples clear? Are the connections between my examples and key points evident?

4. If I have used statistical evidence, was this evidence compiled by a *disinterested* source?

   If *not*, do I have a good reason for presenting statistics from a source with an established position on my topic?

   Such sources can play a helpful role in your argument as long as you make it clear that the source is a stakeholder with a clearly established position on your topic.

   Are the statistics based on an adequate *sample*, and have I drawn appropriate inferences from them, given the sample size?

   Have I considered *multiple interpretations* of this statistical evidence?

5. What *authorities*, if any, do I draw on to support my argument?

   Are these authorities *qualified* to comment on my topic?

   Why?

   Are any of them likely to be *biased*?

   Are their comments *timely*?

   If they are not — if I am citing an ancient authority on a contemporary topic, for instance — do I have a clear reason for why this authority's comment is relevant?

   Do I need to share the authorities' *credentials* with readers, or can I assume that readers already know and respect these sources?

There are a number of ways to discover counterarguments. You could imagine dialogues with one or more "devil's advocates," or you could discuss your subject with a group of classmates. You might even interview someone who holds a different position. Being aware of your own values and beliefs can also help you identify counterarguments. The student arguing against the Forest Service plan might consider the views of someone with different values, perhaps a person who believes in the importance of economic development, such as the owner of a lumber company or individuals living in towns supported by the timber industry. Finally, reading and research can expose you to the ideas and arguments of others.

How you use counterarguments will depend on your subject and rhetorical situation. In some instances, counterarguments can play an important structural role in your essay. After introducing your topic and indicating your thesis, for example, you might present the major counterarguments to your position, addressing each in turn. You might also group the counterarguments, responding to them all at once or throughout your essay.

In his essay in Chapter 5 (pp. 129–34), which is organized around a point-by-point analysis of Amitai Etzioni's text, Stevon Roberts acknowledges counterarguments to many of the issues raised in his analysis. He is careful from the beginning to affirm the strong credibility that Etzioni, a former senior adviser to the White House, brings to his subject. He takes care, as well, to identify those elements of Etzioni's argument with which he is in agreement. On p. 130, for instance, Stevon comments that Etzioni's position on prenatal HIV testing represents "a well-documented and compelling argument." Although Stevon is critical of Etzioni's discussion of biometrics, he acknowledges that "to his credit, Etzioni is quick to follow up the drawbacks of biometrics with compelling statistics about the potential benefits" (p. 131). In these and other ways, Stevon makes it clear that rather than simply looking for reasons to disagree with Etzioni he is working hard to engage his ideas seriously and respectfully. The effect is to strengthen the presentation of his own position.

---

for **collaboration**

This activity will help you recognize possible counterarguments to the thesis that you have been developing in this chapter. To prepare, be sure that you have a clear, easy-to-read statement of your working thesis and of the major evidence you would use to support it. Now spend five to ten minutes brainstorming a list of possible counterarguments.

Bring these written materials to your group's meeting. Determine how much time the group can spend per person if each student is to get help. Appoint a timekeeper. Then have each writer read his or her working thesis, evidence, and possible counterarguments. Members of the group should then suggest additional counterarguments that the writer has not considered. As you proceed, avoid getting bogged down in specific arguments; instead, focus on generating as many additional counterarguments as possible. Continue this procedure until your group has discussed each student's work.

FRAMING YOUR ARGUMENT AS PART OF THE SCHOLARLY CONVERSATION

The previous discussion has emphasized the basic elements you need to understand in order to compose an effective academic argument. Whatever your topic or discipline, to argue effectively you need to do the following:

- Understand the role of values and beliefs in argument
- Determine whether a claim can be argued
- Develop a working thesis
- Provide good reasons and supporting evidence
- Acknowledge possible counterarguments

This section will discuss additional essential rhetorical "moves" that successful academic writers regularly employ—moves that signal to readers that the writers are familiar with the scholarly conversation of which their essays are a part.

In one way or another, for instance, most academic writers must find a meaningful way to *enter the conversation* that grounds or motivates their topic. In her essay in Chapter 5, for instance, Hope Leman begins her discussion by contrasting the "mirror" and the "flashlight" models of media theory, making it clear that her essay will represent her own take on this ongoing controversy. In her essay synthesizing the views and positions of Clay Shirky and David Croteau on the role of technology in the classroom, also in Chapter 5, Elizabeth Hurley uses the opportunity to engage essays by these authors to remind herself "that student-teacher relationships and engaged learning remain the most important aspect of education despite all of the technological changes" (p. 141).

Fostering the ability of students to enter into and contribute to the academic conversation is a major goal of this book. Chapter 5 and this chapter provide essential information on such topics as analysis, synthesis, and making and supporting claims. Daniel Stiepleman's essay, at the end of this chapter, provides a detailed example of how one student moved from an initial mixed response to a public service announcement (PSA) on literacy to a final position on this topic, one that required him to do a careful, in-depth reading of both the text and the visual design of that PSA. The material in Chapter 7, "Doing Research: Joining the Scholarly Conversation," will also help you master such strategies as summarizing, quoting, and interpreting sources that are integral to the scholarly exchange on your topic.

Although you may not realize it, you already have considerable experience with the kind of rhetorical strategies, or "moves," that play a key role in academic arguments. Imagine that you and a group of friends are trying to decide where to go out to eat one night. One friend explains that since she had pizza for lunch she doesn't want that for dinner. Another suggests the new Ethiopian restaurant in town, which she tried a few weeks ago. The others aren't sure they're feeling that adventurous, so the friend who wants to go to the Ethiopian restaurant uses her phone to check some online reviews of the restaurant and reads selected observations to the group, commenting as she reads. Other friends respond, raising issues about the cost, the atmosphere, and the spiciness of the food. In so doing, they add their own perspectives to the conversation. Finally the group agrees to try the restaurant.

You've had countless conversations like this. What you may not have realized is that in these conversations you are enacting some of the fundamental rhetorical moves of academic writing:

- Explaining
- Synthesizing
- Responding

In the previous example, for instance, the first friend *explained* why she didn't want pizza for dinner. The friend arguing for the Ethiopian restaurant went online, found reviews of the restaurant, and *synthesized* those evaluations of it. The rest of the group *responded* by raising additional issues and, finally, agreeing to give the restaurant a try.

Of course, in academic argument these moves can be a bit more complicated. A student who is *explaining* the ins and outs of a topic or an argument may do so by summarizing her own ideas or those of others by paraphrasing or quoting. In academic writing, the process of *synthesizing* most often involves identifying connections and contradictions within a text or group of texts that you have analyzed. And *responding* can take a wide variety of forms—from agreeing or disagreeing to granting part of an argument or a position but resisting another part and so forth. In academic argument and analysis, writers rely on these moves to locate themselves in the scholarly conversation to which they wish to contribute.

Chapter 3 includes an essay by Alia Sands titled "A Separate Education" (pp. 58–61). In the excerpts below, notice how the highlighted words call attention to the moves Alia makes as she articulates her response to Richard Rodriguez's chapter "Aria," from *Hunger of Memory: The Education of Richard Rodriguez*.

> While some argue that students benefit from learning in their native languages, others, like writer Richard Rodriguez, argue that bilingual education deprives students of a shared public identity, which is critical to their full participation in civic life. (par. 1)

Explains two major positions on bilingual education she will address

> Unfortunately, our instructor did not speak Spanish and assumed that none of us spoke English. In fact, more than three-fourths of the students in the class were bilingual, and those who weren't bilingual only spoke English. (par. 5)

Responds to incorrect assumption her teacher made about students in her class and provides correct information

Distinguishes her
experience from
Rodriguez's and thus
responds to his argument

      Unlike Rodriguez, before that class I had always had a sense of myself as part of the public community. (par. 12)

Synthesizes her
experience and
Rodriguez's

    As my experience and Rodriguez's demonstrate, schools play an active role in shaping students' sense of themselves as individuals. (par. 13)

Those engaged in scholarly conversation recognize that the ability to summarize the views of others accurately and fairly is an essential skill. In the following excerpt from Stevon Roberts's essay "The Price of Public Safety" (pp. 129–34), Stevon demonstrates this ability. Notice how the highlighted words and phrases call attention to the logic and organization of his summary.

Etzioni opens his argument by discussing recent HIV testing procedures in hospitals that may infringe on the rights of pregnant women. He then shifts gears and takes a brief look at public outrage from the Coalition for Constitutional Liberties regarding driver's license availability. Next, he gives us a crash course in "biometrics," a controversial new technology that could save billions of dollars lost to fraud every year. Finally, Etzioni addresses our fears (and those of other civil libertarians) that these and other procedures that are designed to increase our public health and safety will not be implemented justly and ethically. Etzioni admits, however, that a growing number of people and interest groups are not convinced that old laws—such as the Fourth Amendment, which protects the United States from becoming a military state—can protect us from new technology. We are left to wonder: Is Etzioni justified in making his unconventional claims despite such well-founded opposition?

Stevon's careful and respectful summary leads clearly to the major question he addresses in his analysis of Etzioni's argument and plays a central role in his effort to engage the scholarly conversation on public safety.

A final essential move in academic writing involves *showing what's at stake in your argument*—explaining why the issue you are discussing is important and why readers should care about it. In her essay on the "mirror" and the "flashlight" models of the role of journalists in Chapter 5, for instance, Hope Leman closes her essay by emphasizing that the power of the media makes it important for readers to have the richest possible understanding of the kinds of choices journalists make.

Whereas Hope makes this move at the end of her essay, Stevon Roberts emphasizes the significance of his argument early in his essay, when he comments that the events of September 11, 2001, "give an increased sense of urgency to Etzioni's message and consequently might make Americans more receptive to protocols that afford protection from public risks in general" (p. 129). Given this situation, this statement by Stevon suggests, it is all the more important to analyze clearly and carefully Etzioni's proposals to curtail protections of personal privacy.

This chapter began by discussing the model of argument that informs academic writing and emphasized that this model is based much more on inquiry than on debate: Rather than defeating opponents, the goal of academic argument is to enter the many rich scholarly conversations that occur in all the disciplines. The "moves" described thus far can help you enter these conversations in productive and rewarding ways.

---

for **exploration**

In this section, you read an excerpt from Stevon Roberts's essay "The Price of Public Safety" to see how he uses transitions and other sentence-level strategies to write an effective summary. Reread his entire essay (pp. 129–34) with an eye toward identifying other rhetorical "moves" discussed in this section of this chapter. Identify at least three moves that enable Stevon to participate effectively in the scholarly conversation on his topic. Be prepared to share what you have learned with your classmates.

USING MEDIA TO STRENGTHEN YOUR ARGUMENT

Images, sound, and graphics play an increasingly important role in communication today. Everywhere we turn—when we walk down the street, listen to a podcast, watch television, or surf the web—images, sound, and graphics compete for our attention (and, often, for our money: think of the power of such logos as Target's red-and-white bull's-eye or audio jingles such as State Farm Insurance Company's "Like a good neighbor, State Farm is there"). Most news media rely heavily on photographs, audio clips, video clips, interactive graphics, and so forth to heighten the impact of their stories.

The use of digital and oral media and visually rich print texts is not limited to professionals, though: Thanks to user-friendly software, we can all create texts that mix words, images, sound, and graphics. But what role should such texts play in the academic writing you do as a student? Because academic argument typically emphasizes logos over ethos and pathos, rhetorical common sense suggests that you should use digital and audio media and visually enriched alphabetic texts when they strengthen the substance of your argument. Tables, charts, graphs, maps, and photographs can usefully present factual information that appeals to logos and helps the writer build credibility as well.

In writing about the fragmentation of bobcat habitats in the Pocono Mountains of Pennsylvania, for example, biology student Suzanne Chouljian used a number of images and graphics to good effect. In her research proposal, Suzanne hypothesized that urbanization and barriers such as highways have cut off dispersal across urban areas, causing inbreeding among bobcat populations in her area. To help readers visualize her area of study, Suzanne included three maps: the first of the Pocono Mountains; the second of the area around the Tobyhanna and Gouldsboro State Parks, where the study was to take place; and the third of two state-designated Important Mammal Areas (or IMAs) in the study area.

Suzanne also included a table identifying the chromosomal characteristics of domestic cats, Canadian lynx, and local bobcat populations to show the ten characteristics she would be studying in the genomes of local bobcat populations. Through use of these visual elements, Suzanne strengthened her thesis proposal. The guidelines on p. 165 will help you make the most effective use of images and graphics in your academic writing.✳

✳ For more about multimodal composing, see Chapter 11.

Chouljian 8

Research Design and Methods

Study Site

Bobcats will be sampled from an area within Monroe County, located in the Pocono Mountains (Fig.1). The primary study area is approximately 832 km² and is surrounded by a 16.5 km buffer zone, producing a total area of roughly 3,900 km². The entire study site is bordered by heavily populated cities including Wilkes-Barre, Scranton, Pittston, Hazleton, Effort, Stroudsburg, and Tannersville, along with numerous smaller cities. Major roads and highways (I-380, I-80, I-84, routes 115 and 209) bisect the area.

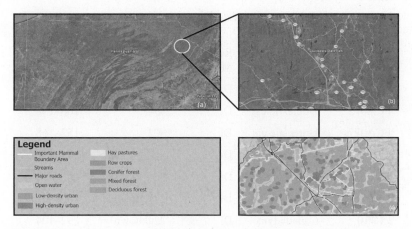

Figure 1. (a) The Pocono Mountains region of Pennsylvania. (b) Area near Tobyhanna and Gouldsboro State Parks, bisected by highways and major roads (I-380, I-80, I-84, routes 115 and 209, etc.) and surrounded by large cities (Wilkes-Barre, Scranton, and Stroudsburg). (c) Most of IMA 36 and a small part of IMA 35, and illustrating the types of land cover across the study site. Source: (a, b) Google Maps, (c) Pennsylvania Game Commission's website (http://www.portal.state.pa.us/portal/server.pt?open =514&objID=814362&mode=2).

Chouljian 15

DNA Analyses

Nuclear DNA will be extracted from hair and tissue samples using the DNeasy purification kit (Qiagen Inc.). Hair samples with at least five follicles are ideal for DNA extraction and will be utilized as often as possible, though Mills et al. (2000) describe successful extraction from samples with at least one hair follicle. Ten primers (Table 1) designed for microsatellite loci in the genomes of the domestic cat, the Canada lynx, and the bobcat will be used in polymerase chain reactions (PCR) to amplify microsatellite loci for each sample (Croteau et al. 2012; Reding et al. 2013).

[a]Table 1

Characteristics of domestic cat, Canada lynx, and bobcat microsatellites

Locus	Species	Repeat Motif	[e]Chromosome	Size range (bp)
[b]FCA023	Domestic cat	Di	B1	151–163
[b]FCA045	Domestic cat	Di	D4	166–178
[b]FCA077	Domestic cat	Di	C2	152–168
[b]FCA090	Domestic cat	Di	A1	117–129
[b]FCA096	Domestic cat	Di	E2	191–219
[c]LC109	Canada lynx	Di	Unknown	182–202
[c]LC110	Canada lynx	Di	Unknown	92–104
[c]LC111	Canada lynx	Di	Unknown	157–217
[d]BCE5T	Bobcat	Tetra	Unknown	257–318

[a]As reported in Reding et al. (2013)

[b]Reding et al. (2013); taken from Menotti-Raymond et al. (1999)

[c]Reding et al. (2013); taken from Carmichael et al. (2000)

[d]Reding et al. (2013); taken from Faircloth et al. (2005)

Student Essay Using a Table as Evidence

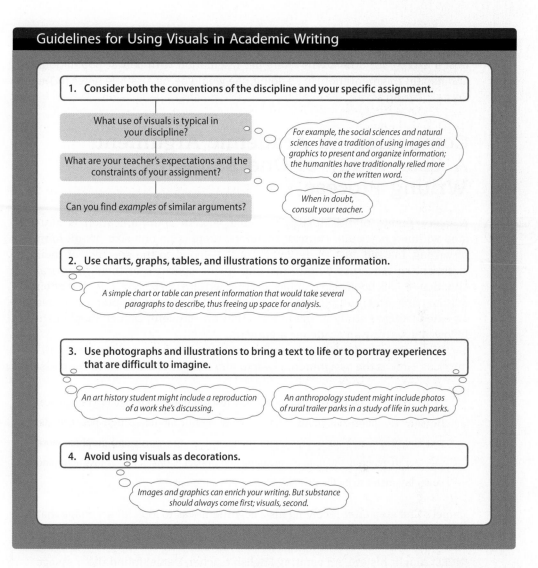

Guidelines for Using Visuals in Academic Writing

1. **Consider both the conventions of the discipline and your specific assignment.**

What use of visuals is typical in your discipline?

For example, the social sciences and natural sciences have a tradition of using images and graphics to present and organize information; the humanities have traditionally relied more on the written word.

What are your teacher's expectations and the constraints of your assignment?

When in doubt, consult your teacher.

Can you find *examples* of similar arguments?

2. **Use charts, graphs, tables, and illustrations to organize information.**

A simple chart or table can present information that would take several paragraphs to describe, thus freeing up space for analysis.

3. **Use photographs and illustrations to bring a text to life or to portray experiences that are difficult to imagine.**

An art history student might include a reproduction of a work she's discussing.

An anthropology student might include photos of rural trailer parks in a study of life in such parks.

4. **Avoid using visuals as decorations.**

Images and graphics can enrich your writing. But substance should always come first; visuals, second.

Suzanne Chouljian was writing a research proposal for a class using the medium of print. But what if she were creating a website to support her undergraduate thesis on this same topic? Her goal? To create a rich repository of information about local bobcat populations that would continue beyond her graduation. In this case, Suzanne might include real-time video of bobcats traversing known travel paths and the results of her DNA analysis of bobcat fur she collected at her study site. She might include links to research reports by other scientists studying bobcat populations or the effects of habitat fragmentation on other animals. She might also incorporate a podcast or video where she explains what attracted her to this project. The possibilities for communicating with others about her interest in this topic are almost unlimited. Suzanne might decide to create a blog on this topic. She could even host a listserv for others who share her fascination with bobcat populations and habitat fragmentation. In so doing, she would be, as Aristotle notes in *The Rhetoric*, taking advantage of all the available means of persuasion.

Composing an Academic Argument: A Case Study of One Student's Writing Process

thinking rhetorically A major theme of this textbook is that written communication is situated within a particular context; therefore, there is no one-size-fits-all form of writing. Instead, just as designers must respond to the specifics of their situation, so too must writers respond to the specifics of their rhetorical situation.✱ This book also emphasizes that writing is a *process*, one that often requires time and multiple iterations. This final section of Chapter 6 provides an extended case study of the process that one student, Daniel Stiepleman, followed in writing an academic argument.

When Daniel composed this essay, he was a student in a first-year writing class. Here is the assignment given to him and other students in the class:

> Write a two- to three-page analytical essay responding to an image of your choice. Be sure to choose an image that involves significant interaction between the text and graphics. Your essay should focus on how the words and graphics work together to generate the image's meaning and impact. Consider your instructor and your classmates to be the primary readers of your essay.

Daniel's first step after receiving his assignment was to look for an image that interested him. While he was flipping through the *Atlantic* magazine, a public service announcement (PSA) for the National Center for Family Literacy (NCFL) caught his eye. An aspiring English teacher, Daniel found the message of the PSA to be powerful, yet something about it that he couldn't quite put his finger on troubled him. In order to explore his initial response to the PSA, Daniel decided to annotate the text and image, using the Guidelines for Analyzing Visual Texts in Chapter 2 (pp. 43–44) as a guide. You can see the PSA with Daniel's annotations on p. 167. Daniel was working on a writing project that he would deliver in print, so his focus was on static visuals. If you were composing a writing project that would be delivered electronically, such as a presentation using PowerPoint or Prezi slides or a video presented online, you would want to consider a broader range of media. But the basic precepts in the Guidelines chart on p. 165 would remain true.

✱   To review the concept of the rhetorical situation, see Chapter 3.

When he first encountered the PSA, Daniel thought that the text's argument was easy to summarize: Literacy improves lives. While annotating, Daniel noticed some details that he didn't catch at first, such as the way the layout and type style underscore the simplicity of the PSA's message. The more he looked at his notes and re-examined the image and words, the more he wondered *why* simplicity was such a central part of the message. He also started to think about what the NCFL was trying to accomplish with the PSA and how other readers of the *Atlantic* might respond to it. And he still wasn't sure what it was about the message as a whole that troubled him.

DANIEL STIEPLEMAN'S ANNOTATION OF THE PUBLIC SERVICE ANNOUNCEMENT

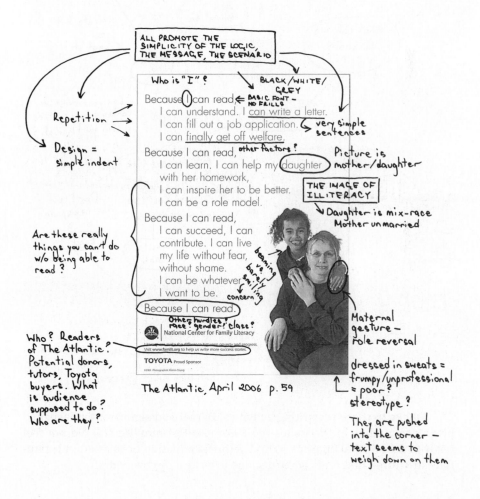

At this point in his writing process, Daniel's primary purpose was to engage as fully and critically as he could with the PSA that he had chosen to analyze. In order to explore his ideas more fully, Daniel decided to create a cluster on the word *illiteracy* to explore his response.✱ After evaluating his cluster, Daniel realized that the causes and effects of illiteracy are more complicated than the PSA acknowledges—and that he had a promising topic for an essay.

DANIEL'S CLUSTER

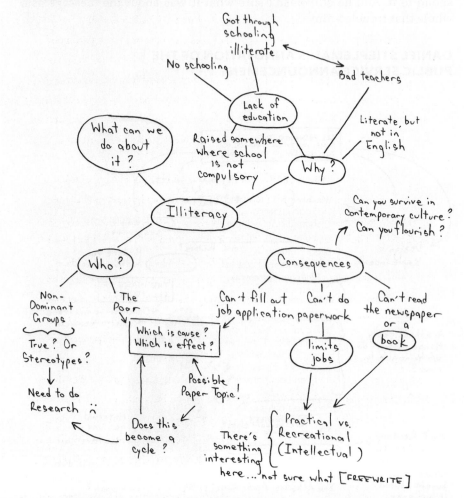

Thanks to these prewriting activities, Daniel had significantly deepened his understanding of the issues the PSA raised for him. He still did not feel ready to do a formal analysis of his rhetorical situation or to attempt a carefully structured first draft, so he decided to write a discovery draft.

✱ For more on invention strategies, see Chapter 9.

DANIEL'S DISCOVERY DRAFT

Literacy, often taken for granted, is a gift. The ability to read text not only offers opportunities for escape and entertainment but gives access to ideas that challenge our own limited worldviews, thus allowing each of us to expand our understandings of our lives on our own terms, at our own pace. The generation of text allows for the further development and sharing of our own ideas with others, at a time when much of the world has lost reverence for oral traditions. Literacy is a gift.

Several organizations exist to help share this gift, but they are underfunded and need help from the public. It is for this reason that groups like the National Center for Family Literacy (NCFL) print public service announcements (PSAs). Obviously these announcements, which appear in magazines and newspapers, are directed toward an educated and literate audience. The task of the men and women who design these advertisements is to convince readers to donate time and/or money toward the cause of literacy training.

In my essay, I want to analyze a PSA that appeared in the April 2006 issue of the *Atlantic* magazine. This PSA uses both text and an image to affect the emotions of the reader. The PSA consists of a series of "Because I can read" statements. The "I" is presumably the woman pictured with a young girl who seems to be the daughter mentioned in the advertisement, though they don't look that much alike. The woman pictured in the PSA stares directly at readers and explains some of the many real-world ways her life has improved because of literacy: "I can fill out a job application . . . I can help my daughter with her homework . . . I can be a role model." By using a first-person narrator, the advertisement is, I think, very successful at adding an emotional element that can inspire people to want to help more illiterate Americans improve their lives. Even though some of the things that are stated in the PSA may not be necessarily linked with literacy, such as when she says, "I can contribute" (certainly there are ways she could contribute to society even without being literate), I think this flaw in the logic of the PSA is subtle enough that an American who is flipping through his or her magazine would probably not notice it.

After reviewing his discovery draft, Daniel realized that while it represented a good start on his essay, he still had considerable work ahead of him. Here's what Daniel wrote about this draft in his journal.

DANIEL'S JOURNAL ENTRY

Now that I've got some distance from this draft, I can see that it really is just a starting point. Right at the end something clicked with me: a flaw in the logic of the PSA. I tried to dismiss it; I even thought about deleting it because it would be easier for me to write about the value of literacy. But the fact of the matter is that the logic behind this ad really is problematic. This is going to be harder to write about, but it's also a more interesting and provocative idea. I think that I need to rewrite with this idea (or something like it) as my thesis. I'm a little frustrated at having to start over, but the truth is that I probably wouldn't have noticed this problem with the PSA if I hadn't written this draft.

Thanks to the preceding activities, which encouraged him to explore his response to the PSA, Daniel now felt ready to undertake a more formal exploration of his situation and goals as a writer. This was the moment, he decided, when it made sense for him to consider his controlling purpose and rhetorical situation and to do so in writing. Here is Daniel's analysis.

DANIEL'S RHETORICAL ANALYSIS

thinking rhetorically

I am writing an analytical essay for my composition class. I want to persuade my readers—my instructor and my classmates—that there are some disturbing assumptions behind the National Center for Family Literacy's public service announcement. If my readers are anything like I am, their first impressions will be that the ad must be good because it promotes literacy. I'm worried this will lead them to resist my argument that literacy isn't, as the ad implies, an easy solution to the problem of inequity. I've got to be convincing by using evidence, both from the text and from other sources.

How will I persuade them to accept my argument? After all, I had to write my way to seeing it. What tone should I adopt—an objective tone or a passionate one? I'm inclined to try the latter, but I know our instructor said that being objective is usually a more effective strategy. Plus that may help it sound less like I'm arguing that the PSA's negative consequences are on purpose. I'll need to be careful in my analysis of the PSA.

Daniel also decided to develop a plan for his essay. As Daniel noted in his journal, he is a visual thinker, and so traditional outlines don't work well for him. So he came up with the visual map below, which helped him imagine how his essay might be organized. It includes several questions he thought he should address, reminders to himself, definitions of terms, and general comments. He used his plan to further explore his ideas and to determine the best organization for his essay. Although probably no one but Daniel could develop an essay from the diagrams and notes he created, the plan fulfilled his needs—and that's what counts.

DANIEL'S PLAN FOR HIS ESSAY

Daniel was now ready to write a formal draft. He had a clear controlling purpose: He wanted to critically examine the logic and design of the NCFL PSA and to convince his readers that although the ability to read and write is valuable, literacy cannot by itself solve the problem of poverty. Here is Daniel's first formal draft of his essay. (Notice that for Daniel's first draft, he has not yet created the necessary works-cited page, and his in-text citations are incomplete.)

DANIEL'S FIRST DRAFT

Literacy, often taken for granted, is a gift. The ability to read text not only offers opportunities for escape and entertainment, but gives access to ideas that challenge our own limited worldviews, thus allowing each of us to expand our understandings of our lives on our own terms, at our own pace. The generation of text allows for the further development and sharing of our own ideas with others, at a time when much of the world has lost reverence for oral traditions. Literacy is a gift.

In recent years educational and other foundations have run literacy campaigns designed to persuade literate Americans to donate their time and/or money to the worthwhile cause of literacy education. These campaigns frequently create public service announcements (PSAs) to convey their message to the general public. One such PSA is produced by the National Center for Family Literacy (NCFL). Published in *Atlantic* magazine, the full-page advertisement essentially sets up a series of linked statements. It begins, "Because I can read," which is followed by a series of "I can . . ." statements, such as, "I can understand. I can write a letter. I can fill out a job application. I can finally get off welfare." At the bottom of the page is an invitation to help the person presented in this PSA and others like her get out of poverty by supporting the NCFL.

When I first read this PSA, I found it persuasive. But the more I thought about it, the more problematic the series of "I can" statements became. By asserting that the ability to read and write is tantamount to the ability to learn, be a role model, and contribute, the text also implies that people who are illiterate cannot learn, cannot be role models, and, worst of all, have nothing to contribute. Such persons, it seems, are utterly worthless without literacy.

The people reading *The Atlantic* are not illiterate. In fact, according to the magazine's website, the average reader of *The Atlantic* is a man in his early fifties with a college degree and a median household income of over $150,000. The image incorporated into the NCFL's "Because I can read" PSA is certainly not that of the typical reader of *The Atlantic*. The image is of a woman with an approximately ten-year-old girl, presumably her daughter, who is significantly darker skinned. The girl's father does not appear in the photograph. The image of illiteracy, then, is a single mother with a mixed-race child.

Can literacy solve this woman's problems? American society is immensely stratified; 58 percent of black and 62 percent of Hispanic children live in low-income households, as opposed to only 25 percent of white children (NCCP). According to the 1999 U.S. Census data, black and Hispanic Americans ("Hispanic" was still classified as a race in the 1999 census data) are twice as likely as European Americans to be unemployed. Those who work have a weekly income far less than whites — over $100 a week less for blacks, and almost $200 a week less for Hispanics (United States Census Bureau).

The NCFL PSA suggests that being able to read will magically get the woman portrayed in the ad off welfare. In reality, more highly educated black and Hispanic people are only slightly more likely to find work (as compared with equally educated whites) than their less-educated counterparts (United States Dept. of Education). Literacy does not equal social equality. Yet that is precisely what this PSA implies.

This PSA presents illiteracy as a problem of others who have not had the same advantages (role models, educational opportunities, membership in a dominant class or sex) as the readers. In so doing, it displays the inherent inequalities of our culture, but also offers an unrealistically simple solution to the problem — literacy. Given its purpose, the PSA is effective — but it is also a lie because it ignores the root causes of illiteracy. Granted, helping more Americans to become literate could be one step toward greater equality. So the question remains: Is the cumulative effect of this PSA harmful or good?

After writing this draft, Daniel knew that he would benefit from setting it aside for a while. After a day had passed, he decided to use the Questions for Evaluating Focus, Content, and Organization to analyze what he had written.✱ Here is his analysis.

See Chapter 10, p. 291. ✱

Focus: I think I do a good job of raising questions about the PSA. I wonder if I come on too strong, however. I also wonder if my focus is narrow and clear enough. I see that I don't write much about how the graphics and text interact. Our instructor specifically mentioned this in the assignment, so I need to pay more attention to that.

Content: I talk about how literacy affects income, and I think that's important. But looking back at the draft, I see that I don't really explain what other factors might cause a person to be poor. I definitely need to do some more research. I wonder, too, if I should include the PSA or describe it more thoroughly so that I can focus readers' attention on the parts of the PSA that are most important. I'd better go back to the PSA to decide which are the most important parts.

Organization: I'm not happy with my intro and conclusion. I kept the same introduction from my discovery draft mainly because I didn't want to worry about it. I'll need to change that. I like how I conclude with a question, but I wonder if it isn't more important to answer that question instead. There's still lots to do, but at least I can see that my ideas are taking shape.

When Daniel analyzed the first draft of his essay, he realized that although he had done a good job of exploring and raising questions about the PSA, his essay wasn't as effective as it could be. He worried that he didn't provide enough evidence to convince readers that his argument was valid, and he was unhappy with his introduction and conclusion. He also realized that he didn't analyze how the words and graphics worked together to create meaning in the PSA.

Fortunately for Daniel, his teacher included in-class peer response sessions for all major writing assignments in their class, so Daniel was able to revise his essay and share it with members of his writing group for feedback. His second draft is presented here, with some of the group members' comments. (Notice that his essay now has a title and that he has revised it in significant ways. This early draft includes some source citations, not yet in final MLA form.)

DANIEL'S SECOND DRAFT WITH PEER COMMENTS

Daniel's second draft had many strengths, which members of his writing group acknowledge. But they had suggestions for improvement as well. A number of them commented on the evidence in paragraph 3, asking for more background on what Daniel meant by "the systematic stratification of American society." Several readers wanted to know more about the PSA's goals and suggested that Daniel's negative tone made his overall argument less convincing than it could be.

Literacy in America: Reading between the Lines
Daniel Stiepleman

A woman and girl look straight at us. Their relationship to one another is unclear, but the girl, maybe ten, stands over the woman with a hand on her shoulder—she seems, unexpectedly perhaps, almost maternal. Huddled together in the lower right-hand corner, they are cradled between a thin border and text. A series of connecting statements takes up the bulk of the page. "Because I can read," it begins in the opposite corner in simple, black font, which is followed, in slightly indented gray, by a series of "I can" statements: "I can understand. I can write a letter. I can fill out a job application. I can finally get off welfare." The call and response repeats: "Because I can read . . . Because I can read . . . Because I can read." This page, a public service announcement (PSA) by the National Center for Family Literacy (NCFL), appears in the *Atlantic* magazine. From its short diction to its basic design to its three-color scheme, everything about this ad reinforces the simplicity of its logic: "Because I can read, I can succeed." This simplicity is reassuring and hopeful, but it's more than that; it's deceptive.

In order for the woman portrayed in this PSA to gain her worth through literacy, we are urged to accept that without reading and writing she is worthless. Asserting that once she learns to read, she can "learn . . . be a role model . . . [and] contribute," the PSA implies that people who cannot read or write cannot learn, cannot be a role model, and, worst of all, have nothing to contribute. It is here where both the simplicity and the logic of the NCFL's message begin to fall apart. The message becomes that people who are illiterate are worthless, and that must be why she is still on welfare. But perhaps even more astonishingly, literacy is supposed to magically solve her problems.

This assertion ignores the systematic stratification of American society. Is illiteracy alone the reason why 58 percent of all black children and 62 percent of all Hispanic children in America currently live in poverty, while only 25 percent of white children do (National Center for

Great opening!
—Parvin

Really compelling description. I like the idea that the simplicity of the design reflects the simplicity of the logic. But I'm having trouble imagining the design: Can you show a picture of it?
—Eric

It sounds like you're saying the NCFL is deliberately insulting the people they help, but I don't think that's what you mean. Maybe you could start by explaining what they're trying to do with the ad?
—Kyong

Good evidence. Are there similar statistics for women?
—Parvin

Children in Poverty)? Will literacy training change the fact that, according to the 1999 U.S. Census data, black and Hispanic Americans are twice as likely as white Americans to be unemployed? Or that those who do work make an average of over $100 a week less than whites if they're black and almost $200 a week less if they're Hispanic? It seems unlikely that simply "Because I [or any illiterate person] can read . . . I can succeed." The NCFL's suggestion otherwise is an unfortunate confirmation of the great American myth that anyone can pull him- or herself up by the bootstraps through simple, concerted effort, with only his or her ability and desire standing as obstacles in the way.

This PSA's potential for success relates directly to the degree to which it does not depict reality. The ad suggests that all the illiterate people in America need to achieve worth—based on its assumption that they are, without literacy, worthless—is to gain the ability to read and write; and it counts upon the readers' inexperience with both poverty and illiteracy to maintain its fiction. This is a safe bet as, according to the *Atlantic*'s website, the magazine's average reader is a man in his early fifties with a college degree and a median household income of over $150,000.

But the Census statistics portray a different image of America; it is a country in which the woman portrayed in the PSA will not so easily change her stake in the American dream. The injustice done by maintaining the myth of equal opportunity outweighs any good the NCFL can hope to accomplish with its ad. Looking at the woman more closely now, she seems somehow to know this. The girl is beaming, but there is a hesitance I see in the woman's smile. Am I projecting upon the image, or is there, in her face, concern? Her concern would be apt; she is shoved into the corner, held there, like so many Americans, beneath the weight of a text that would take the rich and daunting complexity of our multicultural society and give it short diction, basic design, and a three-color scheme. The illusion of simplicity.

Margin notes:

Where does this information come from?
—Kyong

I'm not sure I follow you. What are the other reasons? Why wouldn't being able to read help a person succeed? Maybe you could answer the questions that start the paragraph.
—Eric

This sounds a little harsh.
—Eric

This is a strong conclusion. But your overall argument might be more effective if you acknowledged the positive aspects of the ad — maybe in the introduction?
—Parvin

I love how you circle back to the image in your conclusion.
—Kyong

After Daniel contemplated his readers' responses, he recorded his reactions and ideas in his journal. Daniel's comments indicate that the peer response process helped him gain much-needed distance from his writing.

DANIEL'S RESPONSE TO PEER COMMENTS

At first, I had some resistance to my writing group's comments. I've worked hard on this essay and taken it quite far, given my first draft. But after reading their comments and taking some time to think, I can see that they pointed out problems that I was just too close to my essay to see. Most important, I think I need to work some more on my tone so readers understand that I'm questioning the PSA's assumptions, not the value of literacy itself or the work of the NCFL.

Several readers suggested that I include a new introductory paragraph that sets up the situation and explains what the PSA is trying to do. I thought quite a bit about this and tried out a few new paragraphs, but I kept coming back to the paragraph as it was. I really like this paragraph, so I decided to try to address their concerns by writing a new second paragraph.

Parvin commented that while I have evidence to support my claims, none of it cites the situation of women. Now that I think about it, this is very odd, given the nature of the PSA. I'll check additional sources of information so I can include that.

The rest of the comments seem relatively minor—less revision than editing. I need to fix citations in the text and prepare the works-cited page. Then I'll be really close to a final draft!

In reflecting on his group's responses, Daniel does a good job of taking their comments seriously while also holding to his own vision of his essay. It's not possible to show all the stages that Daniel's draft went through, but the final draft demonstrates that his analysis of his readers' responses enabled him to revise his essay fully, to "see again" how he could most effectively make his point. Daniel's final draft begins on p. 179.

DANIEL'S FINAL DRAFT

In the process of writing his essay, Daniel was able to articulate what was at first only a vague sense of unease about the National Center for Family Literacy PSA. As he moved from his first draft to the second, Daniel was able to identify why the ad concerned him. He clarified the problems with the PSA's logic in his third draft while also attending more carefully to the interplay of words and graphics in the PSA.

Daniel's final draft, you will probably agree, develops an argument that is not only persuasive but also stylish. His tone is more evenhanded, his paragraphs are more coherent, and his language is more polished than in his second draft. The effort that Daniel put into his essay more than paid off. This effort required planning: Daniel knew that he would have to work his way to a clear sense of purpose, audience, and organization, so he built in the necessary time for prewriting, drafting, and revising. The result is an engaged, persuasive analysis and a good demonstration of the inseparable nature of academic analysis and argument.

Stiepleman 1

Daniel Stiepleman
Professor Chang
English 100
21 March 2016

Literacy in America: Reading between the Lines

A woman and girl look straight at us. Though they look nothing alike, they are apparently mother and daughter. The girl, maybe ten, stands over the woman with a hand on her shoulder; it is she who seems maternal. Huddled together in the lower, right-hand corner of the page, they are cradled between a thin border and text. This text, presumably the words of the woman pictured, takes up the bulk of the page. "Because I can read" begins in the upper left-hand corner in simple, black font. This is followed, in slightly indented gray, by a series of "I can" statements: "I can understand. I can write a letter. I can fill out a job application. I can finally get off welfare." The call and response repeats: "Because I can read . . . Because I can read . . . Because I can read."

Stronger introduction focuses readers on image being analyzed

When I came across this page in *The Atlantic* magazine (see Fig. 1), the image of the girl and the woman was what first caught my eye, but it was the repeated statement "Because I can read" that captured my imagination. Its plainness was alluring. But as I read and reread the page, a public service announcement (PSA) designed to solicit donations of time and money for the National Center for Family Literacy (NCFL), I grew uncomfortable. The PSA, with its short diction, basic design, and black-and-white color scheme, reinforces the simplicity of its logic: "Because I can read, I can succeed." This simple message, though it promotes a mission I believe in, I fear does more harm than good.

New paragraph extends context

Copy of PSA included so that readers can judge for themselves

Revised thesis statement is more balanced

The problem is with the underlying logic of this PSA. If we as readers believe the "Because I can read" statements, we must also believe that without literacy the woman in the PSA is worthless. Asserting that because a person can read, she "can learn . . . be a role model . . . [and] contribute," the PSA implies that people who cannot read or write cannot learn, cannot be role models, and, worst of all, have nothing to contribute to society. This is

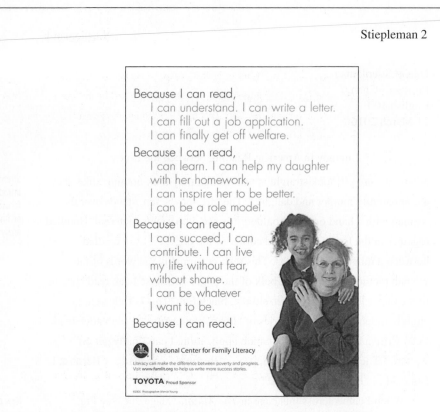

Because I can read,
  I can understand. I can write a letter.
  I can fill out a job application.
  I can finally get off welfare.
Because I can read,
  I can learn. I can help my daughter
  with her homework,
  I can inspire her to be better.
  I can be a role model.
Because I can read,
  I can succeed, I can
  contribute. I can live
  my life without fear,
  without shame.
  I can be whatever
  I want to be.
Because I can read.

National Center for Family Literacy
Literacy can make the difference between poverty and progress.
Visit www.famlit.org to help us write more success stories.
TOYOTA Proud Sponsor

Fig. 1. NCFL Public Service Announcement. *Atlantic*, April 2006.

the real reason, the PSA suggests, why the woman portrayed in the photograph is still on welfare. But perhaps even more astonishing, literacy is supposed to be a quick fix to her problems.

> New evidence added to strengthen argument

> Sources are cited

      This assertion ignores the systematic stratification of American society. Is illiteracy alone the reason why 60 percent of all black children and 61 percent of all Hispanic children in America currently live in poverty, while only 26 percent of white children do (National Center for Children in Poverty)? Will literacy training change the fact that, according to 1999 U.S. Census data, black and Hispanic Americans are twice as likely as white Americans to be unemployed? Or that those who do work make, on average, between $100 and 200 a week less than whites (406)? In the case of the woman pictured in the PSA, should literacy indeed lead her to a job, she is likely to make half as much money as a man with the same demographics

Stiepleman 3

who works in the same position (United States, Dept. of Education). It is
not my intent to undermine the value of being able to read and write, but
given the other obstacles facing the disadvantaged in America, it seems
unlikely that simply because someone learns to read, he or she "can
succeed."

> Less accusing tone
> wins readers over

The benefits and opportunities for success extend well beyond a
person's ability to fill out a job application. Race, class, and gender are
powerful forces in our society, and the obstacles they present are self-
perpetuating (Rothenberg 11–12). Even a well-educated person, if she
is from a minority or low-income group, can find it overwhelmingly
difficult to land a well-paying job with possibilities for advancement. The
lack of simple things that middle-class readers of *The Atlantic* take for
granted—the social connections of a network, the money for a professional
wardrobe, a shared background with an interviewer—can cripple a job
search. The NCFL's suggestion otherwise is an unfortunate reinforcement
of the great American myth that anyone can pull him- or herself up by the
bootstraps, with only his or her ability and desire standing as obstacles in
the way.

> New paragraph
> provides examples
> of obstacles that
> could prevent a
> literate person
> from succeeding

The PSA suggests that all the illiterate people in America need to
achieve worth is the ability to read and write. But Americans disadvantaged
by race, class, or gender will not so easily alter their position in our
stratified culture. As long as we continue to pretend otherwise, we have
no hope of changing the inequities that continue to be an inherent part of
our society. For this reason, as much as I value this PSA's emphasis on the
importance of literacy, I question its underlying logic.

> Language is
> more balanced

Looking at the woman portrayed in the PSA more closely now, she
seems somehow to know that her and her daughter's lives cannot improve
so easily. Though the girl is beaming, there is a hesitance I see in the
woman's smile and concern in her face. And it is apt; she is shoved into
the corner, held there, like so many Americans, beneath the weight of a
text that would take the rich and daunting complexity of our multicultural
society and give it the illusion of simplicity.

Stiepleman 4

Works Cited

Koball, Heather. "Low-Income Children in the United States (2005),"
National Center for Children in Poverty, Columbia University, Mailman
School of Public Health, Sept. 2006, www.nccp.org/publications
/pub_577.html.

National Center for Family Literacy. Advertisement. *The Atlantic*, Apr. 2006,
p. 59.

Rothenberg, Paula S. *Race, Class, and Gender in the United States: An
Integrated Study*. 9th ed., St. Martin's P, 2013.

United States, Census Bureau. "Labor Force, Employment, and Earnings."
Statistical Abstract of the United States: 1999, Printing.

---, Department of Education, Institute of Education Sciences. National
Center for Education Statistics, 1992 National Adult Literacy Survey,
1992, nces.ed.gov/pubsearch/pubsinfo.asp?pubid=199909.

for **thought, discussion, and writing**

1. This chapter has presented activities designed to improve your understanding of academic argument. The For Exploration on p. 150, for instance, asks you to identify the values and beliefs that have led you to hold strong views on an issue. The one on p. 155 asks you to formulate a working thesis and to list the major evidence you would use to support it. Finally, the group activity on p. 157 encourages you to acknowledge possible counterarguments to your thesis. Drawing on these activities, write an essay directed to an academic reader on the topic you have explored, revising your working thesis if necessary.

2. This chapter focuses on argumentative strategies that apply across the curriculum. Now that you have read it once, take a few moments to review the chapter to remind yourself of the topics and strategies covered. Then take five minutes to list the most important understandings that you have gained as a result of reading this chapter. Be prepared to share your thoughts with others in your class.

3. Newspaper editorials and opinion columns represent one common form of argument. If your college or university publishes a newspaper, read several issues in sequence, paying particular attention to the editorials and opinion columns. (If your school doesn't publish a newspaper, choose a local newspaper instead.) Choose one editorial or opinion column that you believe represents a successful argument; choose another that strikes you as suspect. Bring these texts to class, and be prepared to share your evaluations of them with your classmates.

Doing Research: Joining the Scholarly Conversation

In some ways, learning to write for academic audiences is like traveling to a new country and learning a new culture: You may have to learn new approaches to familiar tasks, find ways to apply what you already know to a new environment, and master skills that are entirely new. And these are not things you will do just once. Since scholars in different disciplines examine similar topics in different ways, what works in one course may not work in another. What's important is developing the strategies and habits of mind that will help you determine how your academic audience approaches issues, frames questions, defines evidence, and uses research tools. These strategies and habits will guide you as you gather, analyze, and interpret the sources that are the backbone of a good academic argument. And they will also continue to serve you well long after you leave college: Strong researchers know how to adapt to new audiences, workplaces, and cultures, so they can communicate effectively in any situation.

In Chapter 1, rhetoric was defined as "a practical art that helps writers make effective choices ... within specific rhetorical situations." Research is also a rhetorical process. Understanding your rhetorical situation will help you make good choices every step of the way, from selecting topics, defining research questions, and developing strategies for exploration to filtering search results, supporting your claims with evidence, and documenting your sources appropriately and ethically. Asking yourself the Questions for Analyzing Your Rhetorical Situation as a Researcher (on the next page) can help you respond appropriately to your situation and assignment.

thinking rhetorically

Habits of Mind for Academic Research

In Chapter 2, you learned about the habits of mind that are essential to success in college. (See pp. 27–31.) These same habits also drive successful researchers. Academic research is a learning process that can be simultaneously frustrating

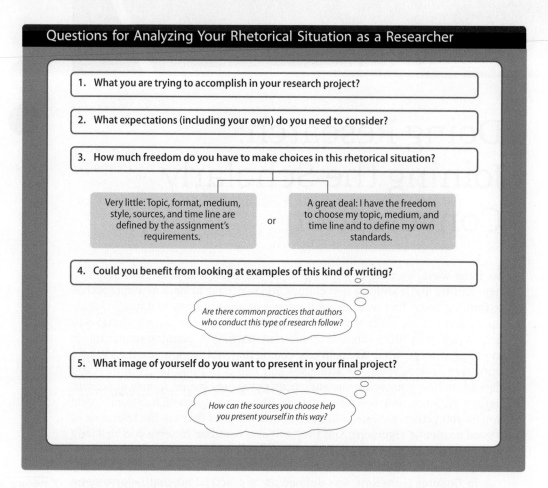

Questions for Analyzing Your Rhetorical Situation as a Researcher

1. What you are trying to accomplish in your research project?

2. What expectations (including your own) do you need to consider?

3. How much freedom do you have to make choices in this rhetorical situation?

Very little: Topic, format, medium, style, sources, and time line are defined by the assignment's requirements.

or

A great deal: I have the freedom to choose my topic, medium, and time line and to define my own standards.

4. Could you benefit from looking at examples of this kind of writing?

Are there common practices that authors who conduct this type of research follow?

5. What image of yourself do you want to present in your final project?

How can the sources you choose help you present yourself in this way?

and rewarding, messy and inspiring. It requires you to take risks, to reconsider things you thought you knew, and to start before you know for sure where your process will lead. It is driven by curiosity, open-minded exploration, and engagement with new ideas. You will need flexibility, persistence, and creative thinking to get through it. And, in the end, you will synthesize your ideas with the ideas, facts, images, and concepts you find to create an argument or interpretation that is uniquely yours.

● EXPLORING A TOPIC AND FINDING A FOCUS

It is natural to feel a lot of pressure to choose a topic and start gathering sources when you are writing on a deadline. Students who choose a topic before they have fully explored their options may find themselves saddled with a boring topic. By staying open to new ideas and perspectives, you are more likely to find a topic that inspires you to do your best work.

Choosing a Topic

Would it surprise you to hear that most undergraduates say that "getting started" is the most difficult part of the academic research process? It takes courage to commit to a topic before you know whether it will work: Will it satisfy your instructor? Will you be able to find sources? Will you find a unique and compelling thesis? Some students try to manage this risk by sticking with topics they've used before (or that they know other students have used before). Fight this impulse! When you use a tired topic, it is unlikely that you will write a paper that really stands out. If you take a risk and go with a topic that you are genuinely curious about, you are more likely to create a project that is interesting to you and to your reader.

You may think that the things you are curious about are not scholarly enough to be the focus of an academic paper. Scholars study the world around them in all its complexity; do not immediately reject a topic because it seems lowbrow, niche, frivolous, or fun. The key is to figure out the types of questions scholars ask about a topic. Think about what makes you curious, and then read some articles to see how scholars approach those topics:

- Are you fascinated by puzzles or problems and interested in how things work? Engineers, scientists, and philosophers are some of the scholars asking these types of questions.

- Do you like to explore the world with your senses, discovering new tastes, smells, colors, textures, and sounds? So do psychologists, artists, anthropologists, and nutritionists — just to name a few.

- Are you motivated to understand other people and their thoughts and feelings? So are scholars in fields like literature, history, marketing, psychology, and sociology.

All of these sparks can lead you to interesting, researchable topics. Curiosity is at the heart of a good research process. It is what drives scholars to discover new things. The amount of freedom you have to choose a topic can vary greatly. When you are allowed to choose your own topic, take the time to analyze your assignment carefully to make sure that your choice is appropriate. Consider the amount of time you have, what you are being asked to do with the topic (to report, to analyze, to argue), and the types of sources you are being asked to use.

Exploring a Topic

Think about the last time you went shopping. Were you looking for something specific, like an outfit for an important event or ingredients for a favorite dish? Or were you browsing — scanning a website or exploring a shop looking for anything that might be attractive, cool, or tasty? How did your goals shape your choices about where to look, what to buy, and when to stop?

Good shoppers know when to do a focused search and when to browse, and they use different strategies in those different situations. Good researchers do this too. It is very difficult to search effectively before you know what your options are. So early in the research process — when you are looking for something to write about or just starting to explore a potential topic area — it is better to browse, keeping your mind open to the possibilities. Here are some potentially useful places to browse:

- Sites like *Science Daily* (sciencedaily.com) or *EurekAlert* (eurekalert.org) aggregate news about new research and new discoveries in all kinds of academic fields. Think about what sparks your curiosity, and then browse research in related fields for ideas.

- Don't forget the analog world. If you are motivated by other people, check out talks or symposia on your campus. If you explore the world perceptually, browse museums, markets, or other environments for things that catch your interest.

- For current events and issues, browse newspaper sites or *Google News* (news.google.com). Even better, use visualization tools like *Newsmap* (newsmap.jp) to explore current news stories.

- If you need to take a side on controversial issue, don't shy away from partisan discussions online while you are thinking about topics. Sites like the liberal *Talking Points Memo* (talkingpointsmemo.com) and the conservative *PJ Media* (pjmedia.com) aggregate news stories from around the web. Look up sites in *Wikipedia* to identify partisan bias and contextualize the information you find.

- Ask your instructor to recommend books, journals, or magazines you can browse for topic ideas.

It can be helpful to set a time limit (like twenty minutes on a website or two hours in a museum) to browse. Look for things that catch your interest. Keep a list of ideas in a notebook or on your phone. Don't worry at this point if they will make good topics. When your time is up, look at your list. See if connections or themes emerge from the list of things that interest you. Eliminate items that interest you primarily because they affirm (or contradict) your beliefs unless you are sure that you can keep your mind open to new ideas during your research process. The themes that emerge can form the basis of an initial, exploratory research question.

CONSIDERING MULTIPLE PERSPECTIVES

Here's another reason to let curiosity drive your research process: Keeping your mind open to different points of view is easier to do when you are learning about a topic than when you already have a specific argument or thesis in mind. Researchers in psychology and communications have actually found that when people feel strongly about an issue, they are less likely to notice sources that contradict their beliefs. As an academic writer, your ethos✱ is closely connected with openness, the habit of mind that welcomes new ways of thinking. When you show that you have critically examined all aspects of a topic, considered different points of view, and taken your readers' perspectives into account, your conclusions are likely to be more persuasive to academic readers.

thinking rhetorically

Think about the types of topics that academic writers address. They are often big questions like "Should the government regulate hate speech?" or "Should there be cooperative international action against global warming?" On the surface, these are yes-or-no questions, but if you dig deeper, you will find that people who answer "yes" (or "no") to questions like these often have very different reasons for their position. You will want to explore all these reasons as you construct your own unique argument. Doing so will help you present yourself as the kind of thinker who carefully considers multiple perspectives, critically evaluates new ideas, and refines his or her ideas in light of new information — in short, as the ideal academic writer.

Remember what you learned in Chapter 2 about interacting with your texts and posing questions as you read. Academic research is iterative; that is, it requires you to repeat steps in the process. As you learn more about your topic, you think of new questions to ask. It is the questions you ask, even more than the answers you find, that move your process forward. Think creatively as you explore.

HANDS-ON RESEARCH

Direct, hands-on experience can be a great way to generate new questions about your topic. Try some of these strategies, particularly if you are feeling blocked or stuck:

- If your curiosity is sparked by how things work or feel, tinker with a piece of machinery or technology related to your topic.

- If you are motivated to understand other people, find an expert on your campus to interview, or survey people who have had firsthand experience with the issue you are exploring.

- Go out into the world and observe or participate in an interaction or event.

For more on Aristotle's appeals of logos, ethos, and pathos, see Chapter 5, pp. 123–25. ✱

Keep track of the ideas, thoughts, and questions that occur to you, and follow up on them when you search the published literature. Contextualize your observations by comparing them to research studies and other accounts. Use the literature on your topic to see if the themes that emerge in your interviews or observations are common or unusual. On the flip side, you can also use these hands-on methods to help you understand and analyze what you find in books and articles. Ask an expert to explain her perspective on a research study you found; ask students to comment on claims made in magazine articles about college life. The guidelines below can help make your hands-on research productive.

Do not expect to use the data you collect using hands-on methods as evidence to support broad claims. Researchers who use these methods to draw generalizable conclusions carefully design their surveys and studies according to established protocols. For example, the survey you do in your

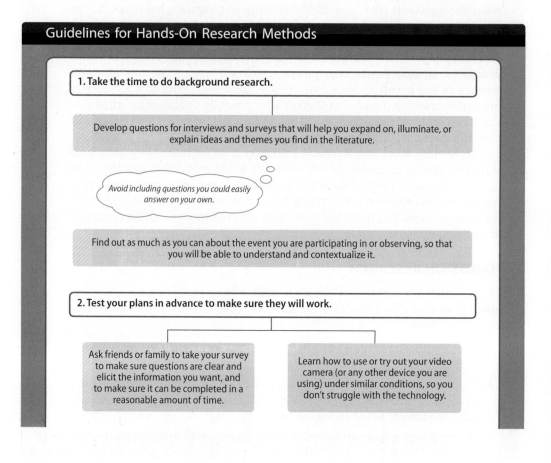

Guidelines for Hands-On Research Methods

1. Take the time to do background research.

Develop questions for interviews and surveys that will help you expand on, illuminate, or explain ideas and themes you find in the literature.

Avoid including questions you could easily answer on your own.

Find out as much as you can about the event you are participating in or observing, so that you will be able to understand and contextualize it.

2. Test your plans in advance to make sure they will work.

Ask friends or family to take your survey to make sure questions are clear and elicit the information you want, and to make sure it can be completed in a reasonable amount of time.

Learn how to use or try out your video camera (or any other device you are using) under similar conditions, so you don't struggle with the technology.

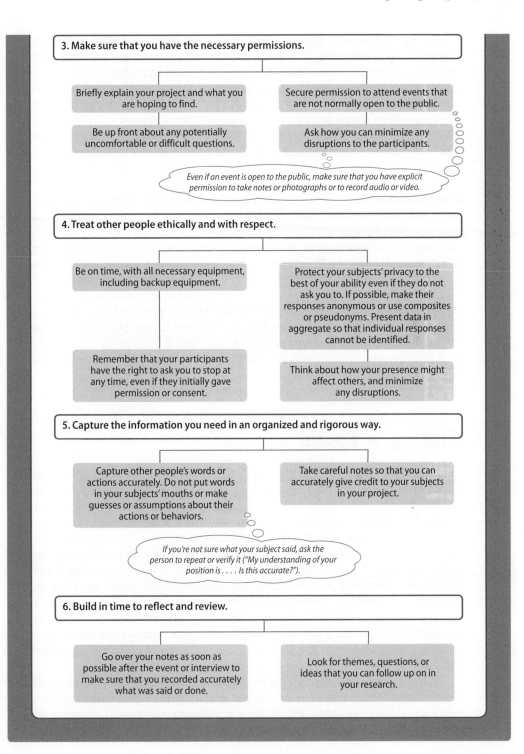

3. Make sure that you have the necessary permissions.

Briefly explain your project and what you are hoping to find.

Secure permission to attend events that are not normally open to the public.

Be up front about any potentially uncomfortable or difficult questions.

Ask how you can minimize any disruptions to the participants.

Even if an event is open to the public, make sure that you have explicit permission to take notes or photographs or to record audio or video.

4. Treat other people ethically and with respect.

Be on time, with all necessary equipment, including backup equipment.

Protect your subjects' privacy to the best of your ability even if they do not ask you to. If possible, make their responses anonymous or use composites or pseudonyms. Present data in aggregate so that individual responses cannot be identified.

Remember that your participants have the right to ask you to stop at any time, even if they initially gave permission or consent.

Think about how your presence might affect others, and minimize any disruptions.

5. Capture the information you need in an organized and rigorous way.

Capture other people's words or actions accurately. Do not put words in your subjects' mouths or make guesses or assumptions about their actions or behaviors.

Take careful notes so that you can accurately give credit to your subjects in your project.

If you're not sure what your subject said, ask the person to repeat or verify it ("My understanding of your position is . . . . Is this accurate?").

6. Build in time to reflect and review.

Go over your notes as soon as possible after the event or interview to make sure that you recorded accurately what was said or done.

Look for themes, questions, or ideas that you can follow up on in your research.

residence hall cannot be used to show what "most undergraduates in the U.S. believe" because the sample of students isn't representative of all the different types of students across the country. But this does not mean that you cannot use what you learn firsthand in your project or paper. A survey of students in your dorm could be mined for data about the students on your campus, and quotations from students in your dorm could be used to personalize national research conducted by another researcher. Just be careful and precise about how you use your hands-on research, and be sure to connect it to the broader conversation.

A note about ethics. When you use any of the hands-on methods described above, you have an important responsibility to treat anyone who agrees to help you with your project with respect. In a research context, this means ensuring that they consent to participate and doing everything you can to protect their privacy. When professional researchers study human subjects, they must prove that the research will be beneficial and adhere to a detailed set of ethical standards to minimize risk to the participants. Before they can even begin research, their projects must be reviewed and approved by their IRB (Institutional Review Board). For most classroom projects, you will not be required to undergo formal review even if you are gathering data from human subjects, but you should still take your ethical responsibilities seriously.

Finding a Focus

Your main goal in exploring a topic is to figure out what you think and what you want to argue — to find a focus for your research. The goal of academic research isn't to find a point of view you agree with and repeat it. You are not looking for a single source that gives you the "truth." Instead, you're *constructing* your argument, building it out of the facts, figures, theories, concepts, ideas, and arguments that have been developed by a community of thinkers over the years. Your argument will still be original and creative, but it won't come out of nowhere. It will be a part of an ongoing conversation in which you have an opportunity to discover connections between new ideas and what you already know. When you do not find a personal focus, academic writing can feel more like editing, paraphrasing someone else's ideas to fit a formula. It is in the connections among ideas that you show your own unique perspective and creative thinking.

In the early stages of a typical academic research process, you will read and consider many ideas that you do not end up using in your final project. Your goal is to explore ideas, and at first you will not know exactly what will be relevant in the end. As your focused argument emerges from your reading and thinking, deciding which sources to consider most carefully will become easier. Expand your perspective by reading widely in many genres. Read actively and critically, asking questions as you go.✱

---

for **exploration**

As you explore, develop a system to capture the ideas that occur to you as you read. Post-it Notes can be very useful for capturing ideas because they are portable and easy to move around, but any method that will allow you to examine and re-examine your thoughts will work: note cards, a spreadsheet, or even a simple text document. Periodically, pull out your collection of ideas, lay it out, and look for connections. If you are a linear thinker, consider using time lines or outlines to organize your thoughts. If you are more visual, use sketches, a mind map, or a cluster diagram. (See Chapter 6, p. 168, and Chapter 9, p. 268.) As you recognize recurring themes or ideas, expand your system so that you can connect sources to themes. For example, you might use a different color or symbol for each theme and then mark your sources with that visual reminder.

Managing Uncertainty

You can expect to feel many different emotions during the research process. Sometimes you will be inspired or invigorated as you learn new things and come up with ideas that move your project forward. At other times, you will be anxious and unsure. You'll worry that you will never find the sources you need or that you'll never figure out what you want to say. Realize that this is a normal part of the research process. All researchers go through these emotional ebbs and flows. In the next section, we will talk about strategies and tools you can use to get through the rough parts.

● GATHERING INFORMATION AND STAYING ORGANIZED

Persistence is one of the most important characteristics you will need to display in an academic research process. Flexible thinking — a willingness to try new things and consider new sources — can help you along the way.

Planning Ahead

One of the best things you can do for yourself is give yourself enough time to deal with unexpected hiccups. When you need everything to work perfectly to finish on time, you can almost guarantee that something will go wrong.

See Chapter 2 for more on genres (pp. 17–20) and reading critically (pp. 31–40). ✱

As soon as you get your assignment, look at the requirements and think realistically about how much time it will take you to work through each stage of the research process. Be sure to give yourself enough time to read your sources carefully and to reflect on and think about them. (Common source types are listed in the chart below.) Scholarly sources in particular can be challenging to digest. You may need to look up additional information just to understand them. Taking a day to think and process what you have read may seem like time wasted, but if you have planned ahead, it is anything but.

Many assignments define the source types you must use, and these requirements can affect your time management. While there are huge amounts of information available immediately on the web, some types of information are more readily available there than others. Current newspaper articles are usually easy to find (though as a story slips off the front page it may be harder to locate). Scholarly books and articles are also easy to find on the web, but accessing the full text often costs money. You can get the same content from your library without these charges, but you may need to factor in delivery time if you request sources from other campuses or from other libraries.

Guidelines for Identifying Source Types

Source Types	Purpose	Audience
Reference sources	Well-organized sources of factual information.	Varies. Some are broadly general (*Wikipedia, Webster's Dictionary*). Others are used by specific communities (*Sax's Dangerous Properties of Industrial Materials*).
Books	Longer, in-depth examinations that frequently place people, places, and events in a broader context.	Varies. Some books are written by experts for scholarly audiences. Others are written for general audiences by professional writers or journalists.
Magazines	A combination of news items and longer features and think pieces on a variety of topics. Usually published weekly or monthly.	Most are written for nonexpert audiences. Some focus on topics of general interest like politics (*Time, Economist*) or science (*National Geographic, Scientific American*). Many focus on narrower interests (*MacWorld, Cooking Light, Field & Stream*).

Source Types	Purpose	Audience
Scholarly journals	Used by scholars to share new research and discoveries. Usually published monthly or quarterly.✳	Written by experts (scholars and scientists) for other experts in the same field. Most scholarly journals focus on work in a specific academic discipline or subfield.
Newspapers and other published news sources	Factual coverage of breaking news in print or broadcast form. Most news outlets also publish reviews and opinion pieces (editorials, op-eds) on a variety of topics. Updated frequently, at least daily and sometimes more often.	Created for general audiences. Some have a national or international audience (*New York Times*, CNN, Al Jazeera). Others are local or regional (*Corvallis Gazette-Times, Syracuse Post-Standard*).
Blogs	Frequently updated websites on a variety of topics. Most blogs also support reader participation on social media and in comments.	Varies. Some are self-published with no defined audience. Some share expert or scholarly information with a broader public (*SciCurious, Archaeological Eye*). Others aggregate information on a topic (*TechCrunch*). Many traditional publications now include blogs on their websites (*Atlantic, New York Times*).
Government documents	Varies. Common purposes include: ● Information and education ● Establishing a historical record of actions taken by the government (*Congressional Record*) ● Reporting the results of expert research and scientific study	Varies. Most U.S. government publications are openly accessible to all citizens (although there are exceptions), but some are primarily used by specialized audiences or communities. ● Educational publications are written for general audiences (*California Driver's Manual*). ● Research reports (*Morbidity and Mortality Weekly Report*) inform the public and support professionals working in relevant fields.

For more about the peer review process, see p. 209. ✳

Searching with Keywords

The most important thing to understand about keyword searching in academic research is this: That there is no such thing as a perfect search. In an academic research process, you will do dozens of different searches. You will try and retry different combinations of relevant keywords, refining your initial broad search in many directions. You will try the same keyword combinations in different search tools, knowing that each tool might yield something new. Some of these attempts will succeed, and some will fail. Persistence is essential.

When you do a keyword search in a database or search engine, the computer looks for exact (or close to exact) matches for your terms in the information it has stored. Although some systems may be programmed to make common substitutions for you, for the most part computers do exactly what you tell them to do. This means that you will need to make some guesses about the specific words and phrases that are likely to be used in the articles, books, and other sources stored in your database. The better educated these guesses are, the more effective the search is likely to be. Thinking in terms of the rhetorical situation(s) that *produced* your potential sources will help. Once you realize that magazines, newspapers, journals, and websites are published with specific audiences or communities in mind, you can tailor your key terms to the communities for whom the texts were written in the first place.✱ The chart "Questions to Ask as You Devise and Revise Your List of Keywords" on p. 195 provides some useful strategies." For example, medical professionals use the term *hypertension* to describe the condition commonly called *high blood pressure*. Thinking rhetorically, you would use the specialized term to search for articles written by and for doctors and the more common term to search for news articles written for the general public.

thinking rhetorically

REVISING AND REFINING KEYWORDS

There are many places you can look for keywords. Academic research tools like databases and catalogs provide a good starting point. Many professional communities (for example, medicine, psychology, and education) have developed specialized *thesauri*, or *controlled vocabularies*, that are embedded into their search tools. Librarians attach subject terms to books and journals as they catalog them. To find these terms, look for a list of limiting or narrowing options next to your search results. (These may also be called subject headings, topics, or descriptors.)

As you find useful sources, you can use those to identify more keywords. Scan article abstracts for important terms. Academic journals often allow authors to add their own keywords to their articles. If you have the article, look for these keywords underneath the abstract. You can also find most of this information without leaving your database. Click on the title of a useful article or book, and you will find an individual item record that is likely to include a variety of keywords and subject terms as well as the article abstract.

✱ For more about genres and source types, see Chapter 2, pp. 17–20.

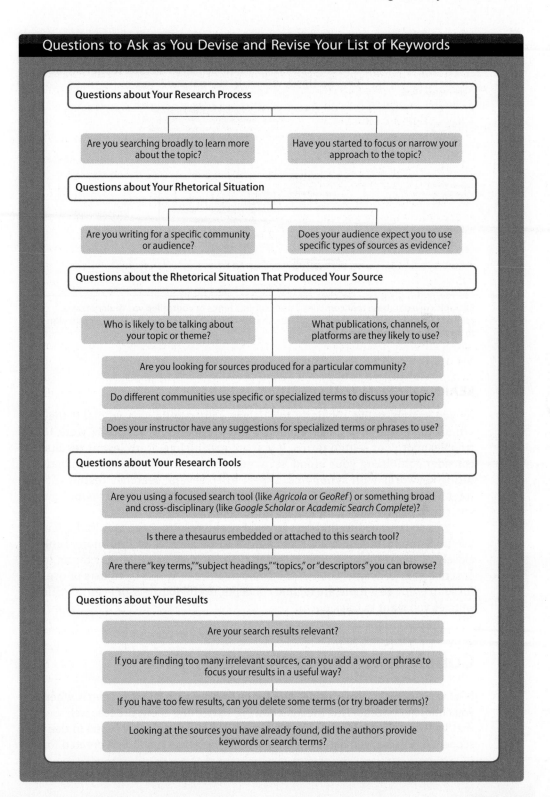

Questions to Ask as You Devise and Revise Your List of Keywords

Questions about Your Research Process

Are you searching broadly to learn more about the topic?

Have you started to focus or narrow your approach to the topic?

Questions about Your Rhetorical Situation

Are you writing for a specific community or audience?

Does your audience expect you to use specific types of sources as evidence?

Questions about the Rhetorical Situation That Produced Your Source

Who is likely to be talking about your topic or theme?

What publications, channels, or platforms are they likely to use?

Are you looking for sources produced for a particular community?

Do different communities use specific or specialized terms to discuss your topic?

Does your instructor have any suggestions for specialized terms or phrases to use?

Questions about Your Research Tools

Are you using a focused search tool (like *Agricola* or *GeoRef*) or something broad and cross-disciplinary (like *Google Scholar* or *Academic Search Complete*)?

Is there a thesaurus embedded or attached to this search tool?

Are there "key terms," "subject headings," "topics," or "descriptors" you can browse?

Questions about Your Results

Are your search results relevant?

If you are finding too many irrelevant sources, can you add a word or phrase to focus your results in a useful way?

If you have too few results, can you delete some terms (or try broader terms)?

Looking at the sources you have already found, did the authors provide keywords or search terms?

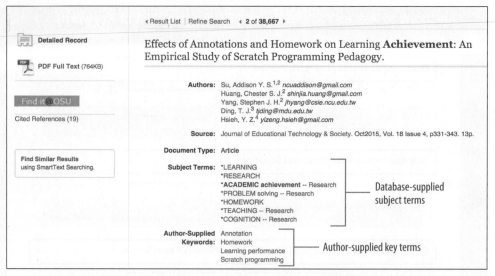

Examples of a database that compiles lists of subject terms or controlled vocabulary terms related to search results. In some databases, the user would need to click an arrow or plus sign to open up a browsable list of terms.

LEARNING FROM YOUR RESULTS

As you search, pause regularly to analyze your results as a whole. If they are useful, great; if not, use what you know about how keywords work to troubleshoot your search terms. If you are getting lots of irrelevant results, consider combining your broad keywords with additional terms or substituting keywords with synonyms. Expect to do several searches testing different combinations. If you are not finding enough results, think about how you can conceptualize your search more broadly.

You do not need to find hundreds of useful results. Once you find a few useful or interesting sources, you can use those sources to find more. Look closely at the results that are relevant to see if they use different terms to describe your concepts. Look at the bibliographies or works cited lists of useful sources to see if there are related concepts, useful journals, or even specific sources you want to track down.

Considering Your Research Tool

It is also important to consider the scope and breadth of your search when you choose keywords. This means knowing something about the research tool that you are using. Internet search engines, like *Google*, are very broad in their scope. With these, you can search for a huge variety of resources, created for all kinds of reasons, by different types of authors, in many languages. There are also research tools that are highly specialized. Some let you search for a specific type of information, like photographs, movie reviews, or historical documents (to name a few). Others give you access to sources written by and for a particular community or discipline.

The scope and coverage of your research tool should affect the keywords you choose. For example, say you were interested in the economic impact of freeway construction. For a *Google* search, you would probably choose to include all of those terms: *freeway construction economic impact*. In a database limited to articles from economics journals, however, the term *economic* would appear in almost every article. In addition, the database itself would be much smaller, meaning that a broader search might still return a focused set of results. In that case, *freeway construction* would be an effective place to start. You will learn more about the different research tools available to you later in this chapter.

Using Common Research Tools

In a typical academic research process, you will use many different types of research tools. Some are broad, and some are specialized. Some are openly available on the web for anyone with an Internet connection, and others are proprietary, requiring a license or access code to use. Here is a brief overview of the tools you are likely to use during an academic research process:

- **Article (or periodical) databases:** These databases store information about articles, sometimes (but not always) including the full text of the articles. Most article databases are accessible only to subscribers or members of an institution that subscribes, so you will need to access these databases through your library's subscriptions. They range from broad collections of published sources (for example, *EBSCO*'s *Academic Search Complete* or ProQuest's *Research Library*) to subject-specific tools (such as *Historical Abstracts* or *PubMed*). In between, you will find databases like *JSTOR* and *Web of Science*, multidisciplinary databases of scholarly research articles, and news databases like *LexisNexis* or *Ethnic News Watch*.

- **Library catalogs:** These databases store information about everything in a library's collection(s). This usually includes books and periodicals (but not the specific articles within those periodicals) and other useful materials specific to the library's user community. A school with a strong music program may collect sheet music, for example, or a chiropractic college may provide bones and skeletons for checkout.

- **Discovery layers:** More and more academic libraries are providing tools that allow you to search for content in several databases, library collections, and catalogs at the same time. The technology that makes these discovery layers work varies from campus to campus, and most of them are customized by the libraries that use them. You will usually find them in the form of search boxes posted prominently on library homepages.

- **Search engines:** Although there are some challengers, *Google* remains dominant in the area of Internet searches because of the huge amount of data it has indexed and because its ranking algorithm continues to deliver results that are perceived to be highly relevant by its users.

    In addition to *Google Search* (google.com), *Google* provides two focused search tools of particular interest to academic researchers: *Google Books* (books.google.com) and *Google Scholar* (scholar.google.com). Both tools allow you to search for specific types of scholarly information and to set your preferences to see if the materials you find are available at your library.

    While *Google* is a very useful research tool, it is not the only option when it comes to Internet search. Some privacy advocates worry about the amount of personal data it collects from its users. *Duck Duck Go* (duckduckgo.com) is a search engine that prioritizes user privacy.

Getting the Most Out of Your Research Tools

A number of strategies will help you get the most out of the databases, catalogs, search engines, and discovery layers you use in academic research and also help you retrieve the documents that look potentially useful. The questions on page 199 can help you assess whether a particular research tool will be useful for your purposes.

FIELD SEARCHING

Computers store information in categories called *fields*. Most of the time when you search a database, the computer does not match your keywords against every word in the articles or books in its index. Instead, it will focus on some fields and ignore others. For example, most article databases will look for your keywords in the title, author, abstract, and subject heading fields but not in the text of the article itself. Why? Because if your keywords appear in those main fields, the chances are good that the article will be relevant to your research. On the other hand, if your keywords appear just once in the text of a thirty-page article, that article might be only tangentially related to your topic.

Most search tools will allow you to specify the field(s) you want to search. This is very useful when you want to focus your results. For example, you can retrieve all the articles written by a specific author or all the articles on a topic published in a particular year. Specialized databases will include fields that are particularly useful to the communities or disciplines they serve. On the flip side, most databases will also allow you to search the full text of articles if you want a broader set of results than you get from the default search.

Questions to Consider When Using a New Research Tool

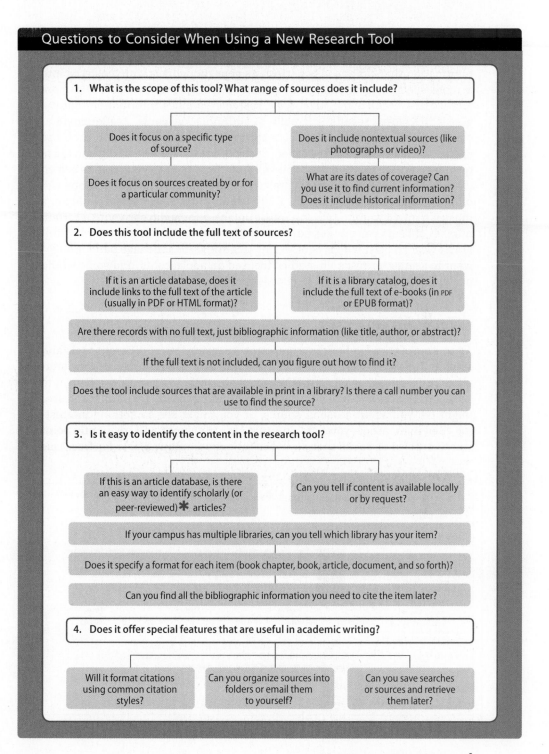

1. **What is the scope of this tool? What range of sources does it include?**

   Does it focus on a specific type of source?

   Does it include nontextual sources (like photographs or video)?

   Does it focus on sources created by or for a particular community?

   What are its dates of coverage? Can you use it to find current information? Does it include historical information?

2. **Does this tool include the full text of sources?**

   If it is an article database, does it include links to the full text of the article (usually in PDF or HTML format)?

   If it is a library catalog, does it include the full text of e-books (in PDF or EPUB format)?

   Are there records with no full text, just bibliographic information (like title, author, or abstract)?

   If the full text is not included, can you figure out how to find it?

   Does the tool include sources that are available in print in a library? Is there a call number you can use to find the source?

3. **Is it easy to identify the content in the research tool?**

   If this is an article database, is there an easy way to identify scholarly (or peer-reviewed) ✱ articles?

   Can you tell if content is available locally or by request?

   If your campus has multiple libraries, can you tell which library has your item?

   Does it specify a format for each item (book chapter, book, article, document, and so forth)?

   Can you find all the bibliographic information you need to cite the item later?

4. **Does it offer special features that are useful in academic writing?**

   Will it format citations using common citation styles?

   Can you organize sources into folders or email them to yourself?

   Can you save searches or sources and retrieve them later?

For more about peer review, see p. 209. ✱

USING FILTERS (FACETS) AND ADVANCED TOOLS

While you are learning about your topic, a broad search that pulls in more information than you need is perfect. As your thoughts start to coalesce into a more specific argument, your questions and queries will become more focused. A search engine, like *Google*, searches so much information that the best way to focus results is usually to add more keywords. Academic databases, on the other hand, let users start with a broad search and then use specific variables, sometimes called *filters* or *facets*, to refine and dig into those results in a more focused way. You will find these next to your results screen (usually on the left). Academic databases that serve specific populations will often include facets that are uniquely useful to their users. For example, a musician might want to search a music database for audio clips with a certain number of beats per minute, so she would add that filter to her search. Similarly, a psychologist who is considering treatment for a teenage patient might want to search for research studies focused on adolescents, and so he would use the *study population* facet to choose *adolescents*.

RETRIEVING FULL TEXT

As you move through your research process, using lots of different tools and services, it is almost certain that you will find yourself in this frustrating situation: You have enough information about an article to know that you want to see it, but you are not sure how to go about finding the full text. Your professor might tell you about a useful source, or you might see something interesting cited in an article you read. Internet search engines will frequently point you to articles or books that seem useful but are not available for free. This

Facets for refining results →

« Refine Results

Current Search ›

Limit To ›

Source Types ⌄

☑ All Results

☐ Academic Journals (1,223,418)

☐ Magazines (55,209)

☐ Electronic Resources (18,549)

☐ Books (6,775)

☐ Conference Materials (4,575)

Show More

Subject ›

Geographical Area ›

Publication ›

Search Results: 1 - 20 of 1,350,464   Relevance ▾   Page Options ▾

1. **Vascular disease** : molecular biology and gene therapy protocols / edited by Andrew H. Baker.

Totowa, N.J. : Humana Press, c1999. xiv, 441 p. : ill. ; 24 cm. Language: English, Database: U of Georgia Catalog

Subjects: Blood-vessels -- **Diseases** -- Molecular aspects -- Laboratory manuals; Blood-vessels -- **Diseases** -- Gene therapy -- Laboratory manuals; Blood-vessels -- **Diseases** -- Genetic aspects -- Laboratory manuals; **Vascular Diseases** -- genetics; Molecular Biology -- methods

See GIL Catalog for more information.

Location	Call No.	Status
Science Library 4th floor	RC691.4 .V36 1999	Available

2. The Portuguese version of Addenbrooke's Cognitive Examination–Revised (ACE-R) in the diagnosis of subcortical **vascular** dementia and Alzheimer's **disease**.

By: Gonçalves, Cátia. Aging, Neuropsychology, and Cognition, Jul 2015, 22 (4). 473-485. (13) (Journal Article), Database: AgeLine

Find it ⊕ UGA

Facets Screen from a Discovery Tool

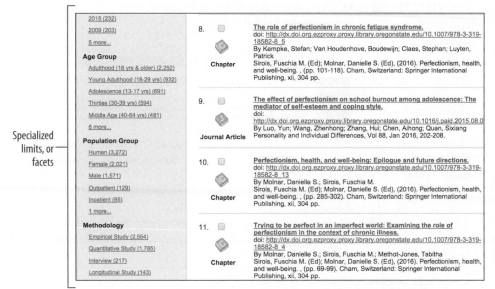

Specialized limits, or facets

Specialized Limits or Facets Available in PsycINFO (American Psychological Association)

situation will also come up when you are searching databases that do not include the full text of sources.

As a member of a college or university community, it is very likely that your library can help you get the books and articles you need. There is not room in this section to describe what to do in every possible scenario, but here are some useful guidelines to keep in mind:

- **Ask a librarian:** Most academic libraries are committed to getting their students access to all the resources they need to be successful in their research projects. If plan A does not work, your librarian will help you figure out plans B and C.

- **Cast a wide net:** To find a specific article in your library collections, you want to search in the broadest, deepest research tool you can find. If your library has a discovery tool, start there. If it does not, try a broad, multi-disciplinary database. If you are not sure where to start, ask a librarian.

- **Try multiple databases:** Just because the full text of an article is not available in one database does not mean that it is not available in all databases. Many libraries will provide tools, called *link resolvers*, that allow you to search quickly for your article in your library's other databases. These tools are usually customized by the libraries they use them. If you are not sure if your library has a link resolver, ask a librarian.

- **Try your luck on the web:** You might get lucky and find a copy of your article on the author's personal website or available for free at the journal's

« Refine Results	Search Results: 1 - 20 of 1,350,464		Relevance ▾ Page Options ▾

Current Search >

Limit To >

Source Types >

Subject >

Geographical Area >

Publication >

Publisher >

Language >

Content Provider >

1. **Vascular disease** : molecular biology and gene therapy protocols / edited by Andrew H. Baker.

Book

Totowa, N.J. : Humana Press, c1999. xiv, 441 p. : ill. ; 24 cm. Language: English, Database: U of Georgia Catalog

Subjects: Blood-vessels -- **Diseases** -- Molecular aspects -- Laboratory manuals; Blood-vessels -- **Diseases** -- Gene therapy -- Laboratory manuals; Blood-vessels -- **Diseases** -- Genetic aspects -- Laboratory manuals; **Vascular Diseases** -- genetics; Molecular Biology -- methods

See GIL Catalog for more information.

Location	Call No.	Status
Science Library 4th floor	RC691.4 .V36 1999	Available

2. The Portuguese version of Addenbrooke's Cognitive Examination–Revised (ACE-R) in the diagnosis of subcortical **vascular** dementia and Alzheimer's **disease**.

Academic Journal

By: Gonçalves, Cátia. Aging, Neuropsychology, and Cognition, Jul 2015, 22 (4). 473-485. (13) (Journal Article), Database: AgeLine

Find It ◇ UGA ——————————— Link resolver button

Example of a Link-Resolver Button in an Article Database

website. You may want to check with a librarian or your instructor to make sure that the version you find this way is a good substitute for the published copy. (Authors may post prepublication [or *preprint*] versions of their articles that may be different from the version that has been peer reviewed and edited.)

- **Use interlibrary loans:** Most academic libraries will help you request articles that they do not have in their collections. These services are usually called *ILL (Interlibrary Loan)*. Today, articles are usually delivered digitally and arrive very quickly. You can also use ILL services to request books, videos, and items in less common formats. (Leave time in your schedule for the items you request to be delivered to you.)

To learn more about accessing articles that are not immediately available, use the Guidelines for Getting the Full Text of Articles on the next page.

Staying Organized

Developing a system to keep organized is one of the biggest favors you can do for yourself as a researcher. There is nothing more frustrating than losing an hour the night before a paper is due because you have to relocate a crucial source. Many students use analog methods like Post-it Notes, binders, note cards, and file folders to keep organized. These methods work just fine,

Guidelines for Getting the Full Text of Articles

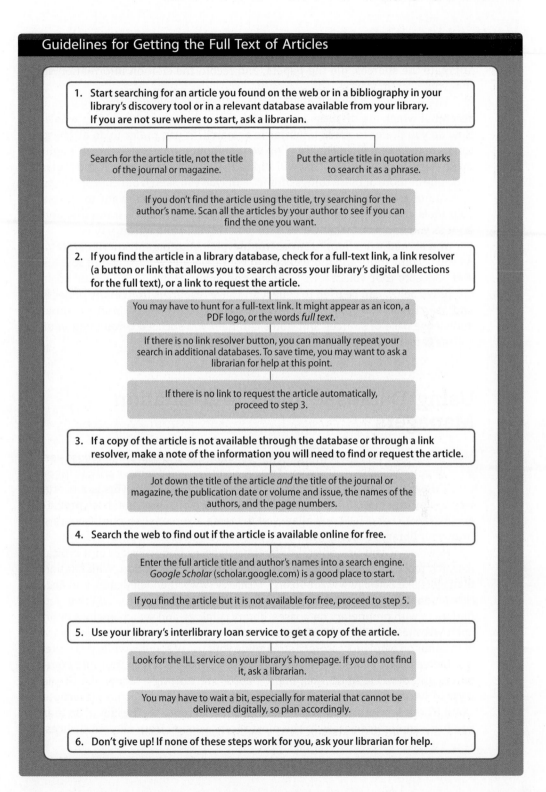

1. Start searching for an article you found on the web or in a bibliography in your library's discovery tool or in a relevant database available from your library. If you are not sure where to start, ask a librarian.

    Search for the article title, not the title of the journal or magazine.

    Put the article title in quotation marks to search it as a phrase.

    If you don't find the article using the title, try searching for the author's name. Scan all the articles by your author to see if you can find the one you want.

2. If you find the article in a library database, check for a full-text link, a link resolver (a button or link that allows you to search across your library's digital collections for the full text), or a link to request the article.

    You may have to hunt for a full-text link. It might appear as an icon, a PDF logo, or the words *full text*.

    If there is no link resolver button, you can manually repeat your search in additional databases. To save time, you may want to ask a librarian for help at this point.

    If there is no link to request the article automatically, proceed to step 3.

3. If a copy of the article is not available through the database or through a link resolver, make a note of the information you will need to find or request the article.

    Jot down the title of the article *and* the title of the journal or magazine, the publication date or volume and issue, the names of the authors, and the page numbers.

4. Search the web to find out if the article is available online for free.

    Enter the full article title and author's names into a search engine. *Google Scholar* (scholar.google.com) is a good place to start.

    If you find the article but it is not available for free, proceed to step 5.

5. Use your library's interlibrary loan service to get a copy of the article.

    Look for the ILL service on your library's homepage. If you do not find it, ask a librarian.

    You may have to wait a bit, especially for material that cannot be delivered digitally, so plan accordingly.

6. Don't give up! If none of these steps work for you, ask your librarian for help.

especially if you tend to do most of your work in one place, like your room. The important thing is that you force yourself to take the time to take the notes, annotate the sources, file the papers, and record the citation information so that your system works!

There are also a host of digital tools available to help you stay organized, several of which are discussed below. Think about your workflow as a whole: How do you prefer to read? to write? to research? If you prefer to do all these things in the same digital space — on your computer or tablet — then it might make sense to find one tool that will support all of those processes. If you prefer to do one or more of these things offline — maybe you sketch out concept maps by hand or take notes in the margins of your books — you'll want to choose your tools accordingly. Each tool has different features; expect some trial and error as you figure out what works with your research and writing style.

You should think long-term as you develop your organizational system. As you become more and more expert in your field, you will likely find sources and concepts that you return to again and again. Many of the digital tools discussed below can be used to collect and save resources from many projects and searches in one place, accessible from all your devices. Your personal knowledge base of sources and notes can help you succeed throughout your college career and beyond.

Using Database Tools and Citation Managers

Most of the research tools designed for academic use — like the databases on your library's website — allow you to save useful sources temporarily, print or email them to yourself, and format the citation information. This is a useful way to stay organized during a single research session. Some database providers (like EBSCO or JSTOR) will allow you to create a personal account (separate from your library account) where you can save sources more permanently.

However, if you use several different databases and websites in a typical research project, you may want to consider a more robust option. With citation managers like *Zotero* (www.zotero.org), *Mendeley* (www.mendeley.com), and *End-Note* (endnote.com), you can save, annotate, and organize sources whether you find them with proprietary databases, library catalogs, and search engines or on open websites like Flickr, YouTube, and Amazon. Citation managers also work with common word processors to streamline your use of sources while you write.

Increasingly, people need to manage information across multiple computers and devices. To do this, many people are turning to tools like *Google Drive* (drive.google.com), *Dropbox* (www.dropbox.com), and *Evernote* (evernote .com). These services allow you to save your documents "in the cloud" so that you have immediate access to the most recent version from all your devices.

Tools like these, and like the citation managers mentioned above, also facilitate collaboration. When you save things online, it is much easier to share them with other people.

Asking for Help

Many students avoid asking for help when they run into research problems because they think they should already know how to use the library or other research tools. Nothing could be further from the truth. Today's information landscape is so complex that everyone needs help navigating it sometimes.

Look for helpful resources on your library's website. Most academic libraries will provide research or subject guides to point you to useful resources for research on a topic or in a discipline. There may also be guides tailored to your specific course or assignment. You probably know that most libraries have a walk-up reference desk where you can ask questions about sources, databases, or the research process. Many libraries also provide these services online, by email, or even via a live chat. Finally, don't forget your instructor, frequently your first resource when you have questions about your research assignments.

● SYNTHESIZING, WRITING, AND CITING

If research is the process of learning about a topic, how do we know when it is time to stop researching and start writing? Can't we keep learning forever? The answer to that is both simple and complex. The simple answer is: It depends when your paper is due! Academic writers are usually working against deadlines, usually deadlines set by someone else. Sometimes, it is time to stop researching because the due date is approaching.

On a deeper level, academic writers know that the learning process does not end when the assignment is due or the paper submitted. They think of their work as a contribution to an ongoing conversation, a conversation they may rejoin later. As an academic writer, your work should reflect your best understanding of your topic, based on your open-minded exploration of a wide variety of perspectives and ideas. But your mind should not close when your paper is done, and you may discover something in the future that sparks you to start reimmersing yourself in your topic.

People who do a lot of research often say that they know it is time to stop gathering information when they see the same themes over and over again in their sources. When that happens, you can be fairly certain that you have been thorough in your exploration and can start to focus on synthesizing the ideas, concepts, facts, and themes that have emerged along the way.

Evaluating Sources

You start evaluating as soon as you start finding sources; sometimes you're not even aware that you're doing it. Every time you say to yourself, "That looks good" or "I think that's a tangent," you're evaluating. Once you decide to click on a source and scan it or download it to read carefully, you start evaluating at a deeper level. Critical reading is an essential part of this process.

In Chapter 2 you learned to question and interact with your sources constantly as you read them.✱ The questions you learned about in that chapter's discussion of analyzing a text's rhetorical situation are at the heart of critical evaluation: Who is the author? Why did he or she write this? What is her or his authority or expertise? What is the central argument? How does this source connect to the broader conversation(s) on this topic? These questions will frequently require you to do further research, and the answers you find may lead you to new questions, but they will help you identify those sources that will push you to learn more about your topic in a complex and meaningful way.

When you are choosing sources to support your own learning on a topic, your needs are your most important consideration. When you start developing an argument, however, you need to include your audience and their expectations in your evaluation process. As you figure out the claims you will be making, start thinking about supporting those claims with evidence. When you choose sources to support your claims, ask yourself, "Which of these sources will be the most convincing to my audience?" A source that is perfect in one rhetorical situation might not work in the next, even if you are writing about the same topic in both cases.✱

(thinking rhetorically)

Choosing Evidence

Students frequently complain that they feel disconnected from academic writing because they have to find experts who agree with their ideas; they are frustrated that teachers won't accept students' reasons and logic alone. But consider what you learned in Chapters 3 and 5 about Aristotle's appeal to ethos, or credibility.✱ The sources you choose to include in your writing say as much about you as a writer as they do about your argument. In other words, you're not just relying on your authors' ethos when you use outside sources; you're also building your own. When you use a variety of source types reflecting multiple perspectives and rigorously gathered information, you are presenting yourself as someone who is careful, thoughtful, thorough, open-minded, and able to deal with complexity. The "Questions to Consider as You Choose Sources" (pp. 207–8) can help you make sure that you are choosing the most appropriate evidence given your rhetorical situation.

✱ Take note of the different ways Twenge uses evidence to convince her three audiences (Chapter 3, pp. 70–82).

Questions to Consider as You Choose Sources

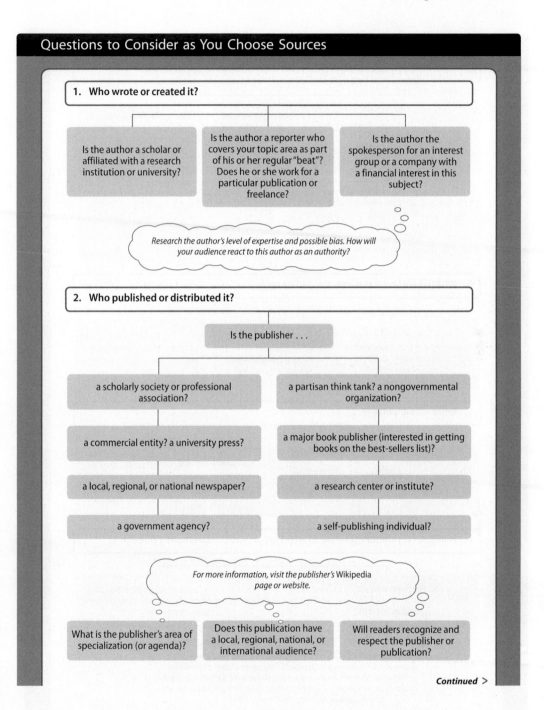

1. Who wrote or created it?

Is the author a scholar or affiliated with a research institution or university?

Is the author a reporter who covers your topic area as part of his or her regular "beat"? Does he or she work for a particular publication or freelance?

Is the author the spokesperson for an interest group or a company with a financial interest in this subject?

Research the author's level of expertise and possible bias. How will your audience react to this author as an authority?

2. Who published or distributed it?

Is the publisher . . .

a scholarly society or professional association?

a partisan think tank? a nongovernmental organization?

a commercial entity? a university press?

a major book publisher (interested in getting books on the best-sellers list)?

a local, regional, or national newspaper?

a research center or institute?

a government agency?

a self-publishing individual?

For more information, visit the publisher's Wikipedia page or website.

What is the publisher's area of specialization (or agenda)?

Does this publication have a local, regional, national, or international audience?

Will readers recognize and respect the publisher or publication?

Continued >

Questions continued

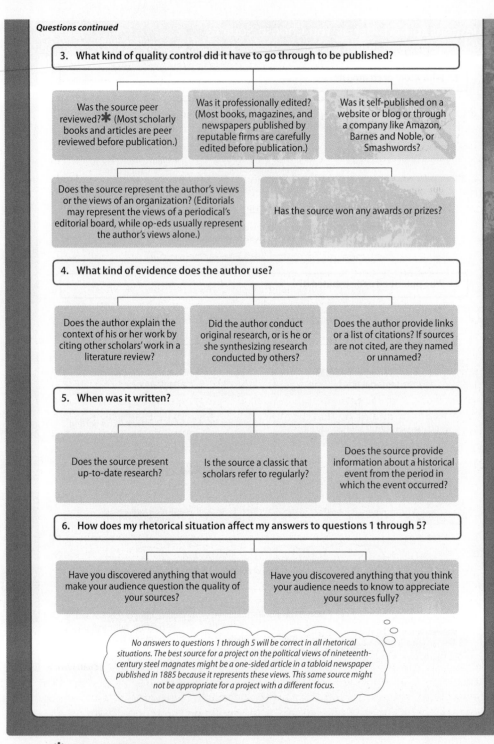

3. **What kind of quality control did it have to go through to be published?**

Was the source peer reviewed?✱ (Most scholarly books and articles are peer reviewed before publication.)

Was it professionally edited? (Most books, magazines, and newspapers published by reputable firms are carefully edited before publication.)

Was it self-published on a website or blog or through a company like Amazon, Barnes and Noble, or Smashwords?

Does the source represent the author's views or the views of an organization? (Editorials may represent the views of a periodical's editorial board, while op-eds usually represent the author's views alone.)

Has the source won any awards or prizes?

4. **What kind of evidence does the author use?**

Does the author explain the context of his or her work by citing other scholars' work in a literature review?

Did the author conduct original research, or is he or she synthesizing research conducted by others?

Does the author provide links or a list of citations? If sources are not cited, are they named or unnamed?

5. **When was it written?**

Does the source present up-to-date research?

Is the source a classic that scholars refer to regularly?

Does the source provide information about a historical event from the period in which the event occurred?

6. **How does my rhetorical situation affect my answers to questions 1 through 5?**

Have you discovered anything that would make your audience question the quality of your sources?

Have you discovered anything that you think your audience needs to know to appreciate your sources fully?

No answers to questions 1 through 5 will be correct in all rhetorical situations. The best source for a project on the political views of nineteenth-century steel magnates might be a one-sided article in a tabloid newspaper published in 1885 because it represents these views. This same source might not be appropriate for a project with a different focus.

✱ For a discussion of peer review, see p. 209.

NAVIGATING SOURCE REQUIREMENTS

As a student, you don't always have complete freedom to choose sources. Some instructors will require you to use specific source types as evidence. Therefore your first step in choosing sources should be to read your assignment carefully. Make sure that you understand any requirements. If you don't know what "scholarly monographs" or "peer-reviewed articles" are, ask! You may have to read between the lines and make sure that you understand the types of sources that will let you do what the assignment is asking you to do. For example, if you have an assignment that requires you to summarize the "current research" on a topic, your instructor probably expects you to find and read research articles in scholarly (or peer-reviewed) journals. If you need to discuss a current political debate, you will need to refer to articles in newspaper or magazines.✳

A note about peer review. *Peer review* refers to a system of quality control commonly used by academic journals. Peer-reviewed articles are usually written by scholars, people who are experts in a specific area of study and who develop that expertise by conducting original research. Before an article or book is published, it is reviewed by the author's peers (other experts in the same research area). These reviewers look at the research and decide if it makes a contribution to the broader conversation in the field. They may comment on the research question or method, or they may consider whether the data gathered supports the researcher's conclusions. They do not repeat the study to check its accuracy. The peer-reviewed (also called *refereed* or *scholarly*) article is one of the most common (and challenging) types of required sources. This is the type of writing that many of your professors do themselves. When you are required to use a peer-reviewed source, ask yourself, "Is this a research article published in a journal that uses peer review for quality control?" If you are not sure, ask your instructor or a librarian.

UNDERSTANDING ACADEMIC AUDIENCES

Occasionally, you may be given an audience to consider in your academic writing. For example, in a course about grant writing, you could be told to write a proposal to a specific funding agency. Most of the time, however, you are writing for your professor (an audience of one) or more generally for an academic audience. In either case, you should find out what you can about your audience — what they do or do not value — and select your evidence wisely.

thinking
rhetorically

There are cultures and subcultures within higher education, and what works well in one course or discipline may not be effective in another. Still, some broad generalizations apply. Most of your instructors are themselves researchers (or training to be). They write about their research, they do presentations about it, and they hope to publish their work in books and journals for other researchers to read. They build on the scholarly work that

For a list of common source types, turn back to pp. 192–93. ✳

has been published before. They analyze, criticize, expand upon, and refine the work that has influenced theirs. They also do research to inspire further inquiry; they want others to build on their work. And many researchers want their work to have a positive impact on the world: to inform policy, professional practice, or cultural expression. What does this mean for you as an academic writer? It means you can assume that research and inquiry, and the kind of expertise that comes from those activities, will be valued by your academic audience. Sources that are based on research and data reflect that value.

In addition, academic audiences tend to value sources that are published in established and recognized outlets like journals, magazines, and newspapers. There are many reasons for this. Researchers ground their work in a broader scholarly conversation; they value sources that are organized and findable, now and in the future. They review one another's work, and they value sources that have also gone through some level of quality control or review. They have published (or hope to publish) their own work and understand the quality control methods embedded in the publication process.

This does not mean that all published sources are equal. As a new academic writer, you will not always know everything you need to know about the publications you want to cite. You should expect to do a little research to ensure that a publication will be credible to your readers. Here are some things to look for. Some newspapers have a national (or international) reputation and are recognized as authoritative sources, while others are written for local or regional audiences. Your local newspaper might be a valuable source if you are writing about a local issue, but you would do better to turn to a newspaper like the *New York Times* for an analysis of a current political event. Similarly, some magazines are widely read and will be familiar to most of your readers, while others are published for niche audiences, and you may need to explain their value. Some magazines are respected as sources of quality information, while others (like the tabloids you may have seen at the supermarket) should be read for entertainment only. Some scholarly journals have a better reputation than others. To find out about the scope, audience, and reputation of the publications you plan to use, you can go the "About" pages on their websites, use *Wikipedia*, or ask your instructor.

Finally, while these guidelines can help you make good choices when writing for academic audiences, they are not hard-and-fast rules. When you know the types of evidence your audience expects to see, you can choose sources that meet those expectations. Sometimes, however, your rhetorical situation will call for another type of source. For example, if a student writing a paper about etiquette in digital environments wanted to make a claim about the differences between Twitter and Tumblr, the best evidence he or she could use might be tweets and Tumblr posts, even though tweets and blog posts are not the type of sources most academic audiences would expect to see. Just be aware that if you are going to go against your audience's expectations, you should have reasons for doing so, and you should communicate those reasons to your reader. If you think you are really pushing the boundaries, talk to your instructor in advance. Academic audiences respect creative and original thinking. If you give your academic readers a good reason to consider an unfamiliar source — a reason that shows you understand and respect their expectations — they likely will agree that the source is appropriate.

Synthesizing Information and Ideas

In Chapter 5, you learned that synthesis and analysis are closely related. In an academic research project, you will do both. As you learned in Chapter 2, effective readers interact with their sources as they read: breaking them down, asking questions, taking notes, and following up on unfamiliar ideas. This is analysis. Synthesis is the process of putting these ideas, facts, concepts, and theories together and creating something new.

Some writers find it much easier to do this as they write; the process of writing helps them make the necessary connections. These writers may write throughout their research process. Others prefer to explore their ideas in a separate planning process, outlining or mapping their ideas and then fleshing them out in a draft.

As you synthesize, you must focus on the connections among the ideas, concepts, and sources you've collected. An outline or chart (like the one below for Aletta Brenner's paper at the end of this chapter, pp. 223–32) is one way to do this. A visual map, like the one on page 171, is another option. And some students use Post-it Notes or note cards that can be grouped and regrouped into categories easily. Whatever method you use, be sure to record the source and page number along with the concept or idea to make attribution and citation easier later.

Claims	Thought/Idea/Fact	Source	Page
Existing laws don't protect these workers	¾ textile manufacturing in NYC = "substandard wages and working conditions"	TTS video	n/a
	61% garment manufacturers in LA violate wage/hour regs	Bonacich & Appelbaum	3
Traffickers prey on vulnerable members of society	⅔ US cases involve foreign-born workers	USDOJ	75–91
	traffickers pretend to help those in need w/ jobs, housing, etc.	Van Impe	114

Structuring a Supporting Paragraph in a Research Project

In most research assignments, your goal is to synthesize information from a variety of reliable sources into a clear and coherent argument that is all your own. Many instructors express frustration with students who borrow their entire argument from a single source or expert or who stitch together quotes from other people without integrating their own ideas. To avoid these problems, consider using this three-part guideline for structuring supporting paragraphs in a research paper.

1. **Introduce the main point of the paragraph in a clear topic sentence.** This sentence should tell your reader what the paragraph is going to be about and how it supports your thesis. It may also make a connection to the paragraph that precedes it.

2. **Integrate your evidence.** This will usually (but not always) be material that you quote, paraphrase, or summarize from your sources. You may synthesize information from several sources to make an original point.

3. **Explain the evidence.** Do not assume that your evidence will "speak for itself." Use your own words to make the significance of your evidence clear to your reader. Use transitional words, phrases, and sentences to link the paragraph back to the thesis and to the paragraphs that precede and follow it. Leaving quotations or facts "dangling" at the end of a paragraph is a good indication that you are asking your reader to build your argument for you.

thinking rhetorically

You will find that this three-part structure will not work in every situation. As always, the choices you make as you write will be shaped by your rhetorical situation. It may be useful, however, to keep this structure in mind as you write and revise your papers. It will prompt you to carefully consider how well you have integrated and explained your evidence and may point out areas where you can improve your argument. Take a look this supporting paragraph from Alletta Brenner's essay, which appears at the end of this chapter. Notice how the paragraph connects to her thesis:✱

Thesis

In the American garment-manufacturing industry, three forces fuel human trafficking: violations by factory owners, an available immigrant labor force, and poor enforcement of laws. Before analyzing these factors, this discussion will take a closer look at the term *human trafficking* and the scope of its practice.

✱ Her thesis appears on page 3 of her essay (p. 225).

Supporting paragraph

Studies of garment manufacturers throughout the United States have found that violations of wage, hours, and safety laws are the rule, not the exception. For example, one study of textile-manufacturing operations in the New York City area found that 75% of them were operating in the informal sector — not legally licensed or monitored — with substandard wages and working conditions ("*Treated Like Slaves*" 5). A different study described in *Behind the Label* found that 61% of garment manufacturers in Los Angeles were violating wage and hours regulations, underpaying their workers by an estimated $73 million every year. Yet another study found that in more than half of firms inspected, workers were in danger of serious injury or death as a result of health and safety law violations (Bonacich and Appelbaum 3).

The topic sentence makes it clear that in this paragraph Alletta will focus on the "first force fuel[ling] human trafficking" referred to in the thesis. Alletta does this by using a key term (*violations*) and synonyms for key terms (*garment manufacturers* instead of *factory owners*) from the thesis in her topic sentence. Alletta synthesizes information from three reliable sources to present the statistics she uses as evidence, building a stronger case than she would have had she relied on a single study. Alletta could strengthen this paragraph by adding a summary sentence at the end, explaining her analysis in her own words.

Quoting, Paraphrasing, and Summarizing

Academic writers integrate ideas and evidence from sources into their writing in three main ways:

- By *quoting*, or borrowing language exactly as it appears in the original source
- By *paraphrasing*, or explaining an idea or concept from a source using their own words and sentences
- By *summarizing*, or restating a source's central argument and main ideas concisely in their own words. (In the example from Alletta Brenner's research project on p. 212, the evidence was summarized.)

Novice academic writers frequently rely too heavily on the first practice: direct quotations. Sometimes this overquoting reflects a lack of confidence or the belief that it's always better to rely on the words of experts. As long as you cite your sources — whether you are quoting, paraphrasing, or summarizing — you can trust that your citation will tell your reader that your ideas are supported, even if you do not use direct quotations.

Sometimes overquoting occurs because transcribing a quotation requires less mental work than identifying or distilling another author's meaning. As you revise, look critically at your quotations. Relying on the words of others instead of integrating their ideas into your own prose can be a sign that you are still not entirely sure what you want to say, how your ideas fit together, or how to move from one part of your argument to another. The guidelines below can help you decide when to use quote, paraphrase, or summarize.

USING SIGNAL PHRASES

Whether you quote, paraphrase, or summarize, it is essential to acknowledge sources accurately, both in the text of your paper and in the *works cited* list at the end. (Depending on your citation style, you may use *bibliography* or *references* to describe this list.) Within the text itself, you'll often want to use

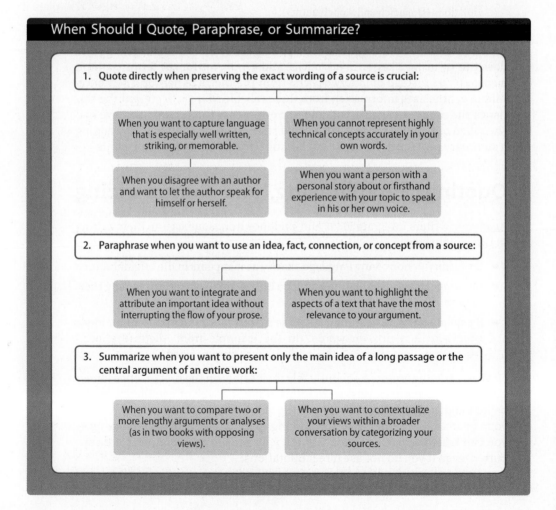

When Should I Quote, Paraphrase, or Summarize?

1. **Quote directly when preserving the exact wording of a source is crucial:**

   - When you want to capture language that is especially well written, striking, or memorable.
   - When you cannot represent highly technical concepts accurately in your own words.
   - When you disagree with an author and want to let the author speak for himself or herself.
   - When you want a person with a personal story about or firsthand experience with your topic to speak in his or her own voice.

2. **Paraphrase when you want to use an idea, fact, connection, or concept from a source:**

   - When you want to integrate and attribute an important idea without interrupting the flow of your prose.
   - When you want to highlight the aspects of a text that have the most relevance to your argument.

3. **Summarize when you want to present only the main idea of a long passage or the central argument of an entire work:**

   - When you want to compare two or more lengthy arguments or analyses (as in two books with opposing views).
   - When you want to contextualize your views within a broader conversation by categorizing your sources.

a signal phrase to introduce a source. A signal phrase includes the name(s) of the author(s) whose ideas you are discussing and a verb that communicates your attitude toward those ideas. For example, let's say that you are integrating a paraphrase of one of linguist Noam Chomsky's central claims into your paper. Consider how the following three signal phrases might help your reader understand how your ideas connect to Chomsky's:

Although Chomsky claims . . .	This phrase suggests that you are going to disagree with Chomsky's idea.
Chomsky clearly shows . . .	This phrase suggests that you agree with the idea you are about to discuss.
Chomsky believes . . .	This phrase is more neutral than the other two and could go either way.

A signal phrase can also help contextualize your source by sharing the analysis you did to evaluate it. For example, to alert readers to the fact that an author is an important voice in an ongoing conversation, with lots of followers, you could communicate that by including a phrase like "In his best-selling book . . ." in your signal phrase. If you were convinced by reading book reviews to use a particular source, you might use a signal phrase like "In her well-reviewed book, Laurel Thatcher Ulrich introduced the concept . . . ." Finally, by "bookending" borrowed ideas or information with a signal phrase and a page reference, you also clearly indicate to readers where your ideas stop and another author's begin.

A note about citations. As an academic writer, you know that you must cite the sources you quote directly, but you may be less clear about whether you must cite reworded information or ideas taken from sources. You must, and here's why: Your ideas are grounded in the conversation represented by your sources, and your citations show how all the ideas — yours and your sources' — work together. Even when you paraphrase or summarize, you want to point to the authors who have informed your thinking, both in the text and in your works cited list.

QUOTING, PARAPHRASING, AND SUMMARIZING APPROPRIATELY AND ETHICALLY

The following original passage is from a classic essay about illiteracy in the United States. Read it closely. We will use this passage throughout the next section to show you how to quote, paraphrase, and summarize appropriately in MLA style.

Original Passage

Illiterates cannot travel freely. When they attempt to do so, they encounter risks that few of us can dream of. They cannot read traffic signs and, while they often learn to recognize and decipher symbols, they cannot manage street names which they haven't seen before. The same is true for bus and subway stops. While ingenuity can sometimes help a man or woman to discern direction from familiar landmarks, buildings, cemeteries, churches, and the like, most illiterates are virtually immobilized. They seldom wander past the streets and neighborhoods they know. Geographical paralysis becomes a bitter metaphor for their entire existence. They are immobilized in almost every sense we can imagine. They can't move up. They can't move out. They cannot see beyond.

— Jonathan Kozol, "The Human Cost of an Illiterate Society," p. 256

Quoting. When you incorporate a quotation into your writing — for any reason — you must include the exact words from the source. Depending on your needs, you will do this in different ways.

USING SHORT QUOTATIONS In the following example, a student only quotes a brief snippet from the original text:

Kozol points out that people who are illiterate often can't leave their own neighborhoods, which is "a bitter metaphor for their entire existence" (256).

This student did three important things when she integrated this quotation:

1. She introduced the source with a signal phrase: "Kozol points out . . . ."
2. She used Kozol's words exactly and indicated the borrowed language with quotation marks.
3. She provided a page reference at the end of the sentence. (She needs to include the full citation for Kozol's essay in the list of works cited at the end of her paper as well.)

USING LONG QUOTATIONS In this example, a student integrates a long quotation into his paper:

Although illiteracy creates serious problems in many aspects of a person's life, its effect on mobility is particularly devastating. Jonathan Kozol puts it this way:

Illiterates cannot travel freely. When they attempt to do so, they encounter risks that few of us can dream of. They cannot read traffic signs and, while they often learn to recognize and decipher symbols, they cannot manage street names which they haven't seen before. The same is true for bus and subway stops. While ingenuity can sometimes help a man or woman to discern directions from familiar landmarks, buildings, cemeteries, churches, and the like, most illiterates are virtually immobilized. (256)

This student did three important things when integrating this quotation:

1. He introduced the quotation with a signal phrase: "Jonathan Kozol puts it this way."
2. He indented the quoted text as a block, without quotation marks.✱
3. He included a page reference at the end of the quotation. (He will also need to include a complete citation in the list of works cited at the end of his paper.)

EDITING A QUOTATION Occasionally you will need to make some slight adjustments to a quotation to fit it into your text grammatically, to add a word, to change a lowercase letter to a capital letter, and so on. Follow these rules to do so:

- Use square brackets ([ ]) when you need to change a quotation to make it fit into your text. For example: "[M]ost illiterates are virtually immobilized."
- Use ellipses (. . .) to eliminate words from the original quotation. For example, "They cannot read traffic signs and . . . cannot manage street names which they haven't seen before" (256).

You should use these techniques sparingly, and always be sure that you do not change the author's original meaning in your edited quotation.

Paraphrasing. A paraphrase should be about the same length as the original text. It must accurately reflect the meaning of that text, without copying or borrowing key words, key phrases, or sentence structure. In this example, a student appropriately paraphrased the Kozol passage above:

> Jonathan Kozol, an expert on literacy, explains that illiterates are unable to travel on their own outside their immediate neighborhoods — and that it is hazardous for them to do so. People who can't read can't figure out most signs — for traffic, unfamiliar streets, bus stops, and so on. Most of the time, illiterates are unable to move very far from where they live. In a way, the inability to travel symbolizes the lives of illiterate people, who are frozen in their economic and social situation and thus lack hope about the future (256).

This student did three important things in this paraphrase:

1. He clearly distinguished his original ideas from the ideas he paraphrased by using a signal phrase and an in-text citation.
2. He used his paraphrase to communicate Kozol's ideas and did not editorialize beyond them.

See the Writers' References appendix, pp. 341 and 376, for rules about indenting quotations as a block. ✱

3. He did not replicate Kozol's language or distinctive sentence structure. Note that this does not mean that the paraphrase doesn't share any words with the original, but instead that student only used common words (*the*, *and*) and words for which there is no ready substitute (for example, variations on the word *illiterate*).

Paraphrasing well is harder than it looks. It requires you to really understand the meaning of a text and to separate yourself enough from the original source so that you are not unduly influenced by it. It is not enough to swap out individual words; you need to make the expression of the idea or concept your own.

If you notice yourself "translating" a passage as you write — swapping in synonyms or turning words around — take a step back. It is likely that you haven't thought enough about the passage to figure out what meaning you really want to capture from it. (Note: Some instructors consider this kind of sloppy paraphrase a form of plagiarism. For more information, see the section on plagiarism on pp. 219–20.)

Summarizing. When you summarize, you condense a long passage by conveying the main idea and key supporting points in your own words and sentence structures. The long passage can be an excerpt, but it is frequently a full article or even a full book. In this example, a student has summarized the Kozol passage:

> Because illiterate people cannot read signs and other directional aids, they have difficulty navigating unfamiliar places and cannot easily move to follow social or economic opportunity (Kozol 256).

This student did four things to effectively summarize the passage:

1. She significantly condensed the initial passage, distilling it into a single, clear message.
2. She used her own language and sentence structure to express Kozol's meaning.
3. She used her summary to communicate Kozol's message, not her own.
4. She clearly attributed the source of the idea in an in-text citation.

You have probably already realized that it is very difficult to do a surface-level summary. To effectively summarize without distorting the original meaning of your source, you must understand the author's message very well. It requires careful, analytic reading. Take the time to summarize your sources as you read them. It is much easier to figure out the main point or points while the source is fresh in your mind; if you wait until you are writing, you may have to reread before you can articulate the main point.

If you get too bogged down in detail or can't help borrowing the original text, try drafting your summary without looking back at the original source or take a short break to let the details fade. You will still want to double-check your work against the original to make sure that you have accurately captured the meaning in your own words.

Avoiding Plagiarism

In academic culture, giving credit to others when you use their work — their ideas, examples, images, facts, theories, and more — is considered the right thing to do. On most campuses, there are also concrete consequences for students who plagiarize. Plagiarism is the intentional or unintentional use of others' words, ideas, or visuals as if they were your own. At some colleges, students who plagiarize fail not only the assignment but also the entire course; at colleges that have honor codes, students may even be expelled. This practice is not limited to academic settings. In recent years, professional authors, journalists, politicians, and news reporters have been caught in plagiarism scandals, leading to public apologies, embarrassment, and sometimes even job loss. On college campuses, a great deal of time and energy is spent adjudicating cases of plagiarism, intentional and unintentional. Some colleges and universities devote resources to plagiarism-detection software like SafeAssign or TurnItIn.

Could it be that plagiarism is more common now than it used to be? It is possible: Taking sloppy notes, forgetting where an idea was first seen, writing a faulty paraphrase, failing to mark a quotation in an early draft — all are easier in the era of copying and pasting from digital texts, and any one of these mistakes can lead to inadvertent plagiarism. Most people who plagiarize do so accidentally. But it is also easier to get caught today than it was in the past. The same tools that make it easy for you to copy and paste text into your paper make it easy for your instructors to copy and paste that same text into databases and search engines to track down the original source. If a text seems familiar or the language in a student's paper doesn't sound authentic, following up on that hunch is quick and easy. In a digital world, keeping track of where sources come from and when and how material from sources gets used is crucial. See the guidelines on p. 220 for strategies for avoiding plagiarism.

---

note for multilingual writers

The concept of plagiarism is central to the modern Western intellectual tradition. It rests on the notion of intellectual property: the belief that language can be "owned" by writers who create original ideas. This is not a universal belief. As a student at a college in the United States, however, you will be expected to follow Western documentation and citation practices. If you have questions or concerns about how to apply them, ask your instructor, a librarian, or a writing-center tutor.

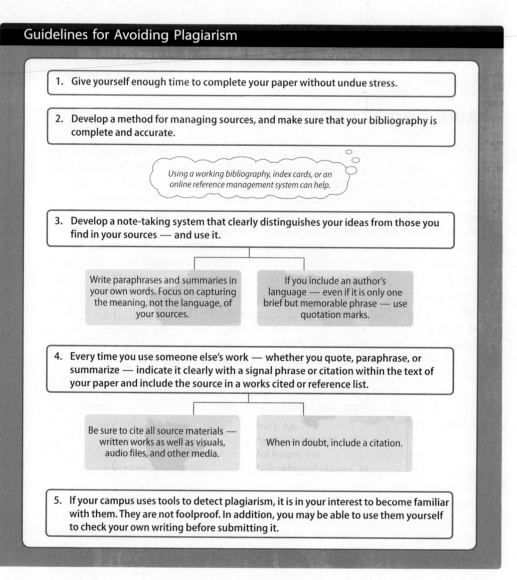

Guidelines for Avoiding Plagiarism

1. Give yourself enough time to complete your paper without undue stress.

2. Develop a method for managing sources, and make sure that your bibliography is complete and accurate.

> Using a working bibliography, index cards, or an online reference management system can help.

3. Develop a note-taking system that clearly distinguishes your ideas from those you find in your sources — and use it.

Write paraphrases and summaries in your own words. Focus on capturing the meaning, not the language, of your sources.

If you include an author's language — even if it is only one brief but memorable phrase — use quotation marks.

4. Every time you use someone else's work — whether you quote, paraphrase, or summarize — indicate it clearly with a signal phrase or citation within the text of your paper and include the source in a works cited or reference list.

Be sure to cite all source materials — written works as well as visuals, audio files, and other media.

When in doubt, include a citation.

5. If your campus uses tools to detect plagiarism, it is in your interest to become familiar with them. They are not foolproof. In addition, you may be able to use them yourself to check your own writing before submitting it.

Using Appropriate Citation Styles and Formatting

Academic communities, or disciplines, have different expectations when it comes to research writing. Some of these expectations are unwritten or tacit, but others have been defined in style guides. MLA (Modern Language

Association) style and APA (American Psychological Association) style are two of the most frequently required styles for undergraduates. (*Chicago* and Council of Science Editors are two other popular styles.) MLA style is typically used in English and other areas of the humanities; APA is common in the social sciences. It is important that you format your papers and your citations in a way that will meet your audience's expectations.

At the end of this chapter, you'll find a sample student essay using MLA documentation and formatting style (pp. 222–33). The documentation guidelines at the back of this book provide examples and explanations for MLA rules (pp. 339–75) and APA rules (pp. 376–99).

Understanding Your Rights as a Content Creator

There is a very good chance that you are already creating content for others to read and publishing it on the web: Every time you tweet, reblog a Tumblr post, or upload a video to YouTube, you're creating content. As an academic writer, you are a creator of information, and as a content creator, you have to decide how much control you want to assert over the things you create. Most social media platforms allow you to decide how public you want your contributions to be. Still, when you sign up for a service, you agree to share the rights to the intellectual property you create and publish on the site, even if you are allowed to adjust your privacy settings.

As you develop your skills as a researcher, you may be in a position to publish your own research, even as an undergraduate. When that happens, you will usually be asked to sign an agreement turning over some, or all, of your copyright to a publisher. You can negotiate with the publishers, keeping some rights to your work. Your professors and mentors can help guide you through this process.

There is no correct answer to the question, "How public should my intellectual property be?" There are arguments for keeping control of your intellectual property and arguments for sharing it. Your individual situation will determine what is right for you. One way that you can assert some control over content you do make public is by attaching a Creative Commons license to it (creativecommons.org). These licenses allow you to define, in advance, whether or not other people have permission to use your work, and they allow you to set conditions on that permission. There are a variety of licenses to choose from. These licenses do not eliminate your copyright, nor do they legally transfer ownership of your intellectual property to anyone else. They simply grant permission, in advance, to others who may want to use your work.

Isn't There More to Say Here on Writing?

This final section might strike you as brief, when there's clearly so much to think about when writing with, and from, sources. Yet the brevity of this section illustrates something important about the recursive nature of the writing process and, indeed, of all rhetorical activities. While there's much to learn about how to do research, and while integrating sources into your writing takes practice, you will not (and should not) throw away everything you know about your writing process when you write with, and from, sources. The strategies you've explored throughout this book apply to research-based writing: Part One leads you to think broadly about reading, writing, and rhetoric; Part Two helps you accomplish specific kinds of reading and writing tasks; and Part Three gives you practical strategies for reading and writing effectively. So the short answer to the question posed in the heading above is that there is more to say — and you'll find it in the rest of the book.

Sample Research Essay Using MLA Documentation Style

Here is a research essay by Alletta Brenner, a student at the University of Oregon. Read it carefully to see how she synthesizes information from sources and skillfully integrates that information to support her own ideas.

Brenner 1

Alletta Brenner
Professor Clark
WR 222
9 May 2016

Name, instructor,
course, and date
double-spaced
and aligned at
left margin

Sweatshop U.S.A.: Human Trafficking in the American
Garment-Manufacturing Industry

Title centered

In early 1999, Nguyen Thi Le, a Vietnamese mother of two, signed a
four-year contract to work for a garment factory in American Samoa.
The island is a US territory with a low minimum wage where enterprises
seeking to benefit from cheap labor costs can produce items with a "Made
in U.S.A." label. Dazzled by the opportunity to live in America and earn
American wages, Nguyen eagerly looked forward to her new job, even
though she would have to move an ocean away from her family and take
out high-interest loans to cover the $5,000 fee for airfare and work permits.
Despite these hardships, the job seemed to offer her the chance to earn
wages more than twelve times those available at home. If she worked

Fig. 1. Two Vietnamese workers after they were beaten at the Daewoosa
factory, American Samoa, 2000 ("Made" cover).

Brenner 2

abroad for just a few years, Nguyen believed, she could dramatically
improve the quality of her family's life (Gittelsohn 16).

However, upon arrival, Nguyen found a situation radically different
from what she had expected. She and the other Daewoosa workers were paid
only a fraction of the wages the garment factory had promised. The factory
owner deducted high fees—sometimes half their monthly paychecks—for
room and board that the contract had indicated would be "free," and when
orders were slow, the owner didn't pay them at all. Kept in a guarded
compound, Nguyen and her fellow garment sewers had to work sixteen- to
eighteen-hour days under deplorable conditions. When they complained,
they were often punished with violence, intimidation, and starvation (see
figs. 1 and 2). According to *The New York Times*, when word of these abuses
surfaced and the factory finally shut down in 2001, the women were left
out on the streets with no means to return home (Greenhouse A14). Stuck
in Samoa, Nguyen learned that back home, loan sharks were hounding
her family to repay the debt she had incurred. Though Nguyen eventually
received US government aid, which allowed her to move to the American

Opens with a narrative to engage readers' interest

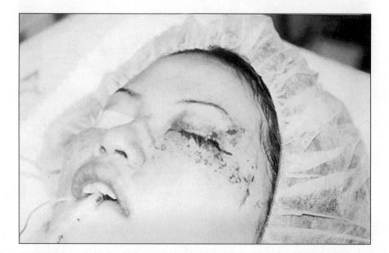

Fig. 2. Daewoosa woman worker who lost her eye after being brutally beaten
on November 28, 2000 (*Vietnamese Workers*).

Brenner 3

mainland and acquire a new job, it will take many years for her to recover from the damage to her personal and financial life (Gittlesohn 16).

Human Trafficking: An Overview

Though what happened to Nguyen and the other workers may seem unusual to you, such occurrences are common in the United States today. Every year thousands of persons fall victim to human trafficking: they are transported either against their will or under false pretenses for the purpose of economic or sexual exploitation. In recent years, politicians as well as the media have paid more attention to human trafficking. Movies, newspaper articles, presidential speeches, and United Nations resolutions portray human trafficking as a negative consequence of globalization, capitalism, and immigration. Yet rarely do such accounts analyze the larger questions of how and why human trafficking exists. This essay will address some of these larger questions. In the American garment-manufacturing industry, three forces fuel human trafficking: violations by factory owners, an available immigrant labor force, and poor enforcement of laws. Before analyzing these factors, this discussion will take a closer look at the term *human trafficking* and the scope of its practice.

The official definition of the term *human trafficking* evolved in 2001 as a part of a United Nations treaty on transnational crime. The UN's *Protocol to Prevent, Suppress and Punish Trafficking in Persons* defines human trafficking as the "recruitment, transportation, transfer, harboring or receipt of persons by means of threat or use of force or other means of coercion, abduction, fraud, deception, abuse of power or position of vulnerability . . . for the purpose of exploitation" (Article 3). According to this definition, human trafficking has three components: (1) movement over geographical space, either across or within national borders; (2) the extraction of profits by the exploitation of victims' bodies or skills; and (3) the coercion of victims, which may include a wide range of tactics and forms (Gallagher 986–87).

How, then, does human trafficking work in practice? It can occur both within and across national borders and may involve a single perpetrator

Side annotations:

Main topic of human trafficking introduced

States thesis and key questions for essay

Definition and background information provided

Brenner 4

or an organized criminal network of recruiters, transporters, sellers, and buyers. The victims of human trafficking usually want to migrate and seek new employment. Van Impe reports that human traffickers typically pose as employers, employment agencies, or smugglers, offering to help victims by assisting them in entering a country or providing a job (114). Once an individual accepts this help, the trafficker may keep up the charade for quite some time, so when victims eventually realize what has happened, they may feel there is no choice but to submit to the trafficker's demands. After individuals have moved and started working, human traffickers use abusive and illegitimate tactics to force victims to work. They may, for example, threaten victims with physical violence, deportation, or debt bondage, wherein traffickers claim that a victim owes them money for transport or other services and then force him or her to work off the debt (*Trafficking* 21).

How widespread is human trafficking in the United States? Both because of its relative wealth, and because it is a destination country for millions of migrant workers every year, the United States is one of the primary destinations for trafficked persons worldwide ("Country Report"). The US Department of State estimates that between fourteen and eighteen thousand persons are trafficked in the United States each year (*Trafficking* 1–4); although the basis for these numbers is unclear, they appear to be consistent with global estimates on human trafficking. Not all victims are foreign-born, but immigrants are particularly vulnerable to such exploitation. In the United States, two-thirds of all human-trafficking cases investigated and brought to court since 2001 have involved foreign-born migrant workers, according to a report by the US Department of Justice (*Report* 75–91).

Human Trafficking in American Garment Manufacturing

Some of the largest human trafficking cases uncovered to date in the United States have occurred in the garment-manufacturing industry. In addition to the Daewoosa factory in American Samoa, investigators have found large sweatshops utilizing human trafficking in California, New

Signal phrase for source at end of sentence, before in-text citation

York, and the Northern Mariana Islands. Police discovered one of the worst cases in El Monte, California, in 1995, where they found seventy-two Thai immigrants in an apartment complex surrounded by razor wire and armed guards. Trafficked from Thailand, the men and women had endured eighteen-hour workdays, seven days a week for seven years, sewing clothing for some of the nation's best-known clothing companies. Constantly threatened by violence to themselves and their families at home, the victims were forced to live in the same tiny, filthy apartments in which they worked. Grossly underpaid and forced to buy food and other necessities from their captors at inflated prices, the workers were in constant debt. To make matters worse, when police discovered and raided the compound, they arrested the workers for immigration violations and put them in jail. Only when local leaders and nongovernmental organizations spurred public outrage over the case were the workers released on bond and able to begin normal lives in the America they had once envisioned (Ross 143–47).

Violations by factory owners are one reason human trafficking such as that in El Monte occurs. Because most American clothing companies outsource the production of their garments to factories around the world, US factories are under constant pressure to lower costs. Unfortunately, this pressure often translates into poorer wages and working conditions for those who produce clothing in this country and illegal activity on the part of their employers (Bonacich and Appelbaum 137). A common violation is the failure of factory owners to pay workers the legally mandated minimum wage. Unlike most US workers, garment workers earn a piece-rate wage rather than an hourly wage. Because the amount of available work and the going rate for items sewed constantly fluctuate, the amount workers earn often reflects downward pressure. Employers, however, are supposed to make up the difference so that workers still make the minimum wage. When employers fail to do so or attempt to comply with the law by forcing workers to speed up production, the result is substandard pay. Some workers in the

First subtopic: violations by factory owners

Brenner 6

American garment-manufacturing industry earn less than $4 an hour, and those who work from home make even less, sometimes as little as $2 per hour.

Studies of garment manufacturers throughout the United States have found that violations of wage, hours, and safety laws are the rule, not the exception. For example, one study of textile-manufacturing operations in the New York City area found that 75% of them were operating in the informal sector—not legally licensed or monitored—with substandard wages and working conditions (*"Treated Like Slaves"* 5). A different study described in *Behind the Label* found that 61% of garment manufacturers in Los Angeles were violating wage and hours regulations, underpaying their workers by an estimated $73 million every year. Yet another study found that in more than half of firms inspected, workers were in danger of serious injury or death as a result of health and safety law violations (Bonacich and Appelbaum 3).

Violations by factory owners, however, are only one part of the picture in the garment industry. Another factor is the availability of an immigrant labor force. Factories that produce clothing in the United States and its territories are heavily dependent on immigrants to meet their labor needs. For example, Bonacich and Appelbaum report that in Los Angeles, which has the highest concentration of garment manufacturers in the nation, 81% of workers are Asian and Latino immigrants (171–75). In American territories, immigrant labor is even more prevalent. In Saipan, the US territory with the largest number of garment factories, almost all garment workers are foreign-born. Because the indigenous populations of many territories are so small, most garment manufacturers could not survive without imported labor. For this reason, territories do not operate under the same immigration laws as the American mainland, where relatively few visas are available to low-skilled workers. Consequently, employers in US territories are able to legally recruit and import thousands of employees from Asia and South America (Parks 19–22).

For a number of reasons, the use of a predominantly immigrant workforce makes it easier for unscrupulous manufacturers to coerce and exploit workers. First, immigrant workers facing economic hardships often

Second subtopic: available immigrant labor force

Brenner 7

have no choice but to take risks and accept poor treatment and pay. A book published by Human Rights Watch quotes one Guatemalan woman who stayed with her abusive employers for many years:

> I am the single mother of two daughters. The salary there [in Guatemala] is not sufficient for their studies, their food, their clothes. I want them to get ahead in life. . . . Sometimes one is pressured by the economic situation. It's terrible what one suffers. . . . Sometimes I ask myself why I put up with so much. It's for this, for my mother and my daughters. (Pier 9–10)

A second reason is that those who enter the country illegally fear deportation. Indeed, as Lelio points out, because of their status, illegal immigrants often work in the informal sector "under the table" in order to avoid authorities, which makes it much easier for traffickers to exploit them (68–69). These jobs may be within individual homes or at businesses owned by other immigrants within tightly knit ethnic communities. The strong fear of deportation that permeates many such communities enables factory owners to effectively enforce a code of silence on their employees, legal and illegal immigrants alike (Bonacich and Appelbaum 144–47).

A third reason is that many immigrants lack English language skills and knowledge of American laws and culture. Thus they find it difficult to do anything about the situation they're in.

Even though most immigrant workers at garment factories in American territories are there legally, they are just as vulnerable to human trafficking. Like immigrant workers in the mainland United States, they are often under a great deal of pressure to support families back at home. Because most immigrant workers in the territories take out high-interest loans simply to get their jobs, they are even more likely to accept deplorable working conditions than are illegal immigrants on the mainland. When employers fail to pay their workers appropriately (or sometimes at all), they can prevent workers from paying off their debts and thereby keep them as virtual prisoners. Indeed, human rights organizations have reported that thousands of garment workers live in severe debt bondage throughout American territories in the Pacific (Clarren 35–36).

Brenner 8

The incidence of human trafficking gets further impetus from the "guest worker" immigration laws. Because such workers' visas depend on their employment with a particular firm, leaving the employer with whom they are contracted would break the terms of their visa. Ironically, this places legal guest workers in a more precarious position than those who immigrate illegally, for guest workers who violate the terms of their visas face deportation. Though some workers do leave and turn to prostitution or other forms of black market work to survive, the fear of being sent back home is a constant one. As a result, most stay with their abusive employers, hoping to someday pay off their debts and leave (Clarren 38–41).

Third subtopic: poor enforcement of laws

A final factor that contributes to human trafficking in the garment industry is that where protective labor laws and standards do exist, their enforcement tends to be lax (Branigin 21–28). Despite the rampant violation of labor and safety laws throughout the industry, most garment manufacturers are able to avoid legal repercussions. Even when human-trafficking cases in the garment industry do occur, they tend to run much longer than other trafficking cases, averaging over six years in duration (*Matrix* 6–9). This occurs for several reasons. First of all, as noted previously, many garment factories operate illegally. Because the Department of Labor only investigates such operations when someone makes an official complaint, traffickers who can control their victims are able to avoid detection. This is generally not a difficult task because victims of trafficking often lack the skills and knowledge required to take such action.

Second, inspectors from the Department of Labor and Occupational Safety and Health Administration rarely visit those factories that do operate legally. Even when workers complain, it can take up to a year for the government to open a case and make inspections. Moreover, when an investigation finally begins, owners often have advance warning, allowing them to conceal violations before the inspectors arrive. Some factory owners under investigation have been known to close up shop and disappear, leaving their employees out on the streets with months of back pay owed to them. These tendencies are especially prevalent in US territories because of the geographic and bureaucratic distance between the islands

Brenner 9

and the governmental bodies that are supposed to regulate them. With the enforcement of most laws left up to local officials and agencies, many of whom stand to profit from arrangements with factory owners, human traffickers find it easy to avoid government interference. The risk for such activity is thus relatively low (Ross 210–11).

Conclusion

In 2001, the same year that Nguyen's case hit the American media, President Bush proclaimed that the United States has a special duty to fight against "the trade in human misery" that human trafficking represents today. Since then, the United States has created a wide range of antitrafficking laws and measures, but little has changed in the lives of human-trafficking victims. Although the owner of the Daewoosa factory was eventually convicted of enslaving more than 250 workers in his factory, other garment manufacturers continue to operate much as they have. Some high-profile American clothing companies, such as the Gap, have promised to stop contracting with factories that violate labor laws; however, the essential setup of the industry remains fully intact. Until these problems are directly addressed, human trafficking will continue to be a blemish on the American dream and, as President Bush recognized in a 2004 speech, "a shame to our country."

Conclusion restates the problem

Works Cited

Heading centered

Bonacich, Edna, and Richard Appelbaum. *Behind the Label: Inequality in the Los Angeles Apparel Industry*. U of California P, 2000.

Branigin, William. "A Life of Exhaustion, Beating and Isolation." *The Washington Post*, 5 Jan. 1999, p. A6.

Bush, George W. National Training Conference on Combating Human Trafficking, Marriott Waterside Hotel, Tampa, 16 July 2004. Address.

Clarren, Rebecca. "Paradise Lost." *Ms.*, Spring 2006, pp. 35–41.

"Country Report—The United States." *The Protection Project*, The Protection Project, 2002, www.protectionproject.org/.

Gallagher, Anne. "Human Rights and the New UN Protocols on Trafficking and Migrant Smuggling: A Preliminary Analysis." *Human Rights Quarterly*, vol. 23, no. 4, Nov. 2001, pp. 986–87.

Gittelsohn, John. "U.S. Sends Strong Message to Those Who Traffic in Human Lives." U.S. Department of State, U.S. Embassy, ILL Digital,

First line of each entry flush left, subsequent lines indented

List double-spaced throughout (single-spaced here for length)

Brenner 10

2003, pp. 14–17, iipdigital.usembassy.gov/st/english/article/2003/07
/20030701160433retropc0.6718408.html#axzz46IFBj1HO

Greenhouse, Steven. "Beatings and Other Abuses Cited at Samoan Apparel Plant
That Supplied U.S. Retailers." *The New York Times*, 6 Feb. 2001, p. A14.

"In the News: US Policy Change Could Aid Daewoosa Trafficking Victims."
Vietnamese Workers Abroad: A Rights Watch, Boat People SOS, 2008,
vietnameseworkersabroad.wordpress.com/2008/12/11/in-the-news-us
-policy-change-could-aid-daewoosa-trafficking-victims/.

Lelio, Marmora. *International Migration Policies and Programmes.*
International Organization for Migration, 1999.

*"Made in the U.S.A."? Clothing for Wal-Mart, J.C. Penney, Target and
Sears Made by Women Held under Conditions of Indentured Servitude.*
National Labor Committee, 2001.

*Matrix of Some of the Major Trafficking Cases in the United States of the
Last Eight Years.* United States, Department of State, May 2003.

Parks, Virginia. *The Geography of Immigrant Labor Markets: Space,
Networks, and Gender.* LFB Scholarly Publishing, 2005.

Pier, Carol. *Hidden in the Home: Abuse of Domestic Workers with Special
Visas in the United States.* Human Rights Watch, 2001.

Report on Activities to Combat Human Trafficking: Fiscal Years 2001–2005.
United States, Department of Justice, 2006, lincolngoldfinch.com
/wp-content/uploads/2015/06/DOJ-Report-on-Activities-to-Combat
-Human-Trafficking.pdf.

Ross, Andrew, editor. *No Sweat: Fashion, Free Trade and the Rights of
Garment Workers.* Verso, 1997.

Trafficking in Persons Report. United States, Department of State, June 2004,
www.state.gov/documents/organization/34158.pdf.

*"Treated Like Slaves": Donna Karan, Inc., Violates Women Workers'
Human Rights.* Center for Economic and Social Rights, 1999.

"Protocol to Prevent, Suppress and Punish Trafficking in Persons,
Especially Women and Children, Supplementing the United Nations
Convention against Transnational Organized Crime." *United
Nations Convention against Transnational Organized Crime and the
Protocols Thereto.* United Nations, Office on Drugs and Crime,
2004, pp. 41–51. www.unodc.org/documents/middleeastandnorthafrica
/organised-crime/UNITED_NATIONS_CONVENTION_AGAINST
_TRANSNATIONAL_ORGANIZED_CRIME_AND_THE
_PROTOCOLS_THERETO.pdf.

Van Impe, Kristof. "People for Sale: The Need for a Multidisciplinary Approach
toward Human Trafficking." *International Migration*, vol. 3, no. 38, 2000,
pp. 113–91. *Wiley Online Library*, doi:10.1111/1468-2435.00117.

for **thought, discussion, and writing**

1. After reviewing this chapter's discussion of paraphrasing and summarizing, select one of the sample essays that appear in Chapter 8, "Writing in the Disciplines: Making Choices as You Write." Choose a paragraph from the essay — one that strikes you as particularly interesting or informative. After reading this paragraph carefully, first write a paraphrase of it, and then summarize the same passage. Finally, write a paragraph explaining why your paraphrase and summary of this passage are effective.

2. Identify an important journal for scholars in your major. You will probably have to ask someone (a major adviser, a professor, or a librarian) to recommend a journal that is important and useful in your field. If you do not have a major yet, ask the person who teaches your favorite class to recommend a journal of interest to scholars in that field.

   Now browse through a copy of that journal, taking note of the articles and the topics it covers. As you browse, ask yourself the following:

   ● How did you gain access to the journal? You might have found the journal online, if access is open. More likely, you needed to access the journal via your library. Think about access as an issue: How easy or difficult is it for people to use the content in this journal? What would the advantages and disadvantages be of changing its level of accessibility?

   ● What do the articles tell you about how scholars in your field write? Do the articles have common characteristics (abstracts, section headings, citation styles)? Do the authors write in first person or third person? Do they place their arguments into a context for you? What are some things they seem to assume that you, as the reader, already know?

   Write a paragraph reflecting on what you've learned.

3. Go to ScienceBlogs (scienceblogs.com) or ResearchBlogging (researchblogging .org). Find a post about an article written by a scholar in your major discipline or a post about an article on a topic discussed in one of your classes. Read the blog post and any responses to it. Take note of important issues or any points of controversy, and try to determine where this scholarly discussion fits within the larger field.

   Now find and read the original article. (If the article is not available for free online — that is, if the link provided takes you to a fee-based site — search for the article through your library instead.) Compare the discussion on the blog about the article to the article itself. What information is available in both places? What information is available only in the post or only in the article? How might each source be useful in an academic research process?

8

Writing in the Disciplines: Making Choices as You Write

thinking rhetorically

Part One of *The Academic Writer* began by asking this question: What does it mean to be a writer today? Despite the increasing prevalence and power of multimodel compositions, writing does indeed still matter. In fact, those with access to computer and online technologies are writing more than ever before.

How can you negotiate the opportunities and challenges of communication in today's world? As Part One emphasizes, you can draw on your understanding of rhetoric, the rhetorical situation, and the writing process. Part Two of *The Academic Writer* builds on the rhetorical approach to writing conveyed in Part One. It applies this approach to the essential intellectual skills needed in college reading and writing. One of the challenges you face as an academic writer is learning how to apply these skills in a wide range of courses—from philosophy to chemistry to psychology. You can use your knowledge of rhetoric and of the writing process to negotiate the demands of academic writing in a broad variety of disciplines. This chapter will help you do so, and it will introduce you to the expectations and conventions of these disciplines.

Meeting these expectations can be a significant challenge, especially when you take courses outside of your major. By thinking rhetorically about the nature and purpose of writing in the various academic disciplines, you can gain confidence, skill, and flexibility as a writer—attributes that will prove very useful when you graduate and begin a career. By learning how writing works in different fields, you can become a successful academic writer in *all* the courses you take in college.

Thinking Rhetorically about Writing in the Disciplines

The conventions of academic writing in different disciplines have histories worth noting. For example, scholars generally attribute the development of scientific writing to the rise of humanism and the scientific method during the Renaissance. When in 1660 a group of scientists in Great Britain founded the Royal Society (a body that still exists), they worked to standardize methods for reporting scientific results. Practitioners refined these textual conventions over time, but, as David Porush notes in A Short Guide to Writing about Science, "the basic outline of the scientific report has changed little in over a century."[1] There is no need for it to change because the scientific report still meets the day-to-day needs of working scientists: It encourages effective and efficient communication among scientists.

Textual conventions in the humanities, too, have a history. One particularly important impetus for those conventions was the desire to interpret religious texts, which has been a strong tradition in most of the world's major religions. Over time, interpretive practices for reading religious texts were applied to secular works as well. This tradition of textual interpretation is particularly important to such disciplines in the humanities as literature, philosophy, religious studies, and rhetoric, but it has influenced such other areas as history, music, and art.

Whereas scientists work to achieve objective and reliable results that others can replicate, those in the humanities often study questions for which there is no definitive answer. What constitutes a just war? How can we best interpret Shakespeare's The Tempest or best understand the concept of free will? Scholars in the humanities take it for granted that there are multiple ways to approach any topic. Although they hope that their writing will lead to a broader understanding of their subject, they don't expect that their research will result in the kind of knowledge generated by the scientific method. Indeed, in the humanities, originality is valued over replicability.

This brief discussion of the development of textual conventions in the humanities and sciences emphasizes that rather than being arbitrary forms to be filled in, the textual conventions that characterize different academic disciplines are deeply grounded in their history, nature, and goals. It is important to remember, however, that even though disciplines in these two broad areas share a number of general assumptions and practices, variations do exist. Moreover, disciplines in the social sciences, such as psychology, sociology, economics, anthropology, communication, and political science, include elements of both the sciences and the humanities, as does much writing in business.

As a college student, you can better understand your teachers' expectations as you move from, say, a chemistry class to a course in art appreciation by thinking rhetorically about the subject matter, methodology, and goals of the disciplines. The questions on the next page can guide this analysis.

---

[1] David Porush. A Short Guide to Writing about Science. Harper Collins, 1995, p. 8.

for **exploration**

Take five minutes to write freely about your experience creating texts in various disciplines. Are you more confident writing for some disciplines than for others? Why? What questions seem most important to you as you anticipate writing in courses across the curriculum?

for **collaboration**

Bring your response to the previous Exploration to class, and share it with a group of students. After each person has summarized his or her ideas, spend a few minutes noting common experiences and questions. Be prepared to report your results to the class.

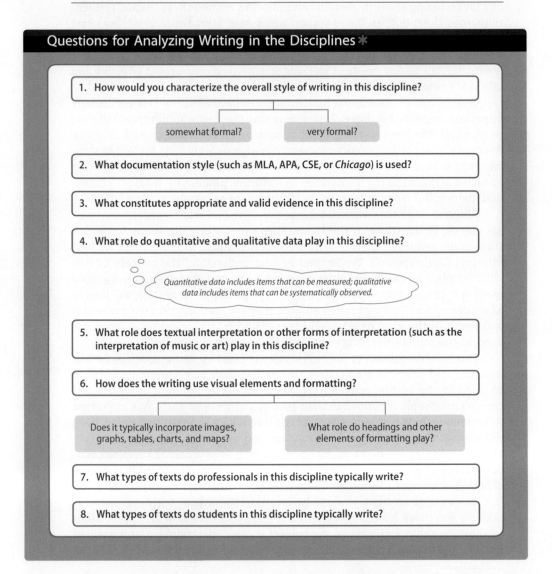

Questions for Analyzing Writing in the Disciplines ✳

1. How would you characterize the overall style of writing in this discipline?

   somewhat formal?   very formal?

2. What documentation style (such as MLA, APA, CSE, or *Chicago*) is used?

3. What constitutes appropriate and valid evidence in this discipline?

4. What role do quantitative and qualitative data play in this discipline?

   Quantitative data includes items that can be measured; qualitative data includes items that can be systematically observed.

5. What role does textual interpretation or other forms of interpretation (such as the interpretation of music or art) play in this discipline?

6. How does the writing use visual elements and formatting?

   Does it typically incorporate images, graphs, tables, charts, and maps?   What role do headings and other elements of formatting play?

7. What types of texts do professionals in this discipline typically write?

8. What types of texts do students in this discipline typically write?

✳ To answer these questions, you'll need to read representative examples of writing from each field; your teacher or your own coursework can provide such examples

Writing in the Humanities

In a general sense, those studying the humanities are attempting to determine what something means or how it can best be understood or evaluated. For this reason, textual interpretation is central to the humanities. Depending on their discipline, scholars in the humanities may read the same or similar texts for different analytical and interpretive purposes. An art critic may analyze paintings by the American folk artist Grandma Moses (1860–1961) to study her use of brush strokes and color, while a historian might study her work to learn more about life in rural America in the mid-twentieth century.

Sample Student Essay in the Humanities*

On pp. 238–40 is an essay written for an in-class exam in a US history course. The author, Elizabeth Ridlington, was responding to the following question: *During his presidency, did Lincoln primarily respond to public opinion, or did he shape public opinion more than he responded to it?* In analyzing her rhetorical situation, Elizabeth commented:

thinking
rhetorically

My teacher phrased this as an either/or question, inviting a strong and clear position statement at the outset. Because this is a history class, I knew that I needed to provide evidence from primary documents we'd read, offering the kind of specific and concrete details that historians value. I also needed to incorporate material from the lectures. In thinking about how to present information, I knew it was important not just to provide evidence but also to explain the logic behind my choice of details. Doing this makes for a more coherent essay in which every paragraph supports my initial thesis statement. Finally, looking at events and actions from multiple perspectives is very important for historians, so I explained Lincoln's decisions in a variety of circumstances essentially as a series of mini case studies.

For a research essay with citations and a list of works cited in MLA style, see Chapter 7, pp. 223–32.

Elizabeth Ridlington

Lincoln's Presidency and Public Opinion

This essay argues that Lincoln shaped public opinion more than he responded to it and examines the issues of military recruitment, Northern war goals, and emancipation as examples of Lincoln's interaction with public opinion.

At the start of the war, Lincoln needed men for the military. Because of this, he could hardly ignore public opinion. But even as he responded in various ways to public opinion, he did not significantly modify his policy goals. Lincoln's first call for seventy-five thousand soldiers was filled through militias that were under state rather than federal control. As the war progressed, the federal government took more control of military recruitment. The government set quotas for each state and permitted the enlistment of African American soldiers via the Militia Act. Kentucky, a slave state, protested, and Lincoln waived the requirement that blacks be enlisted so long as Kentucky still filled its quota. In so doing, Lincoln responded to public opinion without changing his policy goal. Another example of this strategy occurred when the first federal draft produced riots in New York City. When the riots occurred, Lincoln relented temporarily and waited for the unrest to quiet down. Then he reinstated the federal draft. Again, Lincoln responded to a volatile situation and even temporarily withdrew the federal draft. But he ultimately reinstated the draft.

Lincoln's efforts to shape public opinion in the North in favor of the war provide another example of his proactive stance. Whenever he discussed the war, Lincoln equated it with freedom and democracy. Northerners linked democracy with their personal freedom and daily well-being, and therefore Lincoln's linkage of the Union with democracy fostered Northern support for the war even when the conflict was bloody and Northern victory was anything but guaranteed. After the emancipation, Lincoln continued his effort to influence public opinion by connecting the abolition of slavery with democracy. The image of a "new birth of freedom" that Lincoln painted in his Gettysburg Address was part of this effort to overcome Northern racism and a reluctance to fight for the freedom of blacks.

The process that led to the emancipation provides perhaps the clearest example of Lincoln's determination to shape public opinion rather than simply respond to it. Lincoln's views on slavery were more progressive than those of many of his contemporaries. These views caused him personally to wish to abolish slavery. At the same time, Lincoln knew that winning the war was his highest priority. Consequently, retaining the border states early in the war was more important to Lincoln than emancipation, and for this reason he revoked Freemont's proclamation in the summer of 1861. In explaining this decision privately to Freemont, Lincoln admitted that he was concerned about public opinion in Kentucky since it would determine whether Kentucky stayed with the Union. However, in a letter that Lincoln knew might be made public, Lincoln denied that he had reacted to Kentucky's pressure and claimed that emancipation was not among his powers—a clear effort to gain public approval. Even when others such as Frederick Douglass (in a September 1861 speech) demanded emancipation, Lincoln did not change his policy. Not until July 1862 did Lincoln draft the preliminary Emancipation Proclamation. Rather than releasing it then, at the advice of his cabinet he waited for a time when it would have a more positive impact on public opinion.

Several primary sources cited to support third point

Lincoln realized that the timing of the Emancipation Proclamation was crucial. While he was waiting for an opportune time to release the document, Horace Greeley published his "Prayer of Twenty Million," calling on Lincoln to abolish slavery. Lincoln's response, a letter for publication, emphasized the importance of the Union and the secondary importance of the status of slavery. By taking this position, Lincoln hoped to shape public opinion. He wanted Northerners to believe that he saw the Union cause as foremost, so that the release of the proclamation would create as few racial concerns as possible. The Emancipation Proclamation was released on January 1, 1863. Once it was released, Lincoln stood by it despite strong public opposition. In 1864, when Democrats called for an

Final section cites primary sources, gives dates

armistice with the South, Lincoln stood by his decision to abolish slavery. He defended his position on military grounds, hoping voters would approve in the 1864 election.

As the examples I have just discussed indicate, Lincoln could not ignore public opinion, and at times he had to respond to it. But when Lincoln did so, this was always part of a larger effort to shape public opinion and to ensure Union victory.

Conclusion
restates thesis

Writing in the Natural and Applied Sciences

Whatever their skill level, students in the humanities expect that writing will play a key role in their education. Those majoring in other areas, particularly the natural and applied sciences, sometimes assume otherwise. They're wrong. Here's what David Porush tells students to expect if they enter the sciences:

> You will write to report your research. You will write to communicate with colleagues at other institutions. You will write to request financial support for your work. You will write to colleagues, managers, and subordinates in your own institutional setting. You will write instructions and memos, and keep lab notebooks.[2]

Porush's argument is supported by other scientists. Victoria McMillan, author of *Writing Papers in the Biological Sciences*, points out that "no experiment, however brilliant, can contribute to the existing fund of scientific knowledge unless it has been described to others working in the same field."[3]

Because established formats for scientific writing encourage efficient communication and facilitate replication of experiments, scientists use them whenever possible. At the same time, they pay particular attention to the effective presentation of data, often using figures, tables, images, and models. This attention to format and document design is equally important in student writing in the sciences.

---

[2]David Porush. *A Short Guide to Writing about Science*. Harper Collins, 1995, xxi–xxii.
[3]Victoria McMillan. *Writing Papers in the Biological Sciences*. 4th ed. Bedford/St. Martin's, 2006, 1.

Scientists write a variety of kinds of texts. Since maintaining and operating labs can be costly, scientists spend considerable time writing proposals to fund research projects. Most research proposals follow this format: title page, introduction, purpose, significance of the study, methods, time line, budget, and references. The format for research reports and journal articles is generally as follows: title, author(s), abstract, introduction, literature review, materials and methods, results, discussion, and references.

Sample Student Essay in the Natural and Applied Sciences

Scientists value precision, clarity, and objectivity. The following essay, an undergraduate research proposal by Tara Gupta, demonstrates these traits. Note that Tara uses headings to mark the various sections of her proposal. She also uses the documentation style required by the Council of Science Editors (CSE). For details on this reference style, consult its handbook, *Scientific Style and Format: The CSE Manual for Authors, Editors, and Publishers*, 8th ed. (2014).

Complete title,
specific and
informative

Field Measurements of
Photosynthesis and Transpiration
Rates in Dwarf Snapdragon
(*Chaenorrhinum minus* Lange):
An Investigation of Water Stress
Adaptations

Tara Gupta

Proposal for a
Summer Research
Fellowship
Colgate University
March 11, 2016

Water Stress Adaptations 2

Introduction

Dwarf snapdragon (*Chaenorrhinum minus*) is a weedy pioneer plant found growing in central New York during spring and summer. The distribution of this species has been limited almost exclusively to the cinder ballast of railroad tracks[1], a harsh environment characterized by intense sunlight and poor soil water retention. Given such environmental conditions, one would expect *C. minus* to exhibit anatomical features similar to those of xeromorphic plants (species adapted to arid habitats).

However, this is not the case. T. Gupta and R. Arnold (unpublished) have found that the leaves and stems of *C. minus* are not covered by a thick, waxy cuticle but rather with a thin cuticle that is less effective in inhibiting water loss through diffusion. The root system is not long and thick, capable of reaching deeper, moister soils; instead, it is thin and diffuse, permeating only the topmost (and driest) soil horizon. Moreover, in contrast to many xeromorphic plants, the stomata (pores regulating gas exchange) are not found in sunken crypts or cavities in the epidermis that retard water loss from transpiration.

Despite a lack of these morphological adaptations to water stress, *C. minus* continues to grow and reproduce when morning dew has been its only source of water for up to five weeks (R. Arnold, personal communication). Such growth involves fixation of carbon by photosynthesis and requires that the stomata be open to admit sufficient carbon dioxide. Given the dry, sunny environment, the time required for adequate carbon fixation must also mean a significant loss of water through transpiration as open stomata exchange carbon dioxide with water. How does *C. minus* balance the need for carbon with the need to conserve water?

Aims of the Proposed Study

The above observations have led me to an exploration of the extent to which *C. minus* is able to photosynthesize under conditions of low water

Headings throughout help organize proposal

Introduction states scientific issue, gives background information, cites relevant studies

Personal letter cited in parentheses, not included in references

Aims and scope of proposed study

availability. It is my hypothesis that *C. minus* adapts to these conditions by photosynthesizing in the early morning and late afternoon, when leaf and air temperatures are lower and transpirational water loss is reduced. I predict that its photosynthetic rate may be very low, perhaps even zero, on hot, sunny afternoons. Similar diurnal changes in photosynthetic rate in response to midday water deficits have been described in crop plants[2,3]. There is only one comparable study[4] on noncrop species in their natural habitats.

CSE documentation, citation-sequence format

Thus, the research proposed here aims to help explain the apparent paradox of an organism that thrives in water-stressed conditions despite a lack of morphological adaptations. This summer's work will also serve as a basis for controlled experiments in a plant growth chamber on the individual effects of temperature, light intensity, soil water availability, and other environmental factors on photosynthesis and transpiration rates. These experiments are planned for the coming fall semester.

States significance of study

Connects study to future research projects

Methodology described briefly

Methods

Simultaneous measurements of photosynthesis and transpiration rates will indicate the balance *C. minus* has achieved in acquiring the energy it needs while retaining the water available to it. These measurements will be taken daily at field sites in the Hamilton, NY, area, using an LI-6220 portable photosynthesis system (LICOR, Inc., Lincoln, NE). Basic methodology and use of correction factors will be similar to that described in related studies[5–7]. Data will be collected at regular intervals throughout the daylight hours and will be related to measurements of ambient air temperature, leaf temperature, relative humidity, light intensity, wind velocity, and cloud cover.

Water Stress Adaptations 4

Budget

1 kg soda lime	$56.00
(for absorption of CO_2 in photosynthesis analyzer)	
1 kg anhydrous magnesium perchlorate	$280.75
(used as desiccant for photosynthesis analyzer)	
Shipping of chemicals (estimate)	$15.00
Estimated 500 miles travel to field sites in own car	$207.15
@ $0.405/mile	
CO_2 cylinder, 80 days rental	$100.00
(for calibration of photosynthesis analyzer)	
TOTAL REQUEST	$658.90

Itemized budget gives details

References

1. Widrlechner MP. Historical and phenological observations of the spread of *Chaenorrhinum minus* across North America. Can J Bot. 1983;61(1):179–187.
2. Manhas JG, Sukumaran NP. Diurnal changes in net photosynthetic rate in potato in two environments. Potato Res. 1988;31:375–378.
3. Yordanov I, Tsonev T, Velikova V, Georgieva K, Ivanov P, Tsenov N, Petrova T. Changes in CO_2 assimilation, transpiration and stomatal resistance in different wheat cultivars experiencing drought under field conditions. Bulg J Plant Physiol. 2001;27(3–4):20–33.
4. Chaves MM, Pereira JS, Maroco J, Rodrigues ML, Ricardo CP, Osório ML, Carvalho I, Faria T, Pinheiro C. How plants cope with water stress in the field: photosynthesis and growth. Ann Bot. 2002;89(Jun): 907–916.
5. Jarvis A, Davies W. The coupled response of stomatal conductance to photosynthesis and transpiration. J Exp Bot. 1998;49(Mar):399–406.
6. Kallarackal J, Milburn JA, Baker DA. Water relations of the banana. III. Effects of controlled water stress on water potential, transpiration, photosynthesis and leaf growth. Aust J Plant Physiol. 1990;17(1): 79–90.
7. Idso SB, Allen SG, Kimball BA, Choudhury BJ. Problems with porometry: measuring net photosynthesis by leaf chamber techniques. Agron J. 1989;81(4):475–479.

Numbered references relate to citation order in text

Before embarking on her grant proposal, Tara spent time analyzing her rhetorical situation. Here is her analysis:

thinking
rhetorically

I am writing to persuade a committee to grant me funds for working on my scientific project. Because I want the readers (scientists) to notice my ideas and not the medium, and because I want to convince them of my scientific merit and training, I will use the traditional medium and style for scientists—a written research proposal. A research proposal follows a standard format. Hence, I would say that my role as a writer, and my product, is relatively fixed. In the end, I want readers to hear the voice of a fellow scientist who is hardworking, trustworthy, and a creative observer.

To be persuasive, I need to understand the behaviors, motivations, and values of scientists. I expect the readers, as scientists, to immediately begin formulating questions and hypotheses as I present the background information—scientists instinctively do this. My job is to give them the best information to help them form the questions I would like them to be thinking about. In addition, it is important to include all logical steps in proceeding with my idea and background knowledge, especially since the scientists reading my proposal are not all in my research field and cannot fill in the information gaps. Nothing is more boring or painful for a scientist than reading something that has flawed logic which they have trouble following or understanding. I also need credibility, so I will have references for all background information.

Scientists value communication that is succinct, concrete, logical, accurate, and above all, *objective*. For example, if I want to discuss the environmental conditions these plants live in, I will not write a subjective account of how I've grown up in this area and know how hot and dry it can be in the summer. Instead, I will present an objective account of the environmental conditions using specific language (location, temperatures, moisture). In science, the hardest information to write about is ambiguous information, since it can be difficult to be succinct, concrete, logical, accurate, or objective; though in the end, this ambiguity is where the next experiment is and where the real work is to be done.

In reading Tara's analysis, you might be surprised by how extensive and complex her thinking is. After all, scientists just follow the conventions of scientific writing, don't they? Tara's analysis is a powerful demonstration of the kind of rhetorical sensitivity that scientists draw on when they write proposals, lab reports, and other scientific documents.

Writing in the Social Sciences

The social sciences, disciplines such as sociology, psychology, anthropology, communications, political science, and economics, draw from both the sciences and the humanities. Many scholars in the social sciences address questions that interest humanities scholars, but their methods of investigating these questions differ. Consider the topic of aging. An English professor might study several novels with elderly characters to see how they are represented. A philosopher might consider the moral and political issues surrounding aging and longevity. A sociologist, on the other hand, might explore the ways in which the elderly are treated in a particular community and evaluate the impact such treatment has on elders' moods and activity levels.

In general, social scientists explore questions through controlled methods, including the following:

- Surveys and questionnaires
- Experiments
- Observation
- Interviews
- Case studies
- Ethnographic field work

Careful observation is central to all these methods because, like scientists, social scientists value the development of objective and reliable knowledge. As a result, they ground their arguments in quantitative data (data based on statistics) or qualitative data (data based on observations). An economist studying the effect of aging on earning power might gather statistics that enable him to generate a hypothesis about their relationship. A sociologist might use one or more surveys, interviews, and case studies to gain a nuanced understanding of the impact of aging on self-perception and self-esteem.

Writing is as important in the social sciences as it is in the natural and applied sciences and humanities. As Deidre McCloskey, internationally known economist and author of *Economical Writing*, points out, a person trained in economics "is likely to spend most of her working life writing papers, reports, memoranda, proposals, columns, and letters. Economics depends much more on writing (and on speaking, another neglected art) than on the statistics and mathematics usually touted as the tools of the trade."[4] In her book, McCloskey argues for the value of a rhetorical approach to writing in economics.

Sample Student Essay in the Social Sciences

Pages 249–57 present an example of effective writing in the social sciences. Tawnya Redding wrote this essay for an upper-level psychology class in clinical research methods. A major assignment for the class was to write a review of the literature on a possible theoretical experiment. Tawnya chose to write her review on music preference and the risk for depression and suicide in adolescents. Note that this essay uses APA documentation style, required for this course.[5] For details on this reference style, see the APA Documentation Guidelines section at the back of this book.

---

[4] Deidre McCloskey. *Economical Writing*. 2nd ed., Waveland Press, 1999, p. 5.
[5] The formatting shown in the sample paper that follows is consistent with typical APA requirements for undergraduate writing. Formatting guidelines for papers prepared for publication differ in some respects; see pp. 376–99.

Running head: MOOD MUSIC   1

"Running head:" followed by shortened title in all caps and page number

Mood Music:

Music Preference and the Risk for Depression and Suicide in Adolescents

Title, double-spaced

Tawnya Redding

Psychology 480

Professor Bernieri

February 25, 2016

Name and affiliation, double-spaced

MOOD MUSIC 2

Heading, centered

Abstract

The last 25 years have shown a growing concern for the effects that certain genres of music (such as heavy metal and country) have on youth. While a correlational link between these problematic genres and increased risk for depression and suicide in adolescents has been established, researchers have been unable to pinpoint what is responsible for this link, and a causal relationship has not been determined. This paper will begin by discussing correlational literature concerning music preference and increased risk for depression and suicide, as well as the possible reasons for this link. Finally, studies concerning the effects of music on mood will be discussed. This examination of the literature on music and increased risk for depression and suicide points out the limitations of previous research and suggests the need for new research establishing a causal relationship for this link as well as research into the specific factors that may contribute to an increased risk for depression and suicide in adolescents.

Summary of
literature review

Double-spaced

MOOD MUSIC   3

Mood Music: Music Preference and
the Risk for Depression and Suicide in Adolescents

Music is a significant part of American culture. Since the explosion of
rock 'n' roll in the 1950s there has been a concern for the effects that music
may have on those who choose to listen and especially for the youth of
society. The genres most likely to come under suspicion in recent decades
have included heavy metal, country, and even blues. These genres have
been suspected of having adverse effects on the mood and behavior of
young listeners. But can music really alter the disposition and create self-
destructive behaviors in listeners? And if so, what genres and aspects of
these genres are responsible?

The following review of the literature will establish the correlation
between potentially problematic genres of music, such as heavy metal
and country, and depression and suicide risk. First, correlational studies
concerning music preference and suicide risk will be discussed, followed
by a discussion of the literature concerning the possible reasons for this
link. Finally, studies concerning the effects of music on mood will be
discussed. Despite the link between genres such as heavy metal and
country and suicide risk, previous research has been unable to establish the
causal nature of this link.

The Correlation between Music and Depression and Suicide Risk

Studies over the past several decades have set out to establish the
causal nature of the link between music and mood by examining the
correlation between youth music preference and risk for depression and
suicide. A large number of these studies have focused on heavy metal
and country music as the main genre culprits in association with youth
suicidality and depression (Lacourse, Claes, & Villeneuve, 2001; Scheel
& Westefeld, 1999; Stack & Gundlach, 1992). Stack and Gundlach (1992)
examined the radio airtime devoted to country music in 49 metropolitan
areas and found that the higher the percentages of country music airtime,

Full title, centered,
not bold

Opening
sentences set
context for
study, argue for
significance

Questions frame
focus of report

Second paragraph
outlines paper's
purpose,
structure, and
conclusion

Heading, centered
and boldface

Opening sets
chronological
context

APA-style
parenthetical
citation of three
studies

MOOD MUSIC   4

Source named in the body of the text

the higher the incidence of suicides among whites. Stack and Gundlach (1992) hypothesized that themes in country music (such as alcohol abuse) promote audience identification and reinforce preexisting suicidal mood and that the themes associated with country music were responsible for the elevated suicide rates. Similarly, Scheel and Westefeld (1999) found a correlation between heavy metal music listeners and an increased risk for suicide, as did Lacourse et al. (2001).

Headings organize literature review; section discusses studies that fail to establish music as causal factor in suicide risk

Reasons for the Link: Characteristics of Those Who Listen to Problematic Music

Unfortunately, previous studies concerning music preference and suicide risk have been unable to determine a causal relationship and have focused mainly on establishing a correlation between suicide risk and music preference. This leaves the question open as to whether an individual at risk for depression and suicide is attracted to certain genres of music or whether the music helps induce the mood, or both.

Some studies have suggested that music preference may simply be a reflection of other underlying problems associated with increased risk for suicide (Lacourse et al., 2001; Scheel & Westefeld, 1999). For example, in research done by Scheel and Westefeld (1999), adolescents who listened to heavy metal were found to have lower scores on Linehan, Goodstein, Nielsen, and Chiles's Reasons for Living Inventory (1983) and several of its subscales, a self-report measure designed to assess potential reasons for not committing suicide. These adolescents were also found to have lower scores on several subscales of the Reason for Living Inventory, including responsibility to family along with survival and coping beliefs.

Identifies an important psychological measurement tool

Other risk factors associated with suicide and suicidal behaviors include poor family relationships, depression, alienation, anomie, and drug and alcohol abuse (Bobakova, Madarasova Geckova, Reijneveld, & Van Dijk, 2012; Lacourse et al., 2001). Lacourse et al. (2001) examined 275 adolescents in the Montreal region with a preference for heavy metal

MOOD MUSIC   5

and found that this preference was not significantly related to suicide risk
when other risk factors were controlled for. This was also the conclusion of
Scheel and Westefeld (1999), in which music preference for heavy metal
was thought to be a red flag for suicide vulnerability but which suggested
that the source of the problem may lie more in personal and familial
characteristics.

George, Stickle, Rachid, and Wopnford (2007) further explored the
correlation between suicide risk and music preference by attempting
to identify the personality characteristics of those with a preference for
different genres of music. A community sample of 358 individuals was
assessed for preference of 30 different styles of music, along with a
number of personality characteristics including self-esteem, intelligence,
spirituality, social skills, locus of control, openness, conscientiousness,
extraversion, agreeableness, emotional stability, hostility, and depression
(George et al., 2007). The 30 styles of music were then sorted into eight
categories: rebellious (for example, punk and heavy metal), classical,
rhythmic and intense (including hip-hop, rap, pop), easy listening, fringe
(for example, techno), contemporary Christian, jazz and blues, and
traditional Christian. The results revealed an almost comprehensively
negative personality profile for those who preferred to listen to the
rebellious and rhythmic and intense categories, while those who preferred
classical music tended to have a comprehensively positive profile. Like
Scheel and Westefeld (1999) and Lacourse et al. (2001), this study also
supports the theory that youth are drawn to certain genres of music based
on already existing factors, whether they be related to personality or
situational variables.

Reasons for the Link: Characteristics of Problematic Music

Another possible explanation for the correlation between suicide risk
and music preference is that the lyrics and themes of the music have a
negative effect on listeners. In this scenario, music is thought to exacerbate

Transitional sentence announces discussion of new group of studies

MOOD MUSIC   6

an already depressed mood and hence contribute to an increased risk for suicide. This was the proposed reasoning behind higher suicide rates in whites in Stack and Gundlach's (1992) study linking country music to suicide risk. In this case, the themes associated with country music were thought to promote audience identification and reinforce preexisting behaviors associated with suicidality (such as alcohol consumption).

Year distinguishes this study from previously cited study conducted by same researcher

Stack (2000) also studied individuals with a musical preference for blues to determine whether the themes in blues music could increase the level of suicide acceptability. The results demonstrated that blues fans were no more accepting of suicide than nonfans, but that blues listeners were found to have lowered religiosity levels, an important factor for suicide acceptability (Stack, 2000). Despite this link between possible suicidal behavior and a preference for blues music, the actual suicide behavior of blues fans has not been explored, and thus no concrete associations can be made.

The Effect of Music on Mood

Heading and transitional sentence identify problem not yet answered by research

While studies examining the relationship between music genres such as heavy metal, country, and blues have been able to establish a correlation between music preference and suicide risk, it is still unclear from these studies what effect music has on the mood of the listener. Previous research has suggested that some forms of music can both improve and depress mood (Johnson, 2009; Lai, 1999; Siedliecki & Good, 2006; Smith & Noon, 1998).

Lai (1999) found that changes in mood were more likely to be found in an experimental group of depressed women versus a control group. The physiological variables of heart rate, respiratory rate, blood pressure, and immediate mood state were measured before and after the experimental group had listened to music of their choice for 30 minutes and the control group had listened to pink sound (similar to white noise) for 30 minutes. It was found that music listening had a greater effect on participants'

MOOD MUSIC   7

physiological conditions, as decreases in heart rate, blood pressure, and
respiratory rate were greater in the experiment group than the control group
(Lai, 1999). This study suggests that music can have a positive effect on
depressed individuals when they are allowed to choose the music they are
listening to.

In a similar study, Siedliecki and Good (2006) found that music
can increase a listener's sense of power and decrease depression, pain,
and disability. Researchers randomly assigned 60 African American
and Caucasian participants with chronic nonmalignant pain to either a
standard music group (offered a choice of instrumental music between
piano, jazz, orchestra, harp, and synthesizer), a patterning music group
(asked to choose between music to ease muscle tension, facilitate sleep,
or decrease anxiety), or a control group. There were no statistically
significant differences between the two music groups. However, the
music groups had significantly less pain, depression, and disability than
the control group.

On the other hand, Martin, Clark, and Pearce (1993) identified a
subgroup of heavy metal fans who reported feeling worse after listening
to their music of choice. Although this subgroup did exist, there was also
evidence that listening to heavy metal results in more positive affect for
some, and it was hypothesized that those who experience negative affect
after listening to their preferred genre of heavy metal may be most at risk
for suicidal behaviors.

Mentions
seemingly
contradictory
research findings

Smith and Noon (1998) also determined that music can have a
negative effect on mood. Six songs were selected for the particular theme
they embodied: (1) vigorous, (2) fatigued, (3) angry, (4) depressed, (5)
tense, and (6) all moods. The results indicated that selections 3–6 had
significant effects on the mood of participants, with selection 6 (all moods)
resulting in the greatest positive change in mood while selection 5 (tense)
resulted in the greatest negative change in mood. Selection 4 (depressed)
was found to sap the vigor and increase anger/hostility in participants,

MOOD MUSIC 8

while selection 5 (tense) significantly depressed participants and made them more anxious. Although this study did not specifically comment on the effects of different genres on mood, the results do indicate that certain themes can indeed depress mood. The participants for this study were undergraduate students who were not depressed, and thus it seems that certain types of music can have a negative effect on the mood of healthy individuals.

Is There Evidence for a Causal Relationship?

Despite the correlation between certain music genres (especially that of heavy metal) and an increased risk for depression and suicidal behaviors in adolescents, it remains unclear whether these types of music can alter the mood of at-risk youth in a negative way. This view of the correlation between music and suicide risk is supported by a meta-analysis done by Baker and Bor (2008), in which the authors assert that most studies reject the notion that music is a causal factor and suggest that music preference is more indicative of emotional vulnerability. However, it is still unknown whether these genres can negatively alter mood at all and, if they can, whether it is the themes and lyrics associated with the music that are responsible. Clearly, more research is needed to further examine this correlation, as a causal link between these genres of music and suicide risk has yet to be shown. However, even if the theory put forth by Baker and Bor (2008) and other researchers is true, it is still important to investigate the effects that music can have on those who may be at risk for suicide and depression. Even if music is not the ultimate cause of suicidal behavior, it may act as a catalyst that further pushes individuals into a state of depression and increased risk for suicidal behavior.

Marginal notes:

Heading and transitional sentence emphasize inconclusive nature of studies

Emphasizes need for further research and suggests direction research might take

MOOD MUSIC   9

References begin new page

References

Baker, F., & Bor, W. (2008). Can music preference indicate mental health status in young people? *Australasian Psychiatry, 16*(4), 284–288. Retrieved from http://www3.interscience.wiley.com/journal/118565538/home

Bobakova, D., Madarasova Geckova, A., Reijneveld, S. A., & Van Dijik, J. P. (2012). Subculture affiliation is associated with substance use of adolescents. *Addiction Research, 18*(2), 91–96.

George, D., Stickle, K., Rachid, F., & Wopnford, A. (2007). The association between types of music enjoyed and cognitive, behavioral, and personality factors of those who listen. *Psychomusicology, 19*(2), 32–56.

Johnson, F. D. (2009). The effects of music on temporary disposition. Retrieved from http://clearinghouse.missouriwestern.edu /manuscripts/260.php

Lacourse, E., Claes, M., & Villeneuve, M. (2001). Heavy metal music and adolescent suicidal risk. *Journal of Youth and Adolescence, 30*(3), 321–332.

Lai, Y. (1999). Effects of music listening on depressed women in Taiwan. *Issues in Mental Health Nursing, 20*(3), 229–246. doi: 10.1080/016128499248637

Linehan, M. M., Goodstein, J. L., Nielsen, S. L., & Chiles, J. A. (1983). Reasons for staying alive when you are thinking of killing yourself: The Reasons for Living Inventory. *Journal of Consulting and Clinical Psychology, 51*(2), 276–286. doi:10.1037/0022–006X.51.2.276

Martin, G., Clark, M., & Pearce, C. (1993). Adolescent suicide: Music preference as an indicator of vulnerability. *Journal of the American Academy of Child and Adolescent Psychiatry, 32*(3), 530–535.

Scheel, K., & Westefeld, J. (1999). Heavy metal music and adolescent suicidality: An empirical investigation. *Adolescence, 34*(134), 253–273.

Siedliecki, S., & Good, M. (2006). Effect of music on power, pain, depression and disability. *Journal of Advanced Nursing, 54*(5), 553–562. doi:10.1111/j.1365-2648.2006.03860.x

Smith, J. L., & Noon, J. (1998). Objective measurement of mood change induced by contemporary music. *Journal of Psychiatric & Mental Health Nursing, 5*(5), 403–408.

Snipes, J., & Maguire, E. (1995). Country music, suicide, and spuriousness. *Social Forces, 74*(1), 327–329.

Stack, S. (2000). Blues fans and suicide acceptability. *Death Studies, 24*(3), 223–231. doi:10.1080/074811800200559

Stack, S., & Gundlach, J. (1992). The effect of country music on suicide. *Social Forces, 71*(1), 211–218.

First line of each entry begins at left margin; subsequent lines indent ½ inch

Online document identified with URL

Citation follows APA style for print journal article

Article from database identified with the article's DOI (digital object identifier)

References double-spaced (single-spaced here for length)

thinking
rhetorically

In reflecting on her experience writing this essay, Tawnya had this to say:

My assignment was to write a literature review on a topic of my choice. Since the literature review is a fairly standard genre in psychology, my role as a writer was both fixed and flexible. It was fixed in that I had to follow the conventions for literature reviews; this includes conveying the tone of a serious scholar, in part by using the statement-oriented third person rather than the first person. But it was flexible in that I was able to determine what material to include in the review, the conclusions I drew from my analysis, and my suggestions for future research. My professor was the intended reader for this essay, but I also had a more general reader in mind as I wrote. I wanted to encourage readers to think critically about the studies being presented. What are the strengths and weaknesses of the studies? How might they be improved? What information is lacking in the current research? What problem has previous research not yet addressed, and how might future research do so? The constraints of the literature review were actually enabling in that I was able to build on this foundation to go beyond simply conveying information to raising important questions about my topic and the research that has investigated it.

Writing in Business

Historians of business writing emphasize the roles that the spread of literacy in the Middle Ages and the invention of the printing press in the Renaissance played in this history. According to Malcolm Richardson, a contributor to *Studies in the History of Business Writing,* even before capitalism developed in Europe there were scribes and scriveners, who played a key role in both government and private communication.[6] In the fourteenth century, what some historians believe to be the first business writing school opened in England, and in the sixteenth century, Angell Day's *The English Secretary or Method of Writing Epistles and Letters,* one of the earliest texts on business communication (which at that time primarily took the form of letter writing), appeared.

The conventions that characterize modern business writing—particularly the preference for clear, concise, goal- and audience-oriented communication and an easy-to-read visual design—developed slowly but steadily.

---

[6] Douglas, George H., and Herbert William Hildebrandt, editors. *Studies in the History of Business Writing,* Association for Business Communication, 1985.

With the growth of the middle class and the increase of commerce, business-persons needed to be able to communicate with both internal and external audiences. Basic forms of business writing, such as memos, letters, proposals, and reports, became more standard. As layers of management evolved and departments proliferated, written internal communication became increasingly important, as did changes in the technologies of communication. The typewriter and carbon paper (and, later, dictaphones and photocopiers) transformed the office through the mid-twentieth century.

Developments in online and digital communication are once again effecting powerful changes in business writing. Today's business writers communicate online as well as in traditional print environments. They must be able to work effectively in teams, and they need to be able to respond to the demands of working in a global environment. The essential characteristics of effective business writing, however, remain grounded in basic issues of rhetorical sensitivity. When writing for business, it's especially important to consider the differing needs—and situations—of your readers. You may need to consider readers spread geographically or across an organization chart, and, in some cases, you may even need to consider future readers.

Sample Student Email for Business Writing

The email message memo shown on p. 260 was written by Michelle Rosowsky in a business class. The email message presents an analysis and recommendation to help an employer make a decision. As you read, notice how the opening paragraph provides necessary background information and clearly states the email's purpose. Even if this email is forwarded to others, the subject line will make its purpose clear. Michelle was also careful to use bold type to emphasize the most important information.

This assignment took the form of a case study. The student's teacher provided a series of hypothetical facts about a potential business transaction. Michelle had to analyze this information, determine her recommendations, and communicate them in the most effective form possible.

thinking rhetorically

In reflecting on the email message, Michelle commented that the first and most important step in the writing process involved analyzing both the information that she was given and her rhetorical situation.

I first had to analyze the facts of the case to come up with an appropriate recommendation and then present the recommendation within the format of a typical business email. Because it's written for a busy manager, I wrote the email as concisely as possible so that the information would be available at a glance. I also put the most critical calculation, the manufacturing cost, at the beginning of the email and in bold so that the manager could find it easily and refer back to it later if necessary. I go on to make a recommendation about a bidding price and then provide a few other relevant facts since the goal of the email is to enable the manager to make her own decision. The succinctness of the email message also reflects my confidence in the analysis, which gives me a strong and positive ethos and helps establish my reliability and competence.

Subject line clearly indicates topic	**Taylor Nursery Bid – Message (HTML)**
	Message
	Delete Respond Quick Steps Move Tags Editing Zoom
	From: Rosowsky, Michelle Sent: Fri 4/12/2016 1:13 PM
	To: Donahue, Rosa
	Cc: Abernathy, Carina
	Subject: Taylor Nursery Bid

As you know, Taylor Nursery has requested bids on a 25,000-pund order of private label fertilizer. Taylor Nursery is one of the largest distributors of our Fertikil product. The following is my analysis of Jenco's costs to fill this special order and a recommendation for the bidding price.

The total costs for manufacturing 25,000 pounds of private label brand for Taylor Nursery is $44,075. The costs includes the following:

- Direct material
- Direct labor
- Variable manufacturing overhead

Although our current equipment and facilities provide adequate capacity for processing this special order, the job will involve an excess in labor hours. The overtime labor rate has been factored into the costs.

The absolute minimum price that Jenco could bid for this product without losing money is $44,075 (our cost). Applying our standard markup of 40% results in a price of $61,705. Thus you could reasonably establish a price anywhere within that range.

In making the final assessment, we advise you to consider factors relevant to this decision. Taylor Nursery has stated that this is a one-time order. Therefore, the effort to fill this special order will not bring long-term benefits.

Finally, Taylor Nursery has requested bids from several competitors. One rival, Eclipse Fertilizers, is submitting a bid of $60,000 on this order. Therefore, our recommendation is to underbid Eclipse slightly with a price of $58,000, representing a markup of approximately 32%.

Please let me know if I can be of further assistance in your decision on the Taylor Nursery bid.

Michelle Rosowsky ⋮ Sales Associate
❖ Jenco❖

Left-margin annotations:

Subject line clearly indicates topic

Paragraphs flush left

Bold type highlights most important financial information

Double-spaced between paragraphs

Options presented and background given

Final recommendation

Closing offers further assistance

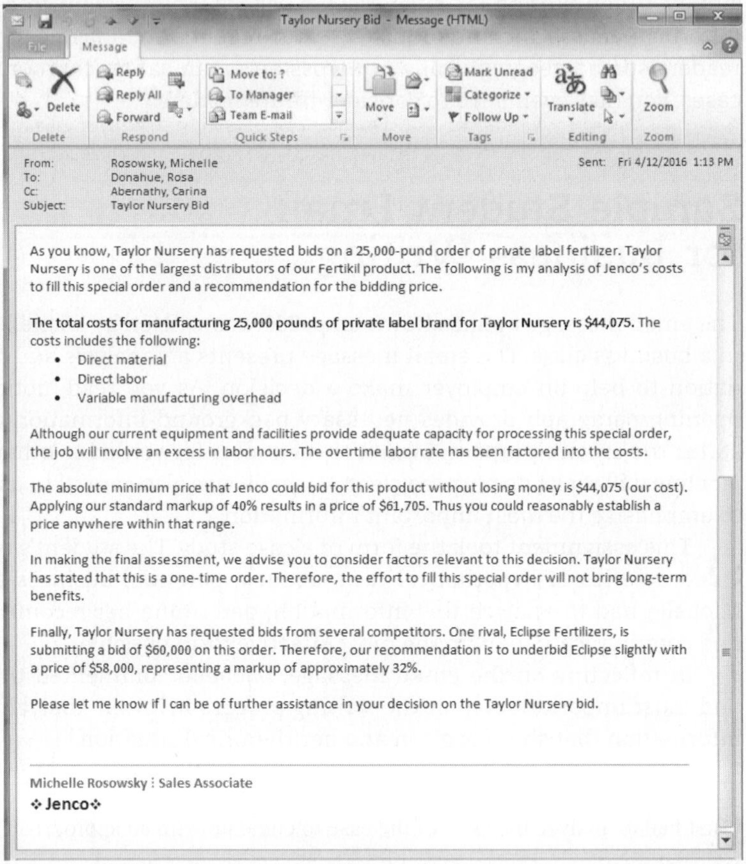

for **thought, discussion, and writing**

1. Although you may not have determined your major area of study yet, you probably have some idea of whether you want to major in the humanities, social sciences, sciences, or business. Meet with a group of classmates who share your general interests. Working together, first make a list of the reasons you all find this area interesting. Next, make a list of the writing challenges that students in this area face. Finally, choose two of these challenges and brainstorm productive ways that students can respond to them. Be prepared to share the results of your discussion with the entire class.

2. Write an essay in which you reflect on the reasons you are drawn to a particular discipline or general area of study. How long-standing is your interest in this discipline? What do you see as its challenges and rewards? (Before writing this essay, you might like to read Brandon Barrett's essay on his decision to major in chemistry, which appears in Chapter 3 on pp. 66–67.)

3. Choose one of the student essays presented in this chapter, and analyze it to determine what features reflect the disciplinary preferences described in this chapter. Alternatively, choose an essay you have written for a class in the sciences, social sciences, humanities, or business, and similarly analyze it. In studying either your own essay or an essay that appears in this chapter, be sure to consider its vocabulary, style, method of proof, and use of conventional formats.

9

Strategies for Invention, Planning, and Drafting

Part Three of *The Academic Writer* provides practical strategies that writers can use when they compose texts. The first two chapters in Part Three provide pragmatic, action-oriented advice about how to meet the challenges of academic writing. They also model strategies that enable writers to move productively through the writing process. Many of these strategies apply to both print texts (or alphabetic texts that look like traditional print texts but are read on screens) and compositions that employ multiple modes. Whether you are writing a print essay for your geography class or creating a Prezi presentation or podcast for that same course, you need to come up with ideas, develop them, and embody them in a print, oral, or digital medium. As Chapter 11, "Strategies for Multimodal Composing," emphasizes, however, students are increasingly creating texts that take advantage of the multiple modes and media available to them. Students who want to share a personal story could write a personal essay, but they could also create a visually rich poster, podcast, collage, or video. Chapter 11 addresses some of the opportunities and challenges that writers face in our world of expanding opportunities for communication.

Strategies for Invention

Like many writers, you may believe that finding ideas to write about is the most mysterious part of the writing process. Where do ideas come from? How can you draw a blank one minute and suddenly know the right way to support your argument or describe your experience the next? Is it possible to increase your ability to think and write creatively? Writers and speakers have been concerned with questions such as these for centuries. Ancient Greek and Roman rhetoricians, in fact, were among the first to investigate the process of discovering and exploring ideas. The classical Roman rhetoricians called this process *inventio*, for "invention" or "discovery." Contemporary writers, drawing on this Latin term, often refer to this process as *invention*.

In practice, invention usually involves both individual inquiry and dialogue with others. In working on a lab report, for example, you might spend most of your time writing alone, but the experiment you're writing about might have been undertaken by a group of students working together; you might look up some related research to be sure you understand the principles you're writing about; you might also ask other students or your instructor for advice in putting the report together. Every time you talk with others about ideas or consult print or online materials for information, you're entering into a conversation with others about your topic, and, like all writers, you can benefit from their support and insights.

The strategies discussed in this section of the chapter aim to help you invent successfully, whether you're having a conversation with yourself as you think through and write about ideas or working with classmates or friends. These methods can help you discover what you know—and don't know—about a subject. They can also guide you as you plan, draft, and revise your writing.

Read this section with a writer's eye. Which of these strategies do you already use? Which ones could you use more effectively? What other strategies might extend your range or strengthen your writing abilities? As you read about and experiment with these strategies, remember to assess their usefulness based on your own needs and preferences as a writer as well as on your particular writing situation. Most writers find that some of the following methods work better for them than others. That's fine. Just be sure to give each method a fair chance before deciding which ones to rely on.

---

note for multilingual writers

When you practice the methods of invention, you're focusing on generating ideas—not on being perfectly correct. There's no need to interrupt the flow of your ideas by stopping to edit your grammar, spelling, vocabulary, or punctuation. Feel free, in fact, to invent in your first or home language—or even to mix languages—if doing so increases your fluency and helps you generate ideas.

FREEWRITING

Freewriting is the practice of writing as freely as possible without stopping. It's a simple but powerful strategy for exploring important issues and problems. Here is a description of freewriting by Peter Elbow, from his book *Writing with Power: Techniques for Mastering the Writing Process*:

> To do a freewriting exercise, simply force yourself to write without stopping for [a certain number] of minutes. . . . If you can't think of anything to write, write about how that feels or repeat over and over "I have nothing

to write" or "Nonsense" or "No." If you get stuck in the middle of a sentence or thought, just repeat the last word or phrase till something comes along. The only point is to keep writing.[1]

Freewriting may at first seem *too* simple to achieve very powerful results, but it can actually help you discover ideas that you couldn't reach through more conscious and logical means. Because it helps you generate a great deal of material, freewriting is also an excellent antidote for the anxiety many writers feel at the start of a project. It can also improve the speed and ease with which you write.

Freewriting is potentially powerful in a variety of writing situations. Writing quickly without censoring your thoughts can help you explore your personal experience, for example, by enabling you to gain access to images, events, and emotions that you've forgotten or suppressed. Freewriting can also help you experiment with more complex topics without having to assess the worthiness of individual ideas. The following shows how one student used five minutes of freewriting to explore and focus her ideas for a political science paper on low voter turnout:

> I just don't get it. As soon as I could register I did—it felt like a really important day. I'd watched my mother vote and my sisters vote and now it was my turn. But why do I vote; guess I should ask myself that question—and why don't other people? Do I feel that my vote makes a difference? There have been some close elections but not all that many, so my vote doesn't literally count, doesn't decide if we pay a new tax or elect a new senator. Part of it's the feeling I get. When I go to vote I know the people at the polling booth; they're my neighbors. I often know the people who are running for office in local elections, and for state and national elections—well, I just feel that I should. But the statistics on voter turnout tell me I'm unusual. I want to go beyond statistics. I want to understand *why* people don't vote. Seems like I need to look not only at research in political science, but also maybe in sociology. (Check journals in economics too?) I wonder if it'd be okay for me to interview some students, maybe some staff and faculty, about voting—better check. But wait a minute; this is a small college in a small town, like the town I'm from. I wonder if people in cities would feel differently—they might. Maybe what I need to look at in my paper is rural/small town versus urban voting patterns.

---

[1]Elbow, Peter. *Writing with Power: Techniques for Mastering the Writing Process.* Oxford UP, 1981, p. 13.

This student's freewriting not only helped her explore her ideas but also identified a possible question to address and sources she could draw on as she worked on her project.

LOOPING

Looping, an extended or directed form of freewriting, alternates freewriting with analysis and reflection. Begin looping by first establishing a subject for your freewriting and then freewriting for five to ten minutes. This freewriting is your first loop. After completing this loop, read what you have written and look for the center of gravity or "heart" of your ideas—the image, detail, issue, or problem that seems richest or most intriguing, compelling, or productive. Select or write a sentence that summarizes this understanding; this sentence will become the starting point of your second loop. The student who wrote about low voter turnout, for example, might decide to use looping to reflect on this sentence: "I want to understand *why* people don't vote."

There is no predetermined number of loops that will work. Keep looping as many times as you like or until you feel you've exhausted a subject. When you loop, you don't know where your freewriting and reflection will take you; you don't worry about the final product. Your final essay might not even discuss the ideas generated by your efforts. That's fine; the goal in freewriting and looping is not to produce a draft of an essay but to discover and explore ideas, images, and sometimes even words, phrases, and sentences that you can use in your writing.

---

for **exploration**

Choose a question, an idea, or a subject that interests you, and freewrite for five to ten minutes. Then stop and read your freewriting. What comments most interest or surprise you? Write a statement that best expresses the center of gravity, or "heart," of your freewriting. Use this comment to begin a second loop by freewriting for five minutes more.

After completing the second freewriting, stop and reread both passages. What did you learn from your freewriting? Does your freewriting suggest possible ideas for an essay? Finally, reflect on the process itself. Did you find the experience of looping helpful? Would you use freewriting and looping in the future as a means of generating ideas and exploring your experiences?

BRAINSTORMING

Like freewriting and looping, brainstorming is a simple but productive invention strategy. When you brainstorm, you list as quickly as possible all the thoughts about a subject that occur to you without censoring or stopping to reflect on them. Brainstorming can help you discover and explore a number of ideas in a short time. Not all of them will be worth using in a piece of writing, of course. The premise of brainstorming is that the more ideas you can generate, the better your chances will be of coming up with good ones.

Alex Osborn, the person generally credited with naming this technique, originally envisioned brainstorming as a group, not an individual, activity. Osborn believed that the enthusiasm generated by the group helped spark ideas. Group brainstorming can be used for a variety of purposes. If your class has just been assigned a broad topic, for instance, your group could brainstorm a list of ways to approach or limit this topic. Or the group could use email, an online discussion board, a wiki, or a blog to generate possible arguments in support of or in opposition to a specific thesis. (See the guidelines for group brainstorming below.)

There are also brainstorming resources available online that you may find useful. Some software, including Thinkature and Bubbl.us, allows you to brainstorm and diagram relationships between ideas.

Those who regularly write with teams or groups cite increased intellectual stimulation and improved quality of ideas as major benefits of brainstorming together, but solitary brainstorming can be just as productive. To brainstorm alone, take a few moments at the start to formulate your goal, purpose, or problem. Then list your ideas as quickly as you can. Include everything that comes to mind, from facts to images, memories, fragments of conversations,

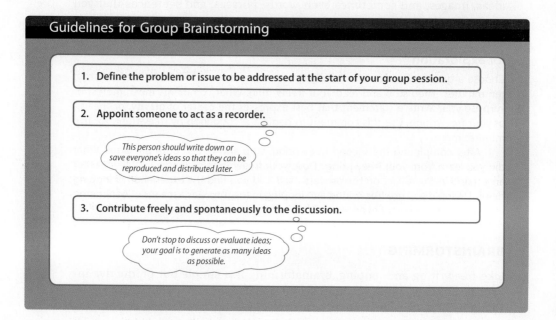

Guidelines for Group Brainstorming

1. **Define the problem or issue to be addressed at the start of your group session.**

2. **Appoint someone to act as a recorder.**

   This person should write down or save everyone's ideas so that they can be reproduced and distributed later.

3. **Contribute freely and spontaneously to the discussion.**

   Don't stop to discuss or evaluate ideas; your goal is to generate as many ideas as possible.

and other general impressions and responses. (You are the only one who needs to be able to decipher what you've written, so your brainstorming can be as messy or as organized as you like.) Then review your brainstorming to identify the most promising or helpful ideas.

After freewriting about low voter turnout, for example, the student whose writing you read on p. 264 decided to brainstorm a list of possible reasons people might not vote. Here is part of her list:

Some people (young people?) mistrust politicians

Alienated from the political process

Many political issues are highly polarized—abortion, research using stem cells, war, drugs, death penalty, health care, etc.

People in the middle may feel left out of the discussion

Don't know enough about the issues—or the candidates—to decide

"My vote won't make a difference"

Her brainstorming also raised several important questions:

What role does voter registration play?

Is the problem getting people to register—or getting registered voters to vote?

What's the connection between voting and other forms of community and civic engagement?

This student will need to explore her ideas further via both analysis and re-search, but her brainstormed list has raised important issues and questions for her to consider.

---

for **exploration**

Reread the freewriting you did earlier, and then choose one issue or question you'd like to explore further. Write a single sentence summarizing this issue or question, and then brainstorm for five to ten minutes. After brainstorming, return to your list. Put an asterisk (*) beside those ideas or images that didn't appear in your earlier freewriting. How do these new ideas or images add to your understanding of your subject?

CLUSTERING

Like freewriting, looping, and brainstorming, clustering emphasizes spontaneity. The goal of all four strategies is to generate as many ideas as possible, but clustering differs in that it uses visual means to generate ideas. Some writers find that it enables them to explore their ideas more deeply and creatively. (The cluster below was done by the student whose writing appears on pp. 264 and 267.)

Start with a single word or phrase that best summarizes or evokes your topic. Write this word in the center of a page of blank paper and circle it. Now fill in the page by adding ideas connected with this word. Don't censor your

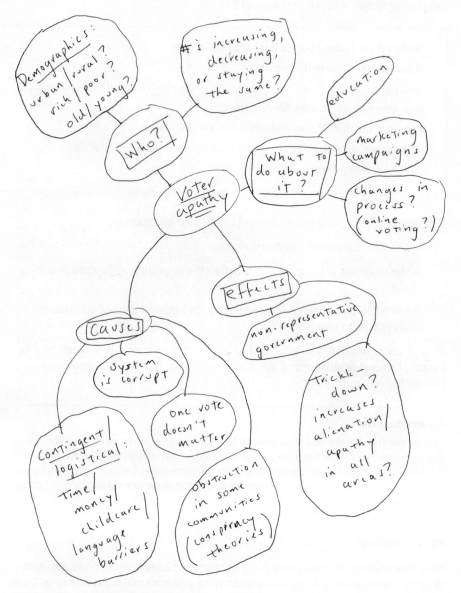

"Voter Apathy" Brainstorming Cluster

ideas or force your cluster to assume a certain shape—your goal is to be as spontaneous as possible. Simply circle your key ideas and connect them either to the first word or to other related ideas. After clustering, put the material you've generated aside for a bit, and then return to it so that you can evaluate it more objectively. When you do return to it, try to find the cluster's center of gravity—the idea or image that seems richest and most compelling.✱

---

for **exploration**

Reread the freewriting, looping, and brainstorming you have written thus far. Then choose one word that seems especially important for your subject, and use it as the center of a cluster. Without planning or worrying about what shape it's taking, fill in your cluster by branching out from this central word. Then take a moment to reflect on what you have learned.

ASKING THE JOURNALIST'S QUESTIONS

If you have taken a journalism class or written for a newspaper, you know that journalists are taught to answer six questions in articles they write: *who*, *what*, *when*, *where*, *why*, and *how*. By answering these questions, journalists can be sure that they have provided the most important information about an event, an issue, or a problem for their readers. And because they probe several aspects of a topic, the journalist's questions can help you discover not just what you know about but also what you *don't* know—and thus alert you to the need for additional research.

You may find these questions particularly useful when describing an event or writing an informative essay. Suppose that your political science instructor has assigned an essay on the conflict in Syria. Using the journalist's questions as headings, you could begin working on this assignment by asking yourself the following:

- *Who* is involved in this conflict?
- *What* issues most clearly divide those engaged in this dispute?
- *When* did the conflict begin, and how has it developed over the last few years?
- *Where* does the conflict seem most heated or violent?
- *Why* have those living in this area found it so difficult to resolve the situation?
- *How* might this conflict be resolved?

Although you might discover much the same information by simply brainstorming, using the journalist's questions ensures that you have covered all the major points.

For another example of a cluster, see Chapter 6, p. 168. ✱

Exploring Ideas

The previous invention strategies have a number of advantages. They're easy to use, and they can help you generate a reassuringly large volume of material when you're just beginning to work on an essay. Sometimes, however, you may want to use more systematic methods to explore a topic. This is especially true when you've identified a potential topic but aren't sure that you have enough to say about it.

ASKING THE TOPICAL QUESTIONS

One of the most helpful methods for developing ideas is based on the topics of classical rhetoric. In his *Rhetoric*, Aristotle describes the topics as potential lines of argument, or places (*topos* means "place" in Greek) where speakers and writers can find evidence or arguments. Aristotle defined twenty-eight topics, but the list is generally abbreviated to five: *definition*, *comparison*, *relationship*, *circumstance*, and *testimony*.

The classical topics represent natural ways of thinking about ideas. When confronted by an intellectual problem, we all instinctively ask such questions as these:

- What is it? (*definition*)
- What is it like or unlike? (*comparison*)
- What caused it? (*relationship*)
- What is possible or impossible? (*circumstance*)
- What have others said about it? (*testimony*)

Aristotle's topics build on these natural mental habits. The topical questions can help you pinpoint alternative approaches to a subject or probe one subject systematically, organizing what you know already and identifying gaps that require additional reading or research. Simply pose each question in turn about your subject, writing down as many responses as possible. You might also try answering the expanded list of questions for exploring a topic on p. 271.

Questions for Exploring a Topic

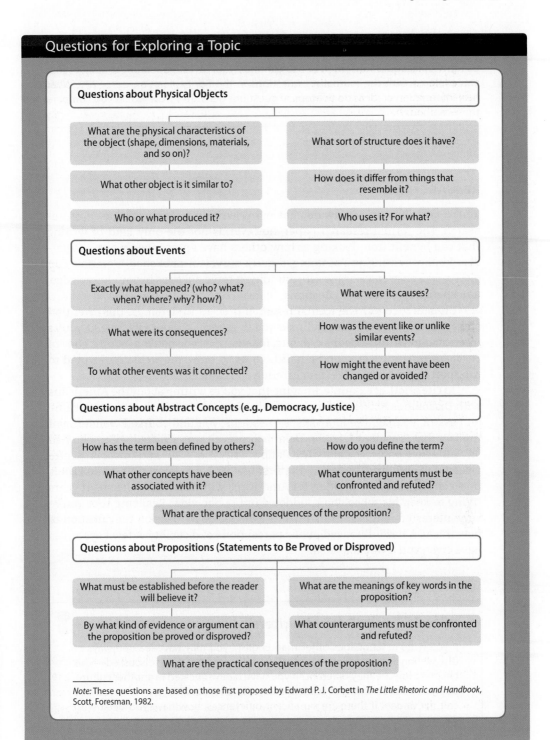

Questions about Physical Objects

What are the physical characteristics of the object (shape, dimensions, materials, and so on)?

What sort of structure does it have?

What other object is it similar to?

How does it differ from things that resemble it?

Who or what produced it?

Who uses it? For what?

Questions about Events

Exactly what happened? (who? what? when? where? why? how?)

What were its causes?

What were its consequences?

How was the event like or unlike similar events?

To what other events was it connected?

How might the event have been changed or avoided?

Questions about Abstract Concepts (e.g., Democracy, Justice)

How has the term been defined by others?

How do you define the term?

What other concepts have been associated with it?

What counterarguments must be confronted and refuted?

What are the practical consequences of the proposition?

Questions about Propositions (Statements to Be Proved or Disproved)

What must be established before the reader will believe it?

What are the meanings of key words in the proposition?

By what kind of evidence or argument can the proposition be proved or disproved?

What counterarguments must be confronted and refuted?

What are the practical consequences of the proposition?

Note: These questions are based on those first proposed by Edward P. J. Corbett in *The Little Rhetoric and Handbook*, Scott, Foresman, 1982.

---

for **exploration**

Use the topical questions on p. 271 to continue your investigation of the subject that you explored with the journalist's questions in the For Exploration on p. 270. What new information or ideas do the topical questions generate? How would you compare these methods?

RESEARCHING

You're probably already aware that many writing projects are based on research. The formal research paper, however, is not the only kind of writing that can benefit from looking at how others have approached a topic. Whatever kind of writing you're doing, a quick survey of published materials can give you a sense of the issues surrounding a topic, fill gaps in your knowledge, and spark new ideas and questions.

Chapter 7 covers the formal research process in detail. At the invention stage, however, loose, informal research is generally more effective. If you're interested in writing about skydiving, for example, you could pick up a copy of *Skydiving* magazine or spend a half hour or so browsing websites devoted to the sport to get a better feel for current trends and issues.

To cite another example, imagine that you're writing about the Americans with Disabilities Act (ADA) for a political science assignment. After freewriting and asking yourself the journalist's questions, you find yourself wondering if the fact that President Franklin Delano Roosevelt was afflicted with polio had any influence on accessibility legislation. You type "FDR" and "disability" into a search engine, and, browsing the first few hits, you learn that while FDR is now considered an inspiration for Americans with disabilities, he spent years trying to keep his wheelchair hidden from public view. Realizing that you're very interested in this shift in attitude, you decide to focus on the question of how the ADA has influenced public perceptions of disability. A few keystrokes have given you a valuable idea.

---

note for multilingual writers

If you write in languages other than English, you may have learned ways of discovering and exploring ideas that are different from those discussed in this chapter. How are they different? If you have been educated in another culture, do the invention methods used in that culture reflect different rhetorical and cultural values? If there are significant differences, how have you dealt with them?

WRITING A DISCOVERY DRAFT

Sometimes the best way to develop and explore ideas is to write a very rough draft and see, in effect, what you think about your topic. This strategy, which is sometimes called *discovery drafting*, can work well as long as you recognize that your draft will need extensive analysis and revision.

Writing a discovery draft is a lot like freewriting, although the process tends to be more focused and usually takes more time. As you write, stick to your topic as best you can, but expect that your thoughts may veer off in unexpected directions. The goal is not to produce a polished—or even a coherent—essay, but to put your ideas into written form so that you can evaluate them. Once you have completed a discovery draft, you can use it to identify and fine-tune your most promising ideas, to clarify your goals, and to determine what remains to be done. In order to do so, you will need to put your draft aside for a bit so you can look at it objectively when you return to it.✱

---

for **collaboration**

Meet with a group of classmates to discuss the methods of discovering and developing ideas. Begin by having group members briefly describe the advantages and disadvantages they experienced with these methods. (Appoint a recorder to summarize each person's statements.) Then, as a group, discuss your responses to these questions: (1) How might different students' preferences for one or more of these strategies be connected to different learning, composing, and cultural preferences? (2) What influence might situational factors (such as the nature of the assignment or the amount of time available for working on an essay) have on the decision to use one or more of these strategies? Be prepared to discuss your conclusions with your classmates.

Strategies for Planning

It may be helpful to think of planning as involving waves of play and work. When you're discovering and exploring ideas, for example, you're in a sense playing—pushing your ideas as far as you can without worrying about how useful they'll be later. Most people can't write an essay based on a brainstorming list or thirty minutes of freewriting, however. At some point, they need to settle down to work and formulate a plan for the project.

The planning activities described in this section of the chapter generally require more discipline than the play of invention does. Because much of the crafting of your essay occurs as a result of these activities, however, this work can be intensely rewarding.

ESTABLISHING A WORKING THESIS

You can't establish a workable plan for your essay without having a tentative sense of the goals you hope to achieve by writing. These goals may change

For an example of one student's discovery draft, see p. 169. ✱

along the way, but they represent an important starting point for guiding your work in progress. Before you start to draft, then, try to establish a *working thesis* for your essay.

A working thesis reflects an essay's topic as well as the point you wish to make and the effect you wish to have on your readers. An effective working thesis narrows your topic, helps you organize your ideas, enables you to determine what you want to say and *can* say, helps you decide if you have enough information to support your assertions, and points to the most effective way to present your ideas.

A few examples may help clarify this concept. Suppose that you're writing an editorial for your campus newspaper. "What are you going to write about?" a friend asks. "The library," you reply. You've just stated your topic, but this statement doesn't satisfy your friend. "What about the library? What's your point?" "Oh," you say, "I'm going to argue that students should petition library services to extend the number of hours it is open each week. The current hours are too limited, which is inconvenient and unfair to students who work long hours to finance their education." This second statement, which specifies both the point you want to make and its desired effect on readers, is a clearly defined working thesis. Further, because the newspaper editorial is an established genre with specific writing conventions, you know before you start that your argument will need to be brief, explicit, and backed up with concrete details.

You can best understand and establish a working thesis by analyzing the elements of your rhetorical situation: writer, reader, text, and medium. This process (which is described in detail in Chapter 3) should give you a clearer understanding of both your reasons for writing and the most appropriate means to communicate your ideas. In some cases, you may be able to analyze your rhetorical situation and establish a working thesis early in the writing process by asking yourself the questions on p. 275. In many other instances, however, you'll have to think and write your way into understanding what you want to say.

A working thesis will help you structure your plan and guide your draft, but you should view it as preliminary and subject to revision. After you've worked on an essay for a while, your working thesis may evolve to reflect the understanding you gain through further planning and drafting. You may even discover that your working thesis isn't feasible. In either case, the time you spend thinking about your preliminary working thesis isn't wasted, for it has enabled you to begin the process of organizing and testing your ideas.

FORMULATING A WORKABLE PLAN

Once you have established a working thesis, you should be able to develop a plan that can guide you as you work. As the discussion of differing composing styles in Chapter 4 indicates, people plan in different ways. Some develop

(thinking rhetorically)

Questions for Establishing a Working Thesis

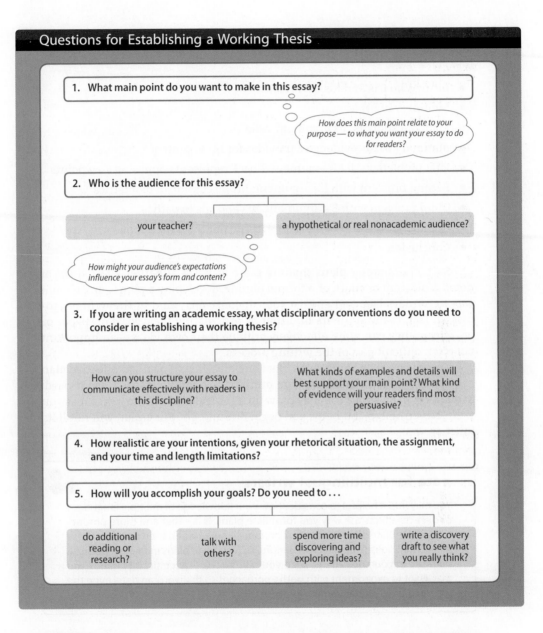

1. **What main point do you want to make in this essay?**

   How does this main point relate to your purpose — to what you want your essay to do for readers?

2. **Who is the audience for this essay?**

   your teacher? | a hypothetical or real nonacademic audience?

   How might your audience's expectations influence your essay's form and content?

3. **If you are writing an academic essay, what disciplinary conventions do you need to consider in establishing a working thesis?**

   How can you structure your essay to communicate effectively with readers in this discipline? | What kinds of examples and details will best support your main point? What kind of evidence will your readers find most persuasive?

4. **How realistic are your intentions, given your rhetorical situation, the assignment, and your time and length limitations?**

5. **How will you accomplish your goals? Do you need to . . .**

   do additional reading or research? | talk with others? | spend more time discovering and exploring ideas? | write a discovery draft to see what you really think?

detailed written plans; others rely on mental plans; others might freewrite and determine their goals by reflecting on their own written text. As a college student, you will often find written plans helpful. Some writers develop carefully structured, detailed outlines. Others find that quick notes and diagrams are equally effective.

Here, for instance, is the plan that Stevon Roberts developed for his essay analyzing Amitai Etzioni's "Less Privacy Is Good for Us (and You)" in Chapter 5 (pp. 117–20).

- Intro: Who E is and his basic claim
- Summary of his argument
- Main question: Is his argument valid?
- Summary of the evidence E provides for his argument
- First problem with E's argument: how E represents opposing viewpoints
- Second problem with E's argument: his discussion of biometrics
- Third problem with E's argument: his appeals to pathos
- Qualification: I'm analyzing an excerpt, not the whole book.
- Conclusion

Still others prefer plans that are more visual.✱ Whether a jotted list of notes, a diagram or chart, or a formal outline, developing a plan is an efficient way to try out ideas and engage your unconscious mind in the writing process. In fact, many students find that by articulating their goals on paper or on-screen, they can more effectively critique their own ideas—an important but often difficult part of the writing process.

There is no such thing as an ideal one-size-fits-all plan. An effective plan is one that works for you. Plans are utilitarian, meant to be used *and* revised. In working on an essay, you may draw up a general plan only to revise it as you write. Nevertheless, if it helps you begin drafting, your first plan will fulfill its function well.

---

note for multilingual writers

You may find it helpful to consider how your knowledge of multiple languages or dialects affects the way you formulate plans. Is it easier and more productive to formulate plans in your first or home language and then translate these plans into English? Or is it more helpful to formulate plans in English because doing so encourages you to keep your audience's expectations in mind? You may want to experiment with both approaches so that you can determine the planning process that works best for you.

---

for **exploration**

If you have ever created a plan for an essay or a school project, what kinds of plans have you typically drawn up? Do you formulate detailed, carefully structured plans (such as detailed outlines or idea maps), do you prefer less structured ones (scratch

✱ Daniel Stiepleman's visual plan appears in Chapter 6 (p. 171).

outlines, lists), or do you just start writing? Use these questions to think about the plans you have (or have not) used in the past; then spend ten minutes writing about how you might develop more useful plans in the future.

Strategies for Drafting

The British writer E. M. Forster once asked, "How can I know what I think until I see what I say?" You can see what he means if you take the writing process seriously: By working through drafts of your work, you gradually learn what you think about your subject. Although your process may begin with free-writing or brainstorming, drafting is the point in the process when you explore your ideas more fully and deeply, and it is through drafting that you create a text that embodies your preliminary goals.

MANAGING THE DRAFTING PROCESS

When you sit down to begin writing, it can be hard to imagine the satisfaction of completing a rough draft. Just picking up pen or pencil or turning on your computer can seem daunting. Once you pass the initial hurdle of getting started, you'll probably experience the drafting process as a series of ebbs and flows. You may write intensely for a short period, stop and review what you've written, make a few notes about how to proceed, and then draft again more slowly, pausing now and then to reread what you've written. It's important to keep your eye on the prize, though: Very few writers, if in fact any at all, can produce anything worth reading without going through this messy, sometimes painful, process. (If, like most writers, you experience moments of writer's block, try the block-busting strategies suggested on p. 278 to get back on track.)

While no two people approach drafting the same way—indeed, even a single person will take different approaches at different times—the strategies discussed in this section can help make your process more efficient and productive.

Overcoming resistance to getting started. All writers experience some resistance to drafting, but there are ways to overcome this resistance. To get started, many writers rely on rituals such as clearing their writing space of clutter, gathering notes and other materials in a handy place, or queuing up a favorite song or playlist. Personal predispositions affect writing habits as well. Some people write best early in the morning; others, late at night. Some require a quiet atmosphere; others find the absence of noise distracting. Some find it easier to draft if they're doing something else at the same time; others

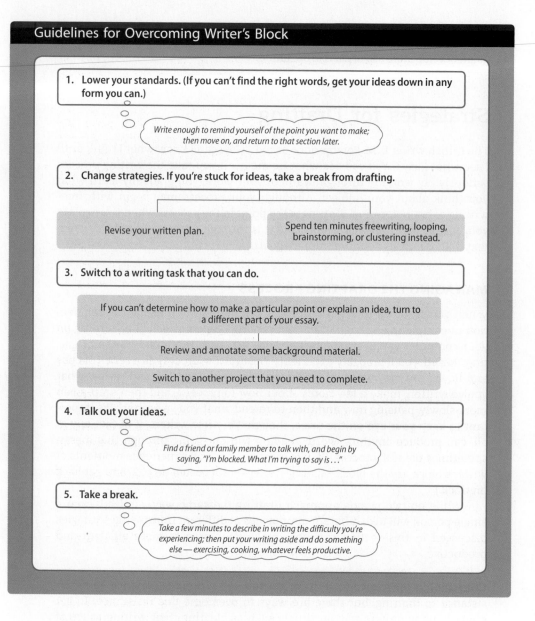

Guidelines for Overcoming Writer's Block

1. **Lower your standards. (If you can't find the right words, get your ideas down in any form you can.)**

   Write enough to remind yourself of the point you want to make; then move on, and return to that section later.

2. **Change strategies. If you're stuck for ideas, take a break from drafting.**

   Revise your written plan.

   Spend ten minutes freewriting, looping, brainstorming, or clustering instead.

3. **Switch to a writing task that you can do.**

   If you can't determine how to make a particular point or explain an idea, turn to a different part of your essay.

   Review and annotate some background material.

   Switch to another project that you need to complete.

4. **Talk out your ideas.**

   Find a friend or family member to talk with, and begin by saying, "I'm blocked. What I'm trying to say is . . ."

5. **Take a break.**

   Take a few minutes to describe in writing the difficulty you're experiencing; then put your writing aside and do something else — exercising, cooking, whatever feels productive.

shut off their devices so they can focus. The trick is to figure out what works best for you.

Reading through early notes is an effective way to begin drafting. It can be reassuring to remind yourself that you're not starting from scratch, and you may find yourself turning fragmentary notes into full sentences or grouping them into paragraphs—that is, drafting—before you know it.

Perhaps the best motivation is to remind yourself that a draft doesn't have to be perfect. Your initial goal should simply be to *get something down*. If you can't think of a way to open your essay, for instance, don't force yourself; just begin writing whatever you're ready to write and return to the introduction later.

Building momentum. While it might seem easier said than done, it's important to keep at it—to keep producing something, *anything*—so that the momentum can help you move steadily toward your goal. Accept that your draft will be imperfect, even incomplete, and just focus on putting your thoughts into words. By giving yourself permission to create a messy draft, you free yourself to explore ideas and discover what you want to say.

Don't try to correct or polish your writing in the drafting stage: Stopping to check spelling or grammar can interrupt your momentum and throw you off balance. Furthermore, it's easier to delete unnecessary or repetitive material when you revise than it is to add new material. If you can't quite articulate an argument or formulate an example, write yourself a note and keep drafting. When you return to your draft, you can fill in these gaps.

Keeping in touch with your "felt sense." You attend to many things when you draft. You stop and reread; you reflect about your topic and assignment; you think about your readers. If you're an effective writer, you also look at what you've written not just to see what's on the page but also to consider what *might* be there—that is, you take stock periodically and evaluate how what you've written so far measures up to the meaning you want to get across. Professor Sondra Perl calls this sort of awareness *felt sense*. This felt sense, Perl argues, encourages us to become aware "of what is just on the edge of our thinking but not yet articulated in words."[2]

The ability to develop and maintain felt sense doesn't require magical gifts. Rather, you need to draft for long enough periods so that you can become immersed in your writing. Additionally, as you write words, sentences, and paragraphs, you need to pause periodically to reflect on the extent to which your draft responds to readers' needs and expectations; it's also a good idea to jot down notes on these reflections.

Allowing time for incubation. Ideally, you'll come to a natural stopping point, a moment when you feel that you've solved a problem you've been wrestling with or concluded a section you've been working on. At this point, take a few moments to jot down notes about what you've accomplished as well as about what you still need to do. You may also wish to ask yourself a few questions: "What's the best transition here?" "Which examples should I use next?" If

---

[2]Perl, Sondra. *Writing with the Body*. Boynton Cook Publishers, 2004, p. xii.

you're like many writers, your subconscious mind will present appropriate answers when you next sit down to draft.

Sometimes it helps to *stop* thinking consciously about your ideas and just let them develop in your mind while you relax, sleep, or occupy yourself with other projects. After this period of incubation, you'll often spontaneously recognize how to resolve a problem or answer a question. (Don't confuse incubation with procrastination, however. *Procrastination* means avoiding the writing process; *incubation* means recognizing and using the fluctuations of the process to your advantage.)

---

for **exploration**

How do you typically draft an essay? How long do your drafting sessions usually last? What do you do when you run into problems? Could one or more of the suggestions presented here enable you to draft more productively? How might you best implement these suggestions? Spend five to ten minutes freewriting in response to these questions.

Developing and Organizing Your Ideas

As you draft, you'll become more aware of what you have to say about a subject. Consequently, you'll also become increasingly engaged with issues of organization and structure. "What do I think about this subject?" becomes less important than "How can I best present my ideas to my readers?" This section of the chapter suggests strategies for responding to the second question. Keep in mind that these strategies are only suggestions; your use of them should be based on your understanding of your assignment, purpose, and rhetorical situation.

USING A THESIS STATEMENT

Academic readers quickly become irritated if writers violate their expectations about how certain kinds of writing should be organized. In general, they expect writing that is straightforward and to the point. For this reason, sharing your working thesis with readers and providing cues about how you will support it are essential.

How to share your working thesis most effectively depends on a number of factors. If you're working on a take-home essay exam for a history class or an analytical essay for a mass media class, for example, you may wish to include in your introduction a *thesis statement*, usually a single sentence that states the main point of your essay.✱ Your introduction may also preview the main lines of argument you'll use to support your position.

✱ For more on thesis statements, see Chapter 6, pp. 151–54.

Much academic writing benefits from the inclusion of a thesis statement, but it is not always necessary or even desirable to include an explicit statement of your main point. If you're writing a personal essay for your first-year writing class about what the word *family* means to you, for example, you might decide that you don't want to articulate the main point of your essay in a single sentence. Instead, you might begin with an example that will create interest in your essay and show, rather than tell, what *family* means to you.

Whether or not you include a thesis statement, what's important is that you have a clear working thesis and that readers can figure it out easily. As you work on your draft, having a working thesis in mind—even if it's not expressed directly—will help you organize your thoughts; it will also help ensure that readers will stay with you.

DEVELOPING IDEAS

It's a good idea to begin each new drafting session by reviewing the material you've already generated, looking for ideas and details to add or develop more fully. Often in rereading these explorations and early drafts, writers realize that they've relied on words that have meaning for themselves but not necessarily for their readers. Learning to recognize and expand, or "unpack," such words in your own writing can help you develop your ideas so that their significance is clear to readers.

Here is a paragraph from one student's freewriting about what the word *family* means to her. While rereading her writing, she recognized a number of general and abstract words, which she underlined.

> When I think of the good things about my family, Christmas comes most quickly to mind. Our house was filled with such <u>warmth</u> and <u>joy</u>. Mom was busy, but she was <u>happy</u>. Dad seemed less absorbed in his work. In the weeks before Christmas he almost never worked late at the office, and he often arrived with brightly wrapped presents that he would tantalizingly show us— before whisking them off to their hiding place. And at night we did <u>fun</u> things together to prepare for the big day.

Words like *warmth* and *joy* undoubtedly have many strong connotations for the writer; most readers, however, would find these terms vague. This writer realized that in drafting she would have to provide plenty of concrete, specific details to enable readers to visualize what she means.

FOLLOWING TEXTUAL CONVENTIONS

When you draft, you don't have to come up with an organizational structure from scratch. Instead, you can draw on conventional methods of organization, methods that reflect common ways of analyzing and explaining information. Your subject may naturally lend itself to one or more methods of organization.

Suppose, for example, that you're writing an essay about political and economic changes in Eastern Europe and Asia in recent decades. Perhaps in your reading you were struck by the different responses of Russian and Chinese citizens to economic privatization. You might draw on conventional methods of *comparing and contrasting* to organize such an analysis. Or perhaps you wish to discuss the impact that severe industrial pollution in China could have on the development of a Western-style economy. After *classifying* the most prevalent forms of industrial pollution, you might discuss the consequences of this pollution for China's economy. In some cases, you may be able to use a single method of organization—such as *comparison, definition, cause and effect*, or *problem-solution*—to organize your entire essay. More often, however, you'll draw on several methods to present your ideas.

thinking
rhetorically

In considering how best to draw on conventional methods of organizing information, remember that you shouldn't impose them formulaically. Begin thinking about how to organize your writing by reflecting on your goals as a writer and on your rhetorical situation. If your analysis suggests that one or more methods of organizing information represent commonsensical, logical ways of approaching your subject, use them in drafting. But remember that the organization or structure you choose should complement your ideas, not be imposed on them.

WRITING EFFECTIVE PARAGRAPHS

If you're freewriting or writing a discovery draft, you may not think consciously about when to create a new paragraph or how to structure it: Your goal is to generate ideas. Additionally, by the time you are a college student, you have probably developed a general understanding of how effective paragraphs work, an understanding that grows out of your previous experiences as a reader and writer. Even so, it is helpful to remind yourself about the nature and functions of paragraphs and the expectations that readers bring to them. In this regard, readers expect the following:

- A paragraph will be unified; it will generally focus on one main idea.
- The opening sentence of a paragraph will often, although not always, state what the paragraph is about. (Sometimes the topic sentence may

appear at the end of the paragraph or even in the middle, acting as a linchpin between ideas.)

- Paragraphs will often, although again not always, have a clear beginning, middle, and end; that is, they will often state the main idea, support that main idea with evidence, and conclude with a sentence that ties the two together and provides a transition to the next paragraph.✱

- There will be a coherent logic to paragraph development; a paragraph will include transitional words, phrases, and sentences or use other strategies (such as strategic repetition) to make clear how it relates to the paragraphs that precede and follow it.

Paragraphs are remarkably flexible textual units. What is essential is that readers can clearly see and follow the logic of the development of ideas within and between paragraphs.

Transitional devices can play a key role in helping readers stay on track as they move through your text. Some transitional words and phrases—such as *for example, therefore, because, in other words, in conclusion, on the other hand, granted,* and *nevertheless*—indicate how ideas relate to one another logically; others—such as *often, during, now, then, at first, next, in the meantime,* and *eventually*—indicate a sequence or progression; and still others—such as *beside, beyond, above, behind,* and *outside*—indicate spatial relationships. Repetition of key terms or synonyms for those terms can also help readers stay on track. Transitional devices help connect ideas within paragraphs. They can also play an important role in clarifying the development of ideas from paragraph to paragraph.

When drafting, be sure to pay special attention to the paragraphs that introduce and conclude your essay. An effective introductory paragraph announces your topic, but it also engages your readers' interest and attention. Analyzing your rhetorical situation can help you determine appropriate ways to introduce your topic. If you are writing a humorous essay or an essay on a casual subject directed to a general audience, you might begin with an anecdote or an attention-getting question. If you are writing an essay about a serious topic directed to an academic audience, a more straightforward approach would generally be more appropriate. While you might begin with a quotation or question, you would quickly state your topic and explain how you intend to approach it.

Your concluding paragraph is as important as your introductory paragraph. Like the introductory paragraph, your concluding paragraph frames your essay. It reminds your reader that your essay is drawing to a close. Depending on your topic and rhetorical situation, concluding paragraphs may vary in their approach. In some way, however, all bring the issues that you have discussed together in a meaningful and emphatic way. Your concluding paragraph is also your final opportunity to emphasize the importance of your ideas and make a final good impression.

Chapter 7 (pp. 212–13) explains the structure of a typical supporting paragraph in a research project. ✱ · · · · · · · · · · ·
· · · · · · · · · ·

Daniel Stiepleman's essay "Literacy in America: Reading Between the Lines" (pp. 179–82) is a good example of effective paragraphing in action. Daniel opens his essay, which analyzes a public service announcement (PSA) from the National Center for Public Literacy, by describing the PSA itself. This description draws the reader's attention and represents Daniel's initial analysis of the PSA. Daniel observes that it is the girl and not the older woman, for instance, "who seems maternal." At this point, this observation seems primarily descriptive, but it will also play a role in Daniel's analysis as his essay progresses. It is important to note that Daniel's essay includes a reproduction of the PSA so that readers can determine whether they think Daniel's description is accurate.

Daniel's second paragraph moves from a description of the PSA to his response. Daniel finds the PSA troubling, but at this point in his essay he is unsure why. He does worry, however, that the PSA's "simple message, though it promotes a position I believe in, I fear does more harm than good." This statement, which is the last sentence of the second paragraph, serves as the thesis statement for his essay.

The initial sentence of the third paragraph establishes a logical connection between the second and third paragraphs: "The problem is with the underlying logic of this PSA." Notice that Daniel does not employ an explicit transitional device. The logic of the relationship between the two paragraphs is already clear. The fourth and fifth paragraphs of the essay explain the difficulties that Daniel sees with the underlying logic of the PSA and provide evidence to support this assertion. The first sentence of the sixth paragraph summarizes Daniel's argument: "The PSA suggests that all the illiterate people in America need to achieve worth is the ability to read and write."

In paragraph seven, his concluding paragraph, Daniel returns to the description of the PSA that opened his essay and extends his description so that it contributes explicitly to his argument. Here are the two final sentences of Daniel's essay as they appear in that paragraph:

> Though the girl is beaming, there is a hesitance I see in the woman's smile and concern in her face. And it is apt; she is shoved into the corner, held there, like so many Americans, beneath the weight of a text that would take the rich and daunting complexity of our multicultural society and give it the illusion of simplicity.

These two sentences evoke the essay's introduction even as they comment in an emotionally charged way on the significance of Daniel's major point. In so doing, they bring Daniel's essay to a powerful conclusion.

Some of Daniel's paragraphs do have topic sentences—the third, fourth, and fifth paragraphs all announce their major point in the first sentence—but others do not. The first paragraph begins with a striking description of the main image in the PSA: "The woman and girl look straight at us." The second paragraph introduces Daniel's troubled response to the PSA: "When I came across this page in the *Atlantic* (see Fig. 1), the image of the girl and the woman was what first caught my eye, but it was the repeated statement 'Because I can read' that captured my imagination." This sentence serves as a transition from the first to the second paragraph, and it also introduces the reservations that Daniel will explore through his analysis. The first sentence of the seventh and final paragraph alludes to the opening paragraph and helps the reader transition to the conclusion.

Daniel's essay is clearly unified, and so is each of the paragraphs in the essay. Daniel does not employ many explicit transitional devices, however. Instead, he creates implicit logical connections. His second paragraph, for instance, is structured around this statement: "When I came across this page in the *Atlantic* . . . I grew uncomfortable." In those body paragraphs that have explicit topic sentences—paragraphs three, four, and five—the remaining sentences in the paragraph support the topic sentence.

Daniel's essay is an excellent example of effective paragraphing. Daniel worked hard on his essay, writing multiple drafts and getting responses from peers. To learn more about how Daniel composed his essay, see the case study of Daniel's writing process in Chapter 6 (pp. 165–82). Reading Daniel's case study will help you see how to draw upon and enact the practical strategies described here and in the following chapter in your own writing.

---

for **thought, discussion, and writing**

1. Early in this chapter, you used freewriting, looping, brainstorming, clustering, and the journalist's questions to investigate a subject of interest to you. Continue your exploration of this topic by conducting some informal research and drawing on the topical questions (p. 272). Then use the material you have gathered to write a discovery draft on your subject.

2. Choose one of the invention strategies discussed in this chapter that you have not used in the past, and try it as you work on a writing assignment. If you have time, discuss this experiment with some classmates. Then write a brief analysis of why this strategy did or did not work well for you.

3. Choose a writing assignment that you have just begun. After reflecting on your ideas, devise a workable plan. While drafting, keep a record of your activities. How helpful was your plan? Was it realistic? Did you revise your plan as you wrote? What can you learn about your writing process from this experience? Be prepared to discuss this experience with your class.

4. Think of a time when you simply couldn't get started writing. What did you do to move beyond this block? How well did your efforts work—and why? After reflecting on your experience, write an essay (humorous or serious) about how you cope with writer's block.

5. Choose an essay that you have already written. It could be an essay for your writing class or for another class. Analyze the essay to determine how effective

your paragraphs are, much as this chapter analyzed the paragraphs in Daniel Stiepleman's essay. Here are some questions to consider as you analyze your essay:

- How effectively does your introduction engage readers? Does your concluding paragraph provide a sense of closure and demonstrate the significance of your topic? How could your introduction and conclusion be improved?
- Which paragraphs in your essay have explicit topic sentences? Which do not? Can you identify the logic behind this pattern? Could any paragraph be improved by adding or deleting a topic sentence?
- Can readers easily follow the movement of ideas within and between paragraphs? What transitional strategies might you use to improve the cohesiveness of your paragraphs and to unify your essay?

10

Strategies for Revising, Editing, and Proofreading

Revising and editing can be the most rewarding parts of the writing process: Together they give you the satisfaction of bringing your ideas to completion in an appropriate form. Revision challenges you to look at your work from a dual perspective: to read your work with your own intentions in mind and also to consider your readers' or viewers' perspectives. Editing provides you with an opportunity to fine-tune your paragraphs and sentences and, along with proofreading, to provide your readers with a trouble-free reading experience. Although revision and editing occur throughout the writing process, you'll probably revise most intensively after completing a rough draft that serves as a preliminary statement of your ideas and edit once you're happy with the focus, organization, and content of your draft. Proofreading usually occurs at the very end of the process.

Revising and editing are medium-specific activities. Revising a video or podcast is very different from revising an alphabetic text—a text composed primarily of black letters on a white page or screen. As you are probably aware, in most cases, multiple programs can be used to revise and edit multimodal digital texts. Someone who wants to edit a video could use Windows Movie Maker, Virtual Dub, Wax, or Wondershare Filmora, to name just a few of the available programs. Programs such as these are constantly being updated, so advice grounded in one version of a program can quickly become out of date. For these reasons, this chapter focuses primarily on the opportunities and challenges of revising and editing alphabetic texts, such as traditional academic analysis and argument.

An important starting point for any discussion of revising and editing involves terminology. In ordinary conversation, the terms *revising* and *editing* are sometimes used interchangeably, but there are significant distinctions between the two. When you revise, you consider big-picture questions about your essay: What are its major strengths and weaknesses? Does it meet the assignment? Are the introduction and conclusion effective given the assignment and your rhetorical situation? Is the essay clearly organized?

Given the topic and assignment, does it cover the most important issues? Can the reader move easily from section to section and paragraph to paragraph?

When you revise, you are willing to make major changes to your text—to revise your thesis significantly or to expand on some analytical or argumentative points while limiting or deleting others. Revising requires you to distance yourself from your text—to read it almost as if you had not written it—which is one reason why getting responses to work in progress from readers, such as other students in your writing class, can be so helpful.

Writers move from revising to editing once they have decided that their essay is working well at a global level. Editing generally involves style and clarity. When you edit your writing, you ask yourself questions such as these: Do your sentences flow smoothly, with appropriately varied sentence length and structure? How about diction or word choice? Could you choose more specific, concrete, or emphatic words? These questions all are aimed at improving the impact of your writing. Editing involves more than attention to style, however. It is also the time to ask yourself whether the logic behind your essay is as clear as possible. Would more effective transitions clarify and enrich your argument and add to its impact? Are there ways that your introduction and conclusion could be improved? Proofreading provides an opportunity to make any final changes to grammar, punctuation, and spelling to provide readers with an error-free reading experience.

Revising and editing can help you transform an essay that is so-so at best to one that engages readers and conveys its ideas powerfully and persuasively. But these processes take time, including the time necessary to gain some distance from your writing. You cannot revise and edit your essay effectively if you write it at the last minute, so effective time management skills are essential. As an example of successful revising and editing, see the case study of Daniel Stiepleman's essay analyzing a public service announcement (PSA) that appears in the concluding section of Chapter 6 (pp. 165–82). Be sure to notice that Daniel's essay benefited from multiple drafts and from responses by his writing group.

Strategies for Revising

You can learn a great deal about revision just by considering the word itself. *Revision* combines the root word *vision* with the prefix *re-*, meaning "again." When you revise, you "see again": You develop a new vision of your essay's logic and organization or of the best way to improve the way it flows.

Revision sometimes requires you to take risks. Often these risks are minor. If you attempt to fine-tune the details in a paragraph, for instance, you need spend only a little time and can easily revert back to the original version. Sometimes when you revise, however, you make large-scale decisions with more significant consequences. You might conclude that a different organization is in order, decide to rework your thesis statement, or consider a new approach to your topic altogether. Trying major changes such as these often requires rewriting or discarding whole sections of a draft, but a willingness to experiment can also lead to choices that make revising less frustrating and more productive. (See the Guidelines for Revising Objectively below.)

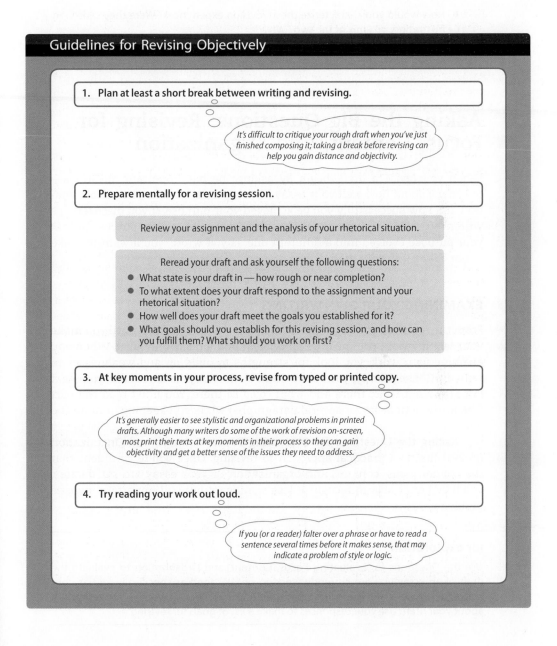

Guidelines for Revising Objectively

1. **Plan at least a short break between writing and revising.**

   It's difficult to critique your rough draft when you've just finished composing it; taking a break before revising can help you gain distance and objectivity.

2. **Prepare mentally for a revising session.**

   Review your assignment and the analysis of your rhetorical situation.

   Reread your draft and ask yourself the following questions:
   - What state is your draft in — how rough or near completion?
   - To what extent does your draft respond to the assignment and your rhetorical situation?
   - How well does your draft meet the goals you established for it?
   - What goals should you establish for this revising session, and how can you fulfill them? What should you work on first?

3. **At key moments in your process, revise from typed or printed copy.**

   It's generally easier to see stylistic and organizational problems in printed drafts. Although many writers do some of the work of revision on-screen, most print their texts at key moments in their process so they can gain objectivity and get a better sense of the issues they need to address.

4. **Try reading your work out loud.**

   If you (or a reader) falter over a phrase or have to read a sentence several times before it makes sense, that may indicate a problem of style or logic.

---

for **exploration**

Think back to earlier writing experiences, and freewrite on them for five to ten minutes.

- When, and for what reasons, have you revised your work instead of just editing it?
- How would you characterize these revision experiences? Were they satisfying, frustrating, or a mix of the two? Why?

Asking the Big Questions: Revising for Focus, Content, and Organization

When you revise a draft, begin by asking the big, important questions—questions about how well your essay has responded to your rhetorical situation and how successfully you've achieved your purpose. If you discover—as writers often do—that your essay hasn't achieved its original purpose or that your purpose evolved into a different one as you wrote, you'll want to make major changes in your draft.

EXAMINING YOUR OWN WRITING

From the moment you begin thinking about a writing project until you make your last revision, you must be an analyst and a decision maker. When you examine your work, you look for strengths to build on and weaknesses to remedy. Consequently, you must think about not just what is in your text but also what is *not* there and what *could be* there. You must read the part (the introduction, say, or several paragraphs) while still keeping in mind the whole.

Asking the Questions for Evaluating Focus, Content, and Organization (p. 291) first is a practical approach to revising. Once you're confident that the overall focus, content, and organization of your essay are satisfactory, you'll be better able to recognize less significant but still important stylistic problems.

---

for **exploration**

Use the Questions for Evaluating Focus, Content, and Organization to evaluate the draft of an essay you are currently working on. Respond as specifically and as concretely as possible, and then take a few moments to reflect on what you have learned about your draft. Use your responses to make a list of goals for revising.

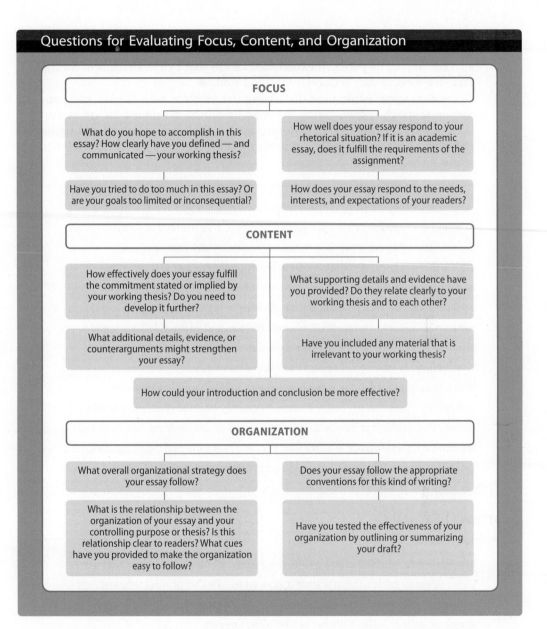

Questions for Evaluating Focus, Content, and Organization

FOCUS

What do you hope to accomplish in this essay? How clearly have you defined — and communicated — your working thesis?

How well does your essay respond to your rhetorical situation? If it is an academic essay, does it fulfill the requirements of the assignment?

Have you tried to do too much in this essay? Or are your goals too limited or inconsequential?

How does your essay respond to the needs, interests, and expectations of your readers?

CONTENT

How effectively does your essay fulfill the commitment stated or implied by your working thesis? Do you need to develop it further?

What supporting details and evidence have you provided? Do they relate clearly to your working thesis and to each other?

What additional details, evidence, or counterarguments might strengthen your essay?

Have you included any material that is irrelevant to your working thesis?

How could your introduction and conclusion be more effective?

ORGANIZATION

What overall organizational strategy does your essay follow?

Does your essay follow the appropriate conventions for this kind of writing?

What is the relationship between the organization of your essay and your controlling purpose or thesis? Is this relationship clear to readers? What cues have you provided to make the organization easy to follow?

Have you tested the effectiveness of your organization by outlining or summarizing your draft?

One Student Writer's Revision for Focus, Content, and Organization

Here is how one writer, Stevon Roberts, used the Questions for Evaluating Focus, Content, and Organization to establish goals for his revision. For an introductory composition class, Stevon was assigned a four- to five-page essay that proposed a solution to a contemporary problem. Stevon decided to write on something he was truly interested in: Internet privacy. This interest was sparked in part by personal experience and in part by his analysis of Amitai Etzioni's "Less Privacy Is Good for Us (and You)." ✳

Stevon spent some time discussing the problem with friends and conducted research online, taking notes as he did so. He reread his notes and then did a freewrite (below) to determine his rhetorical situation and figure out what he really wanted to get across. A draft that grew out of his freewrite starts at the bottom of this page.

> I am writing an essay for my composition class in which I'm supposed to propose a solution to a contemporary problem. I've decided to tackle the problem of Internet privacy. Since my readers—my instructor and classmates—almost certainly spend at least some time online, I think they'll be familiar with the general context of my discussion. Since the things we do online vary so widely, though, I've decided to narrow my focus to social media—Facebook, Instagram, Pinterest, Twitter, and so on. I do have some practical recommendations to make for ways we can protect our privacy, but I've realized in talking with people and doing some research that making concrete recommendations is not always very helpful: rapid changes in technology mean that my suggestions will quickly become obsolete. For this reason, I've decided primarily to raise awareness of the problem, emphasizing the need for every person who uses technology to understand the dangers of providing personal information online and be alert to new threats.

STEVON'S EARLY DRAFT

> My name is Stevon Roberts. I'm a videographer, a blogger, a student, and a tech enthusiast (at least, that's what it says on my Twitter profile). My last known location was on the corner of NW Beca Avenue and NW 20th Street, at a place called Coffee Culture, in Corvallis, Oregon.
>
> In the past, I would have guarded this kind of information to prevent marketers, hackers, and identity thieves from building a profile to exploit. Identity thieves have gotten very good at compiling seemingly innocuous pieces of information and using them for purposes like credit card fraud.

✳ See Chapter 5, pp. 117–20.

These threats are still very real, and I still take some measures to protect myself. You probably do, too. Most of us know by now how to recognize phishing scams and other threats to our personal security. But with the advent of social media, we've seen huge changes in the way this information is obtained.

Most of us just give information away for free on Facebook, Instagram, Pinterest, Twitter, and other social media services, often compromising security. In the same way that the automobile revolutionized transportation, social media have fundamentally shifted the way we manage our personal information. We learned to mitigate our risks on the road by using safety belts and obeying traffic laws, but most of us probably don't have a good understanding of the appropriate precautions for social media. As these services become more integral to our lifestyles, and more revealing of our identities, protecting our identities will become more critical, both online and in real life.

Other security concerns in the digital realm haven't gone away. Spam, for example, has become so pervasive that world spending for anti-spam software was expected to exceed $1.7 billion in 2008, up from $300 million in 2003 ("Anti-Spam Spending Set to Soar," *Global Secure Systems* 24 Feb. 2005). Apart from reducing the annoyance factor, this can also protect from more serious security threats, such as phishing scams, wherein unsuspecting victims will reply to fraudulent emails with personal information—sometimes even giving away bank account numbers!

Clearly, these security issues are still at the forefront of people's minds, and we're taking steps toward better solutions. But let's put the risks in context and compare our relative response. As of the writing of this essay, Facebook had approximately 1.59 billion users. Many of them are content to settle for the default privacy settings, which aren't all that private. Additionally, many Facebook users will add "applications," including games, quizzes, etc., which have access to many parts of your user profile that you may not want to share. In fact, in a twist of irony, the ACLU has added a quiz that you can take to explain exactly what is exposed when you add these sorts of quizzes (aclunc_privacy_quiz/). The quiz offers some suggestions for changing the privacy settings to protect personal information, but many people simply aren't aware, or don't take the time, to make these adjustments.

But let's not focus on Facebook at the expense of an even larger context. Location services, such as Brightkite, allow you to pinpoint your location on a map. You'd probably be happy to share this information with friends whom you'd like to join you, but you likely wouldn't want to share this information with a stalker, or even an angry ex-boyfriend or -girlfriend. Would you broadcast the location of your home address? Most of us would probably think twice before doing that, but the lines can quickly become blurry. Is it OK to broadcast your location from a friend's house? Your classroom, or your office?

With its instructional tagline "What are you doing?" Twitter gives its users 140 characters to broadcast activities, locations, website URLs, and even pictures (via helper services). An individual post, or "tweet," might cost you a job if, for example, you tell your friends you took a job only for its "fatty paycheck" (Snell). You might risk being overlooked for an interview if you posted a picture from a drinking party.

Similarly, your political views and feelings may be called into question if you endeavor to start a blog, as I have. My blog is not especially personal, but it occurred to me when I started writing that this might be another potential vector for increased risk. It bothered me so much that I wrote to one of my favorite bloggers (Leo Babauta of Zenhabits.net), asking him whether he was concerned about security. He wrote back (via Twitter), "No, I haven't faced security or privacy issues as a blogger (yet). My readers are 100% really cool, nice (and sexy) people." It's worth pointing out that his blog has over a hundred thousand subscribers.

Still . . . social media allow you to compromise your own personal identity and security in ways that are unprecedented. And at the same time, participation in all of these environments is almost obligatory. Very few of my friends have not yet succumbed to the peer pressure to be available on Facebook, Instagram, Twitter, and other social media, despite security concerns. And if you're trying to run a business (or promote your blog), avoiding Twitter is tantamount to professional suicide—these venues are key ingredients for successful marketing. In short, your personal name and profile have almost become like a kind of brand that is expected to be proliferated and maintained in cyberspace. And yet censorship levels must be very high to avoid getting passed over for the next opportunity, because heaven forbid that your future employer doesn't agree with you about the last hot political topic (or whatever).

Stevon shared this essay with the members of his peer response group, who used the Questions for Evaluating Focus, Content, and Organization (p. 291) to analyze his draft. The following analysis reflects both Stevon's own observations about the strengths and limitations of his draft and those of his writing group.

Focus: Some of my readers were confused about my main focus. I think I can correct this by revising my introduction and explaining more clearly that we (my instructor, classmates, and I) are all probably too sophisticated now for the "Nigerian royalty" email scams—we've all been there and learned our lessons—but other dangers exist, and we might not all be aware of them: specifically, the dangers presented in giving personal information away while using social media, which many of us are virtually addicted to.

I made one point that readers found really important—the idea that cutting social media off completely is not really an option for most of us, because it's essential for our social and even professional lives—late in the essay; I think I'll move it up closer to the beginning.

Some of my readers wanted more concrete recommendations for what to do to protect themselves. I have to make it clear from the outset that I think awareness and seeking out solutions that work for you are really the only universal solutions anyone can offer—there's too much variety in the kinds of technology people use and it all changes really, really fast. I'm trying to teach them to fish, I guess, instead of giving them fish.

Content: Some of my readers were confused about my opening (where I give away private information about myself—what's my point there, exactly?). I think I just need to make the point more clearly in the second paragraph.

A couple of my readers didn't know what "phishing" was—I have to be careful about assuming too much common knowledge in technical terminology.

I realized on rereading one of my sources that a statistic it offered was a bit out-of-date, so I found a more current source.

I need to provide some more examples of some of the risks that people didn't entirely "get," like how having a blog could cost you a job.

Probably most critical is the fact that my readers didn't like my conclusion: They felt like the discussion just dropped off without really "concluding." I think adding a stronger conclusion, reminding readers of my major points, will make the essay much stronger.

Organization: I outlined my draft so that its organization was especially clear. In general, it's OK, but I realize that I do ping-pong a bit, especially in the beginning, between old threats like spam and new threats like Facebook quizzes. I need to work on transitions to make what I'm doing there clearer (because that's where some of the confusion about my focus crept in, I think).

I also have to add some clearer transitions between the different kinds of risks I discuss (the usual stuff with marketers and scam artists, and then other, even scarier stuff, like losing a job or being stalked). In the discussion of the latter risks (like stalkers), I lost some readers when I started out talking about Brightkite (it uses GPS technology but my readers didn't immediately know what I was talking about), so I think I'll reorder the presentation of topics here, and start with Twitter and blogs (which people are more familiar with).

Stevon used this analysis to completely rework his essay. The result follows below.

Roberts 1

Stevon Roberts
Dr. Mallon
Comp 101
Oct. 17, 2016

Added title to prepare readers for content of essay

Added new epigraph to provide thought-provoking expert commentary

Identity, Rebooted

When you're doing stuff online, you should behave as if you're doing it in public—because increasingly, it is.—Cornell University computer science professor Jon Kleinberg (qtd. in Lohr)

My name is Stevon Roberts. I'm a videographer, a blogger, a student, and a tech enthusiast (at least, that's what it says on my Twitter profile). My last known location was on the corner of NW Beca Avenue and NW 20th Street, at a place called Coffee Culture, in Corvallis, Oregon.

If someone had told me even five years ago that I would one day regularly broadcast this kind of information about myself to people I didn't

Roberts 2

know, I wouldn't have believed it. If someone I didn't know had asked me back then for information like this, I would have refused to give it, to prevent unscrupulous people from exploiting it. I was well aware of how expert marketers, hackers, and identity thieves had become at compiling such seemingly innocuous pieces of information and using them for unwanted sales pitches, or even worse, for credit card scams and other kinds of fraud.

These threats are still very real, and I take some measures to protect myself against them. You probably do, too: Most of us are wary of filling out surveys from dubious sources, for example, and most of us know by now how to recognize obvious email scams like the ones purporting to be from "Nigerian royalty." But with the advent of social media, many of us find ourselves in a bind: We want to be connected, so many of us regularly give confidential—and potentially damaging—information away on Facebook, Instagram, Pinterest, and other social-media services.

In the same way that the automobile revolutionized transportation, social media have fundamentally shifted the way we communicate and share personal information. We learned to mitigate our risks on the road by using safety belts and obeying traffic laws, but most of us probably don't yet have a good understanding of appropriate precautions for social media. As these services become more integral to our lifestyles, protecting our identities from those who might use them for nefarious ends will become even more critical. Given the speed with which social media are developing and changing, it's difficult to give specific recommendations. An important first step, however, is becoming aware of the risks you run in broadcasting personal information.

These new concerns about privacy and safety in the digital realm have arrived on the heels of older problems that haven't gone away. Spam, for example, has become so pervasive that, according to a 2009 estimate by Ferris Research, annual spending that year for antispam software, hardware, and personnel would reach $6.5 billion—$2.1 billion in the United States alone (Jennings). As these figures show, though, in the case of spam, most of us can and do fight back: Antispam software eliminates or at least reduces the amount of unwanted email we receive, and it can protect us well

Revised pars. 2 and 3 to reflect rhetorical situation — writing to media-savvy readers in age of Facebook — and explained focus to make readers aware of privacy concerns

Replaced the term *phishing*, with example that would be more familiar to readers

Moved up important aspect of argument: Social media matter because we want to be connected

Clarified and limited primary goal of essay

Updated statistics and synthesized these with his own experience to provide concrete examples of problems that remain

Roberts 3

from security threats like the "Nigerian royalty" scam mentioned above, wherein unsuspecting victims will reply to fraudulent emails with personal information—sometimes even giving away bank account numbers.

Most of us are not yet doing anything about the threats posed by the information we publish via social media, however, and many of us are not even fully aware of them. In order to put the problem in context, let's take a closer look at the kinds of social media we're talking about and the nature and extent of the risks they pose. Participation in social networks like Facebook, Twitter, Pinterest, Instagram, and others has exploded in the last few years: As of the fourth quarter of 2015, Facebook had 1.59 billion users ("Number"). Most of those who participate don't think twice about privacy issues, or they assume that the systems' default privacy settings will protect them. Yet studies done by researchers at M.I.T., Carnegie Mellon, and the University of Texas have demonstrated that it's possible to determine sexual orientation, match identities to "anonymously" stated preferences, and even piece together Social Security numbers from profile information on Facebook and other social networks (Lohr).

As if putting basic profile information out there weren't enough, many Facebook users will add applications like games and quizzes that allow outside parties unmediated access to unrelated information from their profiles. In an attempt to raise awareness of the issue, the ACLU has added a quiz(!) to Facebook that explains exactly what is exposed when you add these sorts of quizzes (Conley). The ACLU's quiz offers some suggestions for changing Facebook privacy settings to protect personal information.

The risks you take in revealing personal information via social media go beyond its possible misuse by marketers, hackers, and identity thieves. For example, with its tagline, "What are you doing?" Twitter gives its users 140 characters to broadcast activities, locations, website URLs, and even pictures (via helper services). A single post, or "tweet," however, might cost you a job, as it did the woman who openly expressed her concerns about taking a job she disliked for a "fatty paycheck" (Snell). You might risk being turned down for an interview if you post a picture from a wild drinking party.

Clarified transition, moving from spam (older security concern) to social media

Synthesized experience with information about recent studies to specify "threats to privacy"

Added transition to clarify move from one kind of risk to another; also reorganized section, moving Twitter and blogs to beginning as they were likely to be more familiar to readers

Roberts 4

Similarly, your views and opinions, political and otherwise, may become an issue if you start a blog. I have a blog that's not especially personal, but it occurred to me when I started writing that this might be a potential source of risk: What if my boss saw what I wrote, disagreed, and started treating me differently at work? What if my landlord was bothered enough to refuse to renew my lease? I began to worry so much about it that I wrote to one of my favorite bloggers (Leo Babauta of Zenhabits. net), asking him whether he was concerned about security. He wrote back, "No, I haven't faced security or privacy issues as a blogger (yet). My readers are 100% really cool, nice (and sexy) people." It's worth pointing out that his blog has over a hundred thousand subscribers, so maybe I'm worried over nothing. On the other hand, Mr. Babauta lives on the island of Guam, works for himself, and likely doesn't face many of the same identity expectations that I would as a student and young professional.

One last service that's important to consider is the use of Global Positioning System (GPS) technology in cell phones. Many cell phones now have GPS receivers built in, and as with some Twitter applications, location services such as Brightkite allow you to pinpoint your location on a map with startling accuracy. Broadcasting your location is optional, but many people do so because the technology's there and they don't see how it could hurt. It could hurt: When you broadcast your location, everyone, not just your friends, will know where you are. How about angry ex-boyfriends or -girlfriends or potential stalkers? What if someone were casing your home for a break-in and were able to determine via one of these services that you were away?

Clearly, social media allow you to reveal aspects of your identity and (therefore) compromise your security in ways that are unprecedented. At the same time, for many of us participation is almost obligatory. Most of my friends have succumbed to the peer pressure to be available on Facebook, for example. If you're trying to run a business (or promote your blog), avoiding Twitter is tantamount to professional suicide—these venues are key ingredients for successful marketing. In short, your personal name

Provided some examples to clarify kinds of risks he might be taking in posting blog

Responded to question about why readers should be concerned if Babauta wasn't

Added discussion about Brightkite and GPS technology in cell phones because readers of draft are unfamiliar with, or unconcerned about, implications

Added concluding section to clarify purpose and remind readers of key points

and profile have become a brand that you're expected to proliferate and maintain in cyberspace: Without them, you're nothing. Yet, as I have discussed, the risks that accompany this self-promotion are high.

If only because social media are constantly evolving, it is unlikely that a set of specific and concrete best practices for mitigating these risks will emerge. One friend and professional colleague argues that it's simply impossible to manage your identity online because much of it is revealed by others—your friends will post the embarrassing party pictures for you, school or work will post documents detailing your achievements, and Google will determine what appears in the search results when you type your name in. M.I.T. professor Harold Abelson agrees: "Personal privacy is no longer an individual thing. . . . In today's online world, what your mother told you is true, only more so: people really can judge you by your friends" (qtd. in Lohr).

The most positive spin on the current situation is to think of your online identity in terms of a "signal-to-noise" ratio: Assuming you know what you're doing, you are in charge of the "signal" (the information you yourself tweet or allow to appear on Facebook), and this signal will usually be stronger than the "noise" generated by your friends or others who broadcast information you'd rather not share. The key phrase there is "assuming you know what you're doing," and that's where all of us could use some pointers. If you're going to put your faith in your ability to create a strong, positive signal, you need to follow a few key rules. First, realize that there's a potential problem every time you post something private online. Next, make yourself thoroughly acquainted with the privacy settings of any and all social media you interact with. The default settings for any of these programs are almost certainly inadequate because my security concerns aren't the same as Leo Babauta's, and they're not the same as yours. Finally, keep talking (and blogging and Googling) about the issue and sharing any best practices you discover. We need to work together to understand and manage these risks if we want to retain control of the "brand" that is us.

Added quote from expert bolsters claim about ways identities are revealed online

Roberts 6

Works Cited

Babauta, Leo. "Re: Security Concerns?" Received by Stevon Roberts, 11 Oct. 2013.

Conley, Chris. "Quiz: What Do Facebook Quizzes Know about You?" *Blog of Rights*, ACLU, www.aclu.org/blog/quiz-what-do-facebook -quizzes-know-about-you.

Jennings, Richi. "Cost of Spam Is Flattening—Our 2009 Predictions." Ferris Research, email-museum.com/2009/01/28/cost-of-spam-is -flattening-our-2009-predictions/.

Lohr, Steve. "How Privacy Vanishes Online." *The New York Times*, www.nytimes.com/2010/03/17/technology/17privacy.html?_r=0.

"Number of Monthly Active Facebook Users Worldwide as of 4th Quarter 2015 (in Millions)." *Statista: The Statistics Portal*, www.statista.com /statistics/264810/number-of-monthly-active-facebook-users-worldwide / istic. Accessed 12 Oct. 2016.

Snell, Jason. "Think before You Tweet." *Macworld*, www.macworld.com /article/1139480/when_not_to_twitter.html.

The Works Cited page includes all sources in correct MLA format. (*Note*: in an actual MLA-style paper, works-cited entries start on a new page.)

Benefiting from Responses to Work in Progress

You may write alone a good deal of the time, but writing needn't be a lonely process. You can draw on the responses of others to help you re-see your writing and to gain support. When you ask others to respond to your writing, you're asking for feedback so that you can see your writing in fresh and different ways.

Responses can take a number of forms. Sometimes you may find it helpful to ask others simply to describe your writing for you. You might, for example, ask them to summarize in their own words how they understand your main point or what they think you're getting at. Similarly, you might ask them what parts of your draft stood out for them and what they felt was missing.

On other occasions, you may find more analytical responses helpful. You might ask readers to comment on your essay's organization or how well it responds to their needs and interests. If you're writing an argumentative essay, you might ask readers to look for potential weaknesses in its structure or logic.

To determine what kind of feedback will be most helpful, think commonsensically about your writing. Where are you in your composing process?

How do you feel about your draft and the kind of writing you're working on? If you've just completed a rough draft, for instance, you might find descriptive feedback most helpful. After you've worked longer on the essay, you might invite more analytical responses.

As a student, you can turn to many people for feedback. The differences in their situations will influence how they respond; these differences should also influence how you use their responses. No matter whom you approach for feedback, though, learn to distinguish between your writing and yourself. Try not to respond defensively to suggestions for improvement, and don't argue with readers' responses. Instead, use them to gain insight into your writing. Ultimately, you are the one who must decide how to interpret and apply other people's comments and criticisms.

---

note for multilingual writers

If you were educated in another culture, the process of revising multiple drafts may be new to you. Revising is meant to help you rework your writing to make sure it is as effective and clear as possible. If receiving (and giving) comments on drafts is new to you, be assured that the suggestions and questions from peer and other reviewers should lead to constructive collaboration.

RESPONSES FROM FRIENDS AND FAMILY MEMBERS

You can certainly ask the people close to you to respond to your writing, but you should understand their strengths and weaknesses as readers. One important strength is that you trust them. Even if you spend time filling them in, however, friends and family members may not understand the nature of your assignment or your instructor's standards for evaluation; they're also likely to be less objective than other readers. All the same, friends and family members can provide useful responses to your writing if you choose such respondents carefully and draw on their strengths as outsiders. Rather than asking them to respond in detail, you might ask them to give a general impression or a descriptive response to your work. If their understanding of the main idea or controlling purpose of your essay differs substantially from your own, you've gained very useful information.

RESPONSES FROM CLASSMATES

Because your classmates know your instructor and the assignment as insiders, they can provide particularly effective responses to work in progress. Classmates don't need to be experts to provide helpful responses. They simply need to be attentive, honest, supportive readers. Classmates can also read your work more objectively than family members and friends can. To ensure that you and your classmates provide a helpful balance of support and criticism, you and they should follow the Guidelines for Responses from Classmates below.

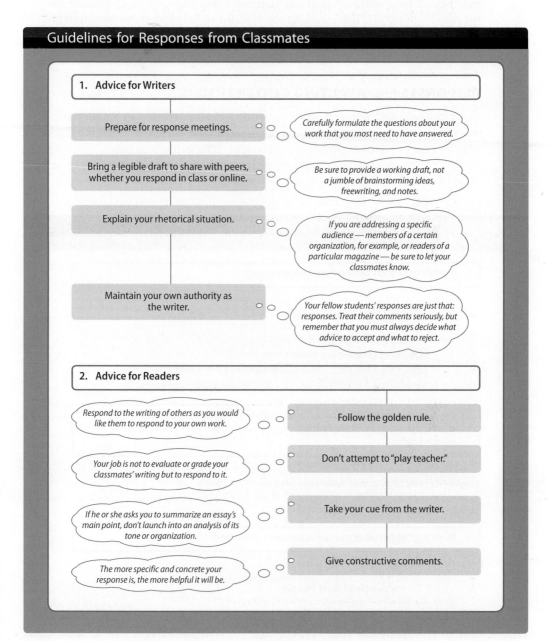

Guidelines for Responses from Classmates

1. Advice for Writers

Prepare for response meetings.

Carefully formulate the questions about your work that you most need to have answered.

Bring a legible draft to share with peers, whether you respond in class or online.

Be sure to provide a working draft, not a jumble of brainstorming ideas, freewriting, and notes.

Explain your rhetorical situation.

If you are addressing a specific audience — members of a certain organization, for example, or readers of a particular magazine — be sure to let your classmates know.

Maintain your own authority as the writer.

Your fellow students' responses are just that: responses. Treat their comments seriously, but remember that you must always decide what advice to accept and what to reject.

2. Advice for Readers

Respond to the writing of others as you would like them to respond to your own work.

Follow the golden rule.

Your job is not to evaluate or grade your classmates' writing but to respond to it.

Don't attempt to "play teacher."

If he or she asks you to summarize an essay's main point, don't launch into an analysis of its tone or organization.

Take your cue from the writer.

The more specific and concrete your response is, the more helpful it will be.

Give constructive comments.

for **exploration**

Freewrite for five to ten minutes about responses to your work from classmates, and then draw up a list of statements describing the kinds of responses that have been most helpful. Meet with a group of your classmates. Begin by having each group member read his or her list. Then, working together, list all the suggestions for responses from classmates. Keep a copy of all the suggestions for future use.

RESPONSES FROM WRITING CENTER TUTORS

Many colleges and universities have writing centers staffed by undergraduate and graduate writing assistants or tutors. If your college or university has one, be sure to take advantage of its services. (The guidelines below can help you get the most from your meeting with a tutor.) Tutors are not professional

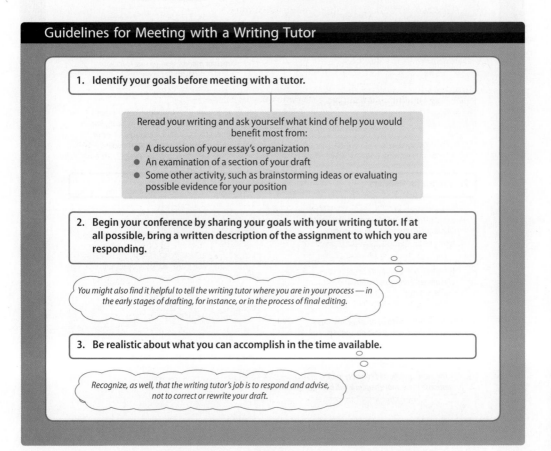

Guidelines for Meeting with a Writing Tutor

1. **Identify your goals before meeting with a tutor.**

   Reread your writing and ask yourself what kind of help you would benefit most from:
   - A discussion of your essay's organization
   - An examination of a section of your draft
   - Some other activity, such as brainstorming ideas or evaluating possible evidence for your position

2. **Begin your conference by sharing your goals with your writing tutor. If at all possible, bring a written description of the assignment to which you are responding.**

   You might also find it helpful to tell the writing tutor where you are in your process — in the early stages of drafting, for instance, or in the process of final editing.

3. **Be realistic about what you can accomplish in the time available.**

   Recognize, as well, that the writing tutor's job is to respond and advise, not to correct or rewrite your draft.

editors, nor are they faculty aides standing in for instructors who are unavail-able or too busy to meet with students, but they are good writers who have been formally trained to respond to peers' work and to make suggestions for improvement. Tutors can provide excellent responses to work in progress.

RESPONSES FROM YOUR INSTRUCTOR AND OTHERS

Because your instructor is such an important reader for your written assignments, you want to make good use of any written comments he or she provides. For advice on making the most of them, see the guidelines below.

Friends, family members, classmates, writing tutors, instructors—all can provide helpful responses to your writing. None of these responses,

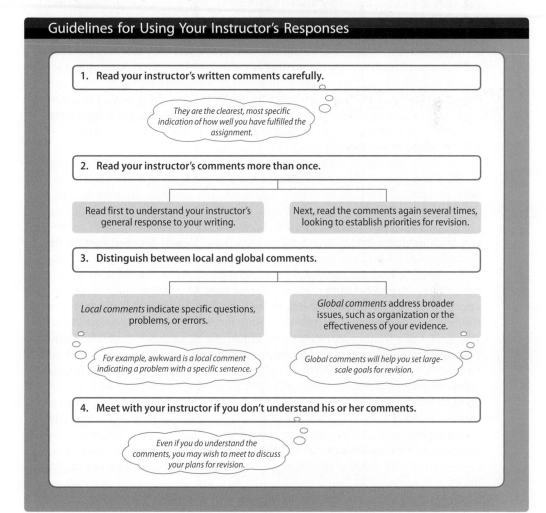

Guidelines for Using Your Instructor's Responses

1. **Read your instructor's written comments carefully.**

   They are the clearest, most specific indication of how well you have fulfilled the assignment.

2. **Read your instructor's comments more than once.**

   Read first to understand your instructor's general response to your writing.

   Next, read the comments again several times, looking to establish priorities for revision.

3. **Distinguish between local and global comments.**

   Local comments indicate specific questions, problems, or errors.

   Global comments address broader issues, such as organization or the effectiveness of your evidence.

   For example, awkward is a local comment indicating a problem with a specific sentence.

   Global comments will help you set large-scale goals for revision.

4. **Meet with your instructor if you don't understand his or her comments.**

   Even if you do understand the comments, you may wish to meet to discuss your plans for revision.

whether criticism or praise, should take the place of your own judgment, however. Your job is to *interpret* and *evaluate* these responses, using them along with your own assessment of your rough draft to establish goals for revising.

Practical Strategies for Editing

While most writers find it helpful to distinguish between revising and editing, they are not completely discrete processes. While you are writing a first draft of your essay, you may decide that one word is just not right and revise it. In so doing, you are editing—or making a local rather than a global change. Similarly, when you are editing your essay, you may discover that the difficulty you are having with writing an effective transition from one section to another is a larger problem than you previously realized. You now see that the two sections function better logically if they are reversed and the relationship between them is clarified. In this instance, when you make those changes—even though you are primarily focused on editing your writing—you are revising.

As these examples suggest, although it is useful to distinguish between revising and editing, the composing process is not rigid or formulaic. Moreover, individuals vary in how they approach this process. Chapter 4, "Academic Writing: Committing to the Process," discusses four general composing styles. (See pp. 91–97.) Heavy drafters, for instance, typically engage in extensive revising and editing. They tend to write long, loosely focused first drafts that are more like freewrites than essays and hence the necessity of considerable revising and editing. Heavy planners do much of the work of invention, planning, and drafting mentally before they sit down at their computer or put pen to paper. Their first drafts are more like heavy revisers' second or third drafts; their second drafts may require more editing than revision. Those who prefer the third composing style, sequential composers, devote roughly equivalent amounts of time to invention, planning, drafting, and revising/editing; they tend to have distinct stages of revising and editing. The fourth composing style, procrastinators, put off their writing so long that all they can do is to frantically pour out an essay at the last minute; many procrastinators are lucky if they can spell-check their essays before printing them. The following discussion of practical strategies for editing will help you meet the demands of editing, whether you are substituting one word for another in an early draft of your essay or analyzing a later draft to determine how you might improve its style.

KEEPING YOUR READERS ON TRACK: EDITING FOR STYLE

"Proper words in proper places"—that's how the eighteenth-century writer Jonathan Swift defined style. As Swift suggests, writing style reflects all the choices a writer makes, from global questions of approach and organization to the smallest details about punctuation and grammar. When, in writing, you put the proper words in their proper places, readers will be able to follow your ideas with understanding and interest. In addition, they will probably gain some sense of the person behind the words—that is, of the writer's presence.

While writers address issues of style throughout the composing process, they do so most efficiently and effectively once they have determined that the basic structure, organization, and argument of their text are working. (Why spend a half an hour determining whether a paragraph is coherent and stylistically effective when that paragraph may be gone in an instant?) At this point, the writer can make changes that enable readers to move through the writing easily and enjoyably.

ACHIEVING COHERENCE

Most writers are aware that paragraphs and essays need to be *unified*—that is, that they should focus on a single topic.✳ Writing is *coherent* when readers can move easily from word to word, sentence to sentence, and paragraph to paragraph. There are various means of achieving coherence. Some methods, such as *repeating key words and sentence structures* and *using pronouns*, reinforce or emphasize the logical development of ideas. Another method involves *using transitional words* such as *but*, *although*, and *because* to provide directional cues for readers.

The following introduction to "Home Town," an essay by the writer Ian Frazier, uses all these methods to keep readers on track. The most important means of achieving coherence are italicized.

> *When glaciers* covered much of northern Ohio, the land around Hudson, the town where I grew up, lay under one. *Glaciers* came and went several times, the most recent departing about 14,000 years ago. *When* we studied *glaciers* in an Ohio-history class in grade school, I imagined our *glacier* receding smoothly, like a sheet pulled off a new car. *Actually, glaciers* can move forward *but* they don't back up—*they* melt in place. *Most likely* the *glacier* above Hudson softened, *and* began to trickle underneath; rocks on its surface absorbed sunlight and melted tunnels into *it; it* rotted, *it* dwindled, *it* dripped, *it* ticked; *then it* dropped a pile of the sand and rocks *it* had been carrying around for centuries onto the ground in a heap. Hudson's landscape was hundreds of these little heaps—hills rarely big enough to sled down, a random arrangement made by gravity and smoothed by weather and time.
>
> —Ian Frazier, "Home Town"

See Chapter 9 (pp. 262–86) for coverage of drafting unified paragraphs. ✳

When you read your own writing to determine how to strengthen its coherence, use common sense. Your writing is coherent if readers know where they have been and where they are going as they read. Don't assume that your writing will be more coherent if you simply sprinkle key words, pronouns, and transitions throughout your prose. If the logic of your discussion is clear without such devices, don't add them.

Editing for coherence proceeds most effectively if you look first at large-scale issues, such as the relationship among your essay's introduction, body, and conclusion, before considering smaller concerns. The guidelines below offer advice on editing for coherence.

FINDING AN APPROPRIATE VOICE

A writer's style reflects his or her individual taste and sensibility. But just as people dress differently for different occasions, so too do effective writers vary their style, depending on their rhetorical situation. As they do so, they are particularly attentive to the *persona*, or voice, they want to convey through their writing.

Guidelines for Editing for Coherence

1. First, read your draft quickly to determine if it flows smoothly.

> *Pay particular attention to the movement from introduction to body and conclusion. How could you tighten or strengthen these connections?*

2. Next, read slowly, paying attention to the movement from paragraph to paragraph.

> *Ask yourself: How do new paragraphs build on or connect with previous paragraphs? Would more explicit connections, such as transitions, help readers better understand your ideas?*

3. Finally, read each paragraph separately.

> *Ask yourself: How do your word choice and sentence structure help readers progress from sentence to sentence? Would repeating key words or using pronouns or adding transitions increase a paragraph's coherence?*

Sometimes writers present strong and distinctive voices. Here, for instance, is the beginning of an essay by the novelist Ken Kesey on the Pendleton Round-Up, a well-known rodeo held every September in eastern Oregon.

> My father took me up the Gorge and over the hills to my first one thirty-five years ago. It was on my fourteenth birthday. I had to miss a couple of days' school plus the possibility of suiting up for the varsity game that Friday night. Gives you some idea of the importance Daddy placed on this event.
>
> For this is more than just a world-class rodeo. It is a week-long shindig, a yearly rendezvous dating back beyond the first white trappers, a traditional powwow ground for the Indian nations of the Northwest for nobody knows how many centuries.
>
> —Ken Kesey, "The Blue-Ribbon American Beauty Rose of Rodeo"

Kesey's word choice and sentence structure help create an image of the writer as folksy, relaxed, and yet also forceful—just the right insider to write about a famous rodeo. In other situations, writers may prefer a less personal voice, as is often the case in informative writing for textbooks, academic articles, newspapers, and the like.

If you think rhetorically, always asking questions about your rhetorical situation, you'll naturally consider such major stylistic issues as voice. By considering how much you wish to draw on appeals to reason (logos), emotion (pathos), and your own credibility as writer (ethos), you will more easily determine your own voice and your relationship with readers.

thinking rhetorically

EDITING FOR EFFECTIVE PROSE STYLE

The stylistic choices that you make as you draft and revise reflect not only your rhetorical awareness but also your awareness of general principles of effective prose style. Perhaps the easiest way to understand these principles is to analyze a passage that illustrates effective prose style in action.

Here is a paragraph from the first chapter of a psycholinguistics textbook. (Psycholinguistics is an interdisciplinary field that studies linguistic behavior and the psychological mechanisms that make verbal communication possible.) As you read it, imagine that you have been assigned to read the textbook for a course in psycholinguistics.

> Language stands at the center of human affairs, from the most prosaic to the most profound. It is used for haggling with store clerks, telling off umpires, and gossiping with friends as well as for negotiating contracts, discussing ethics, and explaining religious beliefs. It is the

medium through which the manners, morals, and mythology of a society are passed on to the next generation. Indeed, it is a basic ingredi-
ent in virtually every social situation. The thread that runs through all
these activities is communication, people trying to put their ideas over
to others. As the main vehicle of human communication, language is
indispensable.

—Herbert H. Clark and Eve V. Clark, *Psychology and Language*

This paragraph, you would probably agree, embodies effective prose style. It's
clearly organized and begins with a topic sentence, which the rest of the paragraph explains. The paragraph is also coherent, with pronouns, key words, and
sentence patterns helping readers proceed. But what most distinguishes this
paragraph, what makes it so effective, is the authors' use of concrete, precise,
economical language and carefully crafted sentences.

Suppose that the paragraph were revised as follows. What would be lost?

Language stands at the center of human affairs, from the most prosaic
to the most profound. It is a means of human communication. It is a
means of cultural change and regeneration. It is found in every social
situation. The element that characterizes all these activities is communication. As the main vehicle of human communication, language is
indispensable.

This revision communicates roughly the same ideas as the original paragraph,
but it lacks that paragraph's liveliness and interest. Instead of presenting
vivid examples—"haggling with store clerks, telling off umpires, and gossip-
ing with friends"—these sentences state only vague generalities. Moreover,
they're short and monotonous. Also lost in the revision is any sense of the
authors' personalities, as revealed in their writing.

As this example demonstrates, effective prose style doesn't have to be
flashy or call attention to itself. The focus in the original passage is on the
ideas being discussed. The authors don't want readers to stop and think, "My,
what a lovely sentence." But they do want their readers to become interested
in and engaged with their ideas. So they use strong verbs and vivid, concrete
examples whenever possible. They pay careful attention to sentence structure, alternating sequences of sentences with parallel structures with other,
more varied sentences. They make sure that the relationships among ideas
are clear. As a result of these and other choices, this paragraph succeeds in
being both economical and emphatic.

Exploring your stylistic options—developing a style that reflects your understanding of yourself and the world and your feel for language—is one of
the pleasures of writing. The Guidelines for Effective Prose Style on p. 311 describe just a few of the ways you can revise your own writing to improve its
style.

Guidelines for Effective Prose Style

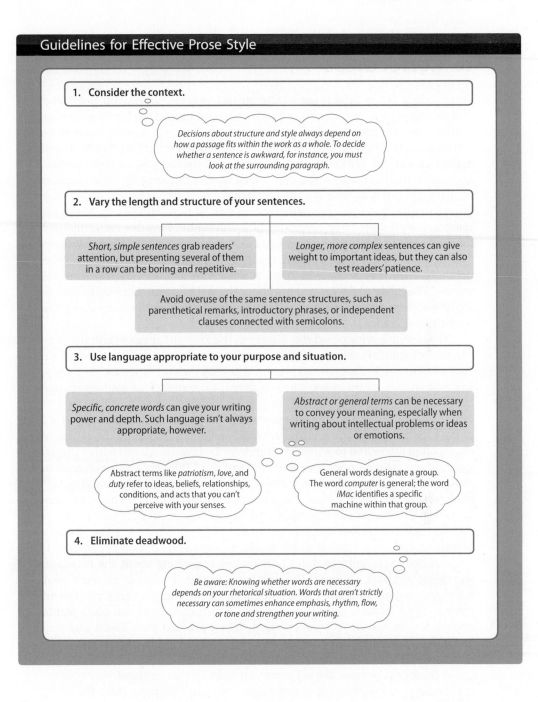

1. **Consider the context.**

   Decisions about structure and style always depend on how a passage fits within the work as a whole. To decide whether a sentence is awkward, for instance, you must look at the surrounding paragraph.

2. **Vary the length and structure of your sentences.**

   Short, simple sentences grab readers' attention, but presenting several of them in a row can be boring and repetitive.

   Longer, more complex sentences can give weight to important ideas, but they can also test readers' patience.

   Avoid overuse of the same sentence structures, such as parenthetical remarks, introductory phrases, or independent clauses connected with semicolons.

3. **Use language appropriate to your purpose and situation.**

   Specific, concrete words can give your writing power and depth. Such language isn't always appropriate, however.

   Abstract or general terms can be necessary to convey your meaning, especially when writing about intellectual problems or ideas or emotions.

   Abstract terms like *patriotism*, *love*, and *duty* refer to ideas, beliefs, relationships, conditions, and acts that you can't perceive with your senses.

   General words designate a group. The word *computer* is general; the word *iMac* identifies a specific machine within that group.

4. **Eliminate deadwood.**

   Be aware: Knowing whether words are necessary depends on your rhetorical situation. Words that aren't strictly necessary can sometimes enhance emphasis, rhythm, flow, or tone and strengthen your writing.

Proofreading: A Rhetorical Approach to Correctness

Proofreading is the final stage of the writing process. When you proofread, you examine your text carefully to identify and correct errors in grammar, spelling, and punctuation. The goal? To ensure that your writing follows the conventions of standard written English. These conventions represent shared agreements about written texts in English and how they can be best received and understood by readers. You may not be used to thinking about correctness in writing in this way. Your teachers (and perhaps also your parents) may have talked about correctness primarily as a matter of right and wrong. There are reasons they did so: They are aware of the potential negative consequences for those whose writing is viewed as incorrect or error-ridden. When a written text violates readers' expectations, readers may find it difficult to focus on its meaning. They may become irritated at what they view as sloppy or careless writing. They may make judgments about the writer's commitment to the assignment (or to their education). They may even make judgments about the writer's intelligence.

Those who have studied the history of the English language and the conventions of standard written English know that such judgments can be unfair. Textual conventions are shared agreements about what is appropriate in spoken and written communication, and these conventions can and do change over time. Decades ago, for instance, schoolchildren were routinely taught that it was an error to end a sentence with a preposition. This convention led to the construction of some fairly awkward sentences, including the sentence that is often attributed to Winston Churchill: "Ending a sentence with a preposition is something up with which I will not put." Over time this convention changed, and most readers find a sentence like "Who were you talking to?" preferable to the more formal "To whom were you talking?" What was once viewed as a matter of correctness is now viewed as a matter of preference.

Textual conventions are also culturally situated. Where the conventions of writing are concerned, in other words, context and community matter. If a friend texts you and you don't understand something about the message, you might text back a simple "?"—perhaps using an emoji to do so. But if your supervisor emails your work schedule for the week and you think you see an error in the schedule, you would be wise to respond using complete words and sentences and correct punctuation. When you text your friend one way and email your supervisor another way, you are making a rhetorical judgment about what is appropriate in that particular context.

thinking rhetorically

A rhetorical perspective on error can help you understand why observing language conventions is about more than just following rules for rules' sake. The conventions of standard written English play an essential role in the creation and transmission of meaning. Imagine trying to read an extended text with no punctuation. (You may be surprised to learn that the system of punctuation that we use today did not exist before the invention of the printing press around 1440.) You wouldn't know (among other things) where a new sentence began or the previous sentence ended. Punctuation can also be critical to meaning, as the following paired sentences, both of which depend on questionable gender stereotypes, humorously demonstrate:

A woman without her man is nothing.

A woman: without her, man is nothing.

The conventions of standard written English help ensure that the message you intend to convey is the message that the reader receives.

To better understand how deviations from the conventions of standard written English can distract, annoy, or confuse readers, let's look at this issue from the perspective of Aristotle's three appeals, as discussed in Chapter 3 (pp. 62–67). According to Aristotle, when speakers and writers communicate with others, they draw on these three general appeals:

Logos, the appeal to reason

Pathos, the appeal to emotion, values, and beliefs

Ethos, the appeal to the credibility of the speaker or writer

What role might deviations from the conventions of standard written English play in the reception of student writing when read by college instructors? As has been discussed throughout this book, academic writing places a high value on logos, or the appeal to reason. Although successful academic writers employ pathos and ethos in key ways in their texts, logos is particularly important. Anything that interferes with an instructor's ability to focus on content and meaning is a distraction. Numerous errors can cause instructors to turn their focus from the writer's message to the form in which the writer expresses it, so the significance of errors becomes inflated.

What about pathos, or the appeal to emotion, values, and beliefs? In academic writing, students employ appeals to pathos when they demonstrate that they share the commitments, values, and practices of the academic community. Instructors believe that correctness is a sign of respect for readers; they also believe that it represents a commitment to the creation and distribution of knowledge. When students turn in written work that is full of errors, instructors may assume that they do not value—and do not want to be a part of—the academic community.

You have probably already realized that error-ridden writing can cause instructors to question students' ethos as well. Ethos refers to the credibility of the writer. When students do not follow the conventions of standard written English valued by their instructors, they risk losing credibility. At best, instructors may view students as sloppy and careless. At worst, they may make negative inferences about students' commitment to the course—and to their education.

As this discussion indicates, a lot can be at stake when students turn in written work that does not meet the conventions of standard written English. This is why it is important to take the time to proofread your writing carefully. Research suggests that students can recognize most errors in their writing if they learn how and when to focus their attention on correcting their writing, which is what proofreading is all about.

Perhaps the major challenge that proofreading poses for writers is the ability to distance themselves from the texts they have written. For most writers, time away from their text is essential if they are to achieve this distance. Time management thus plays a central role in the proofreading process. If you write an essay for your writing, history, or business class at the last minute in a haze of late-night, overcaffeinated exhaustion, you will find it difficult if not impossible to proofread that essay. Thus it is essential to build time for proofreading into your composing process, just as you build in time for research, writing, revising, and editing.

The following guidelines will help you develop the ability to proofread your own writing effectively and efficiently.

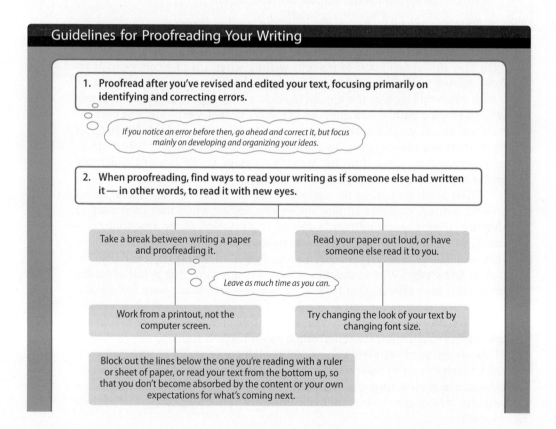

Guidelines for Proofreading Your Writing

1. **Proofread after you've revised and edited your text, focusing primarily on identifying and correcting errors.**

   If you notice an error before then, go ahead and correct it, but focus mainly on developing and organizing your ideas.

2. **When proofreading, find ways to read your writing as if someone else had written it — in other words, to read it with new eyes.**

   Take a break between writing a paper and proofreading it.

   Read your paper out loud, or have someone else read it to you.

   Leave as much time as you can.

   Work from a printout, not the computer screen.

   Try changing the look of your text by changing font size.

   Block out the lines below the one you're reading with a ruler or sheet of paper, or read your text from the bottom up, so that you don't become absorbed by the content or your own expectations for what's coming next.

3. Determine the physical environment and length of proofreading that work best for you. Some writers proofread most effectively . . .

in a quiet place, where they can concentrate.

in a bustling café or public area.

Few people, if any, can proofread effectively in front of a TV.

in several short blocks of time.

in one extended sitting.

4. Know your problem areas.

Pay attention to the errors your instructors identify. Be sure that you understand each error and know how to correct it.

Make a list of your most common errors, and consult it before proofreading.

Copying the corrected sentence by hand could help you build "muscle memory" that will pay dividends in the future.

5. Set priorities for your proofreading.

Focus first on the errors that obscure meaning or violate readers' expectations that a sentence will express a complete thought, like sentence fragments. Then look for less disruptive errors, like typos or spelling errors.

Often, you can correct a fragment by attaching it to the sentence that precedes or follows it.

Example

Sentence fragment: Having worked overtime all day without a break. I was famished and exhausted when I got home.

Complete sentence: Having worked overtime all day without a break, I was famished and exhausted when I got home.

6. Use the search function of your computer to isolate errors you make regularly.

For example, search for opening parentheses if you know that you sometimes forget to include closing parentheses.

Continued >

Guidelines continued

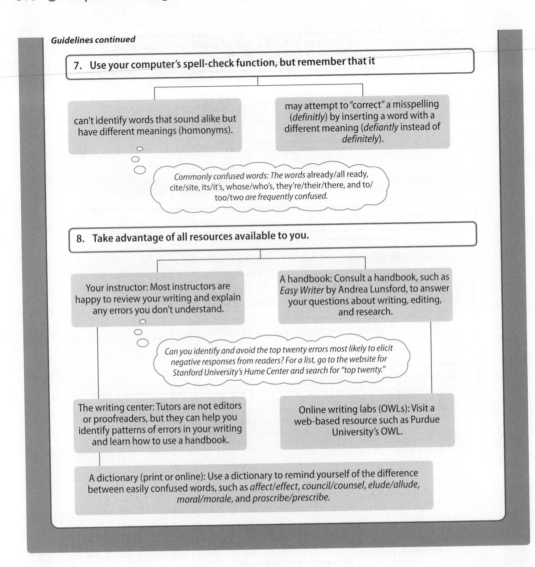

7. **Use your computer's spell-check function, but remember that it**

can't identify words that sound alike but have different meanings (homonyms).

may attempt to "correct" a misspelling (*definitly*) by inserting a word with a different meaning (*defiantly* instead of *definitely*).

Commonly confused words: The words already/all ready, cite/site, its/it's, whose/who's, they're/their/there, *and* to/too/two *are frequently confused.*

8. **Take advantage of all resources available to you.**

Your instructor: Most instructors are happy to review your writing and explain any errors you don't understand.

A handbook: Consult a handbook, such as *Easy Writer* by Andrea Lunsford, to answer your questions about writing, editing, and research.

Can you identify and avoid the top twenty errors most likely to elicit negative responses from readers? For a list, go to the website for Stanford University's Hume Center and search for "top twenty."

The writing center: Tutors are not editors or proofreaders, but they can help you identify patterns of errors in your writing and learn how to use a handbook.

Online writing labs (OWLs): Visit a web-based resource such as Purdue University's OWL.

A dictionary (print or online): Use a dictionary to remind yourself of the difference between easily confused words, such as *affect/effect, council/counsel, elude/allude, moral/morale,* and *proscribe/prescribe*.

note for multilingual writers

Proofreading can be especially challenging for writers whose first language is not English. While students for whom English is their first or only language can certainly have difficulty with the conventions of standard English, they can often notice or "hear" errors more easily than English-language learners. If you find proofreading difficult, try the multiple-reading approach to proofreading. Read your essay first looking for grammatical errors, such as subject-verb agreement, errors involving articles, or pronoun-noun agreement. Then read it again looking for punctuation errors and a third time for spelling errors. Multilingual writers will also find it especially helpful to keep a list of frequent errors.

When you proofread your writing carefully, you demonstrate in the most specific and concrete way possible that you respect your readers and want to do all you can to facilitate communication with them. A rhetorical approach to proofreading—like the rhetorical approach to writing that informs every aspect of *The Academic Writer*—reminds you that writers who think rhetorically apply their understanding of human communication in general, and of texts (whether the medium is print, oral, or digital) in particular, to the decisions that will enable effective communication within a specific rhetorical situation.

for **thought, discussion, and writing**

1. To study your own revision process, number and save all your plans, drafts, and revisions for a paper you're currently writing or have written recently. After you have completed the paper, review these materials, paying particular attention to the revisions you made. Can you describe the revision strategies you followed and identify ways to improve the effectiveness of this process? Your instructor may ask you to write an essay discussing what you have learned as a result of this analysis.

2. From an essay you are currently working on, choose two or three paragraphs that you suspect could be more coherent or stylistically effective. Using this chapter's discussion as a guide, revise these paragraphs.

3. Read the essay by Frank Rose on pp. 33–34 (or choose another essay that interests you), and then answer the following questions.

   - How would you describe the general style of this essay? Write three or four sentences describing its style.
   - How would you describe the persona, or voice, conveyed by this essay? List at least three characteristics of the writer's voice, and then indicate several passages that exemplify these characteristics.
   - Find three passages that demonstrate the principles of effective prose style as discussed in this chapter. Indicate why you believe each passage is stylistically effective.
   - What additional comments could you make about the structure and style of this essay? Did anything about the style surprise you? Formulate at least one additional comment about the essay's structure and style.

4. On the next page is a student's in-class midterm essay exam on Nathaniel Hawthorne's short story "Young Goodman Brown." The student didn't have time to proofread the exam response before turning it in. Correct all the errors you can identify. If you are unsure whether something is an error, put a question mark in the margin next to the line where the possible error appears.

Analysis of A Scene in "Young Goodman Brown"

In the short story "Young Goodman Brown," by Nathaniel Hawthorne the longest (it comprises nearly the entire story) and most influential scene is the one where Goodman Brown ventures into the dark woods with the devil. This scene has multiple elements which make it significant to the story, including setting, irony, and suspense.

The setting of this scene really adds to what is going on with the plot. Goodman Brown has just left his sweet young wife back at home in there quiet town, and is trekking into the dark, gloomy, mysterious woods with a dark stranger, who later on is revealed as the devil himself. The shadows, darkness, seclusion, and wildness of a forest all contribute to a feeling of unease and suspense. Later on, the burning pine trees create a feeling of hell-on-earth and makes the reader feel as though pour Goodman is slipping deeper and deeper into the devil's clutches.

Irony is another thing apparent in this scene. The fact that the main characters name happen to be Goodman ("good man") is ironic in itself given that he has just left his sweet, good pure wife to converse with the devil, at night, in the middle of a creepy forest. Another example of irony is the number of seemingly "good" townspeople that he encounters as he makes his way deeper and deeper into the forest to attend the devil's communion he sees the minister, a Deacon, a pious Christian woman, and the devil tells him that he has known his father and grandfather, even though Goodman Brown argued earlier that he was from a good Christian family.

Finally, the element of suspense plays a large part in the composition of this scene. One of the most suspenseful moments is when Goodman thinks he hears Faith's voice and then sees her hair ribbon flutter to the ground. Later, he sees her face to face and commands her to, "look up to heaven and resist the wicked one," at which time the scene dramatically ends leaving the reader with a sense of suspense and wonderment at whether or not Faith obeyed the command.

11

Strategies for Multimodal Composing

The term *multimodal composing* may be new to you. When you first encounter the term, you may think something like this: "Oh that must refer to forms of digital communication like wikis, blogs, websites, posts to Twitter and Facebook, and so forth." These are examples of multimodal texts, but so is a traditional print essay. "How can this be?" you might wonder. A brief discussion of what modes are should clarify why this is the case.

Understanding Multimodal Composing

There are five primary modes of communication:

- Linguistic: the use of words—written or spoken
- Visual: the use of images of all kinds—both static and moving
- Aural: the use of sound, from tone of voice to musical compositions
- Spatial: the use of design elements, white space, website navigation, and so on
- Gestural: movement of all kinds, from a speaker's facial expressions and gestures (whether seen in person or in a photo or film) to a complex dance performance

There are also three primary media of communication: print, oral, and digital. They are not the only possible media, however. Our bodies can serve as a medium of communication, as occurs in the case of oral presentations and dance. Canvas can serve as a medium for painters. The side of a building or railroad car can serve as a medium for graffiti artists. Print, oral, and digital media, however, are especially important and common in college, the professions, and public life. (Texts that emphasize the linguistic mode and that resemble traditional academic essays do not have to employ the medium of print. You might read an essay for your composition or history class on your laptop or e-reader, for instance. For this reason, some scholars prefer to designate texts that emphasize the linguistic mode as alphabetic texts, a term that acknowledges that these texts are not limited to the medium of print.)

Because print texts draw on a minimum of two modes (the linguistic and the spatial), they are by definition multimodal. It is easy to undervalue the role of the spatial mode when the design elements (margin, spacing, font, and so forth) are standardized (as with traditional academic print essays). Even when students include visuals in print texts, as art history students might do if they insert a reproduction of a painting in their essays, the dominant mode is linguistic, and the dominant medium is print.

In a world of traditional print texts, it was easy for those composing texts to emphasize the role that words (the linguistic mode) play in their development—students and teachers alike would commonsensically say that they *wrote* an essay or report—but in a world where most writers have access to multiple modes and media, design becomes equally important. Students creating a PowerPoint presentation for an oral report or a brochure for a service learning project would probably say that they are *designing, composing,* or *creating* the slide presentation or brochure rather than writing it, even though words would still play an important role in that composition.

Today students live and compose in a world where multiple modes and media abound. While many students continue to compose texts that emphasize the linguistic mode, they are much more likely to include complex visual, gestural, aural, and spatial elements as well. It is quite common for students to create essays with multiple visuals (images, charts, graphs). If they are giving an oral report, they may well create a PowerPoint or Prezi presentation, with sound files and visuals embedded in the slides. They may participate in a class blog, wiki, discussion board, or Facebook page. They may even create films or podcasts to share their ideas.

Students in first-year writing classes are also composing texts that take advantage of multiple modes. An increasingly common assignment in these classes, for instance, asks students to revise, or *remix,* a print text to take advantage of other modes and media. A student might remix a research essay in the form of a Prezi or PowerPoint presentation, an audio essay, or a visually rich poster, for example.

Here are a few additional examples of multimodal assignments from classes at Oregon State University that you can find online with a simple search on Google or YouTube:

- Students in Kristin Griffin's advanced composition class—a class with a focus on food and food writing—created an online magazine, *Buckteeth: Food Writing You Can Sink Your Teeth Into,* to share their visually enriched essays. (The title of the magazine, by the way, is a reference to Benny Beaver, the university's mascot.)

- In 2015, Dwaine Plaza and a group of students spent two weeks in Canada studying that country's economy, society, politics, and culture. One of the assignments for this sociology class was to create brief (three- to six-minute) YouTube videos on the topics of students' final seminar papers. Examples include "Overview of First Nations People and Issues They Face" by Adriana Davis and Marie Davis, "French Canadian Culture" by Amanda Rieskap and Darien Stites, and "Canadian Totem Poles" by Brandi Berger and Madeline Bowman.

- In Ehren Pflugfelder's course on digital literacies, students collaborated to create a twenty-seven-minute video (posted on YouTube), "Does Your Smart Phone Make You Smarter?"

Students also create multimodal texts for their own purposes: To share their experiences with family and friends, students studying abroad might create a blog that combines words, images, and design features. Students involved in campus and community organizations on their own or through a service learning program regularly create brochures, posters, websites, podcasts, videos, Facebook pages, and other texts to promote these organizations and their activities. Multimodal composing is a part of most students' daily lives. Even changing the cover photo on your Facebook page is an act of multimodal composition and represents a rhetorical choice about how you want to represent yourself on that site. The rhetorical nature of Facebook cover photos becomes particularly clear when those who are committed to a cause or who want to express their support after a tragedy employ a filter (such as the colors of the French flag that many Facebook users adopted after the November 13, 2015, terrorist attacks on Paris) to express their position or their solidarity with the victims of a tragedy.

thinking
rhetorically

---

for **exploration**

Think about the texts you have created both in school and out of school. (From the perspective of multimodal composition, a text can be an image or a performance as well as a document created with words.) How many of these texts rely mainly on the linguistic mode that characterizes many print texts? How many incorporate other modes (aural, gestural, visual)? Thinking in terms of a range of multimodal projects — such as collages, posters, brochures, blogs, video or audio texts, and slide presentations — are you more comfortable with some than with others? Take five to ten minutes to reflect in writing on these questions.

The Rhetorical Situation and Multimodal Composing

As the chapters in Part One of this textbook emphasize, a rhetorical approach to communication encourages you to consider four key elements of your situation:

thinking
rhetorically

1. Your role as someone who has (or must discover) something to communicate
2. The audience with whom you would like to communicate

3. The text you create to convey your ideas and attitudes

4. A medium (print, oral, digital)

To make appropriate choices about their writing, effective writers analyze their rhetorical situation. If they are composing a text in a genre with which they are already familiar, they may do so intuitively. But when writers are encountering new genres or undertaking advanced study in their discipline they often find it helpful to do a written analysis.

Chapter 3 provides questions you can use to analyze your rhetorical situation (pp. 53–54) as well as analyses that Alia Sands (pp. 56–57) and Brandon Barrett (pp. 63–65) composed to guide their writing.

Here is an example of a writer's analysis of her rhetorical situation in composing a multimodal digital composition. The writer is Mirlandra Neuneker, whose poster collage about who she is as a writer appears on p. 90. Mirlandra created the collage when she was a student at Oregon State University, using a variety of created and found objects including her favorite pen, sticky notes of all sizes, push pins, a variety of texts, and a hair tie. Since then, Mirlandra has graduated. After working in the financial industry, she decided to embark on a career that would allow more room for creativity while also giving her a flexible schedule. So she created a food blog: *Mirlandra's Kitchen*. Her blog draws on the linguistic, visual, gestural, and spatial modes. As a blog that attracts viewers or visitors from such social media as Pinterest, Facebook, Instagram, and Twitter, *Mirlandra's Kitchen* is an excellent example of a contemporary composition that draws on multiple modes.

"To be successful," Mirlandra wrote, "my blog must make the fullest possible use of social media, and social media are always evolving. Right now, Pinterest is the biggest driver of visitors to my blog, but that could change in the future. The shift from desktop to mobile computing is also really important for my blog. There's a lot to think about, and I'm constantly making choices about where to put my energy and what to do next. Analyzing my rhetorical situation reminds me that these are rhetorical as well as practical choices." The following discussion of Mirlandra's experience with her blog can help you better understand the many challenges and opportunities that those creating multimodal digital texts can face.

thinking rhetorically

Writer: I created my blog to share my love of food and cooking. My blog is also a business venture, one to which I'm deeply committed, so I am happy to put in the time and effort to create a blog that will attract readers. It's been a real learning experience, but a fun one.

In my blog, I want to present myself as knowledgeable about food and cooking, but I don't want to come across as a foodie or someone with extensive

Apple Rose Pie
MirlandrasKitchen.Com

Mirlandra Neuneker

A Screenshot from Mirlandra Neuneker's Blog *Mirlandra's Kitchen* **(mirlandraskitchen.com)**

professional experience. I want my readers to see me as someone who is like them but who has a passion for food and a lot of practice in the kitchen (which they may or may not have). I want every aspect of my blog—from its title to my photo to the font and design to the recipes I create and the photos that illustrate them—to encourage readers to see me as a friend who might be sharing a recipe over tea or across the fence. Some blogs strive for an urban look. I wanted a casual, homey—and yet professional—feel. This is reflected in the cheerful design of my masthead, my blog's subtitle of "homemade happiness," the bright color scheme, and the kind of recipes I share (not too difficult, expensive, or fancy). My goal is to create a uniform image or brand for my blog, one that was inviting but also professional and thus trustworthy.

Reader: Thanks to Google Analytics I have a lot of information about my readers. I know that within a year of starting *Mirlandra's Kitchen* I had 81,000 monthly page views. Over 93 percent of my readers are female; U.S. citizens comprise 88 percent of my readership, with the remaining readers coming from every continent in the world. I keep this in mind when I write. I can track how long someone spends on a post (often less than three seconds) and how many pages of the blog they view before leaving. My goal is to keep them on the blog long enough to capture their attention.

I spend a lot of time researching what my readers are interested in. I check the statistics to see what they are searching for online. I watch food trends. This data helps me craft the right recipes at the right times to appeal to readers. I appeal to readers through format, through photos, through recipes that work the first time, through humor, and through the ability to relate.

I do my best to write honestly about my life. While I don't write about deeply personal matters, I share myself in a way that encourages readers to feel that we have a genuine connection. I want every reader to leave my blog feeling encouraged and hopeful about their cooking life and more willing to try new things and take risks. I love it when readers leave comments—I always respond as quickly and as genuinely as I can. Doing so is part of the personal connection I want to establish with my readers.

Perhaps the biggest surprise for me in terms of readers was how important the photos on my blog are. I have always thought of myself as a writer, rather than a photographer. However, my experience tells me that a food blog lives and dies by its photos. When I take a photo I am crafting an argument for readers as to why they should try to make this recipe for their families. As a blogger, if I don't convey that argument and win it, I lose readers. Many readers spend hours every week scrolling through Pinterest. I have less than a second to capture them with a photo that will get them to the blog.

Text: I could have the best, most inviting design in the world, but if the recipes I post don't meet the needs of my readers my blog will fail. So of course I spend huge amounts of time researching and developing recipes. I also focus a good deal of time and energy on my writing. I was an English major in college, and I also tutored in our writing center, so I am a confident writer. But I still need to work hard to develop a friendly, engaging style and appropriate content. For most posts, I limit myself to roughly 300 words—readers of food blogs don't want extensive commentary—so I need to make every word count.

Food blogs have well-established conventions. Every food blog has recipes, or it's not a food blog. Most food blogs have an "about" category, and many also have FAQs and information about the blogger. But beyond that there are variations, especially in terms of the number and nature of categories. Some food blogs are more lifestyle-oriented. Others, like mine, keep the focus more on food and recipes — though my blog does have a section titled "Zip and Tiger's Corner" where those who share my love of cats can see photos of our cats. (This is another way I try to make personal connections with readers.) **Medium:** Blogs are by definition digital texts, so the decision about what medium to use was easy, but beyond that basic decision, there were still many issues I had to address. I had to consider color choices, type and size of font, navigation, overall design, and how the design and layout affected accessibility. I needed a layout that would make sense to someone in their 20s but would also be logical and easy to use for someone in their 70s who might have less computer experience. Photos needed to be a reasonable size for loading, but they also needed to be big enough to be eye catching and engage my readers.

The fact that my readers use different devices to read my blog is critically important. Mobile users are now 54% of my readership. About 19% of my readers access my blog via tablets, and computer users are now just a quarter of my users. My website must be responsive to any device my readers use. I have to think about how my work appears on screens of different sizes and make sure the advertisements we host are not conflicting with a mobile format. Currently, I am studying the cost of building a more powerful mobile platform that will engage better with mobile readers and streamline the desktop experience. Bloggers must always be looking to the future and thinking about how our work will be read. Will someone be using a smart watch to read my recipe next year?

Social media are a particularly fascinating — and complicated — part of blogging. The biggest challenge by far in creating and maintaining *Mirlandra's Kitchen* grows out of the fact that it is an online blog that depends upon social media to reach readers. If you want to have a successful food blog you need to spend a lot of time promoting your posts. I monitor my blog's performance on Facebook, Twitter, Instagram, and Pinterest. Each has advantages and disadvantages. Each is constantly changing in terms of the platform it provides bloggers. Right now Pinterest is the big workhorse, but that may not be the case in the future.

When Mirlandra was a student writing primarily traditional print essays, her writing process had a definite conclusion: When the assignment was due, she turned her essay in to her teacher and moved on to the next project. As with many people composing online (bloggers, contributors to wikis and social media sites), Mirlandra's composing process for *Mirlandra's Kitchen* is ongoing. Nevertheless, she continues to be guided by her understanding of rhetoric and of the rhetorical tradition.

---

for **exploration**

Mirlandra Neuneker analyzed the rhetorical situation from the perspective of the writer of her food blog. Now analyze how a digital text, such as the homepage of a website, functions rhetorically from the reader's perspective. Choose a website of interest to you, such as a website you consult regularly or the website for your college or university. Then respond to the Questions for Analyzing Your Rhetorical Situation on pp. 53–54, and on the inside covers of this book. (Substitute "the writer," "the composer," or "the author" for "you" in each question; for example, the question "Why are youwriting?" becomes "Why is the author writing?")

for **collaboration**

Bring your analysis and a screenshot of your chosen website's homepage to class. In small groups, have each member briefly summarize the results of his or her analysis. (Be sure to appoint a recorder/reporter to take notes and report the results of your collaborative inquiry.) After each student has spoken, discuss what the analyses have in common, and identify three important insights into multimodal composing your group gained as a result of this discussion. Be prepared to share these insights with the class.

Multimedia Composition and the Importance of Design

As Mirlandra's analysis of her rhetorical situation emphasizes, design plays a key role in the creation and development of her food blog. She writes, "I want every aspect of my blog—from its title to my photo to the font and design . . .—to encourage readers to see me as a friend who might be sharing a recipe over tea or across the fence." The four design principles—*alignment*, *proximity*, *repetition*, and *contrast*—play a key role in all compositions (including images and performances as well as word-based texts). Just as revising and editing are medium specific (revising a film differs greatly from revising an audio essay or a linguistic print or digital text), so too do the opportunities and constraints inherent in design vary depending on medium.

ALIGNMENT

The principle of alignment relates to the way words, visuals, bodies, or sounds are arranged. In linguistic texts, your goal should be to maintain clear and consistent horizontal and vertical alignment so that readers can follow the text without becoming distracted. (In web design, lack of alignment is a very common design problem, so be sure that you don't mix alignments within a design.) In paintings and other graphic arts, strong diagonals can help guide the viewer's eye.

When creating a presentation, consider the alignment preferences built in to the software: PowerPoint assumes a linear alignment; Prezi allows for a nonlinear alignment with a zoom function and variable transitions and movements. Each offers different advantages and disadvantages, so think carefully about your purpose and rhetorical situation before deciding which to use. If you do not already know how to use Prezi, its steeper learning curve may also play a role in your decision.

thinking
rhetorically

More broadly, whatever the medium, alignment involves grouping elements characteristic of various modes of communication in a meaningful way, one that is appropriate to the text's purpose, genre, and situation. Ira Glass, the host and executive producer of the public radio program *This American Life*, for instance, argues that those who listen to public radio have clear expectations about how stories will be organized. In an interview about how his show is designed, Glass refers to this expectation as "the 45-second rule":[1]

> The length of a news spot—if you listen to . . . the news cast at the beginning of *All Things Considered* or *Marketplace*—is 45 or 50 seconds. Usually, there's a couple of sentences from the reporter, then they do a quote from somebody, and . . . two or three more sentences from the reporter, and you're at 50, 45 seconds.
>
> It turns out that we public radio listeners are trained to expect something to change every 45 to 50 seconds. And as a producer you have to keep that pace in mind. For example, in a reporter's story, every 45 or 50 seconds, you'll go to a piece of tape.

As this example indicates, while alignment is often described in visual terms, it functions in powerful ways in other media. Glass's "45-second rule" also calls attention to the interconnections among design principles since it demonstrates the role of contrast in public radio.

---

[1]Glass laid out this and twelve other principles guiding the production of *This American Life* in a lecture called "Mo' Better Radio" given at Macalester College in 1998.

PROXIMITY

A linguistic text makes effective use of the design principle of proximity when the relationships between text elements (such as headings, subheadings, captions, and items in a list) and visual elements (such as illustrations, charts, and tables) are clear. Your goal should be to position related points, chunks of text, and visual elements together so that your reader's understanding of your meaning is unimpeded. An easy way to evaluate a linguistic text's use of proximity is to squint your eyes and see how the page or screen looks. Do your eyes move logically from one part to another? If not, you'll want to work on the internal relationships.

In a more general sense, and in media other than print, proximity refers to how close various elements of a communication are in space or time and what relationships exist among these elements. When those constructing websites consider how users can best navigate their sites, they are considering issues of proximity. Proximity is especially important to a choreographer who is creating or restaging a dance. Dance is all about physical arrangement, or the relationship of bodies to each other. The word *choreography* actually comes from the Greek words for "dance writing."

REPETITION

Repetition is important for creating a sense of coherence: A consistent design helps guide readers through the text, whatever the medium. In linguistic texts, repetition can involve elements that are visual, verbal, or both. For example, those writing linguistic texts need to be consistent in the design of typefaces they choose, the placement and use of color, and the positioning of graphic elements such as a navigational banner on a homepage. One example of repetition in a text-based document is the practice of indenting paragraphs: The seemingly subtle indentation actually signals the start of a new topic or subtopic and helps your reader keep track of your argument.

Repetition in music is crucial to holding listener's attention, but too much repetition can become tedious. (Imagine a song with a refrain that goes on too long or lyrics that get repeated too often.) Repetition—good and bad—plays a key role in oral presentations as well. Listeners can only process and retain so much information—they can't go back and reread something they missed or didn't understand—so effective presenters build repetition by including internal summaries and transitions and by providing brief stories, examples, and analogies that reinforce (and thus in a sense repeat) their major ideas. Repetition can be detrimental, however, when speakers engage in what is sometimes called "PowerPoint karaoke" (or "Death by PowerPoint"): When a speaker's presentation consists primarily of reading words on slides, viewers are quickly bored. Effective speakers understand that they must attend to the relationship between their spoken words (and physical gestures) and the information they share with their audience. Too much repetition makes the audience lose interest.

CONTRAST

A text effectively employs contrast when the design uses difference or surprise to draw the audience in. In linguistic texts, contrast helps organize and orient the reader's interactions with a text, guiding the reader around the elements on a page or screen and making the information accessible. Even the simplest linguistic texts employ contrast in the interplay between white space and text. Margins, double-spacing, and white space around headings or graphics, for instance, frame the text and guide the reader through it. (Take a look at the white space on this page, and try to imagine how difficult the page would be to read if word after word were presented uninterrupted and extending to the borders of the page on all sides.) Visual texts may use contrasting colors or images or fonts to call the viewer's attention.

In both linguistic and visual texts, focal points play an important role in establishing contrast. A focal point—a point that the eye travels to first and that the mind uses to organize the other elements in the composition—may be an image, a logo, or a dominant set of words. When you design a page, flyer, poster, or screen, you should organize the elements so that the focal point makes the relationships among elements clear.

In a medium like film, focal points are constantly changing as camera angles shift from wide angle to close up and so forth. The same is true in dance. At one moment, the focus may be on the lead dancer; the next, it's on the chorus. In aesthetic productions and performances, such as films, opera, plays, or various forms of classical and contemporary dance, the elements of design interact in especially complex and powerful ways.

Managing the Demands of Multimodal Composition

As Chapter 4, "Academic Writing: Committing to the Process," emphasizes, the demands of writing a traditional academic essay for your history or political science class can be considerable. These demands can become even more significant when you add a digital or oral component, as with websites, presentations, films, audio essays, and podcasts.

This chapter can't provide specific instructions for how best to undertake every possible kind of multimodal project. For one thing, all projects need to be considered in the context of their rhetorical situation. Creating a brief video to share a special moment with your family is very different from creating a video that will play an important role in the defense of your honors thesis, the culminating event of your undergraduate education.

thinking
rhetorically

Additionally, the possible technological choices for creating your video are multiple. Someone creating a brief family video would probably use a smartphone; to create a video for a more substantial academic project, he or she might employ a program such as Windows Movie Maker, iMovie, Final Cut Pro, or Adobe Premiere. And, of course, new technologies are being created all the time, even as others fade away.

Some general guidelines nevertheless apply to most multimodal projects, whether it is a relatively simple undertaking (such as an illustrated print essay or a Facebook or Twitter post) or a more complicated project (such as a website or blog, audio essay or podcast, poster, or flyer). See the Guidelines for Multimodal Composing below for details.

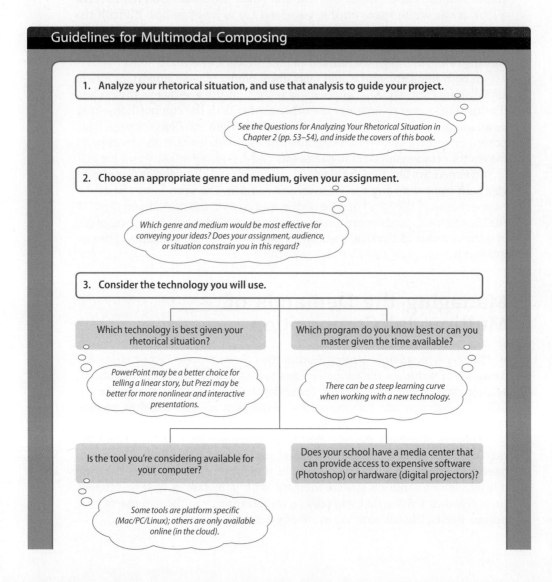

Guidelines for Multimodal Composing

1. **Analyze your rhetorical situation, and use that analysis to guide your project.**

   See the Questions for Analyzing Your Rhetorical Situation in Chapter 2 (pp. 53–54), and inside the covers of this book.

2. **Choose an appropriate genre and medium, given your assignment.**

   Which genre and medium would be most effective for conveying your ideas? Does your assignment, audience, or situation constrain you in this regard?

3. **Consider the technology you will use.**

   Which technology is best given your rhetorical situation?

   PowerPoint may be a better choice for telling a linear story, but Prezi may be better for more nonlinear and interactive presentations.

   Which program do you know best or can you master given the time available?

   There can be a steep learning curve when working with a new technology.

   Is the tool you're considering available for your computer?

   Some tools are platform specific (Mac/PC/Linux); others are only available online (in the cloud).

   Does your school have a media center that can provide access to expensive software (Photoshop) or hardware (digital projectors)?

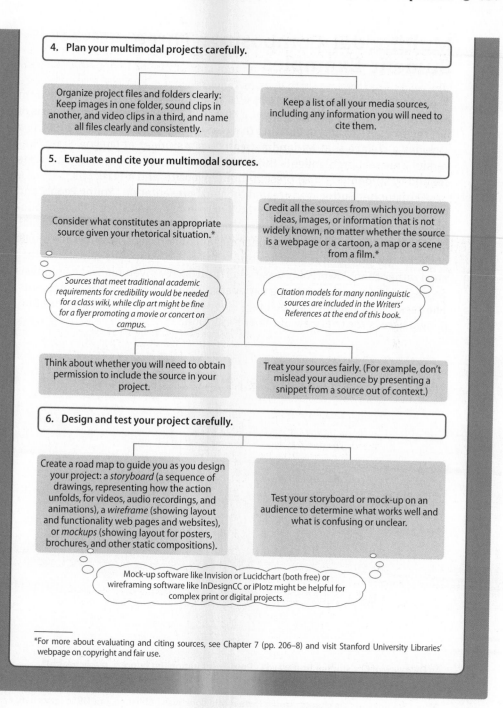

4. Plan your multimodal projects carefully.

Organize project files and folders clearly: Keep images in one folder, sound clips in another, and video clips in a third, and name all files clearly and consistently.

Keep a list of all your media sources, including any information you will need to cite them.

5. Evaluate and cite your multimodal sources.

Consider what constitutes an appropriate source given your rhetorical situation.*

Credit all the sources from which you borrow ideas, images, or information that is not widely known, no matter whether the source is a webpage or a cartoon, a map or a scene from a film.*

Sources that meet traditional academic requirements for credibility would be needed for a class wiki, while clip art might be fine for a flyer promoting a movie or concert on campus.

Citation models for many nonlinguistic sources are included in the Writers' References at the end of this book.

Think about whether you will need to obtain permission to include the source in your project.

Treat your sources fairly. (For example, don't mislead your audience by presenting a snippet from a source out of context.)

6. Design and test your project carefully.

Create a road map to guide you as you design your project: a *storyboard* (a sequence of drawings, representing how the action unfolds, for videos, audio recordings, and animations), a *wireframe* (showing layout and functionality web pages and websites), or *mockups* (showing layout for posters, brochures, and other static compositions).

Test your storyboard or mock-up on an audience to determine what works well and what is confusing or unclear.

Mock-up software like Invision or Lucidchart (both free) or wireframing software like InDesignCC or iPlotz might be helpful for complex print or digital projects.

*For more about evaluating and citing sources, see Chapter 7 (pp. 206–8) and visit Stanford University Libraries' webpage on copyright and fair use.

Multimodal Composing: Three Student Examples

This chapter includes an example of a multimodal text, a screenshot from Mirlandra Neuneker's blog *Mirlandra's Kitchen* (p. 323), as well as her analysis of her rhetorical situation in creating this text (pp. 323–36). Chapter 4 (p. 90) also includes a collage that Mirlandra created as a student at Oregon State University. This section highlights three additional examples of multimodal texts created by students: a Prezi presentation, a website, and a TEDx talk.

Christopher Buttacavoli created the Prezi presentation "Young People and Risky Behavior: Why Prevention Is the Key to Public Health" for a class in public health at Oregon State University. The Prezi employs the linguistic, visual, and spatial modes; when Christopher presented it in class, however, his public performance added aural and gestural modes. Christopher's decision to use Prezi rather than PowerPoint was rhetorically savvy given his text's emphasis on the interconnections among various health-risk behaviors of adolescents. The result is a visually compelling, dynamic, and well-argued presentation. Shown here is the overview of the presentation.

thinking rhetorically

An Overview of Christopher Buttacavoli's Prezi Presentation (bit.ly/prezi_publichealth)*

---

*Note: The links in this chapter worked when this book was published, but URLs may change over time. If any of the links cease to function, try searching for the site online using the creator's name and the title of the project.

Homepage from a Website (savethetrexes.wix.com/gapyear)

Ben Myers, an undergraduate at Oklahoma State University, created a website on the advantages and disadvantages of gap years for college students as the final project in his first-year writing class and as part of a larger research-based project. The homepage for Ben's site is shown above. After first conducting research on his topic, Ben created his website, which represents a preliminary formulation of his argument. After presenting his website in class and getting feedback, he wrote an eight-page research project on the same topic. The organization of Ben's website reflects the research question that motivated his project: "Gap Year: Good or Bad?" Those navigating his site can move easily one subtopic to another:

- What Is a Gap Year?
- Academic Pros and Cons
- Career-Centric Pros and Cons
- Social Pros and Cons
- So . . . What?
- References

Ben takes full rhetorical advantage of the ability to integrate multiple modes and media into his website. Each page includes at least one video and several visuals, including photos, charts, and maps. On the "So . . . What?" page, Ben takes advantage of the potential for interacting with his readers that digital media affords and provides a survey where they can express their own views on gap years.

The final example is a screenshot from a talk that Ben Myers (the creator of the website, above) gave at a TEDx event at Oklahoma State University, TEDxOStateU 2015, designed to share "ideas worth spreading." Ben competed

thinking rhetorically

Ben Myers

A Video Presentation, Delivered April 10, 2015, at Oklahoma State University–Stillwater and Available on YouTube

in an open audition to earn one of the eight spots reserved for students. In his talk "The Disability Conversation," he argues powerfully for the importance of disability advocacy.

His presentation takes advantage of all five modes of communication: linguistic, visual, aural, spatial, and gestural. It is only about eight minutes long, but he uses that time well to share an engaging and thought-provoking mix of personal experience and information with his viewers. At appropriate moments, Ben uses PowerPoint slides to summarize his main points, but they do not dominate his presentation, which is notable for the clarity and persuasiveness of his ideas and his enthusiasm for his topic. Throughout his presentation, his tone is conversational even as he calls attention to the seriousness of his subject. Ben clearly recognizes the rhetorically charged nature of his situation: Many people find discussions of topics like disability uncomfortable. So he begins his talk with a powerful anecdote about his own experience with disability and in so doing puts those attending his talk at ease. Ben then articulates the major point of his talk: "Remaining silent about disability is not helpful." The remainder of his presentation explains why this is the case. Ben concludes his talk with a forceful challenge to his viewers: "Let's start the disability conversation today."

thinking rhetorically

thinking rhetorically

Rhetoric, Aristotle argued centuries ago, is the art of discovering all the available means of persuasion. When Aristotle wrote these words, he imagined a civic space, or *agora*, where the citizens of Athens (who did not include women or the enslaved) would meet face to face to converse and argue. Aristotle could not have imagined the world of print texts that Gutenberg's printing press created, let alone a world enabled by the Internet and World Wide Web. But his emphasis on discovering all of the available means of persuasion applies in all these situations. Thanks to the multiple modes and media of communication available to writers today, new agoras are providing increased opportunities for communication.

for **thought, discussion, and writing**

1. Develop a flyer, brochure, newsletter, podcast, or web page for a community, church, civic, or other group with which you are involved. If you aren't currently involved in such an organization, develop a text that relates to a project that interests you. Be sure to analyze your rhetorical situation before you begin work on your document. After creating your text, make a list of the five most important decisions that played a role in the development of your text, such as the decision to develop a newsletter rather than a flyer. Then explain the rationale for each decision.

2. Evaluate the effectiveness of the three-minute video "Prezi vs. PowerPoint," developed by the Technology and Learning unit of Pepperdine University. (You can find this video on YouTube by searching with the key terms "Pepperdine" and "Prezi vs. PowerPoint.") Watch this video at least three times; during the second and third times you watch it, take notes on the number of modes it employs and the video's effectiveness as a multimodal composition. Then make a list of the video's top three strengths and indicate two ways you think it could be improved. Finally, based on your own experience with Prezi and PowerPoint, indicate whether you think the video provides a fair assessment of the potential strengths and limitations of each program.

3. Write an essay in which you reflect on your own experiences composing multimodal texts. Are you more familiar and comfortable with employing some modes than others? (For example, are you a confident composer of traditional linguistic research essays but a tentative composer of videos or podcasts?) What are your strengths as a multimodal composer? What areas of improvement can you identify? If you prefer, respond to this assignment using a medium other than print, such as a collage, slide presentation, audio essay, podcast, or video.

4. Choose a linguistic text that you have written for your composition class or another class, and remix it using another medium. Possibilities include creating a collage, brochure, slide presentation, audio essay, podcast, or video.

Writers' References

MLA Documentation Guidelines

The *MLA Handbook*, Eighth Edition, published by the Modern Language Association of America, or MLA, offers general principles for citing sources focused on the basic contents of every citation, including the following:

- *Author or authors (followed by a period).*
- *Title of source (followed by a period).* Titles of self-contained works, such as book titles, television series, and website names, are italicized; titles of works contained within other works, such as an article in a magazine or a story in an anthology, are set in quotation marks.
- *Title of the container, or larger work, in which the source appears, if any (followed by a comma).* For example, a newspaper or magazine "contains" the articles that appear within it; a television series "contains" individual episodes. Follow the title of the container with a comma, since the items that follow (other contributors, version, number, publisher, publication date, and location) all relate to the container. If a source has multiple containers— for example, you access an article that appears in a journal (container 1) via a database (container 2)—include information for the second container after the first. Titles of containers are typically italicized.
  - *Other contributors (followed by a comma).* Other contributors may include the editor, translator, producer, narrator, illustrator, and so on.
  - *Version (followed by a comma).* The version may be the edition name or number (revised edition, sixth edition, late edition), director's cut, abridged edition, and so on.
  - *Number (followed by a comma).* The number may include the volume number (for a multivolume work), the volume and issue number (for a journal), the disk number (for a set of DVDs), and so on.
  - *Publication information (followed by a comma).* Publication information may include the name of the publisher, site sponsor, government and agency, and so on.

- *Publication date (followed by a comma).* The publication date may be a year for books or movies; a month and year or day, month, and year for magazines; day, month, and year for newspapers and episodes of daily television or radio shows; and so on.
  - *Source location (followed by a period).* For example, page numbers indicate location for a printed text; the URL or DOI (digital object identifier, a permanent code) indicates location for an online text; a time stamp indicates location for a video or audio file.
- *Additional information (followed by a period).* Additional information may include original publication information for a reprinted book, an access date for an undated online source, or a label for an unusual source type or a source type that readers might not recognize from the citation (as for an editorial or letter to the editor, a typescript, or a lecture).

This appendix helps students make sensible decisions about how to cite sources by providing citation models based on the principles spelled out in the *MLA Handbook.* A number of the models included in the appendix are covered in the *MLA Handbook*; some, however, are not. For example, the *MLA Handbook* provides no model for an editorial or letter to the editor, but one is included in this appendix (p. 360). The model for an editorial is based on that for an article in a newspaper, with an identifying label added at the end of the citation. The appendix provides models for many sources that students consult while conducting research; however, it is not exhaustive. When no model is provided for the type of source you need to cite, base your citation on that for a similar source and add information as needed. Finally, if you are unsure about how to cite a source not included in this appendix, check with your instructor.

Formatting a Research Project

The Eighth Edition of the *MLA Handbook* provides very little guidance for formatting a research-based writing project, but check the MLA's website (mla.org) for more information. The following guidelines are commonly observed in the humanities, but double-check with your instructor *before* preparing your final draft to make sure the formatting advice provided here is appropriate given your rhetorical situation.

- *First page and title page.* A title page is not often required. Instead, type each of the following pieces of information on a new line, flush left, in the upper left corner of the first page: your name, the instructor's name, the course name and number, and the date. On the next line, include your title, centered, without italics, boldface, quotation marks, or any other treatment.
- *Margins and spacing.* Leave one-inch margins at the top and bottom on both sides of each page. Double-space the entire text, including the identifying information at the top of the first page, title, indented (block) quotations, captions, any footnotes or endnotes, and the list of works cited. Indent paragraphs half an inch.

- *Long quotations.* Set off quotations longer than four typed lines by indenting them as a block, half an inch from the left margin. Do not enclose the passage in quotation marks.

- *Page numbers.* Include your last name and the page number in the upper right corner of each page, half an inch below the top margin and flush right.

- *Headings.* Many instructors and students find headings helpful. Make them concise yet informative. They can be single nouns (Literacy), a noun phrase (Literacy in Families), a gerund phrase (Testing for Literacy), or a question or statement (How Can Literacy Be Measured?). Make all headings at the same level consistent throughout your text, for example by using all single nouns or all gerund phrases. Set headings in the same font as the rest of the text, distinguishing levels by typing the first level heading in capitals, second-level headings in boldface, and third-level headings in italics:

  ## FIRST-LEVEL HEADING
  ### **Second-level Heading**
  Third-level Heading

  Position headings consistently throughout your text. Centered headings are common for the first level; for secondary-level headings, you may indent, set flush left, or run them into the text (that is, you can start the section's text on the same line as the heading).

- *Visuals.* Place tables, photographs, drawings, charts, graphs, and other figures as close as possible to the relevant text. Tables should have a label and number (*Table* 1) and a clear caption. The label and caption should be aligned on the left, on separate lines. Give the source information below the table. All other visuals should be labeled *Figure* (abbreviated *Fig.*), numbered, and captioned. The label and caption should appear on the same line, followed by the source information. Remember to refer to each visual in your text, indicating how it contributes to the point(s) you are making.

In-Text Citations

MLA style requires a citation in the text of an essay for every quotation, paraphrase, summary, or other material requiring documentation. In-text citations document material from other sources with both signal phrases and parenthetical references. Parenthetical references should include the information your readers need to locate the full reference in the list of works cited at the end of the text (see pp. 347–75). An in-text citation in MLA style aims to give the reader two kinds of information: (1) It indicates *which source* on the works-cited page the writer is referring to, and (2) it explains *where in the source* the material quoted, paraphrased, or summarized can be found, if the source has page numbers or other numbered sections.

Directory to MLA style for in-text citations

The basic MLA in-text citation includes the author's last name either in a signal phrase introducing the source material or in parentheses at the end of the sentence. Whenever possible, it also includes the page or paragraph number in parentheses at the end of the sentence.

SAMPLE CITATION USING A SIGNAL PHRASE

In his discussion of *Monty Python* routines, Crystal notes that the group relished "breaking the normal rules" of language (107).

SAMPLE PARENTHETICAL CITATION

A noted linguist explains that *Monty Python* humor often relied on "bizarre linguistic interactions" (Crystal 108).

Note in the following examples where punctuation is placed in relation to the parentheses.

1. AUTHOR NAMED IN A SIGNAL PHRASE The MLA recommends using the author's name in a signal phrase to introduce the material and citing the page number(s), if any, in parentheses.

Lee claims that his comic-book creation, Thor, was "the first regularly published superhero to speak in a consistently archaic manner" (199).

2. AUTHOR NAMED IN A PARENTHETICAL REFERENCE When you do not mention the author in a signal phrase, include the author's last name before the page number(s) in the parentheses. Use no punctuation between the author's name and the page number(s).

The word *Bollywood* is sometimes considered an insult because it implies that Indian movies are merely "a derivative of the American film industry" (Chopra 9).

3. TWO AUTHORS Use both the authors' last names in a signal phrase or in parentheses.

For example, Bonacich and Appelbaum report that in Los Angeles, which has the highest concentration of garment manufacturers in the nation, 81% of workers are Asian and Latino immigrants (171–75).

4. THREE OR MORE AUTHORS Use the first author's name and *et al.* ("and others").

Similarly, as Belenky et al. assert, examining the lives of women expands our understanding of human development (7).

5. ORGANIZATION AS AUTHOR Give the group's full name, abbreviating words that are commonly abbreviated, such as *Association (Assoc.)* or *Department (Dept.)*.

Any study of social welfare involves a close analysis of "the impacts, the benefits, and the costs" of its policies (Social Research Corp. iii).

6. UNKNOWN AUTHOR Use a shortened title in place of the author.

One analysis defines *hype* as "an artificially engendered atmosphere of hysteria" ("Today's Marketplace" 51).

To shorten a title, use the first noun in the title plus any adjectives modifying it, leaving out any articles (*a, an, the*), verbs, prepositional phrases, and so on. For example, "The Great Republican Earthquake" becomes "Great Republican Earthquake," and "America's Lurch to the Left" becomes "America's Lurch." If there is no noun in the first part of the title, use the first word (excluding articles) if it will be enough to distinguish the work from other works cited. For example, *Must We Mean What We Say: A Book of Essays* would be abbreviated as *Must*. The word you use in the in-text citation should be the word you use to begin the entry in the list of works cited.

7. AUTHOR OF TWO OR MORE WORKS CITED IN THE SAME PROJECT If your list of works cited has more than one work by the same author, include a shortened version of the title of the work✱ you are citing in a signal phrase or in parentheses to prevent reader confusion.

> Gardner shows readers their own silliness in his description of a "pointless, ridiculous monster, crouched in the shadows, stinking of dead men, murdered children, and martyred cows" (*Grendel* 2).

If two or more works by the same author are referred to, include both titles (abbreviated if necessary) with the word *and* between them: (*Grendel* and *October Light*).

8. TWO OR MORE AUTHORS WITH THE SAME LAST NAME Include the author's first *and* last names in a signal phrase or first initial and last name in a parenthetical reference.

> Children will learn to write if they are allowed to choose their own subjects, James Britton asserts, citing the Schools Council study of the 1960s (J. Britten 37–42).

9. INDIRECT SOURCE (AUTHOR QUOTING SOMEONE ELSE) Use the abbreviation *qtd. in* to indicate that you are quoting from someone else's report of a source.

> As Arthur Miller says, "When somebody is destroyed everybody finally contributes to it, but in Willy's case, the end product would be virtually the same" (qtd. in Martin and Meyer 375).

10. MULTIVOLUME WORK In a parenthetical reference, if you cite more than one volume, note the volume number first and then the page number(s), with a colon and one space between them.

> Modernist writers prized experimentation and gradually even sought to blur the line between poetry and prose, according to Forster (3: 150).

If you cite only one volume of the work in your list of works cited, include only the author's last name and the page number in parentheses: (Forster 150).

11. LITERARY WORK Because literary works are often available in many different editions, cite the page number(s) from the edition you used followed by a semicolon; then give other identifying information that will lead readers to the passage in any edition. For a novel, indicate the part or chapter:

> In utter despair, Dostoyevsky's character Mitya wonders aloud about the
> "terrible tragedies realism inflicts on people" (376; book 8, ch. 2).

For a poem, cite the part (if there is one) and line number(s) (if included in the source), separated by a period:

> Whitman speculates, "All goes onward and outward, nothing collapses, /
> And to die is different from what anyone supposed, and luckier" (6.129–30).

If you are citing only line numbers, use the word *line* or *lines* in the first reference (*lines* 33–34). Omit the word *line* or *lines* in subsequent entries. For a verse play, give only the act, scene, and line numbers, separated by periods:

> The witches greet Banquo as "Lesser than Macbeth, and greater" (1.3.65).

12. WORK IN AN ANTHOLOGY OR COLLECTION For an essay, short story, or other piece of prose contained within an anthology, use the name of the author of the work, not the editor of the anthology, but use the page number(s) from the anthology.

> Narratives of captivity play a major role in early writing by women in the United
> States, as demonstrated by Silko (219).

13. SACRED TEXT To cite a sacred text such as the Qur'an or the Bible, give the title of the edition you used, the book, the chapter, and the verse (or their equivalent), separated by periods. In parenthetical references, use abbreviations for books with names of five or more letters (*Gen.* for *Genesis*).

> He ignored the admonition "Pride goes before destruction, and a haughty spirit
> before a fall" (*New Oxford Annotated Bible*, Prov. 16.18).

14. ENCYCLOPEDIA OR DICTIONARY ENTRY An entry from a reference work—such as an encyclopedia or a dictionary—without an author will appear on the works-cited list under the entry's title. Enclose the title in quotation marks and place it in parentheses. Omit the page number for reference works that arrange entries alphabetically.

> The term *prion* was coined by Stanley B. Prusiner from the words *proteinaceous*
> and *infectious* and a suffix meaning *particle* ("Prion").

15. GOVERNMENT SOURCE WITH NO AUTHOR NAMED Because entries for sources authored by government agencies will appear on your list of works cited under the name of the country (see model 63, p. 374), your in-text citation for such a source should include the name of the country as well as the name of the agency responsible for the source.

> To reduce the agricultural runoff into the Chesapeake Bay, the United States Environmental Protection Agency has argued that "[h]igh nutrient loading crops, such as corn and soybean, should be replaced with alternatives in environmentally sensitive areas" (26).

If the government agency is also the publisher, begin the citation with the source's title, and include the title (or a shortened form) in the in-text citation.

16. ELECTRONIC OR NONPRINT SOURCE Give enough information in a signal phrase or in parentheses for readers to locate the source in your list of works cited. Many works found online or in electronic databases lack stable page numbers; you can omit the page number in such cases. If you are citing a work with stable pagination, such as an article in PDF format, however, include the page number in parentheses.

> As a *Slate* analysis has noted, "Prominent sports psychologists get praised for their successes and don't get grief for their failures" (Engber).

The source, an article on a website, does not have stable pagination.

> According to Whitmarsh, the British military had experimented with using balloons for observation as far back as 1879 (328).

The source, an online PDF of a print article, includes stable page numbers.

If the source includes numbered sections, or paragraphs, include the appropriate abbreviation (*sec.* or *par.*) and the number in parentheses.

> Sherman notes that the "immediate, interactive, and on-the-spot" nature of Internet information can make nondigital media seem outdated (sec. 32).

If using an excerpt from a time-based source (such as an audio or video file), include the time stamp for the section cited.

> Although the Hays Code was written to oust risqué behavior in the movies, its effects were felt in television comedy as well, with shows like *I Love Lucy* and *The Dick Van Dyke Show* depicting their married costars as sleeping in twin beds. But sex did creep in around the edges, if only in the most innocent fashion. For example, much of the humor in the first episode of *Mr. Ed* ("The First Meeting") revolves around Wilbur Post's young wife (Connie Hines) jumping into her costar Alan Young's arms on the slightest pretext (04:22–04:30).

17. ENTIRE WORK Include the reference in the text, without any page numbers.

Jon Krakauer's *Into the Wild* both criticizes and admires the solitary impulses of its young hero, which end up killing him.

18. TWO OR MORE SOURCES IN ONE CITATION Separate the information with semicolons.

Economists recommend that *employment* be redefined to include unpaid domestic labor (Clark 148; Nevins 39).

Explanatory and Bibliographic Notes

Explanatory notes may be used to provide information or commentary that would not readily fit into your text. Bibliographic notes may be used for citing several sources for one point and for offering thanks to, information about, or evaluation of a source. Use superscript numbers in the text to refer readers to the notes, which may be included as endnotes (typed under the heading *Notes* on a separate page after the text but before the list of works cited) or as footnotes at the bottom of the page (typed four lines below the last text line).

SUPERSCRIPT NUMBER IN TEXT

Stewart emphasizes the existence of social contacts in Hawthorne's life so that the audience will accept a different Hawthorne, one more attuned to modern times than the figure in Woodberry.[3]

NOTE

[3] Woodberry does, however, show that Hawthorne *was* often an unsociable individual. He emphasizes the seclusion of Hawthorne's mother, who separated herself from her family after the death of her husband, often even taking meals alone (28). Woodberry seems to imply that Mrs. Hawthorne's isolation rubbed off on her son.

List of Works Cited

A list of works cited is an alphabetical list of the sources you have referred to in your essay. (If your instructor asks you to list everything you have read as background, call the list *Works Consulted*.) The formatting instructions below are consistent with those offered by the Modern Language Association on their website (mla.org). But check with your instructor if you have any doubts about her or his expectations.

- Start your list on a separate page after the text of your essay and any notes. (For works in media other than print, you may need to include documentation elsewhere, such as on a slide or mentioned in your talk for a presentation.)

- Continue the consecutive numbering of pages.

- Center the heading *Works Cited* (not italicized or in quotation marks) one inch from the top of the page.

- Start each entry flush with the left margin; indent subsequent lines for the entry half an inch. Double-space the entire list.

- List sources alphabetically by the first word. Start with the author's name, if available; if not, use the editor's name, if available. If no author or editor is given, start with the title.

- Italicize titles of self-contained works, such as books and websites, but put the titles of works contained in other works (such as articles that appeared in magazines, newspapers, or scholarly journals; stories that appeared in anthologies or collections; or web pages included on websites) in quotation marks.

GUIDELINES FOR AUTHOR LISTINGS

The list of works cited is arranged alphabetically. The in-text citations in your writing point readers toward particular sources on the list (see pp. 341–42).

NAME CITED IN SIGNAL PHRASE IN TEXT

Crystal explains . . . .

NAME IN PARENTHETICAL CITATION IN TEXT

. . . (Crystal 107).

BEGINNING OF ENTRY ON LIST OF WORKS CITED

Crystal, David.

Directory to MLA style for works-cited entries

Continued >

1. ONE AUTHOR Put the last name first, followed by a comma, the first name (and initial, if any), and a period.

> Crystal, David.

2. MULTIPLE AUTHORS For works with two authors, list the first author with the last name first, followed by comma. Then include the word *and* followed by the name of the second author, first name first.

> Bonacich, Edna, and Richard Appelbaum.

For three or more authors, list the first author followed by a comma and *et al.* ("and others").

> Lupton, Ellen, et al.

3. ORGANIZATION OR GROUP AUTHOR Give the name of the group, government agency, corporation, or other organization listed as the author.

> Getty Trust.

> United States, Government Accountability Office.

If the organization or group is also the publisher, start the entry with the title of the source.

4. UNKNOWN AUTHOR When the author is not identified, begin the entry with the title, and alphabetize by the first important word. Italicize titles of self-contained works, such as books and websites. Put the titles of works contained within other works (articles that appear in newspapers, magazines, or journals; web pages that exist within websites; short stories that appear in magazines, anthologies, or collections) in quotation marks.

> "California Sues EPA over Emissions."

> *New Concise World Atlas.*

5. TWO OR MORE WORKS BY THE SAME AUTHOR Arrange the entries alphabetically by title. Include the author's name in the first entry, but in subsequent entries, use three hyphens followed by a period. (For the basic format for citing a book, see model 6. For the basic format for citing an article from an online newspaper, see model 33.)

> Chopra, Anupama. "Bollywood Princess, Hollywood Hopeful." *The New York Times*, 10 Feb. 2008, www.nytimes.com/2008/02/10/movies/10chop.html.

> ---. *King of Bollywood: Shah Rukh Khan and the Seductive World of Indian Cinema.* Warner Books, 2007.

Note: Use three hyphens only when the work is by *exactly* the same author(s) as the previous entry.

BOOKS

6. BASIC FORMAT FOR A BOOK Begin with the author name(s). (See models 1–5.) Then include the title and the subtitle, the publisher, and the publication date. The source map on pp. 354–55 shows where to find this information in a typical book.

> Bowker, Gordon. *James Joyce: A New Biography*. Farrar, Straus and Giroux, 2012.

7. AUTHOR AND EDITOR BOTH NAMED

> Bangs, Lester. *Psychotic Reactions and Carburetor Dung*. Edited by Greil
>   Marcus, Alfred A. Knopf, 1988.

Note: To cite the editor's contribution instead, begin the entry with the editor's name.

> Marcus, Greil, editor. *Psychotic Reactions and Carburetor Dung*. By Lester
>   Bangs, Alfred A. Knopf, 1988.

8. EDITOR, NO AUTHOR NAMED

> Wall, Cheryl A., editor. *Changing Our Own Words: Essays on Criticism, Theory,*
>   *and Writing by Black Women*. Rutgers UP, 1989.

9. ANTHOLOGY Cite an entire anthology the same way you would cite a book with an editor and no named author (see model 8).

> Marcus, Ben, editor. *New American Stories*. Vintage Books, 2015.

10. WORK IN AN ANTHOLOGY OR CHAPTER IN A BOOK WITH AN EDITOR List the author(s) of the selection or chapter; its title, in quotation marks; the title of the book, italicized; *edited by* and the name(s) of the editor(s); the publisher; the publication date; and the selection's page numbers.

> Eisenberg, Deborah. "Some Other, Better Otto." *New American Stories,* edited
>   by Ben Marcus, Vintage Books, 2015, pp. 3–29.

11. TWO OR MORE ITEMS FROM THE SAME ANTHOLOGY List the anthology as one entry (see model 9). Also list each selection separately with a cross-reference to the anthology.

> Eisenberg, Deborah. "Some Other, Better Otto." Marcus, pp. 94–136.

Sayrafiezadeh, Saïd. "Paranoia." Marcus, pp. 3–29.

12. TRANSLATION

Ferrante, Elena. *The Story of the Lost Child.* Translated by Ann Goldstein,
Europa Editions, 2015.

13. BOOK WITH BOTH TRANSLATOR AND EDITOR List the editor's and translator's
names after the title, in the order they appear on the title page.

Kant, Immanuel. *"Toward Perpetual Peace" and Other Writings on Politics,
Peace, and History.* Edited by Pauline Kleingeld, translated by David L.
Colclasure, Yale UP, 2006.

14. BOOK IN A LANGUAGE OTHER THAN ENGLISH Include a translation of the title
in brackets, if necessary.

Benedetti, Mario. *La borra del café [The Coffee Grind].* Editorial Sudamericana,
2000.

15. GRAPHIC NARRATIVE If the words and images are created by the same person, cite a graphic narrative just as you would a book (model 6).

Bechdel, Alison. *Fun Home: A Family Tragicomic.* Houghton Mifflin, 2006.

For a collaboration, list the author or illustrator who is most important to your
research before the title, and list other contributors after the title.

Gaiman, Neil. *The Sandman: Overture.* Illustrated by J. H. William III, DC
Comics, 2015.

William III, J. H., illustrator. *The Sandman: Overture.* By Neil Gaiman, DC
Comics, 2015.

16. EDITION OTHER THAN THE FIRST

Eagleton, Terry. *Literary Theory: An Introduction.* 3rd ed., U of Minnesota P, 2008.

17. MULTIVOLUME WORK If you cite only one volume, give the number of the
volume before the publisher. (You may include the total number of volumes
at the end of the citation if that information would help readers find your
source.) Include the publication date for that volume only.

Stark, Freya. *Letters.* Edited by Lucy Moorehead, vol. 5, Compton Press, 1978.
8 vols.

MLA SOURCE MAP: Books

Take information from the book's title page and copyright page (on the reverse side of the title page), not from the book's cover or a library catalog.

1 Author. List the last name first. End with a period. For variations, see models 2–5.

2 Title. Italicize the title and any subtitle; capitalize all major words. End with a period.

3 Publisher. Use the publisher's full name as it appears on the title page, omitting only terms such as *Inc.* and *Company*. Substitute *UP* for *University Press*. Follow it with a comma.

4 Year of publication. If more than one copyright date is given, use the most recent one. End with a period.

A citation for the work on p. 355 would look like this:

     1   **2**

Patel, Raj. *The Value of Nothing: How to Reshape Market Society and Redefine*

                     3   **4**

   Democracy. Picador, 2009.

THE VALUE OF NOTHING

HOW TO RESHAPE MARKET SOCIETY AND REDEFINE DEMOCRACY

2 Title and Subtitle

Raj Patel

1 Author

PICADOR

New York

3 Publisher

4 Year of Publication

Library of Congress Cataloging-in-Publication Data

Patel, Raj.
   The value of nothing : how to reshape market society and redefine democracy / Raj Patel.—1st ed.
      p. cm.
   Includes bibliographical references and index.
   ISBN 978-0-312-42924-9
   1. Free enterprise.   2. Democracy.   3. Economics.   I. Title.
   HB95.P3185 2009
   330.12'2—dc22

                                                  2009041546

First Picador Edition: January 2010

Printed on recycled paper

355

If you cite two or more volumes, give the number of volumes in the complete work and provide inclusive dates of publication.

> Stark, Freya. *Letters.* Edited by Lucy Moorehead, Compton Press, 1974–82.
> 8 vols.

18. PREFACE, FOREWORD, INTRODUCTION, OR AFTERWORD After the writer's name, describe the contribution. After the title, indicate the book's author (with *by*), editor (with *edited by*), or translator (with *translated by*).

> Bennett, Hal Zina. Foreword. *Shimmering Images: A Handy Little Guide to*
> *Writing Memoir,* by Lisa Dale Norton, St. Martin's Griffin, 2008, pp. xiii–xvi.

> Dunham, Lena. Foreword. *The Liars' Club,* by Mary Karr, Penguin Classics,
> 2015, pp. xi–xiii.

19. ENTRY IN A REFERENCE BOOK If an author is given, begin with the author's name (look for initials and a list of contributors); otherwise, begin with the title. If the entries are alphabetized, you need not include the page number.

> "Ball's in Your Court, The." *The American Heritage Dictionary of Idioms*, 2nd
> ed., Houghton Mifflin Harcourt, 2013.

20. BOOK THAT IS PART OF A SERIES At the end of the citation, include the series name (and number, if any) from the title page.

> Denham, A. E., editor. *Plato on Art and Beauty.* Palgrave Macmillan, 2012.
> Philosophers in Depth.

> Snicket, Lemony (Daniel Handler). *The Bad Beginning.* HarperCollins
> Publishers, 1999. A Series of Unfortunate Events 1.

21. REPUBLICATION (MODERN EDITION OF AN OLDER BOOK) Indicate the original publication date after the title.

> Austen, Jane. *Sense and Sensibility*. 1813. Dover, 1966.

22. BOOK WITH A TITLE WITHIN THE TITLE Do not italicize a book title within a title. For an article title within a title, italicize as usual, and place the article title in quotation marks.

> Lethem, Jonathan. *"Lucky Alan" and Other Stories*. Doubleday, 2015.

> Shanahan, Timothy. *Philosophy and* Blade Runner. Palgrave Macmillan, 2014.

23. SACRED TEXT To cite individual published editions of sacred books, begin the entry with the title. If you are not citing a particular edition, do not include sacred texts in the list of works cited.

> *The Oxford Annotated Bible with the Apocrypha.* Edited by Herbert G. May and
>> Bruce M. Metzger, Revised Standard Version, Oxford UP, 1965.

> *The Qur'an: Translation.* Translated by Abdullah Yusuf Ali, Tahrike Tarsile
>> Qur'an, 2001.

PRINT PERIODICALS

Begin with the author name(s). (See models 1–5.) Then include the article title; the title of the periodical; the volume, issue, and date for journal articles or the date alone for magazine and newspaper articles; and the page numbers. The source map on pp. 358–59 shows where to find this information in a sample periodical.

24. ARTICLE IN A JOURNAL Follow the journal title with the volume number, the issue number (if given), the date of publication, and the page numbers.

> Matchie, Thomas. "Law versus Love in *The Round House.*" *Midwest Quarterly*,
>> vol. 56, no. 4, Summer 2015, pp. 353–64.

> Tilman, David. "Food and Health of a Full Earth." *Daedalus,* vol. 144, no. 4, Fall
>> 2015, pp. 5–7.

25. ARTICLE IN A MAGAZINE Provide the date from the magazine cover instead of volume or issue numbers.

> Bryan, Christy. "Ivory Worship." *National Geographic*, Oct. 2012, pp. 28–61.

> Grossman, Lev. "A Star Is Born." *Time*, 2 Nov. 2015, pp. 30–39.

26. ARTICLE IN A NEWSPAPER Include the edition (*national ed., late ed.*), if listed, and the section number or letter, if given. When an article skips pages, give only the first page number and a plus sign.

> Bray, Hiawatha. "As Toys Get Smarter, Privacy Issues Emerge." *The Boston
>> Globe,* 10 Dec. 2015, p. C1.

> Sherry, Allison. "Volunteers' Personal Touch Turns High-Tech Data into Votes."
>> *The Denver Post,* 30 Oct. 2012, pp. 1A+.

Add the city in brackets if it is not part of the name: *The Globe and Mail* [Toronto].

MLA SOURCE MAP: Articles in print periodicals

1 Author. List the last name first. End with a period. For variations, see models 2–5.

2 Article title. Put the title and any subtitle in quotation marks; capitalize all major words. Place a period inside the closing quotation mark.

3 Periodical title. Italicize the title; capitalize all major words. Follow the periodical title with a comma.

4 Volume, issue, and/or date of publication. For journals, give the volume number and issue number (if any), separated by a comma; then list the date and follow it with a comma. For magazines, list the day (if given), month, and year, followed by a comma.

5 Page numbers. List inclusive page numbers. If the article skips pages, put the first page number and a plus sign. End with a period.

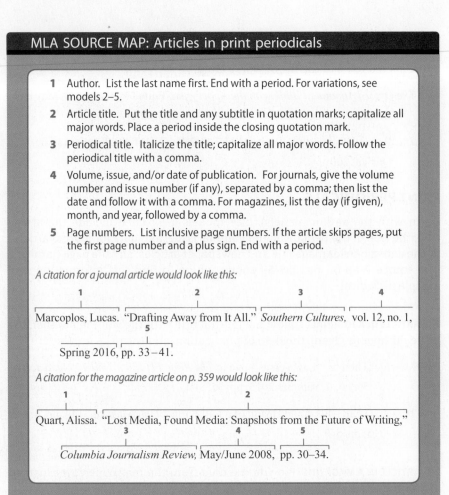

A citation for a journal article would look like this:

    1   **2**   **3**   **4**

Marcoplos, Lucas. "Drafting Away from It All." *Southern Cultures,* vol. 12, no. 1,
                       5

Spring 2016, pp. 33–41.

A citation for the magazine article on p. 359 would look like this:

    1   **2**

Quart, Alissa. "Lost Media, Found Media: Snapshots from the Future of Writing,"
            3   **4**   **5**

Columbia Journalism Review, May/June 2008, pp. 30–34.

4 Date of Publication   **3** Periodical Title

27. EDITORIAL OR LETTER TO THE EDITOR Include the writer's name (if given) and the title (if any). Include a label indicating the source type at the end of the citation.

> "California Dreaming." *The Nation,* 25 Feb. 2008, p. 4. Editorial.

> Galbraith, James K. "JFK's Plans to Withdraw." *New York Review of Books,* 6
>> Dec. 2007, pp. 77–78. Letter.

28. REVIEW

After the title of the review—if the review is untitled, include the label *Review* in its place—include *Review of* plus the title of the work being reviewed (followed by a comma). Then add *By* plus the names of the author(s), director(s), or producer(s) of the original work (followed by a comma). Finally, add the balance of the information you would need for any article within a larger work.

> Walton, James. "Noble, Embattled Souls." Review of *The Bone Clocks* and
>> *Slade House,* by David Mitchell, *The New York Review of Books*, 3 Dec.
>> 2015, pp. 55–58.

> Lane, Anthony. "Human Bondage." Review of *Spectre*, directed by Sam
>> Mendes, *The New Yorker*, 16 Nov. 2015, pp. 96–97.

29. UNSIGNED ARTICLE

> "Performance of the Week." *Time,* 6 Oct. 2003, p. 18.

ELECTRONIC SOURCES

When citing a website or a web page, include all the information you would need to cite any other source (author, title, and "container" information), and add a permalink or digital object identifier (DOI) in the "location" position. If neither a permalink nor a DOI is available, include the URL (omitting *http://*). If accessing a source through a database, add the information about the database as a separate "container": End the information about the journal with a period, and then add the title of the database (in italics, followed by a comma) and the DOI or permalink URL. If you are accessing the source through a database your library subscribes to, include just the basic URL for the database (*go.galegroup.com*), not the URL for the specific article.

30. WORK FROM A DATABASE The basic format for citing a work from a database appears in the source map on pp. 361–62.

> Coles, Kimberly Anne. "The Matter of Belief in John Donne's Holy Sonnets."
>> *Renaissance Quarterly*, vol. 68, no. 3, Fall 2015, pp. 899–931. *JSTOR,*
>> doi:10.1086/683855.

MLA SOURCE MAP: Articles from databases

Library subscriptions — such as EBSCOhost and Academic Search Premier — provide access to huge databases of articles.

1. **Author.** List the last name first. End with a period. For variations, see models 2–5.

2. **Article title.** Enclose the title and any subtitle in quotation marks.

3. **Periodical title.** Italicize it.

4. **Print publication information.** List the volume and issue number, if any; the date of publication, including the day (if given), month, and year, in that order; and the inclusive page numbers.

5. **Database name.** Italicize the name of the database.

6. **DOI or URL.** Include the DOI (digital object identifier) or URL, preferably a permalink URL (minus *http://*). If accessing the source from a subscription database, include only the URL for the database.

A citation for the work on p. 362 would look like this:

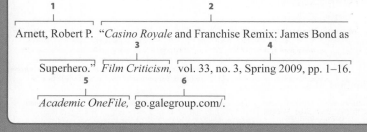

Arnett, Robert P. "*Casino Royale* and Franchise Remix: James Bond as Superhero." *Film Criticism,* vol. 33, no. 3, Spring 2009, pp. 1–16. *Academic OneFile,* go.galegroup.com/.

3 Periodical Title

2 Article Title

Title:	**Casino Royale and Franchise Remix: James Bond as Superhero.**
Authors:	Arnett, Robert P.1 ◄──────── **1** Author
Source:	Film Criticism; Spring2009, Vol. 33 Issue 3, p1-16, 16p
Document Type:	Article
Subject Terms:	*JAMES Bond films **4** Print Publication Information
	*FILM genres
	*BOND, James (Fictitious character)
	*SUPERHERO films
Reviews & Products:	CASINO Royale (Film)
People:	CRAIG, Daniel
Abstract:	The article discusses the role of the film "Casino Royale" in remixing the James Bond franchise. The author believes that the remixed Bond franchise has shifted its genre to a superhero franchise. When Sony acquired MGM in 2004, part of its plans is to transform the 007 franchise at par with "Spiderman." The remixed franchise re-aligns its franchise criteria with those established by superhero films. The author cites "Casino Royale's" narrative structure as an example of the success of the film as franchise remixed for the future. The portrayal of Bond as a superhero by actor Daniel Craig is discussed.
Author Affiliations:	1Associate professor, Department of Communication and Theatre Arts, Old Dominion University
ISSN:	01635069
Accession Number:	47966995
Database:	Academic Search Premier

5 Database Name

Macari, Anne Marie. "Lyric Impulse in a Time of Extinction." *American Poetry Review*, vol. 44, no. 4, July/Aug. 2015, pp. 11–14. *General OneFile*, go.galegroup.com/.

31. ARTICLE IN AN ONLINE JOURNAL Cite an online journal article as you would a print journal article (see model 24). After the page numbers (if available), include the URL or DOI. If you access the article through a database, include the database name (in italics), followed by a comma, before the DOI or URL.

Bryson, Devin. "The Rise of a New Senegalese Cultural Philosophy?" *African Studies Quarterly*, vol. 14, no. 3, Mar. 2014, pp. 33–56, asq.africa.ufl.edu /files/Volume-14-Issue-3-Bryson.pdf.

Rich, Ruby B. "Evidence of Visibility." *Film Quarterly*, vol. 69, no. 2, Winter 2015, pp. 5–7. *Academic Search Premier*, doi:10.1525/FQ.2015.69.2.5.

32. ARTICLE IN AN ONLINE MAGAZINE Provide the usual print publication information for a magazine, but replace the page numbers with the URL.

Leonard, Andrew. "The Surveillance State High School." *Salon*, 27 Nov. 2012, www.salon.com/2012/11/27/the_surveillance_state_high_school/.

33. ARTICLE IN AN ONLINE NEWSPAPER Provide the usual print publication information for a newspaper, but replace the page numbers with the URL.

Crowell, Maddy. "How Computers Are Getting Better at Detecting Liars." *The Christian Science Monitor*, 12 Dec. 2015, www.csmonitor.com/Science /Science-Notebook/2015/1212/How-computers-are-getting-better-at -detecting-liars.

34. COMMENT ON AN ONLINE ARTICLE If the commenter uses a pseudonym (a pen name or screen name), include it; if you know the author's actual name, include that after the pseudonym in parentheses.

pablosharkman. Comment on "'We Are All Implicated': Wendell Berry Laments a Disconnection from Community and the Land," by Scott Carlson. *The Chronicle of Higher Education*, 23 Apr. 2012, chronicle.com/article/In -Jefferson-Lecture-Wendell/131648.

35. DIGITAL BOOK Provide information as for a print book (see models 6–23); then give the electronic publication information, such as the database name (in italics) and the URL, or the digital format (Kindle, Nook). If the book is a reissue of an earlier publication, you may add the original publication information (such as the year of original publication) after the title if it is relevant, given your rhetorical situation.

> Doerr, Anthony. *All the Light We Cannot See*. Scribner, 2014. Nook.

> Goldsmith, Oliver. *The Vicar of Wakefield: A Tale*. 1801. *America's Historical Imprints*, infoweb.newsbank.com.ezproxy.bpl.org/.

> Piketty, Thomas. *Capital in the Twenty-First Century*. Translated by Arthur Goldhammer, Harvard UP, 2014. Google Books, books.google.com /books?isbn=0674369556.

36. ONLINE EDITORIAL OR LETTER For clarity, include the label *Editorial* or *Letter* at the end of the citation.

> "City's Blight Fight Making Difference." *The Columbus Dispatch,* 17 Nov. 2015, www.dispatch.com/content/stories/editorials/2015/11/17/1-citys -blight-fight-making-difference.html. Editorial.

37. ONLINE REVIEW Cite an online review as you would a print review (see model 28), adding or changing information as needed to reflect the digital container, such as by replacing the page numbers with the URL.

> Della Subin, Anna. "It Has Burned My Heart." Review of *The Lives of Muhammad*, by Kecia Ali, *London Review of Books*, 22 Oct. 2015, www.lrb.co.uk/v37/n20/anna-della-subin-it-has-burned-my-heart.

> Spychalski, John C. Review of *American Railroads—Decline and Renaissance in the Twentieth Century*, by Robert E. Gallamore and John R. Meyer. *Transportation Journal*, vol. 54, no. 4, Fall 2015, pp. 535–38. *JSTOR*, doi:10.5325/transportationj.54.4.0535.

38. ENTRY IN AN ONLINE REFERENCE WORK Cite the entry as you would an entry from a print reference work (see model 19), including or changing any information you may need to identify the digital container, such as the URL.

> Durante, Amy M. "Finn Mac Cumhail." *Encyclopedia Mythica*, 17 Apr. 2011, www.pantheon.org/articles/f/finn_mac_cumhail.html.

Hall, Mark. "Facebook (American Company)." *The Enyclopaedia Britannica*,
2 July 2014, www.britannica.com/topic/Facebook.

"House Music." *Wikipedia*, 16 Nov. 2015, en.wikipedia.org/wiki/House_music.

39. WORK FROM A WEBSITE For basic information on citing a work from a
website, see the source map on pp. 366–67. Include the name of the author;
the title of the document, in quotation marks; the name of the website, italicized; the date of publication; the name of the publisher or sponsor if different from the title of the site; and the URL. Include an access date following
the URL only if no publication date is available.

Enzinna, Wes. "Syria's Unknown Revolution." *Pulitzer Center on Crisis
Reporting*, 24 Nov. 2015, pulitzercenter.org/projects/middle-east-syria
-enzinna-war-rojava.

"Social and Historical Context: Vitality." *Arapesh Grammar and Digital
Language Archive Project*, Institute for Advanced Technology in the
Humanities, www.arapesh.org/socio_historical_context_vitality.php.
Accessed 22 Mar. 2016.

40. ENTIRE WEBSITE Follow the guidelines for a specific work from the web, beginning with the name of the author, editor, compiler, or director (if any),
followed by the title of the website, italicized; the name of the sponsor or
publisher, only if different from the author; the date of publication or last
update; and the URL. Include an access date following the URL only if no
publication date is available.

Halsall, Paul, editor. *Internet Modern History Sourcebook*. Fordham U, 4 Nov.
2011, legacy.fordham.edu/halsall/index.asp.

Railton, Stephen. *Mark Twain in His Times*. U of Virginia Library, 2012, twain
.lib.virginia.edu/.

The Newton Project. U of Sussex, 2016, www.newtonproject.sussex.ac.uk
/prism.php?id=1.

Transparency International: The Global Coalition against Corruption. 2015,
www.transparency.org/.

MLA SOURCE MAP: Works from websites

You may need to browse other parts of a site to find some of the following elements, and some sites may omit elements. Uncover as much information as you can.

1　Author.　List the last name first. End with a period. For variations, see models 2–5. If no author is given or if the author and website title or publisher are substantially the same, begin with the title.

2　Title of work.　Enclose the title and any subtitle of the work in quotation marks.

3　Title of website.　Give the title of the entire website, italicized.

4　Publisher or sponsor.　Include the publisher or sponsor only if that name is significantly different from the title of the website. In the example here, the sponsoring organization is the Nobel Foundation, which is not significantly different from the website title (*Nobelprize.org*), so no sponsor is included.

5　Date of publication or latest update.　Give the most recent date, followed by a comma.

6　URL.　Use a permalink if available.

7　Date of access.　Include an access date only if no publication date is available; insert it following the URL. (See model 39 for an example.)

A citation for the work on p. 367 would look like this:

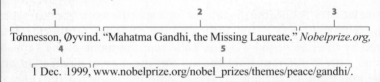

Tønnesson, Øyvind. "Mahatma Gandhi, the Missing Laureate." *Nobelprize.org*, 1 Dec. 1999, www.nobelprize.org/nobel_prizes/themes/peace/gandhi/.

1 Author

3 Title of Website

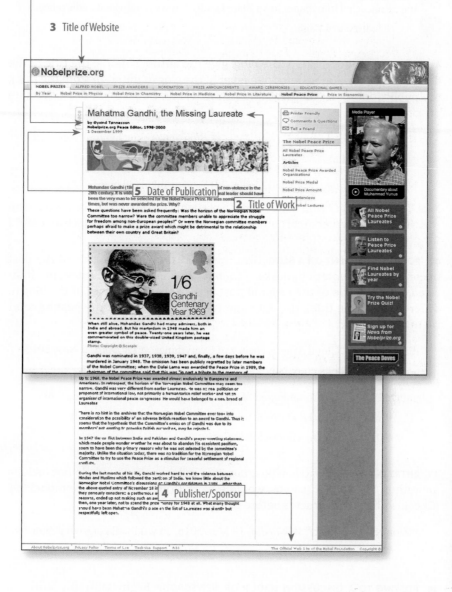

5 Date of Publication

2 Title of Work

4 Publisher/Sponsor

For a personal website, include a description such as *Homepage*, not italicized; the name of the larger site, if different from the personal site's title; the date of the last update; and the URL. If there is no date of publication, add an access date following the URL.

> Bae, Rebecca. Homepage. Iowa State U, 2015, www.engl.iastate.edu/rebecca
> -baedirectory-page/.

41. BLOG (WEB LOG) For an entire blog, give the author's name; the title of the blog, italicized; the sponsor or publisher of the blog (if different from the title); the publication date; the URL; and (if there is no publication date) the date of access.

> Kiuchi, Tatsuro. *Tatsuro Kiuchi: News & Blog,* tatsurokiuchi.com/. Accessed 3
> Mar. 2016.

> Ng, Amy. *Pikaland.* Pikaland Media, 2015, www.pikaland.com/.

Note: To cite a blogger who writes under a pseudonym, begin with the pseudonym and then put the writer's real name (if you know it) in parentheses. (See model 45.)

42. POST OR COMMENT ON A BLOG Give the author's name; the title of the post or comment in quotation marks; if there is no title, use *Comment on*, not italicized, plus the title of the original post, italicized; the sponsor of the blog (if different from the title); the date and time (if available) of the post or comment; and the URL.

> Eakin, Emily. "Cloud Atlas's Theory of Everything." *NYR Daily,* 2 Nov. 2012,
> www.nybooks.com/daily/2012/11/02/ken-wilber-cloud-atlas/.

> mitchellfreedman. Comment on "Cloud Atlas's Theory of Everything," by
> Emily Eakin. *NYR Daily,* 3 Nov. 2012, www.nybooks.com/daily
> /2012/11/02/ken-wilber-cloud-atlas/.

43. ENTRY IN A WIKI Because wiki content is collectively edited, do not include an author. Treat a wiki as you would a work from a website (see model 39). (Check with your instructor before using a wiki as a source.)

> "Zion National Park." *Wikipedia,* 18 Mar. 2016, en.wikipedia.org/wiki/Zion
> _National_Park.

44. POSTING TO A DISCUSSION GROUP OR NEWSGROUP Begin with the author's name and the title of the posting in quotation marks (or the words *Online posting* if untitled). Follow with the name of the website, the sponsor of the site (if significantly different from the name of the website), the date of publication, and the URL.

> Yen, Jessica. "Quotations within Parentheses (Study Measures)." *Copyediting-L*,
> 18 Mar. 2016, list.indiana.edu/sympa/arc/copyediting-l/2016-03/msg00492
> .html.

45. POSTING OR MESSAGE ON A SOCIAL-NETWORKING SITE To cite a message or posting on Facebook, Twitter, or another social-networking site, include the writer's name (or Twitter handle—after the handle, include the author's real name, in parentheses if you know it), the title of the post (in quotation marks), the social-networking site (in italics), the date and time (if available), and the URL.

> Bedford English. "Stacey Cochran explores Reflective Writing in the
> classroom and as a writer: http://ow.ly/YkjVB." *Facebook*, 15 Feb. 2016,
> www.facebook.com/BedfordEnglish/posts/10153415001259607.

> Curiosity Rover. "Can you see me waving? How to spot #Mars in the night sky:
> https://youtu.be/hv8hVvJlcJQ." *Twitter*, 5 Nov. 2015, 11:00 a.m., twitter
> .com/marscuriosity/status/672859022911889408.

> @grammarphobia (Patricia T. O'Conner and Steward Kellerman). "Is 'if you
> will' a verbal tic? http://goo.gl/oYrTYP #English #language #grammar
> #etymology #usage #linguistics #WOTD." *Twitter*, 14 Mar. 2016, 9:12 a.m.,
> twitter.com/grammarphobia.

46. EMAIL Include the writer's name; the subject line, in quotation marks; *Received by* (not italicized or in quotation marks) followed by the recipient's name; and the date of the message.

> Thornbrugh, Caitlin. "Coates Lecture." Received by Rita Anderson, 20
> Oct. 2015.

47. COMPUTER SOFTWARE OR ONLINE GAME Include the author name (if given and different from the title and sponsor); the title, italicized; the version number (if given); the publisher or sponsor; and the publication date.

> *Words with Friends.* Version 5.84, Zynga, 2013.

VIDEO AND AUDIO SOURCES (INCLUDING ONLINE VERSIONS)

48. FILM OR DVD If you cite a particular person's work, start with that name. If not, start with the title; then name the director, distributor, and year of release. Other contributors, such as writers or performers, may follow the director.

> *Birdman or (The Unexpected Virtue of Ignorance)*. Directed by Alejandro González Iñárritu, performances by Michael Keaton, Emma Stone, Zach Galifianakis, Edward Norton, and Naomi Watts, Fox Searchlight, 2014.

> Scott, Ridley, director. *The Martian*. Performances by Matt Damon, Jessica Chastain, Kristen Wiig, and Kate Mara, Twentieth Century Fox, 2015.

49. VIDEO OR AUDIO FROM THE WEB If you cite an online video or audio file, add the URL following the date.

> Fletcher, Antoine. "The Ancient Art of the Atlatl." *Russell Cave National Monument*, narrated by Brenton Bellomy, National Park Service, 12 Feb. 2014, www.nps.gov/media/video/view.htm?id=C92C0D0A-1DD8-B71C -07CBC6E8970CD73F.

> Lewis, Paul. "Citizen Journalism." *YouTube*, 14 May 2011, www.youtube.com /watch?v=9APO9_yNbcg.

50. TELEVISION OR RADIO EPISODE OR PROGRAM In general, when citing a program, begin with the title, italicized. Then list important contributors (narrator, writer, director, actors); the network; and the broadcast date. Include the URL if citing an episode or program you downloaded or streamed. To cite a particular episode from a series, begin with the episode title, in quotation marks, and add the episode number (if available) before the network.

> "Free Speech on College Campuses." *Washington Journal*, narrated by Peter Slen, C-SPAN, 27 Nov. 2015.

> "The Cathedral." *Reply All,* narrated by Sruthi Pinnamaneni, episode 50, Gimlet Media, 7 Jan. 2016, gimletmedia.com/episode/50-the-cathedral/.

51. BROADCAST INTERVIEW Base your citation of a broadcast interview on the citation for a television or radio episode or program (model 50), but add the name of the person interviewed in the author position, and add the interviewer's name (with *Interview by*, not italicized) following the episode title.

> Jaffrey, Madhur. "Madhur Jaffrey on How Indian Cuisine Won Western Taste Buds." Interview by Shadrach Kabango, *Q*, CBC Radio, 29 Oct. 2015, www.cbc.ca/1.3292918.

Tempkin, Ann, and Anne Umland. Interview by Charlie Rose. *Charlie Rose: The Week*, PBS, 9 Oct. 2015.

52. UNPUBLISHED OR PERSONAL INTERVIEW List the person interviewed; the label *Telephone interview*, *Personal interview*, or *E-mail interview*; and the date the interview took place.

Akufo, Dautey. Personal interview, 11 Apr. 2016.

53. SOUND RECORDING List the name of the person or group you wish to emphasize (such as the composer, conductor, or band); the title of the recording or composition; the artist(s), if appropriate; the longer work in which the recording is contained (if any); the manufacturer; and the year of issue.

Adele. "Hello." *25*. XL, 2015.

Bizet, Georges. *Carmen*. Performances by Jennifer Larmore, Thomas Moser, Angela Gheorghiu, and Samuel Ramey, Bavarian State Orchestra and Chorus, conducted by Giuseppe Sinopoli, Warner, 1996.

Note: If you are citing instrumental music that is identified only by form, number, and key, do not underline, italicize, or enclose it in quotation marks.

Grieg, Edvard. Concerto in A minor, op. 16. Conducted by Eugene Ormandy, Philadelphia Orchestra, RCA, 1989.

54. MUSICAL COMPOSITION When you are not citing a specific published version, first give the composer's name, followed by the title (in italics). Do not italicize a work you refer to by form, number, and key.

Mozart, Wolfgang Amadeus. *Don Giovanni*, K527. *William and Gayle Cook Music Library*, Indiana U School of Music, www.dlib.indiana.edu /variations/scores/bhq9391/.

Beethoven, Ludwig van. Symphony no. 5 in C minor, op. 67. 1807. *Center for Computer Assisted Research in the Humanities*, Stanford U, 2000, scores .ccarh.org/beethoven/sym/beethoven-sym5-1.pdf.

55. LECTURE OR SPEECH List the speaker; the title, in quotation marks; the sponsoring institution or group; the place; and the date. Add the label *Address* (not in italics) at the end of the citation.

Smith, Anna Deavere. "On the Road: A Search for American Character." National Endowment for the Humanities, John F. Kennedy Center for the Performing Arts, Washington, DC, 6 Apr. 2015. Address.

If you streamed or downloaded the lecture or speech, include the URL.

> Khosla, Raj. "Precision Agriculture and Global Food Security." *US Department of State: Diplomacy in Action*, 26 Mar. 2013, www.state.gov/e/stas /series/212172.htm. Address.

56. LIVE PERFORMANCE List the title, appropriate names (such as the writer or performer), the place, and the date. To cite a particular person's work, begin the entry with that name.

> *Anything Goes.* By Cole Porter, performed by Klea Blackhurst, Shubert Theater, New Haven, 7 Oct. 2003.

> Snoad, Peter. *The Draft.* Directed by Diego Arciniegas, Hibernian Hall, Boston, 10 Sept. 2015.

57. PODCAST For a podcast, include all the following that are available: the speaker, the title of the podcast, the title of the program, the host or performers (if different from the speaker), the title of the site, the site's sponsor (if different from the site's title), the date of posting, and the URL. You may want to include an access date at the end of the citation, if the date the podcast was posted is not provided.

> McDougall, Christopher. "How Did Endurance Help Early Humans Survive?" *TED Radio Hour*, National Public Radio, 20 Nov. 2015, www.npr .org/2015/11/20/455904655/how-did-endurance-help-early-humans -survive.

> Tanner, Laura. "Virtual Reality in 9/11 Fiction." *Literature Lab*, Department of English, Brandeis U, www.brandeis.edu/departments/english/literaturelab /tanner.html. Accessed 14 Feb. 2016.

58. WORK OF ART OR PHOTOGRAPH List the artist or photographer; the work's title, italicized; the date of composition; and the name of the museum or other location; and the city. To cite a reproduction in a book, add the publication information. To cite artwork found online, add the URL.

> Bradford, Mark. *Let's Walk to the Middle of the Ocean.* 2015, Museum of Modern Art, New York.

> Clough, Charles. *January Twenty-First.* 1988–89, Joslyn Art Museum, Omaha, www.joslyn.org/collections-and-exhibitions/permanent-collections /modern-and-contemporary/charles-clough-january-twenty-first/.

O'Keeffe, Georgia. *Black and Purple Petunias*. 1925, private collection. *Two Lives: A Conversation in Paintings and Photographs*, edited by Alexandra Arrowsmith and Thomas West, HarperCollins, 1992, p. 67.

59. MAP Cite a map as you would a book or a short work within a longer work. For an online source, include the URL. Add the label *Map* (not italicized) at the end of the citation, if the type of work you are citing won't be clear from the context.

California. Rand McNally, 2002.

"Vote on Secession, 1861." *Perry-Castañeda Library Map Collection*, U of Texas, 1976, www.lib.utexas.edu/maps/atlas_texas/texas_vote _secession_1861.jpg.

60. CARTOON OR COMIC STRIP List the artist's name; the title (if any) of the cartoon or comic strip, in quotation marks; and the usual publication information for a print periodical (see models 24–27). If it won't be clear that you're citing a cartoon or comic strip, add an appropriate label at the end of the citation.

Lewis, Eric. "The Unpublished Freud." *The New Yorker,* 11 Mar. 2002, p. 80. Cartoon.

Zyglis, Adam. "City of Light." *Buffalo News*, 8 Nov. 2015, adamzyglis .buffalonews.com/2015/11/08/city-of-light/. Cartoon.

61. ADVERTISEMENT Include the label *Advertisement* at the end of the citation if your readers won't know the type of work that you're citing.

AT&T. *National Geographic*, Dec. 2015, p. 14. Advertisement.

Toyota. *The Root*. Slate Group, 28 Nov. 2015, www.theroot.com. Advertisement.

OTHER SOURCES (INCLUDING ONLINE VERSIONS)

If an online version is not shown here, use the appropriate model for the source, and then end with the URL or DOI.

62. REPORT OR PAMPHLET Follow the guidelines for a book (models 6–23 and 35).

Dead in the Water. Environmental Working Group, 2006. www.ewg.org /research/deadwater.

63. GOVERNMENT PUBLICATION Begin with the author, if identified. Otherwise, start with the name of the government, followed by the agency. If the author and site sponsor are the same, begin the citation with the title of the source. For congressional documents, cite the number, the session, the house of Congress, the report number, and any other information that will clarify the citation for your readers.

> Canada, Minister of Aboriginal Affairs and Northern Development. *2015–16 Report on Plans and Priorities*. Minister of Public Works and Government Services Canada, 2015.

> Gregg, Judd. *Report to Accompany the Genetic Information Act of 2003*. Government Printing Office, 2003. 108th Congress, 1st session, Senate Report 108–22.

> Russel, Daniel R. "Burma's Challenge: Democracy, Human Rights, Peace, and the Plight of the Rohingya." Testimony before the US House Foreign Affairs Committee, Subcommittee on East Asian and Pacific Affairs, *US Department of State: Diplomacy in Action*, 21 Oct. 2015, www.state.gov/p /eap/rls/rm/2015/10/248420.htm.

64. PUBLISHED PROCEEDINGS OF A CONFERENCE Include the editor(s), and information about the conference (including its title, dates, and location). If the conference was sponsored by an organization the name of which is not already included in the title of the conference, include that information at the end of the citation as a separate "container."

> Meisner, Marx S., et al., editors. *Communication for the Commons: Revisiting Participation and Environment*. Proceedings of Twelfth Biennial Conference on Communication and the Environment, 6–11 June 2015, Swedish U of Agricultural Sciences. International Environmental Communication Association, 2015.

65. DISSERTATION For an unpublished dissertation, enclose the title in quotation marks; for a published dissertation, set the title in italics. Add the label *Dissertation* (not in italics), the school, and the year the work was accepted.

> Abbas, Megan Brankley. "Knowing Islam: The Entangled History of Western Academia and Modern Islamic Thought." Dissertation, Princeton U, 2015.

> Kidd, Celeste. *Rational Approaches to Learning and Development*. Dissertation, U of Rochester, 2013.

66. DISSERTATION ABSTRACT Cite a dissertation abstract as you would a dissertation, but add the label *Abstract* (not in italics), followed by information about the "container" in which the abstract appeared.

> Moore, Courtney L. "Stress and Oppression: Identifying Possible Protective
>   Factors for African American Men." Dissertation, Chicago School of
>   Professional Psychology, 2016. Abstract. *ProQuest Dissertations and*
>   *Theses*, search.proquest.com/docview/1707351557.

67. PUBLISHED INTERVIEW Treat a published interview as you would a broadcast interview, with information about the "container" in which the interview appeared at the end of the citation.

> Weddington, Sarah. "Sarah Weddington: Still Arguing for *Roe*." Interview by
>   Michele Kort. *Ms.*, Winter 2013, pp. 32–35.

68. UNPUBLISHED LETTER Cite an unpublished letter as you would an e-mail message (see model 46), replacing the subject line with the label *Letter to* followed by *the author* or the name of the recipient.

> Primak, Shoshana. Letter to the author, 6 May 2016.

69. MANUSCRIPT OR OTHER UNPUBLISHED WORK Treat a manuscript or other unpublished work as you would its published counterpart, adding information after the title that readers will need to understand the nature of the source.

> Arendt, Hannah. *Between Past and Future*. 1st draft, Hannah Arendt Papers,
>   Manuscript Division, Library of Congress, pp. 108–50, memory.loc.gov
>   /cgi-bin/ampage?collId=mharendt&fileName=05/050030/050030page
>   .db&recNum=0.

70. LEGAL SOURCE To cite an act, give the name of the act followed by its Public Law (*Pub. L.*) number, its Statutes at Large (*Stat.*) cataloging number, and the date the act was enacted. To cite a court case, give the names of the first plaintiff and defendant, the case number, the name of the court, the date of the decision, and any other information readers will need to access the source.

> Electronic Freedom of Information Act Amendments of 1996. Pub. L. 104–231.
>   Stat. 110.2048. 2 Oct. 1996.

> Utah v. Evans. 536 US 452. Supreme Court of the US. 2002. *Legal Information*
>   *Institute*, Cornell U Law School, www.law.cornell.edu/supremecourt
>   /text/536/452.

APA Documentation Guidelines

The following formatting guidelines are adapted from the American Psychological Association (APA) recommendations for preparing manuscripts for publication in journals. Check with your instructor before preparing your final draft, however.

For detailed guidelines on formatting a list of references, see pp. 382–99. For a sample student essay in APA style, see pp. 249–57.

- *Title page.* Center the title, and include your name, the course name and number, the instructor's name, and the date. In the top left corner, type the words *Running head:* and a short version of the title, using all capital letters (fifty characters or fewer, including spaces). In the top right corner, type the number 1.

- *Margins and spacing.* Leave margins of at least one inch at the top and bottom and on both sides of the page. Do not justify the right margin. Double-space the entire text, including headings, set-off quotations, content notes, and the list of references. Indent the first line of each paragraph one-half inch (or five to seven spaces) from the left margin.

- *Short title and page numbers.* Type the short title flush left and the page number flush right at the top of each page, in the same position as on the title page.

- *Long quotations.* For a long, set-off quotation (one having more than forty words), indent it one-half inch (or five to seven spaces) from the left margin and do not use quotation marks. Place the page reference in parentheses one space after the final punctuation.

- *Abstract.* If your instructor asks for an abstract with your paper—a one-paragraph summary of your major thesis and supporting points—it should go on a separate page immediately after the title page. Center the word *Abstract* (not boldface) about an inch from the top of the page.

Double-space the text of the abstract, and begin the first line flush with the left margin. The length of abstracts typically ranges from 150 to 250 words, depending on the length of the source it summarizes.

- *Headings.* Headings (set in boldface) are used within the text of many APA-style papers. In papers with only one or two levels of headings, center the main headings; position the subheadings flush with the left margin. Capitalize words of four or more letters, but do not capitalize articles, short prepositions, or coordinating conjunctions unless they are the first word or follow a colon.

- *Visuals.* Tables should be labeled *Table*, numbered, and captioned. All other visuals (charts, graphs, photographs, and drawings) should be labeled *Figure*, numbered, and captioned with a description and the source information. Remember to refer to each visual in your text, stating how it contributes to the point(s) you are making. Tables and figures should generally appear near the relevant text; check with your instructor for guidelines on placement of visuals.

Directory to APA style for in-text citations

In-Text Citations

APA style requires parenthetical references in the text to document quotations, paraphrases, summaries, and other material from a source. These citations correspond to full bibliographic entries in a list of references at the end of the text.

Note that APA style generally calls for using the past tense or present perfect tense for signal verbs: *Baker (2003) showed* or *Baker (2003) has shown.*

Use the present tense only to discuss results (*the experiment demonstrates*) or widely accepted information (*researchers agree*).

An in-text citation in APA style always indicates *which source* on the references page the writer is referring to, and it explains *in what year* the material was published; for quoted material, the in-text citation also indicates *where* in the source the quotation can be found.

1. BASIC FORMAT FOR A QUOTATION Generally, use the author's name in a signal phrase to introduce the cited material, and place the date, in parentheses, immediately after the author's name. The page number, preceded by *p.*, appears in parentheses after the quotation.

> Gitlin (2001) pointed out that "political critics, convinced that the media are rigged against them, are often blind to other substantial reasons why their causes are unpersuasive" (p. 141).

If the author is not named in a signal phrase, place the author's name, the year, and the page number in parentheses after the quotation: (Gitlin, 2001, p. 141). For a long, set-off quotation (more than forty words), place the page reference in parentheses one space after the final quotation.

For electronic texts or other works without page numbers, you may use paragraph numbers, if the source includes them, preceded by the abbreviation *para.*

> Driver (2007) has noticed "an increasing focus on the role of land" in policy debates over the past decade (para. 1).

2. BASIC FORMAT FOR A PARAPHRASE OR SUMMARY Include the author's last name and the year as in model 1, but omit the page or paragraph number unless the reader will need it to find the material in a long work.

> Gitlin (2001) has argued that critics sometimes overestimate the influence of the media on modern life.

3. TWO AUTHORS Use both names in all citations. Use *and* in a signal phrase, but use an ampersand (&) in parentheses.

> Babcock and Laschever (2003) have suggested that many women do not negotiate their salaries and pay raises as vigorously as their male counterparts do.

> One study has suggested that many women do not negotiate their salaries and pay raises as vigorously as their male counterparts do (Babcock & Laschever, 2003).

4. THREE TO FIVE AUTHORS List all the authors' names for the first reference.

> Safer, Voccola, Hurd, and Goodwin (2003) reached somewhat different conclusions by designing a study that was less dependent on subjective judgment than were previous studies.

In subsequent references, use just the first author's name plus *et al.*

> Based on the results, Safer et al. (2003) determined that the apes took significant steps toward self-expression.

5. SIX OR MORE AUTHORS Use only the first author's name and *et al.* in every citation.

> As Soleim et al. (2002) demonstrated, advertising holds the potential for manipulating "free-willed" consumers.

6. CORPORATE OR GROUP AUTHOR If the name of the organization or corporation is long, spell it out the first time you use it, followed by an abbreviation in brackets. In later references, use the abbreviation only.

> FIRST CITATION   (Centers for Disease Control and Prevention [CDC], 2006)
>
> LATER CITATIONS   (CDC, 2006)

7. UNKNOWN AUTHOR Use the title or its first few words in a signal phrase or in parentheses. A book's title is italicized, as in the following example; an article's title is placed in quotation marks.

> The employment profiles for this time period substantiated this trend (*Federal Employment*, 2001).

8. TWO OR MORE AUTHORS WITH THE SAME LAST NAME If your list of references includes works by different authors with the same last name, include the authors' initials in each citation.

> S. Bartolomeo (2000) conducted the groundbreaking study on teenage childbearing.

9. TWO OR MORE WORKS BY AN AUTHOR IN A SINGLE YEAR Assign lowercase letters (*a, b*, and so on) alphabetically by title, and include the letters after the year.

> Gordon (2004b) examined this trend in more detail.

10. TWO OR MORE SOURCES IN ONE PARENTHETICAL REFERENCE List sources by different authors in alphabetical order by authors' last names, separated by semicolons: (Cardone, 1998; Lai, 2002). List works by the same author in chronological order, separated by commas: (Lai, 2000, 2002).

11. INDIRECT SOURCE Use the phrase *as cited in* to indicate that you are reporting information from a secondary source. Name the original source in a signal phrase, but list the secondary source in your list of references.

> Amartya Sen developed the influential concept that land reform was necessary for "promoting opportunity" among the poor (as cited in Driver, 2007, para. 2).

12. PERSONAL COMMUNICATION Cite any personal letters, email messages, electronic postings, telephone conversations, or interviews as shown. Do not include personal communications in the reference list.

> R. Tobin (personal communication, November 4, 2006) supported his claims about music therapy with new evidence.

13. ELECTRONIC DOCUMENT Cite a web or electronic document as you would a print source, using the author's name and date.

> Link and Phelan (2005) argued for broader interventions in public health that would be accessible to anyone, regardless of individual wealth.

The APA recommends the following for electronic sources without names, dates, or page numbers:

AUTHOR UNKNOWN. Use a shortened form of the title in a signal phrase or in parentheses (see model 7). If an organization is the author, see model 6.

DATE UNKNOWN. Use the abbreviation *n.d.* (for "no date") in place of the year: (*Hopkins, n.d.*).

NO PAGE NUMBERS. Many works found online or in electronic databases lack stable page numbers. (Use the page numbers for an electronic work in a format, such as PDF, that has stable pagination.) If paragraph numbers are included in such a source, use the abbreviation *para.*: (*Giambetti*, 2006, *para.* 7). If no paragraph numbers are included but the source includes headings, give the heading, and identify the paragraph in the section:

> Jacobs and Johnson (2007) have argued that "the South African media is still highly concentrated and not very diverse in terms of race and class" (South African Media after Apartheid, para. 3).

Content Notes

APA style allows you to use content notes, either at the bottom of the page or on a separate page at the end of the text, to expand or supplement your text. Indicate such notes in the text by superscript numerals ([1]). Double-space all entries. Indent the first line of each note five spaces, but begin subsequent lines at the left margin.

SUPERSCRIPT NUMBER IN TEXT

The age of the children involved in the study was an important factor in the selection of items for the questionnaire.[1]

FOOTNOTE

[1]Marjorie Youngston Forman and William Cole of the Child Study Team provided great assistance in identifying appropriate items for the questionnaire.

Directory to APA style for references

Continued >

List of References

The alphabetical list of the sources cited in your document is called *References*. If your instructor asks that you list everything you have read—not just the sources you cite—call the list *Bibliography*. Here are guidelines for preparing a list of references:

- Start your list on a separate page after the text of your document but before appendices or notes. Continue consecutive page numbers.

- Center the heading *References* one inch from the top of the page.
- Begin each entry flush with the left margin, but indent subsequent lines one-half inch (or five to seven spaces). Double-space the entire list.
- List sources alphabetically by authors' (or editors') last names. If no author is given, alphabetize the source by the first word of the title other than *A*, *An*, or *The*. If the list includes two or more works by the same author, list them in chronological order. (For two or more works by the same author published in the same year, see model 5.)
- Italicize titles and subtitles of books and periodicals. Do not italicize titles of articles, and do not enclose them in quotation marks.
- For titles of books and articles, capitalize only the first word of the title and the subtitle and any proper nouns or proper adjectives.
- For titles of periodicals, capitalize all major words.

GUIDELINES FOR AUTHOR LISTINGS

List authors' last names first, and use only initials for first and middle names. The in-text citations in your text point readers toward particular sources in your list of references (see pp. 377–80).

NAME CITED IN SIGNAL PHRASE IN TEXT

Driver (2007) has noted . . .

NAME IN PARENTHETICAL CITATION IN TEXT

. . . (Driver, 2007).

BEGINNING OF ENTRY IN LIST OF REFERENCES

Driver, T. (2007).

1. ONE AUTHOR Give the last name, a comma, the initial(s), and the date in parentheses.

Zimbardo, P. G. (2009).

2. MULTIPLE AUTHORS List up to seven authors, last name first, with commas separating authors' names and an ampersand (&) before the last author's name.

Walsh, M. E., & Murphy, J. A. (2003).

Note: For a work with more than seven authors, list the first six, then an ellipsis (. . .), and then the final author's name.

3. CORPORATE OR GROUP AUTHOR

> Resources for Rehabilitation. (2003).

4. UNKNOWN AUTHOR Begin with the work's title. Italicize book titles, but do not italicize article titles or enclose them in quotation marks. Capitalize only the first word of the title and the subtitle (if any) and proper nouns and proper adjectives.

> *Safe youth, safe schools.* (2009).

5. TWO OR MORE WORKS BY THE SAME AUTHOR List two or more works by the same author in chronological order. Repeat the author's name in each entry.

> Goodall, J. (1999).

> Goodall, J. (2002).

If the works appeared in the same year, list them alphabetically by title, and assign lowercase letters (*a*, *b*, etc.) after the dates.

> Shermer, M. (2002a). On estimating the lifetime of civilizations. *Scientific*
> *American, 287*(2), 33.

> Shermer, M. (2002b). Readers who question evolution. *Scientific American,*
> *287*(1), 37.

BOOKS

6. BASIC FORMAT FOR A BOOK Begin with the author name(s). (See models 1–5.) Then include the publication year, the title and the subtitle, the city of publication, the country or state abbreviation, and the publisher. The source map on pp. 385–86 shows where to find this information in a typical book.

> Levick, S. E. (2003). *Clone being: Exploring the psychological and social*
> *dimensions.* Lanham, MD: Rowman & Littlefield.

7. EDITOR For a book with an editor but no author, list the source under the editor's name.

> Dickens, J. (Ed.). (1995). *Family outing: A guide for parents of gays, lesbians*
> *and bisexuals.* London, England: Peter Owen.

To cite a book with an author and an editor, place the editor's name, with a comma and the abbreviation Ed., in parentheses after the title.

> Austin, J. (1995). *The province of jurisprudence determined.* (W. E. Rumble,
> Ed.). Cambridge, England: Cambridge University Press.

APA SOURCE MAP: Books

Take information from the book's title page and copyright page (on the reverse side of the title page), not from the book's cover or a library catalog.

1. **Author.** List all authors' last names first, and use only initials for first and middle names. For more about citing authors, see models 1–5.

2. **Publication year.** Enclose the year of publication in parentheses.

3. **Title.** Italicize the title and any subtitle. Capitalize only the first word of the title and the subtitle and any proper nouns or proper adjectives.

4. **City and state of publication.** List the city of publication and the country or state abbreviation followed by a colon.

5. **Publisher.** Give the publisher's name, dropping any *Inc.*, *Co.*, or *Publishers.*

A citation for the book on p. 386 would look like this:

Tsutsui, W. (2004). *Godzilla on my mind: Fifty years of the king of monsters.*

New York, NY: Palgrave Macmillan.

2 Publication Year

GODZILLA ON MY MIND
Copyright © William Tsutsui, 2004.
All rights reserved. No part of this book may be used or
reproduced in any manner whatsoever without written permission
except in the case of brief quotations embodied in critical articles
or reviews.

First published 2004 by
PALGRAVE MACMILLAN™
175 Fifth Avenue, New York, N.Y. 10010 and
Houndmills, Basingstoke, Hampshire, England RG21 6XS.
Companies and representatives throughout the world.

4 City and State of Publication

PALGRAVE MACMILLAN is the global academic imprint of
the Palgrave Macmillan division of St. Martin's Press, LLC and of
Palgrave Macmillan Ltd. Macmillan® is a registered trademark in
the United States, United Kingdom and other countries. Palgrave
is a registered trademark in the European Union and other
countries.

ISBN 1–4039–6474–2

Library of Congress Cataloging-in-Publication Data
Tsutsui, William
Godzilla on my mind : fifty years of the king of monsters / William
Tsutsui.
    p.   cm.
    Includes bibliographical refer
    ISBN 1–4039–6474–2
    1. Godzilla films—History a

PN1995.9.G63T78   2004
791.43'651—dc22

A catalogue record for this boo
Library.

Design by Letra Libre, Inc.

10 9 8 7 6 5 4

Printed in the United States of

3 Title

GODZILLA®
ON MY MIND

*

*Fifty Years of the
King of Monsters*

3 Subtitle

WILLIAM TSUTSUI

1 Author

palgrave
macmillan

5 Publisher

8. SELECTION IN A BOOK WITH AN EDITOR

Burke, W. W., & Nourmair, D. A. (2001). The role of personality assessment
in organization development. In J. Waclawski & A. H. Church (Eds.),
*Organization development: A data-driven approach to organizational
change* (pp. 55–77). San Francisco, CA: Jossey-Bass.

9. TRANSLATION

Al-Farabi, A. N. (1998). *On the perfect state* (R. Walzer, Trans.). Chicago, IL: Kazi.

10. EDITION OTHER THAN THE FIRST

Moore, G. S. (2002). *Living with the earth: Concepts in environmental health
science* (2nd ed.). New York, NY: Lewis.

11. MULTIVOLUME WORK

Barnes, J. (Ed.). (1995). *Complete works of Aristotle* (Vols. 1–2). Princeton, NJ:
Princeton University Press.

Note: If you cite just one volume of a multivolume work, list that volume, not
the complete span of volumes, in parentheses after the title.

12. ARTICLE IN A REFERENCE WORK

Dean, C. (1994). Jaws and teeth. In *The Cambridge encyclopedia of human
evolution* (pp. 56–59). Cambridge, England: Cambridge University Press.

If no author is listed, begin with the title of the article.

13. REPUBLISHED BOOK

Piaget, J. (1952). *The language and thought of the child.* London, England:
Routledge & Kegan Paul. (Original work published 1932)

14. INTRODUCTION, PREFACE, FOREWORD, OR AFTERWORD

Klosterman, C. (2007). Introduction. In P. Shirley, *Can I keep my jersey?
11 teams, 5 countries, and 4 years in my life as a basketball vagabond*
(pp. v–vii). New York, NY: Villard-Random House.

15. BOOK WITH A TITLE WITHIN THE TITLE Do not italicize or enclose in quotation
marks a title within a book title.

Klarman, M. J. (2007). Brown v. Board of Education *and the civil rights
movement.* New York, NY: Oxford University Press.

PRINT PERIODICALS

Begin with the author name(s). (See models 1–5.) Then include the publication date (year only for journals, and year, month, and day for other periodicals); the article title; the periodical title; the volume and issue numbers, if any; and the page numbers. The source map on pp. 389–90 shows where to find this information in a sample periodical.

16. ARTICLE IN A JOURNAL PAGINATED BY VOLUME

> O'Connell, D. C., & Kowal, S. (2003). Psycholinguistics: A half century of
> monologism. *The American Journal of Psychology, 116*, 191–212.

17. ARTICLE IN A JOURNAL PAGINATED BY ISSUE If each issue begins with page 1,
include the issue number after the volume number.

> Hall, R. E. (2000). Marriage as vehicle of racism among women of color.
> *Psychology: A Journal of Human Behavior, 37*(2), 29–40.

18. ARTICLE IN A MAGAZINE

> Ricciardi, S. (2003, August 5). Enabling the mobile work force. *PC Magazine,
> 22*, 46.

19. ARTICLE IN A NEWSPAPER

> Faler, B. (2003, August 29). Primary colors: Race and fundraising. *The
> Washington Post*, p. A5.

20. EDITORIAL OR LETTER TO THE EDITOR

> Zelneck, B. (2003, July 18). Serving the public at public universities [Letter to
> the editor]. *The Chronicle Review*, p. B18.

21. UNSIGNED ARTICLE

> Annual meeting announcement. (2003, March). *Cognitive Psychology, 46*, 227.

22. REVIEW

> Ringel, S. (2003). [Review of the book *Multiculturalism and the therapeutic
> process*]. *Clinical Social Work Journal, 31*, 212–213.

23. PUBLISHED INTERVIEW

> Smith, H. (2002, October). [Interview with A. Thompson]. *The Sun*, pp. 4–7.

APA SOURCE MAP: Articles from periodicals

1 Author. List all authors' last names first, and use only initials for first and middle names. For more about citing authors, see models 1–5.

2 Publication date. Enclose the date in parentheses. For journals, use only the year. For magazines and newspapers, use the year, a comma, the month (spelled out), and the day, if given.

3 Article title. Do not italicize or enclose article titles in quotation marks. Capitalize only the first words of the article title and the subtitle and any proper nouns or proper adjectives.

4 Periodical title. Italicize the periodical title (and the subtitle, if any), and capitalize all major words.

5 Volume and issue numbers. Follow the periodical title with a comma, and then give the volume number (italicized) and, without a space in between, the issue number (if given) in parentheses.

6 Page numbers. Give the inclusive page numbers of the article. For newspapers only, include the abbreviation *p.* ("page") or *pp.* ("pages") before the page numbers. End the citation with a period.

A citation for the periodical article on p. 390 would look like this:

   1   2   3

Etzioni, A. (2006). Leaving race behind: Our growing Hispanic population

                                      4   5   6

   creates a golden opportunity. *The American Scholar*, *75*(2), 20–30.

2 Publication Date

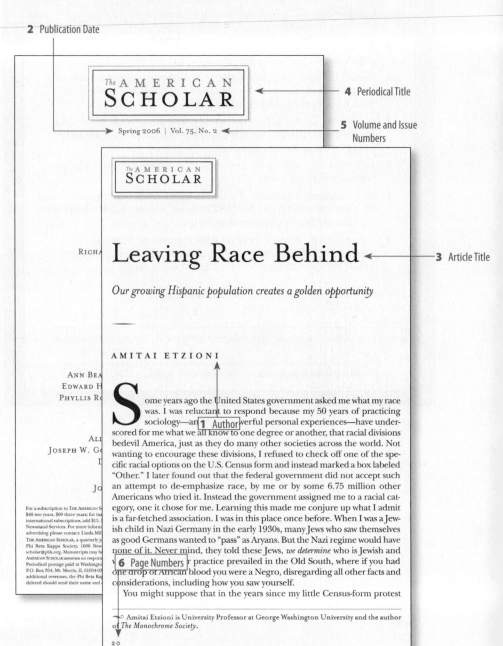

4 Periodical Title

Spring 2006 | Vol. 75, No. 2

5 Volume and Issue Numbers

3 Article Title

Leaving Race Behind

Our growing Hispanic population creates a golden opportunity

AMITAI ETZIONI

1 Author

Some years ago the United States government asked me what my race was. I was reluctant to respond because my 50 years of practicing sociology—and powerful personal experiences—have underscored for me what we all know to one degree or another, that racial divisions bedevil America, just as they do many other societies across the world. Not wanting to encourage these divisions, I refused to check off one of the specific racial options on the U.S. Census form and instead marked a box labeled "Other." I later found out that the federal government did not accept such an attempt to de-emphasize race, by me or by some 6.75 million other Americans who tried it. Instead the government assigned me to a racial category, one it chose for me. Learning this made me conjure up what I admit is a far-fetched association. I was in this place once before. When I was a Jewish child in Nazi Germany in the early 1930s, many Jews who saw themselves as good Germans wanted to "pass" as Aryans. But the Nazi regime would have none of it. Never mind, they told these Jews, *we determine* who is Jewish and

6 Page Numbers r practice prevailed in the Old South, where if you had one drop of African blood you were a Negro, disregarding all other facts and considerations, including how you saw yourself.

You might suppose that in the years since my little Census-form protest

Amitai Etzioni is University Professor at George Washington University and the author of *The Monochrome Society*.

20

ELECTRONIC SOURCES

When citing sources accessed online or from an electronic database, include as many of the following elements as you can find:

- *Author.* Give the author's name, if available.
- *Publication date.* Include the date of electronic publication or of the latest update, if available. When no publication date is available, use *n.d.* ("no date").
- *Title.* List the document title, neither italicized nor in quotation marks.
- *Print publication information.* For articles from online journals, magazines, or reference databases, give the publication title and other publishing information as you would for a print periodical (see models 16–23).
- *Retrieval information.* For a work from a database, do the following: If the article has a DOI (digital object identifier), include that number after the publication information; do not include the name of the database. If there is no DOI, write *Retrieved from* followed by the URL for the journal's homepage (not the database URL). For a work found on a website, write *Retrieved from* followed by the URL. If the work seems likely to be updated, include the retrieval date. If the URL is longer than one line, break it only before a punctuation mark; do not break *http://*.

Updated guidelines for citing electronic resources are maintained at the APA's website (www.apa.org).

24. ARTICLE FROM AN ONLINE PERIODICAL Give the author, date, title, and publication information as you would for a print document. If the article has a digital object identifier (DOI), include it. If there is no DOI, include the URL for the periodical's homepage or for the article (if the article is difficult to find from the homepage). For newspaper articles accessible from a searchable website, give the site URL only.

> Barringer, F. (2008, February 7). In many communities, it's not easy going green. *The New York Times.* Retrieved from http://www.nytimes.com

> Heintzelman, S. J., & King, L. A. (2016, March). Meaning in life and intuition. *Journal of Personality and Social Psychology*, 110(3), 477–492. Retrieved from http://dx.doi.org.proxy.wexler.hunter.cuny.edu/10.1037

25. ARTICLE FROM A DATABASE Give the author, the date, the title, and the publication information as you would for a print document. Include both the volume and issue numbers for all journal articles. If the article has a DOI, include it. If there is no DOI, write *Retrieved from* followed by URL of the journal's homepage (not the URL of the database). The source map on pp. 392–93 shows where to find this information for a typical article from a database.

APA SOURCE MAP: Articles from databases

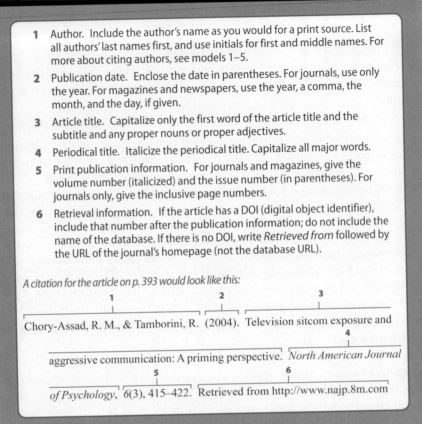

1. **Author.** Include the author's name as you would for a print source. List all authors' last names first, and use initials for first and middle names. For more about citing authors, see models 1–5.

2. **Publication date.** Enclose the date in parentheses. For journals, use only the year. For magazines and newspapers, use the year, a comma, the month, and the day, if given.

3. **Article title.** Capitalize only the first word of the article title and the subtitle and any proper nouns or proper adjectives.

4. **Periodical title.** Italicize the periodical title. Capitalize all major words.

5. **Print publication information.** For journals and magazines, give the volume number (italicized) and the issue number (in parentheses). For journals only, give the inclusive page numbers.

6. **Retrieval information.** If the article has a DOI (digital object identifier), include that number after the publication information; do not include the name of the database. If there is no DOI, write *Retrieved from* followed by the URL of the journal's homepage (not the database URL).

A citation for the article on p. 393 would look like this:

           1   2   3

Chory-Assad, R. M., & Tamborini, R. (2004). Television sitcom exposure and

aggressive communication: A priming perspective. *North American Journal*

                  5   6

of Psychology, *6*(3), 415–422. Retrieved from http://www.najp.8m.com

3 Article Title

1 Author

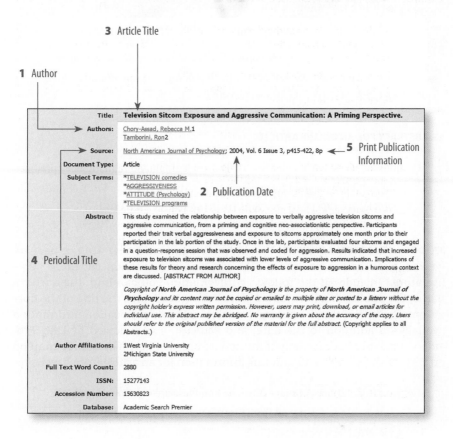

Title:	**Television Sitcom Exposure and Aggressive Communication: A Priming Perspective.**
Authors:	Chory-Assad, Rebecca M.1
	Tamborini, Ron2
Source:	North American Journal of Psychology; 2004, Vol. 6 Issue 3, p415-422, 8p
Document Type:	Article
Subject Terms:	*TELEVISION comedies
	*AGGRESSIVENESS
	*ATTITUDE (Psychology)
	*TELEVISION programs
Abstract:	This study examined the relationship between exposure to verbally aggressive television sitcoms and aggressive communication, from a priming and cognitive neo-associationistic perspective. Participants reported their trait verbal aggressiveness and exposure to sitcoms approximately one month prior to their participation in the lab portion of the study. Once in the lab, participants evaluated four sitcoms and engaged in a question-response session that was observed and coded for aggression. Results indicated that increased exposure to television sitcoms was associated with lower levels of aggressive communication. Implications of these results for theory and research concerning the effects of exposure to aggression in a humorous context are discussed. [ABSTRACT FROM AUTHOR]
	*Copyright of **North American Journal of Psychology** is the property of **North American Journal of Psychology** and its content may not be copied or emailed to multiple sites or posted to a listserv without the copyright holder's express written permission. However, users may print, download, or email articles for individual use. This abstract may be abridged. No warranty is given about the accuracy of the copy. Users should refer to the original published version of the material for the full abstract. (Copyright applies to all Abstracts.)*
Author Affiliations:	1West Virginia University
	2Michigan State University
Full Text Word Count:	2880
ISSN:	15277143
Accession Number:	15630823
Database:	Academic Search Premier

5 Print Publication Information

2 Publication Date

4 Periodical Title

Hazleden, R. (2003, December). Love yourself: The relationship of the self with
   itself in popular self-help texts. *Journal of Sociology, 39*(4),
   413–428. Retrieved from http://jos.sagepub.com

Morley, N. J., Ball, L. J., & Ormerod, T. C. (2006). How the detection of
   insurance fraud succeeds and fails. *Psychology, Crime, & Law, 12*(2),
   163–180. doi:10.1080/10683160512331316325

26. ABSTRACT FOR AN ONLINE ARTICLE

Gudjonsson, G. H., & Young, S. (2010). Does confabulation in memory predict
   suggestibility beyond IQ and memory? [Abstract]. *Personality & Individual
   Differences, 49*(1), 65-67. doi: 10.1016/j.paid.2010.03.014

27. DOCUMENT FROM A WEBSITE The APA refers to works that are not peer reviewed, such as reports, press releases, and presentation slides, as "gray
literature." Include all the following information you can find: the author's
name; the publication date (or *n.d.* if no date is available); the title of the document; the title of the site or larger work, if any; any publication information
available in addition to the date; and *Retrieved from* followed by URL. Provide your date of access only if an update seems likely. The source map on
pp. 398–99 shows where to find this information for an article from a website.

Behnke, P. C. (2006, February 22). The homeless are everyone's problem.
   Authors' Den. Retrieved from http://www.authorsden.com/visit
   /viewArticle.asp?id=21017

Hacker, J. S. (2006). The privatization of risk and the growing economic
   insecurity of Americans. *Items and Issues, 5*(4), 16–23. Retrieved from
   http://publications.ssrc.org/items/items5.4/Hacker.pdf

What parents should know about treatment of behavioral and emotional
   disorders in preschool children. (2006). *APA Online.* Retrieved from http://
   www.apa.org/releases/kidsmed.html

28. CHAPTER OR SECTION OF A WEB DOCUMENT Follow model 27. After the chapter
or section title, type *In* and give the document title, with identifying information, if any, in parentheses.

Salamon, A. (n.d.). War in Europe. In *Childhood in times of war* (chap. 2).
   Retrieved April 11, 2008, from http://remember.org/jean

29. EMAIL MESSAGE OR REAL-TIME COMMUNICATION Because the APA stresses that any sources cited in your list of references be retrievable by your readers, you should not include entries for email messages, real-time communications (such as instant messages or texts), or any other postings that are not archived. Instead, cite these sources in your text as forms of personal communication (see p. 380).

30. ONLINE POSTING List an online posting in the references list only if you are able to retrieve the message from an archive. Provide the author's name, the date of posting, and the subject line. Include other identifying information in square brackets. End with the retrieval statement and the URL of the archived message.

> Troike, R. C. (2001, June 21). Buttercups and primroses [Electronic mailing list message]. Retrieved from http://listserv.linguistlist.org/archives /ads-l.html

> Wittenberg, E. (2001, July 11). Gender and the Internet [Newsgroup message]. Retrieved from news://comp.edu.composition

31. BLOG (WEB LOG) POST

> Spaulding, P. (2010, April 27). Who believes in a real America? [web log post]. Retrieved from http://pandagon.net/index.php/site/2010/04

32. WIKI ENTRY Use the date of posting, if there is one, or *n.d.*, for "no date," if there is none. Include the retrieval date because wiki content can change frequently.

> Happiness. (2007, June 14). Retrieved March 24, 2008, from PsychWiki: http://www.psychwiki.com/wiki/Happiness

33. ONLINE AUDIO OR VIDEO FILE

> Klusman, P. (2008, February 13). An engineer's guide to cats [Video file]. Retrieved from http://www.youtube.com/watch?v=mHXBL6bzAR4

> O'Brien, K. (2008, January 31). Developing countries [Audio file]. *KUSP's life in the fast lane*. Retrieved from http://kusp.org/shows/fast.html

34. DATA SET

> U.S. Department of Education, Institute of Education Sciences. (2009). *NAEP state comparisons* [Data set]. Retrieved from http://nces.ed.gov /nationsreportcard/statecomparisons/

APA SOURCE MAP: Works from websites

1 Author. If one is given, include the author's name (see models 1–5). List last names first, and use only initials for first names. The site's sponsor may be the author. If no author is identified, begin the citation with the title of the document.

2 Publication date. Enclose the date of publication or latest update in parentheses. Use *n.d.* ("no date") when no publication date is available.

3 Title of work. Capitalize only the first word of the title and the subtitle and any proper nouns or proper adjectives.

4 Title of website. Italicize the title. Capitalize all major words.

5 Retrieval information. Write *Retrieved from* followed by the URL. If the work seems likely to be updated, include the retrieval date.

A citation for the web document on p. 397 would look like this:

    1   **2**   **3**

Alexander, M. (2001, August 22). Thirty years later, Stanford Prison

                               4   **5**

Experiment lives on. *Stanford Report.* Retrieved from http://news

-service.stanford.edu/news/2001/august22/prison2-822.html

4 Title of Website

5 Retrieval Information

2 Publication Date

Stanford Report, August 22, 2001

Thirty years later, Stanford Prison Experiment lives on

BY MEREDITH ALEXANDER

Thirty years ago, a group of young men were rounded up by Palo Alto police and dropped off at a new jail -- in the Stanford Psychology Department. Strip searched, sprayed for lice and left **3** Title of Work around their ankles, the young men were part of an experiment to test people's reactions to power dynamics in social situations. Other college student volunteers -- the "guards" -- were given authority to dictate 24-hour-a-day rules. They were soon humiliating the "prisoners" in **1** Author break their will.

Psychology Professor Philip Zimbardo's Stanford Prison Experiment of August 1971 quickly became a classic. Using realistic methods, Zimbardo and others were able to create a prison atmosphere that transformed its participants. The young men who played prisoners and guards revealed how much circumstances can distort individual personalities -- and how anyone, when given complete control over others, can act like a monster.

"In a few days, the role dominated the person," Zimbardo -- now president-elect of the American Psychological Association -- recalled. "They became guards and prisoners." So disturbing was the transformation that Zimbardo ordered the experiment abruptly ended.

A "guard" leads a "prisoner" down the hall in a 1971 Stanford psychology experiment. The experiment explored power dynamics by creating false distinctions among college student volunteers. Credit: Chuck Painter

Related Information

- Prison Experiment Website

- Psychologist puts the 'real' into reality TV;

35. COMPUTER SOFTWARE

> PsychMate [Computer software]. (2003). Available from Psychology Software
>> Tools: http://pstnet.com/products/psychmate

OTHER SOURCES (INCLUDING ONLINE VERSIONS)

36. GOVERNMENT PUBLICATION

> Office of the Federal Register. (2003). *The United States government manual*
>> *2003/2004*. Washington, DC: U.S. Government Printing Office.

Cite an online government document as you would a printed government work, adding the URL. If there is no date, use *n.d.*

> U.S. Public Health Service. (1999). *The surgeon general's call to action*
>> *to prevent suicide*. Retrieved from http://www.mentalhealth.org
>> /suicideprevention/calltoaction.asp

37. DISSERTATION If you retrieved the dissertation from a database, give the database name and the accession number, if one is assigned.

> Lengel, L. L. (1968). *The righteous cause: Some religious aspects of Kansas*
>> *populism*. Retrieved from ProQuest Digital Dissertations. (6900033)

If you retrieve a dissertation from a website, give the type of dissertation, the institution, and the year after the title, and provide a retrieval statement.

> Meeks, M. G. (2006). *Between abolition and reform: First-year writing*
>> *programs, e-literacies, and institutional change* (Doctoral dissertation,
>> University of North Carolina). Retrieved from http://dc.lib.unc.edu/etd/

38. TECHNICAL OR RESEARCH REPORT Give the report number, if available, in parentheses after the title.

> McCool, R., Fikes, R., & McGuinness, D. (2003). *Semantic Web tools for*
>> *enhanced authoring* (Report No. KSL-03-07). Stanford, CA: Knowledge
>> Systems Laboratory.

39. CONFERENCE PROCEEDINGS

> Robertson, S. P., Vatrapu, R. K., & Medina, R. (2009). YouTube and Facebook:
>> Online video "friends" social networking. In *Conference proceedings:*
>> *YouTube and the 2008 election cycle* (pp. 159–176). Amherst, MA:

University of Massachusetts. Retrieved from http://scholarworks.umass
.edu/jitpc2009

40. PAPER PRESENTED AT A MEETING OR SYMPOSIUM, UNPUBLISHED Cite the month
of the meeting, if it is available.

Jones, J. G. (1999, February). *Mental health intervention in mass casualty
disasters*. Paper presented at the Rocky Mountain Region Disaster Mental
Health Conference, Laramie, WY.

41. POSTER SESSION

Barnes Young, L. L. (2003, August). *Cognition, aging, and dementia*. Poster
session presented at the 2003 Division 40 APA Convention, Toronto,
Ontario, Canada.

42. FILM, VIDEO, OR DVD

Nolan, C. (Director). (2010). *Inception* [Motion picture]. United States: Warner
Bros.

43. TELEVISION PROGRAM, SINGLE EPISODE

Imperioli, M. (Writer), & Buscemi, S. (Director). (2002). Everybody hurts
[Television series episode]. In D. Chase (Executive producer), *The
Sopranos*. New York, NY: Home Box Office.

44. TELEVISION SERIES

Abrams, J. J., Lieber, J., & Lindelof, D. (2004). *Lost*. [Television series]. New
York, NY: WABC.

45. AUDIO PODCAST (DOWNLOADED AUDIO FILE)

Noguchi, Yugi. (2010, 24 May). BP hard to pin down on oil spill claims. [Audio
podcast]. *NPR morning edition*. Retrieved from http://www.npr.org

46. RECORDING

The Avalanches. (2001). Frontier psychiatrist. On *Since I left you* [CD]. Los
Angeles, CA: Elektra/Asylum Records.

Acknowledgments

Page 28, Excerpt from *Framework for Success in Post-secondary Writing*: Courtesy Council of Writing Program Administrators.

Pages 33–34, Frank Rose, "The Selfish Meme": Courtesy of Frank Rose.

Page 37, Excerpt from "Less Privacy Is Good for Us (and You)": Courtesy Amitai Etzioni, Georgetown University.

Pages 72–73, from the Introduction to Jean M. Twenge's *Generation Me*: Reprinted with permission of Atria, a division of Simon & Schuster, Inc., from *Generation Me: Why Today's Young Americans Are More Confident, Assertive, Entitled—And More Miserable—Than Ever Before* by Jean M. Twenge, Ph.D. Copyright ©2006 by Jean M. Twenge, Ph. D. All rights reserved.

Pages 74–75, Jean Twenge, "Generation Me on Trial": Used with permission of *The Chronicle of Higher Education*. Copyright© 2016. All rights reserved.

Pages 76–77, Jean M. Twenge, et al., from "Generational Differences in Young Adults' Life Goals, Concern for Others, and Civic Orientation, 1966–2009": Copyright © 2012 American Psychological Association. Reproduced with permission. The official citation that should be used in referencing this material is Jean M. Twenge, Elise C. Freeman, W. Keith Campbell, Personality Process and Individual Differences, *Journal of Personality and Social Psychology*, 2012, Vol. 102, No. 5, 1045–1062; DOI: 10.1037/a0027408. No further reproduction or distribution is permitted without written permission from the American Psychological Association.

Page 117–20, Amitai Etzioni, from "Less Privacy Is Good for Us (and You)": Courtesy Amitai Etzioni, Georgetown University.

Index

List of Easy-Reference Guidelines and Questions

Essential Writing Strategies

Working Collaboratively

Analyzing and Composing Arguments

Reading Critically and Working with Texts

Multimodal Composing and Design

Research

Inventing, Planning, Drafting

Revising, Editing, and Proofreading